received

May 4 : I have a   3. 13.

31. 125. 17. 174. 14. different 288. 12. and

265 - 11

H̶T̶   ̶2̶6̶9̶.̶ ̶8̶.̶ T. 261. 23. —

61. 33. 270. 7. 394. 31. 257. 5. 300. 16. of ▢

39 ing to ·1· — 0 — ÷ 1 — to 49. 20. with

11. at ̶H̶H̶H̶H̶ ▢ — 96. of ▢ ·1· ▢ . 30

180. 34. to my 174. 14 and 169. 37 — It will

call be 334. 17. to 13, 265. 21. and 45 sha

264. 29 —

. 15. — never to 320. 7. with him 182.

husband will 169. 36. in 264. 30. with

98. 10. 174. 14. with whom 13. 242. 38. 98

The

BURR

CONSPIRACY

Even as suspicions grew, Burr and his agents, according to Hinde, continued to build support for their "Conspiracy *plot*, or *intrigue*, (or whatever name it be called by)." Burr's recruiters "were numerous and powerful." They kept lists of the men "in every town or Hamlet" who supported or opposed him. They also tried to secure arms and men by winning over army and militia officers at western posts and towns. Burr himself worked diligently "to enlist the feelings of the youth of the Country"; his "fascinating manners," as Hinde recalled, were "well calculated to win [their] affections."[9] Hinde even admitted that he had nearly been won over by Burr as they rode together one day that fall.

In the midst of these efforts, in November and December 1806, "Col Burr was [twice] arrested" by Joseph Hamilton Daveiss, the federal district attorney for Kentucky. Many of Kentucky's most prominent Republicans defended Burr, who insisted that his projects would advance the nation's interests. When Daveiss failed to secure an indictment, Burr's local popularity soared. But success in Kentucky was quickly followed by a setback in Ohio. In early December, the state government moved to seize "Burrs flotilla at Marietta." When combined with the probability of a war with Spain on the western border and "the plausibility of Col B's aiding Gnl Wilkinson [and] his plans [having] the Sanction of Goverment," the contradictory developments in Kentucky and Ohio left the public "in a state of uncertainty." This confusion was dispelled by the arrival of a presidential proclamation against the western conspiracy in mid-December. After reading Jefferson's proclamation, no one could doubt that the administration opposed Burr's project. It soon became easy, Hinde remembered, "to distinguish the *partizans* of Burr from the Citizens friendly to the *peace* and *permanency* of our *Union*."[10]

Hinde's narrative ended there, with much of the story of the Burr Conspiracy left untold. From his perspective, after "the arm of Goverment" had moved to quell the conspiracy, "all the [subsequent] transactions [were] matters of [public] record" that did not require his particular evidence. Thus, Hinde's account for Madison did not include the movement of Burr's men and boats down the Ohio, Cumberland, and Mississippi Rivers, nor the steps taken by Wilkinson to defend New Orleans, nor the weeks waiting for western news in Washington, nor the abortive trial of Burr in the Mississippi Territory, nor Burr's arrest in the wilderness above Spanish Mobile, nor his celebrated trial and stunning acquittal in the court of Chief Justice John Marshall in Richmond, nor his self-imposed exile in Europe. Beyond noting that "many innocent persons" who had "associated with Col Burr" were long viewed with suspicion, Hinde said little about the crisis's lingering effects on Burr, Wilkinson, Jefferson, or the many subordinate figures who had played parts in the drama.[11]

Hinde's narratives of the Burr Conspiracy, whether written for Madison or others, coupled what was, in many ways, a very narrow view of past events with a very broad sense of their continuing relevance. Each of his accounts related events almost entirely from his own point of view. So much of Hinde's story concerned his own actions that he became the protagonist rather than Burr. When he included information from beyond his own experience, he usually identified his sources. Many were friends or acquaintances; but Hinde also referred to Wilkinson's 21 October 1806 letter to Jefferson and to the cipher letter from Burr to Wilkinson. The vicissitudes of human memory and authorial selection also made Hinde's account distinct. Only he seems to have cared, for instance, that Burr's western tour of 1805 coincided with a travelling "exhibition of Wax figures representing the fatal *duel*" with Hamilton.[12] Within these limits, however, Hinde wrote for larger purposes, not merely for self-serving ends. Believing that an accurate account of the conspiracy was still needed decades after the event, he worked to record and publicize aspects of it that might otherwise be lost. Between 1825 and 1843, he sent a file of old newspaper essays to the State Department, prepared two versions of his story for Madison, and had his narrative and other documents published in the *Daily National Intelligencer* and the *American Pioneer*. And Hinde hoped that his tale could serve didactic purposes as the country seemingly moved away from its founding principles. "Let not the attempts of . . . almost beardless boys of the west, who overturned the great western conspiracy, be buried in oblivion," he charged the editors of the *Intelligencer* in 1838. With a new "conspiracy" threatening to bring a slaveholding Texas into the union, Hinde hoped that publishing his narrative would inspire "our youths [to] *unite* and save their country."[13]

This book examines the much-studied Burr Conspiracy from a new perspective, focusing more on the crisis and on the efforts to make sense of the conspiracy than on the conspiracy itself. What makes a crisis a crisis is not a particular series of events or state of affairs, but the relationship of those developments and conditions to a people's existing hopes and fears. Barely four decades after the Declaration of Independence, and not even two decades after the Constitution, that embodied many of their aspirations, Americans felt great anxiety not just about whether their political institutions could survive, but also about whether they were one people who could live together as one nation. Between the spring of 1805 and the winter of 1807, the Burr Conspiracy, and the response to it, seemed to imperil their hopes for an independent, republican, united, and expanding country. And it inflamed their fears of foreign influence and domestic strife, of a shattered union and a failed republic. These fears showed people what might happen and, in doing so, helped them make sense of what was happening.[14] They not only generated the air of crisis, but also fixed, for many at the time, the nature of the conspiracy itself in a way that the vague rumors, incomplete reports, and conflicting claims about Burr's intentions and actions could not.

Rather than retelling the story *of* the Burr Conspiracy, this book focuses upon the stories *about* the Burr Conspiracy that were told at the time and over the next few decades. These stories appeared in rumors and conversations, in diaries and letters, in newspaper articles and magazine essays, in pamphlets and books, and even in presidential messages and judicial rulings. Some represented little more than an effort to sort through uncertain information and events; they were written for their authors and, perhaps, a few readers. But others embodied a belief that, properly told, the story of Burr's or Wilkinson's or Jefferson's intentions and actions could serve various ends. Some influenced later stories; others had little lasting impact. Taken together, the stories point to the various forces that influenced how people at the time worked through conflicting accounts to decide what to believe—to the uncomfortable but growing impact of political partisanship and the consoling but diminishing force of public reputation, to the alarming prospects of disunion and tyranny and the tenuous balancing of local, state, regional, and national identities. In doing so, they reveal a people who were struggling to make sense of themselves and their world.[15]

Thomas Spotswood Hinde's story of the Burr Conspiracy was just one of many—differing from any other almost by necessity, yet sharing important characteristics with nearly all of the rest. No one else wrote, or could have written, precisely his story for precisely his reasons. But Hinde's account shared some basic characteristics with almost all of the narratives of the conspiracy that were prepared, at the time and afterward, by those who had experienced it. Like Hinde, most authors wrote about themselves as well as about Burr. Like Hinde, they tried to establish their veracity by naming their sources and citing, or even including, supporting documents. Like Hinde, they wanted to preserve what they viewed as an accurate statement of events, yet, as with Hinde, not all of what they wrote was accurate. And, like Hinde, they recognized that the story of the Burr Conspiracy, if properly constructed and employed, could serve a wide range of purposes: personal, partisanal, local, regional, and national.

Hinde's narrative differed most strikingly from many other accounts in the certainty with which he related Burr's plans. For Hinde, there was no question that Burr intended to divide the union at the Appalachians. All of the other plans that were attributed to Burr—launching an illegal invasion of Spanish Mexico, organizing a volunteer company in case of a declared war against Spain, winning election to Congress from a western state or territory, building a canal around the falls of the Ohio at Louisville, Kentucky, or settling the so-called Bastrop Grant on the Ouachita River in the Louisiana Purchase—were merely cover for his real purpose. Hinde's certainty had not developed gradually in the two decades after the Burr crisis, moreover, but had shaped his earliest essays in the *Scioto Gazette* and the *Fredonian*.[16] Many of Hinde's contemporaries, in contrast, described Burr's plans and actions as "enveloped in mystery." In letters, diaries, and newspapers, this phrase appeared repeatedly as men and women tried to make sense of the swirling rumors and conflicting reports about Burr. At the peak of the crisis, in late 1806 and early 1807, it is not surprising that "Colonel Burr's mysterious movements" prompted such language.[17] But many continued to express uncertainty about Burr's plans even after the crisis had abated. To Abigail Adams, for example, Burr's "projects" were "enveloped in as many Mystery as Mrs. Ratcliffs castle of udolphus" as late as mid-March.[18] Burr's trial in Richmond brought countless, drivers also carried letters along their route. Finding alternative ways to transmit letters was attractive for a number of reasons. Postage was relatively expensive, with charges based upon the number of sheets of paper and the distance travelled. Entrusting a letter to a known bearer could also be more reliable than sending it by mail. And using private carriers allowed writers to expect a greater degree of privacy by setting conditions for delivery. Mail was delivered not to homes, but to local post offices. Its arrival was a public event. Letters were frequently read aloud a number of times—at the post office, in a tavern or coffee-house, and at home. Writers used various tactics to avoid both exposing what they wished to keep private and placing recipients in the awkward position of refusing to read a letter. Letters might be labelled "private" or "confidential" on the wrapper or the first page. Writers could also enclose a separate sheet that was to remain private or specify that *"what is on this side is of a private nature."*[19] Some letters included even more detailed instructions for the recipient: "you must not [let] any of the old-folks or the girls lay hands upon this," a medical student insisted in a letter home relating the many opportunities for dissipation in Philadelphia.[20]

For official correspondence, the counterpart to the private bearer was the express rider. When government officials wanted "to save time [or] secure [a letter's] safe arrival," they used expresses.[21] Between October 1806 and February 1807, as he first disclosed and then opposed Burr's project, Wilkinson sent most of his dispatches to Washington by express. The governors of the Orleans and Mississippi Territories also occasionally used expresses during these months. In mid-December 1806, the postmaster general ordered the use of expresses on all of the mail routes from the South and West whenever "the Mail Carrier [was] not prepared to leave" on time.[22] Expresses travelled from Washington, as well. In late December, a Virginian reported that an express "from the president" had passed his home going to the Mississippi Territory "charged to ride 120 miles every 24 hours."[23] Obviously, one man could not complete this trip; the postmaster general provided his expresses with letters urging postmasters, contractors, and citizens to find a "faithful and Vigilent" replacement when a rider could not continue.[24] He also pledged that the riders would "be liberally rewarded . . . in proportion to [their] vigilance and security and dispatch."[25]

What often delayed the mail riders was the great burden of printed matter, primarily newspapers, in their portmanteaus. With the Postal Act of 1792, the federal government committed itself to subsidizing the movement of newspapers in two ways. Newspapers sent to private subscribers paid just one cent for trips of less than one hundred miles, and one and a half cents for longer journeys (mailing a one-sheet letter less than thirty miles cost six cents). The act also made law what had been custom—the free shipment of exchange copies of newspapers between editors. This act promoted the free movement of information among a large number of primarily local newspapers. But it also left mail riders carrying dozens of free and reduced-rate newspapers on each trip. In the early nineteenth century, newspapers accounted for well over half of the weight of the mail and well under one-tenth of the revenue. During the Burr crisis, Postmaster General Granger sent "men & horses into Virginia, to seperate the letters from the Newspapers, in the western mail—in order to have [the letters] in season."[26]

In the three years between Burr's departure for the West in April 1805 and his departure for Europe in May 1808, more than 370 newspapers were published in the United States. Many were short-lived; some were extremely short-lived. But 170 (roughly 46%) remained in operation throughout this period. Most newspapers consisted of a single sheet of paper printed on both sides and folded once to make four pages. Most were weeklies, though there were biweeklies, triweeklies, and even some dailies. And most relied heavily on advertising, which generally filled one, one and a half, or more of the four pages. Other than advertisements, newspapers contained a mix of material, much of it clipped from other newspapers that had been received as exchange copies. The original content was quite diverse. Each issue included a few news items, either concerning local affairs or relating information from travellers, and a few letters that had recently arrived in town, whether addressed to the editor or to others who were willing to share them. There were often editorial comments and perhaps a pseudonymous essay or two on a local or national controversy. And there might be marriage and death notices, a poem or song, and even a recipe. Newspapers did not employ reporters, though a few hired stenographers to record legislative debates and, in exceptional cases, court proceedings. Many editors wrote relatively little, spending much of their time reading other newspapers, selecting items to reprint, finding advertisers, dunning delinquent subscribers, and managing the printing operation, which usually included job printing.[27]

At the peak of the Burr crisis, in the winter of 1806–7, each of the sixteen states and three of the five territories had active newspapers. The most populous states supported as many as fifty. But even the newest state, Ohio, had five newspapers. Only the Michigan and Louisiana Territories lacked newspapers entirely. Large cities always supported multiple prints; New York City, for example, had fifteen newspapers in this period. But most of the newspapers were printed in smaller cities and towns, many of which had at least two, often struggling, prints. Partisanship explained, at least in part, the distribution and multiplication of newspapers. In the eastern states, even small towns typically had a Republican newspaper and a Federalist newspaper. Since the Federalists typically had less support in the West, the appearance of a second newspaper in a western town or city often signalled a struggle between Republican factions or, in the territories, opposition to the federally appointed governor.[28]

These newspapers were far from equal. Most served a local audience and relied heavily on material from other prints. Only rarely did any one of these newspapers provide content for distant newspapers. But a few served a very different role. The leading Republican prints—Philadelphia's *Aurora*, Washington's *National Intelligencer*, and, increasingly, Richmond's *Enquirer*—operated as national newspapers in support of the administration. The *Intelligencer* was widely viewed as "more than half official," in part because it provided the most complete records of congressional debates.[29] But the comments of one Republican editor about the *Aurora* could have been written about each of these newspapers: "*that* paper possesses the confidence of the executive of the United States, receives the most prompt information from the seat of government—and is therefore well qualified to be the source from which to draw *correct* information."[30] These newspapers provided not only news, but also political essays and editorials that could be clipped and reprinted in smaller Republican prints. In the spring of 1807, a Federalist newspaper neatly captured this relationship by referring to "the ministerial presses"—the *Aurora, Enquirer, Intelligencer,* and *Virginia Argus* (Richmond)—and "their echoes."[31] The principal Federalist newspapers—Boston's *Columbian Centinel*, the *New-York Evening Post*, Philadelphia's *United States' Gazette*, and the *Charleston Courier*—served the same functions for the opposition party.

But what about Burrite newspapers? Burr and his allies had long supported a newspaper in New York City, the *Morning Chronicle*; during the Burr crisis, however, people worried that Burr had gained control of or influence over some western prints. The editors of some key western newspapers—the *Pittsburgh Gazette*, the *Kentucky Gazette* (Lexington), and the *Orleans Gazette*—were accused of being at least lax about Burr's plans. Thomas Spotswood Hinde considered Chillicothe's *Ohio Herald* to be a mouthpiece for Burr and believed that Burr had arranged for James B. Gardener, "a mere hirling," to start a newspaper in his interest in Marietta. In early 1807, it was widely thought that Burr had purchased the services of John Wood. After spending the summer and fall of 1806 warning of a new conspiracy under Burr and Wilkinson in Frankfort's *Western World*, Wood left Kentucky for Washington, where he started the *Atlantic World* to defend Burr. According to Hinde, "*Burrs notes*" had funded Wood's new print.[32] During his trial in Richmond, Burr provided money to revive the local *Impartial Observer* as his press outlet.

Burr's control over a handful of newspapers mattered little compared with his potential to gain control over the mail, though, and that is precisely what many people, in and out of government, began to worry about in the fall of 1806. Months earlier, John Randolph had warned that, in Burr's hands, the post office could serve as "an admirable engine"; with it, the conspirators could "make men, who despise them, subservient to their schemes (without knowing it)." Having learned that Burr and Granger had "been closeted for days together" in Washington, Randolph's concerns focused upon the postmaster general.[33] But the corruption of the postal system did not need to reach so high to serve Burr's purposes. Properly placed, a few "treacherous postmaster[s]" or mail riders could have ensured that the conspirators could coordinate their actions freely and that the government could not organize its response.[34] In October, Wilkinson predicted that Burr would move quickly to "cut off" "communication by mail" between Washington and the West.[35] When the western mails failed in December 1806 and January 1807, people had little doubt who was to blame. "The public voice," one Kentuckian noted, "attributes to Burr's machinations" "three successive failures in the Orleans mail."[36]

These reasonable and widespread fears led the administration to secure the postal system. In December, Jefferson and Granger decided to send "a confidential agent" to investigate and rectify delays in the western mail.[37] Granger chose Seth Pease, his brother-in-law, and "secretly clothed" him with considerable power: "all the powers which by law I could confer on him," Granger later remarked. Sent on the route through Nashville to New Orleans, Pease was ordered "to expedite the mails, to correct all errors, [and] to remove the disaffected and substitute others in their place."[38] A letter conferring similar powers on Mississippi's territorial governor made clear that "the disaffected" meant anyone who was involved "in the transmission or handling" of the mail who was "inimical to the Unity of this Nation or attached to the Conspiracy."[39] Although such measures resulted in the removal of a few postmasters, Granger ultimately decided that the failures of the western mails had resulted from "the uncommon Severity of the Weather," not Burr. Whatever their cause, they "had been truly distressing."[40]

Oral, written, and printed forms of communication, while analytically separable, often merged in practice. Information that was received in conversations with travellers appeared in letters and newspapers, while letters and newspapers were often read aloud in public places. Extracts from private letters appeared in newspapers. And letter writers frequently enclosed newspaper clippings to save time and paper; others just admitted, "I have nothing to say more than you will find in the public newspap[ers]."[41] Together, these forms of communication created a powerful and effective system for the circulation of information in the early American republic.

"FROM A GENTLEMAN OF VERACITY"

The circulation of information is a cultural, as much as a technological or institutional, accomplishment. Each society develops its own practices and expectations about sharing and spreading information. Who shares news with whom? What kinds of information are shared with family, with friends, with acquaintances, with political allies, with the general public? To what extent is the exchange of information reciprocal? How does one signal that the information one shares should or should not be shared with others? How does one indicate the quality of one's news—the degree of confidence that can be assigned to it? What costs are involved in spreading inaccurate information? Early nineteenth-century Americans shared information within a system of rules and customs that answered these questions—a system that was largely shaped by English practice as it had developed in the seventeenth and eighteenth centuries. No less than mail routes and exchange copies, this cultural system shaped the flow of information in the early American republic.[42]

This cultural system exerted powerful effects on the educated and genteel, in particular, though there is evidence that it extended into other ranks of American society. It is easiest to see among the elite largely because of the nature of the sources. Gentlemen and, to a lesser extent, gentlewomen wrote most of the letters; they were literate and could afford the expense of paper and postage. And their letters are more likely to have survived and been preserved in archives. For gentlemen, status and honor were profoundly involved in the acts of providing and receiving information. Gentility created an expectation of trustworthiness. As a provider of information, a gentleman was expected to state only the truth; as a recipient, he was relied upon to maintain confidences. How deeply these expectations penetrated through society is not clear. Men and women of all sorts clearly joined in the circulation of public information. If they did not know how to read and write, they relied upon others to read and write for them. They followed political developments and conversed, if they did not correspond, about them. And they travelled and, in doing so, shared news and views across long distances. That the gentry did not equally value their information does not mean that such men and women were not equally committed to appearing honest, accurate, and discreet.

Information flowed most freely when the correspondents or conversants knew each other well and held similar views. Who communicated with whom depended heavily upon bonds of kinship, class, and politics. Family members were especially free in their correspondence, discussing subjects and sharing opinions with each other that they exposed to few others. William Barry's letters to his brother John not only related the news and rumors about Burr around Lexington,

Kentucky, but also included cutting remarks about some of the most powerful men in the community—a community in which William hoped to make his future. He compared the *Kentucky Gazette*'s editor Daniel Bradford to a "solemn Owl [who] says nothing [and] does not even make a noise after night" and condemned, by name, some of the city's leading merchants as "servile, syncophantic, parasites" who would watch "their Country go to ruin" as long as it did not "touch [their] strong box."[43] Family correspondence could convey information across great distances. Sons and brothers, daughters and sisters all across the West wrote to parents and siblings who remained in the eastern states to inform them of recent developments and to convey their views on events and people.

Shared class or status also facilitated an open exchange of information. Gentlemen and gentlewomen communicated most, and most freely, with others among the elite. Certainly, gentlemen regularly spoke and wrote to tradesmen, artisans, and other working men and women, occasionally seeking—or trying to shape—their opinions on political matters. But gentlemen did not do so as equals, with all of the respect for their views or information that they would have accorded other gentlemen. When "2 or 3 Kentucky horse drovers" passed through his town in late 1806, for example, the South Carolina gentleman Edward Hooker "scraped a sort of Yankey acquaintance with them" in order "to learn the feelings of that class of people respecting Col. Burr's projects in the west."[44] Gentlemanly correspondence on public affairs relied upon a common shorthand of ideas, terms, and references drawn from sources as diverse as Shakespeare's plays and the Bible (both of which would have been familiar to many working people), ancient and modern history, Enlightenment philosophy and science, and English law. Such was the stuff of a gentleman's education. One could refer to Burr as a Catiline or a Don Quixote or to Wilkinson as a Leonidas or a "Don Adriano de Armada" and expect the reference to be understood correctly.[45] If this common stock of knowledge facilitated genteel communication, so did the gentleman's outward display of confidence in his own opinions and abilities. "In this country," an English tourist noted after discussing Burr with a group of gentlemen in western Pennsylvania, "every man thinks for himself, or at least imagines he does." As long as gentlemen recognized the culturally fixed limits on how to assert their own views and challenge others', they could have conversations that were "amusing and instructive" and arguments that "were conducted with cool, dispassionate reasoning."[46]

But political partisanship could close, and open, lines of communication. At the time of the Burr crisis, most Americans remained uncomfortable with the idea of lasting party divisions. Parties challenged the ideal of a single American nation and a single public good. Intense partisanship also inverted the desired relationship between nature—society—and artifice—government. Within each party, individuals with common loyalties and principles exchanged information to coordinate action or sentiment. Among Federalists or among Republicans or among Quids, a whole body of shared perspectives on individuals, events, and policies ensured that this information would be read as the writer had intended. Across these political lines, successful communication on political topics often proved difficult. At moments of crisis, it was not just communication across party lines that collapsed, but also normal social relations. One foreign traveller was "astonish[ed]" by the intensity of the "mutual animosity" between Federalists and Republicans in early 1807. Men "who might otherwise be on terms of friendship . . . [were], merely on account of their diversity of sentiment on politicks, avowed and illiberal enemies"; women "carr[ied] the spirit of party into their coteries, so far as to exclude every female whose husband is of a different political opinion."[47] In New Orleans, Richmond, and elsewhere, individuals complained that "all the bonds of society [had been] torn asunder" by the intensification of partisanship due to the Burr crisis.[48]

Partisanship's impact on the flow of information becomes especially clear when looking at the press. Republican readers seem to have principally read Republican newspapers; Republican editors typically exchanged copies with other Republican editors. Clipped articles from the Federalist press occasionally appeared in Republican prints, but rarely without editorial comments to ensure that Republican readers understood them correctly. Thus, the *Enquirer* warned readers to "estimate the degree of truth due" to one account "by the fact" that it came from "a rank federal print."[49] Some even worried that, because of party, what should have been "vehicles of useful information [had] lost their credit and cease[d] to be believed."[50] Even Jefferson, whose faith in the transformative power of free-flowing information often seemed unbounded, could complain in June 1807 that "nothing can now be believed which is seen in a newspaper."[51] Perhaps more nakedly than anything else, partisan newspapers registered the inability to create the kind of common understanding and common sentiment that had been the goal of the institutional commitment to a national exchange of information.

Among men and women who shared ties of kinship, class, and politics, there was generally an expectation of reciprocity in exchanging information. News flowed in both directions, with each correspondent relied upon to contribute whatever he or she could. Territorial judge Harry Toulmin expected "a full statement of the posture of public affairs at New Orleans" from one gentleman, "in payment for the scrawles" that he had sent from the Mississippi Territory.[52] In August 1807, Virginia's William Wirt apologized to his Kentucky friend Ninian Edwards for failing in this regard. When Burr was in the West, Edwards had "obligingly . . . detailed [his] operations"; but Burr had been "near four months" in Richmond, Wirt admitted, "and you have not had a word from me."[53] No such expectation seems to have existed between people of different social standings. Even the correspondence between gentlemen and their commercial agents was typically one-sided. Gentlemen sent instructions about what to buy and what to sell, in what quantities and at what prices, but they also wanted to know "what is doing on the political theater."[54] In the spring and summer of 1807, for example, many letters to Richmond's Ellis and Allan Company closed with requests for the latest information about Burr's trial. Merchants' and agents' replies covered necessary commercial matters and often provided whatever news had recently occurred or arrived in their port.

Even within these networks of kinship, class, and politics, what was communicated depended upon considerations of confidentiality and trustworthiness. Letter writers often made these considerations explicit, particularly when they worried about the security of the mail: "I dare not commit my sentiments & opinions to paper"; "I have [more] that I can't trust to paper"; "I cannot write, but I could tell you, some circumstances that [would] astonish you."[55] Such comments, which appeared at all times in letters on public and private affairs, became more common during the Burr crisis when it seemed possible that both Burr's supporters and federal officials were intercepting letters. Writing from New Orleans in June 1807, James Sterrett assured one correspondent that he could send the "Very long letter" that he had promised and "need not be affraid of *Spies* nor Letter breakers now."[56] Men who had been publicly linked with Burr long believed that the government opened their mail. Ohio senator John Smith insisted in December 1807 that he still could not "write by post, because [his] letters [were] arrested."[57] Some responded to such fears by using elaborate ciphers; others found simpler ways to disguise their information. The editor William Duane asked an administration figure to answer a delicate question "by some reference to one or two words in a Dictionary—or to some line and page in Tucker's Blackstone or by any arbitrary mark."[58] And, from New Orleans, Elizabeth House Trist sent Virginia's Mary Gilmer "a kind of short hand so far as related to names" by a private bearer before trusting her attacks on Wilkinson and Claiborne to the mail.[59]

But concerns about confidentiality and trustworthiness extended far beyond the mail itself. To commit something to paper was to hazard not just the security of the mail, but also the responsibility of the recipient. Bonds of kinship, class, and politics facilitated the circulation of information largely by creating an expectation of trust. They offered some assurance that the writer's information and opinions would be used only as expected or directed. While there were, as Jefferson put it, "general principles of law & reason which render correspondences . . . sacredly secret," writers often provided explicit guidance.[60] Some insisted that their letters were "to remain entirely inter nos."[61] Others placed limits on the use of the information, typically to prevent it from being attributed to its source. From Detroit, a correspondent sent the *Aurora*'s Duane a long letter full of suspicions with clear instructions that they were "not to be published by any means, nor even shewn to any person." If Duane "allude[d] to them, or any part of them," in his newspaper, the writer insisted, "it must be done intirely in *[his] own way* and *language*."[62]

In general, such expectations of confidentiality encouraged a free flow of information. As president, Jefferson understood this function in a broad, national sense. He informed men who wanted to know who had denounced them to the government that it was "essential for the public interest that [he] should receive all the information possible respecting" public men and affairs. This could only happen, he believed, if letter writers felt sure that their news would be treated as "secret and sacred"; otherwise, "honest men" would "withold information." And they would be justified in doing so, in Jefferson's opinion, "if they expected the communication would be made public, and commit them to war with their neighbors and friends."[63] Expectations of confidentiality served similar purposes in communications between private citizens, allowing them to share information that might jeopardize their place in their community—whether by undermining their claims to gentility or by embroiling them in disputes.

But, in the context of the Burr Conspiracy, the reluctance of gentlemen to betray confidences formed a great obstacle to uncovering the truth. A federal land officer in Ohio reported that "all who engage to enter into the Scheme are obliged to take an oath, or pledge their *honor* not to devulge the *real* object in view."[64] Whether or not such oaths were actually required, many men who had learned of Burr's plans through conversations or correspondence hesitated to break even an implied confidence. Burr, the English architect Benjamin Henry Latrobe reflected, had "placed a confidence of a more sacred nature in me" by speaking in a frank, friendly manner "than if he had bound me by the strongest oaths to conceal what he should tell me."[65] Few seemed to have believed, as William Eaton insisted, that "when innocence is in danger, to break faith with a bad man is not fraud, but virtue."[66] Thomas Truxton likewise became willing to "betray" Burr's confidences only when he decided that Burr was "either a traitor to his Country or, a Scoundrel otherwise."[67]

From New Orleans to Washington, government officials worked to overcome the widely held view that informing gave one an "infamous" character.[68] For example, John Graham—the agent whom Jefferson sent west after Burr in October 1806—had to manage Virginia's Alexander Henderson Jr. gingerly to get him to disclose what he had learned of Burr's project from Harman Blennerhassett in "confidential conversation[s]." Henderson quickly revealed the fact of the conversations but initially stated that "he did not feel himself Justified in disclosing" confidences that placed "Mr Blennerhassets Life . . . in his hands" unless "called upon in a court of Justice."[69] The next day, Graham managed to extract the substance of the conversations, but Henderson, who was "*extremel[y] unwilling to come forward as a witness*," did not allow Graham to provide the administration his name.[70] Three months later, Graham still had not divulged Henderson's name "agreeably to promise." Informing Henderson that he had to do so in his next official dispatch, Graham urged the Virginian to provide a deposition and "appear as a Witness."[71] To overcome Henderson's reluctance, Graham reassured him of his patriotism and gentility. In his own deposition, which he sent to Henderson as a part of this campaign, Graham stated that it had required great persuasion for Henderson (whom Graham did not name and referred to only as a "Gentleman") to break the bounds of "secrecy."[72] As Graham had earlier explained to Madison, Henderson was "a gentleman of nice honor and [was of] course entitled to"—and, Graham might have said, required—"the most delicate treatment."[73]

Gentlemen played crucial roles in circulating information, but doing so created problems for them. Better situated to receive information, they were more able to disseminate it, not only through the mail, but also through published pieces or public speeches. But gentlemen needed ways to spread information that did not imperil their credibility and, thus, their gentility. They hoped not to pass along incorrect information, of course, but what seemed even more important was not to be known for doing so on their own authority. By the early nineteenth century, various techniques had emerged that permitted gentlemen to dissociate their reputations from the veracity of the information that they shared even without an injunction of secrecy. Only rarely did gentlemen share information about the Burr Conspiracy as a matter of fact on their own authority. Truxton went further than most in writing from Richmond: "what I do not see, or hear, I cannot confide in."[74] But most gentlemen hesitated to state in direct language things that they had not experienced. Even when they passed along information in which they were confident, they often phrased it in ways that shifted responsibility away from themselves. "It is certain," as Nicholson wrote to Randolph in May 1805, is quite different from "I am certain."[75] Similarly, stating that "the fact does not admit of a doubt" mobilizes a universe of potential doubters, not just the writer, behind the truth of that fact.[76]

Gentlemen spread information that they considered less than certain but did so in ways that guarded their reputations. Some explicitly distanced themselves from its truth: "I give you these reports without vouching for their correctness," one correspondent wrote from Washington.[77] Similarly, a member of the Ohio state legislature shared "a Number of Reports in Circulation Concerning the Expedition of Burr" with Senator Thomas Worthington but left Worthington to "judge of the Truth of them" since he was unwilling to "assert them for facts."[78] A Virginian was only slightly more committal when he passed along a current report "as hearsay, though I believe the hearsay."[79] Deploying such reservations kept information moving, even when the writer "attach[ed] little credit to it," as Governor Claiborne wisely did to reports that Burr had "committed an Act of suicide."[80]

Gentlemen also shifted responsibility for the veracity of their information away from themselves by providing its source. Some simply enclosed an item from a newspaper or copied a passage from a letter that they had received. Others provided a specific source for each piece of news. These sources did not have to be identified by name, though they often were. Describing a source as "a man in whom the utmost confidence can be placed," "a man of distinction," or a "*high authority*" or conveying information as "rumor says" or "report says" signalled the quality of a piece of information as effectively as naming a known individual.[81] For example, when New Jersey senator John Condit related the current news about Burr to his family in January 1807, he described the contents of three letters that had recently arrived in Washington and identified their authors and recipients—including two senators and a representative—as trustworthy. Usually, letters on public affairs mixed direct observation, secondhand information, and rumor, carefully distinguishing between them. The Kentuckian James Taylor's first warnings to the administration about Burr provided some items that he had seen or heard himself, others that he had learned from named sources, others that he attributed simply to "good authority," and others that he related only as "it is said."[82]

When information did not come directly from an eye- or "earwitness," letter writers often established its veracity—and distributed the responsibility for its accuracy—by identifying the chain of sources that had brought it to them.[83] Such chains might be relatively simple, as when Elizabeth Wirt passed along to her husband news that her sister had learned "from *Duval* of Washington—Brother in law to Gibbons of this place."[84] Even within a short chain, the credibility of each link had to be established or asserted; William Wirt would have known that Gabriel Duvall was a federal official and would have had some sense of how accurately his sister-in-law conveyed information. Naming a known individual served this end, but so did describing an unnamed or unknown link in the chain as "a Gentleman of observation and information."[85] Even among gentlemen, however, reports became garbled. Although he had heard his information directly "from a Gentleman of veracity," Nathaniel Saltonstall Jr. admitted that "the Story may have increased by travelling" before reaching his source.[86] Asked by the attorney general to follow his chain of sources to the actual witness to a remark of Burr's friend Jonathan Dayton, Chandler Price could report only that "the Person who told me, says Dayton did not tell him so, & that he only heard it of one who said he understood Dayton should have said so." The whole matter, to Price's dismay, had become "a say so business."[87]

Editors, many of whom were artisans rather than gentlemen, adopted many of the same techniques to establish and protect the credibility of their newspapers. They did not identify sources out of a punctiliousness about proper citation; in fact, they regularly reprinted items without naming the newspaper from which they came. But their original material employed the same methods for signalling the believability of a piece of information that gentlemen used in their correspondence. Some items were reported on the direct authority of the editor or another writer. Others were attributed to correspondents or travellers; these sources often remained unnamed but were referred to in ways that marked the probable truth of their reports—as "respectable" or as "gentlemen." Other reports were described simply as rumors. Early in the Burr crisis, a writer in Richmond's *Enquirer* urged editors to be certain "to distinguish what is *fact* from what is *rumour*" in their reporting.[88] Publishing one rumor, the editor of Pittsburgh's *Commonwealth* remarked that the "news [was] said to have been written by a member of Congress to a merchant in this city"—a chain that, if correct, would usually have fixed the information's credibility. But the editor remained skeptical since "several other embellishments [had] been added as the story rolled."[89]

A culture that prized the regular movement of accurate information would, almost inevitably, foster suspicion of conspiracies, with their

private characters."[99] Even as gentlemen regularly criticized editors, however, they also relied upon them and found ways to use them, and their newspapers, to manipulate a system that readily credited statements from unidentified "gentlem[e]n of unquestionable character."[100]

Even genteel sources were not necessarily treated equally, however. Someone nearer to actual events or to official circles was expected to have more correct and more current information. Being "at a considerable distance from the scene of action," an Ohioan noted, "it is not to be expected that everything which *we heare* is Gospel."[101] Those far removed from "the fountain of information" in Washington sought reliable reports to counteract the tendency of "rumour [to strengthen] as she flies."[102] It was widely accepted, moreover, that more links in the chain of sources made a piece of information less likely to be accurate. A December 1806 letter from Washington to a New York editor explained how the previous day's alarming news—that Burr had set off with "1000 men"—had originated in the president saying "that a party of 20 had marched to join him." "By the time this [comment] had travelled from the President's House to the Capitol," the author remarked, "it had augmented to 1000."[103] Virginia's Littleton Waller Tazewell accepted one "alarming" report about Burr's projects precisely because it had "[come] so direct that one [could] hardly deny credit to it."[104]

If having come from the right place or through a short chain could make one report seem more reliable than another, coming from the wrong political party could make a report seem less trustworthy. Much of the proliferation of newspapers derived from the belief that the opposing party's editors simply lied, both in recounting events and explaining them. But the same partisan calculations shaped assessments of information that arrived through conversations and correspondence. The Republican editor of Pittsburgh's *Commonwealth* did not say so, but he may have doubted a seemingly well-sourced report because the "member of Congress" and the "merchant in this city" who made up the chain of sources were both Federalists. Writing to the president, the attorney general related the contents of a private letter from a gentleman— a merchant and former state legislator—with a warning that it was "from a Federal source & [might] be part of a system of alarm." "What credit is due to it," he suggested, "is equivocal."[105]

Making sense out of conflicting reports also required weighing stories and sources against each other. "By a comparison of reports," one letter writer explained, "we discover the truth or falsehood." Charles Stewart recognized that anything could "be said to be all report." But, when so many reports of so many different kinds "so well quadrate[d]," they should indicate the truth. "False reports," in his experience, were "usually . . . contradictory." Such reasoning regarding the rumors about Burr convinced Stewart of "the actual existence of a deep, well laid, extensive" conspiracy.[106] But the same flood of reports merely left Georgia's Joseph Bryan in a thick "fog." "When I read statements as matter of fact advanced in the paper of today and contradicted and that repeatedly in the papers of tomorrow," Bryan argued, "I have a right to doubt."[107] New reports were also assessed in the context of what has been called "negative intelligence"—the absence of reports from sources that should have provided information. As part of the official channels of communication, government officials were probably most likely to assess new reports on this basis. Both General Wilkinson and Governor Claiborne, for example, initially rejected the correct report that Burr had been arrested by Lieutenant Edmund P. Gaines in mid-February 1807. The news had come through "Several letters from the Town of Mobile," but, since the same mail did not bring official news from Gaines, they "doubt[ed] its truth."[108]

It was not just the character of the source of a report that mattered, however; it was also the character of its subject. In late eighteenth- and early nineteenth-century British America, people typically thought of public events as products not of anonymous social forces or divine intervention, but of personal action. Things happened because individual men, and occasionally women, made them happen. Such thinking, as historians have long recognized, predisposed revolutionary and early republican Americans to see conspiracies. From the suspected conspiracy of the king's ministers and Parliament to deprive them of their rights in the 1760s and 1770s through the Spanish, Genet, and Blount Conspiracies of the 1780s and 1790s, Americans had traced much of their political history in the decades before the Burr crisis to the machinations of small groups of men who wielded or sought power. What modern historians usually refer to as the Burr Conspiracy was typically called Burr's Conspiracy at the time. This tendency to trace large political developments to individual's intents coexisted, moreover, with the assumption that individual's characters were unchanging. Of all the "pre-existing facts," as Duane called them, that had to be considered when assessing new information, none mattered more than the presumably known characters of the public men who were its subject.[109]

Prior knowledge of Burr's character often influenced how contemporaries assessed new reports about his intentions and actions. Beyond a relatively small group of supporters, most Americans already had concerns about Burr's character even before the first hints about a conspiracy. Burr's killing of Alexander Hamilton, his perceived scheming to reverse the voters' will in the election of 1800, and his earlier machinations in New York state politics or even in the Revolutionary army seemed to many, across party lines, to testify to his flawed character. In early December 1806, John Randolph decided that western reports about Burr should be treated as evidence of a "real & serious" danger based upon various "circumstances, *above all from the known character of the man.*"[110] Others similarly applied the test of Burr's character to the crush of conflicting reports, but they did not necessarily agree on which of his attributes best fit the situation. Few denied that Burr was a man of immense ambition and "a bankrupt in fortune & in character."[111] But was he the kind of man who would risk his life on a treasonous scheme, particularly one with little chance of success? New York's Robert R. Livingston thought that Burr, whom he considered "extreamly sanguine & the dupe on every occasion to his own vanity," might.[112] Others were skeptical. "Colo. Burr's character," one westerner remarked, "forbids the idea that he would engage in a scheme [that] if unsuccessful, would cost him his life, or banish him from his Country, without probable grounds of success."[113]

But it was not only Burr's character that had to be taken into account to evaluate conflicting reports. The characters of Burr's accusors seemed equally relevant. Very quickly, General Wilkinson and President Jefferson became the subjects of reports and rumors that raised doubts, in the minds of some, about their charges. As the crisis unfolded, it became increasingly obvious that at least one, and possibly all three, of these gentlemen must be lying. By the time of Burr's trial in Richmond in the spring of 1807, a fairly clear party division had emerged over whose character was the worst. Republicans generally accepted that the ambitious Burr had at least intended, if not actually committed, treason and had lied repeatedly to cover his tracks. Quids openly charged the slippery Wilkinson, whom Randolph called "the most finished scoundrel that ever lived," with backing Burr's treasonous plans and lying to protect his position.[114] And Federalists often believed that the hypocrite Jefferson, whom they considered every bit as ambitious as Burr, had publicly painted innocent activity as treasonous conspiracy to destroy his one-time rival.

Such thinking about the subject, rather than the source, of a piece of information helps to explain why people regularly, if guardedly, credited items without a known source. The *Intelligencer* hinted at this dynamic when it reported, in mid-November 1806, that "rumors, of which the name of Aaron Burr is made the vehicle, actually swarm around us."[115] That these rumors were attached to Burr's name did not make them true. But preexisting doubts about Burr's or Wilkinson's or Jefferson's character ensured that rumors about these men received attention, if not acceptance. To one New York editor, it seemed to be, "in some measure," precisely because of Burr's "well known character for intrigue that so much suspicion [had] recently been entertained and so much noise made concerning the criminal designs imputed to him."[116]

But men and women accepted news that was attributed only to what one author disparaged as "Rumour with her 100 Tongues" when conflicting, often better-sourced, stories were in circulation for other reasons.[117] Rumor and gossip have been the subject of extensive interdisciplinary study by anthropologists, psychologists, sociologists, literary critics, historians, and other scholars. They have found that rumors often win acceptance and gain importance when they resonate with existing concerns and fears. Many of the rumors about Burr squared perfectly with the nation's profoundest anxieties. Concerned that their relatively weak federal system could not long hold together its disparate and often conflicting interests, Americans readily accepted signs of disunionist sentiment and activity, particularly in the West. Taught by ancient and modern history that republics could not survive, Americans quickly credited evidence of ambitious men using the military or the mob to bring themselves to power. Established fears for the union and the republic ensured that the rumors about Burr carried weight; they also helped to generate new rumors about him.[118]

For months, it seemed to many Americans that "all was rumor and guess" regarding the Burr Conspiracy.[119] Each new piece of information might bring the certainty that they so badly desired. "Public expectation stands on tiptoe," Madison's brother-in-law exclaimed in March 1807, "gaping at every rumor afloat thro' the Country."[120] With relevant developments spread across vast distances, it always seemed that better information must be available elsewhere. Kentucky and Ohio waited for answers from the nation's capital or New Orleans; New Orleans looked for news from upriver; Washington anticipated reports from the West. As one western official realized, "alarms are generally increased in proportion to the distance from correct information." During the Burr crisis, though, nearly everyone thought that they were distant from correct information. As such, it should not be surprising "that surmises which [were] only whispered as probable at first[,] soon [became] propagated, as fear or hope [affected] the narrator, into undoubted facts."[121] During the Burr crisis, as in other times of intense anxiety, a communications system that was intended to strengthen the union, to inform the citizenry, and to form the nation instead undermined those ends by inflaming suspicions across lines of region, class, and party.

Knowing how contemporaries learned about Burr's plans and movements and officials' concerns and responses is essential for understanding how they made sense of the Burr Conspiracy; knowing how their letters, dispatches, official messages, and newspaper editorials were written and read is no less essential if we are to make sense of the conspiracy for ourselves. The sense that contemporaries made was necessarily shaped by the information that they received; the sense that we can make is equally shaped by the documents that they have left us. Information reached them through a communications network whose far-flung post offices, extensive mail routes, and dispersed newspapers reached nearly all of the young country's scattered settlements. But, if technologies and institutions structured the network that moved information, settled cultural practices and unsettling political divisions determined exactly what was written and what was left unwritten, how it was stated, and how it was interpreted. The continuing impacts of those cultural and political forces are felt as historians try to interpret and comprehend documents from this period in order to make sense of the past.[122]

FIRST INTERLUDE

A CRISIS IN THE CABINET

In late October 1806, Washington, D.C., was a "scene of bustle."[1] A recent flurry of activity on the part of President Thomas Jefferson, his cabinet members, and their department clerks could hardly have been kept secret in the small community. With Congress and the Supreme Court in recess, the capital's population of around ten thousand was missing many of its most politically attuned members. Nonetheless, residents and visitors recognized that fresh reports about Burr's plans and movements in the trans-Appalachian West had "occasioned considerable alarm."[2] Burr, one Federalist reported, had "publickly announced his project to seperate the Western Territory from the United States" and had James "Wilkinson[,] at the head of the Army, in league with him." This writer was not simply inventing rumors; he (or she) knew that the cabinet had met "for three days."[3] Another late October letter from the capital wrongly stated that "all the marines at Washington [had been] ordered immediately to New-Orleans."[4]

In the days preceding these letters, Jefferson had met with his cabinet heads—Henry Dearborn (War), Albert Gallatin (Treasury), James Madison (State), and Robert Smith (Navy)—three times to respond to evidence of a growing crisis in the West. On 22 October, they reviewed the available information about Burr and decided that he seemed to be engaged in "a scheme of separating the Western from the Atlantic States, and erecting the former into an independent Confederacy." Equally worrisome, Wilkinson, the commander of the army and governor of the Louisiana Territory, was reportedly "engaged with [Burr] in this design." At this meeting, the cabinet agreed, "unanimously," to send "confidential letters" to the governors or district attorneys of most of the western states and territories "to have [Burr] strictly watched" and, if he "committ[ed] any overt act unequivocally," to arrest and try him. It also decided to

43

FIGURE 3. John Graham, the agent whom the cabinet sent after Aaron Burr.

send gunboats up the Mississippi River to Fort Adams, just above the border with Spanish West Florida, "to stop by force any passage of suspicious persons going down [the river] in force."[5] But it left open the question of what to do about Wilkinson.

Two days later, the cabinet met again, turning its attention to dangers approaching New Orleans from the Gulf of Mexico. It decided, again unanimously, to strengthen the naval detachment at New Orleans, both by sending Captains Edward Preble and Stephen Decatur "to take command of the force" there and by reinforcing the port with the brig **Argus** *and eight gunboats from Charleston, Norfolk, and New York. The cabinet also agreed to warn the governors of the Orleans and Mississippi Territories and the commanding army officer at New Orleans "against any surprise of our ports or vessels." And it decided to send John Graham, who was in Washington preparing to return to his post as secretary for the Orleans Territory, "through Kentucky on Burr's trail, with discretionary powers to consult confidentially with the governors, and to arrest Burr if he has made himself liable." The cabinet again "postponed" a decision on Wilkinson, though it agreed to empower Graham to replace Wilkinson as governor of the Louisiana Territory without further orders.[6]*

The next day, at the last of these meetings, the cabinet "rescind[ed]" nearly everything it had agreed to do. Graham's mission remained unchanged. And letters would still go out to the governors of the Orleans and Mississippi Territories and the commanding officer at New Orleans warning them, more vaguely, "to be on their guard." But the letters directing the western governors and district attorneys to watch, arrest, and try Burr were cancelled. And all of the planned naval movements were revoked. The cabinet abandoned most of its initial decisions, according to Jefferson's notes, in response to a new mail "from the westward," in which "not one word [was] heard . . . of any movements by Col. Burr." In the cabinet's thinking, the "total silence of the officers of the Government, of the members of Congress, [and] of the newspapers prove[d]" that, whatever his intentions, Burr had "committ[ed] no overt act against the law."[7]

More than anything else, the crisis in Jefferson's cabinet in late October 1806 was a crisis of information. Jefferson's notes on the meetings reveal little disagreement within the cabinet about the relevant issues or the appropriate responses. What made these discussions difficult was, instead, an inability to answer critical questions with any certainty. The president and his advisors had long had doubts about Burr, "a Catalinarian character," as Jefferson described him, whose "every motion" "had excited suspicions."[8] And, for more than a year, they had worried that Burr and Wilkinson were "too intimate," leading Dearborn to caution the general "to keep [Burr] at arms length."[9] But such broad concerns could provide little basis for decisions and actions. The cabinet needed to answer basic questions: Was Burr trying to separate the western states and territories from the union? Had he met the constitutional definition of treason by levying war against the government? Had he tried to enlist Wilkinson in his project? Had he succeeded? And would Wilkinson use the army to stop Burr? The administration's willingness to revoke at its last meeting most of its decisions of the previous meetings shows clearly that its answers to these questions were shifting and uncertain.

In trying to make sense of the cabinet's thinking at this moment, however, we face a crisis of information of our own. For us, the critical question is, what did Jefferson and his cabinet know about Burr's plans and movements in late October 1806? In other words, what information led them to the decisions, first, to adopt energetic measures against the threat and, then, to rescind those measures? Trying to answer this seemingly simple question reminds us of the impossibility of fully reconstructing even something as well recorded and well preserved as the thinking of the highest federal officials on a matter of national importance. We can—and should—attempt to reassemble what Jefferson and his cabinet knew and when they knew it from their correspondence and their actions; but, ultimately, we will need to acknowledge the limits to our efforts.

In one sense, Jefferson would seem to have answered our questions by identifying the sources and the timing of his information about the Burr Conspiracy in private memoranda, public messages, and personal letters. His notes on the first cabinet meeting listed various sources of information describing activities from western New York through western Pennsylvania to eastern Ohio. Jefferson named four crucial informants: William Eaton, whose disclosures had arrived in a letter from Postmaster General Gideon Granger; John Nicholson, who had written to the president; Nathan Williams, who had written to the secretary of state; and George Morgan, who had corresponded directly with Jefferson and whose information had also been sent to Madison by Presley Neville and Samuel Roberts. Jefferson's notes also referred vaguely to news from "other citizens through other channels," as well as from the press.[10] The notes did not state when this information had arrived in Washington, but Jefferson's important 22 January 1807 message to Congress stated that the earliest "intimations" had reached him "in the latter part of September."[11] Later letters further clarified the sources and timing of Jefferson's information. Writing to Granger in early 1814, Jefferson identified four letters that had led to the October 1806 cabinet meetings. Three of these—the letters of Morgan, Nicholson, and Williams—had arrived in mid-September. The fourth—Granger's account of "the communications of Genl Eaton"—had reached Jefferson just two days before the first meeting.[12] Nearly a decade later, the former president informed Katherine Morgan that it had been a letter from her father-in-law that "first gave us notice of the mad project of that day."[13]

But trying to reconstruct the state of the administration's knowledge in late October 1806 from Jefferson's lists of sources quickly runs into problems. For one thing, some of these letters have disappeared. Granger's account of Eaton's information from Ohio survives, as do the letters to Madison from Williams (in upstate New York) and Neville and Roberts (in western Pennsylvania). But two of the five letters that Jefferson identified as critical, those from Morgan and Nicholson, have disappeared. We can surmise some of what they might have said by using other sources. What Morgan wrote to Jefferson in late August would have been similar to what he told Neville, Roberts, and William Tilghman over the next few weeks. Neville and Roberts's account of their meetings with Morgan reached Madison before the first cabinet meeting; Tilghman's notes from a meeting with Morgan also survive, though they were never sent to the administration. Clues about Morgan's initial warning can also be gleaned from his testimony at Burr's treason trial in Richmond. These sources suggest, as Tilghman put it, that it was Burr's "expression of the sentiment" that "there must, & would[,] be a separation of the Western from the Eastern people" that had "shocked Col. Morgan" into writing Jefferson.[14]

The information in Nicholson's missing early September letter is harder to recover. But, by working with Jefferson's reply and a second Nicholson letter from mid-October, we can deduce some of its contents. Alone, Jefferson's 19 September reply is almost meaningless, lacking both names and details. Instead, even as he left no doubt about the significance of Nicholson's disclosures, Jefferson referred vaguely to "information," "proceedings," "persons," and "measures."[15] Nicholson's 14 October response to this letter, which arrived on the second day of cabinet meetings, provided what are clearly new details about preparations in New York's Mohawk Valley. It also reported that the explanation that this activity was directed toward settling Spanish Florida through a private land company under Burr had "obtained General Credit." But a careful reading of this letter suggests that Nicholson's earlier letter had probably named Burr as the key figure and had certainly identified Comfort Tyler as Burr's local agent. Close attention also reveals that Nicholson had originally warned Jefferson that the preparations were directed at dividing the union. The mid-October letter downplayed this threat in favor of the Florida land scheme. Still, Nicholson's reference to "an attempt at a separation [as] an event [that was] still somewhat to be feared" shows that his initial letter had warned of a separatist plot.[16]

Another obstacle to reconstructing the administration's knowledge from Jefferson's statements about the sources and timing of the cabinet's information is that those statements are misleading, despite a precision that includes not only the names of the authors, but, at times, even the dates on which Jefferson received the letters. The lists of informants are far from complete, and the claims about the timing of the first warnings are off by at least nine months. There is good reason, moreover, to believe that Jefferson's omissions and misstatements on these issues were intentional, not accidental. While Jefferson's notes on the first cabinet meeting identified five letters, it is easy to discover that there were many more. His surviving papers include two anonymous letters, probably by the same author, that he had received in December 1805—nine months before what he later called the "first notice" in Morgan's letter. Those letters linked "Burr's intrigues" to Francisco de Miranda, the Spanish American revolutionary, and Anthony Merry, the British minister in Washington.[17] And they warned that, though "ostensibly directed against a foreign power," "Burrs Manouevres" actually looked to "the distruction of our Government, [Jefferson's] ruin and the material injury of the atlantic states."[18] More important, Jefferson omitted nine letters—full of suspicions and suspects—that he or Madison had received between February and September 1806 from Joseph Hamilton Daveiss, the federal district attorney in Kentucky. Evidence of additional letters that, like those from Morgan and Nicholson, have been lost can be found in the daily lists of incoming and outgoing correspondence that Jefferson kept. Knowing that these missing letters once existed does not help us establish what Jefferson and the cabinet knew in October 1806, of course.[19]

Trying to reconstruct the administration's knowledge using only incoming letters also ignores other sources of information. In his notes on the first cabinet meeting, Jefferson remarked that information about Burr's movements had also come from "the newspapers."[20] During his presidency, Jefferson himself subscribed to nearly three dozen newspapers, not all of which were active in the fall of 1806; the State Department may have taken even more. Even though the president did not subscribe to any newspapers from beyond the Appalachian Mountains, the common practice of clipping and reprinting meant that at least some of the reports on Burr's plans and actions in the western press had appeared in ones that he did receive. But even if we knew exactly which newspapers the president and the cabinet members took, it would still be impossible to know whether and when they received any given issue or whether they read every issue that they received. To expand our focus to newspapers, moreover, is still to limit ourselves to written information. But we know that Jefferson and the department heads also learned about Burr's plans through conversations, almost none of which were recorded. The potential significance of oral communications is clear; one of the few conversations that was documented—between Granger and Eaton—helped to convince Jefferson to call the cabinet meetings.[21]

Even if we could reconstruct all of the information that was available to Jefferson and his cabinet in October 1806—if we could find all of the incoming correspondence, read all of the newspapers, and recover all of the conversations—we still would not know how this mass of material was evaluated. The contents of just the five letters that Jefferson identified as crucial in his notes on the first cabinet meeting do not harmonize easily. Writing on nearly the same day and from towns that were not even twenty miles apart, Williams and Nicholson must have described some of the same things; for example, both apparently named Comfort Tyler as the principal recruiter of "young, active & enterprising men" in the area. But, whereas Nicholson seems to have warned of a separatist project under Burr's direction, Williams believed that the "extraordinary expedition" might be "nothing more than a speculation, or a project for settling some new country," and named four men, including Burr, as its backers.[22] Based on Eaton's disclosures, Granger confidently stated that there was a secessionist plot, led by Burr and supported by Wilkinson, for which boats were already being built at Marietta, Ohio. But Neville and Roberts described something far less certain. In their account of Morgan's revelations, and perhaps in Morgan's letter to Jefferson as well, Burr expected the West to secede from the union and wanted information about the region's military strength. But there was no suggestion that he planned to lead a separatist movement himself or that it would begin anytime soon.

The administration's evaluation of the information that it had—from letters, newspapers, and conversations—was clearly influenced by the absence of information from sources that should have reported significant developments. Apparently, other than Daveiss, none of the federal government's dozens of officials in the West reported anything alarming before the cabinet meetings. Secretary of the Treasury Gallatin received letters from surveyors, land office employees, and customs agents. Secretary of War Dearborn heard from army officers, Indian agents, and purchasing agents. Secretary of the Navy Smith corresponded with naval officers and purchasing agents. And Secretary of State Madison received letters from territorial governors, district attorneys, and federal marshals. Some of the correspondence from these officials has been lost or destroyed over the years; for example, all of the letters from postmasters—the most numerous and widespread federal officials—to the postmaster general were destroyed. But many letters survive, and none suggested that anything was amiss during the late summer and early fall of 1806. "Through the months of September October and November," Dearborn later reported, "a deep silence so far pervaded the Western States that no information was received from any public character."[23]

The administration's outgoing correspondence does little to clarify either what information it had received by October 1806 or which reports had been accepted and which rejected. Comparing the available material with Jefferson's correspondence logs suggests that more of his outgoing letters have survived, largely because he made copies of most of them. Jefferson's replies to Morgan and Nicholson and Madison's response to Williams are available to us. Unfortunately, these letters provide little insight into the administration's understanding of the developing situation. As we have already seen, Jefferson's 19 September letter to Nicholson could not even be linked to the Burr crisis without reading Nicholson's reply. Madison's 3 November response to Williams is equally ambiguous. Only the president's 19 September letter to Morgan even hinted at its actual subject, with a suggestive reference to "parricide propositions." None of these letters identified the individuals, including Burr, who were involved. None of them demonstrated the extent of the administration's knowledge about the preparations. And none of them discussed the nature of the project beyond Jefferson calling it an "enterprise on the public peace."[24]

The letters that were written as a result of the cabinet's decisions also tell us little about how the administration made sense of its incomplete and incoherent information. Moving swiftly on the initial decision to dispatch Preble and Decatur to New Orleans, Secretary Smith wrote two identical letters on 24 October. But those letters merely ordered them to Washington, where they presumably would have received further written or oral instructions. Smith's letters countermanding these orders the next day said even less. Ultimately, the cabinet decided to meet the Burr crisis in late October with three letters—to the governors of the Orleans and Mississippi Territories and to the commanding officer in New Orleans—and a special agent. In fact, the department heads seem to have done even less than that. There is no evidence that Madison sent the agreed-upon warning letters to Governor William C. C. Claiborne and Acting Governor Cowles Mead in late October. Ten days later, he did order Robert Williams, the governor of the Mississippi Territory, to return to his post. Even this letter referred only to recent "accounts . . . from the South Western Quarter of the United States" as grounds for curtailing Williams's leave, a phrase that also encompassed Spanish troop movements on the unsettled frontier.[25] On 8 November, the cabinet would sit again to discuss new orders for Wilkinson. But, in late October, the only actions to result from the cabinet meetings were Dearborn's letter to Colonel Constant Freeman in New Orleans and John Graham's mission in pursuit of Burr.

Dearborn's 27 October 1806 instructions to Freeman served, at best, as a heavily veiled warning and provide little insight into the administration's information about Burr's project or its assessment of that information. The secretary of war cautioned Freeman to beware of "any open or secret measures hostile to" New Orleans. He suggested "pay[ing] some attention to the movements, and the conduct of suspicious characters, either Citizens, foreigners, or strangers." And he directed the colonel to keep "a watchful eye over all Military Stores." But Dearborn provided none of the specific details that the cabinet possessed in late October. He did not name names, even Burr's. He did not suggest that an attack might come from either upriver or downriver. And he did not even hint at the cabinet's suspicions of Wilkinson; in fact, Freeman was directed to "communicate freely" with the general "in case of any alarm."[26] Dearborn's instructions tell us nothing new about what the cabinet had learned and accepted in late October 1806.

Graham's mission is more revealing, despite significant evidentiary problems. We cannot even say exactly when Graham left Washington for the West. Nor do we have the letter, which Graham later mentioned in court, in which Madison asked him to undertake the mission. Graham probably carried with him three official documents—a letter of instructions from Madison, a cipher key, and a brief cover letter. At least one and perhaps two more letters from Madison followed within days of Graham's departure. Unfortunately, only the least important of these documents—the two-paragraph cover letter—survives.[27]

But from this cover letter and from what we can reassemble of the missing cipher key, we can gain some new insights into the administration's knowledge and assessments at the time of the October meetings. The cover letter does not restate Graham's instructions in full, but it does reiterate what we already know from Jefferson's notes on the cabinet meetings. Graham's mission was to investigate "certain projects said to be on foot in the Western Country, adverse to the Unity and peace of the nation." His goal was to "[ascertain] how far these projects are fictitious, or founded in reality." If they were real, he was to determine "what progress [had] been made in them, and to what precise objects they point[ed]."[28] The cover letter mentioned Graham's full instructions but said nothing about the cipher key that accompanied them. It is only from two of Graham's surviving reports to Madison, dated 12 November from Pittsburgh and 28 November from Chillicothe, that we even know of the existence of this cipher.[29]

The very fact that Graham carried, and used, a cipher key provides early evidence that the administration did not trust the mail. Any letter from Graham to Washington would have passed through the hands of numerous postmasters and postriders. A few well-placed agents would have sufficed to intercept all letters addressed to the president or department heads from the Ohio Valley. By providing Graham with a cipher, Madison revealed that the administration already considered it likely that Burr, or any conspirator, would try to control the flow of information from the scenes of action in the West to the administration in Washington. From the administration's perspective, the cipher ensured that Graham could report his discoveries without them being known to Burr or his agents. From our perspective, knowing that Graham carried a cipher key allows us to date to late October a concern about the postal system that we would otherwise place in mid-December, when Jefferson and Granger sent Seth Pease to investigate the western mails.[30]

We can learn even more from the cipher itself, though not nearly as much as if we had the key (at least two copies of which must have disappeared). The cipher that Graham carried was extremely simple. In the early nineteenth century, most State Department codes assigned three- and four-digit numbers to hundreds of words and letter groups. These codes were not impossible to break, particularly since the diplomats who used them frequently mixed sections of clear text with sections of code in their dispatches. But much of the cipher that was given to Graham was even easier to break since it relied on a simple number-for-letter substitution. In Graham's cipher, each letter was assigned a single digit, from one to eight, with a dot, a single line, or a double line below it. The simplicity of this cipher suggests the administration's haste to get Graham on the road; a more complicated code would have taken longer to devise and to copy.[31]

Graham's cipher did not rely entirely upon number-for-letter substitutions, however. It also included as many as ninety two-digit entries that were keyed to individual words. Some of these entries replaced those common words—"of," "he," "that," "from," and "to"—that, due to frequent repetition, can be used to break simple codes. But others referred to names, places, concepts, and institutions that the administration presumably expected Graham to mention in his letters. If we had the key, it would tell us precisely who and what the administration feared in late October 1806. Even without the key, we can uncover some very intriguing clues. A few of the two-digit entries, including "Burr" and "Blennerhassett," are clear from the deciphered version of Graham's first surviving report to Madison.[32] The undeciphered passages in Graham's 28 November letter include another two dozen two-digit entries. By decoding the number-for-letter substitutions and making a few deductions based on context, we can add to the cipher's list of key words: "union" (or "United States"), "West," "separation," "president," "army," "officers," and "French."[33] This list reveals a bit more about the administration's knowledge and concerns during the October cabinet meetings than we can derive from any other source. It suggests that the cabinet's anxieties extended beyond Wilkinson to the "army" and its "officers" more generally. It points to an otherwise unmentioned concern about the role of the "French," though whether in Europe or in New Orleans remains unclear. And it provides the only clear evidence that the administration already knew of the involvement of Harman Blennerhassett, Burr's principal backer on the Ohio River.[34]

The surviving sources—incoming and outgoing correspondence, Jefferson's notes on the cabinet meetings, Graham's cover letter and cipher—allow us to assemble at least a partial picture of what the administration knew when it made its first important decisions about the emerging crisis in the West. By late October, it had clearly identified Burr as the central figure. Jefferson and his cabinet could also have compiled—*might* also have compiled in the missing cipher key—a list of Burr's supporters that would have included four of the six men who were later indicted with him in Richmond: Harman Blennerhassett, Comfort Tyler, Jonathan Dayton, and John Smith.[35] While its sources offered various explanations for Burr's activities, the administration clearly worried most about a separatist plot that would have divided the union at the Appalachians. It had determined that such a plot would target New Orleans. And it wondered if this plot had spread among federal officials in the West, ranging from the lowliest postrider to the commanding general of the army.

CHAPTER 2

LEXINGTON AND FRANKFORT, KENTUCKY

July through December 1806

IN THE EARLY NINETEENTH CENTURY, LEXINGTON AND FRANKFORT were the cultural and political capitals, respectively, of Kentucky. Lexington was the older, larger, and more prosperous. Founded in 1775 during the initial push into Virginia's Kentucky district, it had been named for the opening battle of the Revolutionary War. The first settlers had arrived four years later, built a fort, and plotted a grid of streets and lots along Town Fork, a tributary of the Elkhorn River. Over the next two decades, Lexington had grown rapidly with a mixed population of Virginia and Pennsylvania migrants—white and black, free and slave—and German, Irish, and Scots-Irish immigrants. Some of the Virginians had brought not only their slaves, but also the expectation that economic, political, and social power would accompany slave ownership. Although their power diminished outside central Kentucky, these slaveholding Virginians had become the dominant group in the state's dominant region before Kentucky separated from Virginia and became a state in 1792. By that time, moreover, Lexington had already established itself as a cultural center, with a public library, a newspaper, fencing and dancing instructors, debating societies, and a seminary (which became Transylvania University in 1799).[1]

Lexington's growth continued into the new century. When the Pennsylvanian Josiah Espy toured the region in the summer and fall of 1805, he found Lexington to be "the largest and most wealthy town in Kentucky, or indeed west of the Alleghany mountains."[2] William Leavy later recalled that Lexington included five neighborhoods in this period: a central business district along Main Street; an artisan section

State-House, Frankfort, Kentucky.

FIGURE 4. The Kentucky statehouse, site of Aaron Burr's trials in 1806.

of Germans and free blacks west of the public square; a similar area of Scots-Irish, Irish, and free blacks east of the square; a middling district of homes, churches, and law offices around the university; and the surrounding "Country," including the large estates of the wealthiest families.[3] In the summer of 1807, the English tourist Fortescue Cuming counted "three hundred and sixty-six dwelling houses" for a population of around 3,000, more than a third of whom were enslaved. He also noted the presence of a nearly completed brick courthouse, a bank, a masonic hall, and at least five churches. What most impressed Cuming, however, was the extent and variety of economic activity. He listed over one hundred separate manufacturing establishments, ranging from nailworks and ropewalks to jewelers and cabinetmakers, who, he noted, made furniture "in as handsome a style as in any part of America." Cultural achievements also received special notice. Cuming mentioned the university and library and recorded the existence of numerous day schools and "no fewer than three creditable boarding schools for female education." Lexington's coffeehouse provided "a reading room," with forty-two newspapers from around the country, and a public garden that Cuming reported was "becoming a place of fashionable resort."[4]

What Lexington lacked was established political weight. The economic, social, and cultural center of early Kentucky, it was not the political center. In 1792, the state legislature had placed the state capital twenty-three miles away in Frankfort, a six-year-old town on the Kentucky River. Despite a more economically viable location than the essentially landlocked Lexington, Frankfort had grown slowly before being named the capital and only slightly more rapidly after, reaching just over six hundred people by 1800 and only eleven hundred a decade later. It could boast some wealthy families but could not begin to rival Lexington as a cultural center. Not until 1798—eleven years after John Bradford started Lexington's *Kentucky Gazette* and six years after becoming the capital—did Frankfort have a newspaper that survived more than a few months.[5]

Frankfort's growth was stunted, in part, by lingering doubts about its future. Nearly every year, the legislature debated moving the capital elsewhere, usually to Lexington. The failure of the last effort in 1805 finally produced some stability. When Cuming toured Frankfort two years later, he found that the growing confidence in its future had made "the proprietors . . . spirited in improvement" with the new buildings "on a scale and of materials worthy of a capital." Still, Frankfort remained a seasonal town that came fully to life only during the legislative sessions each fall. It housed the government buildings, including the statehouse, governor's offices, courthouse, jail, and penitentiary. It supported "four publick inns." And it included "several large houses, where people under the necessity of attending the courts . . . [could] be accommodated with private lodgings."[6] But, as late as August 1807, it could boast just ninety homes, according to Cuming's count from the statehouse cupola. And, unlike in Lexington, Cuming recorded no manufacturing activity in Frankfort other than the workshops of the penitentiary.

Lexington and Frankfort were closely connected. For Lexington's wealthy and powerful elite, Frankfort was as common a destination in the fall and winter as Olympian Springs—about thirty-five miles east of Lexington—was in the summer. At the former, they stayed for a few days or a few weeks to transact their most important legal and political business; at the latter, they visited for a few days or a few weeks to form or renew some of their most important social bonds. In both places, they interacted primarily with people who shared ties not only of landed wealth and slave ownership, but also of Republican politics. In the early nineteenth century, few of Kentucky's prominent men opposed the national and state Republican leaders. Kentuckians, as one informed Secretary of State James Madison in May 1805, seemed "almost unanimously in favo[r] of the present administration of the general government."[7] Perhaps more than any other locale, central Kentucky was the place where the Burr crisis was made.

"A GREAT FERMENTATION WAS OBSERVABLE AMONG THE PEOPLE"

Aaron Burr first appeared in central Kentucky in the unlikely form of a life-sized wax model. In early March 1805, a Mr. Davenport brought his travelling exhibition of wax figures to a Lexington tavern. For fifty cents (half-price for children), patrons could see likenesses of prominent American politicians, *"New-York, Baltimore, R. Island, and Friends' Beauties,"* and others. Davenport also displayed tableaux of a beggar receiving alms, the assassination of Jean-Paul Marat, and "the LATE UNFORTUNATE DUEL" between Burr and Alexander Hamilton.[8] One eighteen-year-old visitor noted that "Colo Burr was represented standing on his feet, with his pistol in his hand[,] . . . looking very Stern at Genl Hamilton as he lay before him."[9] This exhibition, an Ohio editor later recalled, "excite[d] the curiousity of the populace to see the original."[10]

Ten weeks later, Burr arrived in person. In late May, he spent a few hours in Frankfort visiting the Republican senator John Brown and a few days in Lexington. Rumors offered various explanations for Burr's western tour: he was going to replace General James Wilkinson as governor of the Louisiana Territory; he was seeking election to Congress from the Orleans Territory or Tennessee; he was organizing a company to build a canal around the falls of the Ohio River at Louisville. But a late May article in Lexington's *Kentucky Gazette* announced that Burr was "merely travelling for amusement and information."[11] Three months later, after stays in Nashville, New Orleans, and Natchez, Burr returned to Lexington and Frankfort for brief visits before proceeding west to St. Louis. During his May and August visits, he captured the attention of the public and the press. Much of this attention was celebratory, as Burr met and dined with some of the towns' leading families. Still, when Burr finally left Lexington in late August, the *Kentucky Gazette* editor Daniel Bradford admitted that some of the interest derived from the indefensible "duplicity" of his politics and his "unrivalled" "talents for intrigue."[12] In early November, a Kentucky Federalist reported to his Virginia brother-in-law that Republicans had paid "a great deal of attention to Col. Burr"; "it is thought there will be attempts made by him to separate this western country from the Union."[13]

The political and social situation in central Kentucky had changed dramatically before Burr returned in mid-September 1806 to make his final plans for descending the Ohio and Mississippi Rivers. The changes stemmed less from Burr himself than from the convergence of two streams of events. One stream had begun as the merest trickle with the arrival of John Wood and Joseph M. Street in the fall of 1805. Wood and Street had walked to central Kentucky from Richmond, Virginia, on their way to survey part of the Louisiana Purchase for a Virginia land company. Wood already had an extensive reputation. Born in Scotland, probably in the mid-1760s, he had lived in England, France, and Switzerland before immigrating to the United States in 1800. In 1801, Wood had written a highly critical *History of the Administration of John Adams* that had allegedly been first commissioned and then suppressed by Burr. In New York, he had also worked as a school-master and a tutor for Burr's daughter, Theodosia. From there, he had moved to Richmond, where he had continued to teach and had written for a Federalist newspaper. In Richmond, he had met and become attached to Street, a clerk who was fifteen to twenty years his junior. Upon reaching Kentucky, Wood and Street first postponed and later abandoned their original plans and sought work. Wood painted portraits in Frankfort and taught at an academy in nearby Versailles; Street worked at the federal court in Frankfort. By the late spring of 1806, Wood and Street were planning to start a newspaper.[14]

The other stream had emerged a little later, but with much greater force. Between early January and late April 1806, Joseph Hamilton Daveiss, the federal district attorney in Kentucky, sent seven letters to President Thomas Jefferson warning of "traitors among us" and divulging a plot for "a separation of the union in favour of Spain." Daveiss, a

Federalist, opened his disclosures by admitting that he was not among Jefferson's "friends" in Kentucky, but he also warned that those friends were at the center of the plot. Even men "high in office" in the West were "deeply tainted with this treason," according to Daveiss. The first letter provided few details and no names, but, with the next letter in early February, Daveiss included "a schedule of the names of suspected persons."[15] The list named many of the leading men of central Kentucky: James Breckinridge, the brother of Jefferson's attorney general; Senator John Adair; Representative John Fowler; federal judge Harry Innes; state judge Benjamin Sebastian; and Lexington attorney Henry Clay. It also included prominent westerners beyond Kentucky—Ohio senator John Smith and territorial governors William Henry Harrison and James Wilkinson. And it named one easterner, Burr. The accompanying letter discussed Burr's recent tour of the West at length. Burr's "jaunting" about the West—his quick visits to so many men in so many places—had confirmed Daveiss's "suspicions . . . of the plot now existing."[16] Daveiss's later letters added some new names and cleared some from the original list. They provided more details of the developing plot, as well as recounting Wilkinson's and Kentucky senator John Brown's roles in the Spanish Conspiracy of the late 1780s and early 1790s. And they reported on Daveiss's efforts to investigate the new plot, including trips to St. Louis, Natchez, and New Orleans.

While Daveiss investigated and wrote letters, Wood and Street developed connections to some key figures in Kentucky and researched past and present state politics. Wood would later claim that he had known, even before leaving Richmond, that Burr planned to develop a military colony in the Southwest from which he could launch an attack on Mexico in case of a war with Spain. But he insisted that he had not suspected Burr of separatist designs until after learning about the Spanish Conspiracy. The sources of Wood's new knowledge remain unclear, though some of it almost certainly came from Daveiss, either directly or through his brother-in-law, and Wood's landlord, George Brooke. In the late spring of 1806, Wood and Street contracted with William Hunter, the editor of Frankfort's *Palladium*, to have their newspaper printed on his press. They began circulating a prospectus for "an *Independent* News-Paper" that "disclaim[ed] all party principles." Such a statement by a newspaper in a solidly Republican state would surely have raised concerns. Even more worrisome would have been the editors' pledge to "rigidly pursue the path of truth, regardless of the anathemas of political maniacs, or the exhorted denunciations of the servile followers of faction."[17]

On 7 July, the first issue of Wood and Street's *Western World* appeared. It was dominated by a long piece of Wood's titled "The Kentucky Spanish Association, Blount's Conspiracy, and Gen. Miranda's Expedition"—the first of what promised to be an extended series. Wood and Street justified the attention to the events of twenty years earlier on two grounds. First, they claimed that many men who still exercised political power in the state and the nation had cooperated in a treasonable effort to divide the union and place the trans-Appalachian West under Spanish authority. They named some of the same men whom Daveiss had listed for Jefferson: Wilkinson, Brown, Innes, and Sebastian. Second, they asserted that these men had not abandoned their separatist designs in the 1790s, but held them still. Even after Kentucky's admission as a state, Wood and Street charged, these leading Kentuckians had joined the plots of the French minister Edmond Charles Genet in 1793, Tennessee senator William Blount in 1796, and the Spanish American revolutionary Francisco de Miranda earlier in 1806. The editors warned, moreover, that the same men had developed a new disunionist plan that, "if ever brought to maturity, [would] affect the interest, not only of the western continent, but of the known world."[18]

The *Western World* quickly became a sensation in central Kentucky and beyond. Within days, Bradford reprinted the first "Kentucky Spanish Association" essay in his Lexington newspaper, accompanied by editorial remarks warning his readers to treat it skeptically and by four brief attacks on Wood in the form of "communications" to the newspaper.[19] Before the second issue of the *Western World* came off his press, Hunter ran an editorial in his *Palladium* disclaiming "responsibility for any thing which may appear in that paper."[20] A week later, though, he met the demands of his subscribers by beginning to reprint the "Kentucky Spanish Association" series in his newspaper. By late July, at least three of Kentucky's six or seven newspapers were regularly printing Wood's essays. By late August, some eastern newspapers—most importantly Philadelphia's *Aurora General Advertiser*, Washington's

National Intelligencer, and Richmond's *Enquirer*—had also begun to carry the essays on occasion.[21]

The *Western World*'s revelations about the Spanish Conspiracy operated in Kentucky just as the scattered reports about the Burr Conspiracy would soon operate across the country. Like a tree limb swept across a still pond, they produced not a single disturbance, but a complex pattern of larger and smaller eddies as each leaf, twig, and branch broke the surface of the water. Some of the smaller ripples quickly disappeared; others merged with their larger and longer-lasting neighbors. The disruptions began almost immediately. The first issue of the *Western World* "had not been two hours in circulation," its editors announced the following week, before "a great fermentation was observable among the people."[22] And the disturbances continued to trouble the waters of Kentucky politics and society for a century. As with the Burr Conspiracy, the evidence of these disturbances appeared in private conversations and personal letters, in newspapers and pamphlets, in private homes and public spaces, and in histories and biographies.

The men who were named in the "Kentucky Spanish Association" essays employed various means to refute Wood and Street's charges and restore their reputations. In part, they relied upon conversations and letters to undo the damage. While the evidence is necessarily limited, there must have been dozens of conversations in central Kentucky during the summer and fall of 1806 in which John Brown, Harry Innes, John Breckinridge, Benjamin Sebastian, and others reassured family and friends, colleagues and allies, and perhaps coffeehouse patrons and courthouse attendees about their actions. Some of these men enlisted Kentucky's congressmen to defend them to national leaders when they returned to Washington. In early 1807, Innes received letters from at least four of Kentucky's congressmen reporting their efforts to protect his reputation. Buckner Thruston, for example, announced his success at "ward[ing] off from you as far as was in my Power every Imputation which Ignorance Malice or Envy has at any Time been disposed in my Hearing to throw upon you."[23] Others simply wrote their own letters to key men in Washington. Only three issues of the *Western World* had appeared before John Brown sent a long letter to Jefferson. Rather than providing a full refutation of the accusations, Brown simply remarked that he "owe[d] it to [him]self" and to the president "to say that the charges exhibited [were] false & without foundation."[24]

The accused also needed to adopt more public forms of rebuttal and defense. The pages of Lexington's and Frankfort's three newspapers quickly filled with refutations (or elaborations) of the Spanish Conspiracy allegations and condemnations (or approbations) of Wood and Street. Each week, from early July to early November, the *Western World* published another "Kentucky Spanish Association" essay. Each week, the *Kentucky Gazette* and *Palladium* printed editorials, signed letters, and pseudonymous essays attacking Wood and Street and defending the men whom they had accused of disunionism. A dizzying parade of charges and countercharges appeared as numerous individuals contributed dozens of pieces during these months. Some wrote repeatedly and at great length. The *Western World* ran nineteen numbers of the "Kentucky Spanish Association," most of which were written by Wood. Between mid-September and late November, John Coburn published six defensive essays as "Franklin" in the *Kentucky Gazette*, in addition to pieces in his own name; most were republished in the *Palladium*. Writing as "An Observer," "Coriolanus," and other pseudonyms, as well as over his own name, Humphrey Marshall expanded and defended Wood and Street's charges in the *Western World* and *Palladium*. By late September, the editor of the *Palladium* admitted that it was "impossible to find room for all" of the submissions and urged his contributors "to attempt more conciseness."[25]

Even as the accused and their supporters filled the pages of newspapers, they also prepared longer pamphlets to bolster their defense with a combination of explanatory text and exculpatory evidence. A report from St. Louis from early August stated that Wilkinson had been "for some time past busily engaged in preparing for publication a work intended to lash, refute, and expose" Wood and Street's allegations.[26] Wilkinson's departure from St. Louis the same month curtailed this work. In Frankfort, Republican lawyer William Littell worked feverishly on a defense pamphlet. In early August, the *Palladium* was already promising that Littell had "a complete political history" of Kentucky that was nearly ready for the press—something that he must have begun before Wood and Street's attacks.[27] By the time it appeared in print as *Political Transactions In and Concerning Kentucky*, that material had been reworked to meet the "malice and revenge" of the *Western World*.[28] The book defended not Littell, who had moved to the state in 1801, but the men who provided him with information and evidence. John Brown, Harry Innes, Innes's cousin Thomas Todd, and appeals court judge Caleb Wallace spent weeks "collect[ing] Documents, facts[,] Dates &c." for a pamphlet that, as Brown wrote, "we design to have prepared & published before the adjournment of the Legislature." They provided this "*collection*" to Littell, who wrote a narrative introduction, and paid Hunter to print it.[29] Just days after Littell's *Political Transactions* appeared in late November, Innes sent a copy to Jefferson, hoping that it would produce "favorable conclusions toward the accused."[30]

Very quickly, Wood and Street announced their response to the attempted rebuttals. In their second issue, they suggested that, if their accusations were false, those whom they had implicated should sue them for libel. That was the normal course, Street argued, for an "upright and virtuous man, when charged with actions of a base description."[31] By late August, amid ceaseless attacks, Street demanded of those "denounced or to be denounced": "if you intend to sue us for slander, do it." If forced, the editors would "plead justification" and produce their evidence in court, but, Street insisted, "we will go into no paper war about it, with William Littell & William Hunter . . . or any of your hirelings."[32] Some of the accused considered applying "the antidote of the Law" at the July court session.[33] But not until the next court session in October did any of them seek indictments; by that time, the damage had been done.

While specific charges, countercharges, and rebuttals about the Spanish Conspiracy cannot be detailed here, the charged climate that they created had a crucial impact on Burr's reception when he returned to central Kentucky in September. Most important, they intensified party politics by reviving a Federalist minority that had been relatively dormant and threatening a Republican leadership that had seemed unshakably dominant. Almost all of the men, living and dead, who were named by Wood and Street as conspirators were Republicans. Kentucky Republicans quickly concluded that, despite the editors' protestations of political neutrality, the *Western World* was a Federalist newspaper. There were "various conjectures as to the Object of the Editors," one

Lexington Republican remarked in October. But the most widely held was that eastern Federalists had "engaged [Wood and Street] to come here, for the express purpose of sowing discord, lessening our unanimity, and ultimately producing a change in our Political Opinions."[34] Such fears reveal the perceived shallowness of party loyalty in Kentucky, and in the West more broadly. If the public came to distrust locally prominent Republicans, if Kentucky's leading Republicans divided among themselves, its leading Federalists might win the public's trust and gain political preeminence, despite their current weakness. Within weeks of the first revelations, a Virginia Republican in Kentucky could report that "federalism [was] already rearing itself, amid the divisions and controversies of the republicans."[35]

If Federalists were behind the *Western World*, then the prime movers, Kentucky Republicans believed, had to be from the extensive Marshall clan. Wood and Street had come from Richmond, the home of Chief Justice John Marshall, perhaps the most powerful Federalist in the country. Marshall's numerous family connections in Kentucky could have provided the local information that Wood and Street clearly needed. Many of Kentucky's leading Federalists were related to the chief justice by blood or marriage (or both). All six of his brothers lived in Kentucky, though only Louis, a doctor, and Alexander, a lawyer, were openly linked to the *Western World*. More important were three of his brothers-in-law: Joseph Hamilton Daveiss, the district attorney; George Brooke, a lawyer; and Humphrey Marshall, a former United States senator and Kentucky legislator (who was also his cousin). To outsiders, the Marshall family seemed very tightly connected: "if you offend one," Innes noted, "it is like touching a Hornets nest, you raise them all in battle array against you."[36] Various Marshalls had collided with various Kentucky Republicans for two decades before Wood and Street began their accusations. These collisions had been political and personal, playing out everywhere, from polling places to dueling grounds. While many Kentucky Republicans saw Wood and Street as pawns in a Federalist political gambit, John Brown viewed them as agents for little more than "the malevolence of that Vindictive family."[37]

Republican charges of Federalist control over Wood and Street filled the columns of the *Kentucky Gazette* and *Palladium*. In late July, Hunter suggested that the men were "the tools of a *Federal Faction* [and] the instruments of private spleen and personal malice."[38] Writing as "Independence," Innes's son-in-law Thomas Bodley urged Wood and Street to explain their reasons for investigating the Spanish Conspiracy and to identify their sources. Doing so, he insisted, would reveal that they were guided by "a connection of men, who [had] become unpopular on account of their political principles and treacherous conduct" and whose actual goal was "to divide the republican interest in the Western country, and thereby favour a return of the reign of terror"—Republican shorthand for the era of Federalist control in the late 1790s.[39] Littell's first essay for the *Palladium* in mid-August portrayed the *Western World* as the product of a long-standing "negociation between several of the federalists of this state, and some of the leading [Federalists] in Virginia to establish a federal press among us."[40]

Both the editors of the *Western World* and the men who were accused of using them denied that there was any Federalist influence over the paper. Daveiss assured the secretary of state that, though suspected as "a mover of this paper," he had "no hand whatever in it, nor is any of [its] information drawn from me."[41] Humphrey Marshall defended himself in the *Palladium*. Still, Marshall, Daveiss, and other Federalists made little effort to hide their pleasure at the discomfort that the *Western World* caused their political opponents. In February 1807, after the newspaper's revelations had produced sweeping changes in the state courts and state politics, Samuel G. Hopkins rejoiced that "Kentucky federalists hold up their heads in triumph."[42]

The disturbances caused by the revelations about the Spanish Conspiracy reshaped not only the political, but also the social landscape of central Kentucky before Burr's return. In late 1805, when Wood and Street had arrived in Frankfort, a writer in the *Palladium* recalled, "there was no 'schism' in our society." Instead, the people had been "remarkable . . . for the friendly intercourse subsisting between themselves."[43] Inflamed party feeling strained the harmonious relationships among central Kentucky's leading men and genteel families. At the center of the social disruptions stood Wood and Street. Their presence very quickly pushed something that had begun as a newspaper war into Lexington's and, especially, Frankfort's private and public spaces.

Soon after publishing the first issue of the *Western World*, Wood and Street began to face the same problems that confronted many combative newspaper editors in the early American republic—problems that were rooted in the gap between their social status and that of the men whom they criticized and, most importantly, embarrassed. Wood and Street were better educated and more polished than many artisanal newspaper editors, but they lacked the financial resources and social standing of the accused, whom they and their supporters sarcastically called "*the great.*"[44] Republicans saw the same division, without the sarcastic bite, with one describing the conflict as between "our great men" and "two despicable printers." On one side, he explained, were "some of the fairest and most popular characters in Kentucky"; on the other was the notorious Wood with his "abandoned character, his profligate apostacy, [and] his total destitution of integrity."[45] Some commentators admitted that the respectable characters of the accused and the questionable characters of the accusers did not *necessarily* settle the truth or falsehood of the accusations. But this gap made it very difficult for Wood and Street to convince doubters when the evidence was contradictory and inconclusive. They tried to keep attention focused upon the political—the public acts, past and present, of the alleged conspirators—but their opponents worked to redirect it to the social—the status and reputations of the two sides.

Wood and Street launched their assault on Kentucky's leading Republicans in the face of a widely shared belief that, as one Tennesseean remarked, "an attack upon the well earned reputation of an honest politician, is one of the greatest crimes against Society."[46] The accused and their supporters used this belief to their advantage. Even as they employed argument and evidence to reassure the public that their reputations were "well earned," they also charged Wood and Street with various "crimes against Society" to destroy their standing. They labelled the two editors liars, slanderers, and apostates. A brief history of Wood that appeared in the *Palladium* in late August claimed that he had been first "a political pimp and spy" for the British during the French Revolution, then a prison informant in a Paris dungeon who "furnished fresh victims for the bloody *Guillotine*," then a plagiarist in Switzerland, then a retailer "of slander and detraction" for New York and Philadelphia newspapers, and finally an "intimate" of the hated Richmond editor James Callender.[47] As if this catalog of sins was not enough, Wood and Street's opponents also placed them on the wrong side of the most important social cleavage in Kentucky society, race. In one issue of the *Palladium*, four different pieces used race to exclude the men from polite society. Littell, for example, noted that Street had briefly left Frankfort "on a horse borrowed from a negro"—suggesting that he was too poor to have a horse of his own and too despicable to have white friends who would lend him one.[48] "Candidus" simply remarked that Wood and Street only had support among "their *negro* associates."[49]

The social gap between accusers and accused had existed, of course, before Wood and Street began making their accusations. Initially, the two had been well received by many of the region's leading families. Street later doubted that a stranger had ever "[met] with more general attention." Respectable families, one Republican acknowledged, had "cheerfully admitted him to their public assemblies, and invited him to their private parties."[50] Shortly after Wood and Street began their attacks, however, they found themselves almost wholly excluded from polite society. "Those who communicate with [Wood and Street]," a writer in the *Kentucky Gazette* insisted, "only do so at midnight."[51] Respectable Republicans closed their homes to the men. By mid-August, "A Citizen of Frankfort" could claim "that there [was] but one white family which either [Wood or Street] visit, or would be admitted in as visitors."[52]

The leading Republican families also excluded Wood and Street from the public spaces that they could control. In August, one writer remarked that there was not "a set of managers in [Frankfort] who would not immediately lead [Wood and Street] out of a Ball or Assembly room."[53] As Frankfort's fall social and political season began, this assertion was tested. In early November, Street was barred from a public ballroom at what he claimed was the insistence of the "great men." He quickly satirized this incident in a poem: "A Congratulatory Epistle to the Dupes of Innes, Todd and Brown—and an Appeal to a Court of Ladies."[54] The next issue of the *Palladium* included a satirical response under the heading "Law Intelligence" that purported to describe Street's suit against "the Managers of the Frankfort Dancing Assembly" in the "Court of Ladies." Street's counsel, "Miss Hezulphoni Slammerkin," had defended him with "great vehemence." But it was "Miss Narcissa Fenton," the opposing counsel and "advocate of propriety and decency," who won the case. In its ruling, the court admitted "that a difference in political opinion [was] no legitimate cause for exclusion." But it also insisted that "this [was] no *political* question. It [was] a question of delicacy, of decency, and morality."[55] In early December, Street was forcibly removed from another ball; on Christmas Day, he was driven out of Weisiger's tavern.

The social conflict spilled from private homes and public ballrooms into Frankfort's streets, where the weapons were far more dangerous than closed doors and satirical articles. The accused seemed committed to preventing further attacks "by any means," one Virginian noted in August, "even by the pistol and stiletto."[56] The perceived gulf between the editors and the accused shaped these clashes. If Wood and Street were not gentlemen, as the established gentlemen of Lexington and Frankfort insisted, they could not be met as equals in an affair of honor by a John Brown or a Harry Innes. These men, as Wilkinson put it, considered themselves "too high to Notice such poisonous reptiles."[57] As a result, most of the physical clashes were between less-established Republicans and Street—Wood reportedly having stated early on that Street "does all the fighting, I only do the writing"—and were over issues that were somewhat removed from the Spanish Conspiracy allegations.[58]

Only the first near-duel grew out of the substantive issues. On the day that the second issue of the *Western World* was to appear, John Brown's brother, Preston, and other Republicans stopped Street in the capital building and demanded that he publish a partial retraction of the initial allegations. Street refused. Brown and others followed Street to the *Western World*'s offices and continued the argument there. Finally, Brown warned Street that if he "continue[d] to traduce characters by publishing falsehoods [he would] get a broken nose or a lashing." Making clear his sense of the social distance between them, Brown told Street that he would not "dirty his hands with him, but would make a *Negro* lash him."[59] Later that day, Street challenged Brown to a duel. Brown rejected Street for various reasons, most of which turned on the men's relative status. As his second, the visiting editor James M. Bradford, publicly explained, Brown was "a man of established character," whereas Street was new to Kentucky and still had "a character to establish."[60]

With Brown's reasons for rejecting Street's challenge aired in the *Palladium*, it became unlikely that anyone of "established character" would duel the editor. But men who were trying to establish one might. A week after Street's encounter with Preston Brown, George Adams, a young lawyer, asked Street to remove his name from the *Western World*'s subscription list. Street did so but told Thomas Bodley that Adams had explained "that he was dependent on *the great*." Bodley reported this comment to Adams, who went into the streets looking for the editor. When Street confirmed Bodley's account, Adams struck at him with his cane. Street warded off the blow and drew a dagger. Bodley tried to interpose himself between the men but quickly stepped aside when Adams pulled a pistol. Adams fired. The ball passed through Street's clothes and grazed his chest. Street leapt forward with his dagger, and Adams, according to Street's account, threw down his pistol, "turned and run."[61] A public caning was an accepted way for a gentleman to avenge an insult from an inferior; pulling a pistol and taking a shot in the streets was not. Both men were arrested, quickly tried, and freed (Street on self-defense, Adams on a technical error). The men took their dispute to the press, where each tried to blame the embarrassing incident upon the other. Adams, especially, needed the publicity to recover the character that he had sought to establish by dropping the *Western World* and later caning Street. Defending his actions, Adams insisted that, if Bodley had not interposed, he "would have given [Street] a decent caning, and there it would have ended."[62] Instead, he had departed from the proper course for a gentleman by pulling his pistol and had ended up on trial.

Other young men confronted Street even after the Brown and Adams affairs. A number of young Republicans seem to have seen an opportunity to win notice in the politically charged conditions. By going public for the accused and against the accusers, even behind a newspaper pseudonym, they might earn the friendship and patronage of some of the state's most powerful men. But the transparency of such thinking made them easy targets for Street's vituperative editorials and satiric poems. Describing them as "subservient tools" or "the cats-paw of a particular family," Street denied them the independence that underpinned any gentleman's reputation.[63] Some men attempted to undo the damage by challenging the outcast editor to a duel but, by initiating an affair of honor with someone who was not a gentleman, they further undermined their claims to gentlemanly status. Street might have viewed these challenges as validating his status, but, with little interest in fighting, he instead treated his challengers dismissively in print. For a number of young Republicans, what began as a bid for public recognition threatened to become a public humiliation.

Weeks before Burr returned to Lexington and Frankfort in mid-September 1806, John Brown could already write to Jefferson that "the peace & tranquility of this State has lately been greatly disturbed by the establishment of a News paper . . . stiled *The Western World*."[64] The revelations in the "Kentucky Spanish Association" essays sparked conflicts of different types and intensities. Some took place primarily on the pages of the *Palladium*, *Kentucky Gazette*, and *Western World*, filling them with editorials, essays, letters, and other items. Others took place in the private homes and public spaces of Lexington and Frankfort. Together, they invigorated the previously quiescent political division between central Kentucky's Republican majority and its Federalist minority. They also generated unwelcome and unaccustomed social friction along party lines. Frankfort Federalist Samuel G. Hopkins found that, by "exert[ing] every nerve" to continue the revelations, he had drawn upon himself "the vengeance of the whole host of conspirators, with whom [he] had before been on terms of intimacy and friendship." Months after Burr's departure, Hopkins could report that Kentucky had remained "in a continual foment" since the *Western World*'s first appearance.[65]

"HAILED AND HUZZAED . . . , CARESSED AND FEASTED"

Before mid-September, Burr played only a minor role in the drama that unfolded in Lexington and Frankfort in response to Wood and Street's accusations. He had been named in a couple of Daveiss's letters to Jefferson; but they were not publicly known. The first three "Kentucky Spanish Association" essays did not mention him at all, though another item in the *Western World*'s second issue claimed extensive knowledge of Burr's plans that would "be detailed in the concluding part of our narrative."[66] In the fourth essay, Burr's name appeared in a list of prominent men who were involved in an ongoing conspiracy with

Wilkinson. The next issue reprinted an item from an Ohio newspaper that called Wilkinson and Burr "the two men most to be dreaded in the union" and used the much-reprinted "Queries" about Burr that had appeared a year earlier in Philadelphia to suggest their plans.[67] But after those few mentions, Burr's name largely disappeared from the *Western World*. Wood kept the "Kentucky Spanish Association" essays focused upon the old Spanish Conspiracy; Street devoted much of the rest of each issue to his current conflicts—political and personal—with Kentucky's Republicans.

Burr apparently first learned of the *Western World* and the "Kentucky Spanish Association" essays in Philadelphia in late July, just a few days before he left for the West. The English architect Benjamin Henry Latrobe later recalled that he had seen Burr's name in the *Aurora* in an essay "from the *Western papers*" and shown the newspaper to Burr. Burr, Latrobe remembered, had read it carefully, suggesting that he had not seen it before. He had explained "that the family of the *Marshalls* [wanted] to ruin and torment their political and personal enemies" and predicted that the series "would run into great length, and occasion great uneasiness to the Westward."[68]

"Great uneasiness," indeed, awaited Burr when he reached Frankfort on 11 September. Two months of political and social upheaval over the *Western World* made Burr's reception in central Kentucky very different from what he experienced in most places. In general, Burr was most likely to find support among those men who were least attached to the Jefferson administration. In some places, such as Philadelphia and Richmond in the East and Pittsburgh and Natchez in the West, his defenders were primarily Federalists. Elsewhere, they were Republicans who opposed the Jeffersonian wing of the party, as in New York, or the local representatives of the administration, as in New Orleans. Only in some Ohio Valley towns—Nashville, Cincinnati, Louisville, and, especially, Lexington and Frankfort—was Burr well-received by those with the closest ties to the president. Burr had known some of central Kentucky's leading Republicans before his first visit, particularly his former Senate colleagues John Brown and John Adair. Others, including Judges Innes and Sebastian, had long associations with Wilkinson. But what helped Burr in Lexington and Frankfort even more than his old friends were his new enemies—John Wood and Joseph Street.

The polarization of central Kentucky politics and society that had arisen from the "Kentucky Spanish Association" essays benefitted Burr. In the two months before his return, the region's most influential Republicans had banded together to refute Wood and Street's charges, destroy their reputations, and carry the offensive to Kentucky's leading Federalists. Although Burr had not received much attention from Wood and Street, they had clearly linked him to the accused. They stepped up their attacks when Burr returned in mid-September. The *Western World* reported the arrival of "this extraordinary character" in Frankfort and referred to that day's essay on the Spanish Conspiracy for "a key to unravel the views of his mysterious journey." But Wood and Street still refrained from publishing their knowledge of Burr's current plans, stating only that it would appear at the end of the essay series "about two months hence."[69] To many Republicans, Burr seemed to be one more victim of the unjust persecution of Wood and Street, and of the Federalists who wielded them.

Burr stayed busy during the three months between his return to central Kentucky in mid-September and his final departure for the Southwest in mid-December—"dashing about from place to place in this country as if he had matters of great moment on hand," according to one Kentuckian.[70] While he also visited Nashville, Cincinnati, and Louisville, he primarily stayed in Lexington and Frankfort. What he was doing in those places is not always clear. After arriving in Frankfort, he spent an evening and most of the next day "in secret consultation" with John Brown, as reported by the *Western World*.[71] He then rode to Lexington, where he remained for a week or so at Wilson's tavern. We know little about whom he saw and what he did there. But it was during this visit that Burr purchased half of Charles Lynch's interest, about 350,000 acres, in the immense Bastrop grant on the Ouachita River in the Orleans Territory. Lynch's title to this land was tenuous at best. The Baron de Bastrop had never fulfilled the conditions of the 1797 grant, and the Spanish king had never formalized it. Over time, the unsurveyed lands had been used as collateral for Bastrop's debts, with the result that pieces of it were claimed by a handful of

American land speculators. Still, for $5,000 in cash and the assumption of a $30,000 debt that Lynch owed to the New Orleans attorney Edward Livingston, Burr acquired the shadow of a claim to a vast tract near the undefined southwestern border.[72]

After a couple of weeks on the road and in Nashville, Burr returned to Lexington by the second week of October. For about six weeks, he lodged at the home of merchant, postmaster, and naval contractor John Jordan. Early in this stay, he was joined by the Alstons—his daughter, son-in-law, and grandson—and Harman Blennerhassett. The Alstons remained only a short time; Blennerhassett stayed until late October. Burr also entertained Robert Wescott, who had recently married Burr's niece, the daughter of the secretary of the Louisiana Territory. As one Kentuckian put it, "colonel Burr and his friends, as also many of our most influential characters here, [were] for whole days together shut up in close rooms." None "but those of their own party" seemed to know what they discussed.[73] Burr spent some of his time in Lexington writing to westerners whom he believed would support his plans, including the Pittsburgh merchant William Wilkins, Ohio militia general Edward Tupper, Tennessee militia general Andrew Jackson, and Indiana territorial governor William Henry Harrison. And Burr also actively raised money, receiving advances from various local merchants and a loan from the Kentucky Insurance Company by promising funds from New York or providing sureties from Blennerhassett. "Public curiosity is still on tiptoe relating to the object of Colonel Burr's visits to the Western country," the *Kentucky Gazette* admitted in late October, but Bradford considered it likely that Burr's plans were "not unfavourable to the interests of the union."[74]

Shortly after Burr's return to Lexington, Humphrey Marshall renewed the assault upon him in the *Western World*. Writing as "An Observer," Marshall focused his 18 October contribution on a series of essays, signed "Querist," that Blennerhassett had written for the *Ohio Gazette*. "An Observer" presented the old "idea of the *Spanish associates*," the disunionist sentiments of the "Querist," and the "secret and mysterious movements" of Burr as elements of a single package. Marshall admitted that Burr's exact plans—whether attacking "the Spanish mines of Santa Fee, . . . the city of New Orleans, or the Spanish territory on the Gulf of Mexico"—remained unclear. But it appeared likely, given the sentiments of the "Querist," that he hoped "to effect a *disunion of the states*, and a dismemberment of the American republic." In Marshall's thinking, this plan revived the Spanish Conspiracy on "a more extensive scale, and with a more imposing aspect." "An Observer" warned, moreover, that the recent efforts to expose the old conspiracy had made the success of the new one more likely. "To suppress the inquiry [and] destroy the reputation[s]" of their accusers, the accused had organized together, mobilized the press on their behalf, and "prostituted" various writers "to misrepresent the truth, and to impose falsehood on the public mind." As a result, "public opinion" had been "divided," and popular attention had been "diverted from the real object of the inquiry." By sowing confusion, Marshall insisted, the accused had prepared the people "for conspiracy, insurrection and disunion." He hoped "to awaken the people to a sense of their danger" in order to defeat the conspiracy and save the union.[75]

Between late September and early November, anti-Burr pieces appeared regularly in the *Western World*. Street occasionally attacked Burr in editorials, poems, and other pieces. Marshall contributed another essay as "One of the People" that also linked current events—"the operations of col. Burr"—to the Spanish Conspiracy. It similarly urged the people to "combat in every shape . . . the idea of disunion."[76] The *Western World* also reprinted anti-Burr material from elsewhere. One item from New Hampshire's *Farmer's Cabinet*, while not wholly endorsing the *Western World*'s charges about a disunionist plot, conceded that Burr was "well qualified to raise a storm and direct it to his purposes."[77] And in early November, the *Western World* began printing Thomas Spotswood Hinde's "Fredonian" essays from the *Scioto Gazette*, which both attacked the "Querist" and reported Burr's recent meetings, travels, and expenditures.

What was missing from the *Western World*'s assault on Burr, however, was material from John Wood. Hinde later recalled that, "in September," he and his friends had urged Wood to fulfill the newspaper's earlier promise to expose "the plan of Burr and his associates," but "Wood [had] remained Silent."[78] By then, Wood wanted to distance himself from the *Western World*. This process culminated in mid-January 1807, when Wood began a new newspaper, the *Atlantic World*, in Washington, D.C., to defend Burr. Hinde's explanation for this reversal was simple—Wood had "received a *douceur* [a bribe] in Burr's notes."[79] Wood's explanation was quite different. He dated the split between himself and Street to mid-July, long before Burr returned to Kentucky. The second issue of the *Western World* was "no sooner published," he later explained, "than I perceived that my real object would be entirely defeated by the ascendancy which I saw Daveiss and H. Marshall were gaining over Street."[80] Wood's "real object" with the newspaper had been to cement his personal relationship with Street, not to expose past or present conspiracies. He had hoped, as he told Henry Clay in October, "that the arduousness of the undertaking . . . would be the means of binding us closer together." But Daveiss and Marshall had worked against his efforts for their own ends; the "indissoluble union" that Wood sought had been broken. In early October, threatened with libel suits, Wood decided to act, informing Clay on 9 October that he wanted to put "a total stop . . . to the further developement of the Spanish Association, if not to the paper."[81] Wood apparently informed Street of this decision in the next few days. While the *Western World* and the "Kentucky Spanish Association" essays continued, Wood said nothing about current events in his essays.

As Wood worked to distance himself from the attacks, Daveiss decided to expand them to a new arena. In late October, he went to Louisville to investigate Burr's progress and found a bustle of activity. "Boats were building, beef-cattle [were being] bought up, . . . [and] a large quantity of pork and flour [was] in demand," he informed Madison. Efforts were being made "to engage men for six months." And "Burr's accomplices [were] very busy in disseminating the idea of disunion." Daveiss's informants confirmed "that Mexico was the first object, the Mississippi the second, and the Ohio the completion of the scheme." When he returned to Frankfort in early November for the court session, Daveiss heard rumors that the administration was either "in the secret" or behind Burr's activities.[82] To thwart or, at least, expose Burr's plans, Daveiss moved on 5 November that Burr be arrested and examined on the charge of preparing a military expedition against a friendly nation in Judge Innes's federal court in Frankfort. After four days of debating the complicated legal questions with Daveiss in a series of letters, Innes denied the motion and directed Daveiss to proceed in the usual manner: by producing enough evidence for an arrest warrant or requesting a grand jury investigation. As Innes finished reading his opinion, Burr entered the courtroom with his lawyers, Henry Clay and John Allen, and demanded a full investigation. The *Palladium* reported that Burr's appearance produced "evident chagrin" among "his enemies" and brought "the utmost satisfaction" "to the impartial, that is to nine-tenths in the house." A grand jury was appointed to begin hearings on 12 November. That day, Frankfort "was crouded with persons from all quarters, beyond any former example." With the jurors assembled and Innes prepared to deliver the charge, Daveiss requested a dismissal due to the absence of a key witness, Davis Floyd, one of Burr's agents in Louisville. "The ridicule and laughter which followed was universal," the *Palladium* noted. "The public sentiment which had all along been strongly in favor of Col. Burr, now burst forth without disguise."[83]

But how far did this "public sentiment" go? It seems clear that Burr had the support of most central Kentucky Republicans in his conflict with Daveiss and the *Western World*. During and after the court proceedings, he received the attentions of Frankfort's elite. He dined at some of the town's "most respectable houses," including the governor's; he visited and was visited by "the most distinguished members of the Legislature"; and he was even invited to sit in the legislative chambers during the session, "a mark of respect scarcely ever before shewn to a *private citizen*."[84] Daveiss's failure in court only strengthened Burr's position, moreover, by bolstering the view that the "*prosecution*" should be "viewed as a *persecution*."[85] After the abortive proceedings, one Mariettan learned from a visiting Kentuckian in late November that Burr "gain[ed] popularity fast."[86] But this popularity had limits. In the *Palladium*, Hunter insisted that his support for Burr derived from his confidence that "the monstrous tales" about his plans were untrue. If Burr actually intended "to attack Mexico, dismember the union, and erect an independent empire," the editor expected him to find "that nine-tenths of the western people would oppose such a project."[87]

The courtroom activity forced Burr to alter his travel plans. He had been about to leave Lexington for Marietta and Blennerhassett Island when he learned of Daveiss's motion. From there, he had apparently intended to return east through Pittsburgh to Philadelphia—at least that is what he had written to Latrobe in late October. He did not entirely abandon this plan even after the delays occasioned by "the ridiculous proceedings" in court.[88] As late as 18 November, nearly a week after the hearing, Burr wrote two letters from Lexington that suggested that, after visiting Cincinnati for a week or so, he would return to Philadelphia. Whether these plans were genuine is impossible to say. His letters—to Latrobe in Washington, Charles Biddle in Philadelphia, and Edward Tupper in Marietta—may have been intended to mislead. A trip east would not have easily squared with the many recent developments that pointed west: the purchase of Lynch's claim to the Bastrop lands; the building of boats along the Ohio and its tributaries; and the assemblage of men and supplies. Conversely, a *well-publicized* plan to return to the East through Marietta and Pittsburgh might have provided cover if Burr actually intended to meet his boats and men at one of those places or at Blennerhassett Island. But it is not clear that his travel plans were publicized at all. In any event, Burr did not head east. On 19 November, the day after writing to Biddle and Tupper, Burr headed northwest to Cincinnati, staying just a few days. Then, rather than continuing upriver to Marietta or Pittsburgh, he proceeded downriver to Louisville.[89]

During Burr's absence from Frankfort and Lexington, the fuse that had been lit nearly six months earlier by the first issue of the *Western World* finally produced a series of explosions. On 22 November, the Kentucky House of Representatives named a committee to investigate the charge that, for over a decade, state judge Benjamin Sebastian had received a pension from Spain. The same day, Littell's *Political Transactions*—the pamphlet that, as Innes put it, had been written "to rebut the calumnies published by [the] nefarious juncto"—came off Hunter's press and was distributed to legislators.[90] Judge Sebastian asked for more time to prepare a defense; when this request was denied, he abruptly resigned. The committee decided to proceed with its hearings. A parade of witnesses left little doubt of Sebastian's guilt. But the most shocking revelations came from Judge Innes, who produced letters and depositions unfolding the ties between Sebastian and other Kentuckians and Spanish agents but tried to defend these actions by referring to the foreign and domestic context of the times. Innes's admissions, as one local remarked, "astonished the country and established beyond doubt the existence of a former Spanish Association."

The legislature had no authority over Innes, a federal judge, but seemed likely to "unmak[e] two more of the Judges of the Court of Appeals," George Muter and Caleb Wallace, unless they resigned as well.[91] All of the accused's work of the previous six months—the private conversations and letters, the newspaper essays, Littell's pamphlet, the social exclusions—seemed to have come to nothing. In fact, the Republican-dominated legislature "reward[ed] the editors of the Western World for the trouble they had incurred" by giving them the printing contract for the committee report. Even Hunter admitted that, whatever their "original motives," Wood and Street had "undoubtedly rendered their country some service."[92]

In the midst of these startling developments, Daveiss learned that Davis Floyd, the witness whose absence had led him to postpone the grand jury investigation, was nearby. On 25 November, Daveiss requested a new hearing, which Innes scheduled for a week later. Two days later, in Louisville, Burr learned of the new prosecution. He quickly sent off two letters. One went to Governor Harrison in the Indiana Territory. Burr acknowledged that he was "engaged in an extensive speculation" but noted that some of Harrison's "dearest friends" were involved and insisted that "several of the principal officers of our Government" knew and approved of his plans. Burr also assured Harrison that he had "no project or view hostile to the Interest or tranquility or Union of the U,S, [sic] or prejudicial to its Government."[93] The other letter went to Clay in Lexington. Burr asked Clay, who was preparing to leave for Washington to fill a vacated seat in the Senate, to delay his departure and act as his legal counsel in Frankfort. Clay had doubts. To ease them, Burr provided Clay with a letter like the one that he had sent Harrison. In it, he also insisted that he had "neither issued nor signed nor promised a [military] commission to any person" and did "not own a musket nor a bayonet nor any single article of military stores."[94] Burr's letter worked; Clay agreed to act as his attorney.

Burr's second trial in Kentucky began on 2 December, the day that the legislature unanimously concluded that Sebastian had received a Spanish pension. Initially, this trial seemed likely to become another "farce and pantomine," as Daveiss sought an adjournment due to the absence of two witnesses.[95] But Clay and Burr protested, demanding a full investigation so that Burr could resume his travels. Once again, various legal issues had to be addressed, particularly whether Daveiss could go before the grand jury to question witnesses. This time, they were resolved not by a private exchange of letters between Innes and Daveiss but through a courtroom display of forensic talent that pitted Daveiss against Burr's attorneys—Clay and Allen—and even Burr himself. Ultimately, Innes ruled against Daveiss. The district attorney believed that this decision guaranteed Burr's victory. "I knew," he later explained, "the witnesses could never be brought to tell what they knew without close examination."[96] Still, Daveiss asked for indictments against Burr and John Adair on the misdemeanor of preparing a military expedition against a friendly nation.

The grand jury began its work on 4 December, quickly rejecting the indictment against Adair. The next day, it turned to Burr. The jurors worked through Daveiss's list of witnesses. They then asked Innes to call Wood and Street and to provide a file of the *Western World*. Since July, the editors had claimed to have evidence of Burr's intentions and associates. But, testifying before the grand jury, first Street and then Wood admitted that all of their information about Burr had come from inadmissable hearsay. And Wood went much further. The hostility between the two editors had only grown since October. The night before his court appearance, Wood had written Clay that "all hopes of reconciliation" between the two men were "at an end." Street was "advised and supported by certain individuals," Wood explained, who "are inimical to me." Wood wanted to leave town. He asked Clay to loan him money for the stagecoach to Richmond and to arrange a meeting with Burr so he could explain how he had gotten into his "present unfortunate political engagement."[97] In his testimony the next day, Wood severed his ties to Street and the *Western World*. He announced that, although he had once thought that Burr's plans were treasonous, further evidence had convinced him that they were "neither against the government or laws of the U. States."[98] The grand jury refused to indict Burr. Then, in an unprecedented step, the jurors prepared a report stating that they had heard no testimony to "criminate the conduct of" Burr or Adair "in the Smallest degree" and "that no violent disturbance of the Public Tranquility or breach of the laws" had come to their attention.[99] When this report was read, the courtroom erupted with "shouts of applause."[100]

That afternoon, the *Palladium* trumpeted in a broadside Burr's innocence "of all suspicion and improper views."[101] The outcome seemed likely to produce "an increase of his popularity in the Western Country."[102] Soon after the trial, Burr's friends organized a supper and ball in his honor at a tavern for 8 December. A visiting James Taylor recalled that "most of the distinguished citizens of Frankfort attended," as did many of the state's leading Republicans, who were in town for the legislative and court sessions.[103] As Humphrey Marshall later remembered, Burr was "hailed and huzzaed by the undersized, caressed and feasted by the higher order" during the few days that he remained in central Kentucky following the trial.[104]

But Burr's acquittal did not silence his critics. Daveiss held what he later described as a "counter party" on the night of Burr's ball at the same tavern.[105] Daveiss and a small group of men spent the evening "drinking wine[,] laughing heartily," and singing songs to "show [their] contempt of the ball given to a man suspected of inimical views to our government."[106] Nor did Street moderate his attacks, despite his inability to produce legal evidence at the trial. The *Western World* launched new assaults: on Burr, whose projects still seemed "inimical to the perpetuity of the union"; on Hunter, whose *Palladium* had defended Sebastian and still supported Burr; and on Innes, whose "predetermination to thwart the proceedings" had been evident "in his every act." Street even ridiculed the Burr ball, from which he had been removed by force, as limited to "only a very few gentlemen." He juxtaposed this disappointing turnout to a ball "in honor of the *Union*" and in support of Daveiss three nights later at Bush's tavern. The second ball, Street reported, was attended by "about 60 or 70 gentlemen," including "the governor, secretary of state, the speakers of the senate and house of representatives, and many of the leading members of both houses." Notable by their absence were the extensive Innes and Brown families. The company for this "brilliant supper" included "about 30 ladies," many of whom "had positively refused to go to Mr. Burr's party," according to Street.[107]

The success of the "union" ball—even discounting the bias of Street's account—suggests the limits to popular support for Burr following his acquittal. It is not simply that more people attended the union ball than the Burr ball, which may or may not have been the case. What is more important is that people could and did attend both without feeling any conflict. Street, Daveiss, and Marshall may have thought otherwise, but central Kentucky's leading Republicans never equated supporting Burr with opposing the union. They celebrated Burr's acquittal because it proved that the prosecution against him was unjustified and that Burr had no designs against the peace or union of the country, not because it allowed him to proceed with a disunionist plot. They could believe, as Hunter stated, that Burr would use the resulting popularity "in such a manner only as shall promote the honour and interest of the country."[108] Many of these men had made their positions clear on 4 December, the opening day of Burr's trial, when the legislature unanimously resolved "that the people of Kentucky . . . feel the strongest attachment to the federal government, and consider a dismemberment of the union as the greatest evil which could befall them."[109]

The glow of Burr's acquittal did not last long. Burr left just a day or two after the ball in his honor, heading south to Nashville. He stayed there a few days before boarding his boats and floating down the Cumberland River. Wood left Frankfort a few days later, taking the eastbound stage and appearing next in Washington, not Richmond. Within a few weeks, he had begun defending Burr with both a pamphlet account of the second trial and his new *Atlantic World*. Not long after these departures, new reports about Burr's plans reached central Kentucky. On 18 December, the presidential proclamation against Burr's project appeared in Street's *Western World*. The next day, Governor Christopher Greenup sent it to the legislature along with a recent letter from Daveiss that reported Burr's preparations in Louisville and suggested that Greenup stop Burr's boats and men at the mouth of the Cumberland. As the assembly discussed this material, John Graham, the special agent whom Jefferson had sent after Burr, arrived in Frankfort with the evidence that had convinced the Ohio legislature to authorize similar steps ten days earlier. On 23 December, within three weeks of Burr's acquittal, Kentucky passed a law to seize Burr's boats at Louisville. In early January, one visitor to Lexington reported that many "who but a few days before" had been Burr's "warmest advocates" now called him "a rascal, villain, thief and highway robber."[110]

The disturbances caused by the Burr Conspiracy—and by the revelations of the Spanish Conspiracy with which Burr's projects had become entangled—continued to be felt in Lexington and Frankfort long after Burr's departure. Public opinion remained in the "state of considerable f[erment]" that had followed the first appearance of the *Western World*.[111] "All those supposed favorable to [Burr's] views," one Lexingtonian noted in mid-February 1807, "are universally detested"; "the thermometer of Burrism . . . is a great many degrees below 0 here."[112] Local newspapers continued to publish material generated by Burr's relatively brief presence for months. Wood and Street battled in the pages of rival newspapers in the fall of 1807; the following summer, Clay found himself at war with the *Western World* over his service as Burr's counsel. The state legislature continued to discuss issues relating to the Spanish Conspiracy. In early 1808, spurred on by "that prince of devils H[umphrey] M[arshall]," the legislature asked Congress to investigate federal judge Innes, hinting that he should be impeached.[113] Relations between gentlemen remained disordered. James Taylor recalled that he "actually recd two challenges, one from Col. J. H. Daviess & one from John Smith [of Ohio], & some thing like one from Col. Carbury, all growing out of the affairs of Burr and Smith."[114] Taylor did not duel over these issues, but Clay and Marshall did, in January 1809, climaxing a conflict that could be traced to the fall of 1806. And the courts continued to hear lawsuits against the *Western World*. Not until October 1810 did the circuit court finally rule, in favor of the plaintiff, on Innes's 1806 libel suit against Street.

The conflicts over the Burr and Spanish conspiracies passed from Lexington's and Frankfort's courtrooms, legislative chambers, newspapers, and public spaces to histories and biographies. Marshall fired the opening salvo in 1812 with *The History of Kentucky*, which extended only through 1792 but included a full development of the Spanish Conspiracy. In the revised and expanded edition that appeared twelve years later, he carried the story to 1811, elaborating—and, at times, simply reprinting—attacks on Burr and his supporters from the *Western World* from the fall of 1806. In 1832, an aging Marshall published a critique of a campaign biography of Clay that, to Marshall's mind, whitewashed the presidential candidate's involvement with Burr and misstated Marshall's and Daveiss's actions—taking twenty-four pages to correct a half-dozen passages in George Prentice's biography. In 1834, the accused responded at length for the first time since Littell's

Political Transactions in 1806. Writing in support of his friend John Brown, who was the last survivor among the accused, Mann Butler published *A History of the Commonwealth of Kentucky* to replace Marshall's volumes. Even the death of the last of the principals did not end the conflict, however. Descendants of Brown, Marshall, and Innes continued to clash over the Spanish Conspiracy. In just four years around 1890, three books appeared that advanced the opposing positions— John Mason Brown's *Political Beginnings of Kentucky* (1889), Thomas Marshall Green's *Spanish Conspiracy* (1891), and A. C. Quisenberry's *The Life and Times of Hon. Humphrey Marshall* (1892). As late as 1926, Temple Bodley, an Innes descendant prepared an exculpatory introduction for a reprint of Littell's *Political Transactions*.[115]

To a significant degree, what happened in central Kentucky in the late summer and fall of 1806—the publication of the "Kentucky Spanish Association" essays, the allusions to a new separatist conspiracy in the *Western World*, and the abortive attempts to try Burr—transformed the uncertain accounts of Burr's project and activities into a crisis. There, as elsewhere across the country, local struggles for political and social power shaped the response to Burr and the understanding of the conspiracy. In Lexington and Frankfort, however, Burr was supported and defended by the kinds of men—powerful Republicans with close ties to the Jefferson administration—who opposed or condemned him in most places. To Street, Marshall, Daveiss, and other critics of those who dominated Kentucky politics, the explanation was simple: Burr's disunionist project reprised the earlier separatist conspiracy. "The immediate adherents and intimate friends of Col. Burr," Street explained following Burr's second trial, were "the very members, the hangers on, and the advocates of the Spanish Association."[116] Burr's Republican friends saw things very differently, of course. Where Street and Marshall found continuity between the Spanish Conspiracy and the Burr Conspiracy, central Kentucky's leading Republicans perceived a relationship between the *accusations* about a Spanish Conspiracy and the *accusations* about a Burr Conspiracy. By the time that Burr returned to the region in mid-September 1806, these men were unlikely to accept the thinking of Wood, Street, Marshall, and Daveiss on any subject. Kentucky Republicans defended Burr not because they hoped that he would divide the union or even invade Mexico, but because they considered him a victim of the same unjustifiable persecution that they—or their family members or trusted friends or political allies—were suffering from men whose real goal seemed to be "changing the politics of this state from warm republicans to Federalists."[117] The nature of their support—its contingence upon Burr's innocence—made it easy for them to abandon him when faced with new information from outside the region soon after his departure. Indeed, "those who were his friends when he was here," one Republican reported from Lexington in February 1807, became "his most bitter enemies."[118]

CHAPTER 3

GUILT BEYOND QUESTION

The Narrative of Thomas Jefferson

PUBLIC ANXIETY ABOUT AARON BURR'S INTENTIONS AND ACTIVITIES reached its peak in late 1806 and early 1807. Burr had provided copy for newspapers and content for letters for months. But the publication of Thomas Jefferson's presidential proclamation against the unnamed conspirators in late November and the news of Joseph Hamilton Daveiss's second attempted prosecution of Burr in early December made the rumors more concrete and more alarming. As reports of these developments radiated out from Washington, D.C., and Frankfort, Kentucky, newspapers and letters recounted Burr's movements: from Frankfort to Lexington to Nashville in early and mid-December; then down the Cumberland River with one group of men, boats, and supplies to meet another group at the Ohio River in late December; and finally down the Ohio and Mississippi Rivers to Bayou Pierre, thirty miles above Natchez, by mid-January. Indefinite, incomplete, and often incompatible reports about Burr rippled out along roads and rivers. Who could make sense of this chaos? Who could answer the basic questions: What were Burr's intentions? How great was the danger? And what was the federal government doing about it? As the anxiety mounted, the public looked eagerly to "the fountain head . . . at Washington [for] the real truth": to Congress, which met in early December; to the *National Intelligencer*; and to the president.[1]

For nearly two months after Jefferson's proclamation, much of the news in and from Washington remained confusing and contradictory. "As to Burr," one New York congressman reflected in early January, "out of a thousand stories, 999 ought to be disbelieved."[2] Then, on 22 January 1807, the president delivered a lengthy message to Congress that seemed to answer the key questions by "disclosing Burrs

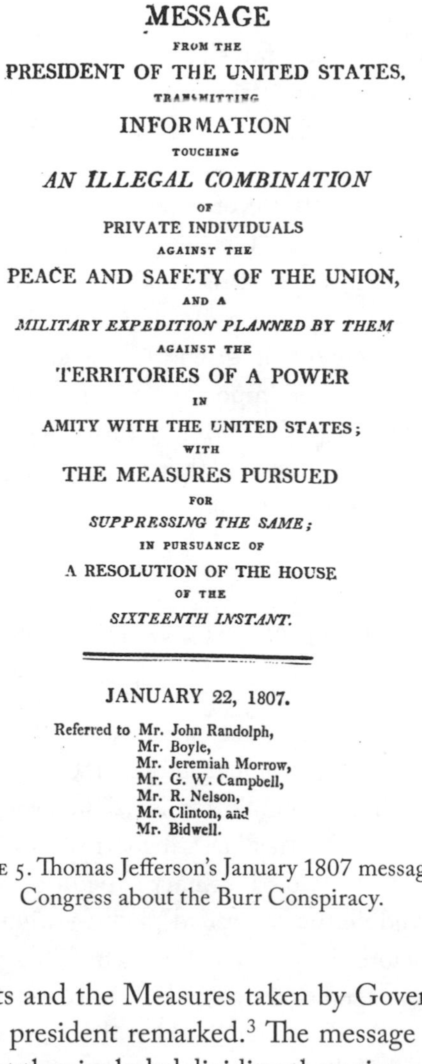

MESSAGE

FROM THE

PRESIDENT OF THE UNITED STATES,

TRANSMITTING

INFORMATION

TOUCHING

AN ILLEGAL COMBINATION

OF

PRIVATE INDIVIDUALS

AGAINST THE

PEACE AND SAFETY OF THE UNION,

AND A

MILITARY EXPEDITION PLANNED BY THEM

AGAINST THE

TERRITORIES OF A POWER

IN

AMITY WITH THE UNITED STATES;

WITH

THE MEASURES PURSUED

FOR

SUPPRESSING THE SAME;

IN PURSUANCE OF

A RESOLUTION OF THE HOUSE

OF THE

SIXTEENTH INSTANT.

JANUARY 22, 1807.

Referred to Mr. John Randolph,
Mr. Boyle,
Mr. Jeremiah Morrow,
Mr. G. W. Campbell,
Mr. R. Nelson,
Mr. Clinton, and
Mr. Bidwell.

FIGURE 5. Thomas Jefferson's January 1807 message to
Congress about the Burr Conspiracy.

treasonous Projects and the Measures taken by Government to defeat them," as the vice president remarked.[3] The message described Burr's plans, insisting that they included dividing the union and that his "guilt [was] placed beyond question."[4] It also discussed the extent of the conspiracy, reassuring the public and Congress that it had never been as widespread as they might have feared. And it detailed the administration's response, demonstrating its competence in a crisis. With its bold assertions and controversial claims, Jefferson's message was challenged from the start, by many people, on various issues. Still, it had a profound impact on contemporaries, and historians, by providing much-needed and long-sought clarity.

But Jefferson's message was never just a means for answering nagging questions or even for shaping popular opinion about the conspiracy and the administration. It was also intended to make the ongoing crisis advance Jefferson's greatest political goal: entrenching republican government as he understood it—limited, decentralized, and nonmilitarized—at a time of deepening Federalist criticism and lingering popular skepticism. "On the whole," he concluded two weeks after submitting the message, "this squall, by showing with what ease our government suppresses movements which in other countries requires armies, has greatly increased its strength by increasing the public confidence in it."[5] To read this important message as simply a record of Jefferson's understanding of the Burr Conspiracy is to misread it. It was, instead, an effort to ensure that the public made sense of the conspiracy—its nature, extent, and failure—in a way that reinforced Jeffersonian principles.

"SO MISTERIOUS THAT THEY CANNOT YET BE UNRAVELLED"

Jefferson's first public statements about the conspiracy came nearly two months before his 22 January message. But neither his 27 November proclamation nor his 2 December annual message to Congress provided the answers that the public and legislators sought. Neither mentioned Burr by name. Neither described the conspiracy as anything more than a plan "to carry on a military expedition against the territories of Spain."[6] And neither indicated that anything had been done to defeat this plan before the proclamation, which "command[ed] all persons whatsoever engaged or concerned . . . to cease all further proceedings," "enjoin[ed] all officers, civil and military, . . . [to prevent] the carrying on such expedition or enterprise by all lawful means within their power," and "require[d] all good and faithful citizens" to provide assistance.[7] The only hint that something more than an "enterprise . . . against a foreign nation" might be afoot appeared in the annual message. The president urged Congress to consider a new law analogous to those that empowered the federal government to arrest private military expeditions against foreign powers. "Would [such laws] not be as reasonable and useful," Jefferson asked, "where the enterprise preparing is against the United States?"[8]

The proclamation and the annual message quickly came under attack. After reading the proclamation, even some Republicans quietly suggested that "the People ought not to have been alarmed or more [energetic] measures taken."[9] Federalists openly denounced *"proclamation-warfare"* as an inadequate response to the western crisis. Rather than sending copies of the proclamation west with one express rider, the editor of New York's *People's Friend* argued, Jefferson "had better sent them by *one thousand expresses*, with orders to deliver them from the mouths of their muskets."[10] Federalist concern that Jefferson would fail to take energetic action in time shaped a savage parody of a Republican defense of the annual message. Appearing in a number of Federalist newspapers in early January 1807, "A Speck of War: or, The Good Sense of the People of the Western Country" rooted Jefferson's policies in his belief "THAT THE GREAT SECRET OF GOVERNMENT IS TO LET EVERY THING TAKE ITS OWN COURSE." The likely outcome, the satirist suggested, was that Burr would seize New Orleans, fortify it, and make it the capital of a new western empire that would soon "be as strong as ourselves."[11]

Federalists reserved their greatest contempt for Jefferson's suggestion that he could not arrest the organizers of a military enterprise against the United States because Congress had not made that illegal. "It is a self evident truth," a writer in the *New-York Evening Post* remarked, "that every nation is under a moral obligation to provide for its self preservation, and as a consequence, that it has a right to make use of all proper means necessary to that end." Even without a specific law, Federalists insisted, the government had "the power & of course the means [for] *preventing* any insurrection or enterprize on the public peace or safety."[12] In fact, Jefferson and most Republicans believed otherwise, rejecting the common-law view that the United States' mere existence as a country sufficed to make some acts illegal. They argued, instead, that the Constitution granted only limited and specified powers to the federal government. It defined treason, for example, but did not make either conspiring to commit treason or preparing to commit treason a crime. In late October, as Secretary of State James Madison was drafting instructions for John Graham to follow Burr through the West, he researched the laws and decided that the administration had no legal recourse if Burr was preparing to levy war against the United

States. "It does not appear," Jefferson noted on Madison's list of relevant laws, "that regular troops can be employed, under any legal provision agst *insurrections*—but only agst expeditions having foreign Countries for the object."[13] "The question will be," Jefferson explained to a Republican editor shortly before issuing the proclamation, "whether we have authority legally to oppose [Burr's project] by force."[14]

Other complaints about the proclamation and annual message concerned their failure to answer, or even to address, the main questions about Burr's operations. Daniel Clark, the delegate to Congress from the Orleans Territory, bemoaned Jefferson's "great Precaution to name nobody" in the proclamation.[15] Massachusetts senator John Quincy Adams criticized the annual message for including "much talk about expeditions undertaken by individual citizens against Spain without naming any body, and a dissertation upon projects against the United States, which *might* be somewhere concerting."[16] After reading the two documents, Virginia's Burwell Bassett, Maryland's Leonard Covington, Ohio's Jeremiah Morrow, and other pro-administration Republicans in Washington agreed that Burr's plans remained mysterious—"so misterious," according to Bassett, "that they cannot yet be unravelled."[17]

Popular and congressional dissatisfaction over the ongoing mystery increased through December and into early January. One Federalist editor considered it positively unrepublican that the people had been "insultingly left by their present rulers . . . in more than Cimmerian darkness."[18] More and more congressmen criticized the administration's failure to keep them informed. "All information on the subject," John Randolph—the leader of the anti-administration Quids—charged in early January, "has been studiously with-held."[19] Some of these complaints may have reflected a justified belief that those who supported the administration, including some moderate Federalists, were better informed than those who opposed it. Midway through the congressional session, most Federalist and Quid congressmen remained largely ignorant of Burr's plans and the government's response. "I [still cannot] add a word to the news contained in the intelligencer," one Quid admitted in early January.[20] The letters of some better-connected Republicans, in contrast, offered valuable information that was "very little known even in Washington."[21] These men could sometimes provide the details of confidential letters that had reached the president or department heads. And they often knew the administration's analysis of developments. Senators Thomas Worthington, an Ohio Republican, and William Plumer, a New Hampshire Federalist, both heard Jefferson describe the nature and extent of "the arch traitor Burr['s]" plans weeks before his 22 January message.[22] Still, even a well-connected Republican senator could confide in late December: "no Republican [in Congress] thinks it Safe to Ask any" information from the administration.[23]

Congressional pressure built to an explosion in mid-January. Sick of the "state of supineness and apathy in which the House [of Representatives had] been satisfied to remain," Randolph decided to act. On 16 January, he offered a resolution calling on the president for information about "any illegal combination of private individuals against the peace and safety of the Union," as well as about "the measures which the Executive has pursued and proposes to take for suppressing or defeating the same."[24] Randolph's resolution and accompanying speech—which one senator called "extremely severe upon the Administration"—provided the session's first indication that "the bickerings of the [previous] Session" between Quids and Republicans would continue.[25] But Randolph's speech attacked congressmen—who were happy to "sit and adjourn, adjourn and sit, take things as schoolboys, do as we are bid, and ask no questions"—no less than the president.[26] The resolution, one supporter reported, "met with the most violent opposition."[27] Fifteen congressmen spoke, most against at least part of it. Some argued that it suggested "a want of confidence in the President."[28] Others opposed the clause requiring Jefferson to provide information about ongoing and future measures to check the conspiracy. When Randolph removed that clause, both parts of the resolution passed easily.

Different people expected different things from Jefferson's reply to Randolph's resolution. Before the resolution, some administration critics had predicted that the president would never publicly address Burr's plans: "Jef. will touch no paper respecting him," a New York Federalist believed.[29] Jefferson, such critics implied, had so mishandled the crisis that he would remain silent—or provide as little information as possible—rather than produce a complete and honest explanation that would reflect badly upon him. A writer in Philadelphia's leading Federalist newspaper spelled out precisely what he (or she) wanted to learn "from the fountain head here at Washington." What was "Burr's object?" Did he have "any military object at all in view" or was it "a mere land speculation?" Was Burr supported by the British, French, or Spanish? Such questions were shared by many—both friends and foes of the administration. But this Federalist had darker concerns as well. Did Jefferson know Burr's plan, "promise [his] support," and then "[disown] it and [pronounce] him a conspirator and a traitor?" Was "all the noise and bluster about Burr" a ruse "to show the vast energy of the present administration?" Had Burr been labelled a traitor to keep him from dividing the Republicans and becoming president? Had the administration focused popular attention on Burr so that it could secretly prepare "some deadly blow at the interests of the nation?"[30] In the days before Jefferson delivered his January message, Abigail Adams remarked that Burr had "led the administration into a labyrinth out of which not even the clue of Adriana will extricate them."[31] Could the president find a way through this maze and satisfy those who hoped that, once he disclosed his "important information[,] we shall know all about Coll. Burr?"[32]

"WITH LITTLE TROUBLE & EXPENSE TO THE UNITED STATES"

"Great anxiety and attention prevailed" on 22 January 1807 as the House of Representatives listened to a clerk read the president's message.[33] Unlike the annual message, which relied upon input from the department heads, this message came "from Mr. Jefferson's own hand."[34] By far the longest special message of his presidency, it provided a full account of events and was supported by a few important documents, including the cipher letter. The message answered, at least implicitly, most of the questions that had been raised in newspaper articles and essays, private letters and conversations, and the congressional debate about Randolph's resolution. Jefferson focused upon the two broad issues in the resolution—the nature and scope of the "illegal combination" in the West and the "measures" adopted by the administration to defeat it.[35] Working within a framework that had been set by the resolution, Jefferson shaped the story of the conspiracy to his own purposes.

"Burr's general designs," according to the message, were never simple. He had "contemplated two distinct objects"—"the severance of the

Union . . . by the Alleghany Mountains" and "an attack on Mexico." These objects could "be carried on either jointly or separately" and could be effected in either order. At the same time, Burr had proclaimed another object—settling what Jefferson called "a pretended purchase of a tract of country on the Washita claimed by a Baron Bastrop"—that was "merely ostensible." The land "serve[d] as the pretext for all his preparations, an allurement for such followers as really wished to acquire settlements[,] . . . and a cover under which to retreat" if his true ends were frustrated. With this combination of real and false goals, Burr had begun recruiting men, building boats, and purchasing supplies. But, as Jefferson explained, he had quickly discovered the impossibility of dividing the union. Westerners would not "consent" to "its dissolution," and Burr's resources were inadequate "to effect it by force." As such, Burr had shifted his focus to New Orleans, where he intended to "plunder the bank . . . , possess himself of the military and naval stores, and proceed on his expedition to Mexico."[36]

Jefferson used the message to demonstrate that, even if extensive and alarming, Burr's plans were never really that threatening. He did so by isolating Burr through a process of exonerating, one-by-one, the key individuals and groups who might have facilitated those plans. He described westerners as unshakeable in their "attachment . . . to the present Union" and noted that, in Ohio and Kentucky, they had moved "with a promptitude, an energy, and [a] patriotic zeal" to thwart Burr. Even in New Orleans, where such loyalty had seemed unlikely, the citizens had "manifest[ed] unequivocal fidelity to the Union and a spirit of determined resistance to their expected assailants." The army, navy, and militias, moreover, had never wavered; General James Wilkinson, the subject of widespread suspicions, had acted "with the honor of a soldier and fidelity of a good citizen." Finally, any concerns that Burr's projects would "receive aid from certain foreign powers," which Jefferson left unnamed, were "without proof or probability." Lacking the support of westerners or the army and navy or foreign powers, Burr had recruited just a handful of desperate men and "seduced" a few "well-meaning citizens" by offering land or hinting of the "secret patronage" of the administration.[37]

Jefferson discussed these matters within a straightforward, chronological narrative told from the administration's point of view. It opened with the administration learning, beginning in September 1806, of a plot that was "unlawful and unfriendly to the peace of the Union" whose "prime mover . . . was Aaron Burr." By late October, new information had suggested the outlines of the plan, but it was "still so blended and involved in mystery that nothing could be singled out for pursuit." In this context, Jefferson reported, he had decided to send a trusted agent "to investigate the plots," to meet with federal and state officials in the West, and, "with their aid," to do whatever appeared "necessary to discover the designs of the conspirators, arrest their means, [and] bring their persons to punishment." Around the same time, he had dispatched warnings to the army and navy commanders in the Southwest and to "the governors of the Orleans and Mississippi Territories." In late November, a fuller disclosure of Burr's plans, including his efforts to corrupt the army, had arrived in a letter from Wilkinson dated 21 October. When combined with "some other information," Burr's intentions had finally seemed clear.[38]

In late November, according to Jefferson's account, the administration had shifted from investigating to thwarting Burr's plans. The new information from Wilkinson and the other sources finally made it "possible to take specific measures" to defeat the conspiracy. Accordingly, the proclamation had been issued and orders had been sent "to every interesting point on the Ohio and Mississippi" to mobilize army, navy, and militia units and to alert civil authorities. Even before these new orders reached their destinations, the cabinet's confidential agent had unfolded Burr's project to the governor of Ohio, who had mobilized the legislature "to crush the combination." Unfortunately, at the same time, "a premature attempt to bring Burr to justice" in Kentucky "had produced a popular impression in his favor." But the arrival of the proclamation and the special agent there had produced another effort to seize Burr's boats and men. As the proclamation and agent checked the conspiracy in the Ohio Valley, General Wilkinson had begun to prepare New Orleans for Burr's arrival. Jefferson admitted that Burr's plot was not yet fully defeated and that he had sent an express rider west with further orders in late December. But he believed that, given Ohio's and Kentucky's actions, the small band of "fugitives from the Ohio, with their associates from the Cumberland, [could] not threaten serious danger."[39]

Jefferson's special message provided exactly the kinds of information for which the public and Congress had been clamoring during the nearly two months since his proclamation. Why had he waited so long to attempt to fix the public's understanding of Burr's project and the administration's response? Jefferson knew much of what appeared in the message long before 22 January. In late November, within days of the proclamation, Worthington reported that Jefferson had told him that "he [had] satisfactory proof" of Burr's objects. Worthington recounted almost exactly what Jefferson described in the January message: a false triad in which an avowed goal—the settlement of the Bastrop lands—"serve[d] as a cover" for two actual goals—"a seperation of the western from the Atlantic states" and "an expedition against the Spanish province of Mexico."[40] Much of the rest of Jefferson's analysis was settled by late December. More than three weeks before submitting the message, Jefferson informed Plumer that "he did not believe either France, Great Britain or Spain were connected with Burr." He also assured the senator "that there was no room to doubt of the integrity, firmness & attachment of Wilkinson." Nor was Jefferson worried about "the loyalty & attachment of the western people to the union," according to Plumer.[41] All of the major points that Jefferson would make in the message about the nature of Burr's ends and the limits of his means had been decided weeks earlier. At any time, moreover, he could have stated when and how he had learned of and responded to Burr's plans, up to that moment.

Worthington and Plumer suggested reasons why Jefferson might have refrained from an earlier public statement, even though his "Silence" left some thinking that there was "no well grounded proof of the mischevious designs of Mr Burr." Both men pointed to the nature of the administration's evidence. Worthington assumed that much of it took the form of "vague reports" that, while reliable, had "been given under such circumstances as to make it improper to publish" them.[42] Plumer put it more bluntly: the evidence had arrived in "confidential letters from individuals." Even if Jefferson provided it to Congress "under an injunction of secrecy," the authors' names would reach the public since "one hundred & forty men cannot, & will not keep a secret."[43] Once these names became known, potential informants would refuse to provide evidence. Furthermore, as Worthington noted, by revealing his evidence, Jefferson would "prejudice the public mind against" the conspirators, making it difficult for them to receive "common justice on their trial."[44] Finally, Plumer saw a trap in congressional pressure for a statement of the administration's information and measures. The president could not make a full disclosure without discouraging future informants and, possibly, "defeat[ing] the measures" that he had "taken to suppress the conspiracy." But a partial disclosure would not help Congress, which could only act with "a *view of the whole ground*." And, if the president provided only a partial account, "his measures [would] subject him to censure, & perhaps contempt."[45]

Some of these considerations do seem to have influenced Jefferson. In the message, he acknowledged that little of his information could be viewed as "formal and legal evidence" since it was not "given under the sanction of an oath."[46] And he did not identify in the message or accompanying documents any of his informants except Wilkinson. But the president's blunt assertion of Burr's guilt indicates that he was not, contra Worthington, concerned about "prejudic[ing] the public mind." And the detailed account of the administration's countermeasures suggests that he was not, contra Plumer, worried about defeating them by publicizing them.

Plumer's suggestion that the president needed to guard against exposing himself to "censure" and "contempt" provides some insight into the message's timing, however. Jefferson began it by explaining why he had not already communicated to Congress about this important matter. "For some time," he reported, he had expected to receive information that would let him "lay before the Legislature the termination as well as the beginning and progress of this scene of depravity." Only recently had he received information—some of it since the adoption of Randolph's resolution—that "brought us nearly to the period contemplated." Of course, Congress and the public had wanted to know what was happening even while everything remained uncertain and unfolding, not when it was resolved. Earlier information might have allowed, or even prompted, Congress to act. But Jefferson did not want congressional action. In the message, he admitted that he had "indulged" his desire to wait for news of the outcome on the Ohio before reporting to

Congress precisely "because no circumstance had yet made it necessary to call in the aid of the legislative functions."[47]

Jefferson had to defend himself against censure and contempt with regard to the timing and content of the message because the administration seemed to have assumed complete responsibility for defeating the conspiracy. The only congressional action that he had requested in the first seven weeks of the session—with Burr and his men on the move and anxiety at its peak—was a law empowering the government to arrest domestic insurrections as they were being readied.[48] Some of Jefferson's closest advisors worried about his approach to the crisis. His former personal secretary, Virginia representative William A. Burwell, later remarked that he had been "struck with the magnitude of the responsibility of the P[residen]t."[49] Within the cabinet, the most outspoken critic of Jefferson's approach seems to have been Secretary of the Navy Robert Smith. He had advocated a strong administration response throughout the fall of 1806 and believed that the countermanding of the decision to send naval vessels to New Orleans in October had been a mistake. Three days after a 19 December cabinet meeting that had adopted more mild measures, Smith urged Jefferson to take drastic steps to "[arrest] the progress of this insurrection by all the means within our power." Most importantly, he suggested that the president immediately send Congress a confidential message with "all the letters in [his] possession conveying any information respecting the movements & designs of Col Burr." The message, Smith argued, should ask Congress to suspend the writ of habeas corpus (to allow civil authorities to hold suspected conspirators without trial) and to appropriate funds "to send promptly a competent naval force into the Mississippi and the adjacent waters."[50] Smith did not think that the ships could still prevent Burr's assault on New Orleans, but he believed that, by "lay[ing] the subject before C[ongress]," the president could "let them take the responsibility upon themselves."[51] Instead, Jefferson chose to wait for news from the West that would show whether Burr and his men had met with "effectual opposition at either Mariette or Cincinnati."[52]

What Jefferson's supporters viewed as assuming an almost-personal responsibility for defeating the conspiracy was actually something far more complicated. Jefferson did not see himself as the only one active against it, as Burwell and Smith seemed to think. He trusted, instead, in popular disapproval and state and territorial government action to crush the conspiracy. With the proclamation and his special agent, he could ensure that everyone knew that the administration did not approve Burr's project. The people and their local governments bore primary responsibility for thwarting it. Jefferson thus made the Burr Conspiracy a test of one of the most famous, and most controversial, assertions of his first inaugural address: that the United States, with its small military and weak fiscal apparatus, was "the strongest Government on earth" because it was "the only one where every man, at the call of the law, would fly to the standard of the law, and would meet invasions of the public order as his own personal concern."[53]

Jefferson's decision to rely upon this uncertain source of strength dictated delaying reporting Burr's plans and the administration's response to Congress. His critics—Federalists, Quids, and even some Republicans—would see only the limits of the administration's approach if its results were not already evident. He had not sent regular troops to the West; he had not ordered naval vessels to the Mississippi. This "apparent inactivity"—as even Burwell put it—would fuel widespread attacks on "the apathy of the govt."[54] Jefferson needed to wait to see whether his reliance upon the loyalty of western citizens and the exertions of western governments, as well as upon the fidelity of Wilkinson and the rationality of foreign powers, produced the expected outcome. In late December, after receiving the much-anticipated news of the seizure of most of Burr's boats at Marietta, Jefferson informed Plumer that he "had no doubt the conspiracy would be crushed, extensive as it was, with little trouble & expense to the United States."[55] The longer Jefferson delayed his communication to Congress and the longer he allowed for favorable reports from the West, the easier it became to defend his decision to defeat the conspiracy through such means. The congressional resolution forced him to respond before the western people and governments had "finish[ed] the matter" in a way that defended "the honor of popular government" and, thus, undermined "all arguments for standing armies."[56] By emphasizing their roles, Jefferson used his message to teach this lesson even though the crisis was not yet concluded.

"CONFOUNDED ENEMIES AND GRATIFIED CONSOLED AND ELATED FRIENDS"

Jefferson's message on the Burr Conspiracy spread rapidly and received widespread attention. The House of Representatives ordered two thousand copies so that congressmen could "scatter them over the Union."[57] Others in Washington likewise "hasten[ed] to enclose . . . the development of Burrs Conspiracy" to distant correspondents.[58] Across the country, Republican and Federalist editors printed the message and accompanying documents, typically in the first issue after they received it. It was published in New York, Richmond, and Boston before the end of January, in Pittsburgh and Charleston a few days later, in Lexington and Nashville by mid-February, and in Natchez and New Orleans by late February. Just a handful of editors failed to print the message at all. Pro-administration Republicans claimed that its impact was almost instantaneous. One of the president's confidants recalled that public opinion was "compleatly quieted" and that John Randolph seemed "mortified" by the evidence that "the govt. had not been idle."[59] Less than a week after the message was delivered and just days after it reached Philadelphia, the Republican editor William Duane reported that it had "confounded enemies and gratified[,] consoled[,] and elated friends."[60] There certainly was a partisan division on the message, but Jefferson's political enemies tended to be energized, scandalized, or amused rather than "confounded." To one Federalist, Jefferson appeared as a "partizan in his own cause, the judge of his own merits[, and] the hero of his own tale" in the message.[61]

Republican correspondents and editors frequently adopted the message's explanation of Burr's projects and its description of the administration's response unquestioningly. Enclosing a copy to an ally in Kentucky, Senator Henry Clay called it "the best development of [Burr's] plans yet presented to the public."[62] Like Clay, many letter writers simply forwarded a copy of the message or merely referred the recipient to the newspapers, rather than summarizing it. As Virginia's Burwell Bassett explained, the message provided "a more copious detail of the insurrection or rebellion or whatever it may be termed than may be condenced into a letter."[63] In the same way, pro-administration editors often reprinted it without comment. Other Republicans employed the message's major points in their own accounts. This practice was adopted, for example, in the circular letters that some Republican congressmen prepared annually for their constituents. Mailed to political allies and friendly editors at home late in the congressional session, these letters typically reported upon key issues and new laws. Of the eight surviving circular letters from February and March 1807, six discussed the Burr Conspiracy. Three—from Tennessee's George Washington Campbell, Virginia's William A. Burwell, and North Carolina's Marmaduke Williams—drew heavily upon the president's message. To explain Burr's designs, Campbell and Williams used the message's false triad of two real goals—the division of the union and "the conquest of Mexico"—and one "ostensible object"—the settlement of the Bastrop grant.[64] Burwell did not mention the Bastrop lands, but listed the same real objects that the message identified. Burwell, Campbell, and Williams, moreover, all followed the president in narrowing the conspiracy's scope by denying that Burr had received support from western citizens, the army or navy, or foreign powers. Instead, the collapse of the conspiracy proved, according to Burwell, that there were "but few men in this country so depraved, so lost to every sentiment of virtue and patriotism, as to join in a plan which, if successful, would draw ruin on the nation."[65]

Pro-administration editors and writers proved especially aggressive— and defensive—in using Jefferson's account of the administration's response to the conspiracy. The Republican editor of Pittsburgh's *Commonwealth* insisted that, if "the disaffected" would simply read Jefferson's message "and then judge of his conduct," they would agree that he had "pursued the course which every virtuous man must approve, and which posterity will applaud."[66] The administration's supporters described its measures as "vigilant," "prompt," "active," and "energetic."[67] They emphasized, as had the president, the measured nature of the response. It had required "neither armies nor statu[t]es written in blood" to defeat the conspiracy; instead, "the ordinary power of the government" had sufficed.[68] For weeks, Federalists had criticized the proclamation's weakness; Quids had denounced the administration's failure to reinforce the West months before the Burr crisis. Jefferson's message provided pro-administration Republicans with evidence that the administration, throughout the crisis, had pursued "proper measures"—ones that were proportioned to the actual danger.[69] "By the vigilance and energy of the government," an "extraordinary project" that had "agitat[ed] the public mind" had been defeated "without the effusion of a drop of blood."[70]

Republicans rarely challenged Jefferson's message in the first weeks after its appearance. Republican editors, essayists, and letter writers almost uniformly accepted its two principal assertions: that Burr had intended to divide the union and attack Mexico and that the administration had addressed the threat effectively. But administration supporters did dispute other elements. Even Senator Campbell—whose reliance on the message in his circular letter bordered on plagiarism—offered subtle revisions on some points. He expanded the message's description of Burr's project by incorporating later information, including William Eaton's claim that Burr had "contemplated the entire overthrow of the present government." And, although the message had proclaimed Wilkinson's innocence, Campbell only said, of Burr's attempt to "corrupt [the army's] commander," that "in this *it seems* he failed."[71] Jefferson's exoneration of Wilkinson quickly emerged as one of the message's most widely contested assertions. Leading Republicans worried that the president had tied himself, his administration, and, thus, his party too closely to the suspect general. After reading the message, one Tennessee Republican sent a pseudonymous letter to Nashville's *Impartial Review* arguing that Jefferson had been "deceived in the character and conduct of Gen. Wilkinson" and that it was "of the utmost importance to the safety and welfare of the union, that he should be rightly informed."[72]

Anti-administration Federalists and Quids found much more to challenge, and even condemn, in Jefferson's message, of course. They considered it contradictory. The message, as John Quincy Adams wrote to his mother, at once "exhibit[ed] Mr: Burr at the head of an expedition to sever the western States and Territories from the Union, *by force*" and asserted "that there [was] no danger to New Orleans."[73] The opposition insisted that it had failed in its fundamental purpose. It gave "nothing," one Federalist editor exclaimed, "either to quiet the fears of the public, or alarm the people to vigorous exertion."[74] They charged that it embodied nothing "more than a jeffersonian Scheme to increase his Popularity"; "the Plot might have been crushed in the

Egg," a South Carolinian remarked, "had it not been foreseen it would produce this Effect upon the many headed Monster [i.e., the public]."[75] They blasted its assertion that "BURR'S *guilt is placed beyond question*."[76] Even if it was "as clear as the noonday sun," John Adams noted, "the first magistrate ought not to have pronounced it so before a jury had tried him."[77] They even complained that it was poorly written, "in a style" that Virginia Quid Beverley Tucker castigated as "worthy of the school of St Omers."[78]

Jefferson's political opponents differed over one of his most important assertions: his account of Burr's plans. Some, including Federalist senators James Hillhouse, Timothy Pickering, and Samuel White, considered the message "the fullest and most correct account" of Burr's project.[79] Others were much more skeptical. After reading the message and accompanying documents, Thomas Boylston Adams concluded that Burr was "*an innocent man.*" "There never was, in any Government, or in any Country that I ever heard of," he concluded, "such ado about nothing."[80] Forwarding a copy of the message to a Federalist editor in Boston, one writer admitted that he was "an unbeliever in the truth of the principal charges."[81] For this writer, as for many other Federalists and Quids, doubts about Jefferson's account of Burr's plans reflected doubts about his sources. Unable to reconcile his belief that Burr was neither "an idiot [nor] a lunatic" with the "extravagant" plans that Jefferson had "imputed to him," John Adams believed that a "lying spirit [had] been at work concerning Burr" that had misled the president.[82] The most important of Jefferson's sources, General Wilkinson, seemed the most dubious. "The evidence of [Burr's] guilt," a Federalist in Washington remarked, "[came] the wrong way[;] it has been, it seems, derived from WILKINSON[,] on whose judgment or solidity I place very little reliance."[83] One Virginia Quid could not decide whether Wilkinson had "been deceived, or [was] attempting to deceive."[84]

Jefferson's political opponents also questioned his effort to narrow the conspiracy by exonerating westerners, Wilkinson, and foreign powers. "Can we believe" Jefferson's portrayal of western loyalty, Beverley Tucker asked, given the long history of separatism that had been exposed by the *Western World*? "The seeds of dissention sown so long ago" had neither been "rooted out" nor died, Tucker insisted, but "occasionally sprout[ed] forth new shoots."[85] Could Wilkinson have been as honest

and faithful as the message asserted? "Burr & Wilkinson were originally concerned together in the plot," the New Jersey Federalist John
Rhea concluded after reading the message and the accompanying documents, "but for some cause, as yet only known to himself, W[ilkinson]
has flinched B[urr]."[86] How could the president think that Burr would
have launched such a "hazardous enterprize without foreign aid," the
Federalist *People's Friend* asked?[87] A project of "so gigantic form" almost had to "[owe] it's birth to some foreign power."[88]

Just like his Republican defenders, Jefferson's Federalist and Quid
detractors turned much of their attention to the message's account of
the administration's response to the conspiracy. Federalists immediately rejected the president's timeline of when he had learned of and
responded to Burr's plans and movements. That Jefferson had received
his first hints about Burr's project "in *the latter part of September* last"
was simply false; he had been "warned of the designs of this Cataline
twelve months ago," a writer in the *Washington Federalist* charged.[89] A
Federalist editor insisted that the president should have taken "immediate measures to frustrate and to get to the bottom of the plans of
Burr" after meeting with Eaton in the spring of 1806.[90] Instead, he had
done nothing for months. When he finally did act, he had merely "sent
a man to ENQUIRE INTO THE AFFAIR" and issued a proclamation.
While Burr was raising "an army to take possession of [Louisiana],"
the administration provided "little or no force to oppose him." Perhaps
the worst offense, from this perspective, was all of the boasting by the
president and Republican congressmen and editors about defeating a
"formidable revolt without expending one dollar."[91] Rather than justifying such pride, Thomas Boylston Adams remarked, "the recent measures of our Rulers at Washington" seemed "happily adapted . . . to
excite mirth."[92]

Writing in his journal shortly after reading the message, Senator
Plumer assembled an account of the Burr Conspiracy that, at once,
adopted and challenged Jefferson's. Though a Federalist and a New
Englander, Plumer's friendly relations with Jefferson had brought privileged access to information during the session. Nonetheless, he had
remained "a long time an infidel" about "Burr's seditious & treasonable
designs." Reading the message and accompanying documents, however,
dispelled these doubts. But Plumer did not accept all of the president's

assertions and conclusions. He calculated that Burr had more support than Jefferson had acknowledged, believing that "Burr [had] had *reason* to beleive [*sic*] Wilkinson would aid him," noting that "some of the officers of our *little* navy were devoted to Burr" and insisting that Burr had arranged foreign assistance through the Spanish minister, the Marquis de Yrujo. Plumer also evinced greater skepticism than Jefferson about popular loyalty. Whereas the president claimed that very few men had joined Burr with a true understanding of his projects, Plumer believed that "the traitor had thousands of men . . . devoted to his plans." Unlike Jefferson, moreover, Plumer worried that Burr would find broad support on the lower Mississippi. Success there, he believed, "would have induced thousands to have joined his standard." To Plumer, these factors made "the chance of [Burr's] success" seem far "more probable" than the message admitted. While Jefferson predicted a speedy and favorable resolution to the crisis, Plumer emphasized how unpredictable the outcome remained. "Who can now say," Plumer wondered despite the message's reassurances, that Burr's "plans are rendered abortive?"[93]

"THE PRESIDENT . . . NEEDS A VINDICATION MORE THAN I"

The most extensive assaults on Jefferson's message came from those whom it implicated in Burr's projects or criticized in other ways. Although the message named only Burr, the accompanying cipher letter mentioned three other individuals—Thomas Truxton, Joseph Alston, and Theodosia Burr Alston. Others also felt injured by the message. Silas Brown, a young man from New Hampshire who had met Burr's agents in upstate New York and travelled with them to Natchez, thought himself included in "the title of fugitives" that Jefferson had used for Burr's followers.[94] And Joseph Hamilton Daveiss saw a criticism of himself in the message's reference to "a premature attempt to bring Burr to justice without sufficient evidence for his conviction" in Kentucky.[95]

The widespread publication of the message and accompanying documents struck directly at the reputations of numerous men. They employed various means to absolve themselves and restore their standing. Some, such as Silas Brown, relied upon private letters to family and friends. Others counted on such confidants to use seemingly private information with the public. Aware that rumors linked him to his friend Burr's "Scheems and designs," Truxton had written to allies in Washington, including Senator Timothy Pickering and naval officer Thomas Tingey, even before seeing the message to deny any impropriety. Closing one of these letters, Truxton suggested how it should be employed: "I have no sort of Objection," he made clear, "to Your giving it publicity, if You Should think it necessary."[96] And others went directly to the public. Upon reading the message, Joseph Alston quickly published a letter denying any involvement in his father-in-law's plans. Though written as a private letter to South Carolina's governor, a "fiction" that Alston readily admitted, the defense appeared in Alston's local newspaper before the governor even received it, and it quickly spread across the country.[97]

Exonerating themselves did not necessarily require these men to challenge Jefferson's account, though. Alston's published letter did not question Jefferson's explanation of Burr's plans. Alston merely insisted that he "had never heard, directly or indirectly, from Col. Burr or any other person, of the meditated attack on New-Orleans." He did not deny that such an attack fit within Burr's project, only that he had known about it. Nor did he question that Burr had written the cipher letter. Instead, he speculated about why his father-in-law would have "introduce[d] my name as he did."[98] Others did attack the message as they defended themselves. Brown insisted that Burr's men were "as friendly to the Government of the United States as Mr. Jefferson ever was, or ever will be." To Brown, the president's inaction for months before the proclamation proved that he was "as well acquinted with the expedition in the West, as Burr himself."[99] But Brown's attack appeared only in a private letter that few beyond his family read. The most extensive assaults on Jefferson's narrative came from Justus Erich Bollman and Joseph Hamilton Daveiss. Bollman's counternarrative challenged the message's version of Burr's plans; Daveiss's refuted its account of the administration's response.

Of all the men who provided firsthand knowledge of Burr's plans to the public or the administration, Bollman was one of the few, and certainly the first, not to use his disclosures to separate himself from Burr's project. A German doctor who had gained international renown fifteen years earlier for trying to rescue the Marquis de Lafayette from an Austrian prison, Bollman had known Burr for years. In July 1806, Burr had sent him to New Orleans with a copy of the cipher letter for Wilkinson. Wilkinson had arrested him in mid-December and sent him to Washington for trial as one of Burr's key agents. Arriving on the day that Jefferson's message went to Congress, Bollman quickly requested a private meeting with the president. On 24 January, Bollman met with Jefferson and Madison. That evening, Madison prepared a lengthy statement of Bollman's comments. The next day, Jefferson asked Bollman "to commit them to writing" himself, assuring Bollman, on "his word of honour[,] that they never shall be used against himself, and that the paper shall never go out of his hand."[100]

Bollman's communications provided a thorough rebuttal of Jefferson's message as it concerned Burr's projects. Whereas Jefferson had described Burr's plans as a false triad of two real and one cover project, Bollman asserted that Burr's "real and sole Object" was "the Conquest, or rather the Emancipation," of Spanish Mexico by force. Rather than being the primary goal, as the message claimed, the separatist project had merely been a cover for Burr's conversations with the Spanish minister and with other "Agents [in] whose Discretion he could less implicitly confide." Bollman claimed that Burr had long been preparing this operation by developing contacts, acquiring "minute geographical Information," and amassing "accurate Intelligence" regarding the opposing military forces. He had assembled men, boats, and supplies on the Ohio and had arranged for ships with military supplies to meet him at New Orleans. Bollman conceded that Burr intended "to take temporary Possession of that City" as a base of operations. And he further acknowledged that Burr planned to seize some artillery pieces that had been abandoned by France and to "put in Requisition all the mercantile shipping" to carry his men to Mexico.[101] But Bollman denied that Burr planned "to seize the money in the Bank" of the United States at New Orleans, as the message asserted.[102]

Bollman also contradicted the message's efforts to narrow the conspiracy. Whereas Jefferson insisted upon the fidelity of westerners to the union and the laws, Bollman claimed that Burr had expected "Seven to Ten thousand" westerners for his Mexican expedition.[103] Whereas Jefferson exonerated the armed forces, in general, and

Wilkinson, in particular, from participation in Burr's schemes, Bollman asserted that Wilkinson had pledged to resign his commission for
a high rank in Burr's army; only the news of Burr's trials in Kentucky
had convinced Wilkinson to abandon him. When asked by Jefferson
and Madison whether Burr had expected Wilkinson to "carry over
with him the army, or any part of it," Bollman remarked that it had
merely been "thought probable" that some officers and soldiers would
"join the corps of Burr." Whatever reassurance that comment might
have provided was surely offset by Bollman's reply when asked whether
the army was expected to "be an obstacle to the progress of Burr?"
"Very little, if at all," Bollman answered.[104]

Even more alarming to Jefferson and Madison may have been Bollman's revelations of the extent of foreign support for Burr's project.
Whereas Jefferson denied any foreign backing for Burr's plans, Bollman
asserted that Burr had arranged both Spanish and British aid. Jefferson
and Madison questioned Bollman on this issue at length. According to
Bollman, the Spanish minister, the Marquis de Yrujo, had been so
excited by Burr's talk of dividing the union that he had sent a special
agent to Madrid and offered Burr the use of "Ten thousand Stands of
Arms." Only Burr's sense of honor, Bollman remarked, had kept him
from capitalizing upon his duplicity, accepting this offer, and using
Spanish muskets to liberate Spanish Mexico. Even as he had deceived
Yrujo, Bollman reported, Burr had communicated his true plan to
British minister Anthony Merry. Merry had been so "struck with the
immense Advantages" to Great Britain from Mexican liberation that
he had tried to secure "the full Approbation and Aid of his Government." Burr had also sent an agent to London to reinforce Merry's
efforts. Only the death of the prime minister, Bollman believed, had
prevented active British support. Still, Burr counted on the "passive
Cooperation" of British naval commanders in the Caribbean Sea to
keep Spanish or French ships from intercepting his transports on their
way to Mexico.[105]

Why would Bollman have volunteered this information? Why would
he have said things freely to the administration that he could not have
been forced to say in court? His counternarrative did deny that Burr's
projects—and, thus, his own actions on behalf of those projects—were
treasonous. But it left no doubt that they were criminal. And, while

Jefferson did pledge not to use the oral or written communications against Bollman, there is no evidence that Bollman had made that pledge a condition of his disclosures. Something that Bollman said in the meeting, and elaborated upon in his memorandum, provides a clue to his thinking. Asked whether he would have accompanied Burr to Mexico, Bollman replied that he had been intended, instead, for "a sort of diplomatic service." Upon Burr's departure from New Orleans, Bollman was to have gone to Washington to try to "induce [the government] to espouse the enterprize, to concert measures with Burr, and thus, by a war, to consummate and extend its objects." He may have arrived in the capital ahead of schedule, under arrest, and without the documents that were supposed "to convince Congress and the Executive," but Bollman clearly saw his communications to the president as consistent with his planned diplomatic mission.[106] His memorandum concluded with a long argument detailing how and why the administration should assist Burr. It still seemed possible to Bollman for the administration "to declare War against Spain, to allow Col. Burr to proceed[,] and to render his Success indoubtable by the loan of a Sum of money . . . and by the cooperation of the naval Forces of the United States."[107]

The administration's failure to recognize or to credit the diplomatic dimension of Bollman's communications helps to explain their limited impact. After the meeting, Madison noted that Bollman's "primary object" had been to distance himself from "Burr's transactions." But, if Bollman remained willing to act—after his arrest and Jefferson's message—as Burr's diplomatic agent, he was hardly trying to separate himself from Burr. To Madison, Bollman's secondary goal seemed to be placing "Burr's plans and proceedings in a light as little criminal as possible," not demonstrating the policy of joining Burr to conquer Mexico.[108] Bollman's counternarrative neither forced a revision of the administration's understanding of Burr's plans nor prompted a reversal of its commitment to thwarting them.

Rumors that Bollman had "turned U.S. evidence" led people to expect that the public would "soon know or hear the whole plan."[109] But the contents of Bollman's communications do not seem to have reached anyone outside of the cabinet for four months. In late May, Jefferson, despite his pledge, sent a copy of Bollman's memorandum to George Hay, the lead prosecutor in Burr's trial in Richmond. Jefferson enjoined

Hay to keep it secret—something to "be seen and known only" by Hay and his colleagues. Having read Bollman's communication, Hay, Jefferson believed, would be able to "draw everything from him" in court, using the promise of a pardon or the threat of exposure.[110] In mid-June, Bollman appeared before the grand jury. Much of his testimony restated what he had communicated in January, but there were important differences. Most importantly, Bollman informed the grand jury that Burr's plan to emancipate Mexico would have been set in motion "only in the event of a war between the U. States and Spain"—a condition that dodged the misdemeanor charge of outfitting an expedition against a nation at peace with the United States. In January, Bollman had told Jefferson that he would have gone to Washington to persuade the government to declare war after Burr's troops departed for Mexico. Similarly, what Bollman had described in January as an intention to "put in Requisition" the merchant ships at New Orleans appeared in June merely as an expectation of "chartering" the ships.[111] Like Bollman's initial communications, however, this revised account was not widely known since the grand jury testimony never became public. Neither side called him as a witness during the stages of Burr's trial that were published.

In contrast, Daveiss's challenge to Jefferson's message received widespread public attention. Over the spring and summer of 1807, Daveiss prepared a sixty-five-page pamphlet titled *A View of the President's Conduct, Concerning the Conspiracy of 1806*, which *Western World* editor Joseph M. Street printed in September. In many respects, it was a classic defense pamphlet; a reader of the draft described it, fittingly, as a "Vindication."[112] Daveiss felt aggrieved by the criticism of his "premature attempt to bring Burr to justice" in the message and by his later removal from his position as federal district attorney. The combination, he noted to open his pamphlet, "presents a suspicion injurious to my honor."[113] Shortly after hearing of Daveiss's removal, his friend John Rowan urged a range of measures to repair his damaged position, including attending the next circuit court meeting in Frankfort and running for a seat in the state legislature. But Rowan also encouraged Daveiss, "in Justice to yourself[,] to publish the correspondence between yourself & the president on the subject of the conspiracy with suitable Strictures."[114]

A View of the President's Conduct went far beyond a defense of Daveiss's actions and honor. It sought to prove, as Daveiss alerted his readers, "that the president . . . needs a vindication more than I, having acted with as much negligence and insincerity towards this nation, as he has towards me." Daveiss especially targeted Jefferson's message as a record of the administration's "vigilant and faithful conduct." The pamphlet included an eight-page "stricture" on the message, in which Daveiss dismantled key parts of it almost line by line. He found especially deceitful and galling Jefferson's chronology of how he had learned of and responded to Burr's plans. Jefferson dated his first intimations about the conspiracy to late September. Daveiss knew that the president had, in fact, received lengthy warnings from him nearly eight months earlier. Much of the pamphlet reprinted, in full, seven letters that Daveiss had written to Jefferson between January and July 1806 and the replies that Jefferson had sent Daveiss in February and September. These letters left little doubt that the president had "render[ed] an unfaithful account" in the message. Daveiss thought the explanation for Jefferson's deceit was very simple. "When you were required to state your doings on the subject of the conspiracy," he charged the president, "you felt how indispensible it was to your popularity, to make such a report as would exhibit . . . *vigilance* and *energy* on your part." To protect his popularity, Jefferson had "state[d] the date of the *warning* . . . in such a manner, as to tally with [his] measures of prevention."[115] Since he had not acted until late October, in other words, Jefferson had considered it necessary to report that he had not learned of Burr's movements until late September.

Throughout the pamphlet, Daveiss juxtaposed his own activity in discovering and defeating Burr's projects with Jefferson's inactivity. Both the reprinted letters and Daveiss's narrative showed his diligence. It was Daveiss who had noticed the ties between Burr and the surviving members of the Spanish Conspiracy. It was Daveiss who had sought reliable information in central Kentucky. It was Daveiss who had visited St. Louis and Louisville, at his own expense, to investigate Burr's preparations. It was Daveiss who had brought Burr before the court, twice, to thwart his plans. And it was Daveiss who had reported all of his suspicions and investigations to the administration. In contrast, Jefferson had done very little. After responding to Daveiss's first letter promptly, he had ignored all of the others for months. When Jefferson had finally replied in September, he had merely acknowledged their receipt without directing Daveiss's efforts to prevent the impending crisis. As Daveiss had raced around the West, exposing himself to "personal risque and hazard," Jefferson had sat "snugly in the corner of his cabinet, wrapped up in his cloak of little cunning prudent reserve." Finally, in late October, having "slept amidst all [Daveiss's] efforts to awake [him]," Jefferson had recognized the peril. In Daveiss's view, Jefferson deserved impeachment "for his negligent and flagitious conduct."[116]

Daveiss concluded the main part of his pamphlet with a final attack on Jefferson's message. Having stripped "the feathers" from the message and revealed it to have been "all plumage" and "no carcase," Daveiss offered what he described as "the first rough sketch of the president's communication to congress, on the subject of the conspiracy." This four-page "sketch" constituted a blistering satire upon the message. It corrected what Daveiss saw as Jefferson's lies, beginning, "About twelve months ago, I was informed by letter from Kentucky, that intrigues were there secretly carried on by traitors." But it also had the president explain his inaction through a combination of party prejudice—"I concluded it might be a mere federal trick of our anti-revolutionary enemies"—and sheer incompetence—"I thought it was all smoke, and still slept quietly." In the revised message, Jefferson admits that his dilatory efforts were too little and too late. His special agent arrived in Ohio only "*after* that state was thrown into commotion." Kentucky did not order its militia to stop Burr's boats at Louisville until a week after they had passed, "so that should any attempt be made to row back the flotilla *up over the falls*, it would fall into the clutches of the [militia] as in a fish trap." Jefferson himself was thrown into "such a *potheration*" by Wilkinson's dispatches that he "sent expresses, couriers, heralds and agents in all directions" with orders "neither to eat nor sleep by the way." "It was a time that tried horses souls," Jefferson admits. In the end, he acknowledges "*that the failure of the enterprize has been wholly owing to [Wilkinson's] betraying Burr, and to no act of mine whatever.*"[117]

In the fall of 1807, *A View of the President's Conduct* was widely sold and discussed. While "not much calculated to please our great man," as one New Yorker noted, it thrilled many of Jefferson's opponents.[118] A number of Federalist newspapers not only advertised the pamphlet, but also mentioned it as a news item. The *Washington Federalist* considered "it well worthy the attention of every American reader," highlighting its "SECRET HISTORY of Kentucky prior to Burr's conspiracy," its clear assertion of Wilkinson's ties to Spain and Burr, and the full correspondence between Daveiss and the administration. Daveiss "severely censures the President for his supineness in relation to this affair," the editor noted, but "grounds his censure on documents which appear well to support and justify him."[119] Harman Blennerhassett, likewise, found much to admire and enjoy in Daveiss's pamphlet. While it had all the marks of "a hasty passionate performance" in its style, it had "great merit in its comments," particularly its exposure of "Jefferson's hypocrisy and neglect." Blennerhassett especially appreciated Daveiss's "parody" of Jefferson's message to Congress, "which," he noted in his diary, "has very much diverted me." The pamphlet, he joyfully predicted, would "mortify Jefferson, by proving to all the world, that he would, at no time open his eyes or ears to Wilkinson's intrigues with the Spa[nish] Govt."[120]

What Jefferson actually thought of Daveiss's pamphlet is not known. He owned a copy, but none of his comments about it have survived. Jefferson's supporters quickly attacked it. The nature of their attacks is revealing. Some traced the pamphlet's origins to Daveiss's "Malice and deep Rooted hatred" of what one writer called "our worthy and inimitable President."[121] Others attacked its style. An Ohio newspaper lampooned its "eloquence," "composition," and "language."[122] A piece in the *Mississippi Messenger* ridiculed the pamphlet as "the poorest attempt at writing we recollect to have seen." Its style, according to the editors, "would disgrace even a school boy"; this piece even provided twenty-six quotes documenting errors of grammar and usage. "If Mr. Daveiss ever had a claim on reputation," the editors remarked, "he has completely forfeited it."[123] William Wirt similarly faulted Daveiss for "mix[ing] such a quantity of trash and sometimes low trash with the sounder parts of his publication."[124] Most critics saw these problems as connected: Daveiss had written so poorly precisely because he was so unjustifiably enraged at Jefferson.

Jefferson's supporters did not, however, try to discredit the pamphlet's most important evidence or analysis. They could attack it as the badly written product of a vengeful man. They could predict, as many did, that it would "do [Daveiss] more harm than it will [the administration]."[125] They could even "defy any one to read [the] pamphlet without thinking the better of Mr. Jefferson."[126] But they could not refute Daveiss's well-documented assertions that Jefferson had known about Burr's plans long before September 1806, had done almost nothing to defeat them for months, and had lied to Congress and the public about his knowledge in his January message. So, they ignored those charges. The Republican-dominated Congress that met in November 1807 did not even challenge the president on this issue, much less initiate the impeachment proceedings that Daveiss argued should attend the "stupendously monstrous" crime of "utter[ing] even a *scintilla* of falsehood" to Congress.[127]

"A FAITHFUL NARRATIVE OF THAT CONSPIRACY"

Jefferson's 22 January message to Congress effectively formed a starting point for two centuries of historiographical debate about two key issues—Burr's projects and Jefferson's responses. Early accounts generally replicated the party divisions of the time. Early Jefferson defenders treated the message as an accurate account of Burr's intentions and the administration's measures; early Jefferson critics often made it the focal point for attacks on Jefferson's handling of the Burr crisis, whether or not they defended Burr.[128] The more scholarly works of the century and a quarter since Henry Adams's *History of the United States during the Administrations of Thomas Jefferson and James Madison* (1889–91) have continued to draw heavily upon some aspects of the message. Jefferson's tripartite discussion of Burr's plans has continued to shape most accounts of the conspiracy. Some scholars have followed Jefferson in arguing that Burr was working toward two real ends—dividing the union and invading Mexico—and covering his activities with a false project—settling the Bastrop grant. Even those who have rejected Jefferson's false triad, however, have often written within a framework that depended upon the message. Starting with these three possibilities, they have compared evidence and weighed arguments to arrive at a single, true goal. In doing so, they, like Jefferson, have entirely ignored or quickly rejected other possibilities that were discussed at the time, including Eaton's charge that Burr planned to overthrow the government in Washington by force.

Jefferson's narrowing of the Burr Conspiracy has not fared as well among modern historians. Most have agreed that few westerners supported dividing the union, though some have found broad support for invading Mexico. But the message's sweeping exonerations of General Wilkinson, of other army and navy officers, and of foreign powers have not stood the test of time. Access to foreign archives, particularly in Spain and Great Britain, has confirmed some of the suspicions that the message discounted. It has demonstrated that the Spanish and British ministers had met secretly with Burr, listened carefully to his talk of dividing the union, and reported it favorably to their governments. Such research has also shown that Wilkinson was a paid Spanish agent who revealed Burr's plans and movements not only to the administration in Washington, but also to Spanish officials in Mexico City (and expected a reward for doing so). Although this confirmation of Wilkinson's duplicity has effectively destroyed his credibility, it has not actually proved that he had joined Burr in a treasonous, or even illegal, conspiracy. Establishing that other army and navy officers had supported Burr did not require access to foreign archives. Within weeks of the president's message, what Secretary of War Henry Dearborn called "the defection [of] so considerable a number of our Officers" was well-known.[129] But the administration's quiet decision to ignore these defections meant that scholars had to rediscover their extent in the War Department's archives.

The message's account of how the president learned of and responded to Burr's activities has carried little weight with modern scholars. Even Jefferson's most fervent defenders have rejected the message's chronology by acknowledging his receipt of warnings from Daveiss beginning in January 1806, though they have not bluntly accused him of lying to Congress, as Daveiss did. Jefferson's most strident critics have gone much further. They have asserted that the president learned of Burr's plans in early 1806 not only from Daveiss, but also from Burr. And they have at least suggested that Jefferson tacitly supported Burr's plan to lead a private military expedition against neighboring Spanish possessions, either West Florida or Mexico. Their evidence is circumstantial at best, though Jefferson did meet with Burr in the spring of 1806.[130]

How should we understand Jefferson's 22 January 1807 message to Congress? Few modern scholars have treated it as a wholly accurate statement of either the nature and extent of the Burr Conspiracy or the timing and content of the administration's response. Too many, however, have viewed it as a correct representation of what Jefferson knew or thought at the time about these issues. Doing so requires us to accept that he genuinely believed that Burr had at least plotted treason and that his "guilt [was] placed beyond question."[131] Certainly, one can find other documents, both private and public, in which Jefferson described Burr's plans as he did in the message and insisted that, given time, "evidence might be collected to convict him."[132] But those documents seem no more reliable as indicators of Jefferson's actual views than the message itself. Ultimately, we are no more likely to discover Jefferson's "true" thoughts on these important issues than Burr's "true" plans for his western activities. Instead, the message needs to be read as a public statement that was designed to serve public ends. Jefferson may have called it "a faithful narrative of that conspiracy," but it did not state everything that he believed on the subject and he did not believe everything that he stated in it.[133]

A letter from Dearborn to Wilkinson, written the day before Jefferson submitted his message, shows that the administration knew much more than it announced to Congress. Even as it echoed Jefferson's description of Burr's goals, Dearborn's account differed from the message on various points. Whereas Jefferson carefully omitted names and details, Dearborn provided them. He wrote of Harman Blennerhassett starting to act "immediately after Burr had reached Ohio," of Comfort Tyler contracting for "$40,000 worth [of] provisions," and of William Eaton and Thomas Truxton "communicat[ing] to the Executive very fully" Burr's proposals. Whereas Jefferson simply exonerated Wilkinson, Dearborn addressed the rumors that the general was "to be first or second in command by land." Dearborn's letter also departed from Jefferson's message in recognizing that Burr's men on the Ohio might still be "augmented by [others from] the Mississippi and Orleans Territories." And it acknowledged, as the message did not, that Eaton's revelations included "some bolder strokes, than had before been suggested."[134] It is not known whether Dearborn had read Jefferson's message before writing this letter, but he was surely aware of it. Knowing that the message would soon reach Wilkinson through the newspapers, Dearborn may have decided to send a letter that would arrive at the same time that would elaborate, clarify, and, at times, correct the public message for the general.

The message not only omitted much that the administration believed, but also included things that it did not. Jefferson certainly knew that he had heard of Burr's activities long before September 1806. He had recorded Daveiss's first letter in his correspondence logs, shared it with at least one cabinet member, and replied to it promptly. His papers included copies of all of Daveiss's letters and of two of his own letters acknowledging their receipt. He must have known that the truth differed from his public statement.[135] On other issues as well, the president—or the administration—did not wholly accept what was asserted in the message. The message flatly denied the "proof or probability" of foreign involvement in Burr's plans.[136] But, in late December 1806, Senator Plumer recorded that the secretary of the navy "was satisfied Burr was connected with a foreign power" and that the president thought that the Spanish minister, but not the Spanish government, was "connected with Burr."[137] Likewise, the message applauded Kentucky's "promptitude [and] energy" for moving to arrest Burr's boats and men after the arrival of the proclamation.[138] But, according to Plumer, Jefferson evinced disappointment "Kentucky did not discover that zeal to aid the views of Government that he [had] expected."[139]

To Jefferson, neither the completeness nor the accuracy of the message mattered as much as the lessons that it taught. He did not merely seek to inform Congress and the public about Burr's projects and the administration's response or even to shape congressional and popular thinking about the conspiracy and his administration. Jefferson's purposes extended much further—justifying not just his governance of the country, but the government itself. The message proclaimed a genuine threat to the union and, then, announced that there was no real danger. Jefferson's critics saw this as contradictory; the president did not. In a republican government, the emergence of a threat, he believed, would always generate the public response that was necessary to defeat it. "A conspiracy which, in other countries, would have called for an appeal to armies," he wrote two weeks after submitting the message, had been "given the mortal blow" by "the hand of the people[,] . . . prov[ing] that government to be the strongest of which every man feels himself a part." The suppression of the conspiracy also provided "a happy illustration . . . of the importance of preserving to the State authorities all that vigor which the Constitution foresaw would be necessary, not only for their own safety, but for that of the whole."[140] With the message, Jefferson told a story of the Burr Conspiracy that confirmed the wisdom of his vision of republican government—one without a standing army or a powerful central state. In private letters, newspaper editorials, and public orations, numerous contemporaries demonstrated that they had learned precisely that lesson. "You have heard much of the strength and energy of the governments of the old world," South Carolina's Eldred Simkins remarked in a Fourth of July address, but the outcome of the Burr Conspiracy afforded "a bright example of the UNION, STRENGTH and ENERGY of a REPUBLICAN GOVERNMENT."[141]

To many Americans, Jefferson's message, particularly when combined with the accompanying cipher letter, answered the most important questions about Burr's intentions and activities. It did not, however, answer these questions in the same way for everyone. For many Republicans, Jefferson's message provided "the real facts from an official source" that one editor had urged them to await before drawing any conclusions in early November.[142] It gave them a story about the Burr Conspiracy that they could adopt and retell as their own without taking personal responsibility for its accuracy. It could serve that function because they trusted Jefferson, both as the president and as a gentlemen. That trust did not exist in the minds of Jefferson's political opponents. His public insistence "that the guilt of colonel Burr *was placed* BEYOND A DOUBT"—and the license that that assertion gave to "all Mr. Jefferson's Intelligencers, Auroras, Chronicles, Citizens," and similar newspapers to attack Burr and anyone who defended him—led many Federalists and other administration critics to accept that Burr's projects had always been innocuous.[143] Jefferson's 22 January 1807 message helped both supporters and opponents to turn the great uncertainty of the preceding months into something approaching certainty. But, as was often the case, partisans on each side embraced different certainties, each of which persisted despite new information and new revelations.

CHAPTER 4

THE THREAT TO THE UNION

FROM THE EARLIEST RUMORS AND SPECULATIONS IN THE SPRING OF 1805 to the latest histories and biographies more than two centuries later, the most resonant questions surrounding Aaron Burr's plans and movements have been: did Burr want to divide the federal union and did the Burr Conspiracy pose a threat to that union? Various historians and biographers have offered sharply opposed answers to these questions. The most respected scholarly history of the conspiracy argued that, in "its potentialities," it "posed the greatest threat of dismemberment which the American Union has ever faced" other than the Civil War.[1] More recent works have generally accepted that Burr never intended to divide the union and that no threat existed. But disputes seem certain to continue. Evidence for Burr's intentions is too ambiguous, incomplete, and conflicting to draw solid conclusions. And the fact that his projects never matured places any assessment of their threat in the realm of counterfactual speculation. Burr's contemporaries had less evidence for deciding what he intended and whether his projects threatened the union, but their answers to those questions mattered much more. From the summer of 1805 through the spring of 1807, the answers of civil and military officials shaped governmental responses to Burr's projects first in the West and later in the courts and Congress; during the same months, the answers of the broader public determined popular appraisals of both Burr's actions and official responses.

Shifting our attention from Burr to the people who sought to comprehend his plans and movements raises questions that can tell us more about the early American republic than the ones that have dominated the historiography. First, why was it so easy, and so alarming, for Burr's contemporaries to see disunionist intentions and dangers in his uncertain projects and actions? By the first decade of the nineteenth century, most Americans had accepted the essentiality of union to their internal

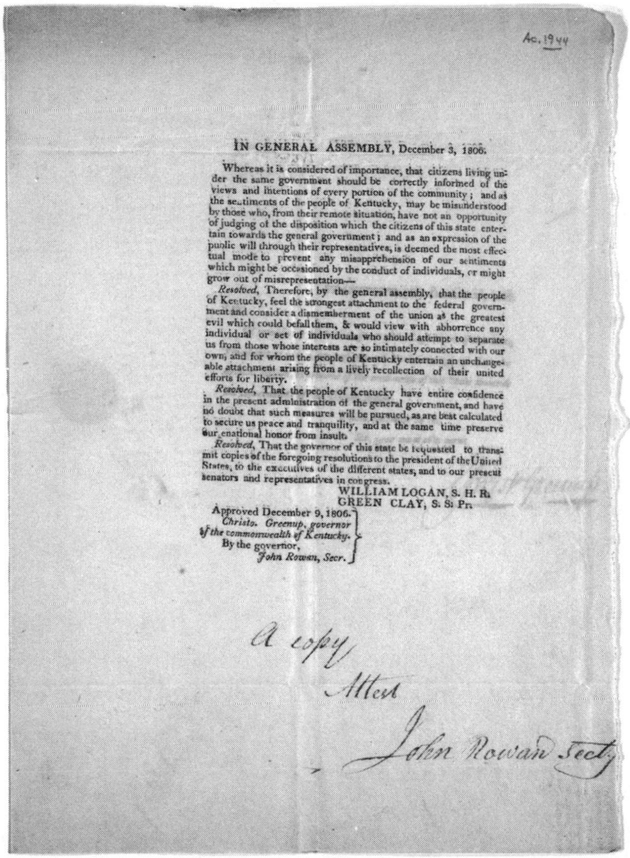

Ac. 1944

IN GENERAL ASSEMBLY, December 3, 1806.

Whereas it is considered of importance, that citizens living under the same government should be correctly informed of the views and intentions of every portion of the community; and as the sentiments of the people of Kentucky, may be misunderstood by those who, from their remote situation, have not an opportunity of judging of the disposition which the citizens of this state entertain towards the general government; and as an expression of the public will through their representatives, is deemed the most effectual mode to prevent any misapprehension of our sentiments which might be occasioned by the conduct of individuals, or might grow out of misrepresentation—

Resolved, Therefore, by the general assembly, that the people of Kentucky, feel the strongest attachment to the federal government and consider a dismemberment of the union as the greatest evil which could befall them, & would view with abhorrence any individual or set of individuals who should attempt to separate us from those whose interests are so intimately connected with our own; and for whom the people of Kentucky entertain an unchangeable attachment arising from a lively recollection of their united efforts for liberty.

Resolved, That the people of Kentucky have entire confidence in the present administration of the general government, and have no doubt that such measures will be pursued, as are best calculated to secure us peace and tranquility, and at the same time preserve our national honor from insult.

Resolved, That the governor of this state be requested to transmit copies of the foregoing resolutions to the president of the United States, to the executives of the different states, and to our present senators and representatives in congress.

WILLIAM LOGAN, S. H. R.
GREEN CLAY, S. S. Pr.

Approved December 9, 1806.
Christo. Greenup, governor of the commonwealth of Kentucky.
By the governor,
John Rowan, Secr.

A copy
Attest
John Rowan Secty

FIGURE 6. The Kentucky General Assembly's formal proclamation of loyalty to the union.

and external peace, their republican governments, and their economic well-being. The logic of union had emerged during the imperial crisis and Revolutionary War in the 1770s and had been elaborated in the ratification debates of the late 1780s. During the partisan battles of the 1790s and the election crisis of 1800–1801, this logic had appeared in speeches, polemics, and letters and guided both Federalist policies and Republican criticisms. The federal union was, as George Washington insisted in his Farewell Address, "the palladium of [Americans'] political safety and prosperity."[2] As such, anything that seemed to threaten the union quickly assumed crisis proportions.

Second, how did widely shared stories about union and disunion shape the efforts to make sense of the Burr crisis? That the union was fragile was as widely accepted as the idea that it was essential. Since independence, Americans had faced a steady stream of what had appeared to be secessionist plots and disunionist dangers in the West, the South, and New England. Knowing from earlier threats to the union how it might shatter, Burr's contemporaries could fit new information—about boats built or supplies purchased or letters sent or men assembled—into preexisting roles in preexisting narratives about union imperilled. "See[ing] the means for effecting some project, not of ordinary magnitude," around them, they turned to these stories because "the end [remained] out of view."[3] Whether Burr actually intended to divide the union was, in a sense, irrelevant; most of his contemporaries could not have known his actual intentions as they struggled to understand his actions. But three decades of paeans to union and fears of disunion had predisposed Americans to see disunionist designs in reports of Burr's movements. Contradictory, fragmentary, and indefinite evidence became coherent, though rarely conclusive, for them by fitting it within stories that they had long heard and told. Each piece of information that could be made to fit these old stories only deepened the sense of crisis.

"HOW IS IT TO BE EFECTED?"

Thirty years of conversations about union and disunion had left Burr's contemporaries with two distinct stories about the union in peril. The first arose from the simple recognition that the extensive federal union included various regions with their own peculiarities of topography and climate, politics and society, economics and culture. Because these characteristics—and the interests and attachments that resulted from them—often followed geographic lines, they could easily strain the fragile bonds of union. For decades, observers across the country had discussed the different and, perhaps, incompatible characters and interests of the union's regions. The second story had been told only about the trans-Appalachian West, where topographical forces steered trade down the Ohio and Mississippi Rivers to the Gulf of Mexico rather than over the Appalachian Mountains to the eastern states and the

Atlantic Ocean. The disunionist pressure exerted by this single, powerful consideration reached its peak between the Revolutionary War's end in 1783 and the Louisiana Purchase in 1803. But memories of this version of disunionism remained fresh as Americans tried to make sense of Burr's plans and movements a few years later.

For late eighteenth- and early nineteenth-century Americans, a threat of disunion inhered in a federal union that combined not only diverse peoples and states, but also distinct sections or regions. Their thinking about precisely how these regions should be defined and exactly how their differences should be weighed changed over time. But, as long as economic activities, political interests, cultural norms, and social structures were segregated spatially, the potential would exist for a geographically defined separatist movement with broad popular support. Responding to the swirl of rumors surrounding Burr's plans and movements, some commentators voiced concerns about westerners' loyalty to the union that embodied this story of the union shattering due to popular separatism.[4]

Over the previous three decades, concerns about popular separatism had taken various forms. In its most basic form, the potential for disunion arose from what seemed to be unchanging, and perhaps unchangeable, conditions. Many worried that the sheer size of the union would bring about its dissolution. The creation of a stronger central government in the Constitution had produced dire warnings of the impossibility of preserving union among such disparate parts. Until the Civil War, moreover, each significant expansion of the union's boundaries sparked new talk of its collapse. In response to the Louisiana Purchase, many leading Federalists warned that attempting to incorporate so much new territory into the United States would "occasion a separation of the union . . . at a time not very remote."[5] If vast extent alone did not destroy the union, the physical barrier of the Appalachians might. "Geographically," Benjamin Tallmadge later recalled, "it seemed that the valley of the Mississippi was, by nature, formed for one nation"—distinct from the one that was east of the mountains.[6] Compounding these geographical forces were the differences in interests and attitudes between regions that resulted from what were often viewed as immutable distinctions of ethnicity, religion, social structure, economic activity, and political preference.

Precisely how such sectional differences would become a popular movement to leave the union was rarely explained. In the fall of 1803, a New England Federalist stressed "the difference of climate, produce, population & manners" between North and South but could offer only a gravitational metaphor to explain the process of disunion itself. At some time "whose whenabouts [are] uncertain," he predicted, "the Northern section will fall off, by force of its own weight."[7] Similarly, Pennsylvania's Josiah Espy found clear differences between East and West as he travelled beyond the mountains in 1805. It seemed certain, if regrettable, "that before many years the people of that [region] would separate themselves from the Atlantic states and establish an independent empire." But he could not explain how this would occur. "What will be the proximate cause producing this great effect," Espy conceded, "is yet in the womb of time."[8]

More fully developed stories about the danger of popular separatism offered more hints about the process of disunion. While differences among sections formed an essential basis for disunion, grievances against the federal government could provide the missing "proximate cause." Whether the West during the Washington and Adams administrations or New England during the Jefferson and Madison administrations or the South leading up to the Civil War, a section that viewed the government as controlled by another section or sections and as negligent of its essential interests appeared ripe for disunion. At the height of the Embargo in 1808, for example, Massachusetts senator John Quincy Adams worried that some New Englanders hoped to foment disunion by "paint[ing their] part of the Union, as under oppression from the rest" through the workings of the federal government.[9]

But without ambitious leaders, even grievances against the federal government might not suffice to transform the differences between regions into a division of the union. The desire of "small statesmen" to acquire power had been, as Adams wrote after the Burr and Embargo crises, "the most powerful operative impulse" for all of the country's "*divisionists.*" Imagining themselves as Caesar, they discovered "that Rome [was] too large an object for their grasp" and decided to "strike off a [portion] where they might aspire to the first station." Ambitious individuals "in every section of the Union," Adams explained, saw "ris[ing] upon a division system" as an "obvious and apparently easy" route to power.[10] Likewise, the Republican editor of Richmond's *Enquirer* considered "the *ambition* of able, cunning, and indefatigable *individuals*" to be the great danger to a union whose permanence might otherwise "[rest] upon the good sense of the people."[11]

This understanding of popular separatism helped some observers process the uncertain reports about Burr's plans and movements. That the West was a geographically distinct region, that westerners had separate interests and concerns, and that Burr was an ambitious individual—all had been widely accepted long before the fall of 1806. Physical barriers of distance and mountains had prevented easy travel, trade, and communication between East and West from the beginnings of trans-Appalachian settlement. During the 1780s and 1790s, westerners had demanded greater control over their own governance, more aggressive protection from Native Americans, easier access to land, lower taxes on their produce, and, most importantly, free use of the Mississippi for their commerce. Easterners had long feared the West's separatist potential. In the mid-1780s, Washington had predicted that westerners would "become a distinct people from us," while Thomas Jefferson had warned that "they [would] end by separating from our confederacy and becoming it's enemies."[12] These concerns had gained force over the next fifteen years, a period rich with activities that were at least incipiently separatist: the Franklin movement in western North Carolina and Virginia, the Spanish Conspiracy in Kentucky, the Whiskey Rebellion across the backcountry and West, and the Blount Conspiracy in Tennessee.[13]

Burr seemed to be exactly the kind of person who could transform such incipient separatism into true disunionism: ambitious enough to try and talented enough to succeed. A reputation for ambition had dogged Burr for years, but, for many, the election of 1800—when Burr had apparently intrigued to steal the presidency from Jefferson— offered the final proof. "Burr's unbounded ambition, courage, and perseverance," Massachusetts's Manasseh Cutler had remarked shortly after the election, might "prompt him to be a Bonaparte, a King, and an Emperor, or any thing else which might place him at the head of the nation."[14] "With a good share of abilities and popular address, and a mind discontented, restless and unprincipled," a New Hampshire newspaper editor opined in the summer of 1806, Burr seemed "well qualified to raise a storm and direct it to his purposes."[15]

At the peak of the Burr crisis, numerous observers showed the impact of long-standing fears of a separatism that involved distinct sectional interests, broad popular support, and ambitious leaders in their accounts of ongoing developments. From upstate New York, one writer predicted "trouble . . . to the Westward"; "the period is not far off," he warned, "when that Country will seperate from us."[16] In late October 1806, with the national capital abuzz with rumors of emergency cabinet meetings, a Virginia Federalist remarked, "if Two Million of People are determined not to be under the Government of the United States, I dont know what King Tom will do."[17] It was not only eastern Federalists who feared western separatism during the Burr crisis, however. A piece in the Republican *Enquirer* considered it obvious "that the Western country, from the very peculiarity of its situation, [would] become the asylum of disappointed ambition, of intrigue, & of conspiracy."[18] Writing to Secretary of State James Madison, a Kentucky Republican confessed his surprise that "the Idea of a separation meet[s] the countenance it does" and suggested "that designing bad men may do a great deal of Mischief in this country."[19] Similar fears about the combination of popular separatism and ambitious leaders informed New Yorker John Nicholson's warning to Jefferson about a "sentiment of disunion" that "pervade[d] many of our western Citizens" and was "probably encouraged by some who might thereby promote their own views."[20]

More often, however, any suggestion that the Burr Conspiracy represented a broad-based, western separatist movement met with great skepticism. Without rejecting the danger of popular separatism in the future, the Federalist Fisher Ames insisted that "the western country [would] not be ripe for such a man as Burr these ten years."[21] Other commentators from across the country discounted all fears about western disloyalty. The New Hampshire Federalist William Plumer believed that it was "not [westerners'] interest nor . . . their disposition, to attempt a seperation from the Union."[22] "From the very nature of their existing situation," westerners must reject any suggestion of disunion, according to Richmond's *Enquirer*.[23] To westerners, Burr's rumored project for breaking the union with broad popular support could only be described as "a *mad, extravagant project*," "chimerical," or a "wild[,] desperate plan."[24] Struggling to rescue himself from the rumors that tied him to Burr's project, Tennessee militia general Andrew Jackson penned perhaps the most overblown denunciation of the idea of western separatism. "It betrays great ignorance in the character of any man," he wrote Secretary of War Henry Dearborn, to "suppose, that two men can be found in the western country willing to form a seperation of the western from the atlantick States."[25]

In part, this skepticism reflected an understanding that the West's position within the union had improved dramatically in recent years. The belief that the West was a distinct region with distinct interests persisted. And the presence of Burr—that "Master piece at Intriague," as one New Yorker described him—provoked concern.[26] But almost all of the grievances that westerners had articulated against the general government in the 1780s and 1790s had been resolved. Local government in the form of statehood had come to Kentucky (1792), Tennessee (1796), and Ohio (1803). Military and diplomatic successes had eased the Indian threat. Common people had gained easier access to the public domain under new laws (1800 and 1804). Most internal taxes, including the tax on distilled spirits that had fueled the Whiskey Rebellion, had disappeared early in Jefferson's presidency. And free use of the Mississippi to the Gulf had been arranged in Pinckney's Treaty (1795) and secured through the Louisiana Purchase (1803). To many, Republican control of the federal government seemed to guarantee a continuing solicitude for western interests. As a Kentucky editor explained in July 1806, "The navigation of the Mississippi secured— peace with the Indians established—and the principles of the present Federal Administration being in unison with their own,—[westerners] have no wish ungratified."[27] During the Burr crisis, many writers could find no grounds of complaint against the government to justify fears of disunion. Westerners, a western Republican asserted in early 1807, "were not a band of ignorant savages who would barter away their rights and the blessings they enjoyed for the paultry baubles of an adventurer."[28]

The near-total absence of signs of popular separatism in the West did not absolve Burr of disunionist intentions, however. Successfully "prevail[ing] upon the people of Kentucky to revolt" may have been "too ridiculous to believe," as the Philadelphia editor William Duane claimed, but that did not mean that Burr had not attempted to do so.[29] Many Republicans thought that Burr had tried to use both private meetings with prominent westerners and provocative essays in western newspapers to encourage popular separatism. Jefferson asserted as much in his important 22 January 1807 message to Congress. Other Republicans had made the same claim weeks earlier. "Desperate and unprincipled men" had tried to promote western separatism, the *National Intelligencer* had charged in early December 1806, but westerners were not "madmen or fools."[30]

If the only stories about disunion that Americans had heard and told in previous years had depended upon popular separatism, Burr's plans and activities probably would not have sparked so much anxiety. A disunionist movement that required that level of popular support might not form even under optimal conditions—distinct interests, regional self-awareness, governmental neglect, and ambitious leaders. "And unless [disunion] becomes a popular measure," as one Kentuckian observed in early 1807, "who is to effect it?"[31] But many of Burr's contemporaries relied upon a different story about disunion, one that did not require such popular commitment, as they tried to comprehend his project. Though developed as early as 1784, when Spain had closed the lower Mississippi to American trade, this story had been most fully elaborated early in Jefferson's presidency when a weak Spain restored Louisiana to a strong France. During the ensuing Mississippi Crisis, many Americans, in and out of government, had recognized that any strong power that held the mouth of the Mississippi could control the trade of the trans-Appalachian West, which had "no outlet to the Sea but thro that River."[32] Offers of special privileges or threats of trade restrictions could be used to draw or drive the West from the union. In this way, even a loyal populace might be pushed to disunion by the manipulation of its economic interests. In late 1806 and early 1807, stories about the Mississippi Crisis led many of Burr's contemporaries to see evidence of disunionist intentions and a threat to the union in the conflicting rumors and reports.

Early in Jefferson's presidency, policymakers in Washington and abroad had quickly recognized the threat that French control over New

Orleans and the mouth of the Mississippi—far more than over the vast territory beyond the river—posed to the union of East and West. In an early report of the retrocession, Rufus King, the American minister in London, informed Madison "that this cession [was] intended to have, and may actually produce, Effects injurious to the Union."[33] As the crisis grew, Jefferson and Madison increasingly worried that France had reacquired Louisiana precisely to gain influence over the West. Instructing his diplomats in Paris in early 1803, Madison expressed this concern clearly. France, he explained, may have calculated "that by holding the key to the commerce of the Mississippi, she [could] command the interests and attachments of the Western portion of the United States." From this position, France would try to "controul the Atlantic portion also, or if that [could not] be done, to seduce the [West into] a separate Government, and a close alliance with herself."[34] Policymakers were not alone in seeing the danger of the retrocession in this way. William T. Barry, a nineteen-year-old law student in Kentucky, perceived the danger as clearly as Madison did. "Having in their possession the sea ports on the Mississippi, which are the only marts for the commerce of these States," he informed his brother, the French would "have hold of a lever with which they can wield and regulate our interests as they please." In time, he predicted, they would "try to separate [the western states] from the Eastern."[35]

In early 1807, Barry told the same story but with Burr taking the place of France. "The first object" was New Orleans, he argued; possessing that, Burr would attempt "to revolutionize the Spanish provinces and establish an independent Govt. distinct from the U.S.[,] and ultimately to bring about a separation of the Union."[36] Others outside of the government described the danger from Burr in similar terms. Wilson Cary Nicholas, a former senator and an administration supporter, warned that losing New Orleans to Burr would bring "the most serious consequences" since "the Western part of America must be connected with, or dependent upon[,] the power that commands the mouth of the Mississippi."[37] The *Enquirer's* editor likewise believed that Burr had intended, "by locking up the mouth of the Mississippi[,] to produce a dissolution of the union and to establish an independent empire to the west of the Alleghany."[38] Such concerns were not limited to Republicans. The Maryland Federalist Charles Carroll informed his son that Burr's plan was "to take possession of New Orleans, and by holding it[,] to compel the western people to come into his views, and to establish a separate State westward of the mountains."[39] And former naval commander Thomas Truxton trusted that any "man of mind" could see "that if New Orleans[—]as the Outlet of the Mississippi, for the productions of the western Country[—]is once Independent of the Union[,] it would Compel the States above to follow [its] Example."[40]

This analysis proved especially powerful among government officials who sought to understand Burr's plans. In one of the earliest warnings, Joseph Hamilton Daveiss, the federal district attorney in Kentucky, remarked, "No doubt all the western waters are calculated on, as falling in with the power possessing the mouths of those waters."[41] After taking "New Orleans with an armed Force," Jefferson's special agent John Graham explained in early 1807, Burr would restrict the West's trade so "as to force it to separate from the Atlantic States."[42] Senator George Washington Campbell offered a similar explanation of the danger in a letter to his Tennessee constituents that was prefaced with an explicit rejection of popular separatism. Having found that westerners were "faithful to the union," Campbell explained, Burr had decided instead to seize New Orleans, invade Mexico, "and if successful in this, shut up the mouth of the Mississippi[,] . . . and thereby compel [the West] to join his newly created empire."[43] The president, as well, returned to the logic of the Mississippi Crisis as he tried to make sense of Burr's plans. Burr intended, Jefferson explained, to "extend his empire to the Alleghany, [by] seizing on New Orleans as the instrument of compulsion for our western States."[44]

"Seizing on New Orleans" would be much easier, Burr's contemporaries believed, than securing the broad support that would have been required for popular separatism. They identified different ways by which Burr could take New Orleans: with a large force raised in the West; with the support of the army and, perhaps, navy; with the assistance of a foreign power; and with the backing of one or more parts of the local populace. Their understanding of the vulnerability of New Orleans and of the fragility of an East-West union that depended upon New Orleans encouraged them to find disunionist intents and disunionist dangers whenever they saw evidence that linked Burr to any of these means. At the same time, their growing anxieties about Burr's uncertain plans and movements led them to imagine, even without evidence, that large numbers of men had been enlisted, that military officers had been corrupted, that foreign powers had been engaged, and that various Orleanians had been mobilized. Speculations about each of these means for "seizing on New Orleans" and imperilling the union echoed across the country in conversations, letters, and newspapers during the Burr crisis.

Unfounded estimates of the size of Burr's force filled contemporary reports. With federal troops in the Southwest totalling just "1165 Men including drummers," according to one account, and closer to 800, according to their commander, it seemed that even a fairly small force under Burr could capture New Orleans.[45] But few of the estimates of Burr's force were even remotely small. Andrew Jackson reported a relatively low figure of 1,000 men. Most accounts gave totals at least three times the size of the regular troops: 3,000 according to Ohio's James Finley; 2,500 to 3,000 with another 1,500 on the way according to Ohio governor Edward Tiffin; and 5,000 and "daily increasing" according to the news that reached Benjamin Hawkins at the Creek agency in Georgia.[46] Other estimates went much higher. From Natchez, in late December 1806, Thomas Freeman alerted the War Department to rumors that Burr "with an armed force of nearly 8000 armed men" would arrive within days; Freeman's repetition of "armed" probably better conveyed his state of mind than his confident assertion that the few soldiers at nearby Fort Adams were determined to "do their duty."[47] From Pittsburgh, Frederick Bates stated, albeit with some amazement, that "the most intelligent" locals "imagine[d] that [Burr's] army [would] be composed of about ten thousand chosen men."[48] Perhaps the highest total, purportedly based upon information that had been "given upon oath," came from Cincinnati in late December: "the number of men already engaged . . . exceeded 20,000."[49]

Many believed that Burr did not need to raise a large force, and might not even need to fire a shot, to seize New Orleans because he had corrupted the army. Officers were always alert for slights to their honor; as little as an improper promotion, one senator remarked, might "have prepared them for Burr & have made them fit for all manner of *Conspiriacies, treasons, & sabots*."[50] But most of these fears centered upon General James Wilkinson, whose loyalties had long been questioned and whose friendship with Burr was well known. The fact that Wilkinson, a man "so eminently worthy of suspicion," headed the troops that might be needed to defend New Orleans and the union fueled widespread concern.[51] As the earliest reports of the conspiracy reached Washington, one Virginian flatly asserted that Burr had "Wilkinson at the head of the Army, in league with him."[52] By mid-January 1807, western accounts provided more details. Burr's men, according to one Tennesseean, would join forces in New Orleans with "Wilkason, and the federal troops there, together, with a detachment from New-York, which [was] to act by water."[53] Even the news that Wilkinson had "denounced B[urr] as a traitor" did not dispel all doubts. Jackson, who had long despised Wilkinson, viewed the general's disclosures as "Deep policy," since he had "obtained thereby the Command of New Orleans [and] the Gun Boats armed."[54] In early January 1807, the Mississippi territorial judge Thomas Rodney likewise thought it possible that Wilkinson was "acting a very Deep part . . . Untill the Important Moment Arrives to Execute the Project in full."[55]

Contemporaries also accepted and circulated rumors and reports that Burr had enlisted a foreign army or navy to help him to seize New Orleans. Relations with both Spain and Great Britain were tense; either power might have hoped to cripple the new nation by promoting disunion. Rumors had long circulated, moreover, about private meetings between Burr and various French, British, and Spanish officials in Washington, Philadelphia, and New Orleans. That he had arranged foreign assistance seemed certain to many; what remained unclear was from which power. Administration supporters generally considered Great Britain "far more probable" than Spain.[56] From Mississippi, Judge Rodney, for example, warned that the conspirators "Expect[ed] a Brittish Fleet to aid them."[57] Administration opponents usually pointed to Spain or France on the grounds, as one Federalist insisted, that there was no "earthly purpose" for Great Britain "to tamper with Louisiana."[58] "The schemes of Burr," according to the Virginia Quid John Randolph, were "carrying on in concert with the cabinet of Madrid & with Spanish money."[59] But general confusion often trumped partisan clarity on this issue. Though confident "that the City of New Orleans was to be Attacked by sea and land," one North Carolinian could not decide "What Nation" would provide the navy.[60]

Even when they could find little clear evidence of a large force on the move from the Ohio Valley or a corrupted army in the Southwest or a supporting fleet or army in transit from abroad, Burr's contemporaries still found grounds for seeing a threat to the union. Even when they viewed westerners as a whole as loyal to the union, they considered the people of New Orleans and its environs to be, at best, loosely tied to a country and government that had only recently acquired their province. Since New Orleans's transfer, each element of the area's mixed population—European, creole, and American, white, mixed-race, black, and Indian—had provoked concern in some way, suggesting to some "that men of different languages and habits, are not calculated to live contented under the same system of laws."[61] Burr had visited New Orleans in the summer of 1805, and it seemed possible that he had arranged enough local support to take the city from within. "Intrigue combined with a dark night might Possess him of it," as one commentator noted.[62] Writing to Madison in August 1806, Daveiss predicted, "you will upon an emergency find the settlement at Orleans perfectly rotten."[63] In mid-November, Wilkinson alerted the secretary of war that "the discontents of some, and villainy of others" would provide Burr with "auxiliaries" in New Orleans.[64] With the crisis upon him in early December, Orleans territorial governor William C. C. Claiborne admitted his doubts about whether "a majority of the People . . . would rally at the call of Government."[65]

Lurking in some minds were fears of another "expedient" that Burr might rely upon to subdue New Orleans, one that Virginia's John Randolph called "as black as Hell."[66] Slaves and free people of color comprised a large and potentially dangerous part of the area's population. The threats that they posed haunted white southerners long before and long after the Burr crisis; many of the statements linking them to Burr reveal these ever-present fears more than this specific context. From western Virginia came a warning that Burr would "stimulate" the South's "white or black caps . . . to insurrection" in order to secure New Orleans.[67] From Nashville came a report that Burr had offered a local barber "(a Mulato) fifty Dollars per month [to] go with him and take fifty or a Hundred Coloured men."[68] And from near Natchez came the news, on "good Authority[,] that certain negroes . . . [had] been heard a few nights ago Huzzarring for Burrs men."[69] Silas Dinsmore, the federal agent with the Choctaws, captured the overblown nature of these fears in an early January 1807 letter to a close friend. "We are all in a flurry here," the New Englander reported from Natchez, "hourly expecting Colonel Burr & all Kentucky & half of Tennessee at his [back] to punish General Wilkinson, set the negroes free, Rob the banks & take Mexico." He urged his friend to "come & help me to laugh at the fun."[70]

Assessing such fears, some historians have argued that Burr, though he owned at least one slave, was considered a proto-abolitionist who would promise slaves freedom in exchange for military service. But Wilkinson and Claiborne, who treated the slave peril very seriously during the Burr crisis, saw something much more complicated. At times, Wilkinson did worry that, if Burr made a successful "Landing at Natchez," he could "draw on the Blacks for any force he may require"; even then, Wilkinson traced Burr's possible use of slaves and free blacks to "desperation" rather than to abolitionism.[71] At other times, however, Wilkinson and Claiborne suggested that the real impact of the slave population was on the size and use of their own forces, not Burr's. They quickly recognized that they could not bolster the meager regular troops with the militias of the Orleans or Mississippi Territories "on Account of the Slaves."[72] Mobilizing the militia from the plantation districts around New Orleans and further upriver to intercept Burr would be "injudicious," Wilkinson warned Claiborne, because of the "danger of an insurrection of the negroes."[73] In their view, the slaves seemed likely to rise in response not to Burr's presence, but to the militia's absence.

In a November 1806 letter to Tennessee senator Daniel Smith, Andrew Jackson assembled uncertain evidence and reasonable suppositions into a coherent explanation of how Burr might seize New Orleans and divide the union. If "a plan for separating the Union is actually on foot," Jackson asked, "how is it to be efected?" Recognizing "the attachment of [th]e western people collectively to the government," he argued, "a designing man" would take advantage of the tensions on the southwestern frontier by "form[ing] an intrigue" with the Spanish minister and adding to it "the general of your army." Under the "pretext" of a war scare, Spanish and American troops would come together "within two hundred miles of New-orleans"—as had recently happened on the Sabine River. As "the two armies . . . forme[d] plans of cooperation," Burr's forces would descend "from the ohio and uper Louisiana." With "two thirds of its inhabitants into the plan," New Orleans would "[fall] an easy pray" to the combination of Burr's men from upriver and the American and Spanish armies from the frontier. Aided by the Spanish navy, Burr would "Shut the Port against the exportation of the west, and hold out alurements to all the western world to Join [in order to] enjoy free trade and profitable commerce." Burr could divide the union at the Appalachians, as Jackson explained, despite near-universal western opposition. In this letter, Jackson blended anxiety and skepticism—a common approach to the disunionist threat of the conspiracy. He detailed a plot that pointed inexorably to a division of the union; yet, he insisted that "no other plan" than this elaborate and improbable scenario "could furnish [a hope] of success."[74]

Stories about the essentiality and the vulnerability of the union—stories that had developed over three decades and that remained compelling nearly twenty years after the ratification of the Constitution and three years after the acquisition of Louisiana—helped Burr's contemporaries to make sense of his uncertain projects and movements. These stories suggested two very different ways in which Burr might hope to divide the union at "the back bone" of the Appalachians.[75] One depended upon a degree of popular separatism in the West that most observers quickly decided did not exist in the fall of 1806. The other centered upon a single spot that might be seized in various ways. At the peak of the Burr crisis, Americans read and heard enough rumors and reports of large collections of men on the Ohio, of alienated army officers, of tensions with foreign powers, of political and cultural clashes in New Orleans, and of slave and free black insurgency for many to accept that Burr intended to divide the union and that the threat of disunion was real.

"HIGH TIME TO VINDICATE OURSELVES"

If the Burr crisis reveals the continuing power of stories about why and how the union might divide, it also exposes the surprising limits of stories about why and how it might remain intact. Behind all of the concerns about the Burr Conspiracy as a threat to the union lay questions of loyalty. Stories that grounded the threat in Burr's seizure of New Orleans raised some relatively narrow questions: Were Burr's men loyal to their leader or their country? Was Wilkinson loyal to Burr or Spain or the United States? Was the army loyal to Wilkinson or the administration? Were Orleanians loyal to their new country? Contemporaries could predict answers to these questions, and could dispute each other's predictions, but they could discover the truth only by waiting for future events, not by turning to oft-told stories. In contrast, stories that located the threat in regional differences and popular separatism raised the broadest possible question about loyalty: would Americans be loyal to the union and its government? One might think that the answer to this question—one that is basic to the existence of any polity—could be found in the stable realm of preexisting stories, not in the uncertain world of future events. But westerners who desperately wanted to absolve themselves of disunionism during the Burr crisis struggled to find compelling stories from the nation's past to justify and explain their unionism and their loyalty.

What was accepted as loyalty in the early American republic included the seeds of disloyalty. Loyalty did not mean the same thing in the late eighteenth- and early nineteenth-century United States that it meant in most contemporary European nations. During and after the Revolution, Americans wrestled with the idea that one's loyalty was unalterably established at birth—an idea that Europeans almost universally accepted. Republicans, in particular, often argued that loyalty should be seen as a matter of conscious choice; this view undergirded their belief that individuals should be able to expatriate themselves from one country and naturalize themselves in another. More than to place, person, or government, Americans usually described themselves as loyal to a body of political principles and to what we might now call an "imagined community" that extended backward and forward in time. During the Burr crisis, a Tennessee militia company expressed this thinking by "declar[ing] to our country and the world . . . that those principles which carried our fathers through the blood & war of a glorious revolution are recorded on our minds, and we intend to bequeth them to our posterity."[76] Such sentiments were widely held. They transformed what might have seemed merely self-serving—a commitment to rights and freedoms that clearly benefitted oneself—into something more selfless—a gratitude for the sacrifices of the past and a solicitude for the happiness of the future. To be loyal in this figuration was to show that "the spirit of '76 [was] still glowing in [ones'] breasts" by "protect[ing the] rights so dearly bought" by revolutionary "fathers" and passing them "inviolate" to "posterity."[77]

But loyalty to a set of political principles and a community that spanned generations did not necessarily mean loyalty to the United States, whether viewed as a union or a government. The same principles could take various institutional forms at the state and national levels. And the line that separated one's own community from others'—"our country and the world," in the words of the Tennessee militiamen— was not fixed. Fundamental American principles, moreover, ruled out an absolute, ineradicable loyalty to the union or its government. As republicans, Americans insisted that all good governments originated in the choice of the governed. As liberals, they believed that individuals were the best judges of their own interests. As the Declaration of Independence asserted, any people had "the Right . . . to alter or to abolish" a government that no longer protected "their Safety and Happiness" and to replace it with a new government that could do so.

In this context, loyalty almost necessarily became a matter of calculation and contingency, of events rather than stories. It only rarely arose from a belief that the existence of union or the structure of the government was perfect and immutable. Instead, it reflected an ongoing evaluation of how well the union and the government protected and promoted interests, whether personal, state, or regional. These interests included everything from physical security to religious freedom, from political rights to economic opportunity. Their specific characteristics and relative importance changed over time, as did the success of the union and the government at defending or advancing them. Philadelphia's Tench Coxe neatly captured the calculated and contingent nature of loyalty in March 1807 as he described the obstacles to Burr's presumed separatism. "After the purchase of Louisiana," Coxe explained, "the people of property or working people of the western country would [not] risk their estates and freedom in a project to place them under a government less free, and less parental."[78] In this brief statement, Coxe named the groups—"the people of property" and the "working people"— that he thought would decide the question of union in the West, identified the interests—"estates and freedom"—that would shape their decision, and recognized the importance of changing conditions—by implying that the same groups, responding to the same interests, might have decided differently before "the purchase of Louisiana." He did not doubt westerners' loyalty to the union. But what Coxe, and many others, accepted as loyalty derived from principles that could also lead to disloyalty.

Across the West, the Burr Conspiracy unleashed a torrent of assertions of loyalty to the union. Territorial assemblies and state legislatures, militia companies and public meetings, newspaper editors and private correspondents—all proclaimed this loyalty to a national audience and to federal officials. From the Orleans territorial assembly came "a solemn testimonial . . . of our firm Determination under all Circumstances and at all hazards to maintain and support that political connexion which has united our Destinies to those of one of the freest and most enlightened people on earth."[79] From a public meeting in central Kentucky came the assurance that the people were "severely attached to our Government and American Brethren" and "deprecate[d] the idea of a disunion from our Sister States."[80] From a letter writer in Lexington came a confident report that Kentuckians were "almost unanimous in their attachment to the union" and "view[ed] with horror the idea of a separation from their Atlantic brethren."[81] Such sentiments reappeared for months in the toasts that were offered at public celebrations, especially on the Fourth of July, and published in local newspapers. Citizens in Nashville, for example, drank to "The Union— may perdition seize those who would sow the seeds of discord between the eastern & western states."[82]

Although they differed in their details, these assertions of loyalty shared a number of characteristics that illustrate the complexities and contradictions of the era's ideas about loyalty. Most arose from the authors' concern that someone—the president, Congress, the eastern states, or the rest of the country—doubted the loyalty of their region, state, or territory. A public meeting in Hartford, Kentucky, began its address to the president by remarking that "the people of the Western Country [had] been often charged with disaffection to the Union."[83] Such doubts followed naturally from American thinking about loyalty. Federalists questioned the loyalty of Republicans; easterners questioned the loyalty of westerners. The Burr crisis even revealed that Kentuckians questioned the loyalty of Ohioans, and vice versa. Kentucky's James Taylor warned that disunionists could accomplish "much more in the state of Ohio than in this," even as Ohio's Wyllys Silliman "fear[ed] that there were *many* in the State of Kentucky, disposed to favor [Burr's] plans, even of dissolving the Union."[84] Resolutions that purported to speak for a broad public might allay such doubts. Citizens meeting in Shelby County, Kentucky, for example, viewed their resolutions as a way to ensure "that their sentiments on political subjects [were] fully and fairly stated to the world" in order to counteract "the slanderous insinuations" of some eastern newspapers.[85]

The Shelby County resolutions reveal another common element in these assertions of loyalty—the linking of political belief and personal honor. Discovering doubts about Kentucky's loyalty in the national capital in late December 1806, Senator Henry Clay assured the doubters, "I would answer with my honor and my life for her attachment to the common cause."[86] In early republican America, one was supposed to be loyal to "principles not men"—one of the era's hackneyed phrases. But, for many, the only language that was available for expressing one's loyalty in this new republican society came from the honor culture of the old aristocratic courts. Even as republican principles eliminated obligation to a person (or family) as a basis of loyalty, they demanded a great investment of personal honor in loyalties that seemed purely volitional. During the Burr crisis, individuals invested their personal honor in their own and their regions' loyalty in various ways. Some signed public statements or private letters asserting it. Since their members' names were widely known or easily discovered, legislative bodies achieved the same effect by announcing that their assertions of loyalty had been adopted unanimously. With loyalty regarded as a matter of personal honor, moreover, doubts were often treated as personal attacks— "slanders . . . derogatory to the character of a people," as a Kentucky editor put it.[87] Some assertions of loyalty even used the language of the affair of honor. They complained of "cruel and unfounded libels," "imputation[s] of ingratitude," and "slander[s] without foundation."[88] They remarked that such comments could no longer be "suffered to pass unnoticed" and that those slandered "[could not] be indifferent."[89] And they proclaimed as their goal the rehabilitation of the author's or region's "just Character."[90] Believing that his territory had "been recently denounced, insulted, and accused of treason," a member of the Orleans territorial legislature insisted that it was "high time to vindicate ourselves."[91]

But, as concerned as the authors of these resolutions and letters were about their questioned loyalty and injured honor, they frequently explained their loyalty to the union in terms of calculated interests and contingent conditions. "No part of the United States is more loyal than the Western Country," Ohio's William Creighton asserted when the Burr Conspiracy had raised widespread doubts. The West's superior loyalty was explained by what he considered "the Strongest motive[,] interest." While "either of the other sections might possibly support their independence," Creighton argued, "the Western Country certainly could not."[92] The citizens of Franklin, Tennessee, also saw "a sure pledge of the fidelity of Western America [in] motives of interest"; only "a union with the maritime states," they noted, could "preserve the navigation and commerce of the gulph with its Northern appendages, which united America [had] recently obtained."[93] And Ohio legislators linked their devotion to the union, in part, to their unwillingness "to hazard by intestine dissensions [their] incalculable advantages," which they described as "enjoying as we now do every blessing which as men and citizens we could desire . . . in a country fertile in natures cherished gifts."[94] Westerners could not be tricked into "withdraw[ing] our affections from that union, on which our prosperity and happiness depends," according to a Nashville newspaper editor.[95]

Each of these statements suggested not only calculations of interest, but also contingency of conditions. How loyal would westerners be if the union no longer seemed to be a source of "prosperity and happiness"? How loyal would Ohio's legislators be if union ceased to bring the blessings that it "now [did]"? How loyal had Franklin's citizens been before "united America" secured control of the Mississippi for western commerce and how loyal would they be if it ever lost control? How loyal would what Creighton called "the Western Country" be once it could "support [its] independence" outside of the union? If the union was "cemented by interest & inclination," as the Shelby County resolutions claimed, what would happen if interests or inclinations changed?[96] One Tennesseean captured, apparently inadvertently, the contingent nature of loyalty in a letter that appeared in the *Intelligencer* in early January 1807. Westerners, he asserted, would not join a disunionist scheme; they were "too well disposed towards the government to indulge the remotest thought of such a measure." "No man of common sense," he concluded, "would attempt such a thing at this time."[97] But what might happen at other times?

Little separated the language of loyalty and unionism from the language of disloyalty and disunionism. During the Burr crisis, such unionists as New York's John Nicholson and Ohio's William Creighton based their confidence in the union on westerners' understanding of "their true Interests" and "their true situation."[98] But the men who were indicted as disunionist traitors alongside Burr in Richmond argued for westerners to separate from the union on the same grounds. According to one account, Ohio senator John Smith defended a division of the union "by the Alleghany mountains" on the grounds "that our interest was entirely different from the Atlantic country."[99] When Harman Blennerhassett published a series of disunionist newspaper essays as the "Querist" in September 1806, he began by urging westerners to consider how "the situation of the Union" affected their "rights and interests."[100] And another alleged disunionist, former New Jersey senator Jonathan Dayton, insisted that the West could leave the union whenever westerners "deem[ed] it essential to their prosperity & happiness" to do so. Disunionist arguments sounded so much like unionist arguments because they derived from the same widely shared principles. Few Americans would have disagreed that westerners, as Dayton argued, must "be the Judges, & [were] the only proper ones," of their own interests. Few Americans would have questioned that interests would ultimately determine western loyalties. And few Americans would have denied that westerners had "a right in common with [them]selves & every other free people to throw off their old connexions, & to form new ones."[101]

Across the country, editors and essayists filled newspapers with attacks on disunion and disunionists during the Burr crisis. Some of the earliest pieces responded to the *Western World*'s "Kentucky Spanish Association" essays; some of the later ones appeared after Burr and his men had started down the Ohio and Mississippi Rivers. But, in the fall of 1806, most of those that appeared in Ohio Valley newspapers answered Blennerhassett's "Querist" essays. At least seven Ohio and Kentucky writers published at least two dozen pseudonymous essays in Chillicothe's *Scioto Gazette*, Cincinnati's *Western Spy*, and Frankfort's *Western World* between October and December 1806; a number of these essays were reprinted in other newspapers. Whether published in Republican or Federalist newspapers, whether written by Republican or Federalist authors, these essays attacked the disunionism that was voiced by the "Querist" and was associated with Burr and Blennerhassett. In general, however, they did so without ever questioning the broad consensus on language and principles that brought disunionism and unionism so close to each other.[102]

The easiest way to counter the "Querist's" disunionism was to challenge the author's fitness for determining western interests. In perhaps the first piece to identify Blennerhassett as the "Querist," "An American" insisted that, as "a foreigner who [had] resided but a few years in our country," the Irish immigrant could not "be supposed a judge of our interests." He needed to be viewed, instead, as "subservient to [Burr's] interest and designs."[103] That Burr—whom many considered the instigator of the "Querist" essays—cared far more about his own than western interests was widely accepted. Anti-"Querist" writers described Burr as "ambitious," "designing," and hoping "to ensnare the people into schemes formed for [his] own aggrandizement, at the expence of their safety, liberty and happiness."[104]

Beyond challenging the fitness of the judge, these writers also challenged the accuracy of the judgments. As the "Querist," Blennerhassett generally presented western interests in economic terms. "Our great western country and the annual produce of our land and labour," he argued, were being used by easterners "as a granary for the Eastern states, and a fund for federal revenue."[105] The federal government required westerners to buy lands that they should have enjoyed by right of conquest. As a result, according to the "Querist," westerners paid three million dollars each year to support a government that was "adverse or indifferent to [their] prosperity," when one hundred thousand dollars would have maintained a western government.[106] Anti-"Querist" writers assaulted Blennerhassett's facts and analysis. Ohio judge Matthew Nimmo, writing as "Regulus," used the latest land sales data to refute the claim that the West paid three million dollars annually. He further insisted that westerners benefitted from federal control over land sales, which kept "land-jobbers, speculators, [and] fortune-hunters" from perpetrating "every species of fraud." Because of the protection afforded by the United States, "Regulus" argued, westerners had been raised "from hopeless prospects of obtaining landed property in the Eastern states, to the possession of fine farms."[107]

But anti-"Querist" essayists also attacked the narrowing of interests to economics. Reviving arguments that had been used to support the Constitution, they insisted that union was essential for securing interests that mattered much more than individual prosperity: national independence and republican government. As obvious as such priorities might seem, the early republic's governing elite generally viewed common citizens as motivated primarily by their personal, economic well-being. Many of the fears about western separatism reflected this belief that economics would dictate individual and regional calculations of interest. The concerns about control over New Orleans, for example, derived from the conviction that westerners would leave the union to preserve their downriver commerce even if they had to subordinate their region to an unrepublican ruler, whether Napoleon or Burr, to do so. By shifting attention from land, trade, and taxes to national independence, republican government, and individual liberties, anti-"Querist" authors challenged the preeminence of economics in calculations of interest.[108]

During the Burr crisis, as during the ratification debates, defenders of union understood national independence as both the continued existence of the nation and its freedom from foreign interference. Combining the North American states into a single union seemed necessary for both aspects of independence. In case of disunion, one anti-"Querist" author warned, the West would "soon become tributary to some powerful neighbor"—Great Britain, Spain, or France. "In the event of a separation of the states," he explained, these powers might work together to "partition the western country among [themselves.]"[109] Similarly, the editor of the Lebanon, Ohio, *Western Star* assured his readers that, as long as East and West remained united, "we need not fear any of the powers of Europe." Disunion would unleash "all the horrors arising from anarchy and confusion," leaving the nation "an easy prey to the ambition of European despots."[110] Writing as "An Observer,"

Kentucky's Humphrey Marshall simply described *"Union"* as part of a divine plan to keep the United States *"free and independent."*[111]

As Marshall and others recognized, an inevitable result of the loss of national independence would be the loss of republican government. But anti-"Querist" authors, like the advocates of the Constitution, warned that the same result would follow no less inevitably from disunion even without conquest. Unless all of its states formed a single union, the original Federalists had argued, North America would replicate Europe's history of perpetual war and monarchical government. A single division—the emergence of a new nation in the West or Southwest under Burr, for example—would almost certainly produce others. The result, according to Marshall, would be a number of "separate confederacies or state sovereignties" that would become "the perpetual rivals, and inveterate enemies of each other." "The dissoluted parts" could not "long retain . . . the republican form."[112] As they competed for wealth, territory, and power, the individual states or partial confederacies would sacrifice personal rights for national security, abandoning republican principles for the advantages of centralized authority, standing armies, and higher taxes. In time, all of the states would adopt the same measures to survive. Although a multitude of states might endure, converting North America into a field of endless warfare, it seemed more likely to some that disunion would ultimately produce a single despot. "Sydney," an anti-"Querist" essayist in Cincinnati's *Western Spy*, predicted that if one region broke from the union, "further division[s] must ensue, war and commotion [would] overspread our land, and our happy country, the only seat of liberty on earth, . . . [would] become the dominions of a sceptred tyrant."[113]

Even as "Regulus," "Sydney," "An Observer," and others tried to elevate political above economic interests, their defenses of union, like those of "Publius" in *The Federalist* two decades earlier, still relied upon an instrumentalism that arose from interests and, thus, accepted calculation and contingency. Such a reliance did not differentiate westerners at the time of the Burr crisis from most other Americans at most other times during the preceding four decades. Union had always been defended by referring to interests and conditions. Union among the thirteen colonies during the imperial crisis had been championed as a way to force Great Britain to rescind the acts that struck at the political rights and economic advantages of the colonists. Union among the states during the Revolutionary War had been defended as a means to provide the manpower and resources that were needed to win independence. And the "more perfect union" of the Constitution had been advanced as a way to secure national independence, republican government, commercial prosperity, and western expansion. But opponents of union—or of specific forms of union—had used the same instrumentalist logic and language at each of these times, just as advocates of disunion had relied upon them during the early republic's separatist crises.

Only rarely did the anti-"Querist" essayists attempt to elevate union above this realm of calculation and contingency where unionism necessarily coexisted with disunionism. They almost never challenged, for example, the starting point for arguments justifying disunion—the presumed right of peaceful secession. The fourth "Querist" essay discussed this right at length, finding support for it in the settled principle "that a sufficient title to all government, legislative & executive, is only derived from the people." Blennerhassett concluded that "the power of peacably withdrawing from the federal partnership is an inherent right" that was "virtually guaranteed by the constitution itself."[114] Only one of the anti-"Querist" authors tackled this claim. In the third "Regulus" essay, Judge Nimmo derided the "Querist's" argument, insisting that secession "from the body politic, without the consent of a majority, at least, of its members, is a violation of the fundamental compact." But rather than disproving Blennerhassett's logic, Nimmo provided a hyperbolic description of secession's consequences. If a state could separate from the federal union as easily as a member could withdraw from "a commercial company," he reasoned, then "every individual, on the same principles, could claim political independence," leading "to a state of nature, in which not only all government, but all society would be dissolved."[115]

Perhaps as a result of the difficulty of arguing against such a widely accepted principle, anti-"Querist" essayists and other defenders of union turned to other ways to elevate union above calculation and contingency. Some tried to reframe it as an interest in itself, rather than a means of achieving political and economic interests, and then raise this interest to the highest level. This claim that union was the paramount interest might be asserted either negatively or positively. One could warn that disunion "must envelope you in inevitable ruin" and that "a separation of these states . . . would ultimately involve the whole country in our common ruin."[116] Or one could insist that "in union" one could find "whatever is most desirable to man, and most amiable in life."[117] According to "Regulus," by preserving the union, the people would ensure that they could "sit down in safety under [their] fig trees, in the peaceful enjoyment of every happiness," and expect to "leave the same measure of happiness and prosperity to [their] children."[118]

Union could also be made "all-important and essential" in the minds of Americans by making it seem sacred. As "An Observer," Marshall took the project of sacralizing the union to its furthest extent, describing it as "an idea inspired by Heaven itself." Union "is to our temporal happiness," he insisted, "what a faith in Jesus Christ is to our future felicity."[119] Other versions of this project sought the same end with a quasi-deity—George Washington—rather than a real one. Washington's defense of union in his Farewell Address had employed the instrumentalist language of the Constitution's supporters, stressing its role in achieving national independence, preventing foreign wars, and securing domestic tranquility. But the Farewell Address had come to be "esteemed," as Governor Claiborne described it, as "a most valuable Legacy." Washington's advice, he assured the Orleans legislature, "is like that of a father to his Children."[120] "Sydney" similarly pointed readers "to the last farewell of our political father," urging them to follow "the pious injunctions of a parent to his children."[121]

Efforts to sacralize the union or to establish it as the paramount interest point to a desire to use the Burr crisis to strengthen its still-fragile bonds. Some believed that that effect had been accomplished even without such efforts, deriving new confidence for the union's future from the failure of the conspiracy and the outcry against it. Writing to the president at the peak of the crisis, one Ohioan predicted that "the agitation produced by [Burr's] scheme of dismemberment" would produce "the best effects to the Union," by "fix[ing] the minds of the present inhabitants, & of the present generation, & render[ing] abortive any similar plan, which might hereafter be proposed."[122] As the crisis abated, more and more commentators emphasized its positive lessons. In early February, a Tennesseean suggested that the failed conspiracy would "more thourily sement every part of the union, and keep it out of the power of any person or persons to effect such attempts again."[123] Some argued that widespread western hostility to disunionism would have beneficial effects far beyond the West. Abroad, news of "the warm, unshaken attachment of the western people to the Union," would convince European powers "of the impossibility of dismembering the Union [and] the futility of tampering with our citizens."[124] At home, "Burr's Affair" would ease sectional tensions by "lulling Jealousies entertained [by easterners] of the Supposed Disaffection of the western People."[125]

Others were not so confident. Should not "the disclosure" of Burr's plans, the Massachusetts Federalist Fisher Ames asked, "awaken . . . fears of the future politics of the transalpine states?"[126] Even if the West could not establish and maintain its independence at present, in ten more years, Ames warned, "a second Burr [could] divide our empire by the Alleghany."[127] The Virginia Quid Beverley Tucker likewise drew little solace from the failure of Burr's disunionist project. There were still many in the West, he stated in late January 1807, "whose attachment to the union [was] wavering" and some "who [were] entirely disaffected."[128]

That the vast majority of westerners remained loyal to the union when faced with Burr's allegedly disunionist project seems clear. There is little evidence that this loyalty even required much thought. What westerners struggled with during the fall of 1806, then, was not deciding on loyalty itself, but finding a language for proclaiming that loyalty when it was questioned. Over the preceding four decades, they, and other Americans, had participated in one of the richest discussions of political principles that the world has ever known. That discussion had left them with new stories about the necessity of both republican government and federal union. But those new stories had not provided them with a way to express their loyalty to a specific government and a specific union that rose above a language of calculated interests and contingent conditions.

The stories about the essentiality and vulnerability of union that structured contemporaries' efforts to make sense of Burr's plans and movements survived westerners' rejection of Burr and proclamations of their loyalty. Americans continued to worry that the West would break, or be drawn, from the union for nearly two decades. In the late 1810s and early 1820s, when depression supplanted prosperity and new grievances arose over federal Indian, statehood, land, and foreign policies, stories of popular separatism reemerged. In 1821, Henry Clay warned that "powerful local causes operating in the West" threatened a "disseverance" of the union.[129] Stories about the power over western loyalties that would accompany control over western commerce also remained compelling long after the Burr crisis, though the focal point of the threat shifted from the mouth of the Mississippi to the mouth of the Gulf of Mexico, between East Florida and Cuba. Cuba "constitute[d] the Key to all Western America," one general explained in August 1816; if it passed from Spain to a strong power, westerners' response would show "that men are oftener governed by their interests, than love of country."[130]

Not until the mid- and late 1820s did the fears for the union between East and West that derived from these old stories finally disappear. The combined impact of the acquisition of the Floridas, the incorporation of Missouri, the completion of the Erie Canal, and the adoption of new land and Indian policies removed the existing grievances. And the solidification of western political power in the federal government—highlighted by the election of Tennessee's Andrew Jackson to the presidency in 1828—seemed to ensure that western interests could be secured within the union.[131] These interests seemed so secure that it became hard to imagine the choices or pressures that might draw or force the West from the union. As the threat of a North-South division over slavery grew, once-common stories about an East-West division were forgotten or ignored. By the 1820s and 1830s, accounts of the Burr Conspiracy, even by those who had lived through the crisis, often dismissed the thinking that had helped so many people understand Burr's projects and movements.

What had not disappeared even two decades after the Burr crisis, and would not disappear until after the Civil War, was the broad acceptance of the idea that loyalty to the union depended upon calculated interests and contingent circumstances. Even western historians and memoirists who dismissed the disunionist threat of the Burr Conspiracy, and the disunionist intent of Burr himself, grounded their accounts in such thinking. In his 1834 memoir, Henry Marie Brackenridge, who had been a law student in Pittsburgh in the fall of 1806, insisted, "It is absurd to suppose that a separation of the Western States entered into [Burr's] plan, when the bare suggestion of it would have excited universal indignation" among westerners. Still, he admitted that similar disunionist projects "might have found partisans" "before the acquisition of Louisiana."[132] Like other Americans between the Revolution and the Civil War, westerners during and after the Burr crisis shared a unionism that, no matter how fervently and frequently asserted, always contained the seeds of disunion.

THE CRIME ON BLENNERHASSETT ISLAND

On 10 December 1806, on Blennerhassett Island in the Ohio River, an assemblage of armed men committed the crime of treason against the United States. Their leader was Aaron Burr, who was not on the island that day. Most of the men had come down the river from western Pennsylvania, where they had been recruited by Burr's agents Israel Smith and Comfort Tyler. They had arrived expecting to find more men, as well as additional boats and provisions, supplied by the wealthy owner of much of the island, Harman Blennerhassett. Instead, they found the people of the surrounding countryside and towns alarmed by the fear that Burr planned to seize New Orleans and divide the union at the Appalachian Mountains.

During their two days on the island, the men displayed a martial appearance. Observers on the Ohio shore saw them walking around with guns. Fires around the island suggested a regular watch, as did the

On 10 December 1806, on Blennerhassett Island in the Ohio River, an assemblage of armed men committed the crimes of robbery and vandalism against the property of Harman Blennerhassett. The men, members of a volunteer corps from Wood County, had come over from the Virginia shore to arrest Blennerhassett and detain a group of men and boats that had arrived on the island two days earlier. Finding that his quarry had departed in the night, Colonel Hugh Phelps took part of his force back to Virginia, where they mounted horses and raced off across the countryside hoping to intercept the slow-moving boats. Perhaps forty of Phelps's men stayed on the island, charged with stopping any additional boats that came down the river and watching its inhabitants—Harman's wife Margaret, their two young sons Dominic and Harman Jr., and their white laborers and black slaves.

use of passwords to hail approaching boats. And the men passed the time preparing for a military campaign by drying corn, casting bullets, and shooting at marks.

Late on 9 December, news came from upriver that the Ohio militia had detained the additional boats and provisions for which Blennerhassett had contracted in Marietta. The men on the island also learned that the Ohio legislature had passed a law for their arrest. Militiamen from Ohio or Virginia seemed likely to descend upon the island the next day. Blennerhassett, Smith, and Tyler decided to ready the men and leave in the night.

Before they could do so, Edward Tupper, a brigadier general in the Ohio militia, arrived. Tupper tried to persuade Blennerhassett to face the accusations against him. When that failed, he attempted to arrest Blennerhassett in the early hours of 10 December, as the men prepared to board the boats. A number of the men levelled their muskets at Tupper, who could only let Blennerhassett, Tyler, Smith, and the roughly thirty men slip off into the current.[1]

The volunteers held the island for a full week, their numbers swelling to eighty at times. Viewing Blennerhassett as a disunionist and traitor, they consumed his provisions and wrecked his property. They plundered the mansion's storerooms and cellars for food and liquor. In their drunken revelry, they stuck bayonets into the furniture; one volunteer fired his rifle into the main room's elegant ceiling. They tore down fences to feed fires around the island, exposing the fine landscaping and unharvested cornfields to the ravages of the cattle. When the slaves refused to serve them, the volunteers locked them in the laundry building.

For a week, the men stopped Margaret and her sons from following Harman downriver. A keelboat that had been built in Marietta especially for their journey was seized. Not until early on 16 December were Margaret and her sons finally permitted to board a boat that had come from Pittsburgh—and had been detained by the volunteers for three days—and slip off into the current.[2]

These very different accounts of the crime on Blennerhassett Island—one ending on 10 December, the other beginning on that day—coexisted and competed for decades after the events that they described. That which alleged a treasonous assemblage of Burr's men on the island

FIGURE 7. The Blennerhassetts' home and grounds.

under the command of Blennerhassett, Smith, and Tyler appeared most clearly in the prosecution's case in Burr's trial in Richmond during the summer and fall of 1807. That which alleged an illegal despoliation of Blennerhassett's property by the Wood County volunteers appeared most forcefully in Margaret Blennerhassett's petition to Congress for redress thirty-five years later. These stories were neither in direct conflict nor mutually exclusive—both treason and robbery could have been committed on Blennerhassett Island in December 1806—but there was a relationship between them. Treason by one side would not have made robbery and vandalism by the other legal. But the more compelling, the more believable, the prosecution's story of treason appeared, the less troubling, the less relevant, the Blennerhassetts' story of despoliation would seem. "The Wood County rabble," Margaret Blennerhassett remarked as her husband awaited trial for treason in August 1807, "only want some pretext to vindicate their plunder."[3] If Blennerhassett could not be shown to have committed treason, however, the violence against his property became harder to excuse.

The origins of both of these alleged crimes dated back more than three months earlier. Around midday on 27 August 1806, Aaron Burr, his travelling companion Julian Depestre, and the Marietta merchant Dudley Woodbridge Jr. arrived at Blennerhassett Island. They stayed one night. When they returned to Marietta, they were accompanied by Harman Blennerhassett, who spent much of the day contracting for boats and supplies on Burr's behalf. On 29 August, Blennerhassett went home; Burr and Depestre headed west to Chillicothe. Burr never returned to the island. Burr and Blennerhassett spent less than forty-eight hours together during these days, much of it asleep or in company. But this encounter set in motion the events that would lead Blennerhassett's Ohio and Virginia neighbors to see treason in the assemblage of men on his island and would propel the Wood County volunteers to occupy, plunder, and despoil his home and property.[4]

Long before Burr's August 1806 visit, the Blennerhassetts had commanded the attention of their neighbors, who viewed them with a combination of admiration and bewilderment. In 1795, the newlyweds Harman and Margaret Blennerhassett had left Ireland, escaping familial censure. They immigrated to the United States in 1796 and made plans to move to the West. In the fall of 1797, Harman purchased roughly 170 acres of Backus Island, an hourglass-shaped island in the Ohio River downstream from Marietta. Since Virginia had retained the whole of the river when it ceded the Northwest Territory, slavery was legal on the island, unlike in Ohio just a few hundred yards away. Over the next three years, the Blennerhassetts lavished money on their home, hiring artisans and laborers, buying supplies and furnishings, and purchasing slaves, livestock, and farm implements. They finally moved into their elegant wooden home in September 1800. The Blennerhassett mansion became a center of social life for the elite of nearby Marietta and Washington County, Ohio, and Wood County, Virginia. The island also developed into an obligatory stop for refined travellers on the river. As early as 1800, the English actor John Bernard could consider a visit to "the fairy creation of Blennerhasset" a "goal of [his] journey."[5] Three years later, Delaware's Thomas Rodney stopped at "Blaney Hazzards" on the way to his federal judgeship in the Mississippi Territory, touring the home and grounds and dining with "Mr. Hazzard" before departing the "inchanted island."[6]

Burr had first visited the island as one of those refined travellers. In May 1805, on his first trip west, he stopped at the island and met its proprietor. After just a few hours, Burr reboarded his keelboat and continued downriver. On his return trip that November, he again visited the island, but the Blennerhassetts were visiting friends in the East. When they returned in December, they found a letter from Burr expressing regret at their absence and making vague suggestions for Harman to improve his fortune and his status. Whether Burr's letter reinforced an earlier decision or prompted a new one is unclear. But, on 15 December, just a week after returning from Baltimore, Harman informed a friend that he had decided to leave his home and asked for help finding a buyer or lessor. Six days later, he informed Burr of his intention to abandon the island and his willingness to join Burr "in any undertaking which [his] sagacity might open to profit and fame."[7] The two men continued their correspondence through the first half of 1806 and planned for Burr to return to the island in late August.

Within days of Burr's final visit to Blennerhassett Island, an essay, dated 1 September 1806 and signed "Querist," appeared in Marietta's *Ohio Gazette*. The weekly newspaper ran three more "Querist" essays before suspending publication due to a lack of paper. These essays examined the West's position in the union, arguing that eastern politicians had always ignored or sacrificed western interests, particularly commercial ones, as they worked to advance those of their own region. In the first essay, the author identified a "severance of the cis and trans-Alleghany States" as the inevitable solution to the West's semi-colonial status.[8] In the next essay, however, he made clear that he would not suggest "either the mode or the time" by which a separation from the East "should be effected."[9] Still, he never retreated from the idea that a separation would occur and could be accomplished without great effort.

That Blennerhassett had written the "Querist" essays was almost immediately assumed, very quickly established, and never really denied. In mid-September, with just two essays in print, one Mariettan reported to his brother that "they [were] supposed to be written by [his] Irish friend B___."[10] A few weeks later, a pseudonymous writer in Cincinnati's *Western Spy* publicly named Blennerhassett as the "Querist." At the same time, private letters and published essays linked Blennerhassett with Burr, with many reporting the latter's recent visit to Marietta and Blennerhassett Island. In mid-October, for example, Kentucky's James Taylor informed Secretary of State James Madison that he had no doubt that Burr, "Blanahazard," and "some other men of talents" were "at the bottom of this publication & a scheme for a division of the Union."[11] That fall, Ohio and Kentucky newspapers teemed with pseudonymous essays answering the "Querist." Most of them attacked the "Querist's" separatism, often naming it treason. And most of them identified Burr and Blennerhassett as the joint projectors of a disunionist plot. In doing so, they inflamed popular anxiety in the Ohio Valley regarding the wealthy Irish immigrant and his ambitious eastern visitor.

In Wood County, this anxiety threatened to explode in early October. "Sundry citizens" met on 6 October to coordinate a response to the "hostile motions and nefarious designs of certain characters." They agreed that the county should form a volunteer corps and selected six prominent residents to recruit men. The corps would be armed and trained in order to repel "any aggression . . . by insurgents inimical to the interest of the U.S." Convinced of the need for haste, the assembled citizens decided that the corps should gather at the county courthouse in just five days. They also appointed a committee of five men, including militia colonel Hugh Phelps, and a secretary, James Wilson, to decide the corps' future actions. Finally, they agreed to publicize the meeting by forwarding its "resolutions" to the president, the governor of Virginia, and the Marietta and Morgantown, Virginia, newspapers.[12] Two events may have helped to precipitate this meeting out of a climate that had become saturated with uncertainty and anxiety. In late September or early October, Burr's daughter Theodosia and son-in-law Joseph Alston arrived at Blennerhassett Island, staying for a few days. This visit certainly raised concerns in Marietta, where, according to one report, "there was a loud talke of [Joseph Alston's] being mobbed by the rabble."[13] After the Alstons left, Blennerhassett—"of a sudden [and] to the surprise of all"—hurried off to meet Burr in Lexington.[14]

The news of the Wood County resolutions and the volunteer corps reached Harman in Lexington by late October. Margaret had grown alarmed by the activity on the Virginia shore and had sent Peter Taylor, the family's Irish gardener, after her husband. Fearing that the volunteers would "land on the island . . . and burn his house," Harman returned home. Arriving on 3 November, he learned that the fear "of an attack on the island from the [p]oint of the Little Kanawha [now Parkersburg, West Virginia] had by no means subsided." He immediately sent a letter to Colonel Phelps, asking to meet to dispel any concerns. At this meeting, Blennerhassett attempted to reassure Phelps that his only involvement with Burr concerned the settlement of the Bastrop lands. He also tried to turn Phelps against the volunteer corps by suggesting that Phelps's political opponents hoped to use it to "overturn [Phelps's] interest." At the same time, he urged Phelps to join the expedition. Though Blennerhassett believed that Phelps was satisfied with his explanation, the volunteers remained alert to developments on the island. Blennerhassett still "receive[d] daily assurances that the people from the Point" planned to seize the boats that he had commissioned at Marietta and the corn on the island.[15]

In mid-November, John Graham, the special agent who had been sent west by the administration after Burr, reached Marietta. Having met Graham five years earlier and having heard that he was involved in Burr's project, Blennerhassett visited him at his tavern. According to Blennerhassett, Graham revealed that he had been ordered to investigate Burr and to oppose any plans that targeted New Orleans or Mexico. Blennerhassett assured him that Burr's destination was the Bastrop grant on the Ouachita River. He believed that Graham agreed that, by avowing a legal purpose, Burr and his supporters had provided legal cover to send boatloads of armed men down the Ohio and Mississippi Rivers. He took leave of Graham convinced he "perfectly [understood] both [Graham] and the government."[16] Graham's recollection of this meeting differed from Blennerhassett's on four important points. First, he testified that Blennerhassett, assuming that Graham was one of Burr's agents, had asked him about the recruitment of men and procurement of boats and supplies upriver. Second, even after being informed that Graham was not "one of the party," Blennerhassett had questioned him about "an association in New Orleans for the invasion of Mexico." Third, Graham insisted that he had never agreed that the legality of the announced project would protect armed men on the river from legal action. "I gave him to understand," Graham recalled, "that when they were collected, they would be arrested."[17] Finally, he testified that Blennerhassett had freely admitted that he and Burr "had sounded the people of the western country" on "a severance of the Union" through the "Querist" essays but had "found them not ripe for the measure."[18]

Within a day or two of this meeting, Graham went to Wood County to speak with the committee that had been created six weeks earlier to direct the volunteer corps. He explained his official mission and recounted his conversation with Blennerhassett. From committee members Hugh Phelps and Alexander Henderson Jr., Graham heard more about Blennerhassett's activities and Burr's plans. Phelps described his recent meeting with Blennerhassett, recounting the effort to entice him to join the expedition. Henderson mentioned a confidential conversation with Blennerhassett that had led him to believe "that it was of the highest consequence to the United States that they should have immediately a very formidable force at New Orleans."[19] After this meeting and additional disclosures from Henderson, Graham informed Madison that he would *now arrest Blennerhassett* if Henderson was not *so extremel[y] unwilling to come forward as a witness.*"[20] Committee secretary James Wilson reported to Madison that the committee "have the wish and they hope and believe the power of stopping Mr. B. from going down the river." All that restrained them was a desire "to proceed with safety"—in other words, with official authorization.[21] Since Blennerhassett had announced his plan to leave on 10 December, the committee members and the volunteers knew exactly how long they could wait for this authorization.

After returning to Marietta, Graham rode west to Ohio's capital, Chillicothe. He immediately informed Governor Edward Tiffin of his mission and his concerns. Tiffin offered to seek more information and "to check any movement which may wear a threatning aspect."[22] With the state legislature convening in a few days, he promised results. Tiffin's official message of 2 December reported the information that he had received from Graham about Blennerhassett's actions and described Burr's plans as attacking New Orleans, seizing the bank and artillery, and establishing a separate government under Spanish protection that would force the West from the union. He requested a law authorizing the seizure of the boats and supplies at Marietta and the arrest of Burr's agents and men on the Ohio. A bill was quickly drafted by Lewis Cass. It took two days to work through the legislature and was delayed another day because the committee chairman "came into the house drunk" and the legislators "adjourned . . . rather than to expose him."[23] Immediately after signing the bill, Tiffin sent an express to Marietta to have Blennerhassett and Tyler arrested and the boats and supplies seized. It took until 9 December, four days after the passage of the bill, for officials in Marietta to execute this order.

As the governor's express rode through the Ohio countryside, Comfort Tyler's four boats and roughly thirty men floated downriver from Beaver, Pennsylvania. They reached Blennerhassett Island on 8 December, "expect[ing] to sail again" the next day.[24] But only ten of the fifteen boats for which Blennerhassett had contracted were ready. Laden with one hundred barrels of provisions, these boats were stopped the next day on the Muskingum River above Marietta. The five uncompleted boats, and another hundred barrels of provisions, were seized on the wharf. Learning of the seizures and of the Ohio law, Blennerhassett and Tyler decided to leave in the night. Phelps and the Wood County volunteers reached the island the next morning, believing that Blennerhassett intended to depart that day. They still lacked any legal authority, the Ohio law having no force in Virginia. They might have derived—and later claimed—some authority from President Thomas Jefferson's proclamation, but they could not have acted upon it on 10 December since it did not arrive in the area until two days later.[25]

In the weeks after the seizures on the Muskingum and the flight from the island, Blennerhassett's finances suffered even greater damages than those wreaked by what he later called the "Wood Co. Myrmidons."[26] On one hand, his creditors and Burr's—some of whose notes Blennerhassett had guaranteed—moved quickly to attach his property to protect their loans. The fifteen boats and two hundred barrels of provisions at Marietta probably would have covered most of these debts, but there was no indication that the state or federal governments would allow them to be sold. Accordingly, in the weeks after Blennerhassett left the island, his creditors—and Burr's—descended upon his house, farm, and store. By late February 1807, two Kentuckians, Robert Miller and Lewis Sanders, had attached much of Blennerhassett's real and "movable property," as well as the debts owed to him by his principal business partners, the Woodbridges, to protect against losses on Burr's notes.[27] To clear these debts, much of the Blennerhassetts' personal property was sold at a sheriff's auction; "a great deal [of it] for near nothing," one of Blennerhassett's correspondents reported.[28]

On the other hand, most of Blennerhassett's slaves seized upon the chaos on the island and the departure of their owner to make the short trip to Ohio and, thus, to freedom. Two slaves, Parson and Jim, did not even wait until Blennerhassett left to effect their escape; their absence was discovered in the final moments before the boats departed. The others, perhaps a dozen or more, appear to have remained on the island at least until Margaret and the children left on 16 December. One slave family, perhaps that of Ransom Reed, stayed long enough to be included in the attachment and sheriff's auction. Those who had escaped to Ohio do not appear to have gone very far. As late as mid-March, four months after Blennerhassett's departure, "there [were] Six or 8 here in Marietta," according to one report.[29] In late July, Thomas Neale, the clerk of the Wood County court, informed Blennerhassett that his slaves were still "on the other Side & . . . scaterd about."[30] Nor do they seem to have made much effort to hide themselves. Neale described them as "Lurking about" in Ohio, but Marietta's Dudley Woodbridge Jr. suggested something quite different when he referred to them as "strolling about on our side of the river."[31] The slaves' own thinking is lost to history. As runaways, they could have been seized under the Fugitive Slave Act of 1793. But they may have felt reasonably secure around Marietta. At least some of them would have known local whites and blacks who must have provided lodging, food, and perhaps work. And they surely recognized that, in Ohio, they were closer to freedom than they had ever been.

Before leaving the island early on 10 December, Blennerhassett had taken steps to protect his property and interests. The previous evening, he had settled his affairs with Woodbridge, his business partner of eight years. He had also written to the attorney James Wilson— secretary of the Wood County committee—asking him to prepare an inventory of his property. Blennerhassett had intended to have some items shipped to him and the rest sold; however, he had not expected the damage that was inflicted by his irate neighbors, desperate creditors, and absconding slaves. Although he knew of the seizure of the boats and provisions at Marietta before he left the island, he did not learn of the "insult and plunder" by the Wood County volunteers until his wife found him at Bayou Pierre, on the Mississippi above Natchez, in late January.[32] And not until mid-April did he learn of the "sequel to the open plunder and destruction of [his] property" that had been carried out "under the cover of legal process, in the shape of attachments."[33]

Between February and May 1807, as he awaited trial in the Mississippi Territory, Blennerhassett labored to recover his property and restore his finances. In February and March, he wrote to Woodbridge, Wilson, and David Wallace "request[ing] their speediest exertions to collect and forward . . . every article of [his] property that [was] worth transportation."[34] Of particular importance were his "Negroes[,] horses and household furniture."[35] At the same time, he asked Woodbridge to look into his prospects "for indemnity fr[om] the Govts. of Ohio and Virginia for any part of [his] property detained or destroyed."[36] Aware only of the damage to his property on the island and the seizure of the boats and provisions on the Muskingum, Blennerhassett wrote with restraint. News of the attachments by Burr's creditors brought a dramatic change in his attitude. Suddenly, all of his wealth and property seemed to be in jeopardy. It was as if "a swarm of Locusts [had taken] wing on the departure of [his] family, to settle upon every Chattel [they] had left behind." Blennerhassett berated Woodbridge for not "attach[ing] every thing fictitiously" as a way to secure his property before Burr's creditors asserted their claims and further chided him for the irregularity of his correspondence. Hoping to prevent "damage to [his] property, or loss of [his] Negroes," he decided to return to Marietta after his expected trial in the Mississippi Territory in May.[37]

But, on the way to Marietta, Blennerhassett stopped in Lexington, where he was twice arrested. First, Burr's creditors filed a civil process against him. Blennerhassett successfully arranged matters with one, Lewis Sanders, by directing him to Joseph Alston, who had agreed to indemnify Blennerhassett for any losses that he suffered as Burr's surety, and further securing this arrangement with a "deed of trust" to the island.[38] Another, Robert Miller, was not in Lexington at the time, but Blennerhassett hoped that he would accept the same terms. These arrangements, he assured his wife, would remove "the greatest part of the incumbrances affecting our property on the Island."[39] Even as

Blennerhassett worked to satisfy Burr's creditors, however, news reached Lexington that the Richmond grand jury had indicted him for treason and misdemeanor. Arrested again, he sent another round of letters to Marietta from jail, hoping to secure slaves, supplies, and funds for his wife and children. On 20 July, Blennerhassett left Lexington under an armed guard bound for Richmond.

Burr's trial in Richmond forced the prosecution to prove its version of the crime on Blennerhassett Island on 10 December 1806. The decision that specified *that* place and *that* date as the location and time of the treason effectively determined the outcome of the trial. It ensured that the case would be tried in the federal circuit court in Richmond by Chief Justice John Marshall. And it very nearly ensured that Burr, who was not on the island on that day, would be found not guilty. If the overt act of treason at Blennerhassett Island was the assembling of men and supplies to levy war against the government, then similar overt acts might have been charged in other locales. At Beaver, Pennsylvania, Tyler had collected and trained men; one participant noted that this group of as many as six hundred men gave "every appearance of a Military Scheme."[40] At the mouth of the Cumberland River in Kentucky, Burr had finally met the men and boats from upriver and, it was widely believed, revealed his actual plans. Across the river from Bayou Pierre, Burr had allegedly prepared his men to resist the Mississippi militia and, after deciding to surrender, ordered them to bury their arms in the swamp. Choosing Blennerhassett Island from these and other options was, as lead prosecutor George Hay later remarked, a "mistake."[41]

But whose mistake was it? The defense claimed that the president had selected Blennerhassett Island to keep the trial in Richmond, where he could most easily wreak his vengeance on Burr. But Hay insisted that Marshall had made the crucial decision. "It was your business," he said to the chief justice, "to select the place for the trial, [as] the examining magistrate." The decision "was not . . . made by the government," Hay remarked, "but by the first judicial officer of the United States."[42] In fact, both Jefferson and Marshall seem to have wanted Burr's trial to be held in Richmond. Marshall replied to Hay's charge by explaining that Burr had been committed for trial in Richmond because there was enough evidence, of the misdemeanor, to try him, but not enough to decide where the offence had occurred. Not knowing where to send Burr, but convinced that he should be tried, Marshall had had "no alternative" in early April "but to bind him over to appear" in his own court.[43] But Jefferson seems to have already decided on the same place. In early March, he informed Senator William Plumer of the difficulty of deciding where Burr "ought to be tried"; "on the whole," according to Plumer, Jefferson "tho't in the State of Virginia."[44] Eighteen days later, the cabinet agreed to order Burr's captors to return south to Richmond rather than proceed to Washington. The Richmond *Enquirer* explained that Burr's trial would probably be held in the city because "the overt act of treason . . . was most probably committed at Blannerhassett's island."[45] Holding the trial in Virginia meant that the offence had to be located in Virginia, leaving Hay with Blennerhassett Island as his only option when he prepared indictments for the grand jury in late May.

Fixing 10 December 1806 as the date of the offence was also problematic. It is not entirely clear how Hay or Attorney General Caesar A. Rodney arrived at that date. The administration had sought information from the West by sending out a set of "Interrogatories" that had been prepared by Rodney, but the replies did not reach Richmond until a week after Hay finished preparing the bills of indictment.[46] Two key witnesses to events on the island were already in Richmond, but Hay had not yet seen them (though his prosecution colleagues may have). And they might not have been very helpful at fixing a specific date; one recalled only that Blennerhassett and the boats had departed in "the fall of the year" with "snow on the ground."[47] There would have been other communications, both oral and written, that could have informed this decision, including some that are now lost. None of John Graham's dispatches between late November and early February have survived in full; one, a mid-December letter from Lexington, seems to be a likely candidate. The best source that we can identify is a published letter from Governor Tiffin to the secretary of war. Tiffin mentioned the presence of armed men on the island and the use of sentries. And he placed the seizure of the boats at Marietta "on the night of the 10th," though it seems to have happened on 9 December.[48] If the assembling of men on the island, the setting of watch fires, the shooting at marks, and the casting of bullets were to constitute the overt act of levying war against the United States, then the indictment was in error. They happened on 8 and 9 December, not shortly after midnight on 10 December.

During the trial, the prosecution's story of a treasonous assemblage on Blennerhassett Island was first built up and then torn down. By indicting Burr, Blennerhassett, Tyler, and four others for treason in late June, the grand jury indicated that the testimony supported the prosecution story enough to merit a trial. That story shaped the prosecution's opening argument to the petit jury in mid-August and its evidence. But the story quickly unravelled. Through cross-examination, Burr and his attorneys elicited how few of the men on the island had guns, how few of the guns were military muskets rather than hunting rifles, and how few of the men were casting bullets. They also attacked the credibility of the main witness to the alleged levelling of muskets at General Tupper just before the boats departed; Blennerhassett's employee Jacob Allbright eventually admitted that he "did not know whether [the men] were in earnest."[49] Another witness said that he had not seen "any arms but those belonging to Blennerhassett" or any "guns presented" at Tupper.[50] And Dudley Woodbridge Jr. testified that Tyler had insisted that the men "would not resist the constituted authorities, but . . . would not be stopped by a mob."[51] Asked by Burr whether the men had been "disorderly," had committed "any mischief," or had been "guilty of any misconduct," Woodbridge answered that they had not.[52]

The final, devastating, blow to the prosecution's story came from Marshall's 1 September opinion that prevented additional testimony on the treason charge and from the jury's not-guilty verdict that followed. After hearing Marshall's opinion, Hay informed Jefferson that the judge had "expressly declared that the transactions and assemblage at Blannerhassett's island, did not amount to an overt act of levying war."[53] In fact, Marshall had left this question open, suggesting that a jury might decide that the assemblage "amounted to a levying of war."[54] Since Burr was not on the island, however, whatever had occurred there could not be charged against him. Not until late October did Marshall close the question of whether any overt act of treason had occurred by committing Burr and Blennerhassett for trial in Ohio only on the misdemeanor of preparing a military expedition against a nation at peace with the United States. In Hay's view, these opinions, in combination, made further treason prosecutions useless—even against

Blennerhassett or Tyler, who had certainly been on the island. As Hay put it in November, Marshall had decided "that the assemblage of men at Blennerhassett island did not amount to a levying of war."[55] Even those who did not accept Marshall's rulings surely recognized that they undermined the prosecution's story of the crime on Blennerhassett Island.

While the prosecution worked to convince the judge, the jury, and the public that the crime of treason had been committed on Blennerhassett Island, Harman Blennerhassett tried to reverse the effects of different crimes—the destruction and confiscation of his property and the flight of his slaves. As he awaited trial in Richmond, he learned of both long- and short-term means to redress his losses. He found that, under Virginia and Kentucky law, he had seven years to have "set aside, or seek redress for[,] a sale made against law or equity."[56] He also learned that Robert Miller and some of the purchasers at the sheriff's auction had agreed to sell back his property, including the slave Ransom Reed, at cost. Sitting in the Richmond penitentiary, Blennerhassett began to calculate how he could repair the damage. If he could raise some money from Alston or Burr, he could go to Marietta, "redeem some few valuable articles of [his] property that [had] been sacrificed at Sheriff's sales," and "get [his] negros away fr[om] Ohio."[57] Squeezing funds from Alston or Burr would not be easy. But it was "in effecting the recovery and removal of the negroes," he later informed Margaret, that he expected to "find great difficulty."[58]

Recovering his old slaves and buying new ones occupied Blennerhassett throughout the fall of 1807. That spring, he had decided that his future lay in the Mississippi Territory; he would become "a Cotton Planter as the surest and easiest means of retrieving [his] shattered resources."[59] On the island, however, most of the slaves had worked within the mansion and its dependencies rather than on the farm. Blennerhassett certainly hoped to recover those slaves from Marietta, but he also recognized that his aspirations required more slaves to work as field hands. When he left Richmond in October, he went to Philadelphia, hoping to arrange a financial settlement with Burr and to raise funds from other sources. He wanted enough cash to recover some of his property in Marietta and "to purchase a dozen slaves" for his new plantation.[60] While he did not reach the arrangement that he wanted with Burr, he did secure credit for his trip through Marietta to Natchez. It is not clear how much of his auctioned property Blennerhassett recovered, but he left Marietta with at least some of the slaves from the island. Within two days of arriving in Marietta, he reported to his wife that he had "seen all the negroes, except Ransom and Clara," and that "they [were] well disposed to accompany [him]."[61] In February 1808, Robert Miller learned that Blennerhassett had "taken his Negroes and Gone."[62] How Blennerhassett got them to abandon freedom in Ohio and return to slavery in the Mississippi Territory is not recorded. We can only wonder about the combination of pressures and incentives that he employed. It does seem, however, that not all of the slaves accompanied him downriver; years later, Blennerhassett asked a friend in Marietta to "recover and send me down my Negro fellow Koger."[63]

Once settled in the Mississippi Territory, Blennerhassett began to explore the long-term solutions for recovering his lost property. He directed his representatives in Ohio and Virginia to sue his former business partner, Dudley Woodbridge Jr., for an outstanding account and to initiate measures to "redress the wrongs [he had] suffer[ed] in Wood Cy." from the volunteers. Through a New Orleans merchant, he tried to arrange a final adjustment with Robert Miller in exchange for the property that Miller still held. In July 1808, he informed his Ohio lawyer, David Putnam, that he wanted to sever all of his financial ties to the region. He offered to sell his interest in the island for "30 prime hands . . . delivered here, allowing two boys or girls not under 13 to go for a hand."[64] A later letter to Putnam complained about how little had been done on his behalf, particularly the continuing failure to begin "a proper suit ag[ainst] Miller and the Sheriff of Wood Co." He wanted an accounting of his property that had been sold at the sheriff's auction and "an action of Waste" against the two men for his losses. He also offered to return to Marietta to complete the suit against Woodbridge or the sale of the island for "$15,000 in produce or Negroes."[65] These efforts seem to have brought little relief. Miller still held the mansion and island in early March 1811, when hemp that was being stored in the once-elegant Blennerhassett home caught fire, burning it to the ground.[66]

Not until the early 1840s, a decade after Harman's death, did Margaret Blennerhassett and her surviving sons, Harman Jr. and Joseph

Lewis, again try to recover the damages that had been caused by the Wood County volunteers. In early 1842, Margaret prepared a petition asking Congress for partial restitution for her family's losses. She had Robert Emmet, a family friend and respected New York attorney, help her assemble the petition and asked Henry Clay, a prominent Senate leader, to present it. Her petition, with supporting documents from eyewitnesses Morgan Neville and William Robinson Jr. and from Dudley Woodbridge Jr., forcefully stated the alternative version of the crime on Blennerhassett Island in December 1806. Margaret's petition described the occupation of the island by the volunteers. Stores of food, wine, and liquor had been "consumed and wasted." A home and grounds that had once "been noted for [their] elegance and high state of improvement" had been left "in a state of comparative ruin and waste." "These outrages" had been committed, moreover, "upon an unoffending and defenceless family in the absence of their natural protector," her husband. Unable to itemize her losses, which she estimated at many thousands of dollars, she asked Congress for a mere $2,000. She reminded Congress that her husband had not only never been found guilty of any crime, he had never been tried. But all of her family had suffered the consequences; they had been plunged into "comparative want and wretchedness," with her sons' prospects "blighted" and herself condemned to live as "a wanderer on the face of the earth."[67]

The petition was well received in the Senate. Clay spoke in its favor, confirming its account from "his own knowledge," having visited the island in the spring of 1807. He recounted the visible "remains of its former beautiful condition" and the imposing evidence of "those dilapidations which constitute[d] the object of the petition." He reported that the damage had been inflicted by soldiers "who were under little or no control, and were consequently very riotous and disorderly in their conduct." In Clay's opinion, it was "incumbent upon this Government to make amends."[68] In mid-March, the petition went to the Committee of Claims, which included Michigan's William Woodbridge, the brother of Harman Blennerhassett's former business partner. Woodbridge's early August report retold Margaret Blennerhassett's story with additional details, many of them incorrect. It presented a similar account of boats seized, stores plundered, and property destroyed. And it left no doubt that most of the damage had been caused by "a tumultuary and armed force." But the report did not "impute any moral wrong" to the Wood County volunteers. Events on the island, when combined with "the dark hints and the thousand rumors to which they gave rise," had agitated the public mind by early December 1806. The arrival of the president's proclamation—which the committee incorrectly assumed had prompted the volunteers' descent upon the island—produced an explosion. "It was not unnatural" that, "on reading such a proclamation," loyal citizens, should "have committed precisely such irregularities." The proclamation could not make legal what was illegal. But the committee argued that it should absolve individuals of any responsibility. "If, obeying the call of the President, and influenced by commendable motives, they had honestly, though unwittingly, invaded private right," the report concluded, "it would seem to be the duty of the Government freely to compensate the party injured for wrongs thus superinduced by its own action."[69]

Thirty-five years after Burr's trial for committing the crime of treason on Blennerhassett Island on 10 December 1806, the Committee of Claims presented a report that accepted that a very different crime had occurred on the island that day. Margaret Blennerhassett, according to the report, had requested "a just, but comparatively small, remuneration." Even if Harman had been guilty, "*mere justice* would seem to demand" that Congress favor her petition. Before the committee could complete its report, however, newspapers announced that Margaret had died in New York City in mid-June. Accordingly, the committee concluded that "no further action" was required. "The injuries of which she complained, [had] become cancelled by the hand of death."[70] Her sons tried to renew the petition with little success. In 1851 and 1852, the Committee of Claims again reported upon it favorably, but the Senate never brought it to a vote.[71]

Even if it did not produce the desired result in Congress, by the mid-nineteenth century, the Blennerhassetts' story carried great weight in popular memory and culture. Mid-century articles about the island or the family regularly mentioned that "the house and grounds . . . had been sacked and destroyed by an infuriated and drunken soldiery."[72] In 1853, a Richmond newspaper even reprinted the recollections of a Blennerhassett slave that stressed "the ramaging and mutilation of his master's elegant mansion . . . and the outrage and insult to his mistress."[73] At least one scene set upon the island became obligatory in the many short stories, novels, and plays that retold, or merely addressed, the Burr Conspiracy. Most lamented the unfortunate destruction of the Blennerhassetts' home and gardens.

What actually occurred and what was alleged to have occurred on Blennerhassett Island in December 1806 made it a special site in nineteenth-century American memory. The events of that fall literally put Blennerhassett Island on the map. No surviving Virginia or Ohio map from before 1806 specifically names the island. But, for decades afterward, Blennerhassett Island was regularly and distinctly identified, even on maps where few other islands were named. As they floated or steamed past, travellers and memoirists often reflected upon what had happened on the island, typically discussing both the alleged treason and the visible devastation. The traveller, one poet remarked, "in descending the river, never fails to request that [Blennerhassett Island] may be pointed out to him."[74] Its "extraordinary history," according to an 1860 magazine article, "mingled . . . the darkest crime [and] the wildest speculation; with Government corruption and Government folly."[75] More than a century and a quarter later, the state of West Virginia established Blennerhassett Island State Historical Park. Even though the steamboats no longer float past, a rebuilt mansion and restored grounds still draw visitors.

CHAPTER 5

THE ENTERPRISE
COMMENCED

The Cipher Letter as a Narrative

AS AARON BURR TRAVELLED THROUGH THE TRANS-APPALACHIAN WEST in late 1806, the public grew increasingly hungry for reliable information about his plans. The West held out numerous possibilities for a man of ambition. Perhaps Burr sought to revive his political fortunes by seeking office in a western state or territory. Perhaps he hoped to restore his financial position by forming a company to construct a canal around the falls of the Ohio River or by opening new lands for settlement across the Mississippi River. Perhaps he wanted to cement his military reputation by raising a volunteer corps for an expected war with Spain over the disputed border. Each of those options seemed perfectly laudable. But rumor and report increasingly linked Burr's ambitions to more alarming plans—an unsanctioned attack on Spanish Mexico or Florida, the military seizure of New Orleans, or even a separatist conspiracy to divide the union at the mountains. Burr did little to ease popular anxieties in these months. Occasionally, he assured prominent citizens and newspaper editors that his unspecified plans promised national benefit and enjoyed official sanction. Even in court in Kentucky in November and December, Burr remained vague about his intentions, relying on his attorneys and friendly editors to defend his activities.[1]

While the court proceedings failed to clarify Burr's plans, they—along with the presidential proclamation of late November—sparked a profusion of new accounts that purported to do so. Some were sent quietly to the administration; others went directly to the press. Many were as speculative as the rumors that had surrounded Burr for months.

(No. 1.)

Table of Hieroglyphicks and Ciphers.

Accompanying the Deposition of Robert B. Taylor.

President,	O	Navy,	96
Vice President,	☉	Peace,	Γ
Secretary of State,	T	War,	1
of War,	Γ	Treaty,	
of Navy,	Л	Convention,	
of Treasury,	L	Commerce.	
Senate,		British Minister,	T
House of Representatives,		French Minister,	T
Congress,		Spanish Minister,	T
Federal,		Appropriation,	V88
Anti-federal,		Reduction,	V88
Administration,		Eastern,	
Military establishment,	88	Southern,	
England,	□	Middle,	
France,		British,	
Minister,	T	Spanish,	
Major General,		French,	
Brigadier,		Canada,	
United States,		Louisiana,	
States,		Posts,	
Republican,	76	Garrisons,	
Aristocratic,	89	Western,	
City of Washington,		Mississippi,	
Election,		Ohio,	
		New Orleans,	

Burr, . . 13, 14, 15, 16.
Wilkinson, ... 45.

ROBERT B. TAYLOR.

JOHN NIRZON, Recorder.

(No. 2.)

a b c d e f g h i j k l m n o p q r s t u v w x y z

1 2 3 4 5 6 7 8 9 0

ROBERT B. TAYLOR.

JOHN NIRZON, Recorder.

FIGURE 8. The "alphabetic" and "hieroglyphic" ciphers as printed in a congressional report.

But a handful took a very different form. Between November 1806 and March 1807, a number of prominent men recounted, for the president or the public, what they had heard from Burr himself about his plans. Though read with great interest, these firsthand disclosures never seemed entirely satisfactory. Taken together, they were contradictory. Treated individually, each seemed incomplete or exaggerated—designed as much to exonerate its author as to provide a full account of Burr's projects.

Everyone awaited an unambiguous statement of Burr's intentions from Burr himself. The document that most nearly met that need was a letter in cipher that Burr wrote to General James Wilkinson in late July 1806. First revealed by Wilkinson that December in New Orleans, most Americans learned of Burr's letter when President Thomas Jefferson submitted it to Congress with his 22 January 1807 message. Over the next few months, what one Philadelphian called "the celebrated cypher'd letter" was widely discussed.[2] But the cipher letter quickly came to seem as problematic as the many firsthand disclosures. Incomprehensible as written, it acquired meaning only in a form that was mediated by Wilkinson, who had deciphered the letter, identified the author, and explained its "very vague terms."[3] Increasingly, Americans wondered if the cipher letter was being made to serve the same exculpatory purpose for Wilkinson that the firsthand accounts seemed to serve for their authors. Was it an accurate statement of Burr's intentions, or should it be read with the same skepticism as other disclosures? Was it more "Wilkinson's letter than Burr's," as New Hampshire senator William Plumer suggested on first reading it?[4] At the peak of the crisis, Americans generally accepted that the cipher letter told a crucial part of the story of the Burr Conspiracy. Over time, they became increasingly divided over whether it revealed more about Burr or Wilkinson.

"COMMUNICATIONS, PARTLY WRITTEN IN CIPHER"

The cipher letter reached most Americans beginning in late January 1807, with its provenance and significance established by Jefferson and Wilkinson. Read alone, the letter seemed vague and imprecise on precisely those matters that contemporaries—and later, scholars—wished were clear and conclusive. But few people read the cipher letter alone. Most first encountered it appended to Jefferson's 22 January 1807 message to Congress and embedded within Wilkinson's 18 December 1806 affidavit supporting his arrest of Justus Erich Bollman in New Orleans. Without quoting the cipher letter, Jefferson's message made clear its importance to the administration's response to the Burr crisis.

It was among the "communications, partly written in cipher and partly oral," that Burr's agents had made to Wilkinson "to engage him and the army in [Burr's] unlawful enterprise."[5] According to Jefferson, Wilkinson had informed the administration of the cipher letter and oral entreaties in a dispatch dated 21 October that had reached Washington on 25 November, prompting the proclamation two days later. Not until 18 January, however, had a deciphered version of the letter itself been received, as part of Wilkinson's affidavit. The affidavit provided a somewhat different history of the cipher letter. While the message stated that Burr's agent had handed the letter to Wilkinson before 21 October, the affidavit reported that "a Frenchman, a stranger," had delivered it on 6 November.[6] A second Wilkinson affidavit, dated 26 December and sent to Congress four days later as a supplement, resolved any conflict. Wilkinson had received two copies of the cipher letter—one directly from Samuel Swartwout in early October, the other indirectly from Bollman in early November. Jefferson's and Wilkinson's accounts of the letter's origins and meaning framed how most readers read and understood it.

But the story of the cipher letter between its composition in July 1806 and its publication in January 1807 is far more interesting than Jefferson or Wilkinson related in these public documents. Assembling that story is complicated both by the usual shortcomings of the historical record and by seemingly deliberate efforts to promote confusion. If we set aside, for the moment, questions about whether Burr actually wrote the letter that Wilkinson received, we are still left with an uncertain tale. In late July 1806, having received a 13 May letter from Wilkinson that is now missing, Burr wrote a long letter to the general from Philadelphia. His New York protégé Swartwout then employed three keys to rewrite the letter as a combination of clear text and code. A Richmond newspaper later labelled these codes: the "*arbitrary alphabet cypher*," in which symbols represented letters and digits; the "*hieroglyphic cypher*," in which symbols or numbers represented words; and the "*Dictionary cypher*," in which a compound number for a page and line in the 1800 Wilmington, Delaware, edition of *Entick's New Spelling Dictionary* indicated a word.[7] After making a second copy, Swartwout headed west with the cipher letter, a letter of introduction from Burr, and other letters to find Wilkinson. Within a few days,

Bollman received the second copy, with an added paragraph of introduction, and went by sea for New Orleans.

Swartwout found Wilkinson first at Natchitoches, near the disputed
western border. In early October, he delivered a sealed packet containing the cipher letter and, according to Wilkinson, two other encoded
letters—one from former New Jersey senator Jonathan Dayton and
another signed "A. Stephens" and addressed to "John Peters[,] Nashville," that Wilkinson believed was from Burr.[8] Wilkinson decoded the
cipher letter during the night and discussed it with Colonel Thomas
Cushing the next morning. But rather than send a copy to Jefferson, he
tried to extract further information from Swartwout. The general did
not write to the president until 21 October—thirteen, or seventeen,
days after receiving the letter and three, or nine, days after Swartwout's
departure, according to different accounts. Even then, he did not mention the cipher letter, as Jefferson later asserted in his message.[9]

Instead, Wilkinson prepared and sent three documents. In a personal letter, Wilkinson defended himself against "the Vile Calumnies"
of Frankfort's *Western World*.[10] A confidential dispatch alerted Jefferson
to the existence of an "Association . . . in opposition to the Laws & in
defiance of Government." It also enumerated the requisite military
measures and announced Wilkinson's decision to "make the best compromise" with the Spanish before leading his "little Band into New
Orleans, to be ready to defend [it] against Usurpation & violence." Despite having deciphered the letters from Burr and Dayton, Wilkinson
was amazingly reserved in this dispatch. He insisted that he was "not
only uninformed of the prime mover, & ultimate Objects of this daring
Enterprize, but [also] ignorant of the foundation on which it rests, of
the means by which it is to be supported, and whether any immediate
or Colateral *protection*, internal or external, is expected." "Forbear[ing]
to commit Names," he did not mention Burr, Dayton, or Swartwout.[11]
The third document—an unsigned and unaddressed enclosure, dated
20 October—provided more details about preparations in the West,
plans to "rendezvous eight or ten thousand men in New Orleans," and
the intention "to carry an Expedition against Vera Cruz" in Spanish
Mexico. A timeline projected an initial assemblage of men and boats
on the Ohio in mid-November, the arrival of "the Van [at] New Orleans in December," and the departure for Veracruz "about the first of

February."[12] Even this more detailed account, however, denied any knowledge of the principal figures or their ultimate goals. Wilkinson selected Lieutenant Thomas A. Smith to take these documents, along with letters to Secretary of War Henry Dearborn and Maryland senator Samuel Smith, to Washington. To avoid suspicion, Lieutenant Smith pretended to resign his commission and concealed the confidential dispatch and enclosure "between the soles of a slipper," in case Burr's men intercepted him.[13]

After concluding the Neutral Ground Agreement with Colonel Simón de Herrera on 5 November and, thereby, removing the threat of immediate war over the disputed boundary, Wilkinson returned to Natchitoches. The next day, an emissary from Bollman arrived with the second copy of the cipher letter and another coded letter from Dayton. On 12 November, Wilkinson prepared another dispatch for Jefferson, again without mentioning or including the cipher letter. It reported his increased certainty about the existence of "a deep, dark and wicked conspiracy" and warned, vaguely, that only "an immediate peace in Europe [could] prevent an explosion, which may desolate these settlements, inflict a deep wound on our republican policies, involve us in a foreign conflict, and shake the Government to its very foundation."[14] It also included an enclosure with additional information, which has been lost. Again, Wilkinson omitted the leaders' names, at least in the surviving dispatch, though he identified Bollman. Additional letters went to Secretary Dearborn and to Orleans territorial governor William C. C. Claiborne. The first detailed Wilkinson's plan to "condense our whole force" at New Orleans to defend it against "a lawless combination of our own citizens."[15] The second warned Claiborne that he was "surrounded by dangers of which you dream not and [that] the destruction of the American Union is seriously menaced."[16] While Wilkinson neither enclosed nor mentioned the cipher letter in his dispatches to Washington, he showed it to the bearer, the federal surveyor Isaac Briggs, and expected him to report its existence and convey its contents.

After arriving in New Orleans in late November, Wilkinson began to use the cipher letter to build support for his measures. In the first week, he showed it to the governor, the federal district attorney, and the ranking naval officer. On 6 December, he produced it in court as he prepared to arrest Swartwout and others. But, when he wrote to Jefferson again three days later, he still forbore to include or mention it. On 18 December, Wilkinson made the cipher letter—decoded in what he called as "substantially as fair an interpretation as [he had] heretofore been able to make"—the centerpiece of his affidavit justifying Bollman's arrest; a week later, he included it in his affidavit regarding Swartwout.[17] The affidavits also provided brief accounts of conversations with Swartwout in Natchitoches in October and with Bollman in New Orleans in late November and early December. According to Wilkinson, both men had believed him to be engaged in the conspiracy and had discussed its supporters, objectives, and progress without reserve. Along with other documents, these conversations settled, in Wilkinson's mind, the two men's guilt of "treason, misprision of treason, or [some] other offence."[18] On 18 December, Wilkinson finally sent a copy of the deciphered letter to Washington.

It would take another month before Jefferson finally saw the cipher letter, though he had learned of its existence and knew some of its contents by then. Lieutenant Smith must not have known of the letter, since he did not mention it when he dramatically drew Wilkinson's October dispatches from between the soles of his slipper in Jefferson's presence on 25 November. But Briggs, the bearer of Wilkinson's 12 November letter, recounted its contents for the president a month later. In a 3 January letter, Jefferson urged Wilkinson "to take the most special care of the two letters which [Briggs] mentioned to me, the one in cypher, the other from another of the conspirators of high standing [i.e., Dayton], and to send them to me by the first conveyance you can trust."[19] Expecting to receive both the deciphered version and the original letter, Jefferson asked Briggs to purchase the correct edition of Entick's dictionary so he could decipher the original himself.

Although the affidavits with the deciphered letters reached Washington within a few weeks, Wilkinson never forwarded the original of either letter. By mid-February, Wilkinson knew that Jefferson wanted them. On 13 February, he promised to send them "with the Key to the Cypher fully explained" by the next "safe conveyance."[20] For two months, Wilkinson repeated this promise and repeatedly failed to meet it, attributing each failure to something that was beyond his control. He alerted Jefferson to expect it by private bearer, by regular mail, by sea, and through an "officer on furlough who will leave shortly."[21] But, even as he sent other letters to Washington by mail and by ship and by express, Wilkinson retained the cipher letters. Finally, in mid-April, he confessed to Jefferson that having already sent the "Substance of Burrs & Daytons" ciphered letters and "finding that my Honor is staked on the Authenticity of those Documents, . . . I [am] reluctant to trust them out of [my] Possession."[22] He did not give the originals to anyone until he appeared before the grand jury in Richmond in mid-June 1807.

As presented by Jefferson and Wilkinson, the cipher letter answered many of the questions that had troubled the government, the press, and the public for months. It established Burr's central role, beginning, "I, Aaron Burr, have obtained funds, and have actually commenced the enterprise." It provided the plan's timetable: Burr, with his daughter, would "proceed westward, 1st August, never to return"; his son-in-law would "follow in October"; "detachments from different points" would unite "on the Ohio 1st November"; and the first "five hundred or one thousand men in light boats" would arrive "at Natchez between the 5th and 15th of December." It announced that the "protection of England is secured" and that "T."—identified as former naval commodore Thomas Truxton in a footnote to the printed version—had "gone to Jamaica" to have a British fleet sent to "the Mississippi." It also asserted that the "navy of the United States" and as much of the army as Wilkinson—who would be "second to Burr only"—wanted were "ready to join." And it described Burr's supporters as "a host of choice spirits," "a *corps of worthies*," and "the best blood of our country." Finally, the cipher letter made clear Burr's confidence of success by offering his personal guarantee of "the result with his life and honor."[23]

What was not clear in the cipher letter, however, was the ultimate object of this planning and activity. Men and boats and supplies would head down the Ohio and Mississippi Rivers toward the southwestern frontier. Other men and ships would sail from the Atlantic Coast and British Jamaica to the mouth of the Mississippi. But what were they going to do? The cipher letter suggested continuing uncertainty in Burr's mind since Burr and Wilkinson would have decided at Natchez whether, "in the first instance, to seize on or pass by Baton Rouge," the capital of Spanish West Florida. If Baton Rouge was not the primary target, what was? The letter alluded only to "the country to which we are going," reporting that its people were "prepared to receive us" and would do so happily "if we will protect their religion, and will not subject them to a foreign Power." But was the "country" in question Spanish Mexico or the Spanish Floridas or American Louisiana? Were the "people" who were concerned about their religion, but receptive to Burr's plans, Spanish Catholics in Mexico or the Floridas or French and Spanish Catholics in Louisiana? Was the "foreign Power" that they feared Spain or France or Great Britain or the United States itself?[24]

By labeling Burr's project treasonous, Jefferson's message and Wilkinson's affidavits effectively answered these questions. A military expedition against Spanish possessions would have been unlawful, but it would not have been treason. If Burr was guilty of treason, as Jefferson insisted and Wilkinson suggested, then the "country" to which his men were destined had to be the Orleans Territory, the "people" had to be French and Spanish Catholics, and the "foreign Power" had to be, or include, the United States. Jefferson and Wilkinson did not rely on the cipher letter alone to discover Burr's treasonous intent. Both the message and the affidavits acknowledged that other evidence—some oral and some written, some already public and some still confidential—had allowed them to read Burr's true intentions through the cipher letter's vague language. But Jefferson and Wilkinson did not share that evidence with most Americans, who initially saw the cipher letter only as framed by the two men's interpretation.

"VIRTUOUS AND INNOCENT DESIGNS DO NOT STAND IN NEED OF THE CLOAK OF MYSTERY"

From January, when the cipher letter was first publicized in Jefferson's message and Wilkinson's affidavits, until June, when it was literally rewritten by the grand jury, what might be termed the official reading of the cipher letter exerted immense explanatory power. That reading included four tenets—Burr's authorship of the letter, the letter's evidence of a treasonous conspiracy, Wilkinson's innocence of any prior involvement, and the letter's importance for defeating the conspiracy. While acceptance can leave few traces in the documentary record, many Americans seem to have accepted this official interpretation. In letters and in newspapers, writers disseminated accounts of the cipher letter, or the letter itself, without raising doubts about its authorship, contents, or importance.[25] Even during these months, however, some people questioned or rejected the official reading. Some simply ignored the explication that had been provided by Wilkinson and Jefferson and examined the cipher letter on its own terms. Others viewed it with a skepticism that drew upon preexisting doubts about the general or the president. And a few claimed that the cipher letter had either been forged entirely or deciphered incorrectly.

By ignoring Jefferson's and Wilkinson's framing, Chief Justice John Marshall recast the cipher letter's meaning in his February 1807 opinion in the Supreme Court cases *Ex Parte Bollman* and *Ex Parte Swartwout*. In late January, Bollman and Swartwout were committed on charges of treason by the federal circuit court for the District of Columbia. Within days, their lawyers asked the Supreme Court to release them on writs of habeas corpus. The court finally addressed the main question on 16 February. After hearing arguments, it identified Wilkinson's affidavits and the cipher letter as problematic. The defense had made "great and serious objections" to these documents, Marshall noted, based on technical flaws in the affidavits and the lack of the original letter.[26] The four available justices divided evenly on the admissibility of the cipher letter.

To overcome this division, Marshall considered whether the letter, if admitted, would support a charge of treason against Bollman and Swartwout. His opinion offered an especially close reading of the letter that emphasized its vagueness. "The letter," Marshall began, "is in language which furnishes no distinct view of the design of the writer." Over the next eight paragraphs, he carefully dissected it, finding "no expression . . . which would justify a suspicion that any territory of the U.S. was the object of the expedition." Even if one placed the letter— not "one syllable [of] which," according to Marshall, had "a necessary or a natural reference to an enterprise against any territory of the United States"—in the context of what Swartwout had allegedly told Wilkinson, confusion would remain. Some of Swartwout's reported comments clearly identified Mexico as the object, implicating him only in a misdemeanor. Other comments were indefinite and had been seen by some of the justices as revealing an "unquestionably treasonable" intent. But, the court agreed, "there [was] not sufficient evidence of [Swartwout or Bollman] levying war against the United States to justify [their] commitment on the charge of treason" and no grounds for trying them in Washington even for the misdemeanor.[27] The Supreme Court granted the writs of habeas corpus; Bollman and Swartwout went free. In late February and early March, Marshall's opinion appeared in newspapers across the country, discussing the cipher letter in a very different way than Jefferson's and Wilkinson's official reading.

Whereas Marshall reached a new understanding of the cipher letter by ignoring the official reading, others acted upon their suspicions of Jefferson or Wilkinson to question key elements of that reading. They rarely challenged either Burr's authorship of the letter or the letter's evidence of a treasonous conspiracy. Instead, doubting the president's honesty or the general's loyalty, they questioned the letter's importance to the administration's response and Wilkinson's innocence of any prior involvement.[28]

By January 1807, Wilkinson's record of questionable behavior and no less questionable loyalty extended back three decades. During the Revolutionary War, Wilkinson, after a quick rise to brevet general, had supported the infamous Conway Cabal, which schemed to dislodge George Washington from command of the army. In the late 1780s, Wilkinson had been a key figure in the Spanish Conspiracy in Kentucky. The special trade permits that he had negotiated for himself with Spanish officials in New Orleans at that time fueled suspicions that he had sold himself to Spain; rumors of an ongoing Spanish pension lingered for the rest of his life (and beyond). In the early 1790s, Wilkinson, in the army again as a brigadier general, had fallen out with commanding general "Mad" Anthony Wayne and then succeeded Wayne on his death. Late in the decade, Wilkinson's continuing Spanish connections had raised the suspicions of Andrew Ellicott, the surveyor of the border between the Floridas and the United States, who sent warnings to President John Adams. After Jefferson's inauguration, Wilkinson's Federalist politics became a source of concern. Named governor of the Louisiana Territory in the spring of 1805, Wilkinson had quickly generated fierce opposition from American settlers who believed that he favored Spanish residents and their often-fraudulent land claims. Finally, as the Burr crisis broke, Wilkinson had been freshly painted as disloyal and conspiratorial when the *Western World* revived the story of the Spanish Conspiracy and announced the existence of a new conspiracy that included Wilkinson and Burr. Few men, as the editor of Richmond's *Enquirer* asserted in September 1806, "seem[ed] so eminently worthy of suspicion."[29]

Early reports that Wilkinson had denounced Burr as a traitor often failed to convince western Republicans and eastern Federalists and Quids of his innocence. In Tennessee, it was "generally believed," according to militia general Andrew Jackson, "that if Burr is guilty, Wilkeson [had] participated in the treason."[30] Too many rumors, too many newspapers had linked the two men in a common project to make accepting Wilkinson's noninvolvement easy. From Pittsburgh to New Orleans, many suspected that Wilkinson had conspired with Burr and then "acted traitor to [Burr]" merely to save himself.[31] Some westerners even worried that Wilkinson had denounced Burr in order to concentrate the region's military under his control, intending "at the Critical moment [to] join Burr, when there would be no force left to oppose them."[32] But it was not westerners alone who initially believed that Wilkinson had been leagued with Burr. In mid-January, Senator William Plumer noted in his diary that "all parties, & all classes of people who are informed, appear to distrust Genl Wilkinson."[33] When the Virginia Quid Littleton Waller Tazewell closed an early January letter reporting the latest western news with the statement "you know Wilkinson," he surely intended to convey suspicion.[34] The suspicions could reach as far in the East as they did in the West. One of New York's Federalist editors shared the fears of the most alarmist westerners. As "to the resistance at New-Orleans," he sneered, "it may be! General Wilkinson may resist.—It is said nothing is impossible."[35]

Reading Jefferson's 22 January message, which praised Wilkinson for acting "with the honor of a soldier and fidelity of a good citizen," did not always assuage these suspicions.[36] Westerners remained especially likely to believe "that our great general Wilkison [was] as deep in the mud as little Burr."[37] An anonymous piece in a Nashville newspaper noted that "no one seem[ed] to doubt" that Wilkinson and Burr had communicated about the project before the cipher letter.[38] Similarly, in central Ohio, "every body seems to believe," Republican senator Thomas Worthington informed the administration, "that

[Wilkinson] was fully acquainted with Burr's plans before the receipt of the letter in cypher[,] found he was playing a dangerous game[,] and endeavoured to extricate himself by exposing his associates."[39] In the early months of 1807, letters from Lexington, Pittsburgh, and New Orleans similarly reported not just personal doubts, but widespread skepticism. "A general suspicion that[,] whatever there may be of treason or other offence in Burr, Wilkinson [was] not innocent" could be found in the East, as well.[40] Federalists from Connecticut to Virginia agreed, as a New Jerseyite put it, "that Burr & Wilkinson were originally concerned together in the plot, but for some cause, as yet only known to himself, W[ilkinson had] flinched B[urr]."[41] Despite the president's seemingly unequivocal support for the general, even eastern Republicans occasionally voiced doubts. Virginia's William Wirt considered it possible "that nothing had been understood between [Wilkinson] and Burr"; if that was true, then Burr, by sending the cipher letter, had "assailed [Wilkinson's] virtue with as little ceremony as if he had been a common prostitute, and was always ready when the money was offered."[42]

While much of the continuing skepticism about Wilkinson did not rely upon or refer to it, the cipher letter appeared to provide evidence of his prior involvement in Burr's plans. Those who knew Burr often insisted that he would not have sent such a letter as a mere overture. For such people, the very existence of the letter seemed to testify to a prior connection since "Burr's habits," as Plumer remarked, had "never been to trust himself on paper, if he could avoid it."[43] It was not just the existence, but also the tone of the letter that raised questions. "The familiar and confident manner" with which Burr addressed Wilkinson suggested at least prior knowledge, if not prior involvement, to Delaware senator Samuel White. Such phrases as "*the* enterprise—the concert—harmony of movement—forwarding provisions to points *Wilkinson* should name—*the* project being brought to the point so *long desired*—the people where *we* are going prepared to meet *us*" suggested such a connection to White.[44] A writer in a New York newspaper also pointed to the phrase "*the enterprize*" in the letter's opening sentence, demanding that Wilkinson answer the question, "which enterprize did you suppose it to be?" The very vagueness of the cipher letter led some to the conclusion that Wilkinson "perfectly understood [Burr's] object [and was] well acquainted with the means of attaining it."⁴⁵ The contrasting position—that "the whole letter" was in "the language of a man who was making proposals for the first time to the person to whom it was addressed"—was rarely advanced.⁴⁶

More important than the fact or the tone of the letter was the cipher itself. The defining quality of the cipher letter was its illegibility to anyone without the key. Marshall considered this aspect of the letter very carefully when he ruled in the federal circuit court in Richmond in early April against charging Burr with treason. As in the Bollman and Swartwout cases six weeks earlier, the cipher letter and Wilkinson's affidavits underpinned the prosecution case. "Exclude this letter," Marshall insisted, "and nothing remains in the testimony, which can in the most remote degree affect Col. Burr." And there were still good reasons to exclude the letter, including Wilkinson's admission that there might be flaws in his deciphering. Most importantly, though, the only evidence for Burr's authorship was Wilkinson's assertion, but Wilkinson had not provided any reasons for this assertion. Searching for grounds for believing that Burr had written the letter, Marshall found them in the cipher itself. "When we perceive that Col. Burr has written in cypher, and that General Wilkinson is able to decypher the letter," he argued, "we must either presume that the bearer of the letter was also the bearer of its key, or that the key was previously in possession of the person to whom the letter was addressed." The affidavit did not resolve this issue, but Marshall surmised that Wilkinson had already possessed the key. If so, he concluded, the fact that the letter had been "written in a cypher previously settled between [Wilkinson] and Col. Burr" was, for the present, "a circumstance which sufficiently support[ed] the assertion, that the letter was written by Col. Burr."⁴⁷

Although Marshall did not think that a shared cipher implicated Wilkinson in Burr's project, many did. Plumer recognized the necessity of a shared key on first reading Wilkinson's affidavit, leading him to wonder whether "Wilkinson [had given] Burr assurances?"⁴⁸ Another writer put it very simply: "W. had the key to B__s cyphers, this alone proves my supposition" that he was a party to the conspiracy.⁴⁹ The strength of the popular belief that "virtuous and innocent designs do not stand in need of the cloak of mystery" left Wilkinson's defenders scrambling to explain his ability to decipher the letter. Rejecting

Marshall's supposition, some assumed that Swartwout had delivered the key along with the letter. It simply did not seem possible, even for a firm supporter, to think that Wilkinson "was not concerned in Burr's conspiracy, or at least, that he had not consented to assist him in some illegal project," if one accepted that the two men had previously "agreed to correspond in *cypher*."[50]

For many contemporaries, the cipher letter—by its very existence, its familiar tone, and its intrinsic illegibility—deepened suspicions about Wilkinson's involvement, even as it provided answers to their questions about Burr's plans. At least initially, most found it far more valuable for understanding Burr than Wilkinson. But its value as a window into Burr's project depended on two crucial assumptions: the original letter had to have been written by Burr and the published version had to be an accurate deciphering. Some doubted one or both of those fundamentals from the start. "Did [Burr] write that cyphered incoherent scrawl to Wilkinson," Thomas Boylston Adams asked on first reading the published letter?[51] Others resolved any problems with reconciling Burr's authorship with the published version by assuming that Wilkinson had deciphered it incorrectly. Plumer quickly warned his son "not [to] place implicit confidence in Genl Wilkinson's account of the contents of Col Burr's letter"; he was certain that Wilkinson had "not accurately decyphered it."[52]

These doubts about the authorship of the original letter and the accuracy of the deciphered version strengthened over the next few months. A few days before Jefferson made public Wilkinson's version in the nation's capital, Burr, hundreds of miles away in the Mississippi Territory, denied that he had written the original letter. On 10 January 1807, Burr had arrived at Bayou Pierre with the first of his boats and men from the Ohio. Soon after, he had been shown a local newspaper that reported Wilkinson presenting the cipher letter to the New Orleans court in mid-December. Burr had then negotiated an agreement with acting territorial governor Cowles Mead that made him subject to civil authority. On 20 January, after meeting with Burr, territorial judge Thomas Rodney reported to his nephew, who coincidentally was named Jefferson's attorney general the same day, that Burr had told him "that the Letters the General had Charged on him were fictitious or forged" by the Marquis de Yrujo, the Spanish minister, or "his

Agents and Emisaries."[53] News of Burr's denial spread quickly, reaching New Orleans before the end of January and central Kentucky and the nation's capital in mid-February. A private letter from Natchez in the *Western World* reported that Burr had declared "that the letter which Wilkinson pretends to have received from him, is a forgery."[54] A similar letter in the *National Intelligencer* included, as well, Burr's charge that the cipher letter, and other letters to Wilkinson, had "emanated . . . from the Marquis Yrujo[,] who fabricated these letters to injure him."[55] As these letters spread in western and eastern newspapers, a barely disguised letter from Wilkinson damning Burr for "descend[ing] to the vulgar baseness of telling palpable lies" began to radiate out from Baltimore.[56]

After these initial denials, however, Burr grew circumspect. At the initial hearing in Richmond in late March, neither Burr nor his lawyers claimed that the cipher letter was a forgery, though he did describe the evidence against him, including Wilkinson's affidavits, as "abounding in crudities and absurdities."[57] A few days later, Burr apparently assured his longtime friend Charles Biddle that he had not written the cipher letter. But, when Commodore Truxton, whose name had appeared in the published letter, requested such assurances, Burr tried to use Biddle to stall their mutual friend. Writing to Biddle, Burr acknowledged Truxton's "right to make the enquiry" and even to publish Burr's reply to clear his name. But, through Biddle, he asked Truxton to wait until after the trial, pledging "full Satisfaction on the Subject" then. Burr did not explain how providing Truxton with such assurances risked "very serious inconvenience and injury" when a similar denial—admittedly not in his own words—had been widely publicized.[58] Burr's uncertainty about how to handle the cipher letter on the eve of his trial is also suggested by its treatment in Richmond's *Impartial Observer*, the newspaper that he paid to write on his behalf. The *Observer* said little about the cipher letter, invoking only the weakest grounds for doubting the published version—Wilkinson's admitted uncertainty about his accuracy—without denying that Burr wrote it.

Through the spring of 1807, doubts about Wilkinson's version of the cipher letter lingered. Men who knew Burr and his habits raised questions about the letter's contents and language. In a published letter, Truxton insisted that Burr would never have used the initial "T" in the letter and then provided a note that gave his name. But what seemed inconsistent to such men probably did not register with many readers of the deciphered letter. For doubts about the accuracy of Wilkinson's version to spread, it would take other kinds of inconsistencies— between the original letter and the deciphered version or between different versions of the deciphered letter. In mid-April, Maryland judge Joseph H. Nicholson predicted trouble for Wilkinson "when Burr's original Letter . . . , of which a decyphered and *mutilated* Copy was sent to the Executive, [was] presented to the public Eye."[59] A few weeks later, published accounts from New Orleans identified differences between the printed version of the cipher letter and the version that Wilkinson had allegedly read to the city's merchants in December, including "substitut[ing] the name of Alston [for Dayton] and omitt[ing] a long paragraph relating to former correspondence between himself and Burr."[60] Rumors that either the cipher key or "the *famous cyphered letter*" itself had been lost deepened suspicions of Wilkinson on the eve of Burr's trial.[61]

By early June, with Burr's trial in Richmond already begun and Wilkinson's arrival from New Orleans imminently expected, questions shrouded the cipher letter. Would the original letter differ from the published version in important ways? Would Burr's authorship of the letter be proven or refuted? Could Wilkinson account for his ability to decipher the letter without implicating himself in the conspiracy? Would the kind of prior involvement of Wilkinson that seemed necessary to explain the fact and tone of the letter be established? Ultimately, would the cipher letter reveal more about Burr's treason or Wilkinson's perfidy?

"IF BURR HAS MADE . . . THOSE OVERTURES TO THESE MEN, HE HAS ACTED UNLIKE HIMSELF"

Wilkinson's earliest exposure of the cipher letter in New Orleans in December 1806 came amid a series of disclosures of Burr's plans by men who claimed to have heard them from Burr himself. Each of these firsthand accounts has a distinct history. Their authors had interacted with Burr in diverse circumstances; made their disclosures for different reasons, in different ways, and at different times; and experienced varied

184 | CHAPTER 5

public and official reactions. Some of the revelations were prompted by news from the West, others by developments in the East. Some were made initially, or exclusively, to the administration; others went directly to the press. Some were ultimately important to the administration's or the public's efforts to make sense of Burr's project; others were unknown or ignored. All promised more reliable information about Burr's intentions and movements than the rumor and speculation that filled conversations and newspapers; but each revealed, as well, its author's anxieties about being associated with Burr's alleged treason. Taken together, these firsthand disclosures presented problems not only for Burr, but also for Wilkinson.

Between August 1806 and March 1807, eight men volunteered accounts of conversations or correspondence with Burr to help to clarify his project—John Adair, Joseph Alston, Justus Erich Bollman, William Eaton, Benjamin Henry Latrobe, George Morgan, Benjamin Stoddert, and Thomas Truxton. It was a striking group. All were known, respected, and could be called, in the words of the cipher letter, "the best blood of our country."[62] Seven of the eight were military men. Only the English architect Latrobe lacked military experience, but his engineering skills could be put to military purposes. Most also felt disaffected from Jefferson or the Republicans, for personal or political reasons, when Burr met with them. The timing of their disclosures were revealing. Only Eaton and Morgan exposed Burr's plans to Jefferson soon after hearing them, though Eaton's initial warnings were as ambiguous and guarded as Morgan's were explicit and direct. The others disclosed Burr's communications weeks or months afterward. In the fall of 1806, the growing sense of crisis prompted clearer revelations by Eaton to the administration and the press and the first disclosures by Truxton to the president. In late November, Jefferson's proclamation led Latrobe to reveal his meetings with Burr to the administration. But it took the naming of the others as Burr's associates in newspapers and, more importantly, in Jefferson's message and Wilkinson's affidavit to spark the final flurry of disclosures. Between January and March 1807, Bollman, Alston, Stoddert, Truxton, and Adair provided accounts to the newspapers or the administration or both. Some of these disclosures became public during Burr's trial; others did not reach the public for years. But, before the Richmond grand jury hearings began in May, Eaton, Alston,

Stoddert, Truxton, and Adair had each made public one or more accounts of his meetings with Burr.[63]

The content of these disclosures ranged widely. Alston insisted that Burr had never said anything to him about either dividing the union or attacking New Orleans, while hinting that his father-in-law's real "objects [were] of a very different nature from those attributed to him."[64] Latrobe revealed that Burr had asked him to arrange for a large group of Irish laborers to go west to build a canal around the falls of the Ohio, but the Englishman worried that that project might have been a cover for other schemes. Of those who described Burr's true intentions, only Morgan and Eaton presented them as unquestionably treasonous. After his conversations with Burr, Morgan had no doubt "that he meditated a separation of the Western side of the mountains from the Eastern."[65] Adair, Bollman, and Truxton stated that Burr had revealed nothing more than a plan to liberate Mexico, with only Bollman saying that Burr's force would have moved before or without war being declared in Washington. Truxton's published letter reported that Burr's plan was *"to attack Vera Cruz and Mexico, give liberty to an enslaved world, and establish an independent government in Mexico,"* but only *"in case of a war between the United States and Spain."*[66] Stoddert told two very different stories. In his published letter, he insisted that "Burr [had] never communicated any scheme of any kind," but had merely offered "speculative opinions respecting our government."[67] Privately, he informed the administration that Burr had claimed "that with 500 men [he] could put himself at the head of [the federal government] . . . without bloodshed, or the appear[ance] of a revolution."[68]

Of the firsthand disclosures, Eaton's were the best known and the most shocking. Eaton seemed a perfect candidate for Burr's confidences— a military figure (he was often called General Eaton) who had fallen out with the administration. In November 1805, after years in North Africa, he had returned home to a hero's welcome. Six months earlier, the former consul at Tunis had led a small band of United States Marines and a motley army of North African and European recruits against Tripoli, with whom the United States was at war. Eaton's assault on the fortress at Derne had driven the pasha of Tripoli to seek peace. But American consular officials and naval officers in the region had thwarted Eaton's efforts to settle the terms. He had returned home hoping to restore his honor, arrange a pension for his North African ally, and secure the reimbursement of his immense expenditures. Eaton's criticisms of the administration and its North African agents helped to make the treaty controversial, assured him Federalist attention, and probably slowed a resolution of his financial claims. Shortly after Eaton returned to Washington, Burr called upon him for the first of a series of meetings.[69]

Eaton's disclosures took different forms and said different things over time. He claimed to have met with the president during these meetings with Burr, probably in the early spring of 1806, and at least hinted at Burr's plans. That October, he provided more complete information first to Postmaster General Gideon Granger and then to Secretary of State James Madison. Newspapers reported the fact of his disclosures, with a brief account of their content. In late November, the first published statement of Eaton's information appeared in a Boston newspaper in a form that he had approved before publication. This statement was re-printed, and commented upon, across the country. But the deposition that Eaton provided in late January 1807 for the Bollman and Swart-wout case became the best known and most influential of his many accounts. The various stories were not entirely consistent with each other. "The more distant the time, the more distant from Burr, & the louder public opinion is expressed agt Burr," Senator Plumer noted, "the fuller & stronger are the declarations of Eaton."[70]

Eaton's deposition described Burr's plans as they had been revealed during numerous meetings. Initially, Burr had told Eaton that "he was organizing a secret expedition against" Mexico with the government's backing and "was authorized to invite [him] to take the command of a division." Eaton admitted that he had immediately agreed to join this expedition. In subsequent meetings, the two men had studied maps and reports and discussed "the feasibility of penetrating to Mexico." Then, in February, Burr had begun "to unveil himself." While Burr's criticisms of the administration had left Eaton suspicious of the claim of government backing, he had feigned continued interest to obtain information. Thus duped, Burr had "laid open his project of revolution-ising the western country, separating it from the Union, establishing a monarchy there, of which he was to be the sovereign [and] New Orleans to be his capital[,] organizing a force on the Mississippi, and extending [his] conquest to Mexico." Rather than immediately denouncing this plan, Eaton explained, he had suggested various "impediments"—"the republican habits" of westerners, "their affection" for the administration, a lack of funds, and the opposition of "the regular army." According to Eaton, Burr had insisted that he had removed these obstacles on his western tour by "secur[ing] the attachment of the principal citizens of Kentucky, Tennessee and Louisiana," arranging "inexhaustible resources as to funds," winning the support of the army, and contacting "powerful agents in the Spanish territory." Offered "the second command in [Burr's] army," Eaton had been told that Wilkinson would have "the chief command." According to Eaton, Burr had repeatedly stated that "the plan of separating the union . . . had been communicated to and approved by Gen. Wilkinson"; in his deposition, Eaton dismissed this claim as "an artful argument of seduction."[71]

According to his deposition, Eaton had finally denounced this project only upon learning that Burr's "ambition was not bounded by the waters of the Missisippi and Mexico." Eaton had appeared acquiescent as Burr spoke of creating an independent nation in the trans-Appalachian West. He had listened as Burr asserted that the feebleness of the government "and the divisions of political opinions" presented "a circumstance of which we should profit." And he had remained silent as Burr argued that "there were very many enterprising men among us who aspired to something beyond the dull pursuits of civil life." Then, Eaton had learned that Burr also "meditated overthrowing the present government of our country." Burr, Eaton stated, had eventually claimed that, "if he could gain over the Marine Corps, and secure the naval commanders, . . . *he would turn Congress neck and heels out of doors; assassinate the President; seize on the treasury and navy; and declare himself the protector of an energetic government.*" Burr had presented such a coup as the only way to restore the honor and "energy" of the country and had insisted that it would be supported by "the best blood of *America.*" At that point, Eaton had finally spoken out against Burr's plans. Burr had continued his visits, with less frequency and greater reserve. But, to the end, according to the deposition, Burr sought "to engage" Eaton in a separatist project, though he had "abandoned the idea of a general revolution."[72]

Eaton's firsthand disclosures, to the Boston *Repertory* in late November and in the deposition two months later, produced mixed reactions in the nation's newspapers. For very different reasons, Republican and Federalist newspapers generally accepted his accounts as true. Republican editors reprinted Eaton's statements without questioning his accuracy, even when they expressed amazement at Burr's audacity. In the *Intelligencer*, a series of essays titled "The Conspiracy" treated "the damning deposition of Eaton" as a starting point for judging other accounts.[73] Federalist editors often accepted Eaton's tale but rarely discussed what they said of Burr's plans. For them, the most useful part of what one editor called "the plain unvarnished narrative of Gen. Eaton" was the revelation that he had warned the president about Burr's disunionist project but had been ignored.[74] Eaton's accounts confirmed their belief that Jefferson had "most shamefully and woefully neglected" "his duty."[75] But the accounts could only serve this purpose if they were taken as true; "no doubts are entertained of his veracity," a contributor to the *Washington Federalist* insisted in late February.[76] As such, the attacks on Eaton's veracity came from outside the regular party newspapers, such as John Wood's newly established *Atlantic World*. Wood dismissed "Gen. Eaton's story of Col. Burr proposing to assassinate the President, and turn Congress *neck* and *heels* out of doors" as "wild and romantic."[77]

The skepticism about Eaton's disclosures that was largely absent from the newspapers was readily apparent in private letters and diaries. Some readers accepted Eaton's account as an accurate, if alarming, statement of Burr's views. Even one of Burr's most trusted New York allies privately admitted that he was "disposed to believe the greater part of" the deposition.[78] But many people, across party lines, discounted Eaton's story, believing that he had "used too lavishly the pencil of fancy" or "blended, what was said in Jest & [in] earnest."[79] Skeptics often based their doubts about Eaton's disclosures on their view of him as "imprudent, wild, & raving"—something that was wholly absent from the newspaper coverage.[80] Privately, his reputation was savaged. "I believe Eaton is a liar," one Georgian bluntly wrote, and "a man who by any means will be talked of as something remarkable."[81] In mid-December, Louisa Catherine Adams reported from Boston that Eaton had fallen "quite out of fashion," which she considered less surprising than "his ever having been thought any thing of any where." Eaton "indulges in intoxication to such an excess," she added, that "he is not conscious of what he says."[82] The same linkage between perceptions of the person and acceptance of his story operated in the nation's capitol. "Considering Eaton as a weak & vain man," Thomas Tudor Tucker explained, many "disregard every thing that comes from him."[83]

Taken together, the published disclosures of Eaton, Alston, Stoddert, Truxton, and Adair—and the lesser-known accounts of the three men who provided information only to the administration—posed problems for both Burr and Wilkinson. The sheer number of firsthand accounts lent support to the charge that Burr had planned and launched a massive enterprise. Furthermore, the revelations came from the same kind of men, men whose military backgrounds might have suited Burr's project and whose political frustrations might have left them "capable of avenging, on their *country*, affronts received from its *government*."[84] The sense that these men fit together made it easier to accept each one's story. Having already read that Burr had offered Eaton "a command by land," for example, increased the likelihood that he "had made overtures to Truxton to take a naval command."[85] Even as this aspect of the disclosures weighed against Burr, it also injured Wilkinson. He seemed to fit the type, strengthening suspicions of his prior involvement.

But Burr appeared not only to have approached the same kind of men, but also to have proposed the same scheme to them. Although the disclosures differed on many points, contemporaries saw enough consistency among them to view them as confirming each other. One newspaper reported that Eaton's and Stoddert's accounts agreed upon "the most serious and sanguinary points," including "the very number of men which Burr conceived to be competent to the expulsion of the President and of both Houses of Congress."[86] Similarly, an editorial in Richmond's *Enquirer* expounded upon the similarities in nature and content between Eaton's and Truxton's disclosures. "The course that [Burr] pursued with Commodore Truxton was the counterpart with his intrigue with gen. Eaton," the editor remarked, "and most probably with many others." To both, Burr had "ridicule[d] the *pretended* weakness of the present administration" and "first baited his hook with [the] ambiguous scheme" of invading Mexico.[87] The firsthand disclosures also included elements that echoed the cipher letter, reinforcing the official contention that it presented Burr's plans in his own hand. Even as

Truxton publicly denied that Burr had proposed a division of the union or an attack upon New Orleans to him, he presented what Burr had said in ways that accepted both the cipher letter and the treason that it was understood to include. The strongest confirmation of the cipher letter came from Eaton's deposition. Both documents placed Burr at the head of a military expedition in the Southwest. Both spoke of the men and monies that Burr had raised and claimed that the army would join his efforts. And both described Burr's supporters as among "the best blood" of the country.

It would have required a very selective reading of the firsthand accounts, however, to see them simply as confirming either the cipher letter or each other, particularly since some flatly denied that Burr intended anything criminal. Together, the firsthand disclosures did not tell a single, coherent story and certainly did not cohere around the story in the cipher letter and Wilkinson's affidavit. Whereas the cipher letter noted extensive British support for Burr's project, most of the other accounts never mentioned foreign backing. Whereas the cipher letter left unclear Burr's ultimate intentions, Eaton's deposition identified not one, but three somewhat distinct projects: establishing an independent monarchy in the trans-Appalachian West; leading a revolutionary force against Spanish Mexico; and overthrowing the government in Washington. After reading Eaton's deposition, Truxton pledged to a friend that Burr's proposals to him had been "very different" from those that Eaton described.[88] Greater consistency among the firsthand disclosures, and between them and the cipher letter, might have bolstered Wilkinson's claims of innocence. But one of their most frequent commonalities—their identification of the general as Burr's main ally—only made his situation worse. Adair clearly implicated Wilkinson in Burr's plan. And Eaton's assertion that Burr had told him that Wilkinson would *act as Lieutenant to me* squared perfectly with the cipher letter's statement that "Wilkinson shall be second to Burr only."[89]

Setting Wilkinson's narrative, as told in his affidavits and his rendering of the cipher letter, alongside the firsthand disclosures both reinforced and undermined the credibility of the official reading. That Burr had attempted to engage a number of men of the same type, had spoken to them during the same months, and had said to them some of the same things suggested that the various pieces fit together to reveal a single picture. That is certainly how the president saw it by late April. "Eaton, Stoddart, Wilkinson, and two others whom I must not name" would establish Burr's guilt, Jefferson insisted, situating the general's evidence among the firsthand accounts.[90] But the similarities between Wilkinson's narrative and these accounts could work the other way, as well. That Alston's and Stoddert's public statements were widely viewed as more exculpatory than revealing strengthened the belief that Wilkinson had disclosed Burr's plans and defended New Orleans to cover his own prior involvement. That Eaton's, Alston's, and Stoddert's public statements could seem unbelievable fueled doubts about Wilkinson's claims. That Wilkinson could be grouped with Truxton and Eaton—as "hasty, imprudent, unguarded[, and] incapable of retaining a secret," according to Plumer—raised questions about Burr's actual role. "If Burr [had] made . . . those overtures to these men," Plumer concluded, "he [had] acted unlike himself."[91]

"WE ARE ATIPTOE TO HEAR WILKINSONS EVIDENCE"

By 13 June 1807, when Wilkinson and the original letters arrived in Richmond for the grand jury phase of Burr's trial, the official reading of the cipher letter seemed imperilled. In newspapers and courtrooms, in private letters and diaries, people had questioned Burr's authorship of the letter, Wilkinson's rendering of its contents, the treasonous nature of Burr's plans, and Wilkinson's noninvolvement. New information from Natchez and New Orleans had fueled doubts about the official reading, but so had the disclosures of Adair, Alston, Eaton, Stoddert, and Truxton. As with so many other aspects of the Burr Conspiracy, the truth about the cipher letter seemed certain to emerge in Richmond. "We are atiptoe to hear Wilkinsons evidence," one Virginian remarked on the eve of his testimony.[92]

Wilkinson's four days of testimony transformed the grand jurors'— and, in time, the public's—impressions of the cipher letter. Wilkinson tried to dispel most of the existing doubts about the cipher letter and himself and to preempt some of the new questions that he must have known would arise once he produced the original letter. His story began with a warning letter about Burr that he had sent to a cabinet member from St. Louis in October 1805. After recounting the grounds for—and limits of—his early suspicions, Wilkinson claimed that he had continued to correspond with Burr to learn his intentions. The first day's testimony ended with his receipt of the cipher letter at Natchitoches, his initial effort to decipher it, and his decisions to defend New Orleans and to communicate with Jefferson "as soon as he could draw from [Swartwout] the whole of the plan."[93] At that point, he surrendered the original letter and the cipher keys; there is no indication that the grand jurors immediately deciphered the letter or even read the parts in clear text. The next day, Wilkinson resumed the story of his efforts to discover and defeat Burr's plans, carrying it through Bollman's arrest in mid-December. His final full day of testimony described his measures in New Orleans and explained his orders to seize Burr after his surrender in the Mississippi Territory.[94]

Its placement in the notes of the juror Joseph C. Cabell suggests that a newly deciphered version of the cipher letter became available to the grand jury only after Wilkinson's third day of testimony. The first deviation from the published version was obvious and portentous. Where Wilkinson's version began "I, Aaron Burr, have obtained funds, and have actually commenced the enterprise," the original opened instead with a sentence in clear text that read, *"Your letter post marked 13th. May is received."*[95] In the original, the next sentence no longer included Burr's name and added "at *length*" before "obtained funds." At two points, Wilkinson had omitted second-person plural pronouns ("our" and "us").[96] And, as Cabell noted, "in place of *our project my dear friend,*" he had substituted "the words *The Project.*"[97] In his notes, Cabell highlighted those discrepancies that suggested Wilkinson's prior involvement in Burr's plans; but there were many other differences between Wilkinson's rendition and the new version. The next day, Wilkinson was recalled by the grand jury and asked to explain "the variation between his copy of Burr's cyphered letter, and that of the Committee," and to relate the contents of his 13 May 1806 letter to Burr.[98] Cabell's notes suggest that his answers were brief and unsatisfactory. Wilkinson raised further questions that day by providing, perhaps "accidentally," the other original of the cipher letter, which he had "altered" by trying to scratch out the opening sentence.[99] Of Wilkinson's final appearance, grand jury foreman John Randolph reported that "all was confusion of language & of looks."[100]

It would take months for the grand jury's new version of the cipher letter and new doubts about Wilkinson to become widely known. But some hints, some fragments began to appear within a few days, first in court, then in conversation, and eventually in newspapers. Two days after recalling Wilkinson, the grand jury requested that the court ask Burr to produce Wilkinson's 13 May letter. Marshall rejected this request. But Burr responded, as well, shifting attention from the letter to his honor. "It would be impossible," he declared, "to expose any letter which had been communicated to him confidentially."[101] The prosecuting attorneys George Hay and Alexander McRae instantly recognized Burr's reply as a master stroke that placed him above everyone, including Wilkinson, who had divulged private conversations and correspondence. "The attitude & tone assumed by Burr Struck every body," Hay informed Jefferson.[102] To undo the damage, McRae asked Wilkinson whether he would waive his rights of privacy and then announced Wilkinson's willingness "that the whole of the correspondence . . . be exhibited before the court."[103] Burr announced that he could not produce the letter because it was not in his possession and further claimed that Wilkinson had known that the letter was not available when he invited Burr to reveal it. Hay believed that this effort to return suspicion to Wilkinson had failed. Although the importance of this exchange would have been clear to anyone who witnessed it in the courtroom or read about it in a newspaper, its meaning would not; they could not have linked the 13 May letter to the cipher letter. But they should have recognized that the grand jury had doubts about the general.

A few days later, an item in Richmond's *Virginia Gazette* suggested the depths of these doubts. It reported that the grand jurors had divided evenly—eight for, eight against—on a vote to indict Wilkinson for treason. Wilkinson immediately denied this report, writing anonymously in the *Enquirer* "that no such motion was even spoken of in the Jury."[104] Richmond's other Republican newspaper also leapt to Wilkinson's defense. And a grand juror "of the most respectable character . . . unequivocally declared" to a group of Richmond gentlemen "that no question of Treason was ever taken against Wilkinson."[105] The truth seems to have been more complicated than either Wilkinson or his accuser, the grand juror Munford Beverley, allowed. The jurors considered three indictments against Wilkinson: for treason; for misprision of treason for failing to apprise the administration of Jonathan Dayton's role in Burr's project; and for the vague charge of violating "the laws and constitution of the United States" with his actions in New Orleans.[106] The votes on these charges are unknown, but a number of jurors recalled that the closest was seven for, nine against on the charge of misprision of treason. Throughout July and August, Wilkinson, Beverley, and other grand jurors disputed this matter in Virginia's newspapers, repeatedly publicizing the jurors' suspicions of the general. Even though Wilkinson had escaped indictment, his reputation suffered from this newspaper battle.

If ordinary readers could derive only vague impressions of the grand jury's proceedings from the newspapers, those close to the trial—and their correspondents—often knew much more. Late on 23 June, Ohio's Dudley Woodbridge Jr. reported that the grand jury had spent the "day in deciphering intercepted letters among others one from Genl Dayton."[107] By the close of the hearings, Truxton knew that the original cipher letter was "a very different thing" from what Wilkinson had provided, with its reference to Wilkinson's letter of 13 May and discussion of various "matters in the plural number."[108] In late June, Randolph detailed the discrepancies to one confidant, and Cabell loaned his notes to prosecuting attorney William Wirt. Asked by Wirt for the jurors' "objections to General Wilkinson," Cabell prepared a list of eight questions, many with multiple parts, that the prosecution should ask Wilkinson before the trial resumed. Three of them concerned the cipher letter: Why had Burr "address[ed] Wilkinson in terms which indicate that he was at least privy to [his] schemes of misdemeanour and treason?" Why had Wilkinson "omit[ted] certain words and phrases which tended to implicate himself" in the published version and then sworn "that the copy was as correct as he could make it?" And "whence came the erasure of the words 'yours of the 13th May post marked has been received'" and their reinsertion into the altered copy in a different hand?[109] Writing to the president's private secretary, Cabell explained that it was Wilkinson's "omission of certain words & phrases . . . tending to implicate himself [that] did him particular injury."[110] Long before Burr's trial resumed in early August, there were growing doubts about "how Wilkinson [stood] as to the Treason."[111]

During the treason trial, a shocking incident thrust the general and the letter into the newspapers again. Late on 24 August, an attempt was made to poison Abner L. Duncan, a New Orleans attorney who had come to Richmond as a witness. News of this crime spread quickly. Rumors hinted darkly that Burr had arranged to have Duncan "take[n] off" before he could testify, while newspapers noted Duncan's value for proving "Wilkinson's innocence."[112] To counter these stories, Swartwout sent a letter to the *New-York Gazette* that claimed that Wilkinson had ordered the murder to damage "Burr's reputation" and to "save himself from exposure." According to Swartwout, Duncan had sworn in a deposition that he had seen Wilkinson *"erase and alter the original"* cipher letter in New Orleans *"and then forge a letter"* that he called *"a true and faithful copy."*[113] Swartwout's charge sparked a newspaper war that lasted for weeks. In New York, Boston, and Baltimore, Wilkinson's friends sprang to his defense. In Philadelphia, Duncan authorized a local editor to denounce the "infamous attack," describing Swartwout's account of his deposition as "a tissue of base falsehoods."[114] In Richmond, Wilkinson denounced Swartwout in the *Enquirer*, while Burr's attorney Luther Martin used the *Virginia Gazette* to call Wilkinson "the instigator to that damnable attempt" on Duncan's life. Writing after Duncan's deposition had appeared in newspapers, Martin also described it as "fix[ing] on Wilkinson the *guilt* of altering the letter in cypher, and of having deliberately sworn to what he knew to be false."[115] Whether they accused or exonerated the general, however, these pieces publicized the charge that he had committed "forgery" by altering the original cipher letter.[116]

Amid this newspaper war, Wilkinson took the stand for five days of testimony in late September and early October that Harman Blennerhassett predicted would be "a spectacle of depravity seldom equalled."[117] The general had not testified in the abortive treason and misdemeanor trials; nor had the cipher letter been produced as evidence. Wilkinson's appearance in the final phase of Burr's trial provided his only chance to tell his story in open court. He tried to present his tale as he had done before the grand jury, bolstered with nearly two dozen depositions, letters, and other documents—many of which were ruled inadmissable. But to a far greater degree than in June, his testimony centered on the cipher letter—its different versions, the uses to which they had been put, the age of the cipher keys, and the reference to a 13 May letter. The defense attorneys focused on these issues, while also pressing Wilkinson about his actions in New Orleans and his orders to arrest Burr near Natchez. They intended, as the attorney John Wickham explained, to "impeach General Wilkinson's credibility."[118] Would not proof that Wilkinson had "made erazures in letters, and then sworn that translations of them were true copies, . . . affect his credibility," another defense attorney asked?[119]

The defense forced Wilkinson to detail the process by which the cipher letters had been deciphered, altered, and publicized. Asked to explain the erasure of the sentence acknowledging his 13 May letter, Wilkinson admitted the change, introducing Duncan's deposition as an explanation. In it, Duncan described serving as Wilkinson's attorney and counselor in New Orleans in December. He admitted that, working with the original letters and the cipher keys, he had prepared Wilkinson's two affidavits, "intentionally omitting every thing which was calculated to inculpate the General, or which might by exciting suspicion, have a tendency to weaken his testimony." Wilkinson, according to Duncan, had "strongly and repeatedly objected to the omissions." In his deposition, Duncan insisted that it was "absurd to impute any sinister intention to the omission," since Wilkinson had always known that the originals would be required in court.[120] Wilkinson further testified that he had never fully deciphered the letter, having made only an imperfect and incomplete effort "hastily and by piece-meal at Natchitoches" shortly after its delivery by Swartwout. Instead, it was Duncan's version, which had been prepared "the 25th or 26th of December," that had been made public.[121] Wilkinson also stated that he had never sworn that Duncan's version was true, "only [that it was] substantially so."[122] And he insisted that he had conveyed the contents of the cipher letter to the president only through Isaac Briggs's "oral communications."[123] None of the defense attorneys seem to have reminded Wilkinson that the best-known version of the cipher letter was his affidavit of 18 December—a week before Duncan had allegedly prepared it—that he had sent to Jefferson himself.

In cross-examination, the defense sought to show that Wilkinson had something to hide when he prepared and presented, either by himself or through Duncan, an incomplete version of the cipher letter. The

13 May letter—whose acknowledgment Wilkinson had tried to scratch from one of the original letters and had omitted from the deciphered versions—became evidence of his prior involvement. The defense asked about it on all five days of Wilkinson's testimony, wanting to know whether he had written that there would be "a war with Spain."[124] Wilkinson repeatedly insisted that he had "not the most distant recollection of its contents."[125] The defense also called one of the grand jurors, Littleton Waller Tazewell, to ask about the jury's knowledge of the 13 May letter. Tazewell reported that Wilkinson had professed the same inability to recall its contents in June, but also revealed that Swartwout had remembered that it included the statement, *"I am ready."*[126] The defense openly admitted that its goal was not to discover the contents of the letter—Burr had it in his possession and could have produced it if it suited his purposes. Instead, as the attorney John Baker explained, they wanted "to shake the credibility of General Wilkinson, and to make him produce the shake himself."[127] Wilkinson and the prosecuting attorneys called upon Burr to produce the letter. The general insisted that it was "the insinuations and innuendoes" that had been attached to the letter, not the letter itself, that threatened his reputation.[128] Even as he demanded that Burr produce it, however, Wilkinson fueled "insinuations and innuendos" of his own by announcing that, by doing so, Burr would "release [him] from all obligation to withhold [Burr's] confidential letters."[129] Since Wilkinson's 13 May letter to Burr does not survive and since Burr's previous letters to Wilkinson exist only as published in the general's memoirs, it is impossible to decide who would have suffered more from a joint exposure. But the revelation of a "secret Correspondence" that both Burr and Wilkinson wanted to keep secret injured them both.[130]

Defense questioning also focused upon the age of the cipher. For months, commentators had recognized that the more recently the key or keys had been devised, the more damaging the cipher letter was to Wilkinson. In late February, a New York newspaper rhetorically asked him, "How long have you been possess'd of that cypher? did col. Burr give it to you, when you were friends at Washington, or did he confide it to you, when you met last year at Louisville?"[131] Wilkinson saw this problem, as well. In a mid-February letter to Jefferson, he stated, unasked, that the cipher had been "designed in 1786 & imparted to

Mr. Burr in 89 at his request."[132] Testifying first before the grand jury and later in open court, Wilkinson abandoned this claim. He dated the book cipher to the fall of 1800—the earliest year possible—and the alphabet cipher to the spring of 1801. But he stated that the hieroglyphic cipher had been devised by himself and Captain Campbell Smith in the mid-1790s. With depositions and letters, Wilkinson tried to establish that he had used that key for over a decade. Through cross-examination of Wilkinson and questioning of Tazewell, the defense suggested that the key must have been more recent because certain hieroglyphs did not fit with Wilkinson's dating. Why was *city of Washington* included, but not "Philadelphia," Wickham wondered, when the national capital had not moved until 1800? Why was *navy* represented by "'96"—the year of the creation of the Navy Department—in a key that had allegedly been prepared in 1794 or 1795?[133] Tazewell identified three other entries, including New Orleans and Louisiana, as "somewhat singular" for the mid-1790s.[134] Wilkinson could explain these aberrations only by insisting that the entries had "originated in [Smith's] caprice, without my privity or participation."[135]

The testimony and cross-examination, argument and counter-argument form of the court proceedings could not provide the kind of final assessment of Wilkinson and the cipher letter that many Americans sought. Efforts at an accounting appeared, instead, in Marshall's official opinion, the press's published analysis, participants' private letters, and rumor's many-tongued reports. Both rumors and letters often concerned the opinions of the prosecuting attorneys. News quickly spread that two of the three—Hay and Wirt—had "washed [their] hands of [Wilkinson]," as Blennerhassett put it, by the end of his testimony.[136] John Randolph shared his knowledge of both men's views with a confidant, having learned from an unnamed source that Wirt had never believed the general and having heard from Hay's "own lips" that Wilkinson was "the most artful scoundrel in existence."[137] In their own letters, Hay and Wirt acknowledged their doubts. Writing to Jefferson in mid-October, Hay admitted that his "confidence in [Wilkinson was] shaken, if not destroyed," and suggested that the president would regret his past support for the general. "You did not know then what you will soon know," Hay remarked, as Wilkinson's testimony began appearing in newspapers.[138] Neither Hay nor Wirt wanted their suspicions to be made public, however.

What did become public knowledge, beginning in late October, were the assessments of the judge and the press. Of Richmond's two Republican newspapers, the *Enquirer* and the *Virginia Argus*, only the latter actively defended Wilkinson by the end of the trial. The editor of the *Enquirer* promised to discuss him in a series of "cursory reflections" on the trial's three central figures. But, after devoting two articles to Burr and four to Marshall, the *Enquirer* abandoned the series without providing the corresponding "portrait" of Wilkinson.[139] While it avoided any sweeping assessment of Wilkinson, though, the *Enquirer* accepted some of his most important claims about the cipher letter in a widely republished discussion "of the *cyphers* which have been exhibited to the court." In describing the three keys, the *Enquirer* piece adopted Wilkinson's testimony about their age and dated his "correspondence in cypher" with Burr to "1800 or 1801."[140] The *Argus* proved much more useful to Wilkinson's cause. In two long pieces, it attempted to dispel the "vague and indefinite suspicions against gen. Wilkinson" that might have arisen from his testimony.[141] The first condemned Burr for denying Wilkinson's request to put all of their correspondence, including the 13 May letter, before the public. The second piece addressed "the charge of *forgery*," using Duncan's deposition to "[acquit] Gen. Wilkinson of any evil intention."[142] But such comments could hardly have counterbalanced the impact of even something as simple as the technique, employed by Virginia's *Norfolk Herald* and other newspapers, of printing together the cipher "letter as decyphered by Wilkinson" and the cipher "letter as decyphered by the Grand Jury . . . from the *original* which Wilkinson would not permit to go out of his own hands."[143]

In a sense, the most important contemporary assessment appeared in Chief Justice Marshall's October opinion committing Burr and Blennerhassett for trial in Ohio on the misdemeanor of preparing an invasion of Spanish territory. After all of the testimony and argument, Marshall concluded that "the authenticity of [the cipher] letter [could not] now be questioned." In the testimony of Swartwout, Truxton, and Wilkinson and in the fact that the letter had been "written in a cypher previously established between gen. Wilkinson and col. Burr,"

Marshall found too much evidence of Burr's authorship to doubt, "at least for the present," that the cipher letter was what Wilkinson claimed. He did not discuss the circumstances by which the cipher letter had been deciphered and disseminated, but accepted enough of Wilkinson's testimony to treat it as a statement of Burr's intentions. As he had eight months earlier when it had first come before him in the Bollman and Swartwout cases, however, Marshall read the cipher letter only as evidence of a military expedition that would have been "intended against Mexico." He also stated that the letter showed that Burr had "calculated on [Wilkinson's] co-operation with the army which he commanded," without deciding whether Burr's calculations had been made "with or without reason."[144]

"HE HAD MADE CERTAIN ALTERATIONS IN THE LETTER RECEIVED FROM ME"

Marshall's "for the present" is, now, two hundred years in the past. How should we assess the cipher letter, given the information that was known at the time and has become available since? How has the official reading of the cipher letter that Wilkinson and Jefferson shaped fared across two centuries? What elements of this reading—Burr's authorship of the letter, the letter's evidence of a disunionist plot, and Wilkinson's innocence of any prior involvement—remain believable? As we have seen, the official reading had been challenged on each of these points even before Marshall handed down his final opinion in October 1807. How have later revelations altered Marshall's interpretation?

Until recent decades, most historians and biographers presented the cipher letter in terms very similar to Marshall's and, thus, somewhat different from Jefferson's and Wilkinson's. They accepted that Burr had sent a cipher letter to Wilkinson, though some authors insisted that Wilkinson's alterations of the originals were so extensive that exactly what Burr wrote would "never be known."[145] They also agreed that the letter provided valuable insights into Burr's thinking, though few writers joined the historian Henry Adams in seeing it as "the key to the whole conspiracy."[146] That does not mean that they agreed on the insights that it offered, of course; exactly what kind of project was described in the cipher letter has always been debated. Before the 1980s, the most important scholarly revisions of the official reading concerned the question that Marshall left open in his final opinion: was the cipher letter evidence of Wilkinson's prior involvement in Burr's project?

Wilkinson's reputation, which one newspaper described as "a carcase" whose "rotten members" were ready to "drop to pieces" in October 1807, crumbled due to later revelations.[147] This process began during his lifetime as he was investigated three times by Congress and three times by military courts before being discharged from the army in 1815. Together, these investigations unearthed new evidence of Wilkinson's crucial role in the Spanish Conspiracy, lasting ties to Spain including a pension, and early involvement in Burr's projects. They suggested that Wilkinson had cooperated both with Spain in efforts to protect Mexico and with Burr in an attempt to revolutionize the Spanish colony. After Wilkinson's death in 1825, the evidence for these betrayals of his responsibilities as the commander of the army only grew. In 1836, Burr's biographer published documents showing that, even as he had sent Lieutenant Smith to Washington with his initial revelations of the Burr Conspiracy, Wilkinson had also dispatched his aide, Walter Burling, to Mexico City to request a reward from the Spanish governor for thwarting it. Nearly twenty years later, the Louisiana historian Charles Gayarré presented extensive evidence from Spanish archives of Wilkinson's efforts to divide the United States on Spain's behalf. In the late nineteenth and early twentieth centuries, scholars working in Spanish and Mexican archives found conclusive proof that Wilkinson, as Agent 13, had carried on a prolonged correspondence with Spanish officials in various colonies and had received generous payments for protecting Spanish interests.[148]

Suspicions about such ties between Wilkinson and Spanish officials had seemed to clarify why he might have first engaged with Burr and then denounced his project. Burr's attorneys believed that, if they could prove that Wilkinson "was receiving a Spanish pension," they would "explain his conduct." "He defeated the enterprize of Burr by hatching a charge of treason against the United States," Wickham argued, "to serve the king whose money he was receiving."[149] One who knew of Wilkinson's pension drew a similar conclusion. Writing to his superiors in Madrid after the publication of the cipher letter, the Marquis de Yrujo explained that Wilkinson had been willing to cooperate with Burr as long as the project aimed at "the separation of the Western States"—long "his favorite plan." When Burr redirected it into "a wild project against Mexico," Wilkinson abandoned him, knowing that it would fail and, in failing, would cost him both "the honorable employment he holds" under the United States "and the generous pension he enjoys from the King."[150] For many historians and biographers, Wilkinson's lucrative connections to Spain provide the key to his actions during the Burr crisis.

But access to additional sources in other archives has also revealed that Wilkinson, on a number of occasions over a period of years, planned and proposed invasions of Spain's neighboring colonies. These documents show that, in the period just before and even during the Burr crisis, Wilkinson was especially active in this respect. He pressed an expedition against Mexico in numerous letters, some to men who would later be publicly linked to the Burr Conspiracy. Writing to Adair in September 1806, for example, Wilkinson announced that "the time . . . [had] now arrived, for subverting the Spanish government in Mexico."[151] He also seized every opportunity to scout routes into northern Mexico and to reconnoiter Spanish troop strengths. Even Walter Burling, whom he sent to Mexico for his Spanish reward, was charged with "examin[ing] every step of the route, with a military eye."[152] During the Burr crisis, Wilkinson repeatedly argued to Jefferson and Dearborn that conditions were perfect for moving against Mexico or West Florida. In his first disclosure of the conspiracy, he argued that Burr's recruits could easily be turned away from the disunionist project and "engage[d] in the service of their Country" against Spain's colonies.[153] From New Orleans in mid-December, Wilkinson even joked with one confidant about "being Crowned Emperor of Mexico, in place of Burr."[154] While such statements undermine Yrujo's claim that Wilkinson was wholly committed to Spanish interests, they fit easily with a different argument—that Wilkinson had joined with Burr in a plan to liberate Spanish Mexico and betrayed him only when success seemed impossible.

Two centuries of revelations about Wilkinson have neither settled nor overturned the official reading's position that Wilkinson was not involved in Burr's project. The evidence still leaves open a number of possibilities. He might have joined what he believed was only a separatist project, as Yrujo reported. Or he might have backed what he thought was only a military invasion, as his letter to Adair suggested. But he might also have merely feigned engagement with Burr to better protect either Spanish interests, as Burr's attorneys sometimes argued, or American interests, as Wilkinson often claimed. Ultimately, Wilkinson did not concede even that much, returning to a firm assertion of his innocence. In 1811, he provided his last and fullest discussion of the cipher letter in *Burr's Conspiracy Exposed*. "Plac[ing] the thing on its just grounds" required nearly five printed pages that addressed ten enumerated points ranging from discrepancies between the original letter and the deciphered version to specific statements in the letter. In the end, Wilkinson insisted that the cipher letter only made sense if "the affair *was still to be* harmonized and concerted" between author and recipient. "The letter is calculated to seduce Wilkinson from his duty, if possible," the general explained; "but if the attempt failed, and the letter should be exposed, to afford no clear evidence of the whole extent of Burr's real designs. Look at the letter in any other light, and the writer must appear a blockhead."[155]

The official reading of the cipher letter faced its most sweeping challenge in the early 1980s, when the editors of the two-volume *Political Correspondence and Public Papers of Aaron Burr* asserted that there was "good reason to believe that Burr wrote not a word of it." In a thirteen-page editorial note, Mary-Jo Kline and Joanne Wood Ryan argued that Dayton, not Burr, "was the author of the cipher" letter. While they presented their case only as a "hypothesis," they insisted that their careful deciphering of the original letters was "almost certainly not a reconstruction of any words that [Burr] encoded for James Wilkinson's eyes."[156] Even before its publication in 1983, Kline and Ryan's argument began to transform the historiography. The previous year, the Burr biographer Milton Lomask incorporated their thinking into his work, detailing their evidence for a "reversal of more than a century and a half of Burr scholarship." Writing for a popular audience, Lomask eliminated every element of scholarly hesitancy from Kline and Ryan's note: "The cipher letter as we know it today was not written by Aaron Burr," he flatly asserted, but by Jonathan Dayton.[157] Since 1982, it has been impossible for scholarly or popular accounts of either Burr's life or the Burr Conspiracy simply to assume Burr's authorship of the cipher letter. Most have accepted Kline and Ryan's contention with as little doubt as Lomask did. "In fact," Burr did not write the cipher letter, his most recent and most scholarly biographer states; "Jonathan Dayton did."[158]

Kline and Ryan based their argument for Dayton's authorship largely upon the handwriting of the original letters. Both copies were in the same hand, but it did not seem to be that of Burr, Swartwout, or Burr's secretary, Charles Willie. Instead, it looked like Dayton's handwriting. The idea that a ciphered letter from Dayton had replaced a ciphered letter from Burr gained support from Swartwout's June 1807 testimony before the grand jury. Swartwout stated that he had left Philadelphia with letters for Wilkinson but had been overtaken by Peter Ogden, Dayton's nephew, with a message from Burr to destroy them and deliver a sealed packet in their place. Seeing the cipher letter as Dayton's work rather than Burr's "resolve[d] many questions" for the editors. It explained the inclusion of Truxton, whom Dayton might have believed supported the project, while Burr would have known otherwise. It explained the mention of Burr's daughter, son-in-law, and grandson; the editors considered it unimaginable that "a doting grandfather [would have] risked the life of a four-year-old child on a military expedition into the wilderness." And it explained the references to Burr in the third person. The editors believed that both Wilkinson and Burr knew that Dayton was the true author, but, they argued, Wilkinson's "purposes" were better served by ascribing the cipher letter to Burr and "Burr's sense of honor would not have allowed him to expose Dayton."[159]

While very influential, Kline and Ryan's hypothesis has faced challenges over the past three decades. Most skeptics have been willing to accept a weak version of their claim—that Dayton penned the cipher letters—but have rejected a stronger reading—that Dayton authored them. In this assessment, the cipher letter is no more Dayton's letter than it would have been Swartwout's or Willie's letter had it been in their handwriting. It certainly does not require another author to explain the components of the cipher letter that the editors identified. Burr frequently wrote about himself in the third person, and it seems unlikely that anyone else would have written about him in the first person, as the cipher letter sometimes did. The Alstons did follow Burr to the

West, though they fell behind the cipher letter's projected timetable. And Burr seems to have been as capable of lying about Truxton and the British fleet to attach Wilkinson to his cause as Dayton was.[160]

In contrast, accepting Dayton as the actual author requires us to ignore the innate characteristics of an encoded letter. Kline and Ryan made the process sound easy; the method for using the dictionary cipher, they remarked, "was almost transparently simple."[161] That was not how Wilkinson saw it. After receiving an earlier ciphered letter from Burr, Wilkinson told Joseph Browne, Burr's brother-in-law and the secretary of the Louisiana Territory, that "the Key [was] such as nobody could ever find out but himself and Burr." The dictionary cipher had required the two men to purchase the same edition, paginate them "*exactly alike*[,] and [number] all the words in each column *alike*."[162] The other two ciphers had their own keys and rules. Kline and Ryan provided no evidence that Dayton possessed the required keys or owned the correct edition of the correct dictionary and knew how to use it to write to Wilkinson. The difficulty of encoding the letter into a form that Wilkinson could later decipher supports the idea that, even if Dayton penned the cipher letter, he did so under Burr's guidance.

Investigating Kline and Ryan's hypothesis about the cipher letter's origins reveals what seems to have been a deliberate effort by Burr, Swartwout, and Bollman to construct a story that could be used to deny Burr's authorship if doing so became necessary. Separated by hundreds of miles, these men could not coordinate their first responses to the publication of the letter as deciphered by Wilkinson. Burr quickly claimed that it had been forged by the Spanish minister, but he probably had not even seen Wilkinson's version when he made that claim—a claim that he does not seem to have ever made again. Swartwout appears to have limited his initial challenge to Wilkinson's version of the cipher letter to one specific point—the missing acknowledgment of the receipt "of a letter from Wilkinson."[163] He does not seem to have denied, in court or in private letters, that the published version of the cipher letter matched, in essence, what he had encoded for Burr. Nor did he tell the story of the substituted packet before reconnecting with Burr. Bollman did not dispute Burr's authorship when he met with the president and secretary of state a day after the publication of Wilkinson's affidavit in Washington, though he may have never seen the original. And he admitted that Burr had asked him "to convey a letter to [Wilkinson] in which he intended to give him some Details respecting his intended Proceedings on the Western Waters, the Time when he intended to be down at New Orleans, the measures he had taken to prevent Interruption from British Ships of War on his Passage through the Gulf, the Rank he—Wilkinson[—]was to hold in Burr's Army," and other issues.[164]

Not until Burr, Swartwout, and Bollman were reunited in the spring of 1807 did any real uncertainty enter into the story of the cipher letter. Before the grand jury, Bollman and Swartwout testified, for the first time, that someone other than Burr had given them the letters that they delivered to Wilkinson, creating the break in the chain of possession that would permit a denial of Burr's authorship. Bollman claimed that, while waiting to set sail in Delaware, James Alexander had handed him "a sealed letter for Genl. Wilkinson" and told him that it was from Burr.[165] Swartwout admitted that he had encoded a "harmless" letter for Burr in Philadelphia but insisted that he had destroyed it in Pittsburgh after Peter Ogden gave him the sealed packet that Swartwout "supposed to be from Colo. Burr."[166] Burr does not seem to have challenged the cipher letter in court, though he frequently spoke as his own counsel. In the trial's final stage, Burr and his attorneys grilled Wilkinson about his alterations of the letter without ever suggesting that they were irrelevant since it was not Burr's letter. The story of a substitute packet reappeared only when Swartwout took the stand on the final day of the trial. Although this story seems to have had little impact at the time, its acceptance by the editors of Burr's papers has made it crucially important in recent decades.

The most intriguing comments about the cipher letter in the fall of 1807 came from Burr himself. After the first day of Wilkinson's testimony in late September, Burr wrote his daughter that his principal accuser had "*acknowledged, very modestly, that he had made certain alterations in the letter received from me, by erasures, &c., and then swore it to be a true copy.* He has not yet," Burr continued, "acknowledged the substitution of names."[167] What Burr meant by "the substitution of names" is unclear to us, though it may have been clear to his daughter. The cipher letter included just three names—Burr, Wilkinson, and Truxton. The first two appeared multiple times, always represented by a number from the hieroglyphic cipher (13, 14, 15, or 16 for Burr and 45 for Wilkinson). Truxton's name appeared only once in a somewhat mangled form. Working with the letter that Bollman delivered, Kline and Ryan decoded the symbols as "T_UAVUN"; I would render it "TVUATUN." It is easy enough to find "Truxton" in those seven characters in a sentence about someone "going to Jamaica to arrange with the admiral there."[168] Most of the symbols in the hieroglyphic cipher could have been changed by adding a line or dot, but it is difficult to get from this particular group to another name that makes sense—such as Stoddert, Alston, Dayton, or even Stephen Decatur, the navy commodore whom both Truxton and Wilkinson worried was connected with Burr. Nor is it easy to imagine why Wilkinson would have replaced any of those names, most of which he later provided in other letters or testimony.[169]

If the meaning of Burr's comment about "the substitution of names" remains elusive, his reference to "the letter received from me," however, seems clear. That statement can hardly be read as a denial of authorship. And Burr could hardly have known that Wilkinson had effected a "substitution of names" if he had not written the original letter. Burr's letter to his daughter suggests that the cipher letter was authored by Burr and altered by Wilkinson; the actual writer—whether Swartwout or Willie or Dayton—seems immaterial. Three decades later, Burr's handpicked biographer took this view. In *Memoirs of Aaron Burr*, Matthew Livingston Davis consistently discussed the cipher letter as something that had been "written in cipher by Colonel Burr," "*altered*" by Wilkinson, "and then deciphered."[170] Whether or not we accept the story of the substituted packets, the original letter seems to have been Burr's letter, expressing Burr's thoughts, to Burr's chosen recipient. But Wilkinson seems to have altered that letter in ways that we still cannot fully identify.

For most contemporaries, and for most scholars, the cipher letter became the crucial document for making sense of the Burr Conspiracy. Still, it never produced the clarity that contemporaries sought. Even if we accept Burr as the author of something approximating the cipher letter as deciphered by either the Richmond grand jury or the modern editors of his papers, it remains imprecise and vague about his intentions. Reading it in the context of the firsthand disclosures of Adair, Alston, Eaton, Truxton, and Stoddert did not provide contemporaries with clear answers either, because those accounts conflicted with each other. Reading it in the context of other firsthand accounts that were not widely known at the time—including those of the British and Spanish ministers—does not offer us any greater clarity for the same reason. The cipher letter lies at the center of a web of outright lies and distorted truths that Burr and Wilkinson spun. To some extent, it was recognized as entangled in prevarications and manipulations as soon as it came before the public—unreliable about both Burr's intentions and Wilkinson's involvement. But that did not prevent people from considering it essential for understanding the Burr Conspiracy, even though they differed about what it actually revealed and about whom it was revealing. "It rarely happens that a single letter is fated to make two men immortal," one writer reflected in 1820; "yet such is the destiny of this [one]."[171]

CHAPTER 6

NEW ORLEANS, ORLEANS
TERRITORY

November 1806 through May 1807

IN NOVEMBER 1806, NEW ORLEANS WAS THE MOST IMPORTANT CITY IN the trans-Appalachian West. Its location near the mouth of the Mississippi River had fixed its role as an entrepôt for the commerce of the interior of a vast continent. Within five years of its founding by the French in 1718, it had become the political capital of the immense province of Louisiana. In five decades under France, New Orleans had grown slowly but steadily. In 1762, as a result of the Seven Years War, the city had passed to Spain. When Spain took control, New Orleans's population had been around three thousand, some thirteen hundred of whom were free or enslaved Africans or their descendants. Over the next four decades, the city's growth had accelerated, driven primarily by increased settlement in its hinterlands—first by British colonists across Lake Pontchartrain and on the lower Mississippi and later by American settlers in the Ohio Valley hundreds of miles upstream. In 1800, New Orleans had been restored to France by treaty, but actual French control had lasted just three weeks before the city passed into American hands in late 1803 through the Louisiana Purchase.[1]

Both the layout and the life of New Orleans centered on the river. The original city, the Vieux Carré, sat at a sweeping curve in the Mississippi that accommodated a rectilinear plat eleven blocks wide and six blocks deep. To the west along the river, at an angle to the old quarter, lay the Faubourg Ste. Marie, the new suburb that provided a home for many American immigrants. By the time of the Burr crisis, the city stretched for about a mile along the river but remained less than a half-mile deep. The most important public spaces were along the riverfront:

A VIEW of NEW ORLEANS TAKEN FROM THE PLANTATION OF MARIGNY

FIGURE 9. View of New Orleans from the plantation where
James Wilkinson was headquartered.

the government building, the Cabildo; the church, St. Louis cathedral;
and the public square, the Place d'Armes. East of the square along the
river could be found a market house. On the broad levee that protected
the city from the river, vendors sold meats, fruits, vegetables, and "articles of every description."[2] The last city before the river's mouth, New
Orleans formed the key site for transferring agricultural staples from
upriver—rice, sugar, and cotton from the lower Mississippi Valley or
tobacco, corn, whiskey, and pork from the Ohio Valley—onto ocean-
going vessels. When Kentucky's John Stuart arrived in early June 1806,
he found "more than 150 Ships & sailing Vessels" along with "upwards
of 300 Flat[boat]s" from upriver.[3] Numerous merchant houses, two
banks, various manufacturing establishments, and such ancillary businesses as boardinghouses, ships' chandlers, and coffeehouses supported
this activity.

By the time of the Burr crisis, New Orleans's population of around
eight thousand was, as an English visitor put it, among "the most motly
grope[s] of human beings ever assembled togeather."[4] The white population included French and French creoles, Spanish and Spanish creoles, Germans, English, Irish, and Americans. Common usage divided
whites into two groups—"Ancient and modern Louisianians"—based
on whether someone had arrived before or after the purchase.[5] Most of

the "modern" Louisianians were Americans; most of the Americans were "modern" Louisianians. But there were exceptions in each case. Combined, whites accounted for slightly more than two-fifths of the population. More prevalent were people of African descent, who were at least as divided as whites by status and skin color and by language and place of origin—some creoles, some from Caribbean islands or the United States, some from Africa. About two-thirds of the black and mixed-race population was enslaved; the remainder, nearly a fifth of the city's population, was free. Also in New Orleans, but uncounted in the census, were native peoples of a half-dozen different nations.

A divided population made for a divided society. The market and levee formed the most significant common spaces. With "no public gardens or promenade," one traveller explained, "the Levee after sunset is crowded with company" in search of "a little fresh air." Elsewhere, "the whites, the quarteroons or coloured people, and the blacks" had "their separate amusements." The whites' balls excluded anyone "in the least degree tainted with the blood of Africa"; those of the mixed-race "coloured people" barred all "who [had] not some white blood in their veins." White society fractured along lines of language and religion. "The manners and amusements" of New Orleans differed greatly from those familiar to most Americans.[6] It had two theaters, with seating following the racial lines of the balls and performances in French. And, as a French visitor noted, the numerically dominant French and the newly arrived Americans rarely even dined together, since they took their meals at "different hours" and consumed different food and drink.[7] With so few social bonds, it is not surprising that, as the Kentuckian Stuart recorded on his second day in New Orleans, there were "frequent disturbances between different parties & sorts of People here."[8]

In the nearly three years between the transfer of Louisiana and the peak of the Burr crisis, political disputes tore at New Orleans. Within a year of the transfer, the city already had four newspapers: one in French, the *Moniteur de la Louisiane*; two in English, the openly Federalist *Louisiana Gazette* and the nominally Republican *Orleans Gazette*; and one bilingual, the *Télégraphe*. The mostly French and Spanish "ancient" Louisianians quickly criticized the gap between the promises of the purchase treaty and the realities of territorial governance. The early appointments to the territorial government elicited dismay; "all those positions that Louisianians could fill much better than foreigners," a French visitor complained, "are given by an odious preference to the Americans."[9] Everything from the legal code to French and Spanish land claims to a ban on importing slaves from abroad produced discontent. In time, the "modern" American immigrants divided among themselves, but their cleavages did not generally follow the political lines elsewhere. "I assure you we scarcely know the difference" between "*Federalist* or *Democrat*," one American reported in October 1806.[10]

Instead, the sharpest line divided supporters and opponents of territorial governor William C. C. Claiborne. Claiborne, a Virginian, had governed the Mississippi Territory before joining General James Wilkinson in taking possession of the province at New Orleans in December 1803. Initially seen as temporary, Claiborne's new assignment had become permanent when President Thomas Jefferson's three preferred candidates refused the post. Claiborne's early reports and letters to Jefferson and Secretary of State James Madison showed that his backing rarely extended beyond his own appointees. He ascribed his weak position to "the Jealousy which exists between the Ancient and modern Louisianians" and "the Intrigues of . . . unprincipled adventurers from every Country."[11] This was an optimistic assessment. The letters of many Americans in New Orleans who supported the Jefferson administration described Claiborne as "inadequate to the task of governing." "His imbecility," the territory's federal district attorney, James Brown, despaired, "was incurable."[12] Political divisions often led to violence, with affairs of honor generally pitting the governor's supporters against his opponents. In February 1805, Claiborne's brother-in-law died in a political duel. The same month, one American reported that "*duelling is all the rage*"; in his thinking, political life in New Orleans after fourteen months of American rule resembled a "war."[13] More than a year and a half later, New Orleans was the place where most of the fears that surrounded the Burr crisis became focused.

"THE MOST COMPLEAT SCENE OF CONFUSION AND ALARM"

On 26 June 1805, Aaron Burr made his only visit to New Orleans, seventeen months before Wilkinson's arrival from the disputed border. That evening, Claiborne apprised Madison of Burr's arrival. Two days later, the two English-language newspapers noticed the event. John Mowry's *Louisiana Gazette* limited itself to two sentences. But James M. Bradford's openly anti-Claiborne *Orleans Gazette* was more effusive, mentioning Burr's Revolutionary War service, celebrating his Republican politics, and describing him as "a man of splendid talents, and pleasing manners, a profound lawyer, and an elegant scholar."[14] Burr stayed in the city for two weeks, describing its society as "cheerful, gay, and easy." He found it to be "larger than [he had] expected," with more families "living in handsome style" than he had imagined.[15]

Exactly what Burr did and whom he met during these two weeks cannot be reconstructed. He certainly saw Edward Livingston, a fellow New Yorker who had moved to New Orleans in 1804 after official improprieties left him deeply indebted to the federal government. Burr also spent time with both Daniel Clark, an Irishman who had lived in the city since 1786 and had served as the United States consul before the purchase, and Juan Ventura Morales, the highest Spanish official in the city before the purchase. But he rejected a dinner invitation from the Marqués de Casa Calvo, a former governor of the province who was still overseeing its transfer for Spain. Burr also visited the bishop of St. Louis cathedral and "passed an hour" with the sisters of the Ursuline convent.[16] He surely saw his stepson John Bartow Prevost, a judge of the territory's superior court. And he probably met Livingston's new brother-in-law, Auguste Davezac, a French refugee from St. Domingue, and Clark's political ally Evan Jones, a New York merchant who had long traded in New Orleans. Burr's "habits of intimacy with Livingston, Clark & Jones"—some of Claiborne's principal opponents—made this brief visit a source of concern to the governor.[17]

But the concern of the summer of 1805 had barely hinted at the alarm that engulfed New Orleans beginning in the fall of 1806. The social and political tensions had only grown in the interim. Conflicts over political appointments, courtroom practices, the legal code, land claims, and slave importations continued. Many still doubted Claiborne's fitness for office, considering him "entirely too Credilious & Weak a man to be placed where he is."[18] These old issues gained force in the new context of rising tensions with Spain, particularly along the undefined borders with Texas to the west and West Florida to the north and east. Fearing war, Claiborne frequently reassessed the loyalties of the polyglot population, worrying about how much support he would receive from each racial and ethnic group. In early 1806, the territorial secretary alerted Madison that New Orleans and its environs could not provide "*more than five hundred men fit for* service," which would include "*all those whose language is not french or Spanish.*" The rest could only be expected "*to remain neutral in case of a war.*"[19] Throughout 1806, Claiborne braced for war by attending militia musters, courting support from the territorial legislature, working with other western governors, and visiting the western frontier. Nonetheless, his critics continued their attacks in letters and newspapers. In May, the legislature displayed its doubts by choosing Clark, whom Claiborne described as "a conspicuous and zealous member" of the opposition, as the territory's delegate to Congress.[20] In newspapers and in the assembly, in the coffeehouse and on the levee, people openly and fully discussed the Spanish threat and the defensive preparations during these months.

News that Wilkinson had temporarily resolved the boundary dispute reached New Orleans in mid-November, just as reports about Burr's movements in the Ohio Valley began appearing in local newspapers. Days later, a group of engineers and two companies of infantry arrived from the frontier and began "repairing the forts and breast works for the reception of the [rest of the] troops."[21] Claiborne knew why the troops were coming to New Orleans in such haste and why the engineers were rebuilding fortifications that had fallen into disrepair since the transfer, but most residents did not. Two days earlier, he had received a confidential letter from Wilkinson warning that "the destruction of the American Union [was] seriously menaced" and that the governor was "surrounded by dangers of which you dream not."[22] Claiborne took this warning seriously—even though things in New Orleans were "apparently tranquil"—writing to Secretary Madison and acting Mississippi territorial governor Cowles Mead the next day.[23] But he followed Wilkinson's advice to "make no *News paper* publication of [the] expected dangers," allowing it to be believed that "the troops [were] going into winter quarters in New Orleans and that the President [had] ordered the old fortifications to be repaired."[24] Wilkinson reached New Orleans on 25 November, nearly a week after the first of his troops, and met with Claiborne and other civil and military officials the next day.

"From the 26th Novem[ber] . . . until about the 10th of February," according to Nathaniel Cox, a recent immigrant from the Ohio Valley, New Orleans experienced "the most compleat scene of confusion and alarm I ever beheld."[25] The events of these months—the peak of the Burr crisis in New Orleans—have formed a chapter of every book on the Burr Conspiracy from Walter Flavius McCaleb's *Aaron Burr Conspiracy* (1903) to David O. Stewart's *American Emperor* (2011). They have been addressed, as well, in biographies of Wilkinson and Claiborne and in histories of New Orleans and territorial-era Louisiana. Together, these works have clarified that Wilkinson's actions far more than Burr's plans produced the crisis in New Orleans and galvanized the responses of different individuals and groups. They have revealed the intense conflicts between Wilkinson and Claiborne over imposing martial law and suspending the writ of habeas corpus. And they have shown that, during the crisis and after, anti-Claiborne "moderns" suffered for opposing the general's measures and that "ancients" benefitted from backing the governor's efforts. These works have differed over some matters, including the extent of Burr's local support and the motives for Wilkinson's high-handed actions, but, in approach and argument, they have agreed on a wide range of issues.[26]

Much of what has been of interest to their authors, however, was not known at the time to most New Orleanians. The Burr crisis in New Orleans was not confined to government offices, courtrooms, and assembly halls. It engulfed the streets and coffeehouses, the levee and wharves. The air of crisis touched much of the public, not just local, territorial, and federal officers. We can attempt to reconstruct the public experience of the Burr crisis in New Orleans—the events and the rumors, the anxiety and the relief—from private and published letters, along with scattered comments in official dispatches and local publications. For most New Orleanians, the winter of 1806–7 included periods of great uncertainty that were punctuated by moments of often-shocking activity.

For two weeks after the general's arrival, Wilkinson and Claiborne kept quiet their fear that Burr and hundreds, or thousands, of men were descending the river. During those weeks, "the operations of [the territorial] government," as one resident noted, were "entirely enveloped in mystery."[27] That there was a bustle of military preparation was obvious.

That "Wilkinson [was] going to fortify the town on a grand scale" was clear.[28] That hundreds of soldiers from the army and the western militias were headed to New Orleans was soon accepted; "it is said," one local reported, "that we shall . . . have One thousand men at this place" by late December. That Captain John Shaw, the ranking naval officer, was readying boats and men on the river and the lake was evident. But why the fortifications were being repaired, why the local militia were mustering, why "an immense quantity of cartridges" had been ordered, why the troops were coming, why Shaw had purchased two ships remained a matter of "much conjecture."[29] "The whole City," as Shaw informed the secretary of the navy, was "struck with terror."[30]

On 9 December, Wilkinson and Claiborne finally dispelled the mystery. The previous day, Claiborne had requested a meeting of the city's chamber of commerce, which included "every respectable Merchant."[31] According to the *Louisiana Gazette*'s report, the governor explained "the object of the military preparations" as defending the city against an attack from upriver that was headed "by some of the first characters in the union." He also asked the merchants to provide enough sailors from their ships "to man the Gun boats and other crafts." He then turned the meeting over to Wilkinson. The general provided more details about the plot—naming Burr as its leader, recounting how he had learned of it, and outlining his defensive plans. These details included a timetable that placed Burr and two thousand supporters at Natchez on 20 December. After Claiborne and Wilkinson left, the merchants agreed unanimously to request an embargo that, by stopping all commercial voyages, would ensure an adequate supply of sailors for the naval vessels. By the end of the day, the embargo had been imposed, and the Battalion of Orleans Volunteers had been ordered "to hold themselves in readiness for duty at a moments warning."[32] Very quickly, news of the danger spread through the city. "The bubble is out," one resident reported, "and everybody knows it!"[33]

Even after this meeting, even with the recent military activity explained, there was still "as much doubt and eagerness displayed in all classes of people as" before, according to the *Louisiana Gazette*. But the diligence with which Claiborne, Wilkinson, and Shaw were readying the city remained apparent. Repairs continued on the fortifications. There was a "bustle [of activity] at the Arsenal." And, two days after the meeting, "several companies" of troops arrived from the frontier.[34] At the same time, according to a militiaman, there were indications that the men directing these preparations were "all at variance with one another" and "hardly on speaking terms."[35]

At the meeting, Wilkinson had also insisted "that there were several persons in New Orleans concerned in the plot" whom he "would have arrested" already, if he had the power.[36] On 14 December, Wilkinson acted, ordering the arrest of Justus Erich Bollman, who had been in New Orleans since September. The next day, James Alexander, an attorney who had travelled with Bollman (and, thus, with the cipher letter) from Philadelphia, applied for a writ of habeas corpus in the Superior Court. Two days later, Alexander and Edward Livingston appeared in court on Bollman's behalf, and the writ was granted. On the same day, news arrived that Samuel Swartwout and Peter Ogden had been arrested in the Mississippi Territory on Wilkinson's orders and were being held aboard a naval vessel nearby. Lewis Kerr, an attorney who had moved to New Orleans as part of Claiborne's retinue, applied for a writ of habeas corpus on their behalf, which was also granted. Although Ogden was freed, Wilkinson had Bollman and Swartwout sent to the nation's capital in defiance of the court's ruling. In his formal response, he informed the court that, after consulting with the governor and two territorial judges, he had "[taken] on himself all responsibility" for the arrests and for defying the writs.[37] On 18 December, Wilkinson denounced Alexander and Livingston as Burr supporters. The following day, Alexander was arrested and Ogden was taken up again.

The courtroom drama between 14 and 19 December combined with developments in the government offices, on the riverfront, and in the streets to "[agitate] the public mind to a violent degree."[38] On Tuesday, 16 December, Claiborne issued a proclamation warning the territory's citizens against supporting the "Traitorous Project."[39] He also took steps to bring the militia companies to full strength and to provide the naval vessels with sailors. On 19 December, the ketch *Ætna* and two of the gunboats headed upriver to intercept Burr's men. Every action, one resident reported, seemed "indicative of an expected attack."[40] In the streets, rumors circulated that martial law had been or was about to be proclaimed and that Claiborne had rebuffed Wilkinson's pressure for this step. The general's insistence that there were many in New Orleans who were "deeply concerned in the Plott" and his decision to have Alexander and Ogden marched through "the streets at noon-day under a strong escort of Dragoons" fueled the alarm.[41] But so did his assumption of "powers that are not given to the Presdt. himself [in] seting aside the Habeas Corpus." "There is nothing talked or [thought] of but Secret expeditions, plots, [p]lans & conspiracies," an American merchant wrote on 19 December.[42]

The celebration of the third anniversary of Louisiana's transfer the next day only temporarily eased the growing anxiety. That morning, the Battalion of Orleans Volunteers "paraded at the *Place d'Armes*" before Wilkinson and Claiborne. At noon, "a federal salute was fired." Afterward, Wilkinson and his officers retired to the government building, where, according to the *Louisiana Gazette*, civil and military officials spent the afternoon "with hilarity and harmony." That evening, "there was a splendid ball . . . , attended by a large and brilliant company."[43] But, while the military display of the volunteers might have added to the celebration, it could not disguise the continuing failure to organize the city's militia, something that Claiborne again tried to rectify four days later. Nor could the festive air improve commercial conditions in New Orleans, where "business [was] quite at a stand" due to the embargo and the uncertainty.[44] Nor did the apparent harmony between Wilkinson and Claiborne improve matters with the court. Wilkinson continued to take depositions from his subordinates, from territorial officials, and from citizens, seeking evidence of Burr's local support. And, hoping to free Alexander and Ogden, Livingston applied to Judge James Workman of the Orleans County court for writs of habeas corpus. When Wilkinson neither released the men nor explained his reasons for not doing so, Livingston called on the court to force him to act.

The conflict between Livingston and Wilkinson exploded into public view in late December when both the *Louisiana Gazette* and the *Orleans Gazette* published a lengthy statement by the attorney. Livingston's main goal was to defend himself against Wilkinson's accusation—made "in the hearing of hundreds"—that he supported Burr's conspiracy. But he embedded his efforts within a larger story of "the extraordinary scenes now exhibited in this territory." He accused Wilkinson of assuming "a dictatorial power," using the military to arrest men charged with civil crimes, and "attempt[ing] to overawe, by denunciations, those who . . . assert[ed] the authority of the law." He also suggested that Claiborne had cooperated in these violations. Livingston's defense detailed the events in court since Bollman's arrest, presenting Wilkinson's actions as unjustified and inexplicable. Local courts and prisons were fully competent to try and secure the guilty, Livingston insisted; sending the accused "to the United States," where there was no evidence against them, could only result in their being freed.[45] Others shared these concerns. "Denunciation and arrest," one writer stated, "appear to have become the order of the day."[46]

The new year began amid great confusion: "all [was] doubt, uncertainty, rumor, conjecture and surmise." In the last days of December, two Army officers had been arrested; why was not known. According to "public rumor," eight or ten more would "be arrested in a few days."[47] In early January, Mayor John Watkins had a list made "of all the strangers, boarders &c." in the city by sending officials to boardinghouses and private homes. He also required that vessels that arrived in New Orleans provide the "names of their Passengers."[48] New reports from outside the city exacerbated the "great alarm about Burr and his party" by proving that the panic was not merely local. On 2 January, the *Louisiana Gazette* ran a proclamation by Governor Mead warning the people of his territory of the impending danger; the next issue included Jefferson's proclamation against the conspiracy. On 5 January, the editor of the *Orleans Gazette* returned to the city with news that Burr had "issued Arms & Amunition to 12,000 Men."[49] "The crisis must end one way or another immediately," one writer asserted. The river was flowing as rapidly as ever seen at that time of the year; if Burr and his men were coming, he concluded, "they [would] come like lightning."[50]

These reports and rumors unleashed a new round of activity. On 6 January, Claiborne called on the area's planters to provide "one tenth . . . of their labouring negro's" for a few days to help complete the fortifications.[51] Over the next few days, militia companies were ordered to continue their twice-weekly training, and the governor even moved to revive a battalion "of Freemen of Colour" that had been dissolved by the legislature.[52] On 7 January, the white Battalion of Orleans Volunteers was mustered into federal service and placed under Wilkinson's command. The next day, the schooner *Revenge* and one of the gun barges left the city. Amid this activity, Wilkinson posted at the coffeehouse a warning to the city's merchants and ships' captains to be prepared "to haul off into the stream . . . on the shortest notice." He reported that he had learned, through an intercepted letter from Burr, that Burr with two thousand men would halt at Natchez to await as many as four thousand more men. But Wilkinson also assured the merchants that, "with moderate exertions only, and the decisive expulsion of traitors, the storm [would] burst over the head of its authors, . . . whilst the inhabitants of this city shall dwell in security." Wilkinson's confident claims and measured tone—he described readying the ships as "a salutary precaution," for example—may have been lost on the public.[53] One account of his announcement stated that Wilkinson himself had received the letter from Burr, that Burr was already at Natchez seeking the general's permission "to pass *New-Orleans*," and that Wilkinson had expressed "his determination to oppose Burr's passing." According to this report, Wilkinson's announcement had "occasioned great confusion" in New Orleans.[54] As Wilkinson informed the secretary of war on 9 January, it was "impossible" to describe public sentiment. "Confidence is fled and hope is almost extinguished," he warned.[55]

On Monday, 12 January, the territorial legislature opened its session, adding another important player to the already crowded cast of territorial and city officials, Army and Navy officers, and judges and attorneys who shaped and contested the city's response to the crisis. The same day, another new actor, the grand jury of the Superior Court, handed down indictments against Lewis Kerr, the attorney who had sought writs of habeas corpus for Bollman and Swartwout, and James Workman, the county court judge who had granted writs for Alexander and Ogden. The indictments stemmed from their roles in organizing a military expedition against Spanish possessions a year earlier—the so-called Mexican Association. On Tuesday, Claiborne addressed the legislature. While he focused on the state of the territory, he also discussed the current situation, choosing his words carefully. He reassured the legislators that, despite present dangers, the territory would "ultimately experience a great share of political happiness and prosperity." He reiterated the importance of union with the American states to that future. And, while admitting that "many well meaning and honest Citizens [might] have been seduced" into supporting an expedition against Mexico, he insisted that few had "approved the traitorous de-sign" of Burr.[56] But Claiborne said nothing about Wilkinson's recent clashes with himself or the court. This omission became especially clear the next day when the assembly's speaker read a letter from Judge Workman announcing that he had shut his court in response to "the illegal arrest and transportation of certain persons" and "the overthrow of the civil authority."[57] For the rest of the week, the assembly deliber-ated behind closed doors.

Workman was arrested the same day that his letter was read before the assembly. What seems to have precipitated Workman's arrest, and Kerr's on the same day, was not the indictments for organizing the Mexican Association, but the welcome that the men gave to Kentucky militia general John Adair when he arrived in the city that afternoon. Barely an hour after his arrival, Adair was seized on Wilkinson's order by "about 100 Regulars & all the Officers of the Garrison." Workman, Kerr, and the *Orleans Gazette* editor Bradford were arrested the same day by cavalrymen from the Battalion of Orleans Volunteers. "The or-dering to arms and beating of the Alarm for the Volunteers to assem-ble," one resident reported, "was truly terrifying," since it suggested that New Orleans was in "immediate danger."[58] By eight o'clock in the evening, a Superior Court judge had issued writs of habeas corpus for the prisoners. The next morning, Wilkinson released Workman, Kerr, and Bradford. Adair remained in custody, joining Alexander and Ogden as military prisoners outside the city.

The arrests of 14 January triggered an onslaught of new activity and "greatly agitated the public mind."[59] The next day, the assembly ordered the general to explain his actions; Wilkinson appeared before a closed-door session two days later. On 16 June, Captain Shaw had published in the *Louisiana Gazette* recently arrived instructions from Secretary of the Navy Robert Smith that authorized a firm response, including orders "to take, and if necessary to destroy[,] the boats de-scending under the command of Col. Burr."[60] Shaw also posted at the coffeehouse a statement that no vessels bearing military supplies would be allowed to ascend the river without a pass and that any vessel de-scending the river with such cargo would be seized. As a result, men with no connection to Burr were taken from approaching vessels, their "papers seized," and their persons "brought to town for examination."[61]

It was believed that even more sweeping orders had been received in the same mail by Claiborne; he shared them with the legislature early the next week. On 21 January, Bradford made clear his views of "the alarming state of public concerns" in New Orleans by announcing that, "until the troubles . . . [were] at an end," the *Orleans Gazette* would "cease to be a political paper." It would publish foreign reports, advertising, and shipping news, but not local coverage. "We cannot deceive the world by the *affectation of A FREE PRESS, when it does not exist*," Bradford insisted.[62]

On 21 January, the day of Bradford's statement, a posting at the coffeehouse stated that Burr's boats and men had arrived at Bayou Pierre above Natchez and that a detachment of Mississippi militiamen had been sent to stop him. But the early reports were "so numerous and contradictory, that it [was] impossible to separate truth from falsehood."[63] As a result, the news did little to alleviate public anxiety. When the upper house of the legislature adopted its official reply to the governor's session-opening message on 22 January, it still feared "that a horrible civil war [might] desolate our country."[64] Nor did the news ease the tensions over recent events. With the assembly again meeting with open doors, the public must have known that many of its members remained alarmed at Wilkinson's "flagrant abuses of power" and at Claiborne's failure to address them in his message. On 23 January, the two houses met together, reelected Daniel Clark as the territorial delegate, and agreed to send a memorial to Congress about "the present situation of this territory."[65] Rumors flowed from New Orleans in these days, including a report of "a serious quarrel" between Claiborne and Wilkinson "in the court house" that had culminated in "the Govr. slap[ping the general] in the face."[66]

This uncertainty continued for two more weeks. Every few days, new reports from upriver spread through the city as rumors or appeared in local newspapers. On 27 January, the *Louisiana Gazette* reported that, according to "a gentleman of intelligence" who had just arrived from Natchez, Mead had met with Burr near Bayou Pierre and persuaded him to go to Natchez. Rumors held, moreover, that "Burr had pledged himself not to leave . . . until every thing was adjusted and cleared up" to Mead's satisfaction.[67] Three days later, New Orleanians learned that Burr had signed a formal agreement with Mead that subjected him to civil authority. On 5 February, the *Orleans Gazette* reported that Burr had posted bond to appear before a grand jury. It also announced that Burr had just thirteen boats at Bayou Pierre, with "no troops . . . and not more than forty or fifty persons."[68]

Even as the crisis eased, however, public anxiety remained high. Downriver and oceangoing commerce—the basis of the city's economic life—remained "almost stagnant," as they had been for two months.[69] Even wholly local businesses suffered. "Every thinge has been and still is dull on account of rumours of Mr Burr," James Johnson, a free black grocer and stable owner, wrote to his former master in Kentucky in early February.[70] The battle still raged within the territorial government. In late January, Representative Joseph Parrot announced plans to move a bill for the better protection of "the rights and liberties of the citizens of the territory . . . and for the punishment of offenders against the same."[71] John W. Gurley, the territory's attorney general, introduced resolutions calling on the governor to report how many militiamen had been placed under federal authority and to provide any new evidence "relative to the danger with which this territory is said to be at present threatened."[72] On 29 January, these resolutions were adopted and delivered to Claiborne. The same day, the *Orleans Gazette* leaked the news that, on 24 January, the grand jury of the Superior Court—fifteen prominent "ancient" and "modern" Louisianians—had adopted a presentment against Wilkinson and Claiborne for "the late unprecedented exercise of military power."[73] With this measure, the grand jurors, headed by the governor's longtime opponent Evan Jones, required the justices to call the two officials into court to explain their actions.

The Burr crisis in New Orleans did not end with an official announcement from Claiborne or Wilkinson or on an identifiable day. It took until early May before Nathaniel Cox could date its end to "about the 10th of February."[74] On 10 February, such a judgment would have been impossible. That day, the governor sent a secret message to the territorial legislature, asking it to suspend the writ of habeas corpus precisely because the danger did not seem to have ended. We might say that the crisis had passed by 3 March, when it became known in New Orleans that Burr had been arrested and sent east for trial, or at least by 8 March, when the Battalion of Orleans Volunteers was dismissed from federal service. Even after those developments, however, tensions remained high for at least two months as the governor, the general, legislators, editors, and others battled over the meaning of the winter's events. Not until Wilkinson sailed for Virginia on 22 May to testify in Burr's trial did the crisis in New Orleans come to a definite end.[75]

"HOSTILE AND CLASHING STATEMENTS"

As an account of the public experience of the Burr crisis in New Orleans, the preceding story is both incomplete and too complete. It certainly omits incidents that would have seemed significant at the time, as well as the sights, sounds, smells, and other sensations that would have enriched the incidents that it includes. At the same time, not everyone in New Orleans would have known of all of these events as they unfolded. But most locals knew more about these events than about the behind-the-scenes disputes between the general and the governor, much less the individual calculations of Wilkinson, Claiborne, and Shaw or Livingston, Workman, and Kerr or Bradford, Alexander, and Adair. It is these more private and more concealed matters, however, that have most captivated historians and biographers. The obstacles to getting from the many and varied documents that the Burr crisis in New Orleans generated to such matters were well understood at the time. In an early attempt by someone outside of New Orleans to reconstruct the crisis there, an author in a Philadelphia periodical identified his principal sources as the "letters of the commander in chief to the government, . . . the legal depositions of a few officers and magistrates," and the copious writings of "those who incurred suspicion and persecution." "As usual among hostile and clashing statements," the author remarked, "the truth . . . is not easily discovered." An impartial historian had "to proceed with caution," but even caution could "[lead] to no certainty."[76] Having access to many more sources than this early author did does not produce greater certainty.

Those who experienced the crisis recognized the problematic nature of the letters, reports, articles, and other documents that it produced. The press seemed corrupted. The accused believed that "the greatest Efforts were [being] used by the Govr. &c. to Suppress the publication" of hostile commentary, even as territorial officials warned distant readers "not to credit all the Reports and publications" from New Orleans as "many [were] erronious."[77] The mail seemed no more reliable than the press for conveying the truth to the rest of the country. Stoppages in the mail to and from New Orleans led both supporters and opponents of the territorial administration to warn outsiders "not [to] trust it."[78] Either Burr's agents or Wilkinson's, many assumed, stopped letters that revealed what was really happening in the city. At the peak of the crisis, Livingston charged that, as a result, those who were suspected of supporting Burr were "farther removed from the Communication of their friends in the U.S. than if they were in Greenland."[79]

The kind of impartial and cautious reading of the sources that the author in the *American Register* called for reveals less the reality of what happened in New Orleans than the awareness on the part of nearly all of the authors of these sources that the most meaningful audiences for their letters, essays, articles, speeches, or dispatches were elsewhere— in Washington and around the country. What was happening in New Orleans mattered, of course, and individuals and groups there battled over the nature of the crisis and the response to it. But they struggled no less fiercely over how outsiders understood their actions, recognizing that the most important judgments about their loyalties or principles or abilities would be made outside of the city and the territory. The weapons for this struggle were many and varied, and the best of them were not available to everyone. The story of this struggle is at least as meaningful a story of the Burr crisis in New Orleans as those of the public events and the private battles.

Over the course of the crisis, Burr's threatened invasion and Wilkinson's excessive response altered the existing political divisions in New Orleans. In April 1807, the recent immigrant Nathaniel Cox described the city's ethnically diverse populace as divided into three groups. Some people, he believed, "were no doubt the friends of Burr and the revolution"; "others [were] friends to the General"; and "a distinct party feared and dreaded both, but were friends to their country."[80] As Burr had few open defenders in New Orleans, it is probably safer to categorize what Cox called Burr's friends as Wilkinson's enemies. But Cox was correct that, in response to Burr's alleged disunionism, some of the formerly anti-Claiborne "ancients" began supporting the territorial administration. And, in response to "Wilkinson's Winter of horrors," some of the formerly pro-Claiborne "moderns" turned against it.[81] The crisis created opportunities for New Orleanians to advance their goals or injure their opponents in ways that had little to do with Burr's plans.

In the Burr crisis, the "ancients" saw a chance to gain influence within the territorial government and to hasten statehood. Disaffected and unified, they had seemed open to any plan that would free them from distant authority, making them the logical audience for a disunionist project. Before leaving for Washington in late October, Clark, one of Claiborne's most ardent foes, had urged leading French immigrants and creoles, as one recalled, "to forget any personal animosity towards the Governor, and to rally round the government, and die, if necessary, in its defence."[82] Providing such support, another later remembered Clark arguing, "would be the best method of convincing the government of the U.S. of the attachment of the inhabitants of Louisiana."[83] Whether acting on Clark's advice or on their own assessments, key Francophone "ancients" gave essential support to Claiborne and Wilkinson throughout the crisis. While they could advance their goals simply by making this support clear locally, even more might be achieved, as Clark realized, if it was known in Washington and elsewhere.

Divided over Claiborne, the "moderns" had never formed a unified political force and entered the Burr crisis with varied goals. By November 1806, Claiborne's most consistent supporters in New Orleans were officers of the territorial and city governments. Anti-Claiborne "moderns" tended to be merchants and lawyers who relied upon business, social, and political ties to the "ancients." Suspected of involvement in Burr's plans, some of Claiborne's long-standing opponents faced public denunciation and even military arrest. But, over time, some of Claiborne's most trusted supporters—including New Orleans mayor John Watkins, county court judge James Workman, and the attorney Lewis Kerr—found themselves facing Wilkinson's wrath, propelling them into opposition. The effect, as Claiborne later explained to Jefferson, had been "to estrange from the Interests of the Government, *Men*, who not long since were viewed as its best supporters."[84] For anti-Claiborne "moderns," new and old, the Burr crisis demanded efforts to protect their reputations from the general's attacks and provided opportunities to prove the governor's incompetence. Neither defending themselves nor displacing Claiborne could be achieved in New Orleans alone.

As such, Claiborne's "modern" opponents sought to construct a story of the crisis that could convince a national audience of their interpretation of events.

Claiborne and Wilkinson found opportunities, and dangers, in the Burr crisis, as well. Claiborne quickly saw a chance to display his abilities and to undermine his local opponents. What was unclear to him, from mid-November until early January, was where Wilkinson fit with those goals. Of the three important November letters that alerted Claiborne to the threat from Burr, two also warned that "Wilkinson is the soul of the conspiracy"; the one that did not came from Wilkinson himself.[85] Claiborne seems to have dismissed such warnings quickly; by 8 December, he could express "entire confidence in [Wilkinson's] firmness and patriotism."[86] Still, for another month, he continued to doubt Wilkinson's information, about both the size of Burr's approaching force and the extent of Burr's local support, and to question Wilkinson's actions, in terms of both his military plans and his extralegal measures. This uncertainty led the governor to reject the general's requests—later, demands—that he suspend the writ of habeas corpus, declare martial law, and place the territorial militia under federal control, even as he worked to defend New Orleans. In early January, acting on new reports that Burr's "forces when collected would exceed six thousand," Claiborne finally decided "to give all the support in [his] power to" Wilkinson rather than risk losing the city by "enfeebl[ing] his Arm."[87] While holding firm on martial law, Claiborne threw himself behind Wilkinson during some of the general's most extreme measures. Claiborne wanted his decisions to be understood, even celebrated, in New Orleans, but he knew that, ultimately, his political future depended upon whether they were approved in Washington.

Wilkinson clearly identified all sorts of potentialities in the Burr crisis in New Orleans, as well. But exactly what he saw eluded his contemporaries—and, later—scholars. Some accepted that he genuinely believed that Burr's men from upriver and his supporters in New Orleans posed so great a threat that energetic, even extralegal, measures were needed. Others thought that his actions reflected, instead, an effort to manufacture a crisis to prove his loyalty in order to overcome the suspicions of his involvement in Burr's schemes—"mak[ing] the most of the [situation] in the expectation of being deemed the very prince of patriots," as one skeptic noted.[88] Still others thought that Wilkinson initially hoped to postpone any decision until he could gauge the size of Burr's force on the Mississippi and the extent of his support in New Orleans. "If Burr passes this Territory with two thousand men," Mead warned Claiborne, "I have no doubt but the Genl. will be your worst enemy."[89] And some found no coherence in Wilkinson's behavior, attributing it, instead, to some combination of isolation, intoxication, anxiety over his situation, and concern for his sick wife (who died in New Orleans on 23 February). One can find evidence for and against each of these explanations. With his rank and reputation dependent upon the administration in Washington, though, Wilkinson always needed to justify his actions to a distant audience.[90]

When it came to shaping how outsiders understood the crisis, Wilkinson and Claiborne possessed a uniquely powerful tool—the official dispatch. Between arriving in New Orleans in late November and reporting Burr's arrest in early March, Wilkinson sent at least twenty-one official letters to Secretary of War Henry Dearborn. During this period, Claiborne dispatched at least twenty official letters to Secretary of State James Madison. The only other person who made such use of official dispatches was Shaw, who sent at least eight to Secretary of the Navy Robert Smith in these months. Each man would probably have corresponded more fully if he had not worried, as Wilkinson explained, that "the State of Affairs" precluded "communicating by Mail," rather than by express or ship.[91] Through their dispatches, these officers could explain their actions to the men, including the president, whose judgments mattered the most—something that was especially important given their lack of specific instructions for much of the crisis. Wilkinson's dispatches to Dearborn included long justifications of the arrests and deportations that he ordered, while Claiborne's reports to Madison provided full accounts of his contributions to the territory's defense. Dispatches could also carry a variety of enclosures. Wilkinson and Shaw sent copies of their orders to subordinates; Claiborne forwarded public testimonials and his official address to the legislature. Wilkinson also enclosed at least eleven depositions from civilians and subordinates that described the conspiracy itself, the actions of Burr's local supporters, and the involvement of army and navy officers.[92] The frequency of these official reports allowed their authors to record the context in which decisions had been made, freezing the chaos of information and incident at crucial and not-so-crucial moments.

Official correspondence took another form, as Claiborne, Wilkinson, and Shaw also wrote to each other. The very existence of this correspondence, totalling more than three dozen letters, reveals the desirability of an official record since the men lived and worked relatively close to each other and met, formally and informally, fairly often. Some of these letters may have seemed necessary for clarity. Wilkinson's 3 January 1807 letter to Claiborne, for example, discussed his plans for defending the city with the army, navy, and militia; proposed five measures for the governor to adopt; addressed various other issues; and urged Claiborne again to "Proclaim Law Martial."[93] But, just as frequently, these officials' letters and memoranda reveal purposes beyond the local and the current. Why else would Claiborne and Shaw have prepared and signed a formal record of their "best recollection" of Wilkinson's first communication about the conspiracy on the day that he made it?[94] Why else would the governor have responded in writing to a two-day-old letter from the general after having dined with him on the intervening day? A few letters made their thinking explicit. In late December, Claiborne ended a brief note to Wilkinson by acknowledging, "I have before communicated verbally these opinions, and I now deem it proper to give them in writing."[95] And, in mid-January, he sent a long letter to the general that enumerated twelve steps that had been or should be taken to prepare for Burr's arrival. "Not one" of these proposals was new, as Claiborne noted, but the letter would serve other purposes. "By stating them in writing," he explained, "it will be hereafter seen, that we act in concert."[96] Some of this internal correspondence made it to Washington as enclosures in official dispatches when its author needed to explain or justify his actions. Shaw, for instance, enclosed his early correspondence with Wilkinson and Claiborne in a dispatch to the Navy Department to explain the "considerable" "expences in [his] department."[97]

Claiborne, Wilkinson, and Shaw clearly recognized that these official documents, whether dispatches or enclosures, could enjoy a broader reach and longer life than many other sources. Placed in department files, they could be utilized for the president's messages to Congress or the secretaries' answers to committee inquiries or other public purposes. Occasionally, recipients showed them to political allies, who might recount their contents to distant correspondents, including newspaper editors. Some were shared with the *National Intelligencer*, which sometimes printed or summarized official dispatches. And they could be requested from the department by their authors in the future if private or public controversies over official acts required them.

Not all of Wilkinson's and Claiborne's letters to Washington during the crisis took the form of official dispatches, however. The characteristics that made official documents so valuable for explaining one's actions to the public also made them inappropriate for conveying some material. Claiborne and Wilkinson responded by directing two streams of correspondence to the national capital. Along with the twenty or more official dispatches that he sent to the secretary of state between late November and early March, Claiborne wrote at least four more letters to Madison that he labelled "private" or "private & unofficial." He also sent at least one letter to "Several Member[s] of Congress."[98] None of Wilkinson's unofficial correspondence with Dearborn seems to have survived. But he wrote private letters during the crisis to his "confidential friend[s]," Robert and Samuel Smith, the secretary of the navy and an important senator, respectively; the letters, or their contents, were sometimes shared with the president or other cabinet members.[99] And Wilkinson continued the private correspondence with Jefferson that included his October and November 1806 letters revealing the conspiracy. Between late November and late May, Wilkinson wrote at least two dozen letters to the president from New Orleans, none of which were placed in the official files. In this period, Claiborne sent four letters to Jefferson. The letters' recipients clearly understood the distinction between official and private; an earlier letter from Jefferson to Claiborne had opened by clarifying that it was "confidential, but not official."[100]

Claiborne and Wilkinson carefully considered whether to designate letters official or unofficial. In his first official dispatch to Madison after Wilkinson's arrival, Claiborne asked to have his previous two letters reclassified "as confidential," removing them from the department files.[101] A long letter from Wilkinson shows the care with which both men managed their correspondence with the administration. Wilkinson began the letter on 8 January as an official dispatch to Dearborn. Having raised his conflicts with Claiborne, he decided to enclose their recent correspondence and asked that it "be Submitted to the President." After detailing this dispute, Wilkinson set aside the letter. When he returned to it the next day, he began in a more measured tone, restoring it to the realm of the official dispatch. Within a couple of paragraphs, however, Wilkinson was decrying Claiborne's "imbecility and indecision." Reading over the completed dispatch, the general "[found] it so tesselated in Matter & so abundant in personalities" that he asked Dearborn to consider it as "address[ed] to the private Cabinet of the President" rather "than the office of a Public Department."[102]

We can see how the different audiences and purposes of these forms of communication shaped Claiborne's and Wilkinson's letters to Washington through the often-tense relations between the men. Claiborne barely hinted at their clashes in his official letters; even his private letters to Madison and Jefferson mentioned little more than his initial distrust of Wilkinson's "fidelity" and his final assessment that Wilkinson's "zeal [had] betrayed him into some errors."[103] But "*Conscious Rectitude*" about his stances in the disputes over the writ of habeas corpus, martial law, the impressment of sailors for naval service, and other issues ensured that Claiborne would want them known to those who judged him.[104] A more complete record of these battles reached Madison in the still-official, but less-public, form of enclosures with his correspondence with Wilkinson. The general, perhaps not surprisingly, was less circumspect. In private letters to the Smiths, he described Claiborne as "a mere Puppet" and "uncertain in all things except his insuperable Vanity."[105] He showed only slightly more restraint in his private letters to Jefferson, insisting that Claiborne's decisions had left him expecting "nothing . . . from the civil authority, which does not depend on the broad letter and tardy course of the law."[106] Still, Wilkinson's official dispatches, other than the one that he asked to have redirected to the president, rarely named Claiborne as the source of his troubles, even as they complained of matters that were often under the governor's control.

Claiborne's and Wilkinson's local opponents recognized the power that came from such access to the administration. In early April 1807, the territory's federal district attorney, James Brown, an anti-Claiborne "modern," complained to his brother-in-law, Kentucky senator Henry Clay, that the "weak Governor and despotic General" had "Slander[ed] all the principal men of the western Country." "These miscreants have not dared to assail me *here*," Brown explained; instead, they had worked "to blast [his] character abroad."[107] Other local critics denounced the depositions that had been hunted for in New Orleans with so much avidity "by the partizans of the general, and by the general himself."[108] No credence, they insisted, should attach to the statements of men who were "unknown, . . . of little consideration, . . . [or] publicly lost to reputation, and actually infamous." Yet, depositions from such men had been sent to the administration and, in some cases, had appeared in "the public prints" as if they accurately reported on Burr's support in New Orleans.[109]

To Claiborne's and Wilkinson's opponents, Congress seemed a more accessible and more receptive audience for their concerns than the administration. The territorial delegate Daniel Clark could assert the loyalty of "ancients" and anti-Claiborne "moderns" to Congress and voice their criticisms of local officials. Having left New Orleans long before Wilkinson's arrival, however, he could speak only of the general situation, not the specific crisis. In late December, as the crisis peaked in Washington, Clark boasted of his territory's attachment to the union and insisted that, if there was a secessionist conspiracy, "there would be no Louisianan concerned in it." But he also warned the House of Representatives that "the militia were in an unorganized state—there were, indeed, no militia in the Territory." Clark attributed this situation to the neglect of "the man put over them," who had preferred "another corps."[110] Other published versions of Clark's comments made clear that "the man put over" the militia was Claiborne and the other "corps" was "a corps of blacks."[111] Some of Congress's earliest firsthand information about the crisis in New Orleans came, instead, from John Adair. While under arrest, the Kentuckian wrote a letter to his state's delegation, mailing it shortly after his discharge in Baltimore in mid-February 1807. Even though much of this letter asserted his innocence, explaining his movements and damning Wilkinson as Burr's "infamous co-intriguer," Adair also detailed his military arrest and imprisonment.[112] Some of the letter's recipients quickly shared it with other members of Congress, and accounts of its contents soon spread across the country.

Clark, Adair, and others in and near Washington also used the press to try to repair their damaged reputations, providing accounts of events in New Orleans that criticized Wilkinson and Claiborne in the process. In late January, Clark turned to the *National Intelligencer* to deny an accusation in Philadelphia's *Aurora General Advertiser* that he was "concerned in [the] conspiracy."[113] Soon after writing to the Kentucky delegation, Adair reiterated his comments in a public letter in the *Intelligencer*. Around the same time, first ensign W. C. Mead and then the attorney James Alexander published lengthy statements in Baltimore's *Federal Gazette*. Mead revealed that Wilkinson was not only collecting depositions in New Orleans, but also sending his subordinates to Washington bearing recommendations that they be arrested as parties to the conspiracy. Alexander recounted his efforts, with Kerr and Livingston, to free Bollman, Ogden, and Swartwout from arrest under the "illegal order[s] of the general." In his view, his own arrest by the cavalry had followed "as if it were the necessary consequence of performing [his] duty." He further described being confined in a "miserable shed" and barred from receiving visitors or gifts for a week before being sent with Ogden to Baltimore. "All this has happened," Alexander insisted, "not in the heart of a despotic empire, not at a period of foreign war, or intestine trouble, but at a moment of profound peace and domestic tranquility, . . . and under the eye of an American governor."[114]

With greater difficulty and delay, people in New Orleans similarly used distant newspapers to influence how the public and the government understood the crisis in their city. Letters from New Orleans to family, friends, and editors ran in major national newspapers, such as the *Intelligencer* and *Aurora*, and in important western prints, such as Lexington's *Kentucky Gazette* and Nashville's *Impartial Review*. But they also appeared in such minor newspapers as the *North Star* of Danville, Vermont. Some of these letters may not have been written for publication. Many were unattributed; some do not provide enough information for us even to situate their authors amid the city's political and social divisions, though "modern" Louisianians, or visitors, seem more likely than "ancients." Some of these letters defended Claiborne, Wilkinson, and what one writer called "the prompt and decisive measures that [had] been used."[115] Others reported events without endorsing or criticizing them. But many denounced Wilkinson's "military government" and anticipated his departure "as a delivery from the greatest evil that ever befel the people of this part of America."[116]

Andrew Marschalk, the editor of the *Mississippi Herald*, attributed his receipt of material from New Orleans "to the fetters which appear[ed] to have been thrown over [its] press."[117] Among other pieces, Marschalk published two satirical reports describing the activities of New Orleans's women. The first noted that the leading women—all of whom had English names—had met as a "female parliament" to discuss "the alarming posture of affairs" and to charge the governor, general, and federal government with mishandling the threat.[118] The second reported that the women had voted to form a military corps and "take the field to oppose Mr. Burr."[119]

Unattributed letters could convey to distant readers the state of affairs in New Orleans but did little to protect or restore the reputations of those who had come under suspicion. Some of these men sent signed letters for publication in eastern cities. Soon after learning that he had been linked to Burr's project in the *Aurora*, Burr's stepson, Orleans territorial judge John Bartow Prevost, wrote to the *Intelligencer* declaring that he had "never had any communications either directly or indirectly, with Mr. Burr on the subject of the charges exhibited against him."[120] Livingston employed various New York newspapers to restore his reputation and to attack Claiborne's and Wilkinson's measures, using them to republish his lengthy public appeal that had appeared in New Orleans in late December. Later, "a Gentleman at New-Orleans," probably Workman, sent two letters as "Aurelius" to New York's *People's Friend*.[121] The first explained the circumstances that had led the territorial legislature to prepare a memorial criticizing the governor and the general. The second defended Livingston, who had "been illiberally and cruelly assaulted," and condemned Wilkinson for his "unconstitutional measures and lawless usurpation."[122]

But Wilkinson also employed distant newspapers to spread his version of events and protect his reputation. His letters appeared in eastern newspapers in various forms during and after the crisis. He sent signed letters to the *Intelligencer* and the Baltimore *American* in April to defend himself against Adair's charges of prior involvement in Burr's schemes. Other, unattributed Wilkinson letters also appeared in the eastern press, including one in the *Aurora* that enclosed an address to Jefferson from "the ancient and honorable inhabitants of Louisiana" praising Wilkinson.[123] Since the *American* was, as the *Aurora* put it, "in the hands of" Senator Samuel Smith, Wilkinson's letters to his confidant could be presented in different guises, as the occasion demanded.[124] Some appeared essentially as written, with or without attribution; others ran in revised forms; and still others became the basis for pieces by Smith or the editor. In late February, for example, the *American* printed a full account of Wilkinson's defense of his decision to ignore the writ of habeas corpus regarding Bollman that probably came from Smith. This statement not only praised Wilkinson and condemned Bollman, "the prime agent of Colonel Burr in this city," and his attorneys, Livingston and Alexander, but also included ten paragraphs of direct quotation from Wilkinson and three depositions that he had read in court.[125]

Wilkinson and Claiborne needed to use newspapers in the East partly because they received little support from those in New Orleans. Only scattered issues of the four New Orleans newspapers survive between late November 1806 and late May 1807. This incomplete record suggests that the governor and the general turned to Claudius Beleurgey's bilingual *Télégraphe* and, perhaps, Jean Baptiste Le Sueur Fontaine's French-language *Moniteur de la Louisiane* more than the English-language gazettes. Locally, this relationship may have served them well, because it both embodied and bolstered the growing support of the "ancients" for the territorial administration; a year earlier, Claiborne had viewed the *Télégraphe* as an opposition newspaper. On the more significant national level, however, this reliance on the Francophone press was problematic. The dearth of items from the *Télégraphe* and the *Moniteur* in other newspapers suggests that they did not exchange copies with many distant editors. Material that Claiborne or Wilkinson placed in those newspapers would need help to reach a national audience. In early April, Wilkinson used the *Télégraphe* to defend himself locally against Adair's charges by publishing a pseudonymous piece signed "Veritas," two depositions, and a letter. But, to ensure their republication in the East, he sent copies of the *Télégraphe* to the editors of the *American* and the *Intelligencer* ten days later.[126]

The two English-language newspapers—the Federalist *Louisiana Gazette* and the Republican *Orleans Gazette*—provided crucial local outlets for the opposition early in the Burr crisis in New Orleans. John Mowry's *Louisiana Gazette* had long backed Clark, Claiborne's most powerful local foe; James Bradford's *Orleans Gazette* had long attacked the governor. Both newspapers quickly challenged Claiborne's and Wilkinson's actions. Both newspapers circulated well, moreover, and their local coverage appeared around the country. In late December, both newspapers printed Livingston's anti-Wilkinson appeal "To the Public." Then, in mid-January, both newspapers succumbed to pressure and largely ceased their criticism. The arrest of Bradford on 14 January, which produced his announcement that the *Orleans Gazette* had "cease[d] to be a political paper," was only the most obvious of Wilkinson's pressures.[127] Locals later attributed the silencing of the English-language press to the fact that "every American printer in New Orleans belonged to some company of [the] battalion" of volunteers. When Claiborne placed the battalion under Wilkinson's command on 7 January, the printers became subject to military discipline. "The printers," according to one pamphlet, "were plainly told that the soldier's back [i.e., their own] should smart for the printer's insolence" and "particularly warned of that article of war which protects superior officers from the calumnies of those under their command."[128] Printing a piece from Wilkinson in late February, Bradford explicitly stated that the paragraph had "[come] from [his] superior officer" and had been included because refusing would have "subjected [him] to arrest, imprisonment, and the degrading punishments incident to the state of a soldier."[129] Under this threat, a writer in the *Louisiana Gazette* recalled in early May, both newspapers became "so meek, so prim, so prettily behaved, and so dull" as to offer little challenge. For two months, the Battalion of Orleans Volunteers, including nearly the whole workforce of both gazettes—editors, "journeymen and all, down to the lowest . . . [printer's] *devil*"—remained in federal service.[130]

While hostile editorials and essays seem to have disappeared from their pages during these months, the two gazettes could publicize at least some accounts and critiques of local developments by covering the courts and legislature. They reported the legislature's decisions to reelect Clark as the territory's congressional delegate and to send a memorial to Congress, as well as one representative's intention to introduce a bill to protect the rights of citizens; those measures had to be read as critical of Claiborne's and Wilkinson's handling of the crisis. Of necessity, such coverage also afforded space to Claiborne to publicize his account of recent events, in the form of messages to the legislature. But, perhaps more importantly, it gave voice to the judges, grand jurors, and legislators who enjoyed more latitude to question and criticize Claiborne and Wilkinson than the editors themselves. In this way, the otherwise-silenced *Orleans Gazette* could publicize the legislative council's insistence that there was no local support for Burr, along with its concern that the recent intrusions on citizens' rights had created "the most serious alarm." It could print a paragraph, which had been excised from the assembly's reply to Claiborne's opening message, expressing surprise that he had said nothing about "the flagrant abuses of power which [had] been committed for about six weeks past."[131] And it could spread the grand jury's denunciation of the prostration of "the law and civil authority . . . before a military force" "as a most dangerous and alarming evil."[132]

With the volunteers released from federal service on 8 March, the English-language newspapers quickly resumed their overt attacks on Wilkinson and Claiborne. Within two weeks, Wilkinson could complain to Jefferson of "the scurrility which issues from the press" and urge him to revoke Bradford's contract as government printer.[133] In the weeks before Wilkinson's departure, "Livingston, Brown, Workman, and indeed all the talents of the country . . . dipped their pens in gall and [vented] their sentiments as freely and bitterly as language [would] permit."[134] Mowry's *Louisiana Gazette* seems to have adopted a more balanced approach. It reprinted such anti-Wilkinson pieces as Adair's letter to the *Intelligencer* and Alexander's to the *Federal Gazette*. And, on 31 March, it printed lengthy extracts from a new letter that Alexander had sent from Washington decrying "the degrading hand of tyranny which had reduced [him] to the condition of a slave."[135] But the same issue included a piece from the *American* defending Wilkinson under the heading, "published by request."[136] Local items attacking and defending Wilkinson and Claiborne appeared, often side by side, in the *Louisiana Gazette* for the next few weeks. In early May, a lengthy essay by "Centurio" recognized that, because "the press once more breathe[d] in freedom," the public could again criticize Claiborne and Wilkinson for mismanaging the crisis, suppressing the press, and misusing the volunteers in print.[137]

Even as editors and essayists exercised their restored freedom in the gazettes, a series of pamphlets began to issue from Bradford's press on what one reviewer described as "very villanous paper of the coarsest and dirtiest quality."[138] Two of these pamphlets—*The Trials of the Honb. James Workman, and Col. Lewis Kerr* and *Debate in the House of Representatives of the Territory of Orleans, on a Memorial to Congress, Respecting the Illegal Conduct of General Wilkinson*—exploited the same space that had remained available in January and February, by covering judicial and legislative proceedings. The trial report showed clearly that such coverage could be far from neutral. Kerr and Workman had been accused of planning a military expedition against Spanish Mexico, not of joining in the Burr Conspiracy. Their trials had played out in two phases in mid-February and early March, ending in acquittals. In the published report, Auguste Davezac, Livingston's brother-in-law, included both phases, allowing him to publicize both the defendants' and their attorneys' attacks on Wilkinson and Claiborne from February and the jury's exonerations in March. To strengthen his message, Davezac simply omitted much of the prosecution's case. The pamphlet thus advanced the defense argument that "the true motives" behind the charges could be found in "the fury of disappointed despotism."[139] Kerr's and Workman's roles in liberating Peter Ogden in mid-December, not their talk of liberating Mexico the previous April, had exposed them to Wilkinson's rage. Before the court, the defense attorneys Edward Livingston and William Duer, along with the two defendants, assaulted the general for violating "our most valued civil rights . . . with impunity" and the governor for "not only remain[ing] a calm and submissive spectator of our oppression, but actually step[ping] forth [as] the ready and open vindicator of the usurpation." For distant readers, the pamphlet would have provided a fuller account of the military arrests of December and January. And it would have revealed that "the season of alarm, disorder, mistrust, violence, and terror" had persisted into mid-February.[140]

Bradford's most effective pamphlet may have been the *Debate*. Early in the legislative session, Claiborne's and Wilkinson's opponents secured support for a memorial to Congress about "the illegal conduct of General Wilkinson."[141] Speaker of the House, and New Orleans mayor, John Watkins's initial proposal received "unanimous" backing, but the memorial was delayed when the drafting committee "dilly dally[ed for] forty days."[142] Another committee was named, but it was an outsider,

Livingston, who almost certainly wrote the memorial. Not until mid-March, after the crisis had passed and near the end of the session, did the House of Representatives consider it. The two days of debate and the fourteen-to-seven vote rejecting the memorial revealed the territory's increasingly complex politics. "Ancient" and "modern" Louisianians appeared on both sides. But the memorial's most vocal opponents included some of Claiborne's most reliable friends—William Donaldson, Alexander Fulton, and John W. Gurley—and its most vocal advocates included some of his most fervent foes—Joseph Parrot and the recently replaced mayor, Watkins. By publishing the *Debate*, Bradford gave broad circulation not only to the defeated memorial, but also to these critics' views.[143]

Together, the memorial and the debate provided an often-strident history of Claiborne's and Wilkinson's handling of the Burr crisis. The six-page memorial began with the troops' return from the western frontier in late November and continued through the military arrests of Kerr and Workman in mid-January. It described the military preparations that had "filled the city with alarm," the official warning to the merchants of Burr's impending attack, the hasty adoption of the embargo ("a serious evil to our country"), the courtroom battle over Bollman, and other key incidents. Throughout, it highlighted the assault on those rights that had supposedly been secured to Orleanians by the territorial ordinance and the federal Constitution, rights that had been "violently torn from our grasp" by Wilkinson "while [their] constitutional guardians looked tamely on."[144] In the debate, the memorial was criticized both for factual errors and for a "vindictive" tone that "went to defeat" its purpose.[145] But its defenders countered that it actually omitted "many important causes of complaint." In their speeches, they retold and elaborated the story in the memorial. They also suggested that, even in mid-March, "the bayonets of military despotism [were still] at [the] door" and the "worse than palsied" "executive of the territory" remained "enlisted in the service of [their] oppressor."[146]

The other pamphlet to come off Bradford's press that spring took the form of a defense pamphlet, rather than the seemingly neutral reportage of court or assembly proceedings. Like most examples of the genre, Workman's *Letter to the Respectable Citizens, Inhabitants of the County of Orleans* tried to restore the author's reputation by narrating a history and providing documents to support it. In forty pages, the judge recounted his efforts to resist the despotic measures of the previous winter and justified his adjournment of the county court. The numerous documents proved particularly damning, especially four letters that Workman had sent in January and February to "the then nominal governor."[147] The first letter showed that, as Claiborne had struggled to decide his response to Wilkinson's demands and actions, Workman had urged him "to maintain the laws of [his] country, and protect its citizens against the unexampled tyranny exercised over them."[148] The last letter charged that, "from the moment [the governor] abdicated the command of" the Battalion of Orleans Volunteers, "the General became [his] and our master."[149] We cannot gauge the impact of this pamphlet, or any of the others, within or beyond New Orleans. But Workman's *Letter* was being sold in New York by late July, as was Davezac's trial report, and was reviewed in a periodical there in September.

The origins of what may have been the most widely available pamphlet, *A Faithful Picture of the Political Situation in New Orleans*, are shrouded in mystery. We do not know who wrote it, who published it, or when it was published. No copies survive of the 1807 New Orleans edition, and the 1808 Boston edition did not identify the original publisher. The pamphlet is undated but includes incidents from Burr's trial in Richmond that were not known in New Orleans until late summer. Both Livingston and Workman have been advanced as its author, but former mayor John Watkins could also have written it. Livingston was certainly writing a history of the Burr crisis in New Orleans in early 1807; in late January, he informed his brother that he was readying an account of the "political situation"—a phrase that appeared in the pamphlet's title—"for the press which will be printed in about ten Days."[150] But Livingston soon became very ill. In mid-March, the *Louisiana Gazette* reported that he still intended to publish an account "of the late extraordinary occurrences."[151] *A Faithful Picture* may be the belated fruits of his efforts. But Workman had stated in his *Letter* that he planned "to answer the charge [against him] more fully than [his] occupations at this moment" allowed.[152] And Watkins's long speech in support of the memorial raised many issues that later appeared in *A Faithful Picture*, even describing the memorial as "a faithful picture."[153]

Any of these men would have fit the anonymous author's self-description as "an eye witness" to "nearly all the transactions."[154]

A Faithful Picture's author set himself two goals—providing an account, "free from misrepresentation," of events that raised grave doubts about the future of republican government in the United States and "do[ing] justice to the country which was chosen to be the theatre of these extraordinary scenes." Its history began with the frontier tensions during 1806 and ended with Wilkinson's departure from New Orleans in May 1807. Throughout, Claiborne appeared as an incompetent—a man who could neither comprehend nor command the people whom he governed, who had refused to challenge military tyranny, and who had effected an "oppressive and arbitrary impressment" of the Battalion of Orleans Volunteers by placing them under federal control. But Wilkinson received the brunt of the attacks, with nearly every one of his public acts assailed. His terrifying revelations about Burr's preparations and movements were presented as lies that "never had even a shadow of existence, except in [his] fables." His military preparations were wrong-headed at best and designed to advance Burr's plans at worst. His "lawless usurpation[s]"—the military arrests, his refusal to respect writs of habeas corpus, his "vile system of *espoinage*"—amounted to a "reign of terror." For months, these measures had kept the city "in painful and unnecessary alarm, suspending all manner of business and depreciating property of every kind." Wilkinson's "visit to New-Orleans was like that of a pestilence," the author concluded; "at his departure every countenance brightened as at a sure symptom of the returning health of society."[155]

We can see many of these tools for shaping distant opinion being utilized by both sides when Wilkinson, as *A Faithful Picture* remarked, "set about, through his friends, to collect evidence" "that all his measures had been popular in the extreme, even in New Orleans, among the well affected."[156] In early February, Wilkinson, or his supporters, secured a statement from thirty-one local shipmasters that justified the recent "military ascendency" as necessary for "preserv[ing] the peace of the country, and maintain[ing] inviolate the real interests of the United States."[157] Six weeks later, two broader statements of praise—one addressed to Wilkinson, the other to Claiborne—were prepared, and an announcement appeared in the *Louisiana Gazette* that they were available for signature. The first described the general's "extraordinary measures" as "not only justifiable, by the extremity of the case, but . . . essential to our preservation."[158] The second approved the governor's stance as "well calculated to stifle the flame of civil discord, and to *defeat* the machinations of base and designing men."[159] Nearly one hundred and fifty of what Mowry called "the most wealthy and respectable inhabitants"—a mix of "ancient" and "modern" Louisianians—signed the addresses.[160] After a few days, these testimonials, along with the lists of signers and Wilkinson's and Claiborne's replies, appeared in the *Louisiana Gazette* and perhaps other local newspapers. Wilkinson and Claiborne quickly put this material to work. Claiborne enclosed copies in an official dispatch to Madison in Washington and in a private letter to Andrew Jackson in Nashville. Wilkinson probably sent the address to him to the *Intelligencer* and the Richmond *Enquirer*, in which they appeared in May.

Concern that distant readers would view these testimonials as legitimate expressions of local sentiment brought a quick response from Claiborne's and Wilkinson's opponents. Letters went to distant editors. One to a New York newspaper described the addresses as a "stale trick" that Wilkinson had "employed to save himself from sinking." Securing so many signatures had required, according to the author, a combination of "importuning[,] coaxing[,] flattering, threatening[,] and deceiving," including telling some French speakers that it was "an address of *condolence*. . . , for the death of Mrs. W."[161] A letter to a Nashville editor explained the willingness of many who knew better to sign as deriving from "the same principles of humanity which induce men to petition for the pardon of a penitent criminal."[162] The local press entered into the battle, as well. In the *Orleans Gazette*, Bradford decried the "undue influence" that "Wilkinson and his 'little band'" had exerted to secure the signatures of a relatively small number of men.[163] And the author of *A Faithful Picture* devoted three pages to exposing the "scheme." Given "the activity, intrigue and perseverance exerted to enlist names," he remarked, it was notable "only that the number was so small," particularly since Wilkinson had considered the address "of such importance to his future fate in life."[164]

Ultimately, Claiborne sought more than such public praise. By late May, he decided to try to force his greatest opponent, Daniel Clark, to acknowledge his competence, which would have served, locally and nationally, to bolster his reputation and to shape popular understanding of the crisis. On 20 May, two days before Wilkinson's departure, Clark returned from Washington. Three days later, Claiborne demanded a retraction of Clark's disparaging comments about the management of the territorial militia in Congress six months earlier, signalling that he viewed the matter as an affair of honor. With Clark adamant that he would "never retract" his charge of "a general neglect of the militia," the men's seconds—Richard Raynal Keene and John W. Gurley— began meeting and exchanging letters to arrange a duel.[165] On 8 June, the four men crossed into Spanish West Florida. Clark's first shot passed through Claiborne's right thigh and struck his left leg, leaving him in "considerable pain" for weeks.[166] The governor had wanted a gratifying retraction, not an embarrassing duel. Locally, opinion after the duel seemed to favor Clark: "prepare yourself to be *congrat[ulated] to death*," Keene warned.[167] Even worse, because it produced a duel and an injury, the Claiborne-Clark affair became national news. In the East, the news fueled calls to replace Claiborne "whether [he] lives or not."[168] Perhaps most damagingly, Claiborne had injured himself with Jefferson, particularly since there had been no obvious replacement if he had been killed. In early September, after many unanswered letters to the president, the governor forwarded copies of his correspondence with Clark, hoping to justify his "rashly imprudent" act. He insisted that he had felt that he "could not decline noticing" "an attack upon [his] conduct & character, *by a Member of Congress, in the face of the Nation*."[169]

With the nation's attention fixed upon their city, New Orleanians faced new opportunities and new necessities not just to meet the impending crisis, but also to expose and explain their measures to a distant audience. Many of the city's groups and individuals responded, employing various tools to influence distant outsiders. But they were not equally successful. Most eastern Republicans, most importantly the president and cabinet, accepted that Wilkinson's and Claiborne's accounts provided the true story of the Burr crisis in New Orleans. The Burr crisis would probably have changed the politics of the city and the territory in any case, but the administration's endorsement reinforced the changes, strengthening Claiborne and those "ancients" who had backed his and Wilkinson's measures and weakening those "ancients"

244 | CHAPTER 6

and "moderns" who had opposed them. As national attention turned away from New Orleans—to Burr's trial in Richmond, to the threatened war with Great Britain, to the presidential election of 1808—Claiborne used both his local power in the territory and his access to national power in Washington to solidify this shift. For years after the crisis, he described "the ancient Inhabitants of the Country" as "the best supporters of the American Government," appointed them to the offices that he controlled, and recommended them for the positions that the president filled.[170] In contrast, Claiborne denied offices and recommendations to his local opponents, whom he grouped under the damning name "Burrites" in his official and unofficial correspondence for years.[171]

Looking back on the events of the previous year in late November 1807, James Brown, the territory's district attorney, reflected that Burr's "bold and unprincipled machinations against the Union and the meditated attack on this country" seemed "to have been fostered by a contempt for the talents of our Governor, . . . a belief in the corruptibility of our General," and the lack of "a sound *American population*."[172] A year earlier, many Americans across the country had worried that the arrival of Burr's forces at New Orleans would expose the weaknesses of a place that seemed crucial to preserving the union—a foreign population, an incompetent governor, and an unreliable general. For months, New Orleans looked like the key not just to Burr's plans, but also to his ultimate success or failure. Due to its vulnerability and its importance, it served as the focal point for their sense of crisis. But Burr and his men never reached New Orleans. In time, they became "a stale story," as one visitor noted, and the "Governor, and military chief," emerged as "the principal topics of conversation."[173] No less than Burr's project, Wilkinson's and Claiborne's responses also seemed full of significance, both locally and nationally. Some people in New Orleans began to view themselves as key players in a different crisis, one of republican government rather than federal union.

It is not easy to reconstruct the story of the Burr crisis in New Orleans. There are gaps in the source record, especially the loss of so many issues of the local newspapers. And there are conflicts among the sources that survive, reaching even to basic statements of fact. Still, recapturing many of the events that would have been known to many New Orleanians at the time is not difficult. The greater problem comes when we try to shape that progression of events into a story. A story requires that causes have effects and that effects have causes. A story about individuals and institutions demands intentions, achieved and un-achieved, and expectations, met and unmet. The problem is not that this internal dimension is absent from our sources. But the men who provide us with that dimension—Claiborne, Wilkinson, and Shaw, or Clark, Livingston, and Workman, or Bradford, Mowry, and Watkins—did not simply leave us with sources. They told stories of their own for their own purposes, and those stories often conflicted. In one narrative, the true story of the Burr crisis in New Orleans was the story of the federal union saved from Burr, his forces on the Mississippi, and his local supporters. In the other, it was the story of republican govern-ment threatened by Wilkinson's despotic actions and Claiborne's meek acquiescence. These stories so shaped the sources that, in the end, we cannot paint the "faithful picture" that their authors claimed to want.

CHAPTER 7

<hr>

THE THREAT TO
THE REPUBLIC

TO MANY AMERICANS, THE BURR CRISIS POSED A GRAVE THREAT TO their young republic. History, both ancient and modern, and theory had taught Americans that all republican governments were fragile and fleeting. They suffered a military disadvantage relative to their more despotic and more dynamic neighbors. At the same time, they promoted the internal divisions that sapped them from within. By empowering the people and restricting the state, republican governments unleashed various pressures even as they surrendered many of the tools that more energetic governments used to control them. Only wise governance and virtuous citizens could restrain the forces that threatened to set republics on the road to democracy, mob rule, and ultimately anarchy, on one hand, or to aristocracy, oligarchy, and finally tyranny, on the other. But a system that relied on wisdom in its governors and virtue in its citizens was always susceptible to such human failings as ambition and jealousy, greed and vindictiveness. "Mankind have pretty nearly the same dispositions whether they live under a monarchy, or in a republick," one contemporary observed, but those dispositions were "more curbed in the former."[1] Americans had worried that their republican government would share the fate of past republics even before it was fully established.

Widely shared narratives about how and why past republics had failed helped Americans to make sense of the uncertain events and reports of the Burr crisis. As such, their efforts highlight for us the nature and range of their continuing fears, even four decades after independence. The rich histories of ancient and modern governments offered Americans various and conflicting lessons about the current situation. For some, Aaron Burr fit perfectly into old stories about the dangers

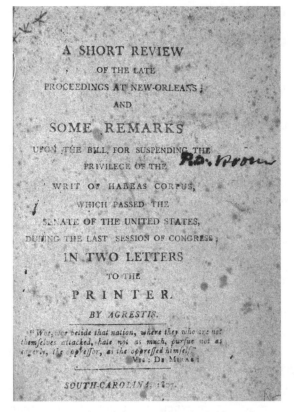

FIGURE 10. A pseudonymous work attacking the
government's response to the Burr crisis as
threatening the republic.

from men of disappointed ambition. In past republics, such men had
conspired with others of their own class or faction to topple elected
governments and claim power. But, for others, General James Wilkinson,
or even President Thomas Jefferson, embodied the real threat to the
American republic during the Burr crisis. From ancient Rome to revolutionary France, civil and military officials in republican governments
had used real or imagined crises to strengthen themselves at the expense of the rights and liberties of the people. Even at the peak of the
crisis, some already wondered, as Massachusetts senator John Quincy
Adams asked, "whether the supposed Traitor, or those who oppose him
[were] the greatest offenders against the Country?"[2]

Interpreting ongoing events through these historically informed frameworks helped contemporaries to process new events and information. Seeing Burr as a Catiline or Wilkinson as a Bonaparte provided clues about their motives, giving observers additional tools for understanding what they had done and predicting what they would do if left unchecked. These old stories imparted deeper meaning to rumors and reports about Burr's movements in the West, Wilkinson's actions in New Orleans, and the administration's and Congress's efforts in Washington. And it was not just individuals who possessed what one Delaware assemblyman called "refinement of understanding" who viewed the Burr crisis with such tools. Even people "of plain common sense" employed foreign and historical analogies.[3] In a letter that was replete with misspelled words and grammatical errors, New Jersey's Henry Guest drew not only on English history, but even on "the State of Holand Long Since," as he urged the president to "make Exampels of All incendreys."[4] Such historical perspective also made each new incident seem portentous for the future of the American republic. In republican Rome, as one westerner noted, "conspirators [had] appeared" only when "every spark of public virtue was extinguished." What did it say about the American republic, contemporaries wondered, that such dangers had emerged "in the infancy of our national existence?"[5] What did it mean for its future when, to remove those dangers, those in power embraced the very measures that had "preceded the downfall of every republican government?"[6]

"A CATALINE IN EVERY SENSE OF THE WORD"

"How like ancient Rome is the present state of affairs," an essayist remarked in an Ohio newspaper as the crisis deepened in the fall of 1806.[7] During the crisis and beyond, many Americans relied upon what a Virginia editor called "parallel[s] drawn from Antiquity" to understand the conflicting reports about Burr.[8] Worried about the permanency of their republic, they looked to "the republics of Rome, Carthage, and Greece" to anticipate the dangers that they would face. Those republics, as another Ohio essayist noted, had "lost their liberties" through the efforts "of designing, ambitious demagogues."[9] Burr seemed to be just such a person, uniting real ability "with corruptness of principle" and a devotion to "ambition, wealth & power." The same qualities that had made possible his political elevation in the 1790s—"a heart of steele, the most engaging address, and fascinating eloquence"— now made him dangerous. To countless observers, Burr seemed to be "the *modern Cataline*."[10]

To early republican Americans, Cataline, as one judge asserted, was "not merely the name of a conspirator, but of conspiracy itself."[11] The story of Cataline and his conspiracy against the Roman republic in 63 BCE was widely known. Many well-educated men, and some well-educated women, had read Sallust's *Bellum Catilinae* or Cicero's orations against Cataline in Latin or in translation. Other men and women had encountered the story in popular histories and schoolbook accounts, such as the English author Oliver Goldsmith's multi-edition *Roman History* (1772). But anyone whose schooling or reading had not already included Cataline could have learned about him from various newspapers during the Burr crisis. A reader of the most recent edition of Goldsmith's history would have learned that "Sergius Cataline, a patrician by birth, [had] resolved to build his own power on the downfal of his country." Goldsmith emphasized Cataline's complex character, describing him as, at once, eloquent and courageous and "ruined in his fortune, profligate in his manners, and . . . insatiable after wealth." With his "debauched associates," Cataline conspired to unleash local insurrections across the Italian peninsula. In the resulting confusion, Cataline and his army would take possession of Rome "and massacre all the senators." Cicero, the legendary orator of republican Rome, posed the greatest obstacle to this plan. He learned of Cataline's scheme, acted to defend Rome, and denounced the conspirator in the Senate. Cataline defended himself before the Senators, "but when confronted by the eloquence of Cicero, he hastily withdrew." He fled Rome, leaving many of his supporters to be seized and executed, and "raised an army of twelve thousand men" including "slaves, who had flocked to him in great numbers." As the Roman army approached, Cataline tried to lead his troops to Gaul but found the mountain passes blocked. Ultimately, "with nothing left him but either to die or conquer," Cataline turned to fight. His troops were destroyed, Goldsmith related, "to the last man."[12]

As early as 1800, Burr had been called "as true a *Cataline* as ever met in midnight conclave" by Alexander Hamilton, and references to Burr as "the American Cattaline" had appeared again after his duel with Hamilton four years later.[13] But the widespread, public discussion of Burr as Catiline began in the fall of 1806 in such newspapers as Frankfort's *Western World,* Chillicothe's *Scioto Gazette,* and Cincinnati's *Western Spy.* In their pages, newspaper editors and pseudonymous authors drew comparisons between what was coming to be called Burr's Conspiracy and Catiline's conspiracy. They charged that Burr's character was like Catiline's. To see a mix of attractive and repellent qualities like Burr's, according to one essayist, one need only "view the life and actions of the Roman Catiline." In both men, one would "find the utmost depravity of intellect blended with the sternest courage, and the liveliest feelings of love and friendship."[14] These writers also claimed that Burr's followers resembled Catiline's. Both conspirators won admirers among young men and married women. Both attracted those whose "indulgence of what are called the genteel vices[—]prostitution, dissipation, and extravagance of show and luxury"—"require[d] means far greater than can be derived from common industry."[15] These essays were widely republished in the West and beyond that fall.

But it was in a Virginia newspaper early the next year that the "parallel" between Burr and Catiline was drawn most fully. Thomas Ritchie, the editor of Richmond's *Enquirer,* considered himself a learned gentleman, something quite different from the artisan printers of many Republican newspapers. In numerous editorials and essays, Ritchie linked Burr to Catiline. An early January 1807 piece developed the similarities between "the man who [was] now attempting to disturb the repose of the American people" and "one of the worst characters of antiquity." In their characters, plans, and tools, the men seemed so similar that one had to wonder, Ritchie noted, whether Burr had "pored over the pages of Sallust to make Cataline his model." In a single essay, Ritchie addressed all of the comparisons that had been scattered across the Kentucky and Ohio pieces. He treated each point at greater length than the earlier writers. And he relied heavily on quotes from Sallust to make the comparisons. In the end, he provided an account of Catiline's conspiracy that was nearly as long as the one in the young-readers' edition of Goldsmith's history. Throughout, Ritchie's account incorporated recent and current events to show the "many points of parallel between the Roman conspirator and [the] American" one.[16]

Perhaps inspired by such publications, the Burr-as-Catiline trope began appearing in private and public writings in late 1806. As early as October, Jefferson privately described Burr as "a Catalinarian character."[17] In November, the Kentucky federal district attorney, Joseph Hamilton Daveiss, reported that Burr's conspiracy was "like Cataline's"; "the same means and address are used . . . and the same kinds of desperate characters engaged in the scheme."[18] At the peak of the Burr crisis, use of the Burr-as-Catiline analogy crossed lines of region, class, and party. To the Ohio editor Wyllys Silliman and the New Jersey teacher Daniel Mulford, Burr was an "American Cataline"; to the Virginia student John Campbell, New York City mayor Dewitt Clinton, and the Delaware attorney Caesar A. Rodney, he was a "modern Cataline."[19] In mid-January, the Philadelphia Federalist Thomas Truxton described Burr as "a Cataline in every sense of the word."[20] At the same time, the Philadelphia Republican Thomas Leiper urged Jefferson to fill the vacant attorney general position with someone who could be a Cicero to Burr's Catiline since it seemed that "we must have some *Hanging.*"[21]

While Burr-as-Catiline was certainly the most compelling, other analogies suggested themselves to contemporaries. Some writers saw Burr as "the Caesar of the west."[22] Others implied something similar when they related that, like Caesar on his march to overthrow the Roman republic, Burr had "passed the *Rubicon.*"[23] William Eaton claimed that Burr had likened himself not only to Julius Caesar, but also to Oliver Cromwell and Napoleon Bonaparte when discussing his plan to usurp governmental authority. Virginia's William Wirt explained Burr's behavior by surmising that "the examples of Sylla, Cataline, Caesar, Augustus, Buonaparte &c. . . . [had] had the same effect on his brain, which those of Orlando Furioso & other knights errant had on that of [Don] Quixote."[24]

With such an array of antirepublican conspirators available to them from ancient and modern history, contemporaries could imagine various ways in which Burr threatened their republic. The one that most resembled Catiline's conspiracy was publicly attributed to Burr by Eaton on various occasions beginning in January 1807. According to Eaton, Burr's plans included "overthrowing the present government of our country" by winning over the only military force in Washington, the

Marines and the Navy. With their assistance and "the support of the best blood of *America*," according to Eaton, Burr expected to *"turn Congress neck and heels out of doors; assassinate the President; seize on the treasury and navy; and declare himself the protector of an energetic government."*[25] After reading Eaton's disclosures, an essayist in the *National Intelligencer* claimed that there had never been "a more ferocious plot engendered since the creation of the world."[26] Ohio senator Thomas Worthington agreed; Burr's plan was "the most extraordinary which was ever exhibited to any people."[27] But, whereas these writers viewed Burr's schemes as unprecedented and, thus, devoid of historical antecedent, Wirt saw "the extended and magnificent project" that Eaton had ascribed to Burr as providing the best evidence that Catiline's example, and others, had shaped Burr's plans.[28]

Americans could easily accept that Burr wanted to "create an empire in which he could display power," but they did not agree upon the location of this new unrepublican government.[29] Perhaps he expected to establish *"a very energetic Government within the United States,"* with or without a military coup.[30] For Republicans and Quids, such an understanding of Burr's plans raised persistent fears about the Federalists' antirepublican views. They quickly linked "Burr's plots" to "the plots of a federal or anglo-monarchico-aristocratic faction" within the United States.[31] Some thought that Burr's ambitions merely coincided with Federalist desires; as Jefferson explained, Federalists "would have joined him to introduce his object, their favorite monarchy."[32] Others hinted that the Federalists had set Burr in motion. Despite *"hating Burr,"* as one Republican explained, the Federalists would seize upon anyone *"to bury [the Republicans] under the ruins of the constitution."*[33] A writer in one of Richmond's Republican newspapers agreed. "Burr was a great rascal when he killed Hamilton," the anonymous author had Federalists say, but having set out "to divide the Union, destroy the Constitution, turn Congress out of doors, assassinate Jefferson, and establish a Monarchy—he is a pretty clever fellow again!"[34]

But there were other places where Burr could achieve his goal "of raising himself to a powerful station over a separate government and an independent territory," as the *Aurora General Advertiser* editor William Duane described it.[35] Burr might accomplish this end by "conquering Mexico & establishing an empire under his own dynasty as Emperor or

King."[36] To many Americans, conquering Mexico seemed almost as easy to accomplish as to imagine. Although luring the western states from the union or usurping the constituted government in Washington were unlikely at best, according to the *Enquirer's* Ritchie, "the conquest of Mexico by a very small force [was] practicable."[37] And many contemporaries would have agreed with Burr's view, as related by Justus Erich Bollman, that any independent government in Mexico would have "to partake of monarchy" since the people there were not "fit for a republican Government."[38]

Burr might also hope to become the *"Emperor of the West"*—the ruler of a place that did not yet exist as either country or colony.[39] Many observers believed that Burr planned to erect an immense empire in the center of the North American continent. Its borders would have been the natural barriers of the Appalachian and Rocky Mountains and the Gulf of Mexico. Did not "Nature . . . [design] the western continent for many distinct governments," one Ohio essayist asked?[40] Its capital would "be fixed at New Orleans."[41] Even if it encompassed only the American possessions on both sides of the Mississippi watershed, Burr's new empire would have been far larger than the remaining United States. But it might have included not only the states and territories between the Appalachians and the Mississippi River *and* the vast immensity of "Louisiana of America" beyond the river, but also all or part of Spain's possessions on the Gulf of Mexico—the Floridas, Texas, and Mexico.[42] Through "force and seduction," Burr might try to establish "an imperial, *confederated* country" from "the U.S & Spanish territories" in the west.[43] In late November 1806, the uncertain reports led New Hampshire senator William Plumer to wonder if Burr sought something even larger. Perhaps Burr's "new empire in the western world" was to include "South America & the western States of North America."[44]

Many Americans recognized that either the erection of a western empire or the establishment of a Mexican empire would pose nearly as grave a threat to their republican government as the usurpation that Eaton had described. They had imbibed the lessons of the founding and accepted that an absence of powerful neighbors made possible republican government in the individual states and in the United States. The prospect of a monarchy on the union's western border—whether beyond the Louisiana Purchase or across the Appalachian ridge—inspired alarm. If "future empires" arose in North America, an essayist in the *Scioto Gazette* warned, they would compete with the United States "like rival Sparta and Athens, in Greece, sprinkl[ing] with blood the fair temple of liberty."[45] And, as Philadelphia's Tench Coxe needlessly informed James Madison, "an antirepublican Neighbour under the protection of one or more of the great European Nations" was "what most & *perhaps alone* [could] influence a change of [the union's] democratic government."[46]

Whatever its ultimate goal, conspiracy seemed inherently unrepublican. In a republic, where the people were sovereign, the public good—the only proper end of government—should not require secrecy and intrigue. If Burr's intentions were "lawful or honorable," an essayist in the *National Intelligencer* asked, why were they surrounded "in clouds and darkness?"[47] In a republic, where most men could vote and many could win office, the franchise and elected office offered the only legitimate means to effect political goals. To satisfy their ambitions, conspirators spurned these accepted routes to influence and power. Unable to advance through open and honest means, they tried to "dupe & inveigle" the public "for the aggrandizement of themselves and their minions, to the oppression of the great mass of the people."[48] That the government of the United States was "the freest of any other in the world," as one Ohio Republican stated, only made the Burr Conspiracy that much worse.[49] Similarly, to Mississippi territorial judge Harry Toulmin, Burr's conspiracy seemed to be "one of the most abandoned" ever precisely because it had "threaten[ed] the demolition of the only government on earth, on which the eye of philosophy can fix itself with any degree of complacency."[50]

Americans drew some hope that their republic could avoid the fate of other republics from the ease with which Burr was defeated, even without a new Cicero arising to thwart him. Looking back as the crisis waned, many contemporaries placed the turning point at the time, which varied from place to place, when the people learned through Jefferson's November proclamation that the government opposed Burr's plans. No one saw anything Ciceronian in the proclamation itself. What was important was how the public responded to it. Merely "informing the Citizens of their duty and danger" had been enough to defeat Burr's project, according to a Pennsylvania Republican.[51] At the first *"overt evidences* of the plan," a Fourth of July orator in the South Carolina upcountry proclaimed, "citizens of all denominations flocked to the standard of the UNION," proving that "the ATTACHMENT of FREEMEN to their GOVERNMENT, *was above all price*."[52] The United States seemed "like another Athens" to a student at western Virginia's Washington Academy, in that its republican government depended wholly on "the virtue and patriotism of her citizens."[53]

In mid-February 1807, shortly after the news of Burr's surrender in the Mississippi Territory reached Richmond, a writer in the *Enquirer* predicted that "some Sallust will hereafter record" the history of the Burr Conspiracy.[54] In fact, a number of would-be Sallusts addressed the threat that the conspiracy had posed to the young republic, often returning to the analogy that had helped the public make sense of Burr's plans and movements during the crisis. Perhaps not surprisingly, Thomas Ritchie revisited the Burr-as-Catiline trope. In the three-part "Portrait of Aaron Burr" that he began printing soon after Burr's trial, Ritchie again argued that, to understand Burr's character and "means for enlisting adherents," one needed to turn to "the pages of Sallust." "The resemblance is so striking," he concluded, "that no one can believe but that Burr had made [Catiline] his model."[55] Fourteen months later, a group of Maryland Republicans returned to this analogy as they celebrated the recently retired Jefferson's achievements, including his role in defeating "a Catilinian conspiracy, which [had] aimed a Death Blow at our vitals."[56] Even when they did not mention Catiline, however, early histories regularly saw in Burr's conspiracy a threat to republican government in the United States since it "call[ed] upon the people, to subvert, that by force, which they [had] the power and the right to do without it."[57]

Over time, though, historians, biographers, and others grew more skeptical than contemporaries had been about the idea that the Burr Conspiracy had posed a threat to republican government. The plan of usurpation that Eaton ascribed to Burr, when noticed at all, was rarely described as more than a "visionary notion" or "the madness of the moon."[58] That Burr intended to conquer Mexico and even to establish there "a monarchy, at the head of which would have been King Aaron the First," seemed much easier to accept.[59] But, by the 1820s and beyond, that idea produced little of the anxiety about the impact on republican government at home that so many people had felt two decades earlier. Even as they downplayed the Burr Conspiracy's threat to republican government, however, writers continued to celebrate the people's response to it. "In the restless, distempered masses of some European countries," a Kentucky historian wrote in the 1830s, Burr's "mad enterprise might have succeeded." But it had had no prospect of success "amid the steady attachment of a people for a government of their own choice and workmanship."[60]

"DO WE LIVE IN A FREE COUNTRY, OR ARE WE IN FRANCE?"

Even as many Americans viewed Burr's project as a threat to republican government, some believed that the measures that were adopted to thwart it posed an equal or greater danger. To defeat Burr, as the Massachusetts Federalist John Quincy Adams informed his mother in early February 1807, government officers "adopt[ed] the most violent and extraordinary measures."[61] While some past republics had fallen to internal conspiracies, others had been destroyed by the men who had pledged to secure them against internal and external threats. The Virginia Quid Littleton Waller Tazewell admitted that his real fear during the Burr crisis was of "the consequences resulting from the precipitance, with which executive officers are endowed with dictatorial powers upon such occasions."[62] Tazewell and Adams wrote as the crisis raged. As it abated, it became even easier to worry more about the response to the conspiracy than about the conspiracy itself. "Will not the arbitrary Conduct of our high Officers on the pretext of Supporting Government," a Mississippi territorial judge asked after Burr's surrender, "give the Constitution a more dangerous Shock than Burr or any other Man Could do at the head of ten thousand Men in open Rebellion?"[63] Those who voiced such concerns, moreover, generally agreed that the real danger came not from the specific measures that Wilkinson or Jefferson, the state and territorial governments, or the national legislature adopted to defeat Burr, but from the precedents that those measures would set for future crises, real or imagined. "In a free country," an essayist in a Maryland newspaper warned, "every arbitrary precedent . . . is as pregnant with mischief as the box of Pandora."[64]

Across the trans-Appalachian West, men acted to crush the Burr Conspiracy in ways that seemed inconsistent with republican principles. In western Virginia's Wood County, local militia occupied the island home of Harman Blennerhassett, looted his belongings, and stopped suspicious boats on the Ohio River without warrants. In western Pennsylvania, sheriffs and militia seized men, boats, and goods on the Ohio and its tributaries upon no better grounds. In Ohio, the governor and legislature acted to bring the militia's seizure of persons and property within the law but also suspended habeas corpus—something that only Congress can do under the Constitution. In the Mississippi Territory, federal soldiers arrested a few men, even though "the civil Authority [seemed] fully competent to su[ppress] any disorders," thereby "infring[ing] upon the rights of the people."[65] But the greatest transgressions against republican principles occurred in New Orleans between late November 1806 and early February 1807. Wilkinson violated the law and the Constitution in numerous ways, including military arrests and imprisonments for civilians, restrictions on travel, intimidation of newspaper editors, collection of secret testimony, violations of "the confidence and privacy of the post-office," and defiance of writs of habeas corpus.[66]

No less alarming, in the nation's capital, the legislative and executive branches seemed willing to defend and even expand these outrages rather than denouncing or ending them. On 23 January 1807, the day after Jefferson sent Congress his long Burr Conspiracy message, the Senate met behind closed doors to pass—quickly and with little opposition—a bill to suspend the writ of habeas corpus for three months for anyone charged with treason or other crimes against the United States by the president, any of his officers, or any state or territorial governor. Delivered to the House of Representatives under an injunction of secrecy and with a push for haste, the bill met fierce opposition from all sides. The House decided to debate the proposal openly and defeated it by a large majority (113 to 19). Having recently been reassured by the president that the conspiracy posed no danger, many opponents viewed the suspension bill primarily as an attempt to provide cover for Wilkinson's arrests.[67] In mid-February, the Delaware Federalist James Broom introduced a bill to better protect the writ from the executive branch. Where the suspension bill had been seen as designed to sustain

Wilkinson's measures after the fact, the Broom bill appeared to strike a blow at the general and the administration. "A mighty consternation prevails in the House," one Federalist remarked, "for fear something may be done which may operate against General Wilkinson or hurt the feelings of the President."[68] After two days of heated debate, the bill was "postponed, or in other words, lost" on a close vote of sixty (all Republicans) to fifty-eight (mostly Federalists and Quids).[69]

Jefferson seemed culpable for some of the outrages against republican principles. It was widely, and perhaps incorrectly, believed that he had arranged for William Branch Giles, one of his most loyal Senate supporters, to introduce the suspension bill. Even if he had not, Jefferson evinced support for Wilkinson's measures in other ways in early 1807—a time when many people, across party lines, expected him to remove Wilkinson from his command or to find another equally public mode of disavowing him.[70] Jefferson's 22 January message praised the general, even as it mentioned the irregularities in his arrests. Privately, Jefferson directed Secretary of War Henry Dearborn to assure Wilkinson of the administration's approval; ten days later, he sent his own assurances. In this letter, Jefferson identified the limits to the public's, and his own, acceptance of Wilkinson's measures, though. Arresting and sending to Washington Bollman and Swartwout—and Burr, Blennerhassett, and Comfort Tyler, if possible—would "be supported by the public opinion," the president believed. But, if such actions extended "to persons against whom there is only suspicion," he warned, "the public sentiment would desert" the general.[71] In time, this support became public when Wilkinson used these letters to bolster his position in New Orleans. Jefferson also bore responsibility for his own violations of the Constitution. When he sent John Graham after Burr in late October 1806, Jefferson empowered his agent to do things only the president could do and, as one critic noted, "to do things which [even the president could] not do."[72] And Jefferson permitted, or perhaps ordered, one of Wilkinson's prisoners to be "secretly sent in military custody" from Baltimore to Washington, "confined in the Marine Barracks" under a military guard, "and denied all intercourse and communication" with friends or counsel.[73]

As with the Burr Conspiracy itself, observers turned to historical and contemporary examples to explain how these responses to the conspiracy threatened the republic. No single individual or incident possessed the same explanatory power for this perspective that Catiline held for those who were seeking to make sense of Burr and his plans. One essayist even insisted that Wilkinson's actions in New Orleans were "unparalleled in the annals of any free country, ancient or modern."[74] Others had no trouble finding specific historical analogies for the measures and the justifications of government officials in New Orleans, Washington, and elsewhere. But, whereas the Burr-as-Catiline trope had been used to comprehend ongoing events as well as to denounce those behind them, these analogies were generally employed for political ends. Both Republicans and Federalists had described Burr as a Catiline, and they had done so in private letters as often as in published accounts. But it was primarily anti-administration Federalists, Quids, and Burrites who enlisted well-known narratives to criticize various government officials, and they did so principally in newspaper essays and editorials, speeches, and pamphlets.

The histories of ancient republics, particularly Rome's, offered numerous comparisons. One Federalist worried that the ruling Republicans, like "the Decemvirs" of late republican Rome, would extend the emergency powers that had been justified "under the pretence of promoting public good" in order to establish "an arbitrary system" that could "[trample] with impunity on the rights of their fellow-citizens." In Rome, this writer reminded readers, the result had been "the long and horrible despotisms of Tiberius and Caligula, or Nero and Heliogabalus."[75] To a New Orleans pamphleteer, Wilkinson himself was "the Caligula of Louisiana"; to another writer, he was a Sylla or an Augustus, both of whom had claimed despotic powers as "the only modes of *preserving* Roman liberty."[76] And one of New York's leading Federalist editors considered Wilkinson a Caesar, who had "passed the Rubicon, and [stood] in the eyes of the law as much the object of impeachment as Burr."[77]

Decemvir or Caesar, Sylla or Augustus—those were certainly not the historical comparisons that Wilkinson drew for himself. Instead, he considered himself a Leonidas, the Spartan general who, with just a few hundred Greek soldiers, had attempted to hold the pass at Thermopylae against an immense Persian army under Xerxes I in 480 BCE. Wilkinson invoked this analogy in at least three letters in mid-November

1806 as he prepared to move his troops from the disputed western border to New Orleans. "Emulating the example of Leonidas," he informed Secretary Dearborn, "I will with the force I may be able to collect defend the pass, or perish in the attempt."[78] Writing two days later to Ohio senator John Smith, who held the contract to provision his troops, Wilkinson pledged that he would "throw [him]self in the Gap & defend it or fall."[79] And he even used this image—"I will hurl myself like a Leonidas into the breach, defending it or perishing in the attempt"—in a letter to José de Iturrigaray, the Spanish viceroy of Mexico, requesting a reward for thwarting Burr.[80]

Modern history and contemporary politics also provided a welter of useful analogies. The author of one anti-Wilkinson and anti-administration pamphlet offered an expansive list, finding comparisons for events in New Orleans and Washington in the histories of Ireland and England, the experiences of *ancien régime*, revolutionary, and Napoleonic France, and even the "Oriental despotism" of the Ottoman Empire.[81] Other modern analogies were suggested, including the "absolute military despotism" "of a Russian or Prussian government."[82] But most observers relied upon either English or French history to understand and condemn recent developments in their country. In private letters and in published editorials, essays, and pamphlets, Wilkinson's actions in New Orleans were likened to those of England's Charles I, George III, and the Earl of Camden (who had suppressed the Irish uprising of 1798) and of France's Louis XIV, Maximilien Robespierre, and Napoleon Bonaparte. His arrests resembled those made by the *"Star Chamber"* or produced by *"Lettres de Cachet"*; a "modern bastille" held his prisoners.[83] And his sending them by sea for trial in Washington echoed "that very outrage which was one of the most just grounds of complaint against England" during the imperial crisis.[84] Though it was not fully developed until 1808, perhaps the most apt English comparison for Wilkinson was Titus Oates, whose wild charges had stoked popular and governmental outrages against Catholics in the Popish Plot of the 1670s and 1680s. The Virginian Jonathan Danvers liked this analogy so much that he referred to Wilkinson as "the *American Titus Oates*" throughout his pamphlet, describing the real Oates as Wilkinson's "great predecessor in the manufacturing of plots."[85]

For critics of Wilkinson and the Republican administration, recent French history offered some of the most powerful comparisons; "do we live in a free country, or are we in France?" one writer asked.[86] In a published letter from Washington, one Federalist decried a "new '*reign of terror*'" in which the administration and "its minions" had seized "a moment of alarm . . . to exercise their petty tyranny." "They only want the physical force of BONAPARTE," the writer concluded, "to play the part of ROBESPIERRE to perfection."[87] These three analogies proved very fluid and very effective in anti-administration hands. Wilkinson could be rendered as a "little Bonaparte"—a military chief trying to use an internal crisis to overturn the civil government and install himself above it.[88] But so could Jefferson, who, according to a Federalist editor, seemed willing to "be as arbitrary, as tyrannical, as oppressive . . . as emperor Bonaparte."[89] Wilkinson could be accused of conducting a "Robesperian system of inquisitorial tyranny" in New Orleans.[90] But Jefferson's "persecution" of Burr could just as easily be compared to "the cruelty and savage barbarity of a Robespierean tribunal."[91] Federalists especially relished the opportunity to denounce Republicans for first creating a "reign of terror" in New Orleans and then sanctioning it in Washington. A decade earlier, Republicans had charged President John Adams and the Federalist-dominated Congress with instilling a "reign of terror" during the Quasi-War with France. But, to Federalists, the situation in New Orleans was far worse than anything that had happened under Adams. In New Orleans, the author of one piece charged, the public could "see one citizen after another, seized and shipped off, in defiance of the civil authority, and in open and *avowed* violation of the constitution." That Republicans— who had complained about a "reign of terror" under Adams "when they knew there was none"—remained "perfectly silent" about Wilkinson's abuses only proved their "hypocrisy."[92]

The identification of Wilkinson's measures as threats to republican government like those that had doomed past republics first appeared in New Orleans itself. In a sense, its residents were uniquely positioned to complain. Before the Louisiana Purchase, most had lived under a Spanish colonial rule that many Americans considered a notorious example of despotism. Many of the recent American immigrants had boasted that the purchase would inaugurate a new era of limited government and individual rights. Although the residents of the territory did not enjoy all of the rights of a citizen of a state during the Burr crisis, they could claim basic constitutional protections. "Their privation of those rights" by Wilkinson, the upper house of the territorial legislature insisted, "created among them the most serious alarm."[93] In conversations and private letters, in newspapers and pamphlets, in the courts and the legislature, New Orleanians decried what one judge called an "odious and disgusting tyranny."[94] Residents described Wilkinson as "a little petty tyrant," a "despotic General," and "a military usurper."[95]

When outraged Louisianians found no protection against Wilkinson's measures from Governor William C. C. Claiborne, they looked to Washington. In published letters and pamphlets, in a formal address by the upper house of the legislature, and in a planned memorial to Congress by the lower house, they called upon the federal government to punish Wilkinson for his "acts of high handed military power" and Claiborne for his meek acceptance of this "oppression."[96] When the attorney Edward Livingston sent his lengthy appeal to New Orleans newspapers in late December, he expected it to "find [its] way to the seat of government." Once news of what had transpired "attract[ed] the notice of our representatives," he predicted, "the day of retribution" would soon follow for both Wilkinson's "wanton abuses of power" and Claiborne's "shameful direliction of duty."[97] When the president and Senate instead upheld the general's measures, they became, as one administration critic in New Orleans remarked, "in a great degree accessory to his guilt."[98] Even ardent Republicans in New Orleans shared this view. More than eighteen months after the crisis, James Brown could privately complain that those he trusted in Washington had effectively "advocate[d] the propriety of openly treading [the Constitution] under foot" by supporting Wilkinson and pushing the suspension bill.[99]

Elsewhere in the trans-Appalachian West, observers, regardless of party loyalties, warned about the threat to republican government in Wilkinson's actions. Westerners, in general, had little confidence in Wilkinson. Examining his actions in New Orleans they saw the same thing that many others saw—echoes of past threats to republican governments. In Natchez, a piece in the *Mississippi Herald* bemoaned a "reign of terror" in the neighboring territory that included "military arrests[,] suspension (by absolute power) of the writ of Habeas Corpus[,] Courts of Justice insulted[, and] a bomb ketch prison."[100] Wilkinson's conduct so infuriated Mississippi's territorial legislature that it passed a bill "to annihilate the name of Wilkinson County."[101] In Nashville, one newspaper criticized "the length to which military despotism [had] been carried at New Orleans," while the other described Wilkinson as "a tyrant [and] a usurper," whose actions were "symmetrical to those of Robespierre."[102] And, in Chillicothe, Ohio, an essayist in a Republican newspaper insisted that Wilkinson threatened to "deluge our country with anarchy or despotism." "The miseries of the French" and "the wretchedness of the persecuted patriots of Ireland" were no worse than the sufferings of the people of New Orleans, the author insisted.[103] That westerners shared a sense of outrage over Wilkinson's actions was recognized at the time. "The citizens of the western country," an Ohio editor announced in April 1807, "unanimously condemn him. Not a dissenting voice is heard in his defence."[104]

Across the West, as in New Orleans, calls upon the federal government to redress the situation accompanied the attacks on Wilkinson. In mid-February, one Nashville editor expressed his faith "that some stop [would] shortly be put to the reign of terror carried on" in New Orleans, for the benefit of both its residents and "the United States generally."[105] Similarly, writing to a Tennessee congressman, militia general Andrew Jackson declared that "it [was] expected" that the "stride of military despotism . . . [would] be duly noticed by" Congress. If it was not, he warned, the impact would be "injurious to our goverment and [would] destroy [the] confidence" in the men who controlled it.[106] Travelling in Tennessee later that spring, a South Carolinian saw clear evidence that the administration's support for Wilkinson and the Senate's effort to suspend the writ of habeas corpus had shaken public confidence. "The people here are heartily sick of Mr Jefferson, his friends & their present system of duplicity," Henry Middleton Rutledge reported.[107] From Natchez to Pittsburgh, in the spring of 1807, westerners, even western Republicans, warned the administration about the impact of its continuing support for Wilkinson and seeming endorsement of anti-republican measures. The administration, Mississippi's Cowles Mead informed Madison, risked losing the confidence of "the whole western World . . . by maintaining this man & his measures."[108]

No one could have made such a statement about the East. East of the Appalachians, the administration's supporters often took very different positions on these issues from its Federalist, Quid, and Burrite opponents. Throughout the East, anti-administration editors and essayists, writers and speakers, echoed most westerners in attacking Wilkinson's actions. To one Massachusetts Federalist, the general's arrests and deportations seemed "an alarming procedure in a free country."[109] Federalist senator William Plumer viewed "the imprudent, wild, & I may justly add, *mad conduct* of Genl Wilkinson" "as wanton acts of cruelty & tyranny."[110] The editor of Burr's newspaper in Richmond condemned Wilkinson's "despotic conduct," while a Virginia Quid reported that the general had "violat[ed] with impunity the most sacred privileges of the Citizen & [bid] defiance to their most inestimable Rights."[111] Editorials and essays in Federalist newspapers from Georgia to Massachusetts decried the "self created dictator of N. Orleans."[112]

To many eastern Republicans, in contrast, the firm measures that had been taken to defeat the Burr Conspiracy across the West merited support and praise, at least publicly. Not surprisingly, Baltimore's *American*—the newspaper that was influenced, if not controlled, by Wilkinson's most loyal defender, Maryland senator Samuel Smith—published numerous pieces justifying his actions in New Orleans. If Wilkinson had "*not* adopted any precautionary measures" and had "suffered Bollman, Swartwout, Ogden, and Alexander, to proceed in their project," an early editorial suggested, the consequence would have been "dreadful, past doubt."[113] Equally supportive pieces appeared in other Republican newspapers, including Richmond's *Virginia Argus* and Philadelphia's *Aurora*. In the East's leading Republican newspapers, Wilkinson appeared as someone who had "rendered essential services to his country" and "*out-generaled* the little emperour of the quids."[114] No lover of "our country and its happy constitution," one essayist in the *Argus* insisted, could want to "discourage . . . such exertions as were made by [Wilkinson] to crush what he *knew* was a damnable treasonable conspiracy!"[115]

In the view of the opposition, the staunchness of the administration, its congressional allies, and its "ministerial presses" in defense of illegal and unconstitutional measures dramatically increased the threat to republican government.[116] In the East, Federalists, Quids, and Burrites attacked Jefferson for backing Wilkinson "when he tossed the civil authority at the point of the bayonet."[117] These attacks began as soon as the president's support for the general became clear and continued throughout the spring. Anyone who could "approve such manifest violations of the constitution," a Federalist editor in New York charged, "has already harboured a secret & disguised wish to free his passions from the fetters of the laws."[118] Administration opponents also derided the Senate for approving the suspension bill "with wicked haste" and praised the House for strangling the bill "as a *viper* ought to be strangled."[119] If the suspension bill failed to arouse the public's concerns, a Virginia Quid warned, "a Bastile may be built without a murmur, & its Dungeons filled by Lettres de Cachet."[120]

In both private letters and published editorials and essays, eastern Republicans accepted and defended the administration's decision to support Wilkinson and to praise westerners for their vigilant response to the Burr Conspiracy. And they accused opposition editors of acting from the worst motives when they attacked the administration and its officers. Those who censured Wilkinson, according to one Baltimore Republican, were "a passil of English Irish & Scotch, all Federalists."[121] Eastern Republicans were willing to say that the government had gone too far only on the suspension bill. As one Republican congressman explained to his constituents, the suspension of the writ of habeas corpus when "unnecessary to secure the tranquillity of the country" seemed "extremely dangerous as an example."[122] In an affair "in other respects so honorable to our government," a Virginia student asked his brother, "[is it] not to be lamented" that the Senate "should have stained their anals" by passing that bill?[123]

How do we explain the party divisions of the East given the apparent cross-party unity of the West? How do we account for eastern Republicans' defenses of Wilkinson and the administration given western Republicans' criticisms? Western Republicans do not seem to have been more ardent republicans or more concerned about the fragility of republican government than their eastern counterparts. But westerners, across party lines, had long viewed Wilkinson with suspicion. Pre-existing doubts may have predisposed western Republicans to worry about his measures and prompted them to denounce him publicly. Western Republicans may also have felt more freedom to criticize the general, and even the administration, than eastern Republicans because party tensions tended to be weaker where there were few Federalists and almost no organized Quids or Burrites. In the West, Republicans' criticisms might embarrass party leaders but were unlikely to affect federal or state elections.

More than ideological fervor or past suspicions or partisan intensity, however, the movement of information may have produced the different responses of East and West. In general, westerners learned of the excesses—in western Pennsylvania and western Virginia, in the Mississippi Territory and Ohio, and in New Orleans—before they learned of the administration's reaction to them. They knew of these anti-republican measures through direct experience, travellers' reports, private letters, and western newspapers. Most easterners, in contrast, learned of the excesses at roughly the same time that they learned that Jefferson had defended Wilkinson and praised other western officials in his message to Congress. When they discovered what had been done to suppress the conspiracy, western Republicans expected the Republicans who controlled the federal government to share their concerns and act upon them; most eastern Republicans already knew the response of those in power when they learned what had happened in the West.[124] There are hints, in private letters and diaries, that some eastern Republicans initially shared westerners' concerns about Wilkinson's measures. Administration critics suggested that the influence of what one Federalist called "a few back stairs men" brought Republicans in Washington and beyond into line behind the president.[125] Even a Republican could later admit that "the course of conduct in the great, the good, the enlightened Jefferson had [had] a decisive influence" upon "publick opinion."[126]

That is not to say, of course, that eastern Republicans grounded their defenses of Wilkinson's measures or Jefferson's support for them on party loyalty. Such an idea would have been an anathema to men who prided themselves on their independence of mind. Instead, they argued that the incursions upon civil authority and popular rights in New Orleans and elsewhere had been made necessary by the threat, or supposed threat, of Burr's conspiracy. In doing so, they invoked a doctrine of necessity that derived from the almost-universal agreement that self-preservation, whether of individuals or of states, was the first law of nature. Necessity was precisely the ground on which Wilkinson had justified his actions in his dealings with Claiborne, his dispatches to Washington, and his response to the Orleans territorial court.[127] "Imperious necessity" was also the ground on which the administration understood and defended the general's measures in its letters to Wilkinson and messages to Congress.[128] Republican newspapers echoed this language. "Cases may occur," an essayist in the *American* explained, when "the only mode of securing" rights for the future is through their "temporary infraction." In such cases, "necessity becomes justice."[129] In newspapers up and down the Atlantic Coast, Republican essayists and editors accepted "that the Plea of necessity did actually seem in this particular instance to exist in sufficient force" to "justify *many* of the acts which [Wilkinson] committed."[130]

But the doctrine of necessity held a prominent place in the history of failed republics. From ancient Rome to modern France, the claim that intrusions upon popular rights and legitimate authority were necessary to save the nation had preceded the toppling of republics and the emergence of despots. The administration's opponents repeatedly reminded the public that necessity had been "the constant, hacknied, worn-out plea of every usurper" in history and the "dreadful auxiliary of tyranny in all ages."[131] Some opposition writers admitted that there were times when necessity justified illegal or unconstitutional acts but denied that the Burr crisis was one of those times. "That there are cases of extreme necessity which require an extraordinary vigor in government," one victim of Wilkinson's outrages freely admitted, "but this necessity should be clear, evident, palpable[—]as if Hannibal or Cataline were at the gates."[132] Others took the extreme position that no crisis could justify such measures. Former New Orleans mayor John Watkins did not believe that there could be "a case in which any officer of the government . . . can be justified in a departure from the written laws of his country." To accept the contrary even in principle, he warned, was to "lay the foundation for despotism" by enabling "any ambitious man . . . *to imagine public danger*" and use it as grounds to seize the government, rule "to his own fancy, and finally erect upon its ruins just such a system as Cæsar did in Rome[,] as Bonaparte has done in France."[133]

Republicans certainly knew this history as well as their critics. Their invocations of the doctrine of necessity often included explicit recognitions of its troubled past. "We grant that necessity is too often the tyrant's plea," the editor of the *Virginia Argus* conceded.[134] A western Republican who followed the administration in supporting Wilkinson thought that "nothing [was] so dangerous or abhorrent in a government of laws as the doctrine of expediency," which was "fitting only for the cabinets of St. James [in London] and St. Cloud [near Paris], for a Rajah or a Bey[, and was] the plea of every tyrant."[135] Even one of the general's most ardent defenders acknowledged that, employed unnecessarily or frequently, "the 'plea' of the 'patriot' [could] be artfully converted into that of the 'tyrant.'"[136] But, as the editor of the *Argus* noted, there were countless examples of the doctrine of necessity being employed by "the best patriots and sincerest republicans in all ages" with cause.[137] In fact, an essayist in the *Intelligencer* explained, the more successfully a government protected freedom under normal conditions, the more willing its people had to be to accept "the occasional necessity[,] in periods of uncommon danger, for some of the public functionaries" to overstep the law. "Usurpations of authority[and] violations of the constitution," in other words, would "more frequently fall to our lot than to those of nations less free."[138]

Perhaps the most thoughtful discussion of the doctrine of necessity to emerge from the Burr crisis came from the very person whose decision to support Wilkinson bequeathed such a potentially dangerous precedent to the future. In September 1810, eighteen months after leaving office, Jefferson responded to a request from John B. Colvin for an explanation of his views. Wilkinson had asked Colvin to ghostwrite part of his memoirs, and Colvin wanted to ensure "that the *principles* upon which [Jefferson] approved of [the general's] conduct at New-Orleans should not be mistated nor mistaken."[139] In his reply, which Colvin incorporated with few changes and without attribution, Jefferson articulated his view of the appropriate course for "officers of high trust" during a crisis. While "a strict observance of the written laws [was] doubtless *one* of the high duties of a good citizen," he argued, "it is not *the highest*. The laws of necessity, of self-preservation, of saving our country when in danger, are of higher obligation." "The line of discrimination between cases [could] be difficult," Jefferson admitted, "but the good officer [was] bound to draw it at his own peril." In the end, the officer's decision and actions would be judged by "the controuling powers of the constitution" and the good sense of "his fellow citizens." But, Jefferson argued, these judgments should be based on "the state of the information, correct & incorrect," on which the officer acted, not on what was known at the time elsewhere or was learned later.[140] Jefferson grounded his defense of Wilkinson's actions on that perspective. Most of these ideas—the reference to the "good officer," the reliance upon the regular process of the law and "honest juries" to judge Wilkinson, and the need to do so based upon Wilkinson's "own view of the danger"—had appeared in Jefferson's writings during the crisis; Colvin's request merely provided Jefferson an opportunity to pull them together in a more developed form.[141]

Concerns and charges that measures that had been adopted in New Orleans, Washington, and elsewhere to defeat the Burr Conspiracy threatened republican government in the United States did not persist much beyond the crisis itself. For another year or so, as Burr faced trial in Richmond and Wilkinson underwent investigation by a military tribunal, people occasionally discussed the same issues along the same partisanal and sectional lines that had appeared during the crisis. Eastern Republicans, as the president's elder daughter explained, continued to believe that Wilkinson "deserv[ed] the gratitude of his country in an eminent degree."[142] Westerners and opposition writers continued to decry Wilkinson's "tyrannical persecutions" and to "reprobate a precedent which whatever may be its motive is at all times dangerous to liberty."[143] But the prospective dimensions of the general's measures and the administration's support for them that had seemed so crucial—their significance as precedents for the future—soon faded from view. Increasingly, these events were treated retrospectively—as background for Burr's trial or as evidence of Jefferson's hypocrisy or simply as occurrences in the annals of the year 1807.[144]

That republican government in the United States survived both the Burr Conspiracy and the measures that were employed to defeat it did not lead Americans to stop worrying about it. In 1829, responding to Thomas Spotswood Hinde's offer to provide his recollections of the conspiracy, James Madison described the public's critical role in defeating it as one of the "auspicious pledges given by the genius of Republican institutions and the spirit of a free people, for future triumphs over dangers of every sort."[145] Even as Madison wrote, however, many Americans worried that a new conspiracy, operating behind the secrecy of the Masonic Order, posed a grave threat to their republic. Concerns over the dangers of anti-republican conspiracies persisted long after Burr, just as they had existed long before him. In the late antebellum era, northern Whigs and Republicans often warned of the Slave Power Conspiracy that ruled the country on behalf of southern slaveholders. Farmers and laborers, and their middle-class allies, identified an anti-republican conspiracy among industrial and financial leaders in the late nineteenth century. In ever-changing forms, such conspiratorial thinking continued through the twentieth century. Historians, political scientists, and sociologists have even considered the recurrence of all-consuming efforts to identify and suppress anti-republican conspiracies, or supposed conspiracies, a central feature of American political culture.[146]

At the same time, Americans have continued to see equally grave dangers to republican government in some of the means that have been employed by federal, state, and local governments, the media, and the public to defend the nation against internal and external threats. Just as the Virginia student John Campbell did in the spring of 1807, they have worried that "the splendor of our government will be extinguished, our liberties will vanish[,] and we shall be no longer a nation" if we continued to adopt "such violent remedies to protect ourselves internally [and] to keep our own citizens in order."[147] From the Quasi-War of the late eighteenth century and the Civil War of the mid-nineteenth century to the Cold War of the mid-twentieth century and the war on terror of the early twenty-first century, at least some Americans have considered measures that those in power defended as necessary and temporary incursions against the law or the Constitution to be dire threats to republican government. The prohibitions against seditious speech during the Quasi-War and World War I, the suspension of the writ of habeas corpus to permit the detention of Confederate sympathizers during the Civil War, the internment of Japanese Americans during World War II, the interception of electronic communications in the war on terror—all of these measures were decried in their own time by Americans who worried about the immediate and long-term impact on their constitutional rights and civil liberties.

If the Burr crisis and its resolution did not end Americans' fears about threats to their republican government, it did provide a new historical analogy that helped later Americans make sense of the potential threats of their own times. After the crisis, it became possible to describe someone as "a Burr" in much the same way that it had been common during the crisis to describe Burr as "a Catiline." In 1827, the Jackson supporter Anthony Butler denounced Henry Clay as being "like Burr" in that "he would make any effort, adopt any plan and use any instrument to regain what he has lost, and even jeopardise the integrity of the Union to subserve [that] purpose."[148] Fourteen years later, Pennsylvania's James Buchanan spoke against a proposal before the Senate on the grounds that, in the future, "an ambitious and dangerous man"—"an Aaron Burr"—might be "at the head of the Government."[149] The same thinking could be reversed, with some men, in some cases, considering it necessary to insist that their characters or projects were not like Burr's. "My Country can never make 'A Burr' of me," a dejected Meriwether Lewis wrote the secretary of war in August 1809; "she can never sever my Attachment from her."[150] In the early 1820s, one of the planners of a new settlement in Mexican Texas similarly felt the need to proclaim in a Nashville newspaper, "there are no Aaron Burrs among us [and] no treasonable plans."[151]

THE ARREST OF AARON BURR

Late on 18 February 1807, in the small hamlet of Wakefield in Washington County in the eastern Mississippi Territory (later Alabama), Nicholas Perkins heard "the sound of horses feet" on the road outside the courthouse. Curious, Perkins, the register of the district land office and a major in the territorial militia, went to the doorway to see what he could see in the moonlight. One rider passed by quickly without stopping "or saying a word altho he passed within 20 feet." A second paused to ask directions to Major John Hinson's house. Perkins told him the route but also warned that Hinson was not home and that it would be a difficult trip at night because the bridges had been washed out and the road was poorly marked. He suggested that the riders stay at Wakefield's tavern and proceed to Hinson's home in the morning; the men continued on their way. Such odd behavior—"riding at that late hour of the night in strange country, determined to go on to Major Hinsons at the distance of 7 or 8 miles on a bad road over broken and dangerous bridges, passing by a public house to a private one"—convinced Perkins that either the two men had "some bad design upon Hinson or his property" or "it was Colonel Burr making his escape through that country."[1]

Perkins informed the other men who were in the courthouse— Clerk of the Court Thomas Malone and Sheriff Theodore Brightwell— of his suspicions and urged them to join him in pursuing the riders. Brightwell agreed, rose from his bed, and rode with Perkins to Hinson's. Outside the house, they met the man who had spoken with Perkins at the courthouse door, Robert Ashley. The other man had already gone into the separate kitchen to warm himself at the fire. After some time, he entered the main house, where Perkins watched him closely. "His dress and every appearance [were] extraordinary." "He had on a white hat with a brim rather broad than otherwise[,] a

THE ARREST OF AARON BURR.

J.D.Torrey, Publisher. 13 Spruce St. New York.

FIGURE 11. The arrest of Aaron Burr in the Mississippi Territory in February 1807.

long beard, a checked Hankerchief around his neck[, and] a great coat belted around him to which was hanging a tin cup on one side and a butchers knife on the other." Thinking that this mysterious figure "must be Colonel Burr," Perkins "watched an opportunity of seeing his eyes," eventually glimpsing them.[2] Having heard "Burr's eyes mentioned as being remarkably keen," this glimpse "strengthened his suspicions."[3] The man was Aaron Burr, whom Perkins knew was a fugitive from justice.

Leaving Brightwell with Burr and Ashley, Perkins excused himself and rode south to Fort Stoddert, reaching it before sunrise. There, he related to Lieutenant Edmund P. Gaines the events of the night and his "suspicions that the person with the white hat was Colonel Burr." Gaines assembled a small group of soldiers and returned with Perkins to Hinson's. A few miles from the house, they met Burr and Brightwell, who had agreed to show Burr the "way to the ferry" across the Tombigbee River. Gaines arrested Burr, despite his protests, and took him to the fort. Perkins returned to Wakefield. On the way, he met Ashley and, without telling him of the arrest, informed him that Burr had "requested him to come to Fort Stoddert."[4] The next day, after extracting information from Ashley about Burr's plans, Perkins and Colonel John Callier, a militia commander and county court judge, arrested him in Wakefield.

On 21 February, two days after Burr's arrest, Perkins rode back to Fort Stoddert, where he found Gaines in a quandary. The lieutenant seemed most concerned about the Spanish forces in neighboring West Florida. When a Spanish officer came to the fort and asked to see Burr, Gaines and Perkins decided not to permit a meeting. But they allowed the officer to pass along a verbal message and a written note from Burr to Juan Ventura Morales, a civil official at nearby Mobile. Worried, as Perkins recalled, that "the Spanish would endeavor to rescue Colonel Burr and that he was unable to defend himself, as his pickets were pulled down and some of his men unfit for duty," Gaines decided to send Burr to Washington, D.C., without waiting for instructions.[5] He asked Perkins to assemble a small group of men to escort the prisoner. Two days later, four days after the arrest, Perkins's party of civilians and soldiers took charge of their prisoner and began their journey. They travelled through Creek and Cherokee lands and the southern upcountry with only one significant incident—when Burr broke free from his escort and tried to claim the protection of civil authorities at Chester Courthouse, South Carolina. On 25 March, after a month on the road, Perkins and his party reached Fredericksburg, Virginia, sixty miles from the nation's capital. A messenger from the administration met them there and redirected them south to Richmond, where they arrived the next evening.[6]

The drama of this event—of the sequence of incidents that began with Burr and Ashley's late-night ride into Wakefield and ended with Burr and Perkins's arrival in Richmond—ensured it a central place in stories of the Burr Conspiracy. Unfounded rumors and barely grounded suppositions about Burr's arrest radiated out from Fort Stoddert, staying a few days ahead of Burr and his captors as they traversed the southeastern states. It seemed that everyone wanted to know not just that Burr had been arrested, but when and where and by whom and how. The first full account of this event—published in the Richmond *Enquirer* the day after Burr's arrival and based upon secondhand information from "a gentleman, who travelled with [Burr's escort] in the stage" from Fredericksburg—was widely reprinted.[7] Beginning with the early reports and culminating in the histories and biographies of the mid-nineteenth century, the story of Burr's arrest emerged as one of the most heavily embellished and romanticized elements of the larger story of the conspiracy. The discrepancies between what happened and what was said to have happened, between event and memory, reflect changes in the broader culture.[8]

Identifying these discrepancies—discerning embellishments and revisions in the memory of an event—is possible only when one can recover the event itself. Relying on Perkins to reconstruct this dramatic event, or succession of incidents, is both essential and problematic. Only a handful of people could have provided firsthand accounts of the key incidents: Ashley, Burr, Perkins, Malone, and Brightwell for the initial encounter at Wakefield courthouse; Ashley, Burr, Perkins, Brightwell, Mrs. Hinson, and perhaps some of the Hinsons' slaves for the time at the Hinson home; Burr, Perkins, Brightwell, Gaines, and a few soldiers for the arrest itself; and Burr, Perkins, Malone, the other members of Burr's escort, and a few locals for the failed escape at Chester Courthouse. Only Burr and Perkins were present for all of these moments. While Burr said little, at least for the record, Perkins said and wrote a lot. Much of what Perkins said and wrote, moreover, took the form of sworn testimony or informal deposition and was recorded relatively shortly after the incidents themselves. And much of it became widely and quickly available, to contemporaries and historians, in newspapers and in the published records of Burr's trial.[9] Finally, many of the key questions about this event have turned upon Perkins's thinking: What led him to suspect that one of the riders was Burr? Why did he decide to follow them to the Hinson place? And why did he involve Gaines in the arrest?

But there were other firsthand accounts and other questions about these incidents. Burr addressed some issues briefly during the opening phase of his trial in Richmond. Gaines sent one report east to Secretary of War Henry Dearborn in Washington and others west to General James Wilkinson in New Orleans and Governor Robert Williams in Natchez within days of Burr's arrest; some of these reports made it into the press. In early April, Ashley told his story in a letter to a South Carolina newspaper that was widely reprinted. And, more than forty years later, Malone and Mrs. Hinson provided their own accounts in interviews with the Alabama historian Albert James Pickett.[10] Comparing these firsthand accounts reveals numerous inconsistencies. Some concern purely factual matters and are relatively unimportant: When did Burr and Ashley ride into Wakefield? Who was in the courthouse? Did Burr or Ashley come up to the courthouse door or did Perkins go out to the street? Who was in the Hinson home? Others emerge from the necessarily different perspectives of their authors. And still others point to more significant questions that were contested, at the time and since: Did Ashley know Burr's plans, whether his larger project or his immediate destination? Was Burr in flight from the court and the law in the Mississippi Territory or from the flagrant disregard for courts and laws in Wilkinson's New Orleans? Was Burr going to Spanish Pensacola or to the eastern United States?[11]

But perhaps the most fascinating point of contestation, throughout the nineteenth century, concerned Burr's appearance. This interest in Burr's clothing derived from early reports that he had been "discovered in disguise," detected while dressed in what one South Carolinian who saw him on the road described as "a very mean apparel of homespun."[12] Everyone from private citizens and newspaper editors to the attorney general and the president commented upon Burr's clothes, usually treating them as a failed disguise. It is easy to understand both the interest in and the disputes over questions about Burr's associates or his intentions or his destination. In the short term, such issues might have legal relevance for his pending trial; in the long term, they could provide important clues for biographers and historians about the conspiracy and its suppression. But it was Burr's appearance and clothing that became the central elements in the heavily embellished and romanticized accounts of his arrest, accounts that highlighted nineteenth-century Americans' concern with visual markers of class and status in a republican—and, increasingly, a democratic—society.[13]

Assumptions that derived from ideas of class and status shaped even the earliest rumors of Burr's arrest. In the first accounts, however, the misconstructions and romanticizations concerned Burr's captors, rather than Burr himself. Both administration officials and newspaper editors shaped the first fragments of information about the arrest into a narrative of republican purity foiling aristocratic treason. In doing so, they invoked, at least implicitly, the most famous arrest in American history to that time—that of Major John André, the British major who had helped Benedict Arnold plan his treason. In September 1780, André had been seized by three common farmers in New York. The motives and nature of André's captors would later be viewed with some suspicion, but, at the time of Burr's arrest, the three young men figured in histories, plays, and popular memory as simple yeomen who had acted entirely out of a virtuous republican attachment to the public good. The earliest descriptions of Burr's captors echoed this story. On the basis of vague information obtained from someone who had been in Fredericksburg when Perkins's party arrived, Attorney General Caesar A. Rodney apprised the president that Burr had been apprehended by "some countrymen who knew him."[14] Thomas Jefferson's first letter on the subject consequently described Burr's captors as "country people."[15] The earliest items on the arrest in the *National Intelligencer* and some other newspapers used similar language and suggested its implications. According to rumor, the *Intelligencer* reported, Burr had been "apprehended by a plain countryman, who had not even heard of [Mississippi territorial] Governor Williams's proclamation"—which not only announced Burr's flight, but also offered a two-thousand-dollar reward for his capture.[16] Republican virtue, not personal gain, had motivated Burr's "country" captors.

The ease with which Rodney, Jefferson, the editor of the *Intelligencer*, and others imagined Perkins and the civilians in his party as "country people" contrasted sharply with the effort that the latter exerted to present themselves as gentlemen, despite their residence on a remote frontier. From the start, Gaines and Perkins had agreed that the task of escorting Burr required "respectable men."[17] Before departing for the capital, Perkins and the other civilians had proclaimed their respectability by solemnly drafting and signing a document that "pledge[d] our lives[,] our honour[,] each to the other for the safe conducting and Delivery of Aaron Burr."[18] Perkins explained his thinking on this issue to an administration official soon after reaching Richmond. The escort, he noted, "consist[ed] of seven persons besides myself"—two soldiers and five "gentlemen . . . , as men of that description only could be trusted" with such an important duty.[19]

Whatever reflex led at least some contemporaries to cast Burr's captors as simple and virtuous "country people" was soon brought under control as more accurate information from Richmond established Perkins's claims to respectability. The *Enquirer*'s first report on the arrest already referred to Perkins as a "gentleman"; a more accurate account in the next issue described him as well as "the register of the Land-Office."[20] Three weeks later, the editor made a special point of noting that the escort had included "the most respectable men in the country, some of them possessed of very considerable property, and others much distinguished in their districts."[21] A narrative of simple republican virtue thwarting aristocratic corruption no longer seemed appropriate. But, accompanying the new information about Perkins was new information about Burr's detection and arrest. The attention of letter writers and newspaper editors quickly shifted from the captor to the capture and the captured, particularly to Burr's appearance and clothing.

Burr's apparent flight from the Mississippi territorial court and decision to do so in disguise raised legal and cultural issues. Recognizing the legal weight of the details of Burr's arrest, one Richmond newspaper refused to describe "the manner in which he was apprehended" in order not to prejudice the case.[22] Burr's appearance was discussed at his initial examination before Chief Justice John Marshall, with Perkins describing Burr as "in disguise" and defense attorney John Wickham insisting that Burr had "assumed no disguise."[23] In legal terms, though, flight mattered more than disguise. Blackstone's commentaries on English common law said little about adopting a disguise but clearly stated that flight when "accus[ed] of treason, felony, or even petit larciny" created "a strong presumption of guilt."[24] Even before leaving Natchez, Burr had insisted, in a letter to Governor Williams, that he had fulfilled his obligations to the territorial court. Williams's proclamation calling for Burr's arrest after his failure to appear in court on 5 February evinced his rejection of Burr's view and stated the official position in this dispute. In late March in Richmond, Burr's flight remained a key issue. "Why did he fly," the federal district attorney, George Hay, asked at the examination, "but from a consciousness of guilt?"[25] Burr insisted that he had fled not the territorial court, but "the arm of military power." Knowing that Wilkinson had sent officers and agents "to seize [his] person and property," Burr had "abandoned a country where the *laws* [had] ceased to be the sovereign power" once the territorial grand jury had cleared him.[26]

Ultimately, the cultural implications of Burr's actions far surpassed the legal ones. "The disgrace of flight," even more than the "presumption of guilt," one writer speculated, would "have deterred [Burr] from the measure" if he had not, in fact, been guilty.[27] In cultural terms, however, Burr's apparent decision to disguise himself to facilitate his escape mattered more than flight itself. Simply put, a true gentleman would never need a disguise. Gentlemen might wear costumes in theatrical settings, such as balls, skits, or tableaux vivantes, with no risk to their honor and status. At much greater risk, they could go about with their identities "masked" in ways, including women's dress, that would have been humiliating to have exposed. But it was something very different to attempt to conceal one's identity to avoid the law. By disguising himself, especially as a person of low rank, and by having that disguise pierced, Burr undermined his claims to gentility. Finally, being conveyed across the country "under guard . . . , like a felon or murderer convict," inflicted another blow to his status.[28] "How very different was [Burr's] entry last evening," a "respectable gentleman" wrote from Fredericksburg, "from what it was seven or eight years ago." Then, Burr had been bound for Jefferson's home on his way to the vice presidency; now, he was "mean and dirtily dressed, guarded like a felon, and apparently much depressed and sunk in spirits."[29]

Many who saw Burr during these weeks commented upon his appearance in great detail. The briefest accounts simply said that he was "in disguise" or "shabbily dressed."[30] Other witnesses provided lengthy descriptions. Perkins's account for the attorney general included Burr's hat and coat, the bandana around his neck and the belt around his waist, and his beard. In a letter for a Charleston newspaper, the postmaster at Chester Courthouse described Burr's apparel as "very coarse homespun, an old hat, great coat, with a tin cup to his side."[31] After seeing Burr in Fredericksburg, the federal surveyor William Tatham described him for the president as wearing "an old White Hat, a pair of Checked Virga. Cloth Pantaloons & an old Virginia Leggins, & an old Virginia Cloth Coat."[32] Even four decades later, one of Pickett's interviewees could describe every item of Burr's outerwear in terms of material and color. Having travelled with Burr as part of the escort, Malone could recall his "round about of drab cloth," "pantaloons . . . made of plain cotton cloth with coperas stripes going round his legs," "boots & spurs," and "white hat which floped."[33]

But men who had not actually seen Burr also described his disguise, often as fully as those who had. Even as he admitted that he had not seen Burr when the escort "passed by [his] door," Virginia's John Randolph still reported upon Burr's "shabby suit of home-spun" and the "old white hat [that] flapped over his face."[34] From New Orleans, General Wilkinson informed Jefferson that Burr had been "taken in an old Blanket Coat begirt with a leathern Strap, to which a Tin Cup was suspended on the left & a scalping Knife on the right."[35] Rodney's description, which had originated with the innkeeper in Fredericksburg, had Burr "dressed in a pair of striped Virginia cloth trousers, a white country man jacket, an old drab surtout & an old white hat."[36] It was rare indeed for someone with any knowledge of Burr's apparel to admit, as one letter writer did: "I cannot describe his dress." Even this author, however, could not resist writing that what he had heard had conveyed the impression "of an Indian countryman carricatured."[37]

Almost unspoken in these descriptions was the universal understanding that a gentleman such as Burr should not have been wearing clothes such as these. Most of those who described his appearance stated that he was in disguise, before detailing his clothes. But it was hardly necessary. Simply describing his appearance sufficed to establish to anyone who read or heard the description that Burr was in disguise. Burr, one newspaper account explained, was clothed in "all the habiliaments of a man so perfectly different from those in which he commonly appeared."[38] Frequent references to his clothes as "mean" (as in "average") neatly captured this sense that he was dressed as a commoner.[39] The specific details of Burr's appearance differed in these accounts: Were his pants striped as Rodney reported, checked as Tatham described, or a copperas color as Malone remembered? Did he look like a hunter, a farmer, a fisherman, or a boatman? Different people read his appearance in different ways, but none of them doubted that he was dressed as a commoner rather than a gentleman. And none disputed that this fact raised questions about his claims to respectability. A man whose usual attire "was fashionable and rich, but not flashy," Burr temporarily abandoned a crucial marker of status when he donned the coarse homespun and floppy hat of a commoner.[40]

We can see the power of these assumptions about dress, self-presentation, and status in Robert Ashley's efforts to defend Burr. Ashley, a shadowy figure whom Wilkinson described as "a most desperate Villain & a great Woodsman," had led Burr from Natchez through the forests of the Mississippi Territory as far as the Hinson home.[41] According to Ashley, Burr had known that he had been recognized by Perkins at Hinson's and had sent Ashley back to Wakefield "to ascertain the sentiments of the people," with the hope of bringing "700 men down . . . to Mobille."[42] Instead, Ashley had been arrested in Wakefield on 20 February, the day after Burr's arrest, and held until after Burr left Fort Stoddert. "Two days after Burr's departure," according to Gaines, Ashley "made his escape." A few days later, a mail carrier met Ashley "in the Wilderness about Sixty miles in the rear of Burr, riding a very fine Horse, and determined to overtake the party."[43] Crossing the South Carolina upcountry a few days behind Burr's escort, Ashley read an account of the arrest in the *Georgetown Gazette*. As "an act of justice" to Burr, Ashley wrote a rebuttal for publication. In particular, he insisted that Burr "was neither in disguise nor was he going to the Spaniards." "His dress was as usual," Ashley asserted, "except that he had on a pair of coarse overalls to preserve his pantaloons from being soiled."[44] Ashley's letter appeared in numerous newspapers but seems to have had little impact upon the popular understanding of Burr's arrest or appearance.

The process of restoring Burr's claims to gentility began almost as soon as he replaced his disguise with gentleman's dress. When he was arrested, Burr had no other clothes with him, having sent his German secretary, Charles Willie, with his baggage, papers, and slave by another route. As a result, as a number of writers between Fort Stoddert and Richmond reported, he was escorted "the whole way in the very dress in which he was taken."[45] Burr clearly understood the importance of acquiring proper attire. Within a day or two of his arrest, he already had the tailor at Fort Stoddert "doing some work" for him; the new clothes were not ready when he left the fort.[46] Once in Richmond, he quickly outfitted himself with a new wardrobe when visitors to his guarded room "offer[ed] him a change of linnen &c."[47] When he appeared before Marshall for his examination a few days later, Burr already wore clothes that were appropriate to his station; Governor William H. Cabell reported that he "looked as little like a criminal as any man in the room."[48] As Randolph remarked during a later phase of the trial, Burr's "nice linen & black silk suit" made it much harder to see him as a criminal; "felons [were] generally ragged lousy fellows."[49]

Increasingly, accounts of Burr's detection and arrest showed that the inherent conflict in the idea of a gentleman in disguise could be resolved in two ways. In the earliest versions, Burr's disguise compromised his gentility; later accounts insisted that his gentility had compromised his disguise. Accepting the incongruity of a gentleman in disguise, these accounts concluded not that someone in disguise must not be a true gentleman, but that a gentleman could never truly disguise himself. His innate quality, they suggested, would subvert any effort at concealment. Only one version of Perkins's narrative—in the *Enquirer*—provided any grounds for resolving the conflict in this manner. Recalling his efforts to persuade Gaines to return with him to Hinson's, Perkins remembered having said that, if neither of the men he had seen "proves to be Co. Burr, [and] the one I suspect, is a gentleman, he will think himself flattered for being mistaken."[50] In every account, though, Perkins made clear that his suspicions had been aroused not by any discrepancy between the first rider's appearance and his character, but by the two riders' decision to ride to a private home, over bad roads, in the middle of the night. And the only physical clue of Burr's identity that Perkins ever mentioned, Burr's eyes, had served only to confirm what he had already deduced from Burr's actions.

Even as the first accurate accounts of the arrest began to circulate, the potential for the story to slip into the realm of the fanciful became clear. As the editor of the *Intelligencer* remarked on reprinting the first, uncorrected, version from the *Enquirer*, the particular circumstances of Burr's arrest read like something from "the page of romance."[51] Soon, new explanations for Perkins's suspicions that were based on Burr's appearance rather than his actions began to appear. An early April letter from Richmond suggests how quickly the question arose of whether it was "the *'fire of his eyes,'* or his *'white slouched hat,'* a letter from Washington[, Mississippi Territory,] or the *surprising fact* of his leaving the comfortable enjoyment of a tavern and a fire, at a late hour of night, to encounter hazard of land and water [that] betrayed him to Perkins."[52] By the end of 1807, the triumph of romance over reality seemed assured. Though generally hostile to Burr, William Thompson's *A Compendious View of the Trial of Aaron Burr* (1807) developed at length the idea that Burr's gentility had trumped his disguise. "Through [his] disguised appearance," Thompson insisted, "there was still something that marked him for more than an ordinary man." Burr's "appearance formed a contrast with his manners, which could not be reconciled." Thompson began a process of embellishing the "romantic circumstances" of Burr's arrest that reached its apex in mid-nineteenth-century histories and biographies.[53]

In the mid-nineteenth century, accounts of Burr's detection and arrest four decades earlier seemed to be everywhere, from Montgomery's *Alabama Journal* to Tallahassee's *Floridian and Journal*, from the *Ladies' Repository* to the *North American Review*, from William H. Safford's *Life of Harman Blennerhassett* (1850, revised 1853) to James Parton's *Life and Times of Aaron Burr* (1858), and from Albert James Pickett's *History of Alabama* (1851) to Orville J. Victor's *History of American Conspiracies* (1863). Despite the wide range of publications and the long span of years, the mid-century story of this event was remarkably consistent. In its embellishments and its romanticism, moreover, this story looked very different from the one that had been told by Perkins in the spring of 1807. And it has continued to shape popular and scholarly works more than a century and a half later.

Central to this new story was an inversion of the common understanding of the relationship between Burr's gentility and his disguise that had shaped the early accounts. The new story, like the old, detailed Burr's appearance. Pickett, for example, described Burr's "disguise-dress" as "coarse pantaloons, made of homespun, of a copperas dye, and a round-about, of inferior drab cloth," accompanied by "a flapping, wide-brimmed beaver [i.e., hat], which had, in times past, been white, but now presented a variety of dingy colors."[54] But the new story preserved Burr's gentility by having it defeat his efforts to disguise himself. In Victor's retelling, Perkins quickly perceived that Burr, "though outwardly dressed in the rough garb of a common planter, was a person of mark."[55] Burr's clothes, according to Pickett, could not hide eyes that "sparkled like diamonds" and "a pair of exquisitely shaped boots." Nor did his disguise square with "his splendid horse, . . . fine saddle[,] and new holsters."[56] An article in the *Ladies Repository* had Burr spotted by first Mrs. Hinson and later Perkins largely because his "character and attire . . . by no means corresponded." "Though coarsely dressed," Burr "exhibited a lofty and gentlemanly bearing utterly inconsistent with his apparent condition."[57] Although Parton at least mentioned the real issue—"the lateness of the hour"—that had aroused Perkins's suspicions, he still emphasized Burr's physical appearance and refined presence: his "striking features," "the incongruity of his dress, [and] his superior air."[58] Even a wildly erroneous account from this period that excluded Perkins entirely still had Mrs. Hinson seeing through Burr's disguise due to "the vivacity of his countenance and his courtly demeanor."[59]

Such a romanticized tale could also easily accommodate discussions of Burr's ability to "fascinate" men—something that had been mentioned repeatedly before, during, and after the Burr crisis, but not in the specific context of Burr's arrest. In the new story, Burr's powers of fascination appeared most clearly in his relations with his captors. Most of the longer versions spun a tale in which Perkins never entered the Hinson home, instead sending Sheriff Brightwell inside to confirm that the mysterious traveller was Burr. As Perkins "shiver[ed] with cold" outside the home, according to Pickett, Brightwell "became fascinated with Colonel Burr" and grew "sorry that he had sought to arrest him."[60] As Parton described the scene, "the traveler with the sparkling eyes led the conversation in so sprightly a manner, was so polite and grateful to the lady, and made himself so agreeable generally, that the heart of the sheriff relented."[61] Pickett, Safford, Parton, and other mid-century authors further highlighted Burr's powers of fascination in recounting his journey from Fort Stoddert to Richmond. They recast the pledge that had been made by Perkins and the party's civilians as an attempt to guard against Burr's seductive influence. This tale had more basis than that of Perkins outside the Hinson home. Gaines had feared that Burr could corrupt the soldiers at the fort, who were "almost continually intoxicated," though he had worried not about Burr's commanding presence, but about his bribing the sentinels.[62] Gaines and Perkins had considered it crucial, moreover, that the party consist of men in whom they had confidence—what Gaines called "confidential young men."[63] But there is nothing in Perkins's accounts, or in other contemporary sources, to support the fancies of the mid-century writers. In the later retellings, as the article in the *Ladies' Repository* explained, Perkins "knew the fascinations of Burr, and feared their power upon his men and also upon himself."[64] Before leaving for Washington, according to Pickett, Perkins "obtained the most solemn pledge" that his men "would not suffer the prisoner to influence them, in any manner, in his behalf."[65] Each man had to agree, as Parton put it, "to steel his soul against the prisoner's winning arts, and indeed to avoid all conversation with him."[66]

A single, brief incident effectively captures the new story's inversion of the early stories of Burr's arrest. After more than a week on the road, Burr's escort stopped in a remote village in Georgia. According to a contemporary account, the innkeeper "asked the officer, in a tone expressive of his honest indignation, 'if he knew what had become of that *rascal* Burr and his army.'" Still in disguise, Burr announced: "I am the man they call Burr." To which, the innkeeper sarcastically replied, "why really I did not think he was as likely a fellow as you are." Burr, according to this report, was "mortified by receiving the execrations of his [host]."[67] In mid-century accounts, this story was reversed. No longer did the simple innkeeper humiliate the well-born Burr. As related by Pickett, when the innkeeper asked about "the traitor," Burr's guards were "annoyed and embarrassed, hung down their heads, and made no reply." But Burr "majestically raised his head, and flashing his fiery eye upon [the innkeeper], said, 'I am Aaron Burr!—what is it you want with me?'" According to Pickett, the innkeeper "trembled like a leaf"— "struck with the keenness of [Burr's] look, the solemnity of his voice and the dignity of his manner."[68] As first reported, this incident fit with the early story of republican virtue triumphing over aristocratic treason; in Pickett's hands, it preserved Burr's gentility at the expense of both his guards and the innkeeper.

In one sense, the emergence of a new story about Burr's detection and arrest that was so consistent when read across different authors and so inconsistent when compared with the earliest accounts is easily explained. All of the mid-century works ultimately derived from a common author, Pickett. Both Safford and Parton drew heavily from Pickett's history. In both the *Life of Harman Blennerhassett* and the *Blennerhassett Papers* (1864), Safford simply acknowledged in his chapter on the arrest that "the whole of the incidents" came from Pickett's work, "the exact language" of which he had adopted "with but few exceptions."[69] While Parton did not go so far as to quote Pickett in full and even added his own inventions, he did state that "most of the facts and incidents relating to Burr's arrest" in his work came from Pickett's history.[70] For his *History of American Conspiracies*, Victor started with Parton's account, "stripp[ed] it of embellishment," and, in doing so, ended up with something very close to Pickett's story.[71] The mid-century magazine versions appeared either in reviews of one of the book versions or as narratives that were derived from those works. And the newspaper accounts generally excerpted the eleven-page pamphlet that was Pickett's first published version.

Tracing the new story of Burr's arrest through the array of mid-century articles and books to Pickett's account explains why the various versions looked so similar to each other, but not why the new story looked so different from the old ones. Toward that end, we need to look more closely at Pickett's account, whether as a separate pamphlet, a newspaper article, or a lengthy chapter in his *History of Alabama*. In addition to being a cotton planter near Montgomery, Alabama, Pickett was a serious historian. Like a number of early historians of the trans-Appalachian West, such as Samuel P. Hildreth in Ohio and John Dabney Shane in Kentucky, Pickett worked diligently at mid-century to record the history of his state before the pioneer generation disappeared. He not only read government documents, private memoirs, and old newspapers, but also identified men and women from key moments of Alabama's past and arranged to see their papers or to interview them. For his chapter on Burr's arrest, Pickett tried to contact Nicholas Perkins, only to learn that he had died in Tennessee in January 1848. He also wrote to Edmund Gaines, only to discover that the former commander had lost most of his early papers in "the wreck of a boat in Mobile, in the year 1813."[72] As a result, his account of Burr's arrest relied heavily upon interviews with two men, Thomas Malone and George Strother Gaines, and two women, Mrs. Hinson and a Mrs. Howse.

Pickett's most distinctive sources for Burr's arrest were inherently problematic. Each of his interviewees was being asked to recall an event that had occurred four decades earlier and been written and talked about ever since. None of them had witnessed every incident of Burr's detection and arrest, from his late-night ride into Wakefield on 18 February until his arrival in Richmond more than a month later. Malone was the best situated of Pickett's sources, but he had stayed at Wakefield courthouse when Perkins and Brightwell left for the Hinson home and had not seen Burr again until the escort took charge of the prisoner. Mrs. Hinson had witnessed some of the interactions among the four men at her home. George Strother Gaines—the brother of the commander at Fort Stoddert—had been at the fort when Perkins arrived seeking assistance and had remained there throughout Burr's stay. Mrs. Howse had merely seen Burr with the escort. Finally, in neither of the surviving accounts, Malone's or Gaines's, did the interviewees limit themselves to their own experiences. Gaines's recollections, for example, included a full account of Perkins's thoughts and actions that drew on the conversation between Perkins and his brother that had awoken him "about sun up" on 19 February 1807.[73]

Many of the simple, factual errors that made it into the new story of Burr's arrest had their origins in Pickett's interviews. A comparison of Pickett's surviving notes from the interviews with Perkins's three accounts reveals numerous discrepancies, many of which Pickett avoided in his publications. Malone placed Burr and Ashley's arrival in Wakefield in January, rather than February, and had Burr asking Perkins for a tavern, rather than Perkins asking Ashley about the riders' destination. Gaines's recounting of the incidents in Wakefield and at the Hinson home, relying as it did on memories of an early-morning conversation that he had merely overheard, is replete with mistakes. His version had Burr and Ashley arriving in Wakefield at "a little after dark," rather than near midnight; Burr riding up to the courthouse door, rather than continuing down the street; and Burr asking Malone or Brightwell for directions, rather than Perkins questioning Ashley. Even when discussing things that he had experienced himself, Gaines's memory also failed, perhaps because he had been "suffering from sickness" during Burr's stay at the fort. His recollection that Burr remained at Fort Stoddert for "about three weeks" seems to have been the source of Pickett's incorrect, but still-accepted, statement that Burr departed on 5 March, rather than 23 February.[74]

Some of the romantic fancies that figured so prominently in the new story of Burr's arrest also derived from Pickett's interviewees. Malone claimed that the sworn agreement among the civilians of the escort party had included a promise "that none of them were to converse with [Burr] except when it was absolutely necessary because he was a fascinating man & might lead some of the party to befriend him." He also provided some foundation for Pickett's inversion of the story of Burr's encounter with the Georgia innkeeper. And he remembered that Burr's "eyes looked like 'stars' [with] large projecting pupils."[75] But Malone also recalled, correctly, that it was Burr's actions that had roused Perkins's suspicions, not his appearance. Gaines, in contrast, claimed that Perkins had been struck first by Burr's "large black penetrating eyes" and then by his clothes and horse. According to Gaines, Perkins had instantly recognized that Burr's "coarse grey round about & pantaloons of the same" squared with neither his "fashionable hat & boots" nor his fine horse with its "elegant saddle & bridle."[76]

Tracing the embellishments and romanticizations in the mid-nineteenth century story of Burr's arrest back through Pickett's publications to his interviews with Malone and, especially, Gaines only takes us so far. Pickett did not simply disseminate Malone's and Gaines's fancies to a larger audience. Working with a group of differing and even conflicting accounts, presumably including one or two of Perkins's statements, Pickett assembled a story that made Burr's genteel refinement shine through his plain clothes and his aristocratic qualities triumph over his common antagonists. Pickett's narrative choices strengthened his interpretation, describing Burr's disguise six pages after detailing the eyes, boots, and horse that allowed Perkins to see through it. More importantly, he decided to devote a lengthy chapter of his state history to an event that, as one reviewer remarked, "in no way . . . affect[ed] the history of Alabama, the events in her career, or the features of her people."[77] And Pickett left no doubt that he sought to redeem Burr in popular thinking, especially in the pamphlet version. Believing that Burr had intended only to liberate Texas, Pickett claimed that his principal failing was that he had lived "at too early a period." Accordingly,

Pickett charged "young Alabamians" to remember "Col. Burr's brilliant military and civil services."[78]

In Burr, Pickett seems to have found a perfect embodiment of the characteristics that Romantic-era southerners celebrated. In painting, literature, architecture, and other arts, Romanticism displayed a fascination with the past, with cultural forms and practices that had been lost or that survived only as ruins and fragments. By the mid-nineteenth century, many elite southerners saw themselves as the true, even the only, inheritors of the values of medieval courts. In their view, the rest of the nation, and much of Europe, had abandoned the once-admired traits of bravery, gentility, chivalry, and adventurousness in a misguided dream of egalitarianism and an all-consuming pursuit of profit. It is easy to see how Burr—with his military service, his deadly duel, his western project, and his polished manners—could have embodied this lost culture for Pickett.[79]

But the new story of Burr spread far beyond the South and was repeated or expanded by authors who were not southerners, such as Safford and Parton. And the rise of a Romantic sensibility—which was not limited to the South, though it was especially strong there—was not the only cultural change in the decades after Burr's arrest. Even at the time of the arrest, some Americans had been attracted to an aristocratic culture that seemed to conflict with their republican politics. The democratization of American politics by mid-century made an aristocratic culture seem even more appealing to some people, partly because it made a truly aristocratic politics less likely and less threatening. The accompanying social and economic changes of these decades—the growth and dispersal of the population, the emergence of new class lines, the instability of wealth and position, and other factors—also fueled new anxieties about masks and deceptions. At mid-century, the personification of these anxieties was the "confidence man," who exploited the social and economic fluidity to present himself as something better than he actually was, whether to win the hand of a respectable woman or to fleece the pocketbook of a wealthy victim. The new story of Burr's arrest both drew upon and played with these cultural changes. In an inversion of the confidence man, Burr tried to present himself as something worse than he actually was; he failed only because of the intensity of his aristocratic qualities. "Even under the most desperate circumstances," Pickett insisted, Burr "was ever . . . the man of lofty dignity and noble bearing."[80]

"The circumstances attending [Burr's] arrest," as the editor of the *Intelligencer* immediately recognized, were "so strikingly singular, that they could scarcely fail . . . to excite the interest of the reader."[81] While this event continued to capture readers' interest throughout the nineteenth century, many of its "singular" characteristics were lost over time. People, and peoples, misremember past events. At times, they do so through simple error. At other times, they do so in ways that make for better stories—stories that are more coherent as narratives, more entertaining to their readers and auditors, and more relevant for their times. Simple errors are accidental. Better stories—the qualities that make some stories more coherent, entertaining, and relevant than others— are cultural. For new authors and new audiences, shifting ideas of gentility, aristocracy, class, and self-presentation between early republican and mid-nineteenth-century America made the new story of Burr's arrest seem better than the old. Both stories, old and new, recognized a problem when dress and status did not match; they resolved this problem in opposing ways, first challenging and later reaffirming Burr's gentility.

CHAPTER 8

RICHMOND, VIRGINIA

March through October 1807

BY THE TIME THAT AARON BURR AND HIS CAPTORS ARRIVED IN LATE March 1807, Richmond had become the most important city in the nation's most powerful state. First plotted at the fall line on the James River in 1737, Richmond had grown slowly but steadily, becoming Henrico County's political center after 1752. Still, at the start of the Revolution, it had remained a small cluster of homes, shops, and tobacco warehouses below the falls along Shockoe Creek. In 1779, the General Assembly had made Richmond the new state capital. Over the next three decades, the city grew in extent and population. By 1810, with nearly ten thousand inhabitants, three-eighths of whom were enslaved and another eighth of whom were free blacks, Richmond would overtake Norfolk as Virginia's most populous city. As it expanded up the river and away from the bottomlands, the city entered a broken terrain of steep hills and deep gullies. One early nineteenth-century traveller described its location as "much the finest site in Virginia"; another called it "a beautiful place" with an impressive view across the falls.[1] The difficulties of actually making one's way around such a landscape on a daily basis were better captured by a resident. In 1858, former president John Tyler recalled that, fifty years earlier, Richmond had been "untamed and broken," with "almost inaccessible heights and deep ravines."[2] This topography long divided the city.

In 1807, Richmond's economic core remained the river. The original settlement along Shockoe Creek still served as its primary link to distant markets, though a state-owned warehouse and improved port facilities at Rockett's Landing, further downriver, provided another center for ocean-going commerce. Just as the river below the falls tied Richmond to the Atlantic world, the river above the falls connected it

A View of Richmond from Below Mayo's Bridge, 1807.

FIGURE 12. View of Richmond, with the capitol building and
state penitentiary on the horizon.

to an agricultural hinterland. From the Piedmont's plantations and
farms, products flowed toward Richmond. In 1800, the James River
Canal Company had brought these goods into the city itself with a
canal around the falls that ended in a basin in west Richmond. Various
businesses sprang up around the basin, while gristmills and an armory
appeared along the falls. White, free-black, and slave carters and dray-
ers carried goods between river bateaux in the basin and ocean-going
vessels at Shockoe Creek and Rockett's Landing. The bottomlands
along the river developed into a largely working-class, mixed-race
district of small homes, boardinghouses, drinking and gambling dens,
and brothels; such districts commonly emerged among the warehouses
and wharves of port cities.

On the heights above stood what one traveller called "the pleasantest
part of the town," with most of the public buildings and the finest
homes.[3] Some impressive homes and buildings had been built on
Church Hill, east of Shockoe Creek, beginning in the 1740s. More
were constructed on Shockoe (later Capitol) Hill, west of the creek,
after the 1770s. Towering above the city and "of great importance to
[its] beauty" was the capitol building, which Thomas Jefferson had designed.[4] The planned Capitol Square was to include the state courthouse and the governor's residence, but, after three decades, as Tyler
recalled, the area "was *ruda indigestaque moles* [a rude, undigested mass],

and was but rudely, if at all, enclosed." Between Capitol Square and the river stood the brick storefronts of Main Street, "the chief pride of the city."[5] On the opposite side of the square was Richmond's finest neighborhood, the Court End, where many of the men who played prominent roles in Burr's trial lived. The defense attorneys Benjamin Botts, Edmund Randolph, and John Wickham, the prosecuting attorneys George Hay and Alexander McRae, and Chief Justice John Marshall—all lived within a few blocks of each other.

Richmond's elite shaped a society that one traveller described in 1805 as "very hospitable"; "the refinements & pleasures of its inhabitants," another visitor wrote that year, "more than keep pace with [its] growth."[6] Early nineteenth-century Richmond had dancing masters, painting and drawing instructors, and various schools and tutors, but no college, since its elite sent their sons to the College of William and Mary in the old capital. Social outlets abounded, as well. In 1807, Richmond's elite could stroll in pleasure gardens, dance at public balls, bet on horse races, and attend theatrical or musical performances. Gentlemen gambled at quoits at Buchanan's Spring a mile west of Capitol Square; many of Richmond's ladies had been caught up in a craze for the card game loo a few years before Burr's trial.

The roughly equal balance of Federalists and Republicans in the Court End belied the political imbalance in Richmond as a whole. Republicans dominated city, as they did state, politics. The balance of political power in Richmond appeared in its newspapers. Before Burr's arrival, three of Richmond's four newspapers—the *Virginia Argus*, the *Enquirer*, and the misleadingly named *Impartial Observer*—were Republican. In December 1806, the editor of the *Observer* had described the *Argus* as "first in rank" and its editor, Samuel Pleasants Jr., as "an inflexible republican." The *Argus* may have carried more weight locally, but it was Thomas Ritchie's *Enquirer* that was becoming one of the country's leading Republican prints. The *Observer* itself had a troubled existence. Samuel Brooks had begun it in May 1806, pledging that it would be open to all parties and tied to none. Barely a month later, it had passed to Thomas Manson, who "unequivocally avow[ed] democratic principles" and preserved the stance of impartiality only by declaring that "the democratic republicans [were not] *a party*."[7] Manson published the *Observer* until January 1807, when Brooks tried to revive the failing newspaper with a former governor vouching for its "genuine republican principles."[8] Only one newspaper, the *Virginia Gazette*, served the Federalists. It was poorly run, functioning primarily as "a mere copying machine" of Federalist material from elsewhere.[9] "The poor Federalist is poor indeed," a visiting Massachusetts Federalist lamented; "his voice is no more heard, and he lives only at the mercy of his enemies."[10] Richmond was the place where the Burr crisis was to be justified and the Burr Conspiracy proven.

"THE FAR FAMED TRIAL OF AARON BURR"

Between late March and late October 1807, Burr's trial in Richmond became the nation's first great legal spectacle, with a famous defendant, high-profile lawyers, a significant crime, and intense media coverage. The defendant was no mere celebrity, but a former vice president. The lawyers were not just renowned litigators but included a former attorney general and secretary of state (Edmund Randolph), the lieutenant governor of Virginia (Alexander McRae), and a renowned belletrist (William Wirt). The crime was the highest imaginable, treason. And the coverage was so pervasive that the trial was said to "[engross] the attention of the country to the exclusion of every other subject."[11] But Burr's trial had even more. The grand jury's foreman was John Randolph, the congressional leader of the anti-administration Quids; its members included the governor's brother and some of Virginia's most prominent men. And the judge was the country's highest ranking and most influential jurist, Chief Justice John Marshall. "Whether we consider the nature of the crime or the character of the criminals[,] the witnesses who will be brought up, the council by whom it will be argued, or the eager curiousity of the nation," the *Enquirer* asserted just days after Burr's arrival, "this will be one of the most impressive spectacles which this or any other city in the U.S. has ever witnessed."[12]

Burr's trial attracted so much attention, in part, because such critical issues seemed to be at stake. What those issues were, however, varied from person to person and party to party. Both the Delaware Republican George Read and the Maryland Federalist Luther Martin considered the trial "of infinite importance"; Martin, one of Burr's attorneys, described it as "infinitely the most important of any which ha[d] ever taken place in this Country."[13] Attorney General Caesar A. Rodney captured a common Republican perspective when he wrote that "the safety peace & happiness of the Country demand[ed] that examples should be made of Burr" and his key supporters.[14] In contrast, Martin voiced a common Federalist assessment when he insisted that the trial would answer the crucial "question whether any Citizen can be safe when Government from the basest of Motives wish to hunt him down."[15] The fundamental question in Burr's trial could be seen as either: does the Constitution provide adequate means to protect the government from individuals, *or* does the Constitution provide adequate means to protect individuals from the government? Most accounts of the trial focus upon the central legal issues. Often written by lawyers or legal scholars, these works typically highlight the attorneys' arguments and the judge's opinions. Some emphasize the important precedents that emerged from the trial more than the verdicts. Others assess the various steps and missteps taken by the prosecution, defense, and judge that produced its outcomes. These works generally mention each of the trial's five distinct stages but emphasize the grand jury hearings and treason trial. Such works rarely ignore the drama in the courtroom; there are too many fascinating characters and absorbing moments for that. But it generally remains secondary to the legal issues.[16]

The first stage ended before most of the country even knew it had begun. Just days after arriving in Richmond, Burr was examined by Marshall, as judge of the federal circuit court, in a private room at the Eagle Tavern. With "multitudes" wanting "admission to this secret conclave," the examination resumed the next day at the capitol before an immense "concourse of citizens."[17] It concluded the following day, 1 April, when Marshall handed down his ruling. Wickham, Randolph, and Burr himself served as defense counsel, while Attorney General Rodney and district attorney Hay appeared for the prosecution. The examination would determine whether there was enough evidence to hold Burr on charges of treason or misdemeanor. While the administration had rushed Rodney to Richmond, it had not had time to compile and organize its evidence. Marshall had to base his decision primarily upon what he had seen six weeks earlier, when the Supreme Court had heard the cases of Justus Erich Bollman and Samuel Swartwout: the cipher letter, General James Wilkinson's affidavits, and William

Eaton's deposition. The only new testimony came from Nicholas Perkins and concerned Burr's arrest. Marshall decided that there was no evidence of a treasonable act, even if there might be evidence of treasonable intent. He charged Burr with organizing a military expedition against a friendly nation and scheduled his trial for the court's next session in late May. The government could also present a case for treason then. Burr arranged bail for the misdemeanor and went free, remaining in Richmond until late April before travelling to Philadelphia.[18]

The second stage of Burr's trial was everything that the first was not: anticipated, protracted, and complicated. Even before the court met on 22 May, observers speculated about the outcome. Some predicted that Burr would not return to Richmond; others calculated that Wilkinson would not leave New Orleans for fear of exposure. Some trusted that Burr would be indicted; others expected the whole thing to "end in Smoke," with Burr emerging unscathed.[19] Some viewed the entire proceeding as a "political prosecution"; others considered it "a mere farce."[20] It certainly seemed doomed to become one as the grand jury waited more than three weeks for the arrival of Wilkinson and the original cipher letter before hearing testimony. During those weeks, the attorneys battled over various issues, and Marshall ruled on a half-dozen points. After news arrived on 11 June that Wilkinson had reached Virginia, the grand jury began its secret proceedings. For the next fifteen days, the trial proceeded on two fronts—in open court, where the attorneys argued various questions and the judge issued opinions, and behind closed doors, where witnesses testified and the grand jurors considered bills of indictment.[21]

The first battle concerned the grand jury's size and composition. Joseph Scott, the federal marshal, had carefully selected "the ablest and most respectable men in our Country to Serve as grand Jurors."[22] Problems had arisen nonetheless. Scott had summoned twenty-four men, as required. When some had failed to show, he summoned more. The defense objected. Marshall agreed that Scott could not call replacements until the pool fell below the legal minimum of sixteen. He also accepted a defense argument that jurors could be removed for cause, allowing Burr to strike three Republicans who seemed especially inveterate against him. These decisions shocked many Republicans and left the grand jury with just sixteen men. One Federalist viewed the jury as composed "of 14 Members, not Federalists—but they are not Jacobins—& 2 Federalists."[23] But Jefferson counted "2 feds, 4 Quids & 10 republicans" and questioned whether such a jury was "a fair representation of the state."[24] Since any indictment would require twelve votes, the jury's size and composition favored Burr. The "violent opposers of the administration"—the Federalists and Quids—seemed likely to cooperate to prevent an indictment.[25]

After this initial dispute, the trial proceeded slowly—"*Inch by Inch*," according to one Virginian.[26] Much of the court's time was filled "with the sparring of the counsel"; as one witness noted, "decisions on the most trifling points do not take place in less than a day."[27] A major conflict erupted in early June when the defense asked the court to subpoena the president to produce Wilkinson's letter of 21 October 1806, which Jefferson had mentioned in his message to Congress, and any administration letters and orders that had responded to it. This motion produced four days of bitter debate that included some of the ugliest invective of the entire trial, particularly from defense attorney Martin and prosecuting attorney Wirt. In his ruling, Marshall charged "both sides [with] act[ing] improperly in the style and spirit of their remarks."[28] He decided that a sitting president could be subpoenaed and issued a subpoena duces tecum for the papers. That decision put Jefferson in a difficult position and produced an early statement of what would later be called executive privilege. Jefferson approved the release of the Wilkinson letter but instructed Hay to withhold any parts that were "not directly material for the purposes of justice." He refused to provide the administration's ensuing correspondence, which "would amount to the laying open [of] the whole executive books."[29] Additional papers would be made available, Jefferson pledged, but the defense would have to specify which documents it sought. He insisted, moreover, that the court could not compel his own or his cabinet members' attendance, because "comply[ing] with such calls" across the United States "would leave the nation without an executive branch."[30]

On 13 June, with the courtroom proceedings drawing huge crowds and filling newspaper columns, the grand jury commenced its secret hearings. Nearly four dozen witnesses had been brought to Richmond to establish the prosecution's case; almost all of them testified. Most could either speak to Burr's intentions—including William Eaton, the

Hendersons (Alexander and John), the Morgans (George, John, and Thomas), Benjamin Stoddert, and Thomas Truxton—or describe the events on Blennerhassett Island—including Jacob Allbright, Peter Taylor, David Wallace, and Dudley Woodbridge Jr. Some testified at great length; Wilkinson required two full and two partial days "to discharge" what the New Yorker Washington Irving described as his "wondrous cargo" "of *words*."[31] But most spoke only briefly. The grand jury heard from half of the witnesses on just two of the ten days of testimony. To everyone's surprise, the jurors kept the testimony secret. "Not the least particle of evidence," one Richmonder noted, "has been suffered to leak out."[32] As a result, no one could confidently predict the outcome. Some expected that Burr would be indicted, others that he would not, at least on the treason charge. But no one had solid ground for their predictions. Accordingly, even "the knowing ones" were surprised when the jurors handed down indictments for treason and misdemeanor against Burr and Harman Blennerhassett on 24 June and against Jonathan Dayton, Davis Floyd, Israel Smith, John Smith, and Comfort Tyler the next day.[33]

Burr's treason trial, the third stage, was scheduled for 3 August. After a grand jury hearing unlike any "from the beginning of the world to this day," in Hay's words, many predicted a long, difficult, and controversial trial, first for Burr and then for each of the other six.[34] Marshall expected to be called upon to make critical decisions. He asked other Supreme Court justices for their views on three "points of difficulty." The most important concerned "the doctrine of constructive treasons," a broadening of the constitutional definition of treason that had been adopted in the Bollman and Swartwout decision and relied upon by the grand jury; without it, the jurors could not have returned four of the seven treason indictments, including Burr's. The others addressed evidentiary questions: Could "the declarations or confessions" of one party to a conspiracy be used against other parties? And could an overt act of levying war outside of Virginia be used as evidence of treason in Virginia?[35] Like Marshall, Wirt expected that the trial would "be perpetually interrupted by questions to the court." After "struggl[ing] through this thorny labyrinth for four or five weeks," he predicted, "then the court & bar are to be annoyed for just as long a time by motions to the court to instruct the jury in the doctrines of evidence & treason and all this before the argument can begin to the jury."[36] When Wickham wrote in mid-July that the trial "cannot last many Days," he voiced a rare perspective indeed.[37]

In many ways, the four weeks of the treason trial fulfilled Wirt's fears by reenacting the worst aspects of the grand jury stage. The proceedings were again delayed waiting for witnesses; with one hundred and forty of them, Eaton predicted in early August that he would return to Massachusetts "by Sleighing."[38] There was another battle over the jury's composition. Marshal Scott had called four dozen potential jurors, including a dozen from Wood County, the site of Blennerhassett Island; Burr rejected forty-four of them for cause. None of the twelve jurors who were finally sworn on 17 August came from west of the Blue Ridge; more than half were from Richmond and its environs. With the jury selected, Hay opened the case for the prosecution. "With great anxiety," according to one witness, the audience "attentively listened to the Prosecutor & the greatest silence prevailed."[39] The prosecution proceeded to call witnesses, intending first to establish Burr's treasonable intentions and then to prove that the needed military preparations had occurred on Blennerhassett Island. The defense quickly challenged this approach. It demanded that the prosecution first produce two witnesses to the same overt act, the constitutional requirement, before addressing whether Burr's designs were treasonous. Marshall granted the prosecution some leeway but cautioned it to stick to the offense that was named in the indictment—the levying of war on 10 December 1806 on Blennerhassett Island. Hay resumed with his witnesses, interspersing those who could speak to Burr's intentions with those who had been on the island. In general, the witnesses reiterated what they had told the grand jury, making public what had remained secret since June.

After just a few days of testimony from barely a dozen witnesses, the defense again objected. Everyone agreed that Burr was not on the island on 10 December. Therefore, the defense argued, evidence about either his intentions or the activities there was irrelevant. He simply could not have committed the overt act that the Constitution required at the place and time that the indictment specified. This motion curtailed further testimony and sparked more than a week of argument. Everyone understood that Marshall's decision would determine the trial's outcome. If the defense motion succeeded, one observer explained, "the effect will be a suspension of all further testimony as to the Guilt of the prisoner and his acquital of Course." Nearly every attorney spoke to the motion—Wickham, Randolph, Martin, Charles Lee, and Benjamin Botts, for the defense, and Hay, Wirt, and McRae, for the prosecution. Wickham gave "a very learned speech" of seven hours, before Randolph spoke for three more.[40] McRae answered with a day-long argument, and, on 25 August, Wirt produced the most famous argument of the entire trial. Botts and Martin answered Wirt, with Martin speaking for fourteen hours over two days. If the presidential subpoena had produced the harshest comments of the trial, this motion summoned forth what Marshall described as "a solidity of argument and a depth of research" that were "embellished" by "a degree of eloquence seldom displayed on any occasion."[41]

With the issue "argued in a manner worthy of its importance," Marshall handed down his decision on 31 August. In a long and labored opinion, he tried to clarify the Supreme Court's ruling in the Bollman and Swartwout cases. If that ruling had seemed to broaden treason by adopting the English common law view of constructive treason and accepting a loose definition of "levying war," Marshall's opinion marked a return to the language of the Constitution, strictly construed. As such, it formed a critical contribution to American treason law. Marshall did not wholly adopt the defense's position but did accept its ends. He suggested that no overt act of levying war had taken place on Blennerhassett Island and agreed that, whether one had or not, Burr could not be guilty of it because he was not there. "Of consequence," Marshall concluded, "all other testimony must be irrelevant."[42] Marshall's ruling, one observer immediately reported, "puts an end to the Trial for Treason."[43] The judge left the final decision with the jurors but provided no room for a guilty verdict. In Wirt's view, Marshall had "stepped in between Burr and death."[44] The prosecution had predicted this result weeks earlier. Even as the jury was being selected, Hay had warned Jefferson: "There is but one chance for the accused, and that is [a] good one because it rests with the Chief [Jus]tice," who might not consider the Bollman and Swartwout ruling "binding."[45]

With Burr's treason trial ended, the prosecution faced a choice. It could press the misdemeanor charge against Burr or ask Marshall to commit Burr and perhaps others for a new treason trial in another jurisdiction; both options might be pursued if the misdemeanor trial came first. The prosecution's hopes for the fourth stage of Burr's trial were always limited. "We Shall be defeated there too," Hay bluntly informed Jefferson.[46] The misdemeanor trial seemed certain to founder on the same shoals as the treason trial—Burr's absence from Blennerhassett Island on 10 December. But pressing the misdemeanor charge could serve other goals. Hay clearly viewed it as a way to buy time to receive further direction from the administration. Jefferson's instructions made clear that the administration saw it as a way to produce and publicize more testimony against Burr. In a condensed form, the misdemeanor trial reenacted elements of the earlier stages. Once again, Marshall heard defense motions that were designed to frustrate or humiliate the prosecution, including another request to subpoena a document—in this case, Wilkinson's letter to Jefferson of 12 November 1806. Once again, the defense tried to limit the evidence that could be introduced. Once again, the attorneys on both sides bolstered their positions with argumentation and eloquence. Once again, Marshall's rulings generally supported the defense; "as in the trial for treason, so in this," one Virginian remarked, "every point of importance is decided in favor of Burr."[47] And, once again, the trial ended suddenly with Burr's acquittal. "Marshall," Wirt wrote on 14 September, "has again arrested the evidence."[48]

Burr's trial entered its final stage on 16 September when Hay moved to have Burr, Blennerhassett, and Israel Smith committed for treason in Kentucky, the Mississippi Territory, or elsewhere. Contemporaries considered the committal hearing an anticlimax; early in the process, one observer noted that "the Court, Bar, Witnesses & byestanders appear[ed] to be entirely worn out & wearied with the subject."[49] And historians have rarely paid it much attention. But the committal hearing developed into one of the longest and most interesting stages of the trial, finally ending on 20 October. It also raised an important legal question: how would the constitutional prohibition against "double jeopardy" work in a federal system? Did Burr's acquittal of treason in one jurisdiction mean that he could not be tried for the same treason in another jurisdiction? Could assembling men and arms to levy war against the United States at the mouth of the Cumberland River in Kentucky or at

Bayou Pierre in the Mississippi Territory even be considered the same treason as the one for which he had been acquitted? The defense argued that Burr could not be tried for treason in another jurisdiction. The prosecution insisted that he could, particularly since Marshall had barred testimony about overt acts at places and times other than those in the indictment. Marshall had foreseen this problem in late June but had not settled the matter in his own mind even in mid-September.[50]

Unwilling to answer this "constitutional question . . . unless it [became] absolutely necessary," Marshall agreed to hear all of the evidence first; only if it established an overt act of treason somewhere would he decide.[51] With this ruling to open the committal hearing, the court displayed a new willingness to support the prosecution over the defense. Other than accepting a defense argument that the circuit court could not commit someone for trial in a territorial court, Marshall repeatedly ruled in the prosecution's favor. The change was widely noted. Writing to his daughter, Burr complained that Marshall had "gradually relaxed from former rules of evidence, and [would] now hear any thing, without regard to distance of time or place."[52] Accordingly, the prosecution enjoyed free rein to elicit evidence. Close to fifty witnesses took the stand, most of whom had not testified in the earlier stages. Most were called by the prosecution, but some appeared for the defense. Their testimony appeared in newspapers in the fall of 1807, achieving one of the administration's goals. On 20 October, Marshall finally ruled that, while there may have been treasonable intent, there was no overt act of treason to require a new trial. Still, he committed Burr and Blennerhassett for trial in Ohio on the misdemeanor, though it seemed unlikely that the cases would ever be prosecuted.

What one Virginian called "the far famed trial of Aaron Burr"—a trial that had "jostled the public mind from one end of the union to the other [and had] been the subject of speculation for all ranks of people from the sage politician do[wn] to the ignorant mechanic, and the simple and unlettered ploughman"—was finally over.[53] It had produced treason and misdemeanor indictments for Burr and six others. Burr had been acquitted on both charges; no one else had even been tried. All that remained from the Richmond trials were misdemeanor charges against Burr and Blennerhassett in Ohio. "The result of this trial," as one contemporary remarked, "seems to have pleased neither party."

Burr's "enemies" thought "he should have been convicted of treason, and censure[d] Judge Marshall for having decided many preliminary questions" in his favor. At the same time, his "friends" insisted "that after the acquittal at Richmond, he should [have been] exempt from further prosecution." In any case, after nearly seven months of examinations, hearings, and trials, "the public curiousity" appeared to be "completely satiated."[54]

"A RICH FIELD OF CHARACTER AND INCIDENT"

To focus upon the legal dimensions of Burr's trial, as most histories do, is to miss much of what contemporaries found so captivating. Before the grand jury stage concluded, the *Argus*, in a satirical piece that was modelled on a price current list, reported that the market was "overstocked" in "*Law Slang*" and "*Quibbling*."[55] Disputes over legal technicalities were not just uninteresting to most people; they were incomprehensible. Only a small fragment of those who followed the trial through newspapers or letters understood the issues that dominate most historical accounts. It was not only "ignorant mechanic[s]" and "unlettered ploughm[e]n" who were confused by the "very important law point[s] before the Court," moreover.[56] Reporting Marshall's 31 August opinion to the secretary of state, John Graham—the former secretary of the Orleans Territory—admitted that he could not explain it: "I did not hear him distinctly and if I had I could not have followed his reasoning as it was bottomed on legal principles which I did not understand."[57] Precedent-setting decisions and trial-changing maneuvers meant little to most contemporaries, who regularly downplayed even the verdict in favor of uncovering the truth. "Bewildered" by the "unaccountable proceedings" in the courtroom, one witness simply sought "a full and clear development of truth in the case."[58] The *Enquirer* captured a common view when it reflected that, "whatever . . . may be the consequence of this arduous trial, there is one great sentiment which every honest heart will re-echo[:] May mystery expire; may the light of truth beam upon us; and may justice be faithfully rendered to every man."[59]

This widespread interest in uncovering the truth rather than securing a verdict ensured that the contemporary fascination with Burr's trial turned less on questions of law than on matters of character; the trial was expected to be, as author Washington Irving put it, "a rich field of character and incident."[60] Sorting truth from falsehood inevitably involved an evaluation of characters since a gentleman's veracity was central to his honor, and his honor was central to his character. Gentlemen rarely faced criminal charges and even more rarely faced equally genteel accusers. Long before Burr's trial began, it seemed clear that too many gentlemen had told too many conflicting stories. Some of them had to be lying. After hearing the indictments, Tennessee's Andrew Jackson reported "strong and bold Swearing before the grand jury, by three persons"; Burr raised Jackson's number tenfold, informing his daughter that "thirty at least have been perjured."[61] It was not just the characters of witnesses and defendants, but also of attorneys and judge, that could be helped or harmed by their statements and actions, moreover. For contemporaries, the most significant aspects of Burr's trial were those that revealed, counterposed, and confirmed or destroyed characters.

Establishing or undermining the characters of witnesses was critical for both sides throughout the trial. To Thomas Truxton, it seemed crucial "for the honor of the Govt" that "bad men or loose witnesses should be avoided." Writing to a friend with access to the administration, Truxton warned that press, public, and court would maintain "a watchful eye" and that "the validity of witnesses [would be] measured by integrity."[62] A variety of witnesses testified during the trial's different stages. Most of those with firsthand information about Burr's intentions were at least presumptively gentlemen. Some of the witnesses to events on and near Blennerhassett Island were likewise respected lawyers, merchants, planters, and officials from western Virginia and southern Ohio. But gentlemen regularly faced attacks on their honesty throughout the trial. One Federalist newspaper charged the administration with "destroying the character of the witnesses supposed to be favourable to [Burr]" through the press.[63] Conversely, shortly after being indicted, Burr prepared to undermine the stories of George, John, and Thomas Morgan, members of one of the most respected families in western Pennsylvania. Burr urged a New Jersey friend to send the names of "some men of higher grade" who could testify that "the characters of

George & John, whilst inhabitants of [his] State, were rather light & to say the least, equivocal in point of credit."[64]

William Eaton's experience as a witness is illustrative. Eaton could certainly claim the status of gentleman, with his high rank and government service. His accounts of Burr's plans had contributed to both popular understanding and legal proceedings, including Burr's initial examination, long before he appeared in Richmond. In Richmond, he testified in the grand jury, treason, and committal stages, confronting a skeptical audience each time. According to Burr, Eaton left the grand jury "in such rage and agitation that he shed tears, and complained bitterly that he had been questioned as if he were a villain."[65] Although the defense had no opportunity to challenge his grand jury testimony, Eaton was "exposed to the sarcasms and severity of [Burr's] attornies" throughout the trial, and Burr warned that he would destroy Eaton's character when he got the chance.[66] An opportunity finally arose during the committal hearing. Through its cross-examination of Eaton and its own witnesses, the defense sought "every possible resort," Eaton remarked, "to invalidate my testimony," including revealing an old arrest in Georgia and a court-martial.[67] Eaton claimed "a complete victory" in this battle, but many observers thought otherwise.[68]

Much of the crucial testimony about events on the island came from witnesses with no claim to genteel status, men that one wealthy merchant disparaged as "tag rag and bobtail."[69] Blennerhassett's servant William Love, hired hand Jacob Allbright, and gardener Peter Taylor, as well as the Marietta printer Samuel Fairlamb, all came to Richmond to testify. The very idea that "Blannerhassetts domestics" could testify against him unsettled elite observers.[70] "A man of [Blennerhassett's] refined sentiments," Botts argued, "would never have expressed himself on such a subject in such a manner to any man, and much less to such a man as Taylor."[71] The lack of respect for such men is apparent in something as basic as terms of address. One Federalist newspaper listed the first witnesses to appear before the grand jury as "Capt. *Decatur*, Commodore *Truxton*, Mr. *Eaton*, [and] *Peter (Blannerhasset's* gardener)."[72] Peter Taylor was denied not only a "Mr."—a mark of respectability, though not necessarily gentility—but even a surname. Without personal knowledge of many of the western witnesses, the grand jurors tried to use them to fix each other's characters. While questioning Edmund Dana about conversations with Blennerhassett and Tyler, for example, the jurors also asked him about Dudley Woodbridge, Simeon Poole, Peter Taylor, and Jacob Allbright. Dana praised the merchant Woodbridge and the magistrate Poole but described Taylor as "a labourer [who] called Bl[ennerhassett] master" and Allbright as one of "the most ignorant men he ever saw, [who] might be easily wrought upon," though he considered "both honest."[73] Attacks on the reputations of men from "the lowest order of Society" extended beyond the courtroom.[74] In early June, the *Observer* announced that Fairlamb had been discovered trying to incite a slave rebellion outside Richmond, managing, in just four sentences, to mention twice that "the offender" was a prosecution witness.[75]

Allbright and Taylor had important roles in Burr's trial as the "two positive witnesses to the fact of an armed assemblage" that the Constitution required.[76] As such, the prosecution worked hard to establish their honesty. After the grand jury hearings, it summoned extra witnesses from the West to support their "good, fair or honest character" in the treason trial.[77] The defense, in contrast, sought to destroy Allbright's and Taylor's characters, acting on the principle, as Burr explained in court, that "the object of cross examination is to degrade a witness if he merits it."[78] When Hay tried to defend Allbright as "a very honest man," though "a very ignorant" one, Burr responded: "ignorance is of the same nature as dishonesty in the hands of men who are artful."[79] This battle over Allbright's and Taylor's characters continued for months after the trial. Implicated in Burr's project by Taylor's testimony, Ohio senator John Smith assailed Taylor's veracity as he fought expulsion from the Senate in early 1808, while Smith's critics offered paeans to "the humble and honest gardener."[80]

Burr's trial also tested the characters of the attorneys. The trial brought together an amazing assemblage of legal talent, including most of what Wirt called "the grand climacteric characters of the American bar."[81] The strength of the attorneys' arguments, the eloquence of their speeches, the composure with which they faced the unexpected and unwelcome—all would reflect upon their characters. They would need to "[act] like men & . . . [acquit] themselves with honor."[82] Lapses were noticed and noted. One stenographer captured a near explosion when

Botts charged Wirt with trying "to prove a fact which he knew had no existence"; the "warm and animated" exchange that followed this assault upon Wirt's honor ended only when Marshall reassured the attorneys, and the assembled crowd, "that the evidence was such that different gentlemen might draw different inferences from it."[83] And Blennerhassett recorded in his diary a momentary slip by Hay, who, having been interrupted by his colleague McRae, "plainly exhibited his contempt for his coajutor . . . and then endeavour[ed] fruitlessly to compose" himself.[84]

Throughout the trial, the attorneys understood that their battles were being waged not only before the judge, but also for "the people behind the bar" and for the press.[85] "Two thirds of our Speeches," Hay informed Jefferson during the grand jury phase, "have been addressed to the people."[86] Blennerhassett even believed that one of Burr's counsel, John Baker, had been employed "more for the benefit of his influence out of doors" than for his impact in the courtroom, "where he [was] only of use thro' his humour and the freedom with which he lavishe[d] his abuse."[87] As the attorneys played for the crowds, the observers evaluated their talents. Countless letters included assessments of their merits and demerits. Governor William H. Cabell ranked all four of the attorneys who participated in the initial examination in a letter to his brother. Ohio's Elias Glover sent home his impressions of five attorneys early in the grand jury stage. Nathaniel Saltonstall Jr. evaluated six in a letter during the subpoena battle. These assessments varied widely. While Glover described Hay as "a man of talents & a handsome speaker," Saltonstall reported that Hay said "a great deal to little purpose." Conversely, even as Saltonstall viewed Randolph as "a Jiant of the Law [with] a most impressive manner," Glover considered him "incapable of nice discrimination."[88] Only Wickham and Wirt were uniformly praised for their courtroom performance; only Rodney was unequivocally criticized. After making an argument during the examination that Cabell described as "without form, & void," Rodney did not appear again in the trial.[89]

Of all of the attorneys, seven for the defense and four for the prosecution, during the five stages of Burr's trial, none provoked more comment than Luther Martin. Sketches of his character and assessments of his abilities appeared in diaries, letters, newspapers, and, later, books.

A non-signing member of the constitutional convention and former attorney general of Maryland, Martin had long been prominent in the Maryland bar. Even his bitterest foes admitted his extensive legal knowledge; even his greatest friends acknowledged his ungentlemanly personal habits. And everyone knew of his prodigious drinking, since he was intoxicated, as one witness remarked, "the most part of his time."[90] Martin's formal arguments defied every contemporary expectation for eloquence. "Never at a loss for ideas such as they are," one elite Richmonder remarked in a published letter, Martin was "often at a loss for words, his stock of which does not appear to be copious, nor his selections from that stock made with judgment." Still, even this critic noted that Martin's legal "reading appear[ed] to have been great."[91] In contrast, to Blennerhassett, Martin comprised "the whole rear-guard of Burr's Forensic Army"; yet even he described Martin as "rude" in manner, "ungrammatical" in language, and verbose in style, with habits that, "even upon the most solemn public occasions," were "gross and incapable of restraint."[92] Writing soon after the trial, William Thompson provided an apt summation of the controversial attorney: "I will not pretend to say, that the selection of this man was unfortunate for the prisoner; but I will say, that none could have been chosen, whose manners, whose habits, or whose principles, are less consonant to those of a Virginia gentleman."[93]

While the characters of witnesses and attorneys received careful attention, the characters that were most clearly on trial in Richmond were Burr's, Wilkinson's, and Marshall's, as the three crucial components of the trial—accused, accuser, and adjudicator. Those who commented upon the trial, privately and publicly, paid great attention to the appearance and actions of these men. Contemporary thinking about sensibility posited a direct relationship between one's internal state—one's emotions—and one's external appearance—one's countenance, composure, and movements. One's face and body could be expected to reveal one's true character, especially in stressful situations. When the *Enquirer* launched a series of essays on the recently concluded trial in late October, it promised "three great portraits" of these men. According to their author, everything about the trial that required comment could "very properly fall under one of these heads."[94]

Observers watched Burr throughout the trial, expecting his body language and facial expressions to provide evidence that might be more reliable than that of the witnesses. Facing both his accusers and "the finishing cord" of the hangman's noose, Burr could not help but physically manifest his guilt or innocence.[95] Whether defenders of Burr or not, most observers admired his composure. Supporters filled their letters with praise of his appearance and behavior. To Irving, Burr seemed to wear "the same serene and placid air that he would show were he brought there to plead another man's cause, and not his own."[96] Burr's critics charged that these repeated exclamations of "how collected; how composed; how elegant his language; . . . how graceful and commanding his attitudes" were merely intended to redeem his reputation as a "*Great Man*."[97] But even those who questioned Burr's innocence often acknowledged his composure. "Nothing that is said (and there has been some severe things) affects a mustle," one observer reported during the grand jury stage.[98] Decades later, Winfield Scott, who had witnessed the trial as a young law student before achieving fame as an army officer, remembered Burr standing "on the brink of danger, as composed, as immovable, as one of Canova's living marbles."[99]

But Burr was not merely a defendant, he was also an attorney of great renown. His legal talents provided a way for him to assert his character and "restore his fame." As Blennerhassett put it, Burr seemed to hope that "the Little Emperor at Cole's Creek [might] be forgotten in the Attorney at Richmond"—that the display of Burr's forensic skills at the trial might supplant memories of his miniscule force and humiliating surrender in the Mississippi Territory.[100] Burr sought to put the prosecution, in general, and its key witnesses, in particular, on trial. Before the grand jury stage, he assured his daughter that, if he had "the same means," he "could not only foil the prosecutors, but render them ridiculous and infamous," destroying not only their case, but also their characters.[101] Whenever Burr (or his attorneys) excoriated the administration or exposed a weakness in its case, supportive newspapers proclaimed victory. When it followed news of Burr's acquittal of treason with a report of his effort to force Jefferson to surrender more papers, for example, the *New-York Evening Post* announced: "the pig got loose and killed the butcher."[102] But Burr's reliance on what were seen as legal technicalities could work against him. The motion to stop testimony in the treason trial, according to one Richmonder, was "viewed by some people as a dishonorable attempt in Burr to *clean off*."[103]

If Burr tried to conceal the shame of being the defendant behind the triumph of being an attorney, Wilkinson's role unexpectedly oscillated between accuser and accused. To the administration and its allies, Wilkinson was the crucial witness. His disclosures had produced Jefferson's proclamation against the conspiracy; his rendering of the cipher letter had shaped the popular understanding of Burr's plans and movements. He had met with Burr's agents in the Southwest, acquiring additional information about the project. His testimony before the grand jury, a writer in the *Enquirer* predicted, would "give some degree of form and symmetry to [the] rude undigested mass" of conflicting accounts.[104] Because the cipher letter was often read as an overture from Burr to commit treason, however, Wilkinson's "own character" seemed "deeply implicated in the investigation."[105] "I am as much on trial as Burr Himself," Wilkinson wrote the secretary of war soon after arriving in Richmond.[106] Wilkinson seemed vulnerable on two questions: Why would Burr have seen him as a willing accomplice in treason? And why had he acted with so little regard for civil authority in New Orleans? While the grand jury showed relatively little interest in the latter question, it was very curious about the origins of the cipher letter, particularly once it discovered that Wilkinson had altered it to hide prior communications with Burr. This interest nearly led to an indictment for misprision of treason and produced an embarrassing newspaper battle.[107]

As they deliberated between accuser and accused, observers sought clues in Wilkinson's appearance and behavior. Such clues produced "a great change" in Hay's view of Wilkinson during an hour-long conversation on the general's first day in Richmond. Recounting this meeting for the president, Hay did not mention a single thing that Wilkinson had said. Instead, he described how Wilkinson's "erect attitude, the serenity of his countenance, the composure of his manners, [and] the mild but determined expression of his eye" had led him to believe that the general "had been most grossly calumniated."[108] Over the course of the trial, however, Wilkinson's actions and attitudes in court and around town tended to alienate rather than endear. By "putting on Airs, *he is Not intitled to*," Truxton warned Jefferson, "Wilkinson [had]

Contrived . . . to make himself enemies."[109] When he finally took the stand during the committal hearings, Wilkinson, according to Blennerhassett, "exhibited the manner of a sergeant under a Ct. Martial rather than the demeanor of an accusing Officer confronted with his Culprit."[110] While the direct examination by the presumably friendly prosecuting attorneys left him perplexed, the cross examination of "the Little Upstart Brigadier" by the defense a few days later was even more humiliating.[111]

That Burr's and Wilkinson's characters would be on trial in Richmond was expected; that Marshall's came to be was surprising. Both detractors and defenders saw the trial as a test of the chief justice's character. The former doubted that Marshall could restrain his political loyalties to the Federalists and personal enmities toward the president enough to permit the exposure and punishment of treason. They predicted "undue exertions to screen the traitor from the pains of the law."[112] His supporters wondered if Marshall could withstand the tide of administration pressure, newspaper opinion, and popular sentiment that favored hanging Burr regardless of the evidence or law. They feared that he might "bear too hard on the Prisoner . . . for fear of clamour." To one Federalist, Marshall seemed trapped from the beginning. So many people expected him to tilt toward Burr that any error "in favor of the Prisoner" would unleash a torrent of abuse. But "an error against [Burr]," at least in this view, would "be even more fatal to his Character."[113] "The character of a Judge," as a Republican editor insisted, "ought not only to be upright, but unsuspected."[114]

Many people, including Marshall himself, explained his decisions with references to his character. After reviewing Marshall's actions during the grand jury stage, one Republican remarked that he was "now perfectly satisfied of the corruption & depravity of the Chief Justice."[115] Early in the treason trial, Hay reported that Marshall seemed to be trying "to work himself up to a State of [*illegible*] which will enable him to aid Burr throughout the trial." The district attorney could explain this attitude only by noting that the judge "seems to think that his reputation is irretrievably gone, and that he has now nothing to lose by doing as he pleases."[116] After Marshall's ruling ending the treason trial, a Richmond Federalist reported that he had "act[ed] in all matters with pure uprightness & integrity," while one of the Ohio witnesses insisted that Marshall could not have "give[n] a corrupt opinion from personal or party motives when it would at once destroy his character as a man."[117] In the ruling itself, Marshall had forcefully asserted his claims to character grounded not on the ephemeral sentiments of public esteem, but on the eternal demands of sacred trust. "No man is desirous of becoming the peculiar subject of calumny," he explained of his own situation. But, if the only alternatives were "a dereliction of duty or the opprobrium of those who are denominated the world," any man would "[merit] the contempt as well as the indignation of his country who [could] hesitate which to embrace."[118]

The emphasis upon character gave greater resonance to some of the trial's significant legal developments. In legal terms, the grand jury's decision to indict Burr and six others for treason and misdemeanor concluded the second stage of the trial and necessitated the ensuing stages. But that is not what many witnesses emphasized when they described the moment, on 24 June, when Burr's indictment was announced. Even Wirt remarked upon not the legal implications, but the "shocked faces."[119] "The consternation visible in the faces of Col. Burr and his friends," a handbill reported, was "beyond description."[120] While he saw something very different, Bollman agreed on this moment's importance as a test of Burr's character, assuring Burr's daughter that "not a Feature in his Countenance [had] changed" to "the astonishment and admiration of all who beheld him."[121] While most observers watched for Burr's reaction, Wirt also noticed the indictments' impact upon Marshall, who "shrunk back with horror upon his seat." According to Wirt, Marshall watched Burr "with an expression of sympathy so agonizing and horror so deep & overwhelming, that he seemed for two or three seconds to have forgotten where & who he was." Only a "consciousness that he was giving way too much to his feelings," Wirt believed, had "start[ed Marshall] from his reverie."[122]

But seeing the trial as a test of character also imparted great weight to events that meant little when viewing it as a battle of legal tactics and arguments. What was widely considered one of the most important moments of the trial had no legal significance whatsoever. On 15 June, Burr and Wilkinson faced each other in court, the first time that they had been together since the revelation of the cipher letter. This event, which Washington Irving called "the first interview," was widely anticipated, and he, like many others, carefully positioned himself to view it. It is impossible for us to know exactly what happened. Few of the witnesses were neutral, and those who left accounts presented their side in the better light. Irving described Wilkinson as "swelling like a turkey cock, and bracing himself up for the encounter of Burr's eye," while Burr, at the mention of Wilkinson's name, "looked him full in the face with one of his piercing regards, swept his eye over his whole person from head to foot, . . . and then coolly resumed his former position." Burr's "whole look was over in an instant," Irving noted, "but it was an admirable one."[123] Wilkinson's supporters described this moment very differently. According to a Republican newspaper, Wilkinson's "countenance was [not] flushed with apprehension or 'sicklied over with the pale cast' of fear and guilt"; "had he but fainted or betrayed the least timidity," the author admitted, "it would have been a luscious banquet for federalism."[124] Writing to Jefferson, Wilkinson offered his own overblown version of the encounter. On entering the courtroom, he reported, his "Eyes darted a flash of indignation at the little Traitor," which the "Lyon hearted Eagle Eyed Hero" tried to meet with his own "haggard Eye." But, "under the weight of conscious guilt," Burr "averted his face, grew pale & affected passion to conceal his perturbation."[125]

Wirt provided perhaps the most perceptive description of this moment. No defender of Burr, obviously, Wirt also had his doubts about Wilkinson, particularly when he recorded his account in early August. Wirt had been "curious to mark the interview between Burr & Wilkinson" but had been greatly disappointed because, like everyone else, the two men "had anticipated the meeting." They had prepared themselves by, as Wirt put it, "resolv[ing] on the countenances which they would wear." Thus, neither Burr's "look of scorn & contempt" nor Wilkinson's return gaze, which had "all the sullenness and protervity of a big black bull," actually revealed the men's characters because "there was no nature in it."[126] Even though they disagreed with Wirt's analysis, Irving and Wilkinson certainly shared his assumptions about nature and artifice. Looking to the impact of their accounts, each presented his hero as natural and his foe as artificial. Irving portrayed Wilkinson "bracing himself up" for Burr's gaze, even as he insisted that "there was no appearance of study or constraint" in Burr's actions.[127] Conversely, Wilkinson reported that it was only "in spite of [him]self" that he had even looked at Burr, while describing Burr as having to "[make] an effort to meet" his eyes and "affect[ing] passion to conceal" his true feelings.[128] Wirt, Irving, and Wilkinson each accepted that natural actions and reactions revealed true character and suggested that artificial ones had been adopted to conceal that character.

The easy slippage between different meanings of the word "character" led some to discuss the trial as a play. The *Argus* occasionally commented on the trial under the heading, "Dramatic Intelligence," as in mid-June when it reported that "the arrival of Mr. *Wilkinson*, a performer of long standing, has excited much curiosity" and that "the engagement of Mr. Martin, from the Theatre at Baltimore, appears to have been made upon a supposition that the taste of the Richmond audience was for *Low Comedy*."[129] In mid-October, the *Argus* reviewed the "drama" that had finally reached its "last scene." While the "play" had been criticized "as rather too long," "the Characters were extremely well cast, and performed to the admiration of the audience." The review included a "*Dramatis Personæ*" of fifteen characters, including Marshall as "Chief Justice"; Wilkinson and Eaton as "Gen. Trueman" and "Gen. Hardy," respectively; Blennerhassett as "Squire Dupe"; and Burr as "Mahomet Volpone, the Grand Impostor." Three prosecuting and two defense attorneys were assigned the names of renowned British orators. Martin was cast as "Lawyer Ardent" and likened to Shakespeare's Falstaff, "a character truly inimitable" and "not averse to a cheerful glass." The review favorably evaluated the leading characters. But it was Mahomet Volpone's (Burr's) "low craft, his innumerable falsehoods, his callous effrontery, his remorseless treachery, . . . and his strange tricks and manoeuvres," according to the review, that "form[ed] the chief entertainment of the piece, which (take it all together) was certainly the most extraordinary that ever was exhibited in this or any other country."[130]

"THE STATE OF ANXIETY AND AGITATION"

Just as the forensic battles composed only a part of the courtroom drama for contemporaries, the courtroom itself formed only a part of the full experience of Burr's trial in Richmond. The trial temporarily transformed the city. It brought hundreds of people to Richmond as attorneys, witnesses, and curious on-lookers, creating new opportunities for business and pleasure. It also inflamed political divisions in the city, leading to newspaper wars and social tensions. "You cannot conceive," a resident wrote in late April, "the state of anxiety and agitation . . . in our metropolis."[131] And it challenged men's characters in ways that spilled beyond the courtroom and rippled through Richmond society. In private homes, public taverns, and even prison cells, through public statements, published letters, and affairs of honor, the trial's participants worked to secure, revise, or reverse its impacts on their characters. Since the gentleman's final recourse for protecting his character was the duel, moreover, events within and beyond the courtroom threatened violence. On the opening day of the treason trial, a Federalist merchant warned that "irritation must be the Consequence of social intercourse amongst the Citizens here" and predicted that the resulting "altercations will lead to Bloodshed."[132]

Burr's trial drew tremendous throngs from beginning to end. The crowd of would-be spectators outside the Eagle Tavern on the first day of the examination prompted the shift to the courtroom of the capitol the next day. The "impossib[ility] of accommodat[ing] the spectators in the court room" that morning forced an immediate move to the assembly's chambers, where the trial remained until its end.[133] While most of the earliest spectators must have been Richmonders, the later stages drew attorneys, witnesses, and others from great distances, filling not just the makeshift courtroom, but also the taverns and homes of the city. "Our City," the *Argus* announced in May, "is at present full of strangers from various and very distant parts of the United States."[134] A resident reported that Burr's trial had "brought together a greater concourse of people from difrent parts of the United States than was ever known to be in Richmond before."[135] The crowds thinned after the grand jury stage but returned a few weeks later for the treason trial. "The Concourse of people," a government witness wrote in mid-August, "is great."[136] Only in the final weeks of the trial's final stage did the crowds dwindle.

This influx of people brought a short-lived boom with "the bustle of business, and crouding of curiousity . . . observable in every street."[137] Those who could provide lodging and meals for visitors benefitted the most. By late May, according to a published letter, "the taverns and houses [were] occupied by so many people, that new comers [could] with difficulty procure accommodations."[138] Having arrived late, Wilkinson found himself forced to live in "the same House" as the Burrites Robert Ashley, Peter Ogden, and Samuel Swartwout.[139] But it was not tavern keepers and boardinghouse owners alone who hoped to share in the promised bounty; other entrepreneurial locals and outsiders also sought to profit from the temporary crowd. In late July, John Pryor advertised that he would rent his "public garden for the remainder of the season" to anyone who saw an opportunity in "the great concourse of strangers that [might] be expected to assemble in this city."[140] A number of artists tried to tap the market of well-heeled locals and visitors. In July, the French immigrant Charles B. J. Févret de Saint-Mémin brought his physiognotrace, pantograph, and graver to Richmond. Over the next year, he prepared nearly photographic images of dozens of Richmonders and visitors, including Justice Marshall, attorneys Wickham and Wirt, and witnesses Eaton and Wilkinson.[141]

The genteel men and women who filled the city's finest taverns and private homes and sat for portraits by Saint-Mémin and other artists enlivened Richmond society during the normally dull summer months. "Serious as the occasion," Samuel Mordecai remembered half a century later, "the concourse that assembled in Richmond . . . made it a gay time."[142] The local elite paid visits and issued invitations to visiting ladies and gentlemen. After ten days in Richmond, Truxton reported that, even if he stayed another month, he would "not be able to get through the dinner and evening invitations."[143] Irving's letters from Richmond reveal a similarly crowded social life. Having gotten "the character, among three or four novel read damsels[,] of being *an interesting young man,*" Irving found himself immersed in a social whirl of early morning rides and "moonlight walks[,] . . . red hot strolls" and "romantic walk[s] along the canal," and "routs and tea parties."[144] This activity apparently slowed by late summer, when elite Richmonders often travelled over the mountains for the cool air and restorative waters of the Virginia Springs resorts. In mid-August, with the treason trial just beginning, John Graham complained that the visiting witnesses had "neither Business nor amusements to employ [their] time."[145]

Usually, this genteel social landscape rested fairly easily upon a complex political world. Alongside the usual Federalists and Republicans,

Richmond and its environs provided a stronghold for the anti-administration Quids. Political tensions probably would have increased even if the trial had been held elsewhere, as Virginians looked ahead to the presidential election of 1808. By the spring of 1807, Virginia's Quids and Republicans were already divided over whether James Monroe, the Quid's preference, or James Madison, the president's choice, should succeed Jefferson. By quickly becoming "a party question," however, Burr's trial inflamed partisan tensions in the city on numerous issues.[146] The one thing that Federalists, Republicans, and Quids could agree on was that "party spirit rage[d]" in Richmond during the trial.[147]

The city's newspapers became a crucial site for partisan sparring. Burr's trial filled the pages of the *Argus*, *Enquirer*, *Gazette*, and *Observer* in various forms: an abbreviated account of the latest developments; a fuller record of the proceedings that, because of its length, appeared after a long delay; and editorials, letters, and other pieces that responded to the trial and its local repercussions. The editors, and their stenographers, provided much of this content. Republican or Federalist, editors struggled with the often-conflicting duties of informing the public without influencing the trial. Early promises by the editors that they would do nothing to "prejudic[e] the public mind" fell prey to equally early assurances that they would report "every circumstance" of the trial "with such observations upon [it], as, in our opinion, the public good may require."[148] For the Republican editors, this standard permitted blasts at Burr, his associates, his counsel, his friends among local Federalists, and Marshall. For the Federalist Augustine Davis, it accommodated encomiums upon Marshall, condemnations of Wilkinson, and calls upon the administration "to defend itself against the high charges of persecution and tyranny."[149] The newspapers also remained open to the community, including those who were involved in the trial; thinly veiled by pseudonyms, Martin provided eight essays for the *Gazette*, while Wilkinson published a lengthy piece in the *Enquirer*. Davis, especially, relied upon others to fill the columns of the *Gazette*, reprinting editorials and other pieces from leading Federalist newspapers and publishing letters and essays by local and visiting Federalists. Over the course of the trial, the newspaper attacks grew in intensity, but the editors continued to disclaim any intention of "inflam[ing] the public mind."[150]

The Federalist/Republican division in Richmond's newspapers was complicated not by a Quid newspaper, but by the *Observer*. Samuel Brooks's late January 1807 efforts to revive the *Observer* as a Republican print had failed after a handful of issues. When it resumed publication in mid-April, the *Observer* was effectively Burr's newspaper. Brooks claimed impartiality; contemporaries rejected his claims. Wilkinson complained of the attacks he received from "the prints of Burr [i.e., the *Observer*] & the Federalists [i.e., the *Gazette*]."[151] And Republican editors, in Richmond and elsewhere, denounced Brooks as an apostate and a hireling. These charges appear well founded. In late September, long after the *Observer* had again folded, Harman Blennerhassett noted that Burr was trying to raise three hundred dollars so that "the press of the Impartial Observer, which had been obliged to stop for want of funds, could be again set to work." In Burr's view, according to Blennerhassett, its "editor was bold and ingenious, passed for a good Democrat, [and would] represent things right and print everything that was required of him."[152] Burr's funds had revived the *Observer* in mid-April but must have been exhausted fairly quickly. Brooks's renewed efforts to keep the newspaper in operation failed, as well. The *Observer* permanently suspended operations in early July, managing just one issue after Burr's indictment.

During this brief run, the *Observer* went far beyond the *Gazette* in defending Burr and attacking his denouncers. In the first issue after he resumed publication, Brooks described Burr as a "victim of the despotic fury of prejudice"—a prejudice that derived from "party malice" with "not a particle, not an atom, not even the shadow of an atom of proof" to justify it. He directed much of his fury against "the newspapers [that had] succeeded so well in destroying the popularity of Col. Burr." Brooks also blasted the *Argus*'s Samuel Pleasants for refusing to attack Wilkinson's "arbitrary conduct" in New Orleans.[153] He then denounced Ritchie and the *Enquirer* for "veer[ing] about with every popular breeze" rather than helping to "[fix] the public will upon that which is right."[154] Editorials and other pieces assailed the integrity of government witnesses, particularly Wilkinson and Eaton. In mid-May, Brooks published an open letter calling on Jefferson to show that he was not "the persecutor of Col. Burr and the protector of Gen. Wilkinson in his tyranny and usurpation."[155] As one of his last acts for Burr,

Brooks printed a revised version of the anti-Wilkinson *A Short Review of the Late Proceedings at New Orleans*, which had recently been published in South Carolina and was believed to have been written by Burr's son-in-law, Joseph Alston.

From early April until late June, Burr's trial dominated the pages of Richmond's newspapers, as "the affairs of the world [seemed to] stand still to let this great affair of armed rebellion pass."[156] Then, on the morning of 25 June, the day that the grand jury finished its work, news arrived from Norfolk that the British ship *Leopard* had fired upon the American frigate *Chesapeake*, killing three crew members before removing four men as deserters from the British navy. The emerging details of the *Chesapeake* Affair and the growing prospect of an Anglo-American war quickly supplanted Burr's trial as the principal topic of political conversation and press coverage during the long recess between the grand jury stage and the treason trial. "Burr & his associates in infamy," one Republican admitted as the trial resumed in early August, "have been almost forgotten in the indignation that has been excited by the outrage on our frigate."[157] According to many observers, the *Chesapeake* Affair produced an almost-instantaneous and almost-complete end to the party divisions that the trial had stoked. War, as one Richmonder explained in late June, "has seemingly buried all party distinctions except that of Whig & Tory."[158] By mid-July, it was reported that "all here are soldiers—from boys of 8 years, to men of 65."[159] But this easing of party tensions did not last very long in Richmond, in part because it never extended very deep. Both Quids and Republicans worried that "federalists and Burrites," by "tak[ing] the lead in offering their service for defense," were merely trying "to lose their political names, mix with the democrats, retain their principles, and wait for an opportunity to carry them into execution."[160] Shortly after Burr's trial resumed in earnest in mid-August, Richmond's party divisions seemed as intense and as pervasive as they had in the spring.

To many, the heightened political tensions that resulted from Burr's trial mattered most because of their impact on social relations. For six months, partisan divisions reshaped social life in Richmond, which is hardly surprising since the trial reportedly formed "the only topic of conversation in all Companies," especially before the *Chesapeake* Affair.[161] Still, the encroachment of politics on society was disturbing since Enlightenment thought generally viewed society as desirable and government as, at best, necessary. In Richmond, during Burr's trial, the necessary seemed to trump the desirable. Within the gentry class, social relations displayed the corrosive effects of political divisions. "Distrust & suspicion generally prevail in the intercourse between man & man," the Quid John Randolph lamented.[162] More than one observer perceived in Richmond during Burr's trial a return to the superheated political atmosphere of the late 1790s. "Since this trial commenced," Governor Cabell wrote his brother even before the grand jury stage began, "I have had feelings which I have not experienced since 1798," when fierce party divisions over the Quasi-War, the Alien and Sedition Acts, and other measures had warped social relations.[163] The destructive impact of politics on society appeared most clearly in matters of hospitality: how should genteel Richmonders treat those visitors whose characters were at stake in the trial? Hosting genteel visitors in one's home, calling upon them at their lodgings, inviting them to private dinners and public functions—such were the usual forms of elite hospitality in the early American republic. Such acts, at other times, had made Virginia, according to the *Gazette*, "a state far-famed for the hospitality of its inhabitants."[164] Such acts, during the trial, became freighted with political meaning. In newspapers, letters, and conversations, Richmonders and others disputed the political implications of social interactions—of visits and gifts, of dinners and barbecues.

Ultimately, the central question was, should Burr be treated as a gentleman despite the accusations against him? Truxton faced this question when Burr visited Philadelphia in early May. Ever alert to the impact of others' perceptions of his actions on his honor, Truxton decided that any social interaction with Burr would be improper. In his view, "gentlemen and men of honor must all think alike on such a subject[;] *scoundrels only can differ.*"[165] Richmond Republicans tended to share the Federalist Truxton's views: "gentlemen" would abjure social relations with Burr; only "scoundrels" would accord him hospitality. Most Federalists argued that Burr should be treated as a gentleman. "Till Colonel Burr be legally found guilty," a Federalist newspaper explained, "it is no more reprehensible to shew him hospitality than it would be to be civil and polite to any gentleman concerned in his prosecution or in his defense."[166] In late July, one of Burr's supporters reported that, in his view, "to wish [Burr] well or not almost formed the line of Demarcation between Gentlemen and those who were not it."[167] While they behaved differently, both sides accepted that showing hospitality to Burr divided "gentlemen" from "those who were not" gentlemen. Divisions over how to behave toward Burr strained elite Richmonders' relations with each other.

Hospitality toward Burr took different forms at different points in his seven-month stay in Richmond as he moved between public taverns, private homes, and prison cells. He spent his first nights in the city under guard at the Eagle Tavern; after arranging bail, Burr moved to the Swan Tavern. Following his trip to Philadelphia, he shared a rented home near the Swan with Luther Martin. After being indicted for treason, Burr was confined again, spending two nights "in the common jail—of all holes the most horrible and desolate."[168] His attorneys moved that Burr be placed in "some comfortable and convenient place of confinement" that would be both healthier for him and more accessible for them.[169] Marshall agreed, ordering that the dining room of the house that Burr and Martin shared be barred and guarded. When the prosecution protested, Marshall sent Burr to the state penitentiary on the city's western edge until the treason trial. In early August, Burr returned to the barred and guarded room that he had briefly occupied in late June. After his acquittal of treason, he rented another house nearby, where he remained until he left Richmond in late October.[170]

It was not immediately apparent that the social act of offering hospitality to Burr would be viewed as the political act of displaying antipathy to the administration. At the Eagle Tavern in late March, Burr received "many presents" from "many ladies of rank."[171] He also had visits from "4. or 5 [people] other than *Council*," though they could "only [speak] into the door in [the] presence of the Guard." The Richmond Federalist Robert Gamble did not mention the visitors' politics, describing them simply as "those who [had] rece[ived] Civilities from him in former days."[172] In other words, he suggested that they had merely acted according to the usual rules of hospitality. But two incidents quickly made the political dimensions of such hospitality clear. First, the five Richmonders who offered themselves as securities for Burr's bail came under attack for what one Republican sarcastically denoted their "federal *sympathy and benevolence.*"[173] The Federalist *Gazette* immediately sprang to the men's defense. In saving "this unfortunate and distinguished prisoner from the horrors of a dismal dungeon," the editor asserted, they had done "honor [to] themselves" and upheld Virginia's reputation for "civility and attention towards strangers."[174] Six weeks later, he returned to this issue, using it to attack the Republicans in Richmond and elsewhere who had criticized the five men. Under Republican rule, Davis charged, acts that had been "honored and cherished, [had] become the watchwords for detraction and abuse." The result, he warned, would be a "complete prostration of all those ties which unite men as citizens of the same country."[175]

Then, within days of the examination, Wickham hosted a dinner for Burr at his home that Marshall attended. Wickham's hospitality toward Burr was "loudly censured" by the public and by the Republican press, which dubbed this dinner the "Feast of Treason," but was generally excused by gentlemen, who accepted that attorneys could have social as well as professional contact with their clients.[176] Marshall's willingness to dine with Burr could not be justified so easily. Defending the justice, Federalists insisted that he had not known that Burr would be there; Republicans countered that, even if that had been true, Marshall should have left immediately upon seeing him. Republican newspapers exploded with editorials and letters attacking Marshall for "the extreme indelicacy and impropriety" of attending the dinner. These attacks helped to define the limits of acceptable hospitality toward Burr. A piece in the *Argus* accepted that "the rites of hospitality ought not to be refused to this *unfortunate gentleman* by those who believe him innocent," making such acts a mark of political loyalties.[177] Perhaps the most significant statement on this issue appeared in the *Enquirer* over the signature "A Stranger from the Country." Its author, Benjamin Watkins Leigh, blasted Marshall for "a willful prostration of the dignity of his own character." But he did not limit his attacks to the justice. Leigh accepted some forms of hospitality toward Burr, considering it proper that, "on his arrival in Richmond, [he had been] readily furnished with the supplies necessary to his comfort" and that his counsel were treating him "with civility and tenderness." But he rejected the suggestion that Burr could be "admitted to the familiarity of private friendship, much more to the house and table, of any man, but Mr. Wickham."[178]

Such public attacks succeeded in politicizing and minimizing hospitality toward Burr between early April and late June. Burr remained "intirely dormant" after the Wickham dinner; "I do not understand that he pays visits," Hay reported in mid-April, "and I believe that he receives very few." Hay attributed this situation largely to "A Stranger from the Country," which had "made a great impression [in Richmond] on men of all parties."[179] Irving, who arrived in Richmond a month later and stayed through late June, reported much the same thing and explained it in much the same way. While Burr's position, in Irving's view, should have "appeal[ed] eloquently to the feelings of every generous bosom, . . . the reverse [had] been the fact." "It has almost been considered as culpable," he explained, "to evince towards [Burr] the least sympathy or support," particularly among those who had been his Republican friends.[180] Such sentiments lasted for months. In late September, nearly a month after Burr's acquittal, John Chevallié, the French consul, complained to Blennerhassett about "the restriction imposed on the hospitable dispositions of the families of this town." Chevallié believed that this restriction was enforced through "a system of espionage which is kept up by [the] Govt."[181]

The shock of Burr's indictment for treason and return to confinement in late June brought a new wave of hospitality, in the form of frequent visits and gifts. According to an account in a New York newspaper, Burr invited these visits. "When he got into his carriage to drive off to prison," an anonymous writer related, "he bowed and said pleasantly, my friends will always find me at home, and I shall be glad to see them at all times."[182] Even if apocryphal, this incident harmonized with Burr's diligent efforts to maintain his gentility despite his imprisonment. This project appeared most clearly in letters to his daughter, Theodosia Burr Alston. "I may be immured in dungeons, chained, murdered in legal form," he assured her, "but I cannot be humiliated or disgraced."[183] His first letter to her from the penitentiary described his lodgings and reported that various "servants [had] arrived with messages, notes, and inquiries, bringing oranges, lemons, pineapples, raspberries, apricots, cream, butter, ice, and some ordinary articles."[184] In his next letter, Burr explained that "friends and acquaintance of both sexes are permitted to visit me without interruption, without inquiring their business, and without the *presence of a spy*"; he invited his daughter to stay with him if she reached Richmond before the treason trial.[185] Fearing that the Alstons would not arrive before he was returned to Martin's rented house, Burr, in a final letter from the penitentiary, urged his daughter to "drive directly out here" since he had "a great desire to *receive you all in this mansion*."[186] She did, "spen[ding] several days and one night" and finding his rooms to be "cool, clean, and retired from all unpleasant *company*."[187]

Harman Blennerhassett, who moved into the same rooms on 4 August, had a similar experience during his month at the penitentiary. "I was not half an hour here," he wrote his wife, "when I had a lively note from Col. Burr, a present of tea, sugar and cakes from Mrs. Alston," and visits from Joseph Alston, Edmund Randolph, and, later, Charles Fenton Mercer.[188] The next day brought a stream of visitors that included friends from the West and acquaintances from an earlier stay in Richmond. The stream abated a bit in time, but a day without any visitors was rare enough for Blennerhassett to note in his journal. And he continued to receive gifts, including "fruit, good butter[,] and fine calf's feet jelly," from Theodosia Burr Alston and various Richmonders throughout his stay.[189] Still, Blennerhassett's journal shows the realities of a gentleman's life in the penitentiary—its privileges and limits—in ways that Burr's letters do not. At least some of the company, Blennerhassett noted, took the form of "idle visitors" who were merely curious "to survey [his] countenance and [his] Quarters."[190] And, while the rooms were "large and convenient," they were "very warm" and "in no small degree tainted from the effluvia of a certain necessary fixture."[191] They were also unfurnished, forcing Blennerhassett to rent "indispensable necessaries . . . from the tavern."[192] But he could buy his meals from the tavern and "[hire] a servant @ $13 a month" for his personal needs. And he had "every liberty . . . but those of passing fr[om] under the *roof* of this building by day, or out of *my room*, at night."[193]

The rich social life that Burr enjoyed in the penitentiary continued during the treason trial in the barred room in Martin's rented house. He "lives in great style," Blennerhassett learned, and "sees much company within his gratings, where it is as difficult to get an audience, as if he were really an Emperor."[194] Republicans insisted, as they had for months, that "all the attentions paid to" Burr represented Federalist hatred of Jefferson rather than "real respect" for Burr.[195] But

Blennerhassett understood that the crowds in Burr's room and in court—"at the Levé and the Bar"—served Burr's purposes by forming the audience before which he could display "the vivacity of his witt" and "his *proper* talents."[196] Such thinking may have led Burr, after being acquitted of treason, to host "an amazing frolic at the Eagle (tavern)" and, soon after being released from confinement, to take a long, evening stroll with his daughter, "in which he exhibited his person thro' the greater part of the town."[197] The circle of Burr's social life seems to have narrowed shortly after his release, however.

The suspension or politicization of social interactions during the trial extended beyond the accused. Some of the departures from customary hospitality probably resulted from the sheer number of witnesses and other visitors. The crowds clearly overwhelmed Richmond's taverns and boardinghouses and probably overwhelmed its social networks, as well. While Marietta's Return J. Meigs Jr. was pleased to have found a room in a private home where he could "retire from the Noise & Bustle," he was dismayed at not having "receive[d] that pointed attention that [he] expected—not having dined out" even after a month in Richmond.[198] But other visitors were nearly as politically charged as Burr. Wilkinson raised many of the same questions for Federalists that Burr did for Republicans. On his first day in Richmond, Wilkinson attended, by invitation, a dinner party for some of the government witnesses that was held by the Barbecue Club at the Haymarket Gardens. Such events were common for distinguished visitors. Nonetheless, some Federalists decried this "*barbacue*" as politics rather than hospitality. One described the Richmonders who hosted and attended it as "parasites of the administration," who hoped "to pave the way to a share of the 'loaves and fishes,' by joining in the *hue and cry* against Burr."[199] But Republicans insisted that Wilkinson, who had "risked all . . . to save his country from bloodshed and civil war," merited hospitality, particularly if Burr was going to be "treated by the federal nobility, more like a Roman general returned from a triumph, than like a great culprit."[200]

One family provides a striking example of the ways in which the political could overwhelm the social during Burr's trial. In mid-May, James Gibbon, the federal customs collector in Richmond, invited Truxton to stay at his home during the trial—a common form of hospitality among friends and even acquaintances. Though he was a government witness and a Federalist, Truxton himself managed to avoid controversy, being entertained by everyone "from the Governour down, throughout the Society of 'Worthies,' of all politics."[201] But Truxton's visitors included Burr's most notorious attorney, Luther Martin. As Martin and Truxton exchanged visits, Martin's daughter Maria befriended Gibbon's daughters, Mary and Elizabeth. On her frequent visits to the Gibbon home, Maria Martin "brought also company with her, that under circumstances, could not be agreable"—the young Burrites who often gathered at her father's rented house.[202] Such visits made James Gibbon a subject of Republican reproach; even Jefferson heard "that the most conspicuous accomplices of Burr were at home at [Gibbon's] house."[203] By early July, Gibbon worried that he might lose his lucrative position. After Truxton returned to Philadelphia, Gibbon implored prominent Richmond Republicans to intercede on his behalf with the president. To former governor John Page, Gibbon confided that he had "been intruded on to his mortification, . . . by Puppies, who mis[took] him" for an opponent of the administration.[204] Gibbon also informed Truxton that he would need to find other lodgings for the treason trial. And, because Truxton's absence would not end Maria Martin's visits, Gibbon sent his daughters to stay with their aunt in Washington so that they would "not again be the innocent means of bringing Miss Martin, her Father, & some of Burr's young friends to his house."[205]

As the case of the Gibbon sisters suggests, politicized hospitality could be heavily gendered. With such politically charged visitors as Burr, Blennerhassett, and Wilkinson, it was typically men who hosted the public dinners, visited the prison cells, and extended—or withheld—the invitations to dine with the family. Women could send gifts to prisoners through male relatives or servants. They could bring less controversial visitors into the social whirl that so occupied young Washington Irving. Bollman reportedly "courted every lady in the place," while Swartwout apparently "floated on the very surface of the Beau Monde."[206] And women could openly display their sympathy even for an accused traitor. "The ladies alone have felt, or at least had candor & independence sufficient, to express" their true support for Burr, Irving remarked.[207] But, with Maria Martin and the Gibbon sisters as seemingly rare exceptions, women did not display hospitality in the ways that carried the greatest political—or, in James Gibbon's case, financial—risks. That is not to say that women were not political. Blennerhassett mentioned conversations about politics with various Richmond women, including Catherine Gamble—the wife of the Federalist merchant Robert Gamble and mother-in-law of the prominent Republicans William H. Cabell and William Wirt—and Mary Randolph—the sister-in-law of the president's daughter, Martha. Randolph, Blennerhassett noted, voiced "more pungent strictures upon Jefferson's head and heart . . . than any I had ever heard before"; "she certainly uttered more treason than *my wife* ever dreamed of."[208]

In dining rooms and prison cells, in newspaper essays and editorials, in courtroom testimony and arguments, the characters of defendants, witnesses, and attorneys—both locals and visitors—were challenged and defended during Burr's trial. For most of these men, the final recourse for protecting one's character was not society or the press or the courts, but the affair of honor and, if necessary, the duel. Before Burr's trial had fully begun, contemporaries predicted that it would produce duels. Too much was at stake to imagine otherwise. Too many men who had already assailed each other's honor and, thus, character, would be assembled in one place. Too many new slights and offenses would be created in the courtroom, the newspapers, and society. Such predictions began early and spread widely. Talk of "*daggers* and *stilettos*" filled the air before Wilkinson's arrival, according to the *Argus*.[209] Early in the grand jury stage, a Boston newspaper reported that "the southern bloods calculate on some *duels*," since Burr, Wilkinson, Swartwout, Eaton, John Adair, William C. C. Claiborne, and other men would "all be on the spot."[210] "Rumour," according to a South Carolina newspaper, had already "singled out the parties": "*Burr* against *Wilkinson*, [Benjamin] *Stoddard* and *Eaton*—*Adair* against *Wilkinson*—and *Swartwout* against *Claiborne*."[211] Events that had occurred outside of Richmond and before the trial undergirded such predictions.

Wilkinson's heightened sense of honor and critical role in exposing and suppressing the conspiracy made him a central figure in these predictions. Most of the early comments about the trial as an occasion for violence looked to his arrival from New Orleans. Those whom Wilkinson had denounced and arrested had good cause to challenge him; some of

328 | CHAPTER 8

them had dueled for lesser reasons before. Wilkinson, moreover, came to Richmond ready to issue and to receive challenges; "an Affair or two," he wrote one confidant, "must Ensue."[212] Before leaving New Orleans, Wilkinson had assured his "very dear Friend" Samuel Smith that he would challenge John Randolph: "The World is too small for us both."[213] Other men, Wilkinson trusted, would challenge him. "I am informed several persons lay claim to [my life]," he wrote Secretary of War Henry Dearborn within a week of reaching Richmond.[214] Initially, no one seemed more likely than Wilkinson to bring about a duel.

New affronts that arose from interactions in society and in court soon complicated and compounded the old injuries. Though it did not produce an affair of honor, Truxton's "cutting" of Wilkinson at the Barbecue Club's dinner was clearly intended by the former and understood by the latter as a slight. Truxton later described this incident as "My Contemptious Treatment of [Wilkinson] at Richmond, in presence of More than 100 Gentlemen, *at a public Dinner.*"[215] Furious that Wilkinson had attached his name to the decoded cipher letter and had never apologized for doing so, Truxton turned away as the general approached. Wilkinson's account reads like a battle report: "Approaching Him with some caution I found he changed his front as I came near Him, on which I flanked Him & he again faced, & thus I turned Him on his pivot."[216] Though they did not press this matter in Richmond, both Truxton and Wilkinson wrote to their mutual friend Charles Biddle about the incident "in such a manner," Biddle later remarked, "that they would have fought had they seen each other's letters."[217] An erroneous account of Andrew Jackson's first meeting with Wilkinson in Richmond did spark an affair of honor. On his way back to Tennessee, Jackson learned that Virginia's Andrew Hamilton had said that, despite vilifying Wilkinson before his arrival, Jackson had been "the first man that Took him by the hand when he (Wilkingson) reached Richmond." "Never having a wish to condemn any unheard," Jackson gave Hamilton a chance to deny that he had "made such a statement."[218] He dropped the matter only after being assured that Hamilton had "[given] *the Lye* to this report."[219]

As we have seen, men's characters were deeply implicated in the conflict of testimony, argument, and will in the courtroom throughout Burr's trial. By late June, according to Ohio's Dudley Woodbridge, the grounds had been "laid for 2 or 3 duels already."[220] During the treason trial, Wirt used the language of an affair of honor in reaction to a statement of Botts's that seemed to challenge his veracity; Marshall's intervention may have prevented a challenge. Three weeks later, in mid-September, Hay issued a formal challenge to Wickham for "some remarks, as unjust as they were unexpected," that struck Hay as "a direct attack upon [his] integrity, both as an individual and a public officer." Hay interpreted one of Wickham's comments as asserting that the prosecution "averred a *belief* of that which *we could not believe*"—in other words, "that we had told a wilful & deliberate falsehood." Hay stated that he had considered replying to Wickham in court but had accepted—using language that makes clear that he considered the matter an affair of honor—"the necessity of pursuing a different course, to obtain the redress to which [he was] intitled."[221] And, during the committal hearing, Wilkinson assailed Swartwout's character, even as his own was besmirched by Wickham. Swartwout and Wilkinson each looked to duels to repair the damage.

Ultimately, no blood was shed in Richmond during the long months of Burr's trial. Characters were attacked; honor was impugned; and challenges were issued. But no duels were fought. Various factors combined to prevent expected violence from becoming actual violence. For one thing, men outside of Richmond used their influence to prevent it. In addition to keeping Wilkinson and Truxton from seeing each other's letters to him, Philadelphia's Charles Biddle also wrote to Burr and Wilkinson urging them not to duel. "I should be sorry to hear of your having a meeting with G[eneral] W[ilkinson]," he informed Burr in early August; "it wd. in my opinion be highly improper & perhaps involve you in new difficulties."[222] And, though the letters do not survive, Baltimore's Samuel Smith clearly tried to dissuade Wilkinson from challenging John Randolph. By assuring the recipients that their honor was already secure, such letters could alleviate the greatest impetus to a duel—fears for one's reputation among other gentlemen. Such efforts did not always work, however. Wilkinson answered Biddle's counsel of restraint by declaring: "*I will* have the most ample reparation, or I will wash out the blemish with my own Blood or that of my Traducers, (I have two selected)."[223] Still, he foreswore any intention of dueling Burr, satisfying Biddle's principal goal.

Another factor that worked against actual violence was the sheer length of the trial. No one wanted to duel until it was done. The grand jury stage had barely begun when a published letter from Richmond reported that "General Eaton [had] been insulted—and the conjecture is, that something of a serious nature will take place." But it would only take place, the author continued, "as soon as the storm of Burr's trial is over."[224] Blennerhassett similarly noted that it was expected that Wilkinson would "have to settle his private accounts with Gen. Jackson, and four or five other persons," but not until "immediately after the trial."[225] Wilkinson always couched his plans to seek redress as something that would await the outcome of the trial. "I only regret," he wrote Smith in mid-June, "that the period should be so remote."[226] Such delays allowed new developments to ease the conditions that had made a duel likely. Wilkinson's early intention to duel Randolph, for example, subsided due to the respect that Randolph showed him as grand jury foreman; the fury of two weeks earlier—when Wilkinson had responded to learning that Randolph was the foreman by writing, "I am glad to *find* Him so exactly in my Way"—abated.[227] This fury soon returned, with added force, when accounts of the grand jury's deliberations about Wilkinson appeared in print, but Randolph had left Richmond by then; Wilkinson would eventually challenge Randolph in late December, when the two men were again together in Washington.

With both old grievances and new complaints held in abeyance until the trial's end, its final days emerged as an especially dangerous period—one rife with challenges and expectations of challenges. By mid-October, Eaton had forgiven or forgotten whatever insult had made him so anxious to duel five months earlier and had no plans to challenge anyone before leaving Richmond. But he expected others to challenge him. To avoid suspicions about his bravery, he announced his planned departure date well in advance; "I feel," Eaton wrote one confidant, that "I have discharged my duty and acquitted my honor."[228] A few days later, however, he informed the same person of a change of plans: "It has been since intimated to me that my *honor* dictates delay." Eaton's calculations are revealing. "If I go away," he explained, "every *coward* in Richmond will take the merit of having challenged me—by staying the *reality* may occur from one or *two* brave men."[229] After a few more days, Eaton left town without being challenged. In the same weeks, however, Wilkinson became involved in two affairs of honor, receiving a challenge from Swartwout and issuing one to Wickham.

The resolution of the Wilkinson-Swartwout affair points to another factor that prevented expected violence from becoming actual violence—uncertainties about the character of men who had been associated with treason. The rules were very clear. Affairs of honor and, especially, duels should occur only between equals. The disputants had to be equals not in age, rank, or wealth—certainly not in dueling ability—but in character. Both had to be gentlemen. When men who were not gentlemen were the sources of insults and affronts, gentlemen dealt with them in other ways, most commonly by whipping or caning the offender in public; in early June, the *Observer* reported that Eaton had "mentioned a horsewhip" as the appropriate response to some of the editor's attacks.[230] Shortly after arriving in Richmond, Wilkinson made clear how these assumptions shaped his thinking. Writing to Samuel Smith, he explained that there were some—presumably Randolph and perhaps one other—from whom he would "ask [redress] in the manner of a Gentlemen." But there were others—Burr "& his satellites & associates Jackson, Adair[,] Dayton &c:"—who had "sunk below [his] consideration & [would] be treated as ruffians." "I shall hold their invitations [to duel] in contempt," Wilkinson remarked, "& be always prepared to punish in an examplary manner [e.g., a public caning] the first who may dare to insult me."[231] Burr apparently had no higher view of Wilkinson. When the general charged him in court with "a gross and groundless untruth," Burr ignored it; Blennerhassett attributed Burr's response to his belief that "he [was] not bound to give Wn. a meeting out of c[our]t."[232]

Such assessments dictated Wilkinson's response when, on the last day of the trial, Swartwout sent him a challenge through Israel Smith. Swartwout's exact complaint is unclear, though the timing suggests a response to a recent reminder—his testimony the previous day—of an old insult—Wilkinson's arrest in December. When Smith tried to hand Swartwout's challenge to the general in a public room of a tavern, Wilkinson "handed back the letter unopened," according to a witness, "and requested Mr. Smith to inform Mr. Swartwout that he held no correspondence with Traitors or Conspirators."[233] Swartwout responded in the only way that might sustain his claim to honor, by publicly post-ing Wilkinson as "a COWARD and POLTRON" in the *Gazette*. But Swartwout's posting undermined his claim to gentility and, thus, con-ceded Wilkinson's reason for rebuffing him. If, as Swartwout claimed, Wilkinson's own "reputation was gone forever," then Swartwout never should have stooped to challenging him.[234] Republican newspapers derided Swartwout's claims to gentility; "the extravagance of the abuse" in his posting, the *Argus* charged, "defeats its own object."[235] Wilkin-son, another Virginia newspaper noted, "has very properly, refused to accept the challenge."[236] Wilkinson knew how to handle insults "from *such* a source." He had the New Yorker's posting, and sworn accounts of his rebuff of the challenge, printed in New York City. In private letters, he described Swartwout as a "Villain" and a coward, claiming that he had refused to fight even after having "his nose pulled by a Lt. Jackson" outside of Richmond.[237] And, expecting to find Swartwout in Balti-more, Wilkinson made plans for the proper treatment; "it was my purpose," he informed Secretary Dearborn after learning of Swart-wout's quick departure, "to have made my Servant flog Him."[238]

The resolution of Wilkinson's challenge to Wickham suggests the final reason that expected violence never became actual violence in Richmond—cultural conventions about the courtroom. By eliciting conflicting statements of fact and opinion, court proceedings could have easily produced affairs of honor and duels. Usually, they did not. The courtroom, like the legislative assembly, seems to have been a protected space where things could be said that would have led to chal-lenges if spoken elsewhere or printed in a newspaper. But the protec-tion did not cover everyone equally. Its extent and its limits emerged clearly when Wickham rebuffed Wilkinson. On the same day that he rejected Swartwout's challenge, Wilkinson initiated the affair by re-questing "an explanation" of a comment that Wickham had made in court. Wilkinson's letter made clear that his honor was at stake and proposed that Wickham redress the "unprovoked & unmerited wrong" by stating that the comment had been made "inadvertently & without design."[239] Wilkinson did not specify Wickham's offense but instead had his second, William Upshaw, do so. Upshaw delivered the letter with a two-week-old affidavit from Miles Selden that recounted how, before Wilkinson's arrival in Richmond, Wickham had "indignantly" thrown his December deposition "on the clerks table and declared that he cared nothing about it, that it was a composition of falsehood from beginning to end."[240] Wickham informed Upshaw that Selden "had misapprehended [his] Meaning" and directed him to the published trial records.[241] After finding that the offensive comments "were not noted or recollected by any person," Wickham wrote to Wilkinson directly, rejecting Selden's account and offering explanations for his confusion. At the same time, he claimed "the right of commenting on Testimony in a Cause in any manner allowable in fair Argument and required by the Interests of those I defend," insisting that "motives of Self-respect as well as regard to the rights of others" would hold him within proper bounds.[242]

The failure of Wickham's letter to resolve the matter suggests that this early incident was merely the grounds, not the reason, for Wilkinson's challenge. More than two weeks before his first letter to Wickham, two days before Selden made his affidavit, Wilkinson had asked fellow officer Jonathan Williams to come to Richmond to act as his second for an "Interview" that could not "be satisfied without ablution."[243] The timing of this letter suggests that what actually precipitated Wilkinson's challenge was his five-day appearance in court, which had ended the previous day. By most accounts, this protracted appearance had gone badly; Blennerhassett even noted that Wickham's "masterly and ingenious" cross-examination on the second day had produced "a general buzz about the General's embarrassment [that] ran thro' the crowd."[244] Wilkinson had always doubted that Wickham would agree to duel. While he had to accept Wickham's rebuttal of Selden's affidavit, he did so with obvious reluctance and immediately took offense at Wickham's claims about his rights and duties as an attorney. With Wilkinson's reply of 24 October, the grounds for the affair shifted from a specific comment that Wickham may or may not have made months earlier to the general conventions that Wickham claimed governed his courtroom behavior.

At the same time, the affair entered a lull due to the absence of Wickham's second and the vagueness of Wilkinson's new complaint. In his 24 October letter, Wilkinson claimed "the right of vindicating his Character against abuse under whatever pretense offered," without specifying any particular abuse.[245] Upshaw's letter that day provided little clarification, stating only that Burr's counsel had taken "liberties frequently unwarranted and oftimes cruel and insufferable."[246] In their view, nothing more needed to be said. On 27 October, Wilkinson informed Williams: "Tomorrow will determine whether [Wickham] is a Coward or a Man of Spirit."[247] But the next day came and went without determining anything because Wickham made no reply. On 29 October, Wickham finally responded to the two letters. Writing to Upshaw, he insisted on being informed in "explicit" terms of the specific "Injuries," so that he could "Shape [his] reply accordingly." But he refused not only to duel, but even to justify the things that he had said in court as part of his "Duty to [his] Client," including "contend[ing] that the Testimony which went to establish his Innocence deserved more credit than that which was offered to prove his Guilt."[248] Upshaw answered the same day, explaining that Wilkinson sought redress from Wickham for "charg[ing] him in open court" with three things: "*felony*[,] *purgery*[, and] *Forgery*." For such "*grievous* attacks on [Wilkinson's] character & honor," the redress would have to "be ample, to be satisfactory."[249] Wickham asked for details and for time for his second to return to Richmond. But Wilkinson was impatient; one of his correspondents reported that he "was endeavoring to bring Mr. Wickham's Courage to the *Sticking place*."[250] A final letter from Upshaw made clear that Wickham could delay no longer.

Wickham's eventual response of 31 October attempted to close the affair without providing the satisfaction that Wilkinson sought. It took shelter behind the accepted duties of an attorney to his client since Wilkinson had complained only of things said by Wickham "in the Fedl. Court while acting as Counsel for Col. Burr." In his lengthy letter, Wickham quickly dispatched with two of those complaints, the charges of felony and forgery. He insisted that he had "no Recollection of having ever made" such charges and was "thoroughly persuaded that he never did." But "the term 'perjury' or its equivalent," he admitted, "certainly was used" in reference to Wilkinson's lying about altering the cipher letter. Burr's counsel, he insisted, acted within their rights in trying "to invalidate the Evidence of Genl. Wilkinson." Wilkinson could have refuted this charge in court but had failed to do so. But Wickham did not rest there. He closed the letter, and the affair, by insisting that "the subject [could] *no longer* be considered as an affair of

Honor"; instead, it was "a charge of a criminal offence made on legal Evidence, and [was] a fit subject for Judicial Decision." Wilkinson had raised an issue that Wickham had intended not to revive. "The General should have reflected," Wickham concluded, "that a person charged with *such* an Offence in the regular Course of Judicial proceedings and on *such* proof has no right to consider the charge as an 'affair' of Honor between himself & the Counsel whose Duty it was to make it, & who was *then* able to maintain it." At the same time, Wickham assured Wilkinson that there had been nothing personal in anything that he had said. He had never "engag[ed] in the controversy in any other Character than as counsel for Col. Burr." Feeling "no animosity" toward Wilkinson, Wickham insisted, he had considered it "a most unpleasant Duty, forced on him by his professional situation," "to be under the necessity of impeaching his Integrity."[251] A week earlier, Wilkinson had denied that there was anything "to justify such license" and claimed a right to "hold any Person (bearing the Character of a Gentleman) personally responsible for such conduct."[252] But he could not make Wickham fight. The Wilkinson-Wickham affair revealed the boundaries of the cultural conventions that kept court proceedings from producing duels: attorneys and judges were covered; witnesses and defendants were not.

The affair should have ended with this letter. That it did not resulted less from the principals themselves than from the political hostilities that Burr's trial had exacerbated. On 2 November, Philadelphia's leading Federalist newspaper, the *United States' Gazette*, briefly noticed Wilkinson's challenge of Wickham "on the authority of a letter from the southward." According to this account, Wickham was "said to have returned [as an] answer, that if [Wilkinson] would clear up his character he would meet him."[253] Wickham had written no such thing, and what he had stated on 31 October could not have made it to Philadelphia so quickly. The author or editor may simply have transferred the logic of Wilkinson's response to Swartwout to Wickham. On reading this piece about his "Affair with that damned Villain Wickham," Wilkinson quickly sent instructions to a friend and fellow officer in Philadelphia. He provided a correction that General William MacPherson was to have printed in the newspaper but also instructed him to "Stop the Gazette from being sent to Richmond."[254] The contents of the unsigned note suggest why Wilkinson wanted to prevent it from reaching Wickham. It asserted that Wickham had not rejected the challenge on the grounds of Wilkinson's character and had "acknowledged the General to stand on a footing with any gentleman."[255] The first claim was correct; the second required a very liberal reading of Wickham's final letter.

Long before the interdicted copies of the *United States' Gazette* could have made it to Richmond, most of the visitors who had been drawn there by Burr's trial had departed. Those who had come just for the show had left first, with some attending only the grand jury stage and others returning for the treason trial. Many of the witnesses had returned home soon after providing their testimony in court or by deposition. By the trial's final week, those who remained either still had parts to play—the judge, attorneys, defendants, and witnesses—or believed that their characters required their presence—Eaton, Swartwout, Wilkinson, and others. Of these men, the Richmonder Marshall left first, "gallop[ing] to the mountains" the day after his final ruling.[256] Swartwout, Blennerhassett, Martin, and Burr departed in separate groups over the next few days, headed for Baltimore. Detained by his affair with Wickham, Wilkinson may have been the last of the visitors to leave Richmond.

Even as popular attention followed these men north, the trial continued to reverberate in Richmond. In the press, editors and others rehashed its developments. The Federalist *Gazette* abandoned the trial first, not surprisingly since it had provided the least original material. It closed its trial coverage by early November with Swartwout's posting of Wilkinson, a pseudonymous letter to the editor, and a final piece from Martin. The *Argus*'s interest in the trial lasted longer and filled more pages. For another month, it published editorials, essays, letters, clipped pieces from elsewhere, and satirical items that apportioned censure and praise among the trial's participants. The *Enquirer* committed even more time and space to dissecting Burr's trial. Between 30 October and 24 November, Ritchie published a six-part series entitled "Cursory Reflections," devoting the first two numbers to Burr and the next four to Marshall; a promised series on Wilkinson never appeared.[257] Then, it reprinted a four-letter series of attacks on Marshall, signed "Lucius," from Philadelphia's *Aurora General Advertiser*.

Scattered among the two series of essays were editorials and other pieces on the trial. Long after new developments elsewhere had displaced the trial from its newspapers, though, Richmond felt the impacts of the final judicial resolution of the Burr Conspiracy.

Reflecting upon Burr's trial a month after its end, Marshall described it as "the most unpleasant case which has ever been brought before a Judge in this or perhaps in any other country."[258] Marshall had hinted at some of the sources of this unpleasantness months earlier, after the grand jury hearing. The case, he had written to Justice William Cushing, "presents many real intrinsic difficulties which are infinitely multiplied by extrinsic circumstances."[259] The difficulties included not just the importance of the alleged crime and the conflicts among the witnesses' accounts, but also the significance of the legal and constitutional questions. They had been intensified by the circumstances that surrounded the case. Some of these—city, state, and national politics, the political differences among the trial's leading figures, the partisan press—would surely have been what Marshall had in mind when writing to Cushing. But other "extrinsic circumstances"—most importantly, the centrality of character in the courtroom and in society—would have been so integral to their culture that neither Marshall nor Cushing may have considered their impact. At the very least, Marshall, Cushing, and their contemporaries may not have been able to imagine a trial that was not shaped by character and similar extrinsic circumstances.

In some ways, the Burr trial was everything that the Burr Conspiracy was not. Ultimately, very little had happened at Blennerhassett Island, on the Ohio and Mississippi Rivers, or in the Mississippi Territory, much less in New Orleans or Mexico, in late 1806 and early 1807. But much of local, state, and national interest had happened in Richmond during the trial. At the climax of the treason trial, Burr's attorney Benjamin Botts had emphasized the great disjuncture between the "terrible war" that had allegedly occurred on 10 December 1806 on Blennerhassett Island and the "much more serious war" that had actually occurred in court. "We have had here," Botts charged, "a carnage of breaths, sour looks and hard words and the roaring of vocal cannon. We have had a battle with the laws and constitution fought courageously and furiously by our enemy [i.e., the prosecution]." Given what had happened in court, he asked, was "it not a mockery to speak of the war on Blannerhassett's island?"[260] Nearly two months of battles remained to be fought in this courtroom war when Botts spoke. Another war had long raged in Richmond's newspapers, pitting the *Argus* and *Enquirer* against the *Gazette* and *Observer*. Still another had already swept through Richmond society, reaching homes and taverns, pleasure gardens and penitentiary cells. And another war loomed as some men looked to the dueling ground to defend their honor and repair their character. But, despite the great interest that it provoked at the time, despite the cultural dynamics that it can reveal to us now, the courtroom war failed to produce the clear answers that so many contemporaries had expected. By failing to justify the Burr crisis or to prove the Burr Conspiracy, Burr's trial inflamed, rather than soothed, the tense political and social climate in Richmond and beyond.

CHAPTER 9

"WHO IS BLENNERHASSETT?"

The Narrative of William Wirt

SEVENTY-FIVE, FIFTY, INDEED, TEN YEARS AFTER THE TRIAL IN Richmond, even literate, engaged Americans would rarely have seen the key documents that had shaped popular understanding of the Burr Conspiracy during the crisis. Aaron Burr's famous cipher letter to James Wilkinson was available in some of the published trial reports, a few government document collections, and a handful of biographies and histories. Thomas Jefferson's crucial message to Congress would have been even harder to find. But, for decades after the trial, another, very different document occasionally appeared in magazines and books and was regularly recited in lecture halls and schoolhouses. This document became so ubiquitous and so powerful that it, perhaps more than any other, continued to shape popular views of a key aspect of the Burr Conspiracy throughout the nineteenth century. Indeed, when an Aaron Burr Legion took shape early in the twentieth century to defend Burr's memory, its enumerated goals included "expunging from all reading books, or other text books used in the public schools of America, . . . the speech of William Wirt during the trial of Aaron Burr at Richmond."[1]

William Wirt's "Who is Blennerhassett?" speech, as it was usually known, differed from the other significant documents that had helped contemporaries make sense of the conspiracy in various ways. The cipher letter and the presidential message were linked to the principal figures in the Burr crisis—the main conspirator, his expected supporter and eventual betrayer, and his powerful denouncer. Their authors and intended audiences fixed the importance of these widely reprinted documents. These documents, moreover, had reached the public when Burr's plans seemed mysterious and his actions seemed portentous.

339

FIGURE 13. William Wirt and Harman Blennerhassett.

Wirt, in contrast, had played no role in creating or defeating the crisis itself. Furthermore, there was nothing inherently significant about the "Who is Blennerhassett?" speech; it formed a small part of one of Wirt's many arguments in Richmond and, as such, comprised just a tiny fragment of the published record of the trial. And Wirt's speech began to reach the public beyond the courtroom only in late September 1807, long after the crisis had passed and after people had learned of Burr's acquittal.

In time, however, Wirt's brief discourse on the Irish immigrant Harman Blennerhassett, his island home, and his relationship with Burr not only became the most celebrated moment of the trial, but also captured the popular mind of nineteenth-century America in a distinct way. Heavily romanticized and largely groundless, Wirt's story developed into the controlling narrative of Blennerhassett's role in the conspiracy, shaping the understanding of both the person and the event for generations. Blennerhassett had his own views of his relationship with Burr and Burr's project—views that he planned to present when his own case came to trial. When the course of the legal proceedings made that unnecessary, Blennerhassett filed his accounts among his papers, where they remained, unseen by any but family and friends, until mid-century. By the time that Blennerhassett's alternative story became widely available, Wirt's fanciful tale had grown so deeply entrenched in the popular, and even scholarly, imagination as to have become almost unassailable. As had often been the case during the Burr crisis itself, the less accurate narrative had a greater impact than the more accurate one.

"SUCH WAS THE STATE OF EDEN, WHEN THE SERPENT ENTERED ITS BOWERS"

Burr's treason trial carried an immense weight of public expectation when it commenced in early August 1807. For months, the public had looked to the trial to "devellope what is now [a] matter of doubt."[2] In late June, the grand jury had indicted Burr, Blennerhassett, and five others on charges of treason and misdemeanor. But only it had seen and heard the evidence that supported those indictments. Now, that evidence would have to be produced before the petit jury in open court. Beyond the jury box, beyond the crowded courtroom, men and women across the country eagerly awaited the revelations about the conspiracy, often expecting that "Some great Secret [would] be devellope."[3] As the *National Intelligencer* had announced after the grand jury hearings, the treason trial needed to produce "a full and satisfactory disclosure of all the circumstances connected with the conspiracy" so that the public would "no longer grope in the dark."[4]

The treason trial started slowly. Not until 17 August did the prosecution—George Hay, Alexander McRae, and William Wirt—finally begin to make its case. Its plan, as Wirt explained, was "to narrate a tale." Through the arguments of the attorneys and the testimony of the witnesses, it would relate the story of the conspiracy in "chronological order . . . , unfolding events as they occurred." This tale would "[develop] this conspiracy from its birth to the consummation[, unravel] the plot from its conception to its denouement, and [trace] Aaron Burr step by step as he advanced and became more bold, till the act was consummated by the assemblage on Blannerhassett's island." The prosecution viewed assembling a coherent, chronological narrative out of the fragmentary evidence as essential. Doing so would provide "the most luminous mode of communicating [the facts] to the jury" and be the "most favourable to a complete comprehension of the subject."[5] Hay's opening remarks embodied this strategy. They included a lengthy section that unfolded the conspiracy from its conception to its collapse as clearly as anything that had been written on the subject. According to one witness, Hay's opening statement was "solemn & impressive," producing "a visible change . . . in the countenance of the accused."[6]

That the defense intended to frustrate this strategy became clear the same day. When Hay called William Eaton as the first witness, Burr quickly objected. The defense asked the court to require the prosecution to demonstrate first, with two witnesses, that Burr had committed an overt act of levying war against the United States at the time and place specified in the indictment—on 10 December 1806 at Blennerhassett Island. This motion would have silenced the prosecution's most damning witnesses, who could speak only to Burr's intentions. Chief Justice John Marshall's ruling rejected the motion's most sweeping implications, but it limited the prosecution's ability to construct a chronological story by insisting that, while witnesses could speak to Burr's intentions, they had to limit themselves to "the intention with which the overt act itself was committed." Wide-ranging testimony about "a general evil disposition" would not be admitted, at least not until after the fact of levying war had been established.[7] The prosecution was not barred from calling witnesses to Burr's intentions, but it was forced to deviate from its original strategy by also calling, from the beginning, witnesses who could speak to events on the island.

After three days of testimony by a dozen witnesses, the defense moved to arrest the evidence on the grounds that Burr had not been on Blennerhassett Island on the specified day. Two more witnesses to the events of 10 December spoke on 21 August. Then, for eight days, the two sets of attorneys argued the motion to arrest the evidence, scouring hundreds of years of English and American case law to find precedents for and against the notion that Burr could have committed treason without being present for the overt act. One strain of the defense's arguments asserted that Burr could not be found guilty even as an accessory until "the person from whom his guilt is derived [i.e., Blennerhassett, had been] shewn to be guilty."[8] Even those who did not understand all of the legal complexities recognized that, if the motion carried, testimony would end and Burr would be acquitted.

With a four-hour argument on 25 August, Wirt anchored the prosecution's response. He carefully addressed the defense's precedents. He attacked every element of its argument. And he advanced his own points in favor of hearing further testimony to prove that, because Burr had assembled the men and supplied their provisions, he could be guilty of treason despite being absent at the time of the overt act. In the midst of this forensic counterattack, Wirt briefly addressed the defense's efforts to present Burr as, at worst, an accessory to Blennerhassett's actions by asking and answering the question, who is Blennerhassett? In a few paragraphs, Wirt set out to "compare the cases of the two men and settle this question of precedence between them." He concluded this passage by insisting that "*reason* declares Aaron Burr the principal in this crime."[9]

The central metaphor of this passage in Wirt's argument came from the Bible. Wirt constructed Harman Blennerhassett as Adam, Margaret Blennerhassett as Eve, their island home as the Garden of Eden, and Aaron Burr as the serpent who tempted them into their own destruction. Thus, in answering his question, who is Blennerhassett? Wirt presented an innocent. Harman had "fled the storms of his own country to find quiet in ours." He was a man of "taste and science and wealth" who had "sought quiet and solitude in the bosom of our western forests." All of his past actions showed "that war [was] not the natural element of his mind" and that an army could not "[furnish] the society natural and proper to [his] character." With him had come his wife, "who is said to be lovely even beyond her sex and graced with every accomplishment that can render it irresistible." In Wirt's account, Harman had created a "paradise" on "a beautiful island in the Ohio." He had erected "a palace and decorate[d] it with every romantic embellishment of fancy." Here, he was surrounded by "a shrubbery that Shenstone might have envied, . . . music that might have charmed Calypso and her nymphs, . . . an extensive library[, and] a philosophical apparatus [that] offer[ed] to him all the secrets and mysteries of nature." In a new country and a wild land, he had built a place of civility, hospitality, and beauty. At his island home, "peace, tranquility and innocence shed their mingled delights around him." As Wirt reminded the court, "Such was the state of Eden, when the serpent entered its bowers."[10]

Wirt left no doubt that, in this analogy, Burr was the "serpent," though "in a more engaging form." It was not simply that Burr was the "author," the "projector," and the "active executor" of the whole conspiracy, whose "brain conceived it [and] hand brought it into action." He was also a tempter and a seducer. The "innocence" of the Blennerhassetts made them easy prey for the wiles of Burr. With "the dignity and elegance of his demeanor, the light and beauty of his conversation, and the seductive and fascinating power of his address," Wirt charged, Burr "[wound] himself into the open and unpracticed heart of the unfortunate Blennerhassett." Burr gradually filled Harman with "the poison of his own ambition" and "the fire of his own courage." Soon, Harman, like Burr, "burn[ed] with restless emulation at the names of Cromwell, Cæsar, and Bonaparte." The "mastering spirit and genius" of Burr, as Wirt declaimed, had "deluded [Blennerhassett] from his interest and his happiness" and "seduced [him] from the paths of innocence and peace." By coming to Blennerhassett Island, the "destroyer" Burr had "turn[ed] this paradise into a hell."[11]

Although one witness found Wirt's account so compelling as to become convinced "that Col B's motion [would] not prevail," the "Who is Blennerhassett?" speech, and the larger argument of which it was a part, failed.[12] A week after Wirt spoke, Marshall accepted the defense motion, stopped the presentation of further evidence in the treason trial, and placed the jury in a position that effectively guaranteed Burr's acquittal. At that time, Wirt's speech was known only to those who had heard it when he delivered it on 25 August. Having failed in its purpose, it might easily have been forgotten long before Thomas Carpenter's and David Robertson's trial reports appeared nearly a year later. In fact, if the administration had decided to try Blennerhassett for treason, it might even have made the prosecution's task very difficult. Instead, the "Who is Blennerhassett?" speech survived long after Burr's trial as the embodiment of what Marshall called "a degree of eloquence seldom displayed on any occasion."[13]

"NO MORE THAN THE CREATION OF THE ORATOR'S FANCY"

Even before Burr's trial, Wirt had earned a solid, if local, reputation for eloquence. The appearance of *The Letters of the British Spy* in late 1803 had established him as a belletrist. His legal work in the courts of Norfolk and Williamsburg between 1803 and 1806 had secured his renown as "one of the most eloquent advocates in the state."[14] By March

1807, Wirt enjoyed such a strong reputation as an attorney and an orator that both sides in the Burr case tried to hire him. Before the trial began, people who had heard Wirt speak or knew his reputation anticipated the opportunities for oratory that it would provide him. Bishop James Madison of the College of William and Mary predicted that the trial would offer "a fine Field for Wirt," who needed "only the opp[ortunity] to display a Store of Talents, as rare as rich."[15] Virginia governor William H. Cabell likewise noted that the young lawyer "never did & never can, in any case, make any but an able speech."[16] Wirt hoped to improve upon this "opportunity of measuring [his] strength with the greatest men of the nation." Writing to a confidant, he admitted that the only consolations in what seemed certain to be a difficult trial were "the glory & the cash."[17]

Throughout Burr's trial, Wirt satisfied these expectations. During the grand jury stage, Nathaniel Saltonstall Jr. described him as "a most eloquent Man," while Wilkinson proclaimed him to be the long-sought "Demosthenes of our Country."[18] A quarter century later, Wirt's first biographer identified passages from three arguments from the trial, in addition to the famous one of 25 August, "as very happy examples of [his] oratorical skill."[19] This list included Wirt's final argument in the trial, a long and often sarcastic speech in support of committing Burr and Blennerhassett for trial elsewhere, that some witnesses considered his finest. "They say Wirt made last monday the most able & eloquent speech ever delivered in Virginia," the governor informed his brother.[20] But it was the 25 August argument, in general, and the "Who is Blennerhassett?" passage, in particular, for which Wirt would long be remembered. Anticipation led to a crowded courtroom, and Wirt did not disappoint many auditors. Reporting upon this argument a day later, the *Virginia Argus*—whose trial coverage appeared in newspapers across the country—called it "one of the most eloquent and argumentative speeches that was ever delivered within the walls of the Capitol."[21]

While many of those attending the trial may have been most interested in deriving "Entertainment" from "pleadings [that were] expected to be energetic[,] eloquent & impressive," Wirt understood that an effective argument had to be solidly grounded in evidence.[22] Within the passage itself, he claimed that his narrative was "substantially capable of proof." He even insisted on the accuracy of his description of the Edenic nature of Blennerhassett Island before Burr's arrival: "The *evidence* would convince you, . . . that this is but a faint picture of the real life."[23] By 25 August, Wirt had seen notes of the evidence from the grand jury hearings and heard a week's worth of testimony. While extensive, though, this material provided little to substantiate his description of Blennerhassett and the island before Burr's first visit or his tale of Burr's corruption of Blennerhassett. The most valuable of these sources was Dudley Woodbridge Jr., Blennerhassett's former business partner. Woodbridge, like most of the western witnesses, had spoken primarily about Blennerhassett's role in recruiting men, building boats, and purchasing provisions for Burr. But he had also commented upon Blennerhassett's character and lifestyle. Burr had opened this line of questioning by asking Woodbridge: "Was it not ridiculous for [Blennerhassett] to be engaged in a military enterprise?"[24] Woodbridge had responded that Blennerhassett "[knew] nothing of military affairs" and, because of his extreme near-sightedness, was physically unsuited for battle. Additional questions by Burr and Wirt had produced answers from Woodbridge that mentioned Blennerhassett's immense library, scientific pursuits, and musical abilities, as well as the vast sums that he had spent improving the island. Woodbridge had also acknowledged that many of Blennerhassett's neighbors viewed him as having "every kind of sense but common sense."[25]

That Wirt drew from sources beyond the trial itself seems clear. He probably had already formed some sense of the Blennerhassetts and their home from the reports—oral and written, published and unpublished—of the many travellers who had visited or passed the island. One published travel account from 1805, for example, had mentioned "the elegant mansion and buildings of Mr. Blennerhasset, on an island of more than one hundred acres [that] possess[ed] all the beauties of a well-cultivated garden."[26] In early 1807, a letter that had appeared in newspapers across the country had even described the island as "com[ing] near [the author's] notion of Eden."[27] Wirt could also have learned a great deal by talking with the Blennerhassetts' Ohio or Virginia neighbors among the witnesses. And he had presumably seen the file of answers to the questions that Attorney General Caesar A. Rodney had directed federal agents in the West to ask of potential witnesses—a body of evidence that seemingly no longer exists. In the early 1830s, Wirt's first biographer pointed to the existence of additional sources as he challenged the supposition that this "well known description of Blennerhassett and his Island" was "no more than the creation of the orator's fancy." Whatever this unspecified evidence may have been, Peter Hoffman Cruse called it "quite as high-wrought" as Wirt's account.[28]

Wirt's narrative seems to have derived primarily from his knowledge of and beliefs about the characters of Blennerhassett and Burr. In the case of Blennerhassett, Wirt's understanding came less from direct experience or firsthand testimony, such as Woodbridge's, and more from vague reports about his home and habits. Wirt had apparently never seen Margaret Blennerhassett and had probably only seen Harman once in the three weeks since he had arrived in Richmond. Wirt had not read any of the letters between Blennerhassett and Burr. And there is no evidence that he had heard even secondhand accounts of how the two had met or interacted with each other. As such, Wirt's account described a meeting between types—the gullible innocent and the seductive fiend—rather than an actual event. Indeed, one of the few solid facts about their relationship in his narrative was incorrect. Wirt mistakenly placed their initial meeting "in the autumn of 1806" rather than the spring of 1805.[29]

Late on 25 August, one of the witnesses reported home to Ohio that "Mr. Wirt delivered today the most eloquent speech I ever [heard]."[30] The "Who is Blennerhassett?" speech's impact on those who heard it that day was both immediate and lasting. When he gave his deposition on behalf of Blennerhassett in mid-September 1807, Charles Fenton Mercer, who had been in court for Wirt's speech, began a long history of echoing Wirt's imagery. Unlike Wirt, Mercer knew the Blennerhassetts and had visited the island just days before the alleged act of treason. Still, his deposition displayed "the same fervour of poetical rapture" as Wirt's passage.[31] It referred to the "shrubs," the "library," the "melodious instruments," and the scientific apparatus that Wirt had highlighted. It commented upon the elegance of the home and "the society of Mr. Blannerhasset and his lively and accomplished lady." And it described "a solitary island in the heart of a desert" that had been transformed into "a terrestrial paradise."[32] Others who witnessed Wirt's speech continued to refer to it months and even years later. In December 1807, the law student John F. May concluded a letter with a long paean to this argument, which he viewed as "a perfect pandect . . . digested, harmonious, consistent, [and] mature as Pallas from the brain of Jove."[33] As late as 1834, one writer noted that "hundreds in [Richmond] still remember these surpassing triumphs of [Wirt's] genius as an orator and advocate."[34]

Repeated publication soon spread Wirt's tale far beyond the court. Important developments in the trial delayed the publication of any of the attorneys' arguments on the motion for weeks. Finally, on 26 September, the *Enquirer*, which had begun printing Wirt's full argument a few issues earlier, reached the "Who is Blennerhassett?" passage. Three days later, the nearby *Petersburg Intelligencer* published it as an excerpt. The extracted passage spread to newspapers across the country, reaching New York City and Raleigh in early October and Pittsburgh, Natchez, and New Orleans in November.[35] The next year, Wirt's entire argument appeared in two reports of the trial: Carpenter's *The Trial of Col. Aaron Burr* and Robertson's *Reports of the Trials of Colonel Aaron Burr*. These somewhat different accounts had been taken down in shorthand in court. Another version that appeared in 1808 used Wirt's "original notes" to revise and supplement a shorthand transcript.[36] A one-volume report of Burr's trial that appeared in 1864 cut hundreds of pages from Carpenter's and Robertson's by "greatly abridg[ing] and condens[ing]," and in some cases "wholly omitt[ing]," the attorneys' arguments. Still, the compiler included the "Who is Blennerhassett?" passage in full as evidence "of the manner and spirit in which the trial was conducted."[37]

The public interest in the Burr Conspiracy, the widespread acclaim for Wirt's oratorical skill, and the ready availability of his argument made it a natural selection when the first collections of American oratory were prepared in the 1810s and 1820s. Long or short, the Wirt excerpts in these anthologies and in schoolbooks invariably included the "Who is Blennerhassett?" passage. Increase Cooke reprinted it in his 1811 instructional manual, *The American Orator*—a work that went through four editions by the decade's end. S. C. Carpenter published a long section from Wirt's argument in his *Select American Speeches* (1816); E. B. Williston included Wirt in his five-volume *Eloquence of the United States* (1827). Similar collections with Wirt's speech appeared throughout the century. Americans not only read Wirt's "Who is Blennerhassett?" passage for decades after the trial but heard it, as well. It was recited as an example of oratorical excellence in various contexts. The William Wirt Societies and Literary Institutes that persisted long after Wirt's death in 1834 often featured this passage in their public presentations. In 1838, a Professor Bronson, an oratory instructor, advertised an evening of recitations in the nation's capital that included Wirt's "Burr and Blennerhassett" among thirteen "*descriptive, patriotic, amusing,* and *tragic* pieces."[38] The most common place to have heard Wirt's speech, though, was in the nation's schools. One 1847 work called it "the favorite of every school-boy."[39] Wirt's depiction of Blennerhassett, according to the *Southern Literary Messenger* in 1858, was "still spouted on many a country school-house floor."[40] Another five decades later, a Burr biographer could still describe the passage as "familiar to every schoolboy."[41]

The "Who is Blennerhassett" passage appeared in other, often stranger places, as well. Wirt's biographer John Pendleton Kennedy reprinted a long extract from the 25 August argument in his *Memoirs of the Life of William Wirt* (1849). An earlier Wirt biographer had decided not to include this "well-known popular passage" only because it had already, by 1832, "shared the fate of many a classic page, of palling by familiar repetition."[42] In 1827, an article, "Intemperance," in a Rhode Island newspaper that included a letter from Harman Blennerhassett's son Dominic—regarding a cure for alcoholism—had reprinted Wirt's passage, even though the editor admitted that it was "somewhat odd to embody it in this article."[43] And, in 1818, George Watterston, the librarian of Congress, had included the "Who is Blennerhassett?" passage as evidence of Wirt's eloquence in his book, *Letters from Washington*. After reading Watterston's work, the artist Charles Willson Peale became so impressed that he transcribed the excerpt into his diary, noting: "I have copied this memorable speach of the orator Mr. Wirt, as worthy of remembrance."[44]

"A LIGHT WHICH SHOULD BE ADMITTED TO FEW EYES"

Peale was not alone in copying Wirt's famous passage into his diary; Blennerhassett had done the same thing a decade earlier. On 25 August 1807, while Wirt spoke in court, Blennerhassett sat in the penitentiary awaiting his trial. Nonetheless, he knew of both the anticipation that preceded and the acclaim that followed Wirt's performance. The next day, Blennerhassett apparently could learn only that Wirt had "paid [him] some compliments" in his long argument. Not until 30 September did Blennerhassett first see what he described as the "curious parallel of Burr's character and my own drawn by Wirt" in the *Enquirer*. Three days later, he transcribed most of the already celebrated passage into his diary. At the time, he offered only a brief assessment: "Whatever may be the defects of this performance, . . . it is remarkable as containing far more real history than fiction, tho' wearing so much the face of the latter."[45]

Blennerhassett quickly adopted elements of Wirt's narrative into his own perspective on past and current events. Long before he read Wirt's argument, Blennerhassett had recognized that the conniving Burr "had duped" him; in late August, he recorded in his journal that he had been "possessed of [this knowledge] these 9. months." But Wirt's biblical metaphor gave Blennerhassett a new language for expressing this perspective. On 30 September, the day that he first read Wirt's speech, he described Burr using his "talents for intrigue" to entangle two "young men" in "snares . . . rashly laid for their credulity." The day after copying the passage into his journal, Blennerhassett made his appropriation of Wirt's trope complete when he recorded that one of these young men was in danger of succumbing to "the fascination of this serpent." Throughout the remainder of the journal, Burr appeared as a "tempter" whose "career" had depended upon "the absurd confidence of so many dupes."[46]

If Blennerhassett found it easy to adopt Wirt's construction of Burr as the serpent, it proved much more difficult to accept Wirt's presentation of himself as an innocent. His cunning in his dealings with Burr, Burr's wealthy son-in-law Joseph Alston, and others formed one of the principal themes of his journal—both before and after he read Wirt's argument. Written for his wife and a few friends, the journal boastingly recorded the various stratagems by which Blennerhassett sought repayment from Burr and Alston for the losses that he had sustained. Its author presented himself not as an innocent dupe, but as a deft manipulator. One lengthy entry detailed his skill at playing on Alston's "vanity of author-ship" by lavishing praise upon a pamphlet that Alston was assumed to have written. During another of Alston's visits,

Blennerhassett tried to show his "perserverance in [his] duties of honour and good faith" toward Burr, hoping that this approach would serve "the interest of [his] pecuniary expectations." With Burr, Blennerhassett chose different "baits," raising the possibility of financial backing for Burr's new projects by hinting at his "ability to introduce him into the first circles in England" and his prospects of inheriting "a large fortune." The night before he put "this plan [into] execution," Blennerhassett predicted that he could gain "thro' [Burr's] vanity and interest" the repayment that seemed unlikely to come "thro' his justice or generosity."[47]

While this self-presentation as a skilled manipulator of men appears throughout the journal, it seems clear that, in other areas, Blennerhassett's construction of himself responded to how he had been constructed at the trial, particularly by Wirt. The implications of Burr's and Wirt's questioning of Woodbridge proved especially troubling. Blennerhassett bristled at their efforts to portray him "as a character less skilled in the ordinary affairs of life than common men" and "to show, that [he] cd. in no sense, be regarded as a military character." Wirt's depiction of Blennerhassett as an innocent Adam raised similar doubts about his competence and manhood. Blennerhassett viewed, and presented, himself very differently. He considered himself a man of honor, unafraid of violence and bloodshed. He went out of his way to demonstrate his bravery following the trial. In early November, he gleefully reported to William Duane, the editor of Philadelphia's *Aurora General Advertiser*, how coolly he had "dine[d] and sup[ped] in public on the day [his] effigy was executed" in Baltimore. "When I told him I was always provided with a brace of pistols," Blennerhassett recorded with obvious pleasure, "he twirled on his seat." For years, Blennerhassett seemed overly ready to suggest duels to settle disputes, even though, as Alston had reminded him in August 1807, his "short sight wd. lay [him] under very unfair disadvantages." With characteristic bluster, Blennerhassett had replied: "I should know how to accommodate the distance to the extent of my sight."[48]

Blennerhassett also seized upon an opportunity afforded by Wirt's metaphor to reconstruct himself as a St. George to Burr's dragon, instead of an Adam to Burr's serpent. After reading Wirt's argument, Blennerhassett began to refashion himself in his journal as a champion who could protect others from Burr's wiles. He quickly assigned himself the task of defending "young men . . . fr. future connections" with Burr. Recognizing, in early October, that Burr was trying "to attach to him some yng. men," Blennerhassett devoted himself to foiling these efforts. Of particular interest to Burr was Bob Robinson, whose "father was *wealthy* and [who was] an *only child*." "To save him," Blennerhassett recorded, "my breast heaved with indignation against his tempter." By preparing Robinson for Burr's lies, Blennerhassett ensured that he "[made] his escape."[49]

Blennerhassett's journal had its purposes, but it could hardly have revised or refuted Wirt's narrative as written. It was principally, as its title claimed, the "Journal of Harman Blennerhassett Esq. Whilst in the Jail at the City of Richmond Va. awaiting his Trial for Treason & Misdemeanor." It began on 20 July, when Blennerhassett was arrested in Lexington, Kentucky, to be taken to Richmond. And it ended exactly four months later, after his final meeting with Burr in Philadelphia. In only a few places did Blennerhassett comment upon the conspiracy itself; these comments were scattered and fragmentary. But, while he said relatively little about his past relations with Burr, Blennerhassett included too much in the journal on other topics to publish it without careful editing. "My reflections are penned for no eye but that of my wife and 2 or 3 confidential friends," he noted at one point. Always aware that those few people formed his audience, he exercised little restraint in commenting upon his antagonists, acquaintances, and allies and was equally free in writing about himself. "Many characters," including his own, were "passed . . . in review, in a light which should be admitted to few eyes."[50]

If the journal held no promise as Blennerhassett's counter-narrative to Wirt's story, another document did. On 7 August, three days after arriving in Richmond, Blennerhassett, a lawyer by training, "began to brief my case for my Counsel." The brief, unlike the journal, covered past events and addressed a broader audience—effectively the jury in his own expected trial. For a week, Blennerhassett worked steadily on the brief; on 13 August, he recorded: "I entered on the 13th folio, bringing the narrative of the case, so far as I hope I can prove it, down to the period of my first interview wth. [John] Graham on Burr's affairs at Marietta, in last Novemr." On that day, or soon after, he stopped writing his still-incomplete brief. Why he set aside a project that had clearly allowed him to feel productive and stay active during his difficult first days in prison is not clear. He may have abandoned it out of frustration over Burr's refusal to recognize his legal abilities. In a note to Burr on 14 August, Blennerhassett tried to claim an active role in the defense by urging the summoning of a particular witness, arguing that he should be involved in "cross-examining all the witnesses that [he] knew," and suggesting that he "shd. at least be in Court, when such witnesses appear." In the same note, he proposed that one or more of his and Burr's attorneys should read his "Brief so far as [he] had written it." Burr's reply—"that he was so surrounded by company he could not make up his mind" about these issues—must have annoyed a man in a prison cell. Burr added that he would send one of their attorneys to read the brief and "confer on other matters"; "but," Blennerhassett noted, "I have recd. no such visit." There is no evidence that the attorneys ever read his brief. He clearly had not shown it to them before 23 August, when he told John Wickham and Benjamin Botts that he "hoped, it wd. not be necessary to trouble them, with [it]."[51] And it seems unlikely that he would have done so later, given the developments in the trial.

Even unfinished, the brief stood as Blennerhassett's most complete narrative of his involvement with Burr. It began with the first meeting between the two men in May 1805 and ended with Blennerhassett's conversation with Graham, the special agent whom Jefferson had sent after Burr, eighteen months later. It was replete with the facts that are so obviously absent from Wirt's speech. Blennerhassett first met Burr during "a voluntary and unsolicited visit made by A.B." to the island; the visit was short and included "no private interview." A correspondence began in late 1805, when Blennerhassett responded to a polite letter from Burr by asking to join in "any speculation" that he might undertake in the West, whether "a commercial enterprise or [a] land purchase" or "a military adventure" against Spain's colonies. Burr visited the island again in August 1806 for one day, "in which not more than 3/4 hour was spent" alone with Blennerhassett. The following day, they went together to Marietta, "where there was no time for organizing treason or military expeditions." Burr and Blennerhassett discussed western sentiment that might produce a division of the union, but only "in a speculative way." They were more interested in the Spanish, whom they agreed should be expelled from "American territory." Although aware that Burr had not divulged "his exact plans," Blennerhassett "tendered his services" on Burr's assurance that the government would ignore preparations for an attack on Spanish possessions if "they were kept secret till their execution should be legalized by a declaration of war."[52] And so on.

Blennerhassett did not write his brief—could not have written his brief—in response to Wirt's famous speech. But it offered a self-portrait that contrasted starkly with Wirt's innocent Adam. In the brief, Blennerhassett presented himself as a man of initiative and action. He may not have invited Burr to the island, but he had taken the first step toward turning a slight acquaintance into something more, even "distinctly mention[ing]" a military enterprise as one possibility. And he claimed for himself "the design of publishing in the Ohio Gazette" the series of essays explaining why the West should separate from the East that were signed "Querist." The brief also showed Blennerhassett to be far more cautious than Wirt imagined. It recounted his doubts about Burr and his repeated efforts to have those doubts removed, whether by pressing Burr for answers or by making his own observations "with views of further certifying himself" that Burr's efforts were approved by the people and ignored by the government.[53]

Nor did Blennerhassett prepare the brief as an accurate account of Burr's project or of his role in it. He wrote it for a particular audience and purpose—to help his counsel secure his acquittal of treason and misdemeanor. That he could have told a very different history of the conspiracy, based on his papers and his memories, than the one in his brief became apparent within a few years. On various occasions in the early 1810s, he tried to use his papers, or the story that they permitted him to tell, to restore his finances. He worked to convince first Alston and later Burr that they could avoid embarrassing disclosures "relative to Mr. Burr's designs upon New Orleans and Mexico" only by making a substantial payment toward his heavy losses on Burr's behalf, which he estimated at $50,000. Otherwise, he would publish a book that he claimed, as early as March 1811, was "ready for the press."[54] Both men ignored these blackmail attempts. In late 1814, having tired of Alston's evasions, Blennerhassett even offered to testify against the then governor of South Carolina before a judge, promising to "unfold a tale 'respecting [his] concern and participation in all the views and designs of Col. Burr.'"[55]

Even as Wirt's account appeared in more places, even as Blennerhassett's finances continued to suffer, he never published his threatened book or his correspondence with Burr, Alston, and others. His own narrative, supported by his papers, might have combatted Wirt's depiction of him as an innocent and dupe with his own self-construction as a man of initiative, calculation, and honor. But a true story would have established his conscious involvement in disunionist plotting, even if it did not prove an overt act of war against the United States. By remaining silent, Blennerhassett allowed something that he considered a misrepresentation to shape his public image. In the first years after the trial, this choice must have seemed more likely to afford him a life of peace and retirement at his Mississippi plantation, La Cache (The Hideaway). After Harman's death in 1831, his widow, his sons, and, eventually, some more remote descendents turned to his papers as they sought both to raise funds and to restore his reputation. A few excerpts from his prison journal appeared in the mid-1830s in Matthew Livingston Davis's biography of Burr. But not until 1845 did the brief and a few letters first appear, and not until 1864 did William H. Safford publish a more complete edition of the Blennerhassett papers.[56]

"IN LANGUAGE WHICH I NEED NOT ATTEMPT TO EMULATE"

Long before Blennerhassett's account began to reach the public in the mid-1840s, Wirt's fanciful narrative had become entrenched in the popular consciousness. For decades, nearly every mention of Blennerhassett seemed to require a reference not just to Burr, but also to Wirt. "The connexion of these two names," the 1845 article "Burr and Blennerhassett" began, "has been made immortal by Wirt's eloquent and beautiful allusion to the latter in his speech on the trial of the former."[57] Wirt's tropes—the "Adamic" Blennerhassett, the "Edenic" island, and the "Satanic" Burr—became so familiar and so accepted as to remain largely impervious to the new evidence in Blennerhassett's papers. In newspaper articles and magazine pieces, in private letters and travel accounts, in novels and plays, in biographies and histories, Wirt's account echoed and reechoed across the nineteenth century.

Newspapers and magazines, in particular, reified the key elements of Wirt's narrative. The very titles of some of the articles—"The Island Paradise" (1855), "And Who Was Blennerhasset?" (1877), and "Who then is Blannerhasset" (1830)—make clear its impact. Again and again, Blennerhassett appeared as a man of refinement and science who had withdrawn from the world's conflicts and constructed a happy domestic life. His island home was repeatedly called "Eden."[58] And Burr's arrival was frequently likened to "the introduction of the serpent into Paradise" or described as having occurred "in an evil hour."[59] At times, the invocation of the link between the three men seems almost reflexive. That Margaret Blennerhassett's obituary in 1842 would recall Wirt's description of her "in the famous passage of his defence of her husband" is perhaps not surprising.[60] That Catherine Wirt Randall's obituary eleven years later would describe her, among other things, "as the daughter of the glorious painter of the quiet and beautiful home of Blennerhassett" is harder to explain.[61] But that Caroline Swartwout's obituary in 1898 would mention "Wirt's famous 'Defense of Blennerhassett'" seems purely gratuitous since Wirt had not mentioned either her father, John, or her uncle, Samuel.[62]

Wirt's speech also provided language and meaning for many of the countless travellers on the Ohio River who viewed or visited Blennerhassett Island during the nineteenth century. Given the Romantic enthusiasm about ruins, and the young nation's relative lack of them, it is not surprising that the abandoned gardens and demolished home drew attention. But, even as the island soon bore little resemblance to Wirt's description, travellers regularly referred to his speech and occasionally quoted from it. An 1874 account in a Cincinnati newspaper, for example, reprinted a few sentences from Wirt regarding the long-gone shrubbery, music, library, and scientific apparatus, even as it insisted that "some allowance must undoubtedly be made for the orator's vivid imagination."[63] Travel accounts regularly emphasized the contrast between the "beauty," "elegance," "gaiety[,] and fashion" of the home and grounds as portrayed by Wirt and the current state of "desolation" on the island.[64] Wirt's well-known passage gave the remains a unique character as "the ruins of a former Paradise [that] told the melancholy tale of the ill-fated Blennerhassett."[65] As early as 1840, when she passed the island on a summer tour, Eliza R. Steele discerned the cultural work it performed due to Wirt's speech. "The saddest part of Herman Blennarhasset's fate," she reflected, "is, that every tourist who passes the island, must mention his name and utter an effecting sentimentality about ambition; it seems like dragging him out of his resting place, to hear our taunts."[66]

For some visitors, the moment seemed to call for more than a passing acknowledgement of Wirt's speech. Writing to his wife in May 1818, Horace Holley reported on a stop at Blennerhassett Island, where he and his travelling companion had recalled "the description of Burr's entrance into this island by Wirt." Holley's companion then "repeated [the passage] on the spot," allowing the men to "[enter] into its spirit."[67] In a published account of an 1820 trip, the magazine editor James Hall quoted, paraphrased, and plagiarized Wirt's depiction of the Blennerhassetts' fall after the "evil hour" in which Burr entered their lives. "That this fairy spot . . . was once the elegant retreat of a philosophic mind," Hall stated as justification for his appropriations, "has already been told in language which I need not attempt to emulate."[68] John Lambert's "biographical notice" of Blennerhassett in his *Travels through Lower Canada and the United States of North America* (1810) went even further. It consisted of just a few short paragraphs of his own, followed by four pages from Wirt's speech. Blennerhassett's fall had "been so ably depictured by Mr. Wirt," Lambert explained, "that I should do him injustice, were I to describe [it] in any other language than his own."[69]

Numerous late nineteenth- and early twentieth-century literary and dramatic depictions of the Blennerhassetts and their island home similarly displayed Wirt's impact. Emerson Bennett's *The Traitor* (1850) drew heavily from Wirt for its depiction of the island as a "Garden of Eden," Blennerhassett as an innocent who was "incapable . . . of doing, or even plotting a base action," and Burr as a tempter who was "full of the flattering deceits of a vaulting, avaricious, reckless ambition."[70] Similarly, in Edwin Bynner's novel *Zachary Phips* (1892), Blennerhassett goes out to meet Burr—"the man come to work his destruction"—as "unconscious as the turtle in the market-place bearing on his back the label 'Soup To-morrow.'"[71] Introducing his 1881 play, *Blennerhassett, or*

The Irony of Fate, Charles Felton Pidgin stated that "more than half the language put in *Burr's* mouth [was] taken from his own letters, speeches, and note books." When he penned the Blennerhassetts' lines, however, Pidgin turned not to their letters and papers, though they had long been available, but to Wirt's passage. In the final act, both Harman and Margaret give voice to Wirt's words, with Harman even asking Wirt's famous question: who *is* Blennerhassett?[72]

Among the first generation of American historians in the mid- and late-nineteenth century, many authors employed Wirt's story of innocence beguiled, even if not his imagery, to explain Blennerhassett's role in the conspiracy. In his 1851 history of the United States, Richard Hildreth described the "excitable imagination" of Blennerhassett, the "little Eden of civilization in the midst of the wilderness," and the captivating "arts of Burr."[73] Orville J. Victor's *History of American Conspiracies* (1863) included just two sentences on Burr's first visit to the island but still related the key components of Wirt's narrative. Burr's "winning discourse and polished manners," according to Victor, "captivated the too-credulous [Blennerhassetts] whose fortunes were to be so intimately and disastrously affected by their relations with [him]."[74] Despite his extensive research, which included Safford's *Blennerhassett Papers*, Henry Adams presented the same basic narrative in his *History of the United States of America during the Administrations of Thomas Jefferson and James Madison* (1889–91). "Of all the eager dupes with whom Burr had to deal," Blennerhassett was, according to Adams, "the most simple."[75]

Even the biographers and historians who focused upon Blennerhassett himself rarely resisted the attractions of Wirt's narrative. Safford quoted Wirt at great length in both *The Life of Harman Blennerhassett* (1850) and *The Blennerhassett Papers*, even though he had Blennerhassett's brief, journal, and letters when he wrote the latter. The Ohio historian Samuel P. Hildreth did not quote Wirt in his biographical sketches (1848 and 1852) but certainly adopted his interpretation. "In an evil hour," Hildreth recounted, "this peaceful and happy residence was entered by Aaron Burr, who like Satan in the Eden of old, visited this earthly paradise, only to deceive and destroy." While Hildreth had access to only a few Blennerhassett documents, including the brief and some letters, he had interviewed many Ohioans. Their reminiscences often echoed Wirt, with one describing "the wily serpent" Burr insinuating himself into Blennerhassett's acquaintance.[76] A scholarly article from 1887 similarly described the "good-natured, credulous, generous, gullible" Blennerhassett succumbing "to the plausible, flattering wiles of the shrewd charlatan" Burr. Its author, E. O. Randall, even presented Burr's first visit to the island as "the entry of Satan into Eden."[77]

Only rarely did nineteenth-century authors openly dissent from Wirt's interpretation; their accounts did not rely upon the new evidence from the Blennerhassett papers. In his 1834 memoirs, Henry M. Brackenridge drew on personal knowledge of the Blennerhassetts, before and after they met Burr, to correct the picture painted by "the elegant Wirt." It was not simply that Wirt's account of "the character and motives of Blennerhasset and his lady [were] almost entirely fanciful" and that "his description of the place, which he had never seen, [was] a beautiful touch of the romantic, drawn from his own teeming imagination." Other commentators had said—and continued to say—as much without challenging the basic story told by Wirt. Brackenridge further insisted that the Blennerhassetts' situation "was not that of Adam and Eve in Paradise, nor was Burr a Satan as to them." Instead, Burr had "found them discontented" and seeking a society that better suited their "aristocratic" sensibilities.[78] In 1847, Cincinnati's James W. Taylor saw Blennerhassett's behavior in the years after the trial, which "exhibited the irritability of [his] Irish character," as evidence of "a violent and restless disposition" that conflicted with Wirt's "florid description."[79] A few years later, the Alabama historian Albert James Pickett presented Blennerhassett as "an extravagant, impulsive man" who had "sought Burr" and "was anxious to engage in his schemes." "Burr did not enter the 'terrestial paradise' as a 'serpent,'" he insisted, "but as a man of bold and brilliant schemes, in which Blennerhassett most eagerly and willingly enlisted."[80] Taylor's account reflected his sense of the evolving local memory of Blennerhassett, and perhaps growing anti-Irish sentiment in Cincinnati; Pickett's emerged from his personal respect for Burr, and possibly from support for southwestern expansion. Neither author mentioned Blennerhassett's account.

Such dissents had little impact on the popular or scholarly understanding of Blennerhassett. Long quotes from Wirt's "Who is Blennerhassett?" speech remained common in magazine articles and books into the late nineteenth century. Increasingly, they might be accompanied by a brief excerpt or two from Blennerhassett's letters, brief, or journal. Nonetheless, the basic story that their authors told remained Wirt's. An 1858 article even quoted Blennerhassett's first letter to Burr asking for "a share in the risks and glories of whatever enterprise he had on foot," before presenting him, once again, as an innocent who had been "captivated by [Burr's] glittering visions."[81]

"SUCH A DISPLAY OF ELOQUENCE"

In a trial that lasted seven months, in an argument that consumed four hours, Wirt spoke for perhaps ten minutes about Blennerhassett and his island. Yet, from the hundreds of pages of testimony, argument, and opinion that the trial yielded, this single passage captured the national imagination and shaped the popular and scholarly understanding of a key dimension of the Burr Conspiracy. Arguing that its ubiquity—in newspapers and magazines, in biographies and histories, in oratory collections and schoolbooks—explains its widespread and persistent impact only forces the question, why was it so ubiquitous? What were the characteristics of American politics and culture that made Wirt's account of Blennerhassett's role in the conspiracy so widely accepted and admired?

We can explain some of the immediate appeal of Wirt's speech by situating it within the larger project of diminishing the Burr Conspiracy. Once the failure of Burr's plans became clear, almost everyone who wrote or talked about the conspiracy joined this project. Naturally, Burr's former and current supporters insisted that his plans had always been legitimate and admirable. Federalists sought to minimize Burr's threat to highlight the excessive reactions of Jefferson, Wilkinson, and the Republican press. And Republicans contrasted the limited backing for Burr with the near-universal support for the administration and the union. By circumscribing the circle of traitors more and more narrowly, the Republican participants in this project, from the president down to local committees and newspaper editors, admitted less and less possibility of popular disloyalty. Wirt's speech suggested that, even within the small band of indicted traitors, one could still distinguish the arch-fiend Burr from his dupe Blennerhassett. The formal language of the indictment had described the accused men, including Burr, as having been "moved and seduced by the instigation of the devil."[82] Wirt's speech metaphorically raised (or lowered) Burr from one seduced by the devil to the devil himself, making his alleged disunionism even more isolated and unnatural.

Wirt's "Who is Blennerhassett?" speech also gained potency by making one of the strongest statements of Burr's guilt at the trial. Just days after Wirt spoke, Marshall handed down the ruling that ensured that Burr would not be found guilty of treason. Newspapers across the country reported Marshall's decision, and often printed his opinion, long before they published Wirt's speech. That the "Who is Blennerhassett?" passage came from a losing argument at the decisive moment in a losing cause only seemed to strengthen its appeal. "Few but the avowed friends of the Prince of conspirators [had] doubts of his guilt," according to one Virginian.[83] Although Burr had been "acquited of high treason," the Philadelphia Quaker Elizabeth Drinker similarly remarked, he could not "acquit himself of guilt."[84] For the many who felt that Marshall had unfairly shielded Burr from justice, reading Wirt's strong assertion of Burr's treason may have offered some measure of satisfaction.

Much of the lasting appeal of Wirt's account derived from his success at building its construction of Blennerhassett upon firm cultural and political foundations. Wirt presented Blennerhassett Island as the very embodiment of the republican idyll of the gentleman's estate—a world within itself that was inhabited by cultivated men and women, managed as a productive farm, tended with great care, and isolated from the political world. In the late eighteenth- and early nineteenth-century Anglo-American world, this idyll was frequently expressed through the biblical image of retiring under one's own "vine and fig tree." While Wirt did not use this hackneyed phrase, his story of Blennerhassett's "retire[ment]" to the "quiet and solitude" of the island invoked this well-established image.[85] Presenting Blennerhassett as an exemplar of this cultural construct served Wirt's forensic purposes. A man who had retired from the world would hardly instigate treason. Writing in late December 1806, Judge Thomas Rodney, who had stopped at the island and met Blennerhassett in 1803, admitted that he could not imagine "what should Induce him to quit a Pallace &

Paradice . . . to Undertake a wild adventure."[86] "Had I been situated as Blennarhasset, litterally insulated, & detach'd from the busy World, & surrounded by every Comfort," one Virginian reflected, "all the Diadems of Europe & asia together should not have enticed me from my Paradise."[87] The force of this construct grounded Charles Fenton Mercer's confidence in Blennerhassett's innocence. "What!" Mercer asked in his deposition on Blennerhassett's behalf, "will a man who, weary of the agitations of the world, of its noise and vanity, has unambitiously retired to a solitary island, . . . start up in the decline of life from the pleasing dream of seven years' slumber" to undertake treason and war?[88] Mercer *insisted* that such a man would not; Wirt merely *suggested* that he would not, unless seduced from his virtuous repose.

Wirt's audience, moreover, would have readily accepted that an honest republican could be duped by a shrewd aristocrat. Americans had adopted Brother Jonathan—the rustic, "true blue son of liberty" who is repeatedly gulled by the worldly, "courtly" Jessamy in Royall Tyler's *The Contrast* (1787)—as a personification of their young nation in plays, almanacs, poetry, and political cartoons.[89] And a dichotomy of republican openness and integrity versus monarchical secrecy and duplicity pervaded the discourse surrounding their diplomatic relationships with Europe. Wirt's speech seems to have benefitted from such thinking, even though he never identified Blennerhassett as a republican. In fact, Blennerhassett was both more aristocratic, being the youngest son of a landed Irish family, and more worldly, having lived in Ireland, England, France, and the Netherlands, than Burr. But many of the Irish immigrants to the United States in the 1790s had been republicans fleeing a British crackdown on reformers and radicals. Blennerhassett's involvement with the Irish republicans seems to have been limited and had ended long before their radicalism peaked in 1798. Still, those who read or heard Wirt's speech could easily have assumed that Blennerhassett belonged to the stream of Irish republicans. Unaware of the family issues that had forced Harman and Margaret's departure, Blennerhassett's nineteenth-century biographers often claimed that it had been his "republican principles" that had driven him from home.[90]

Wirt grounded his construction of Blennerhassett on an even firmer cultural and political foundation by relying so heavily on a classic archetype—the fall of man. His allusions to the republican idyll of retirement from the world would have had the greatest resonance for educated and wealthy men and women, such as Rodney, Mercer, and much of the audience in the courtroom. But his appropriation of the story of the fall would have crossed lines of education and class to reach men and women, boys and girls throughout the country. Almost anyone who was old enough and interested enough to have read Wirt's speech in a book or article or heard it in an oratorical society or schoolhouse could have made the connection. By linking his narrative to one of the most familiar and powerful stories in western culture, Wirt embedded it within an array of preexisting ideas about paradise, temptation, and ruination. For the well-read, Wirt's imagery gained additional meaning by aligning the Blennerhassetts and Burr not only with Genesis, but also with John Milton's *Paradise Lost* (1667). In Milton's poem, Satan had sat at the right hand of God before leading a revolt of angels against Him. One writer developed this potential in Wirt's narrative when he likened Blennerhassett's cooperation with Burr to Adam "join[ing] in the revolt of lost spirits against their Maker."[91]

The power of this archetypal story becomes apparent when we examine a curious reworking of Wirt's narrative. His parallel between events on Blennerhassett Island and events in the Garden of Eden ended with his treatment of Margaret Blennerhassett. In the Bible, it is Eve, of course, who succumbs to the temptations of the serpent and involves Adam in her ruination. Wirt did not assign Margaret any part in the Blennerhassetts' downfall, presenting her, instead, as a victim of Harman's "seduc[tion] from the paths of innocence and peace."[92] Over the course of the century, however, it became increasingly common to extend Wirt's metaphor to its logical conclusion by expanding Margaret's role. By the early 1840s, Margaret had been recast as the initial target of Burr's "smooth and fascinating manners"; once "beguiled," she had used her "great influence over the mind of her husband" to engage him in Burr's plans.[93] The next step removed Harman from the scene entirely, leaving Margaret alone with the tempter Burr when he first visited the island. In 1850, Safford recounted such a story in his biography, even though his book reprinted the brief, which clearly placed Harman at the scene. While not every book and article included this error, accounts with Margaret alone when Burr first arrived reappeared for over a century: in 1858, in James Parton's biography of Burr; in the late 1880s, in Henry Adams's respected history; in 1954, in Thomas Perkins Abernethy's still-standard account of the conspiracy; and in many other works.[94] The frequency of this mistake, particularly given the available evidence of Harman's presence, suggests the power of Wirt's Adam and Eve metaphor.

Even these erroneous accounts did not typically suggest a romantic or sexual relationship between Margaret and Burr, who had a merited reputation for "success with the fair sex."[95] A few writers, however, did describe the relationship in such terms. Ohio's David Wallace later recalled that "slanderous insinuations . . . respecting Mrs B. & Burr," which he flatly denied, had been "promulgated at [the] time" of Burr's visits.[96] Some people interpreted Wirt's speech as referring to a sexual relationship, even though it never mentioned one, at least as published. The defense attorney Benjamin Botts immediately detected a sexual dimension in Wirt's argument. In his reply, Botts charged Wirt with introducing into the trial "a sleeping Venus with all the luxury of voluptuous and wanton nakedness" and turning "our imaginations to the fascinating richness and symmetry of a heaving bosom and luscious waist."[97] Such readings seem to have grown more common over time. In 1902, the new Aaron Burr Legion grounded its call to excise the "Who is Blennerhassett?" passage from schoolbooks, in part, on the "alleged intimacy of Colonel Burr and Mrs. Blennerhassett" that it suggested.[98] A year earlier, in an article in defense of Margaret, Therese Blennerhassett-Adams had traced the confusion to Wirt's use of the phrase "the bowers of Eden."[99] "Bower" could mean either "a place closed in or overarched with branches of trees, shrubs, or other plants," as Wirt probably intended, or a woman's bedroom—"a boudoir."[100] The ambiguity of a crucial word in Wirt's well-known speech encouraged at least some people to imagine a sexual relationship.

But Wirt's success at serving present political purposes and appropriating shared cultural values only partly explains the initial acceptance and lasting force of his narrative. We also need to recognize the power of eloquent argument, both heard and read, in nineteenth-century America. As the author of *The American Orator*—the 1811 instructional manual that included Wirt's passage—explained, "oratory . . . is the most splendid object of all literary exertion, and the highest scope of all the study and practice of the art." The greatest achievements of oratory united a "perfection of composition" and a "perfection of delivery"; they joined "the power of reasoning" and "the various arts of persuasion." Oratorical excellence seemed especially important in a republican government—and in a jury-based legal system—where persuasion, rather than force or fiat, would guide the actions of others. As the histories of the Greek and Roman republics showed, civic-minded orators could move others to act in the public interest through the spoken word. Americans devoted considerable time and effort to studying, teaching, and perfecting oratory. Even those with great natural talent needed "long and laborious exertion" to master the arrangement of argument, ornament, delivery, and movement. The best orators—those who had risen to "the regions of honorable excellence"—managed to make this studied display seem entirely natural.[101]

Wirt's own writings on oratory before Burr's trial set almost impossibly high standards. Four of the ten letters in his *Letters of the British Spy* (1803) concerned oratory and orators, as did a pseudonymous newspaper essay, "On Forensic Eloquence" (1804). Wirt's comments in the *Letters* were quite damning of his countrymen. "Puerile rant" and "tedious and disgusting inanity," in his view, far outweighed "eloquence of the highest order" in the nation's assemblies and courtrooms. Lacking a "sufficent fund of general knowledge," unaccustomed to "close and solid thinking," and uninterested in "original ornaments," American speakers might "pour out . . . a torrent of words," but those words were generally "destitute of the light of erudition, the practical utility of just and copious thought, [and] novel and beautiful allusions and embellishments."[102] Wirt's writings also assessed contemporary orators, including Patrick Henry, whose biography he would write; John Curran, an Irish attorney who had defended Irish republicans in the 1790s; and three men who would become his opponents at Burr's trial—John Marshall, Edmund Randolph, and John Wickham. From reading Curran's legal speeches, Wirt drew the lesson that "the candidate for forensic glory" needed to learn that he should first "rear the great edifice of argument on a rock, before he calls in fancy to gild and to paint."[103]

The Burr trial elevated Wirt to the upper ranks of American orators, earning him a national reputation that was further enhanced by later displays in the Supreme Court and a respected eulogy for John Adams and Thomas Jefferson. Writers on oratory dissected Wirt's famous speeches, examining the reasons for and evidence of his greatness. In doing so, they almost invariably referred to or quoted from the "Who is Blennerhassett?" passage. In his *Sketches of American Orators* (1816), Francis Walker Gilmer, Wirt's former brother-in-law and protégé, insisted that Wirt exemplified the "qualities requisite for genuine eloquence": a "dignified and commanding" form; an "open, manly and playful" face; a "clear and musical" voice; a "prompt, pure, and brilliant" wit; an ease of "action" (i.e., movement); and a "diction [that] unite[d] force, purity, variety and splendour." Wirt's great success, according to his defenders, and his great failure, according to his few detractors, was his balancing of "judgment and imagination."[104] The common practice of excerpting the "Who is Blennerhassett?" passage from the larger argument's legal reasoning and precedents highlighted Wirt's fanciful side. But, as Samuel L. Southard explained in his eulogy on Wirt, "imagination, taste, and fancy" always coexisted in Wirt's mind with "masculine judgment, and close, logical, and lucid argument."[105] In Wirt's hands, an early supporter argued, subjects that were as "barren as the sands of Africa" produced arguments that were "always profound and cogent, [yet] clothed in the richest and most varied imagery."[106]

The most detailed criticism of Wirt's oratory came from Wirt himself, who certainly would have known that the orators of ancient Greece and Rome had assessed themselves with an air of modesty and self-criticism. Forwarding a pamphlet version of his two main arguments from the Burr trial to his confidant Ninian Edwards, Wirt warned that it would reveal "on how small a foundation it is sometimes the pleasure of Fame to stand." Wirt found little to praise in either his delivery or his content. In his view, he spoke "with a tongue two inches thick and an articulation so rapid & indistinct . . . that in the middle of my sentences I am perfectly unintelligible."[107] After "trying all [of his] life to learn to speak in the time of Lady Coventry's minuet," he had written even before Burr's trial, he was still "shuffling" along in "a Virginia jig."[108] Wirt admitted that he had "some briskness & vivacity of fancy," but insisted that it lacked "the originality, the fertility, the boldness and the awful grandeur which the orator requires." "As to moving the heart," he remarked, "I know no more of it than a child." Wirt insisted that these criticisms were "not affectation." Still, his careful delineation of what good oratory required, his insistence that no one "now before the public" in Virginia had reached a level of excellence, and his enclosure of his own celebrated speeches suggest that he thought that he had come as close to meeting his unattainable standards as anyone. By late 1807, Wirt had clearly won the glory that he had foreseen could come from participating in the trial. But he worried that past achievements—and overrated ones at that—would only fuel demands for future successes. "The exertions of mere duty," he lamented to Edwards, "imposed on me a superstructure of character which I know I cannot bear."[109]

This "superstructure of character"—the comparisons of Wirt to the ancients Demosthenes and Cicero and to his contemporary Curran—had little to do with the Burr Conspiracy, with Harman Blennerhassett, or with Blennerhassett Island. Newspaper editors, letter writers, and, in time, oratory collectors seized upon Wirt's speech, celebrated it far beyond its merits, and cemented its status as an example of oratorical excellence for reasons of their own. In the late eighteenth and early nineteenth centuries, Americans desperately sought evidence that their young, coarse nation could contribute to the international "republic of letters." Surely, the nation's first great trial—a trial that combined the blackest crime, a famous criminal, the highest judge, and some of the most respected attorneys—would produce examples of American oratorical genius. But the trial's course limited the opportunities for stirring oratory. Too much of the argumentation turned on narrow technical questions. And Marshall's decision to arrest the evidence deprived the attorneys of the opportunity to make closing arguments to the jury—often the occasion for the most carefully prepared speeches. Wirt's "Who is Blennerhassett?" passage was celebrated because a speech that could be celebrated was needed, because an American Curran or an American Demosthenes was needed. As the editor of the *New-York Evening Post* noted in publishing the excerpt: "Those familiar with the eloquence of the late Lord Chancellor of England and still more with those of the celebrated Curran, will immediately recognize the resemblance, and may possibly think with us, that the American Barrister does not suffer in the comparison with either."[110]

Just a few hundred people heard Wirt deliver his speech, but many thousands read the "Who is Blennerhassett?" passage in articles, books,

and collections that reprinted it precisely because of its oratorical qualities. Print could not always capture the power of oratory. Many oral
performances that were lauded by their audiences seemed bland in
print; other, perfectly average speeches benefitted from being "curtailed & ordered into a Newspaper."[111] Wirt's passage succeeded at its
first delivery (for most of its audience), in printed excerpts, and, presumably, in subsequent performances by countless schoolhouse and literary
society orators. It was long remembered as "one of the most brilliant
speeches ever delivered in this country," and even as "one of the most
splendid forensic displays ever recorded."[112] Presented, over and over,
as an exemplar of oratorical skill, it owed much of its acceptance and
importance to the high esteem that oratory enjoyed in nineteenth-
century American culture. "Seldom had [an] audience listened to such
a display of eloquence," one author explained; they could hardly "believe that the glowing pictures existed chiefly in the vivid imagination
of the orator."[113]

What one historical lecturer in the mid-1840s referred to as "the immortal fancy of Wirt" shaped popular and scholarly thought throughout
the nineteenth century.[114] Its incredible power had been noted, even lamented, decades before the Aaron Burr Legion called for its removal
from schoolbooks in the early twentieth century. Even the gradual appearance of conflicting evidence in Blennerhassett's papers—the journal,
the brief, and the correspondence with Burr—between the mid-1830s
and the mid-1860s had done little to break the hold of Wirt's largely fanciful account. For many nineteenth-century Americans, Blennerhassett
Island had become "a famous spot," as one author recognized, through
the combined effects of "the intrigues of one distinguished individual, the
misfortunes of another, and the eloquence of a third." Wirt's eloquence
seemed no less essential than Burr's intrigues and Blennerhassett's misfortunes in the cultural process through which the island was "made classic ground."[115] Beginning soon after its delivery and continuing through
the end of the century, Wirt's "Who is Blennerhassett?" speech defined
Blennerhassett, his island, and his relationship with Burr. In doing so, it
made sense of an important dimension of the Burr Conspiracy for both
the general public and the first generation of historians for decades.

CHAPTER 10

THE CONFLICT OVER
BURR'S FOLLOWERS

CONTEMPORARIES HAD GOOD REASONS TO ASK AND ANSWER THE
question, who were Aaron Burr's followers? Burr's men, as they were
often called, might be targeted for territorial, state, or federal legal proceedings. Even those who were "too small game" to be hunted in their
own right might provide evidence against Burr or others who were to
be tried.[1] But identifying individual followers often mattered less than
identifying the broad types of men who supported Burr. Identifying
individuals could serve specific legal ends; identifying types could influence the way that people thought about Burr and his project. In an
early description of the conspiracy to the president, General James
Wilkinson reported that it "embrac[ed] the young and the old, the
democrat and the federalist, the native and the foreigner, the patriot of
'76 and the exotic of yesterday, the opulent and the needy, the ins and
the outs."[2] In political terms, such an all-encompassing list served no
one's interests. Commentators usually offered much narrower descriptions or constructions of Burr's followers as they tried to make sense of
his project for themselves and others. They chose terms that drew upon
existing stories and cultural assumptions, reinforcing the power of
those stories and assumptions even as they looked to them for clarity in
an emerging crisis. In the process, they revealed deeper anxieties about
a crucial and disputed question—what kinds of people posed the greatest danger to the new nation?

Ultimately, roughly a dozen individuals became widely known as
Burr's men, though most of them publicly disputed this label. Six were
eventually indicted with Burr for treason and misdemeanor in Richmond (Harman Blennerhassett, Jonathan Dayton, Davis Floyd, Israel
Smith, John Smith, and Comfort Tyler). Five more were sent from

FIGURE 14. Aaron Burr revealing his plans to his followers at the mouth of the Cumberland River.

New Orleans to the East by Wilkinson for trial (John Adair, James Alexander, Justus Erich Bollman, Peter Ogden, and Samuel Swartwout). Another was named in the first printed version of the cipher letter (Thomas Truxton). And one was implicated primarily because he was Burr's son-in-law (Joseph Alston). Some of these men were already known: Blennerhassett, the wealthy and eccentric Irish refugee; Dayton, the former United States senator from New Jersey; John Smith, a current senator from Ohio; Adair, another former senator and a general in the Kentucky militia; Bollman, the German doctor who had tried to rescue the Marquis de Lafayette from an Austrian prison in 1794; and Truxton, a former naval commodore. The others had not been nationally prominent before being linked to the conspiracy.[3]

At most one hundred men, white and black, along with a few women and children, composed Burr's force when he surrendered to civil authorities in the Mississippi Territory in January 1807. But hundreds more had decided to follow Burr and had made it no further than New York, Pennsylvania, Ohio, Kentucky, Tennessee, or the Indiana Territory before stopping due to second thoughts, adverse publicity, state action, or the presidential proclamation. Although some of their names appeared in a newspaper article or official document, most remained entirely anonymous.[4] Their anonymity made them especially useful for anyone who sought to use Burr's followers to make sense of Burr's project, either for themselves or for others. Aggregated and abstracted, these men acted, in the view of contemporaries, not from individual motives, but as members of groups that were defined by age, marital status, class, and other factors. As such, they proved extremely useful for ongoing debates about what kinds of people most threatened the new nation during an era of social and political change.

"ANY ENTERPRISE ANALOGOUS TO THEIR CHARACTERS"

Descriptions of Burr's followers that served to define his project appeared in newspapers, official documents, published letters, private correspondence, and conversations. Burr himself initiated this process as he tried to enlist support. Because it was known to so few, however, his construction did not become contested until his men began to move in the fall of 1806. At that point, newspaper editors from the rival parties attempted to use for partisan advantage the uncertainty about who was involved and the concern about what was happening. As it became apparent that support for and opposition to Burr did not follow clear party lines, the battleground shifted from political loyalties to social typologies. What kinds of men had joined Burr? What were their motives? How had they been enlisted? The opposing sides often answered these questions not by examining the actual participants, about whom very little was known, but by applying their existing views about Burr and his project. Their reasoning was relentlessly circular. Burr and his project were honorable—or, alternately, treasonable—therefore, Burr's men were "choice spirits"—or, alternately, "desperate persons"; the assertion that Burr's men were "choice" or "desperate" was then used to show that Burr and his project was honorable or treasonable.

The public battle over Burr's followers began late in 1806 as an effort to turn something that seemed to be a treasonous conspiracy into a party issue. Federalist and Republican editors seized upon vague and conflicting reports for political purposes. Federalist editors utilized the news from Lexington and Frankfort, Kentucky, where the few Federalists seemed to be working diligently to expose and defeat Burr's plans, while the dominant Republicans defended Burr in the press and in court. Commenting on a report from Kentucky, for example, a Federalist editor in Virginia flatly denied "that any Federalist of respectability is concerned in Burr's plans."[5] In early March 1807, Boston's *Columbian Centinel* printed a letter from the nation's capital that insisted that "*nineteen twentieths* of those implicated as traitors and conspirators are 'exclusive *republicans*.'"[6] "All those who have lately been implicated in the so much talked of Conspiracies, rebellions, &c, are to a man, *rank democrats*, and *high Jeffersonians*," another Federalist account noted.[7] A New York editor simply remarked that, "as usual," this insurrection "originate[d] with the democrats."[8]

Not surprisingly, Republican editors saw something quite different unfolding in the trans-Appalachian West. Initially, they emphasized reports from Pittsburgh, Pennsylvania, one of the few Federalist strongholds in the West. According to a local Republican editor, "not a single democratic republican [had] been led astray" by Burr.[9] An early December 1806 letter from Pittsburgh to Washington that appeared in many Republican newspapers confirmed that "all that have joined the expedition and all who encourage it are of that class of persons called federalists."[10] Another widely reprinted letter from Meadville, in northwestern Pennsylvania, named eighteen men from the area and from neighboring Erie County who had left to join the assemblage of Burr's men at Beaver, Pennsylvania. According to this report, these men were "all federalists, and cordially unfriendly to the government."[11] For weeks, the editor William Duane made the alleged Federalism of Burr's supporters a leading topic in his highly influential *Aurora General Advertiser.*

Over time, however, more and better information suggested that Burr's followers could not be easily categorized along party lines. His supporters and defenders did include Republicans in Lexington and Frankfort, as well as in Nashville. But they also included Federalists in Pittsburgh, as well as in Natchez. Furthermore, in time, the broad consensus that Burr's activities were worrisome began to fracture. Republicans still insisted that Burr had intended to divide the union or destroy the republic, but many Federalists accepted his claim of persecuted innocence. While Republicans never entirely abandoned the effort to connect their opponents to the accused traitor, the focus of the debate shifted from party ties to social types. Two crucial documents heralded this shift: the cipher letter and the president's message to Congress on the Burr Conspiracy.

In the cipher letter, Burr described his "friends and followers" as "a host of choice spirits," "a corps of worthys," and "the best blood of our country."[12] The implications of these phrases are clear. "Choice spirits" was a common phrase, at least in refined discourse. At the Constitutional Convention in 1787, Alexander Hamilton had spoken of the "choice spirits" in any government who could act upon motives more elevated than "their passions."[13] The phrase's origins are unclear, but it probably came from Shakespeare. In *1 Henry VI*, Joan la Pucelle (Joan of Arc) calls down "choice spirits," referring to otherworldly beings, to aid the French against the English. But the more likely source, even though the quote is imperfect, is *Julius Caesar.* On first seeing the fallen Caesar, Marc Antony speaks of the "choice and master spirits" who had murdered him to save the Roman republic. At the time, American audiences often viewed the assassins, not Caesar or Marc Antony, as the heroes of the play.[14] For Burr, as for Hamilton, "choice spirits" clearly had positive connotations. Like "best blood" and "worthys," it referred to men (usually) who were distinguished by family, wealth, education, and manners from the common sort.

Burr apparently spoke of his followers in similar terms in the conversations that gradually reached the public in published depositions and testimony. According to Truxton's testimony at the treason trial, Burr had described the people who would join him on the Bastrop grant as "respectable and fashionable." After one year, he had predicted, there would be "a thousand [such] families[,] . . . some of them of considerable property."[15] Former secretary of the navy Benjamin Stoddert similarly recalled that Burr had counted upon support from "men of energy[,] property & talents."[16] And William Eaton reported that Burr had looked to the "many enterprising men . . . , who aspired to something beyond the dull pursuits of civil life" to join his undertaking.[17]

Burr's supporters and defenders employed similar terms in their descriptions. According to one witness, Ohio senator John Smith had explained that Burr sought "young men of interprise" and was backed by "many of the first characters of the country."[18] Another deposed that Blennerhassett had assured him "that the society" under Burr "would soon become the most select and agreeable in America."[19] Editorials and letters in defense of Burr in some Federalist newspapers adopted this language. Long before the publication of the cipher letter, a piece in Boston's *Columbian Centinel* referred to the "dashing spirits" who followed Burr and were "capable of enterprizes of 'much pith and moment.'"[20] In fact, before the presidential proclamation in late November 1806, even some Republican newspapers had chosen such terms to describe Burr's followers. Writing in early November and defending Burr against the charges in Frankfort's *Western World*, a writer in Richmond's *Enquirer* had considered it perfectly "natural" that Burr had "engage[d] young men of talents and enterprize, not only to become settlers [on the Bastrop grant] but also to promote the general purposes of the plan."[21]

By asserting that such men—men of energy and enterprise, of property and standing, of talents and respectability—had joined their undertaking, Burr and his supporters effectively claimed that neither the project nor the projector should be a source of alarm. Eaton expressed what was, at least for gentlemen, the common sense of the matter before the grand jury. "Men . . . clothed with honor, and independent in their circumstances," he recalled having told Burr, "were not the materials for a revolu[tio]n."[22] Burr, his followers, and his defenders in the press and the courts relied upon this common sense as they described Burr's men. "Office and wealth would have quietly reposed upon their cushions," one early defender argued, "and left the dangers and the profits to such, as had neither the wealth nor the office to lose" if the project had been improper.[23] Men of office, wealth, and reputation simply would not join the kinds of projects that the administration charged against Burr. Another kind of project—such as erecting a new community on the Bastrop grant—better suited them.

With this perspective on the nature of the project and its supporters, Burr's defenders could easily explain why men had chosen to follow him. With a Spanish war looming, some were tempted by hopes of military glory. Writing while Burr visited his Tennessee home in early October 1806, militia general Andrew Jackson voiced his expectation that volunteers would flock to such a war as "a handsome theatre for our enterprising young men, and a certain source of acquiring fame."[24] Others were drawn by the allure of a new social order on the Bastrop grant. Burr apparently enticed a number of potential followers by promising to create a society that was more hierarchical, more refined than the increasingly democratic, increasingly coarse society of the eastern cities or the western frontier. Such talk often appealed to Burr's "best blood." To the architect and engineer Benjamin Henry Latrobe, Burr offered a range of inducements. He promised the English immigrant ten thousand acres of land. But, more importantly, he insisted that he wanted Latrobe's "advice in the establishments about to be made"—presumably new cities for Latrobe to plan, new public buildings for him to design, and new roads, waterworks, and canals for him to build. "In short," Burr concluded, Latrobe was "necessary to [his] settlement."[25] Such appeals would have been difficult for some men to resist.

In his message to Congress, Thomas Jefferson countered this talk of "choice spirits" with an equally powerful description of Burr's followers. According to the president, Burr's men included "all the ardent, restless, desperate, and disaffected persons" "from all the quarters [of the union] where [Burr] or his agents possessed influence."[26] Jefferson's private letters expounded upon this public description, referring to Burr's followers as "adventurers and speculators" and even as "desperadoes."[27] While his writings gave such language the imprimatur of the administration, Jefferson did not invent it. He drew upon a body of largely uninformed speculation about Burr's men that had appeared for months in letters and newspapers. One of Wilkinson's early warnings, for example, had called Burr's men "an undisciplined rabble"; a later letter had referred to them as "Burrs renegadoes."[28] Hostile newspapers had already described Burr's followers as men "of desperate character and fortune" and as "lawless Desperadoes."[29] Other administration members had adopted this language weeks before the president publicly used it. Writing to his officers in the West in December 1806, the secretary of war had called Burr's followers "disappointed, unprincipled, ambitious or misguided."[30]

Reinforcing these earlier accounts, Jefferson's message set the tone for most later Republican descriptions of Burr's men. Burr's followers were painted as "discontented men of desperate fortunes" by a Pennsylvania congressman and as "unprincipled, disaffected and desperate persons" in a letter from a Tennessee congressman to his constituents.[31]

Republican town meetings echoed Jefferson's language back to him in resolutions praising his handling of the crisis. The Republicans of Montgomery County in New York's Mohawk Valley, for example, called Burr's men "a Small band of adventurers of desperate character and ruined fortune."[32] Republican newspapers endorsed this view as well. Within days of printing Jefferson's message, a writer in the *Enquirer* referred to Burr's supporters as "desperadoes," noting that "such only would have joined him."[33] Even William Plumer, a Federalist senator from New Hampshire, adopted Jefferson's language. Burr "had thousands of men of the idle, disaffected, & men of desperate fortunes" behind him, Plumer remarked in his diary, his garbled entry employing two of Jefferson's terms.[34]

According to Jefferson's message, these "ardent, restless, desperate, and disaffected persons" had joined in an "enterprise" that was "analogous to their characters."[35] Like many people, the president assumed that establishing the character of Burr's followers necessarily settled the character of his project. As one New Orleanian explained, no one who was engaged in an honorable undertaking, as Burr claimed to be, would rely upon "low, pitiful, degrading rascally means." Someone capable of projecting "a noble enterprize," Thomas Power argued, "could never have descended for it's execution" to "means that would almost disgrace housebreakers, high-way-robbers, and pick-pockets."[36] Of course, the assumption that "no man, but of the most *desperate* fortunes, [was] cut out for such a desperate design" as plotting to divide the union had fueled the initial, almost entirely groundless, assessment of what kinds of men had joined Burr.[37]

Burr could have led such "desperate persons" to join him, it was broadly accepted, with fairly simple inducements. It was generally assumed that many "bankrupt[s]" had followed him simply to escape their debts.[38] "These men are all like col. Burr," an essayist in the *Western World* insisted; "their every hope in Eastern America is blasted[,] and they are now ripe for any enterprise, which, with employment, will give them the means of a livelihood."[39] Discounting the settlement of the Bastrop grant as mere cover for the real project, Burr's critics did not generally regard access to cheap land as an adequate motive for such men. They often meant something very different when they pointed to material benefits. Some wrote vaguely of the "very flattering prospects

of wealth" that Burr held out; "the needy and desperate," one Pennsylvanian noted, "embark in [his project] with avidity."[40] Other critics
were more precise, identifying "the golden prospects" afforded by the
chance "to dip their hands into the mines of Mexico" as the reward for
joining Burr.[41] Others considered the motives of Burr's men even more
obvious. "The dissolute and unprincipled," one essayist explained, "will
always flock to the standard of rebellion."[42]

But Jefferson's message also offered a third portrayal of Burr's adherents that differed sharply from either Burr's "choice spirits" or his own
"desperate persons." The president conceded that some of Burr's followers were simply "good and well-meaning citizens" who had been
duped.[43] This explanation for at least some of Burr's support was not
new. Two months earlier, it had shaped the presidential proclamation,
which sought to separate the "faithful citizens who [had] been led
without due knowledge or consideration to participate in . . . unlawful
enterprises" from the true conspirators.[44] The same perspective continued
to appear in Jefferson's personal correspondence and other administration documents, in public and private letters, in newspaper editorials
and essays, and in reports from various federal officials. Writing from
Washington, a Kentucky congressman worried that "some well meaning men [had] been duped."[45] From Natchez, the acting territorial governor reported that, in his opinion, most of Burr's men were "the dupes
of stratagems."[46] Jefferson and others who asserted that "many who followed [Burr] . . . were deluded," as one Virginian put it, seem to have
sought to reassure the public that there were few true disunionists.[47]

Contemporaries offered different explanations for how these men
had been duped. Jefferson's message identified various ways in which
Burr had "seduced" innocent men. Some had been promised "land in
Bastrop's claim," even though their real destination was Mexico or
New Orleans. Others had been "assur[ed] that [Burr] possessed the
confidence of the Government and was acting under its secret patronage."[48] Many people viewed such assurances as Burr's most effective
stratagem. By cultivating the belief that he was acting with administration backing, he had been able to enlist men, build boats, and buy supplies
for his real project. To assuage any doubts about this support, according to some reports, Burr even showed—or left "spread open on his
table"—a forged letter from the secretary of war that seemed to prove

administration connivance.[49] It took such "great falsehoods," Indiana territorial governor William Henry Harrison insisted, "to entrap those whose honesty [was] proof against any proposal to violate the Laws of their Country."[50] Mississippi territorial governor Robert Williams claimed that Burr and his agents had not relied upon any one lie. Instead, "innocent" men had been "induced [to join] under a Variety of pretensions Calculated to meet the Necessities, Situations, Views and talents of each."[51] The Federalist James McHenry likewise believed that Burr had "aimed at governing his agents, by springs, calculated to impel them to his object, without their perceiving clearly the whole object or the springs."[52]

While many portrayed Burr as an archdeceiver, weaving a web of lies to ensnare innocent men, others believed that his success in winning followers derived from something more complex. Those who knew Burr even slightly often remarked upon his unmatched ability to sway men and women. It went beyond simply displaying the "manners . . . of the finished gentleman."[53] Burr possessed some other, much rarer, talent of conversation and comportment that gave him power over those around him. At times, contemporaries referred to this ability as "address"; more often, they wrote of his "fascinating manners."[54] The word "fascinate" no longer denotes what it did then. To fascinate someone was to gain "an irresistible influence" over them.[55] The earliest uses of the word had attributed this influence to witchcraft or magic. By the late eighteenth century, "fascinate" had been stripped of its supernatural component and reframed as a natural process, the mechanics of which were unknown. In North America, serpents—particularly rattlesnakes—were often ascribed the power of fascination, which they exercised through their eyes to prevent birds and small mammals from fleeing; according to some accounts, the serpent's power of fascination was so strong that its prey literally ran into its mouth. At the end of the eighteenth century, the American naturalist Benjamin Smith Barton had challenged such claims about the fascinating powers of rattlesnakes. But the idea of fascination remained widespread through the mid-nineteenth century.[56]

Burr's power to fascinate men and women had been noted long before the Burr crisis. After riding with Burr from Baltimore to Philadelphia in March 1805, Massachusetts senator John Quincy Adams wrote that he "def[ied] Man, Woman or Child, so to withstand the powers of his fascination, as to part from him after such a transitory association, without feelings of good-will towards him."[57] A Kentuckian who met Burr that August insisted that "never were there charms displayed with such potency and irrisistible attraction." Neither tall nor large, Burr's imposing presence derived, instead, from his "erect and dignified deportment," command of the social graces, and famed black eyes, which "glow[ed] with all the ardor of venereal fire, and scintillate[d] with the most tremulous and tearful sensibility." Burr's physical presence—his carriage, movement, conversation, manners, and address—embodied his status as a gentleman. In a society that usually prized the conversation of established gentlemen, moreover, Burr seemed to have learned the value of paying more than ordinary attention to the talk of women and young men. And when he spoke, it was "with such apparent frankness and negligence, as would induce a person to believe he was a man of a guileless & ingenious heart."[58] Burr's manners were not just polished, but insinuating. He often won people's affections against their wills. Even the cautious Adams admitted that he had concluded his brief journey with Burr feeling "more kindness" for him "than [was] rightly consistent with the character which on a cool and distant estimate" he truly possessed.[59]

During the Burr crisis, and for decades after, commentators invoked the force of Burr's personality to explain his ability to attach men to a project that they would have rejected on its merits. In the fall of 1806, western newspapers referred to Burr's "most pleasing and fascinating" conversation, his "enchanting manners," and his "most engaging address, and fascinating eloquence."[60] "While we might be sensible he was plotting our destruction," an author in the *Western World* admitted, "yet we can with difficulty refrain from wishing him prosperity, and candidly confessing ourselves to be charmed into his views."[61] Throughout the nineteenth century, biographers and historians, journalists and novelists returned, again and again, to the idea that Burr had won over supporters through such powers. Influenced by the era's Romanticism, these accounts often located those powers not just in Burr's conversation, but especially in his eyes—eyes that were "bright as a basilisk, but whose expression changed as often and as vividly as an opal"; eyes that were "calm, penetrating, [and] masterful in their startling intelligence"; eyes "whose sharp light resembled lightning imprisoned and forever playing in a cloud black as death."[62] "If the victim fully came under the gaze of" Burr's eyes, one author insisted, "he was lost."[63] Remembering encounters with Burr many years later, one westerner recalled that "his eyes were more like those of a rattlesnake than like a human being."[64]

In April 1807, soon after learning that the arrested Burr had been taken to Richmond, Latrobe reflected upon his "acquaintance with & opinion of [Burr]." The Englishman had never agreed to follow Burr west but had been intrigued by what Burr had told him. He had provided designs for boats to carry Burr's men and provisions. And, most alarmingly to himself, he had arranged to send Burr "at least 500 able bodied" Irish laborers to build a canal around the falls of the Ohio River at Louisville; if Burr had actually received this force, Latrobe believed, he "might have defied all opposition." In his self-examination, Latrobe identified various factors that had led him so deeply into Burr's projects. The Ohio canal, he admitted, "offered to my professional ambition, & to my desire to accumulate a provision in good Land for my children[,] every possible temptation."[65] But it was not just about personal rewards. Latrobe had also been captivated by Burr's manner and reputation. Months earlier, he had concluded that Burr had intended for him "to be a most egregious dupe."[66] By April, Latrobe could see his own role in this dupery. "The public opinion of the superiority of [Burr's] talents, and their adequacy to accomplish any thing he might attempt," he admitted, had "imposed upon my own judgement." Only Burr's failure to send the funds to engage the canal workers had saved Latrobe from the compromising position in which he had let himself be placed by "the superiority of [Burr's] character."[67]

Deliberation and calculation often shaped contemporary efforts to answer the question, who were Burr's followers? Newspaper editors, government officials, and even private letter writers often thought more about the political uses of their answers than the actual qualities of Burr's men. Initially, a broad consensus that Burr's designs were dangerous suggested that this question might be answered in ways that served partisan purposes. The vice president highlighted this potential for his nephew, a leading New York Republican, in late December 1806. "If prudently managed," he argued, "Burrs Expedition . . . will contribute to the downfall of Quiddism & Federalism[;] for it cannot be doubted that both were in some measure implicated in it."[68] Even after the consensus about the danger eroded, constructing Burr's followers remained valuable for fixing the popular view of the project and its projector. The effectiveness of these efforts depended upon widely accepted and deeply engrained beliefs about what kinds of enterprises would attract what kinds of people. That honorable men would not engage in dishonorable measures, that desperate men would adopt desperate measures—those ideas were well established and broadly shared. Even if they rejected his conclusions, few people would have disputed one essayist's insistence that "presumptive proofs" of the nature of Burr's project could be found in the kinds of men who were "embark[ed] in his employ."[69]

"CANKERS OF A CALM WORLD AND A LONG PEACE"

Examined more carefully, contemporary discussions of Burr's followers also reveal deeper fears that lay beneath the level of conscious construction. In newspaper essays, in private letters, and in official documents, men and women who were genuinely alarmed by Burr's plans, as they understood them, suggested their answers to a question that arose repeatedly in the first decades of American independence: what kinds of people posed the greatest threat to the new nation? Frequently, their answers did not refer to party loyalties or even to the vague, and potentially overlapping, social typologies embodied in the labels "choice spirits," "desperate persons," and innocent "dupes." Instead, they identified markers of age and gender, occasionally marital status, and, most contentiously, class that linked Burr's supporters and resonated with existing ideas about what kinds of people threatened the political and social order. One set of questions in the list of "Interrogatories" that the attorney general sent to federal officials who were charged with finding witnesses for Burr's trial highlighted these issues: "What number of men, and of what description were they[—]young or old; farmers or mechanics; or what trade, profession, or calling, who embarked on board" Burr's boats?[70]

Observers repeatedly noted that most of Burr's followers were young and male. Burr, Joseph Hamilton Daveiss informed the administration in mid-November 1806, "seems principally to address our young men[,] and with a success at once astonishing and mortifying."[71] According to widely published accounts, "a number of young men" had left Pittsburgh intending to join Burr, and a group of "young men of talents and address" had enlisted with his agent, Comfort Tyler, in upstate New York.[72] Most of the people who made it as far as Bayou Pierre on Burr's boats, the acting governor of the Mississippi Territory reported, were "boys or young men just from school."[73] After months of reading such descriptions, the editor of Nashville's *Tennessee Gazette* asked the obvious question, "Was there no old men in the plot?"[74] The answer, of course, is that there were. In the fall of 1806, Burr was fifty. Adair, Blennerhassett, Dayton, John Smith, and Tyler were middle-aged, as well. But most of the unknown followers and some of Burr's better-known associates—including Floyd, Swartwout, and Israel Smith—were fairly young.

No one saw this issue in simple biological terms. Science did not explain why young men threatened the political and social order; culture did. For many young men, approaching and reaching the age of maturity exposed a huge gap between expectations and reality. Anxious to establish their independence, economically and socially, they often found that they lacked the capital or the connections to do so. Many would-be farmers spent the first years of their adulthood working on their fathers' farm, often thinking that it would eventually become their own, but feeling restless under parental control. Many would-be artisans spent years after their apprenticeships working for wages as journeymen with the skills, but without the funds, to establish their own shops. Many would-be lawyers and doctors struggled through their early twenties to build a sufficient client base to support themselves and a family. Frustrated by their present situations, such men often seemed eager to embark upon new ventures. Most of these ventures seemed laudable—opening new farms in the West or moving to a new town, for example. But other outlets might appeal to them as well. The challenges that inhered in young men must have seemed especially great in the early nineteenth century with a relatively young population and a relatively fluid political and social order. Every year, tens of thousands of young men reached the age of maturity. In a society that was experiencing what one historian has called a "revolution in choices," where established authority of all kinds was being challenged or overturned, there was little to keep these young men in place.[75]

Even as these young men lacked the farms or businesses that might have kept them in check, many also lacked wives and families. Bachelors had long been portrayed as a wild and reckless group. With more freedom to roam and fewer cares for the future, bachelors had always filled armies, naval vessels, merchant ships, and prisons. Transforming potentially dangerous bachelors into virtuous husbands was one of the few political roles imagined for the new nation's young women. Burr himself was single. With his wife long dead and his only child married, one writer explained, Burr could not find "solace in domestic comforts." Instead, he was "entirely under the control of his restless, aspiring disposition."[76] Many of his young followers were also bachelors, and numerous observers noted that his projects would appeal to "an ambitious Batchelor."[77] According to one of his defenders, Burr had explained "that he had taken care to have no women or children" in his party, because, "in a new settlement[,] families were useless lumber."[78] Marriage and family clearly stopped some of Burr's potential followers, as well. Latrobe admitted "that had I been single, or less attached to my family[,] I could not easily have resisted."[79] The fact that a few of Burr's young followers did bring their wives and children suggests that they believed that they were settling land.

If contemporary comments showed a broad agreement about age, gender, and marital status as markers of potentially dangerous groups in American society, they also exposed a serious disagreement about which socioeconomic class posed the greater threat. Did the real danger to the political and social order come from the working classes, the lower orders, the "many?" Or did it come from the nonlaboring classes, the elite, the "few?" Would political liberalization unleash the dreaded mob or would it spark a counterrevolution by would-be aristocrats? Was the greater threat from the bottom or the top? These were among the most significant and most divisive questions facing the early American republic. They had been debated for decades by the time of the Burr crisis, with Federalists worried more about the bottom of society and Republicans more about the top—one might even say, with those who were more worried about the bottom of society *becoming* Federalists and those who were more worried about the top *becoming*

Republicans. The Burr Conspiracy could be seen as confirming each side's fears.[80]

In late 1806 and early 1807, when Burr's project still seemed threatening, Federalist newspapers published numerous essays and letters highlighting the danger of the lower class. In these public writings, unlike in some private letters, Federalists almost never suggested that the mass of the people were inherently vicious. Instead, they identified the characteristics—ignorance, gullibility, and greed—that left ordinary people vulnerable to designing men. According to a writer in New York's *People's Friend*, for example, "the natural cupidity of the people, [which had been] sharpened into avarice by our executive experiments," made them easy prey for anyone who could promise quick wealth.[81] To Federalists, Republicans at the state and federal levels had abdicated the government's responsibility "*to fix the sentiments of the people.*"[82] Instead, Jeffersonian principles had given free rein to the worst instincts of the people and, thus, to those who might inflame and guide them. "The relationship between *Democracy* and *Conspiracy*," Boston's *Columbian Centinel* insisted, "is as nigh almost as that of brothers."[83]

Many elite westerners, both Federalist and Republican, found special cause for concern about the lower classes in their new communities. The late eighteenth and early nineteenth centuries witnessed a struggle over how fully the trans-Appalachian West would replicate the established societies of the East. Elite migrants generally expected to wield the economic, social, and political influence that they had enjoyed in the Carolinas, Virginia, or New England. Small farmers, local artisans, and other workingmen in Kentucky, Ohio, and western Pennsylvania regularly challenged this goal. From the elite perspective, the West's common people seemed to have little respect for wealth, refinement, or education. And the elite accepted, as Wilkinson—a longtime Kentuckian—remarked, that "an unpolished coarse People are apt to be governed by Events, & are easily duped by Artifice & cunning."[84] A wealthy Tennessee Republican sounded like many Federalists when, even as he insisted that "the Mass of the people . . . are virtuous," he noted that the elite needed to "explain to them the error and dangerous tendency of particular measures or opinions [so that] they would avoid them."[85] But the sources of authority that allowed the eastern elite to "explain" things to ordinary people were weak in the West. It was not just the newness of western communities, but also the nature of the western economy that fueled elite concerns. The difficulty of acquiring clear title to good land created a body of men, according to one Kentuckian, "whose circumstances could not be worsted in any event & whose principles would not restrain them from taking any side."[86]

Even as the Burr Conspiracy recharged elite fears about an uneducated, unrefined, and ungovernable people, it also revived popular fears about an overeducated, overly refined, and overpowerful elite. Events seemed to substantiate these fears. The people, the mob, never rose behind Burr. Instead, the increasingly detailed accounts from the West suggested that most of his followers were "of a class superior to the common labouring people."[87] One report referred to young men who were "respectable by birth, education and property"; another wrote of men of "independent fortunes and high standing."[88] The editor of Pittsburgh's *Commonwealth* described the men who had gone off to join Burr as "*single* young men of *character*," meaning, he clarified, "of *conspicuous* parentage."[89] And the commander at Fort Massac on the Ohio reported that Burr's boats were full of "Genteel young men, such as had not been acostomed to hard Labour."[90] William Love, a Marietta workingman who testified in Richmond, agreed. The men that he saw on Blennerhassett Island were "young gentlemen" and looked like those who "live upon their own property"—rents and interest—not "like men used to work."[91] Burr, many accepted, could hardly have needed "so many young gentlemen unacquainted with farming to settle lands."[92]

The evidence from Burr's various trials not only confirmed, but also explained these reports. Thomas Morgan, William Eaton, and Benjamin Stoddert each recalled that Burr had based part of his appeal on a class analysis of American politics and society. Morgan, a young son in one of western Pennsylvania's leading families, testified that Burr had warned that he and other "similarly situated" young men would be frustrated in their efforts to earn reputations as lawyers. "Under our government," Burr had explained, "there was no encouragement for talents."[93] Such frustrations did not face the young alone. Burr had also appealed to Truxton and Eaton—who saw themselves as suffering from unfair treatment by the administration—as victims of a system that ignored talent. According to Eaton, Burr had promised to make them "admirals, gen[era]ls, &c." and to put the government "on a basis

favorable to the reward of merit & enterprize."[94] While Truxton and
Eaton were special cases, they were hardly unique. "The men of energy[,] property & talents," Stoddert recalled Burr arguing, "were every
where disgusted" because they "had less influence in the Public affairs
of this than the same description of men had in the Public affairs of
any other country." Burr expected such men to support his energetic
government because "their influence would be increased."[95]

Did the frustrations of "Men whose manners and whose acquire-
ments [were] superior to the common run" make them natural enemies
of a political and social order in which they faced "growing jealousy
and indeed enmity?" If Burr thought so, he was not alone. Morgan,
Eaton, and Stoddert do not seem to have rejected this analysis, though
each insisted that the people or the government would defeat Burr's
projects. Latrobe certainly thought that "the state of society . . . favored
[Burr's] influence," especially among "well educated young Men" and
men "of superior talents." Government by *an unlettered majority*," he
explained during the Burr crisis, tended to suppress any form of deference, even to "that ideal rank which manners had established"—"the
Gentlemen"—except in the large commercial cities. Among his circle of
acquaintances, Latrobe claimed, "there [were] few young men of genius and cultivated minds" who did not "despair [at] the growing pre-
ponderance of the unlearned in the government of the country."[96] He
could easily see how some gentlemen, especially young ones, would
have been tempted by a project that promised to restore social hierar-
chy and elite governance.

Latrobe's analysis echoed some very old stories about who caused
revolutions in republics. It seemed well established that educated and
privileged young men with higher expectations than could easily be
satisfied would seek to overthrow the social and political order that
constrained them. The Roman conspirator Catiline's followers, according to one early nineteenth-century history, included "all the young
people in Rome, who, [had] been rocked in the cradle of luxury, and
enervated by a continual succession of pleasures," as well as those who
"had ruined themselves by excesses, and were no longer able to support
their extravagancies."[97] In some places, Burr's supporters seemed to fit
perfectly within a category that was defined not simply by age, gender,
and class, but by the combination of those characteristics with specific

behaviors and attitudes. Around Natchez, the "60 or 70" men who were "avowedly the adherents of Mr. Burr," Wilkinson reported, were "Young Gentlemen . . . who live extravagantly."[98] In the eastern Mississippi Territory, those who were "active in the cause of Burr," according to one report, were "such as [had] yet their fortunes to make, and the most extravagant views to gratify."[99] Men whose usual occupations had been to "while away their mornings of a gaming table, dine at the mansion hotel, or sup at [a] coffee-house" seemed unlikely to exchange such a life for carving out a new settlement on a rough frontier.[100]

The perception that what Latrobe called the "state of society" had led would-be aristocrats to join Burr, or had merely led Burr to consider such men his likeliest followers, suggested a new way to make use of the crisis. A number of Republican editors—many of whom were artisans rather than gentlemen—incorporated a class dimension into their pieces on the conspiracy, juxtaposing the republican many against the aristocratic few. The editor of Baltimore's *American*, for example, used testimony from Richmond to show that Burr had recognized that "good, industrious citizens, were not calculated for the purposes of an adventurer, who meditated the ruin of his country." Burr had found no supporters among "the honest yeomanry," the editor insisted. Instead, he had turned to "men of loose priciples [*sic*] & evil habits"—men "in whom the love of idleness had quieted the admonitions of virtue."[101]

Philadelphia's leading Republican editor, William Duane, became an early and frequent exponent of such an analysis. In a series of essays that first appeared in the *Aurora* before being reworked into the book *Politics for American Farmers*, Duane used the elite character of Burr's followers to argue that the working many were the great defenders of the republic and the leisured few were the great danger. "Who are more contented, or who give less cause of uneasiness to their fellow citizens, than the *farmer*?" Duane asked rhetorically. Farmers were both "*temperately pacific*" and "devoted to the *unity and integrity* of these states." In contrast, who had "left Pittsburgh to join Burr?" "Not *farmers*," he reminded his readers, but "a kind of negative beings who call themselves gentlemen, whose business is laziness, and who abhor honest labor." Duane warned that Burr and his elite supporters would have established "*a despotism*" and, with their new power, would have "[made] the *farmers* and *mechanics* toil" to support them. One of Duane's tricks was to turn Burr's reference to "choice spirits," "best blood," and "corps of worthys" against not just Burr, but all elites. What Duane called *"Burr's dictionary"* included each of these phrases, as well as one drawn from the published account of Eaton's conversations with Burr, "men above the dull pursuits of civil life." This dictionary, according to Duane, provided the "true definition of all Burr's adherents," who were *"well born*, all of them."[102]

The ironic twist that Duane gave to Burr's description of his supporters as "choice spirits" became common in public and private writings. Republican newspapers across the country happily conceded that Burr's men were, in fact, "choice spirits," refiguring that phrase to stigmatize an aristocratic elite.[103] Such uses of the phrase appeared in letters and diaries, as well. During the crisis over the *Chesapeake* Affair in July 1807, Virginia's John Page listed "Burr's thousands of choice spirits," along with slaves and Federalists, as auxiliaries that the British could mobilize in case of war.[104] Even Blennerhassett—himself a "choice spirit" at one time—used it ironically in his journal. This ironic usage became so common that William Wirt complained "that Burr [had] polluted" a once-useful phrase.[105] "Particular phrases are at times more fashionable than straw-bonnets in the dog days," a Baltimore editor explained in November 1807: *"Choice Spirit* bears the bell at present. Nothing is done, be it famous, or infamous, that is not ascribed to some choice spirit."[106]

The simple binaries of young versus old and many versus few could not fully explain the sources of danger that the Burr crisis revealed. Contemporaries recognized that young men would, at times, follow old men and that the many would, at times, follow the few. American society had never been as deferential as British society; forty years of political and social upheaval had further eroded whatever deference had existed in colonial America. Still, neither expectations nor exhibitions of deference—to age, to education, to refinement, to power—had disappeared entirely. By linking young and old, many and few, deference raised its own questions. Was it a source of stability or of danger? Did it help older, better-educated, and wealthier men to regulate the young, the uneducated, and the poor? Or did it merely enable the former to manipulate the latter? Many who worried about Burr and his "choice spirits" also hinted at the dangers of deference.[107]

Few questioned that young men owed some degree of respect, and perhaps even obedience, to older men. But one of the most frequently remarked parallels between Burr and Catiline was their "attachment to the Society of the young, the desperate, and the daring."[108] Wherever Burr went, the *Enquirer*'s editor remarked, he "shunned the society of the staid, and the aged," and "sought the intimacy of young men." "Their tender and ductile minds," the editor explained, quoting Catiline's historian Sallust, "are with less difficulty captivated by cunning and specious appearances."[109] Burr's powers of fascination clearly made him more dangerous than most older men; as his biographer later admitted, Burr "possessed, in a pre-eminent degree, the art of fascinating the youthful."[110] But contemporaries worried that there would be other Burrs and other Catilines as long as frustrated young men allowed themselves to be manipulated by ambitious older men who promised easy wealth and instant reputation.

Contemporaries also worried that deference could form a dangerous link between the few and the many. Even as observers commented upon the class bias of Burr's recruiting, they knew that either seizing New Orleans or invading Spanish Mexico or even settling new lands would require many more commoners than gentlemen. A widely reprinted letter from upstate New York resolved the apparent discrepancy between Burr's designs and his followers. If the object was merely to settle the Bastrop grant, the author explained, "farmers, and not gentlemen of talents and address would be wanted[.] But if a dismemberment of the union be contemplated, then the first step would be to draw as many gentlemen of [this] description as possible . . . to assist in the measure by their united influence and address."[111] Armies had long been filled by naming gentlemen officers and requiring them to recruit common soldiers from farmers, laborers, and artisans through their "influence and address." If Burr planned military action against either New Orleans or Mexico, an administration correspondent remarked, the logical first step would be "to engage a number of interprising respectable young men . . . as subordinate officers." "A sufficient number of a lower class," Ohio's Henry Baldwin argued, "can be procured nearer the immediate place of action."[112]

The weight that the young and unestablished gave to the opinions of older and better-situated men appears clearly in the letters of one of

Burr's men, Silas Brown. Brown was neither poor nor uneducated; he left enough property to settle his debts and wrote long letters to explain his actions. But he was young, single, and seeking a way to advance in the world. In upstate New York, in the summer of 1806, Brown—a New Hampshire native—learned from Comfort Tyler about "an Expedition . . . of great importance." Brown's later explanation of his decision to follow Tyler first to Beaver, Pennsylvania, and then down the Ohio emphasized his deference to the opinions of "men of abilities." According to Brown, Tyler had told him that the project was supported by "some of the first men in the United States," mentioning Dayton "and several other Gentlemen of rank" by name. To help him decide, Brown then turned to "a number of men of respectability and good information"; all of them encouraged him to go. He settled his affairs in New York and followed Tyler. Certain that he had joined "a respectable party of men" in "an agricultural and commercial" undertaking, Brown remained with Tyler all the way to Bayou Pierre. Burr's followers were "honest, well-meaning men," Brown insisted even in October 1807, who had been wrongly stamped "with infamy and disgrace" by "men of the lowest Class"—the editors and officials who had denounced the enterprise.[113]

The failure of the Burr Conspiracy did not challenge the view that some categories of people—defined by gender, age, marital status, class, and other characteristics—posed a greater danger to the new nation than others. Few would have agreed with the Spanish minister that the United States had "an infinite number of adventurers, without property, full of ambition, and ready to unite at once under the standard of a revolution which promises to better their lot."[114] But many accepted that, for all of the opportunities that their political and social order created, there remained large numbers of men whose ambitions exceeded their achievements and who chafed at the limits of that order. Thinking back on "Burr's Projects" after the trial, Senator John Quincy Adams, for example, saw a great danger to the new nation in the "*numbers*, of young men, with educations, but without occupations, or projects with which they can be satisfied." Quoting Shakespeare's Falstaff, he concluded that such men were "cankers of a calm world and a long peace."[115] But others continued to see different kinds of men, facing different kinds of obstacles, as the greater danger to the new nation.

Long after the Burr crisis, the phrase "choice spirits" continued to be associated not only with Burr, but also with those who threatened the government or the country. In late 1819, as the Missouri Crisis renewed fears of disunion, former president John Adams worried that "choice Spirits of [Burr's] Stamp might produce as many Nations in North America as there are in Europe."[116] Humphrey Marshall used the phrase ironically in his *History of Kentucky* (1824). In 1838, Thomas Spotswood Hinde mentioned "Burr's 'choice spirits'" in a published letter that warned of conspiratorial designs on Texas.[117] Despite this continuing usage, it was Burr's original meaning of "choice spirits" that increasingly shaped mid-nineteenth-century descriptions of his followers. In an 1820 article, the editor James Hall revived the question, "who were the adherents of Colonel Burr?" "Were they persons of obscure name and desperate fortune," he asked, or "men of good blood and fair fame?" The answer remained unclear. But Hall believed that many of Burr's supporters "were men of high standing, who had reputations to be tarnished, fortunes to be lost, and families to be embarrassed." Others were "high-souled youths," with "proud aspirings after fame" yet to gratify.[118] It became increasingly common to see Burr's followers presented as educated, energetic, cultured, and, often, young men. According to one Mississippi editor and historian, his state had benefitted when many of Burr's men had settled there. The educated and genteel young men on Burr's boats, he claimed, had "supplied it 'with school-masters, singing-masters, dancing masters, and doctors in abundance.'"[119] As the anxieties of the nation's early years receded into the past, the same romanticization of the Burr Conspiracy that reshaped accounts of Burr's arrest often affected portrayals of his followers.

By the last third of the century, Burr's best-known follower may have been Philip Nolan. A "gay, dashing, bright young fellow," Nolan was an army officer in the West. In 1805, he met Burr at Fort Massac. When Burr returned a year later with his boats and men, he lured Nolan away for a private conversation and "enlisted [him] body and soul" in his project. In 1807, as Burr's trial unfolded in Richmond, Nolan and other officers faced courts-martial at Fort Adams in the Mississippi Territory. Found guilty, Nolan cried out in court, "Damn the United States! I wish I may never hear of the United States again."[120] Rather than hanging Nolan, the court condemned him to live out his days on an American naval vessel, cut off not only from friends and family, but even from news about his country. Nolan was afforded every other convenience and civility, living as a gentleman and socializing with the officers on the corvette *Levant*. When he died in May 1863, it was discovered that, while he had outwardly respected the court's sentence and never asked the officers about his country, he had secretly celebrated every American triumph of the previous fifty-five years. He had hungrily sought any news that could be overheard from conversations among the hands or read in newspapers that were brought aboard. He died both a true American and a true gentleman.

Philip Nolan—at least this Philip Nolan—was a fictional character, the protagonist of Edward Everett Hale's 1863 story, "The Man without a Country." There had been a real Philip Nolan, a shadowy figure who had been killed by Spanish officials in Texas in March 1801. Intending to invent a brother for this real person, whom he had learned of from Wilkinson's memoirs, Hale accidentally gave his character the wrong name. Published at the height of the Civil War, "The Man without a Country" was meant to provide a lesson for "young Americans of to-day."[121] The story was reprinted "everywhere without the slightest deference to copyright," as Hale later noted; in the United States and Great Britain, more than half a million copies were printed in the first year alone.[122] Hale intended for his story to show the terrible consequences of turning against one's country. But, influenced by four decades of romanticized portrayals of Burr's followers, it also suggested not only that gentlemen could become traitors, but also that traitors could remain gentlemen.

FOURTH INTERLUDE

━━━━━━━━━━━

A "RISING" IN BALTIMORE

On Monday, 2 November 1807, thirteen days after his trial in Richmond ended, Aaron Burr arrived in Baltimore on the stagecoach from Washington. The previous day, four others—fellow indictees Harman Blennerhassett and Comfort Tyler, Burr's attorney Luther Martin, and defense witness Samuel Swartwout—had arrived from Richmond. Burr settled at the French Hotel on Gay Street, "obscure quarters" if compared to either Martin's home on South Charles Street or the inn where Blennerhassett and Tyler lodged on Baltimore Street.[1] On the day of Burr's arrival, a letter from Martin appeared in Baltimore's Federalist newspaper, the Federal Gazette. *It defended Burr, attacked the administration, and claimed "freedom from censure" for Martin himself.[2] That evening, a local volunteer company led by Captain Leonard Frailey, the printer of the Republican* Baltimore Evening Post, *visited Martin's home, where nearly "all the Burrites in town" had dined. The "fife and drum played the Rogue's march," then the company "gave 3 cheers" and left.[3]*

The next morning, the city's newest Republican newspaper, the Whig, *urged "the young men of Baltimore" to provide the "illustrious strangers" and Martin, "this very DAY, with a suit of tar and feathers."[4] Around noon, a handbill titled "AWFUL!!!" appeared around the city, informing residents "that four 'choice spirits'"— "His Quid Majesty" (Burr), "Blennerhassett the Chemist," "Lawyer Brandy Bottle" (Martin), and Chief Justice John Marshall—would be executed "by the Hang-man on Gallows-hill" at three o'clock according to "the sentence pronounced against them by the unanimous voice of every honest man in the community."[5] Within an hour, Burr, Swartwout, and Tyler left the city—"rather precipitately" in Blennerhassett's view. Certain that Burr would "receive unwelcome obliquy for his flight," Blennerhassett decided to remain at his*

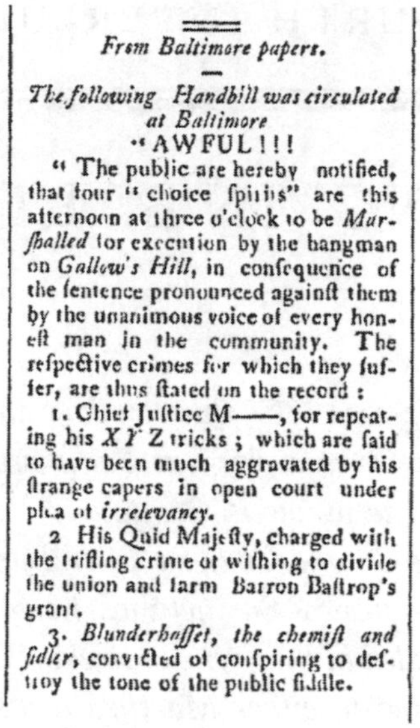

From Baltimore papers.

The following Handbill was circulated at Baltimore

"AWFUL!!!

" The public are hereby notified, that four " choice ſpirits" are this afternoon at three o'clock to be *Marſhalled* for execution by the hangman on *Gallow's Hill*, in conſequence of the ſentence pronounced againſt them by the unanimous voice of every honeſt man in the community. The reſpective crimes for which they ſuffer, are thus ſtated on the record :

1. Chief Juſtice M——, for repeating his *X Y Z* tricks ; which are ſaid to have been much aggravated by his ſtrange capers in open court under plea of *irrelevancy*.

2 His Quid Majeſty, charged with the trifling crime of wiſhing to divide the union and farm Barron Baſtrop's grant.

3. *Blunderhaſſet, the chemiſt and fidler*, convicted of conſpiring to deſtroy the tone of the public fiddle.

FIGURE 15. Newspaper publication of the "Awful!" handbill.

lodgings. Martin also stayed in Baltimore, but not at his home. His law students and some friends occupied his house, arming themselves "to repel an expected assault."[6] Before three o'clock, Mayor Thorowgood Smith and other civil officials decided to call out the constables and two companies of cavalry to prevent personal injury or property damage.

By mid-afternoon, men began collecting in the Fell's Point district to construct effigies and to organize the procession to Gallows' Hill. Each effigy was dressed in white, hooded, and hung with "an appropriate motto," drawn from the recent trial. Marshall's motto, for example, included a pastiche of his comments: "If this trial should terminate as the government wish—but this is not relevant to the case—I wish to hear an argument—I am willing to hear counsel on that point."[7] The four effigies were loaded into two tumbrels and taken to the gallows. The procession "traversed, and traversed again, the principal streets," "followed by [the] two troops of horse" that the mayor had mobilized.[8] When it passed by Blennerhassett's lodgings, it numbered "about 1500" and was "in full huzza, with fife and *drum-playing the rogue's march."*[9] *At Martin's house, it stopped and "gave three cheers."*[10] *After dark, it reached Gallows' Hill. The hanging "was executed like an Irish funeral, . . . by flambeaux," and the effigies were set ablaze.*[11] *By eight o'clock, the city was quiet.*

Burr and those whom the public associated with him had faced similar treatment before. In October 1806, as "Querist" and anti-"Querist" essays filled Ohio Valley newspapers, there had been "loud talke" in Marietta that Burr's son-in-law Joseph Alston would be "mobbed by the rabble" and that Burr himself would be "tar[red] and feather[ed]" if he returned. Near Cincinnati, locals had acted rather than merely talked—assembling at Burr's lodgings "with drums and fifes, beat[ing] the rogue's march, and [making] much disturbance."[12] In late December, soon after Burr and his boats departed down the Cumberland River, residents of Nashville, Tennessee, had reacted to the president's proclamation and William Eaton's disclosures by gathering in the city square. According to one witness, "about three or four Hundred People assembled" at nine o'clock to burn Burr in effigy. With "the American Flag hoisted and the Drum beating," they fired a cannon "until they bursted it," near midnight.[13] Ten days later, a Kentucky newspaper reported that "the same *honours*" had been paid to Burr "at Robinson court house and several other places in the state of Tennessee."[14]

What distinguished the incident in Baltimore from incidents elsewhere was the furor with which its character and meaning were contested, in Baltimore and beyond, for weeks afterward. Of the earlier incidents, only the one in Nashville seems to have received much attention beyond its immediate locale. Private letters and a brief, favorable item in the town's *Impartial Review* had spread the news. Some newspapers had reprinted the *Impartial Review* piece; others had reported the incident either through letters from Nashville or simply by noting that "Burr [had been] burnt in effigy" there.[15] This coverage had not suggested either regional or partisanal differences over the incident, since editors, essayists, and letter writers had rarely used it to address larger concerns. One Republican editor in western Pennsylvania had hinted that Nashville's "example [should] be followed throughout the union."[16] And one Federalist newspaper in Massachusetts's Maine District had decried the incident as an example "of this mobocracy mode of bringing offenders to justice."[17] But such comments seem to have been rare in early 1807.

When Burr's effigy—along with Blennerhassett's, Marshall's, and Martin's—was consigned to the flames in Baltimore on 3 November, the context was very different. The early doubts and anxieties about Burr's project that had made most commentators reluctant to speak or write in his defense had disappeared. By November 1807, the Burr Conspiracy had been the subject of a year of increasingly intense partisan wrangling in Congress and in the courts, in newspapers and in pamphlets, in taverns and on street corners. During that year, people of all political persuasions had discovered that the conspiracy could serve partisan purposes. But these developments had been both gradual and national. Other cities had shown, and would continue to show, greater tolerance for the presence of Burr and his associates than Baltimore. Burr had spent months in Richmond without provoking an incident like the one on what would have been his second night in the city. Leaving Richmond, he had passed through the nation's capital with little trouble, though he had been forced to lodge in Georgetown, rather than Washington proper, when innkeepers refused to house him for fear of losing lodgers. Blennerhassett and Martin had not suffered even that indignity, staying at Stelle's Hotel, one of the most respected public houses in Washington. After leaving Baltimore, Burr and some of the others went to Philadelphia, where, as Blennerhassett correctly predicted, they did not "receiv[e] similar public honours."[18]

Baltimore offered especially fertile ground for conflict over the conspiracy. In late March 1807, some Baltimoreans were already saying that, "If Burr Should be Cleared at the Circute Court in Virginia" and pass through their city, "he Shall have a New Coat of Tar & feathers."[19] A dynamic port city of roughly 40,000 people, Baltimore was widely celebrated for having "made the most rapid progress of any town in the U.S." Like most eastern cities, it was divided by geography, class, race, and politics. The white elite, Federalist and Republican, often had their homes, stores, or offices in the section called "Old Town" or simply "the town," though the wealthiest also owned country estates outside the city.[20] East of Old Town and separated from it by a small stream were the wharves of Fell's Point, home to many of those—white and black, male and female—who performed the manual labor of a busy seaport. Of the workers who enjoyed any sort of political voice, most were Republicans. In late October 1807, party conflict in Baltimore lacked the intensity that had marked the late 1790s or that would re-emerge over the next five years. Some Republicans voiced their frustrations with a political system that often elected Federalists to municipal offices, despite the city's Republican majority. But Baltimore had not yet earned the nickname *"Mob-town,"* which Philadelphia editor Enos Bronson bestowed in the summer of 1812 after some residents destroyed a Federalist newspaper office, attacked the city jail, and murdered one Federalist and beat others.[21]

Baltimore supported a diverse and engaged press in late 1807, including four daily newspapers and, beginning in late November, a short-lived, weekly news periodical. Three of the newspapers—the *American*, the *Baltimore Evening Post*, and the *Whig*—identified themselves as Republican. Often viewed as the mouthpiece of merchant and senator Samuel Smith, William Pechin's *American* functioned as a reliable administration paper with a national reach and a deep commitment to General James Wilkinson, who had local ties and support. Hezekiah Niles and Leonard Frailey's *Evening Post* received less national attention than the *American* but was firmly established locally. The city's newest print, the *Whig*, had been founded by the Democratic Republican Association, also called the Whig Club, in mid-September with an editor, Baptist Irvine, who had worked at William Duane's *Aurora General Advertiser*. These "Democratic printers," according to Blennerhassett, were "but little controlled by one spiritless federal paper," John Hewes's *Federal Gazette*.[22] While Hewes was typically reserved in his editorial comments, he provided space for more spirited Federalist essayists and letter writers. Late in November, John B. Colvin, who would later work in the State Department and ghostwrite part of Wilkinson's memoirs, launched the *Weekly Register of Politics and News*. Although just three issues appeared before Colvin moved it to Washington and re-named it, it briefly provided another Republican voice in Baltimore.[23]

The incident of 3 November consumed Baltimoreans for the rest of the month, and beyond. Editors and essayists, city officials and public assemblies fought to shape how local and distant audiences understood what had happened that day. What became the main points of contention appeared in the diary entry that Blennerhassett wrote as the ashes of his effigy still smoldered. In the course of recording his actions that day, he briefly suggested the three key questions in the battle to construct the incident: Who participated? How should those who participated be described? And how should local officials have responded? Blennerhassett briefly noted that the procession had been "chiefly made up at [Fell's] Point" and distinguished its members from "the respectable part of the city." He also captured the importance of a label when he recorded that the constable, a self-proclaimed "*republican,*" who had been sent to protect him had informed him "that the mob[—](I beg pardon) he said the people[—]were in motion in grt. force." And Blennerhassett remarked that, while the mayor "had promised . . . to make all necessary arrangements to secure the peace," the cavalry had actually "patroled the streets, not to disperse the mob, but to follow—and behold their conduct."[24]

The different local perspectives of what Blennerhassett called the "rising at Baltimore" became evident almost immediately.[25] The *American* and the *Whig*, both Republican, appeared first after the incident. The *American*'s initial coverage would have confused anyone outside of Baltimore. Even as it reported that "Burr's presence in town [had] excited great indignation," it mentioned neither the procession through the city nor the burning of the effigies.[26] In contrast, the *Whig* published a detailed account of the march and its culmination at Gallows' Hill under the title "Reward of Merit." Celebratory in tone, this piece called the incident "a *great* triumph."[27] The *Federal Gazette* appeared next. Its editor had announced his opposition to the "riot" even before it occurred.[28] Then, on 4 November, Hewes published a letter from Martin thanking those who had defended his home and denouncing those who had made up "the Mob of the City."[29] To help "distant readers" understand this letter, Hewes added a brief note about "the affair of last evening."[30] The same day, at least three accounts of the incident were written for Federalist editors and friends in Washington, Philadelphia, and Richmond that were subsequently published. The Republican *Evening Post* ended the day with an account that was generally favorable and slightly longer than Hewes's note, but more reserved and much shorter than the *Whig*'s report.

One of the conflicts in these initial accounts concerned the marchers themselves. Federalists wanted outsiders to know, as Hewes stated, that "the people of Baltimore [had taken] no part in the frolic."[31] With this assertion, he drew the same distinction that Blennerhassett had made in his diary—between the respectable merchants, lawyers, and shop-keepers of Baltimore proper and the rough sailors, dockworkers, and mechanics of Fell's Point. Other Baltimore Federalists echoed this characterization. In a letter to the *Virginia Gazette*, one distinguished "the dregs and rabble of the Point" who had participated in the inci-dent from "the respectable part of our citizens [who] join[ed] in one universal detestation of what has occurred."[32] The *Whig*'s lengthy de-scription claimed something very different. It stressed that the proces-sion comprised not only "an *immense concourse*," but also "a respectable assemblage of citizens." Not everyone had cheered the procession; Ir-vine admitted that there had been "some very 'vinegar aspects' and surly faces . . . at some doors and windows," but they had belonged solely to the "friends" of the condemned.[33] Disputing Hewes's "'auda-cious' falsehood," Irvine insisted on 5 November that the procession had been "planned and carried into execution *chiefly* by the citizens of Baltimore[,] *thousands* of whom [had] gloried in expressing their detesta-tion of traitors."[34] It is impossible to know how many men, and perhaps women, and from which part, or parts, of the city joined the procession or cheered the executions. Of the eight leaders for whom arrest warrants were later issued, however, only three lived in Fell's Point, including "one of the richest men in town," the shipbuilder James Biays.[35]

For Baltimore's Federalists, the key word for understanding the events of 3 November was "mob." In private letters and published writ-ings, they almost invariably called the hundreds of Baltimoreans who had marched through the city and burned the effigies a "mob." Doing so evoked a particular image with a particular place in the era's political thought. Mobs, as one New York Federalist remarked, were "impetu-ous, cruel, [and] relentless." In their "lawless violence," they were "fickle as the wind" and likely to turn against those whom they had once sup-ported.[36] When a local Federalist reported that the Baltimore mob's conduct had been "violent and intemperate," he simply stated that it had behaved as mobs behaved.[37] In contemporary political thought, the mob was the most alarming embodiment of the raw power of the many, the mass, the lower orders and, thus, the most serious challenge to the stabilizing influence of the few, the propertied, the elite. In his published letter of 4 November, Martin captured this perspective when he warned those who sought "the prosperity of this city" that men of property would avoid Baltimore if it became known as a place where the mob held sway. Who would "transfer his person, or his capital to a place where life, liberty, and property [were] held at the will of an infuriated Mob?"[38] Federalists, in Baltimore and beyond, also invested the mob with a partisan dimension. Mob rule, they believed, was the logical, even inevitable, outcome of the Republicans' excessively democratic politics and principles.

In early republican America, "mob" had no positive connotations. No one could defend the participants in the events of 3 November and still call them a "mob." Even the *Whig*, the most democratic of the city's newspapers, insisted that the incident was "not the drunken triumph of a mobbish rabble" and stressed "that *not a single instance of disorder happened from beginning to end*." As suggested by Blennerhassett's diary, where Federalists saw the "mob," Republicans often saw the "people." Irvine repeatedly referred to the incident as an expression of the unanimous, or near-unanimous, sentiments of "the people of Baltimore." "Until the events of yesterday *removed* my scepticism," he exclaimed, "I had disbelieved the adage, '*Vox populi est vox dei*'"—"the voice of the people is the voice of God."[39] The more restrained *Evening Post* likewise made clear that the participants in the procession had not behaved like a mob—"no violence was offered to the person or property of any"—and that those who had applauded the burnings at Gallows' Hill were the "people."[40] Republicans had adopted similar language in describing the earlier displays of popular outrage at Burr. The burning of Burr's effigy in Nashville, for example, had been effected "by the people" and "was all done in cool and sober blood."[41]

If the procession through the city and the burning of the effigies were the work of the mob, as Federalists believed, then civil officials should have exerted their authority and power to control it. The mob's natural inclination to violence and intemperance could be kept in check by external pressures, particularly when applied early. On the afternoon of 3 November, as the marchers assembled at Fell's Point, the *Federal Gazette* announced to those who had seen the *Whig*'s invitation to tar and feather Burr and the handbill's call to burn the men in effigy that "the CIVIL AUTHORITY" had "authorized" it to state "that *Efficient*

Measures have been taken to quell riot and preserve the peace of the city."[42] The next day, Federalists attributed the lack of violence to the quick action of the authorities and the constant presence of the cavalry. Martin began his published letter that day by thanking Mayor Smith and the cavalry for "preserv[ing] the persons and property of myself and others from lawless violence."[43] Other Federalists also claimed that "no violence [had been] offered to any of the citizens" largely due to the "precaution" of ordering out the cavalry.[44] Because the "troops of horse [had] parade[d] the streets," one wrote, the day had "ended in loud huzzas" instead of a "riot."[45]

Seeing the procession and its culmination, instead, as the act of the "people," as Republicans did, made interference by the mostly Federalist civil authorities more problematic. On the day after the incident, all three Republican newspapers suggested that ordering out the cavalry had been unnecessary and inappropriate. "There was *no use* for the two *troops of horse*, or even the *civil* officers, who were assembled to preserve order," the *Evening Post* remarked.[46] The *American* sarcastically charged that, if civil officials had really wanted to "prevent riots" and preserve the peace, they should have put Martin "in a strait waistcoat."[47] The *Whig*'s account of the procession explicitly juxtaposed the people to the civil and military authorities. "So whelming was the popular voice," Irvine reported, "that not a *sabre* [the cavalry's principal weapon] was drawn, or *dare* to be *drawn*," against it.[48] In Irvine's view, the mayor, showing his "strong sympathies for Treason and Traitors," had "exceed[ed] the limits of [his] official duties [by] discountenanc[ing] those *honest* citizens who are friends of the government."[49]

By reprinting and addressing the early accounts from letters and newspapers, editors beyond Baltimore made the 3 November incident the topic of a national discussion. Outsiders found it difficult to dispute the local origins of the marchers, an issue that mattered greatly within the city. But Federalist editors in New York, Philadelphia, Washington, Boston, and elsewhere were as quick as Baltimore's Federalists to see the incident as "a singular riot" and those involved as "a lawless, disorderly rable" or, simply put, a "mob."[50] Far more than Hewes's early coverage in the *Federal Gazette*, they traced the mob to their political opponents, with comments on the incident and its aftermath titled "Baltimore Democrats run mad," "More Democracy at Baltimore," and

"Democracy Unveiled."[51] Using a long-established shorthand for Republican fanaticism, they stressed the role of "the Jacobin prints" in inciting the "riot."[52] And they found it unsurprising "that the good democrats should raise a mob to put down the laws."[53] Tapping into the near-universal condemnation of mobs, these editors used any evidence of apologism or support to blast their foes. "He whose blood does not boil with indignation on the bare perusal of such conduct," the editor of the *Washington Federalist* insisted, "must be too far bewildered in the mazes of folly, or sunk too deep in wickedness, to be reclaimed."[54]

One Republican editor did express such indignation. James Cheetham, a longtime Burr critic and the editor of New York's *American Citizen* and *Republican Watch-Tower*, offered both a clear statement of the broad consensus on the evils of mobs and a rare admission by a Republican that the marchers in Baltimore had constituted one. To Cheetham, mobs were "many headed hydras, which in no one instance can be right, but in all must be wrong." The despicable nature of "Burr and his associate conspirators" did not justify the protest. It was not the place of a mob—"persons tumultuously assembled in our streets," in Cheetham's definition—to judge the chief justice. Nor should editors encourage or defend mobs, regardless of their targets. Instead, Cheetham argued, "the press should in an especial manner reprehend them."[55] Federalist editors seized upon Cheetham's comments, reprinting them as a rare example of "correct and proper" thinking by a Republican and using them to critique "the Aurora, and [the] other jacobin prints, [that] openly advocate[d] the doings of the Baltimore mob."[56]

Although Republican editors did not usually reprint Cheetham's remarks or offer similar views, many took positions that were much closer to the *American*'s or the *Evening Post*'s than the *Whig*'s. Echoing the former's near silence, the *National Intelligencer* waited almost three weeks before even mentioning the incident, despite reporting Burr's reception in Washington and Philadelphia in a timely manner. The editors of Richmond's Republican newspapers, the *Virginia Argus* and the *Enquirer*, never commented directly upon the incident. Instead, they offered what might now be considered balanced coverage by printing two pieces from the *Federal Gazette* and two from the *Whig*—except the items from the *Whig* directly refuted those from the *Federal Gazette*. Elsewhere, some Republican newspapers simply reprinted the *Evening*

Post's brief report, often without any comment. Other editors echoed the *Evening Post*'s Niles and Frailey, presenting the procession and its culmination as the work of "the people" or stressing the absence of "personal violence" or property damage.[57]

But Federalist editors were essentially correct when they charged that at least some Republican newspapers had "openly advocate[d] the doings of the Baltimore mob."[58] Several Republican editors reprinted the *Whig*'s lengthy report with favorable comments. One upstate New York editor, for example, explained that his publication of the *Whig* account was meant to show the harmony in "sentiments respecting the transactions in the federal court at Richmond" between Baltimoreans and his readers.[59] In Philadelphia's *Aurora*, William Duane evinced disappointment that, rather than providing Burr, Blennerhassett, and Martin with "a suit of *Yankee ermine*" (i.e., tar and feathers), "the citizens of Baltimore" "had only erected a funeral pile" for their effigies.[60] Some Republican editors also used the Federalists' denunciations against them. In one widely reprinted piece, titled "Mobs! Mobs! Mobs!," the editor of Boston's *Democrat* sneered: "The delicate nerves of our tories are greatly discomposed . . . at the thought of the proceedings of the people of Baltimore, which they choose to magnify into 'a mob.'" Benjamin Parks then explained that, to Federalists, "mob" covered "any promiscuous collection of the American people, assembled, however peaceably, for any purpose contrary to the interest of George III." Their opposition to Baltimore's "mob" was not based upon "*principle*," he insisted; they would not have uttered "a word of disapprobation," if people had "assembled to execute the effigy of General Wilkinson." The Federalists' "*mob-hating* fit," Parks charged, reflected a combination of "fellow-feeling for Burr, and fear for themselves," since the prospect of a British war made them suspect.[61]

As the early reports of the events in Baltimore spread and as distant editors fueled a national conversation about them, the conflict intensified in the city. On Thursday, 5 November, two days after the procession, Judge Walter Dorsey, a Federalist, issued a warrant for the arrest of eight men, including the *Whig* editor Baptist Irvine and militia captains James Biays and Joseph O'Reilly. The same day, a meeting of "the Democratic Republican Citizens of Baltimore" was proposed for Saturday at the Pantheon, to discuss "the conduct of certain *civil* officers . . . in calling on the *military* to suppress an APPREHENDED riot."[62] On Friday, the *Federal Gazette* printed another letter from Martin thanking a group of men—"not less than an hundred," he claimed—who had "intermix[ed]" with "the Mob" to prevent it from doing any damage.[63] On Saturday, the sheriff served Dorsey's warrant. Six of the eight men provided security and remained free. Biays and O'Reilly refused to do so. O'Reilly alone was imprisoned, being held for seven hours before "the frowns of five hundred citizens" who had assembled at the jail led the sheriff to release him.[64] That evening, "Six hundred" Baltimoreans met at the Pantheon, where "an *illuminated* Gallows was introduced into the Hall, containing Burr and Blent. *strech'd up*."[65] Deciding that the actions of civil officials formed "an example dangerous to the rights and liberties of the people," the meeting appointed a committee to investigate "judicial abuses," to consider whether there was "*something radically wrong in the principles of [Baltimore's] corporation*," and to draft a petition to the state legislature.[66]

The next day, 8 November, Baltimore Republicans found another way to display, on the streets and in their newspapers, their opposition to Burr. Three days earlier, General Wilkinson had arrived in the city. That Sunday, the first of what would become a number of local volunteer and militia companies paid their respects to him. On some occasions, an entire company visited Wilkinson at his lodgings and displayed their martial skills; on others, a delegation of officers represented the company. Each time, the officers formally thanked the general for his efforts, as one group put it, "to defeat the foul projects of Treason, and save a people from the horrors of revolutionary rapine and violence."[67] Each time, Wilkinson delivered a formal answer. On 17 November, nine days after the first of these visits, the *Whig* reported that Wilkinson was still "receiv[ing] additional marks of esteem every day."[68] Finding these "public displays . . . very fatigueing," one of Wilkinson's lieutenants wished that the companies had conducted them "all in one."[69] But doing so would have defeated an important purpose—the creation of not one, but many opportunities to publicize Republicans' pro-Wilkinson and anti-Burr sentiments, in person and in print.

Following Saturday's arrests and meeting, tensions in the city escalated. The *Federal Gazette* and the *Whig* entered into what one New

York editor called a "war" over recent events.[70] For days, nearly every issue of these newspapers included editorials or essays on the burning of the effigies, the calling out of the militia, the arrests of the presumed leaders, the resolutions of the Pantheon meeting, or the developments of the ensuing days. In the *Federal Gazette*, Hewes and various essayists continued to distinguish between the "very limited" number of "*Terrorists*" who had caused the "recent tumult" and the large number of "respectable citizens" who had opposed them, though party largely replaced place in distinguishing between the groups.[71] They also continued to describe those who composed not only the procession of 3 November, but also the crowd at the jail four days later, as a mob. And they began to warn of a grand design by its leaders "to ascertain to what extent the people of Baltimore [would] tolerate the licentiousness of a mob"; "if the men of virtue" did not "strangle and subdue this more than hydra-headed monster," "Senex" warned on 10 November, "they will soon have to bid adieu to their quietness and security." Such concerns fueled a belief that the civil authorities' initial and ongoing response had been inadequate and that "severe punishment" was needed for "the factious and evil-minded men who have planned and organized the recent commotions."[72]

In the *Whig*, Irvine restated and extended the positions of his initial coverage of the procession through the city and the burning of the effigies. He still claimed broad support within Baltimore, though the continuing clamor made it impossible to talk of near-unanimous backing. Instead, Irvine distinguished between the "enemies" and the "friends . . . of traitors" or between "the *real* supporters of the laws" and those who merely claimed to support them. He also continued to insist that the people had not acted as a mob during the original incident—which was "conducted with such *order* and tranquillity as were utterly unprecedented"—or subsequent events.[73] Refuting the language of newspaper editors outside of Baltimore, moreover, Irvine announced that "no riot had happened" and "not a single instance of disorderly conduct [had taken] place (on the part of the Democrats)." Increasingly, Irvine's focus shifted to the civil authority's, and particularly Judge Dorsey's, response. He attacked the judge and mayor personally and attributed their crackdown on the procession's leaders to "fear [of] an enquiry into their conduct."[74] And he criticized Dorsey's warrant, which, as he read it, did not actually charge anyone with a crime. Instead, it seemed designed to prevent the named men from committing future outrages by forcing them to post security in order to avoid arrest. In Irvine's words, the warrant should be read as saying: "YOU MUST ENTER INTO BOND, NEVER AGAIN TO MAKE EFFIGIES, SHOW CONTEMPT FOR TRAITORS, OR BURN IMAGES."[75]

This newspaper war raged amid continuing tensions in the city's streets. On Monday evening, 9 November, rumor suggested "that Judge Dorsey was to be *mobbed*, or outrageously insulted," according to Hewes, "for the part he [had] *dared* to act."[76] The next day, the monthly muster of Captain O'Reilly's company produced a brief panic when it was rumored that the soldiers planned to visit Dorsey's house and "beat the rogue's march."[77] In response, a group that Hewes praised as "a number of gentlemen of respectability and nerve"—and that Irvine disparaged as "a crowd of *gentlemen*, and *no-gentlemen*"—assembled to protect Dorsey's person, family, and property.[78] But O'Reilly had apparently never intended any insult against Dorsey and did not pass his home. Irvine believed that the "infamous tale" of a plan to insult the judge had been concocted by Federalists "for the infamous purpose of endeavouring to *disgrace* republicanism, by exciting a riot."[79] But an essayist in the *Federal Gazette* insisted that the mob's leaders sought "to overawe and intimidate" Dorsey, either to prevent him from maintaining order or to drive him from office.[80]

On Saturday, 14 November, Baltimore's Democratic Republicans met again at the Pantheon to hear "the report of the committee" that had been appointed a week earlier.[81] Of the eight committee members, only James Biays, the chair, had been named in Dorsey's warrant, and just one other, Leonard Frailey, had been named in newspaper accounts of the procession. The other members included attorneys, merchants, and federal officeholders; only Biays lived in Fell's Point. The committee's report began with as full a history of recent events as the authors could assemble. It opened with the publication of Martin's letter in the *Federal Gazette* on 2 November and the playing of "the rogues march" at Martin's home that afternoon but focused upon the events of 3 November. It reprinted the *Whig*'s "Earnest Proposal" and the "Awful!!!" handbill and discussed the decision of Mayor Smith, Judge Dorsey, and others to use the constables and the cavalry to prevent "outrage and riot." Then, it described at some length the procession, whose participants "behave[d] like good and peaceable citizens," and its interactions with the cavalry. It closed with the visit to Martin's house, the hanging and burning of the effigies on Gallows' Hill, and the dispersal of "the people . . . in the utmost harmony and quietness." Of the developments since 3 November, the report said relatively little. It detailed the process by which eight men had been served Dorsey's warrant on 7 November, even though they had violated "no known law." And it dispelled any suggestion that O'Reilly's company had intended to intimidate Dorsey on 10 November, even as it denounced those who had gathered to protect Dorsey's house as the most "dangerous" and "illegal" assembly of all.[82]

The conclusions that the committee drew from this history ranged far beyond the events of the previous two weeks, though not beyond its charge to consider if there was "*something radically wrong in the principles of [Baltimore's] corporation.*"[83] While accepting that "the motives" of the city's civil and military leaders may have been good, the committee insisted that "their conduct was entirely illegal." Under state law, the militia could be called out only by specified officials in a specified manner and only when the people rose in "oppos[ition to] the government" or "insurrection against the constitution." Those procedures had not been followed and those conditions had not been met on 3 November. The committee then rooted the officials' "grand and dangerous mistake" not in the confusion of the moment or even in the incompetence of the officials, but in "radical errors in the principles of the incorporation of the city of Baltimore." The combination of high property requirements for voters and officeholders and the indirect election of the mayor permitted the city's highest official to be "unacquainted with," negligent of, or "even opposed to" "the temper and dispositions of the people." "Can it be supposed," the committee asked, "that a mayor elected by the people . . . would have believed the wonderful tales that were circulated on the day of the procession?" The report also suggested that either the judge had acted illegally in ordering the arrests of the presumed leaders or the law under which he had acted was "a most alarming encroachment" on a cherished right. Accordingly, the report proposed petitioning the state legislature to revise the city's corporate charter by changing the rules for municipal voting, giving the people more influence over local appointments, and reforming the administration of "criminal justice."[84]

The report's publication in the city's Republican newspapers beginning on Tuesday, 17 November, reanimated a local discussion that had quieted somewhat during the preceding week. The meeting and report fueled a new round of editorials and essays in the *Federal Gazette* and the *Whig* that disputed and defended specific points in the committee's history of events. But larger issues were addressed, as well. The *American* editor William Pechin printed the report to counteract the charges by "*federal* editors throughout the Union" of "mob" and "riot."[85] In the second issue of his new *Weekly Register*, John Colvin likewise rebutted the idea that "those who attended the effigies" had formed a mob, even as he suggested that the procession had been unnecessary. But, believing that the mayor had been right to try to preserve peace even if wrong "as to the manner" and doubting that "a democratic mayor" would have acted differently, Colvin also rejected the report's argument for wholesale revisions of the city's charter.[86] The proposed revisions alarmed Baltimore Federalists, who saw "a disposition" "in some of the democrats . . . to break down the characters and standing of some of the most respectable citizens" as part of their project "of LICENTIOUS INNOVATION."[87] "A head-strong, turbulent mob," one essayist warned, had established a committee to propose "a chimerical reform of municipal regulations hostile to tumult and faction."[88]

What the author considered "chimerical," however, became increasingly real in the weeks after the committee reported. On 30 November, the *American* announced that the proposed petition had been drafted and was available for "general signature."[89] After detailing the "antirepublican" character of the mode of electing the mayor and the upper branch of the city council, the petition called for amendments to Baltimore's charter to establish a single, lower property requirement for voting for all elected offices and the direct election of the mayor. It never mentioned the incident of 3 November but stressed, as the report had, the problems arising from there being "no common sentiment between a people and a chief magistrate."[90] By late December, the signed petition had been delivered to Maryland's House of Delegates. Within two weeks, a bill of amendments to the city's charter had been reported out of committee. It did not include the direct election of the mayor but did reduce the property qualifications for holding office and for voting. The bill was adopted, thirty-five to sixteen, four days before the session ended. On 20 January 1808, the last day of the session, the governor signed it into law. The bill did not actually change the charter. On 2 February, Baltimore's voters would elect delegates to a convention whose sole purpose would be to approve or reject the revisions.[91]

The incident of 3 November had hardly been forgotten in Baltimore while the petition was under consideration in Annapolis. In the *Whig*, Irvine pounded away at Mayor Smith, Judge Dorsey, Martin, and others. Various men who had played roles in the incident continued to use the *Federal Gazette* and the *Whig* to attack those who criticized their actions and to defend their own reputations. Baltimore's newspapers also provided space for discussing the proposed revisions to the charter. Very quickly, "Tammany," an essayist in the *Whig*, emerged as the most forceful advocate of reforming a political system in which "the *majority* are subjected to the rule of the *minority*."[92] Enough local Federalists grew frustrated with Hewes's inability to counter the *Whig* that they established another Federalist newspaper, Jacob Wagner's *North American*. Even before the first issue appeared, Irvine denounced the *North American* as "Luther Martin's paper" and traced its origins to Martin's belief that the *Federal Gazette* was "no stronger than 'chicken-broth,' or 'dish-water.'"[93]

When the *North American* published its first issue on 11 January 1808, the proposed revisions to the charter had largely driven the other repercussions of the incident of 3 November from the city's newspapers. The *Whig* had provided the first glimpse of the committee's recommendations two days earlier. Hoping that the assembly would strengthen this proposal, both Irvine and "Tammany" denounced it as inadequate; to Irvine, it "remedied no omission [and] remove[d] no grievance." Once it passed the House of Delegates, however, the *Whig* became the strongest supporter of this "*partial remedy*."[94] In the two weeks before the special election, Irvine and "Tammany" repeatedly urged Baltimore's working classes to "turn out, one and all," to "give a death-blow to foul oppression."[95] The *North American*, along with the *Federal Gazette*, sought to rally opposition to the revisions. At times, both opponents and supporters of the revisions referred to what an essayist in the *North American* called "the riot in November last."[96] On 2

February 1808, the voters showed their support for the revisions. Seven of the city's eight wards chose delegates who supported the changes; across the city, the voting ran more than two to one in favor of the revisions.

What began as a relatively innocuous bit of street theater grew, over the course of three months, into a democratic revision of Baltimore's municipal government. That result was never inevitable. In the weeks after 3 November, some Federalists decided that the procession through the city and the burning of the effigies had arisen from a grand design to remake Baltimore's politics. And there certainly had been earlier efforts to reform the city's charter on the part of the city's working classes and Republican leaders. But it is hard to imagine that the group of men who read Martin's public letter defending Burr and attacking the administration in the 2 November *Federal Gazette* and decided that something needed to be done "to exhibit[,] in the most unequivocal manner, [their] aversion for traitors" could have foreseen the ultimate outcome.[97] In retrospect, even the civil authorities' response on 3 November—the decision to call out the constables and the cavalry— seems less important to what followed than later developments—the attacks in the press and the arrests of the presumed leaders. "The whole mighty matter would have evaporated in one evening's noise and drumming," an essayist in the *American* remarked after two weeks, "if it had passed without offensive notice."[98] Instead, "by raising an outcry," as Colvin explained in early December, "the friends of Mr. Martin" had "invoke[d] popular resentment to something more serious."[99] The incident of 3 November and its aftermath did not create the demands for a revision of the corporate charter, but, in the politically charged atmosphere that followed the Burr crisis and the controversial trial, they may have sparked enough support in Baltimore and Annapolis to produce change.

CHAPTER 11

FINAL ACCOUNTS OF THE
BURR CONSPIRACY

IN MID-NOVEMBER 1838, CHARLES FRANCIS ADAMS, THE SON AND grandson of presidents, began reading Matthew Livingston Davis's two-volume *Memoirs of Aaron Burr* (1836–37) with the idea of reviewing it. Having completed it in early December, Adams decided to wait for "Burr's new work"—Davis's edition of Burr's journals from his European travels between 1808 and 1812—before beginning his review.[1] While Adams found the *Private Journal of Aaron Burr* (1838) disappointing—"a mere parcel of emptiness"—he decided in late January "to go on seriously with Burr and to try to squeeze something out of him."[2] After a week spending most mornings rereading the memoirs in his office and most afternoons reading the journals at home, Adams wrote to John G. Palfrey, the editor of the Boston-based *North American Review*, proposing a joint review of the works. As he awaited a response, he began thinking seriously about Burr, whose history seemed "entirely unexampled in America and perhaps in the world."[3] After hearing from Palfrey, Adams sought various primary sources for some of the key incidents in Burr's life. Over the next few weeks, he completed his research and prepared the review, finishing the draft in early March. Adams spent the next two months working on revisions, except for those days when he "had an insurmountable repugnance to taking up Burr."[4] In early May, he sent the finished manuscript to Palfrey; the unattributed review appeared in the *North American Review* in July.

Although Adams devoted just four of his fifty pages to the Burr Conspiracy, it was the subject of much of his research. In his diary, he listed "the Report of Burr's trial at Richmond" first among the material that he needed.[5] After searching local booksellers, Adams went to

FIGURE 16. Aaron Burr in old age.

Boston's Athenæum, where he "procured the necessary volumes," choosing among its three versions of Burr's trial—the collection that Thomas Jefferson sent to Congress, the two volumes of David Robertson's *Reports of the Trials of Colonel Aaron Burr*, and the three volumes of Thomas Carpenter's *Trial of Col. Aaron Burr*. He also borrowed the second volume of "General [James] Wilkinson's life," two volumes of "Jefferson's letters," the collection of Jefferson's memoranda that had been labelled the *Anas*, and John Quincy Adams's "report upon [Ohio Senator] John Smith" for the Senate.[6] Still, neither his own research nor Davis's memoirs had answered Adams's questions about this "most mysterious incident in our history." Both "the real design" and "the features of [Burr's] plan" remained unclear.[7]

Adams's reading and research may have included what we could call the final accounts of the Burr Conspiracy of the three men who had most shaped the crisis thirty years earlier—Burr, Jefferson, and Wilkinson. Burr had not written his final account himself but had chosen his longtime political ally Davis as its author and had provided letters and guidance as Davis began the *Memoirs*. Jefferson had not written his final account of the conspiracy either. His most important final statement appeared not in the letters and memoranda that Adams perused, but in the record of Burr's trial in Richmond that had been prepared under his direction and sent to Congress in November 1807. Wilkinson had written numerous accounts of the Burr Conspiracy, concluding with the three-volume *Memoirs of My Own Times* (1816) and including an earlier work with the uncompromising title *Burr's Conspiracy Exposed; and General Wilkinson Vindicated Against the Slanders of His Enemies on that Important Occasion* (1811).

Each of these men viewed the Richmond trial as a failure. For Jefferson, it had failed to provide the administration with the expected opportunities to substantiate the treason that he had charged upon Burr in his important 22 January 1807 message to Congress. For Wilkinson, it had failed to redeem his reputation, whether by establishing Burr's treason or by vindicating his acts in defeating it or even by removing any suspicions of his prior involvement in Burr's project. For Burr, it had failed to prove his innocence and clear his name, even as it returned not-guilty verdicts on both the treason and misdemeanor charges. Though they assumed different forms, appeared at different times, and even addressed different problems, these men's final accounts of the conspiracy—Jefferson's trial report, Wilkinson's various statements, and Burr's memoirs—sought to redress what each man viewed as the trial's failure. In doing so, each represented an attempt to control the story of the Burr Conspiracy as it passed into history.

"THE *ANARCHIAD*"

When the trial ended in late October 1807, the story of the Burr Conspiracy seemed less, not more, coherent than it had six months earlier when the trial began. Expectations had been very different. It had been widely assumed that the trial, by producing sworn testimony from the numerous witnesses and eliciting comprehensive narratives from the prosecution and defense attorneys, would clarify what had long been mysterious. But the trial's course had frustrated those expectations, with the treason and misdemeanor stages having been aborted by Chief Justice John Marshall's rulings. "It is generally believed," one government witness wrote from Richmond in early September, "that Burr has escaped by a sort of legal finesse, not only a Condemnation, but a Trial."[8] Additional evidence had been offered during the committal hearing, but newspaper coverage and popular interest had waned by then. Many of those who had followed the evidence believed that it showed treasonable intent, at least. But Marshall had again ruled that no treasonable act had been committed. A month later, Jefferson met the increased uncertainty about the conspiracy and the lingering controversy over Marshall's decisions by putting before Congress and the public a record of Burr's trial. The ideal trial report would be complete, accurate, and impartial; Jefferson's report possessed none of those characteristics.

Before mechanical recording, the ideal of the trial report was unrealizable. In the early nineteenth century, court reporters, "short hand men," employed various stenographic systems to capture witnesses' testimony, attorneys' arguments, and judges' opinions as they were spoken; from these notes, they prepared a final report.[9] It was widely accepted that the reports would be incomplete, as it was almost impossible for reporters to catch every word. But reporters did not necessarily include everything in their final report even when they had good notes. The published reports of Burr's trial, for example, summarized the attorneys' arguments on minor points and occasionally hid personal conflicts behind comments such as: "Here a desultory conversation ensued."[10] The nature of the task also ensured that trial reports would be inaccurate, though this departure from the ideal was not as readily accepted, particularly by those whose words had been "mangled . . . most hideously."[11] Reporters often asked judges, attorneys, and even witnesses to review their notes; still, speakers occasionally complained that they had "been badly copied by the Stenographer."[12] The inherent problems of incompleteness and inaccuracy mattered most because there was no guarantee of impartiality. During Burr's trial, the reporters for the *Virginia Argus* considered it necessary to assure those who spoke in the courtroom and those who read their report in the newspaper: "We never *designedly* will state a word incorrectly."[13]

In the early American republic, trials were reported by private citizens, not public officers. Official clerks prepared formal records of charges and outcomes. But neither federal nor state governments required that the full proceedings be recorded. As such, most trials went unreported. Reports were made only for those trials where private or public interest seemed to justify the high costs of employing a stenographer, preparing a report, and putting it before the public. There was little question that Burr's trial would justify such expense. Newspaper editors dreaming of new subscriptions, publishing houses imagining robust sales, and even individual stenographers foreseeing personal gain predicted that reporting Burr's trial could be "very profitable." In February 1807, William Sampson, a recent immigrant from Ireland who lived in New York, informed his wife that he was considering going to report the trials "in shorthand" since they would be "of infinite importance and interest in this Country."[14] While Sampson abandoned his plan, at least four stenographers attended part of Burr's trial and published their efforts in book form.

Two of the four, William W. Hening and William Munford, worked as a team. Well-regarded in Virginia's legal circles for reporting cases in the highest state court, their presence at the trial is not surprising. They probably began their work as a private speculation. The only stenographers at the trial's opening stage, they quickly published the *Examination of Col. Aaron Burr*, with copies for sale within two weeks. Before the trial's next stage, they had been hired by the *Virginia Argus* editor Samuel Pleasants Jr. to report it for his newspaper. Pleasants announced, moreover, that their reports would ultimately be printed as a book for "such gentlemen as wish[ed] to preserve in [that] form . . . this interesting trial."[15] Near the end of the trial, the federal district attorney George Hay mentioned another source of employment for the men. Writing to the president, Hay stated that he had hired Hening "to take down the evidence," probably meaning both depositions and testimony.[16] If Hening and Munford earned anything from their reporting after the examination, it must have come from the *Argus* or the administration because they never turned their notes into a book.

Another stenographer began reporting Burr's trial in late May during the grand jury stage. Advertised as "one of the most able and correct Stenographers in the United States," Thomas Carpenter had previously reported the debates in the New Jersey legislature and the treason trials of Pennsylvania's John Fries. He had been hired by the printer James D. Westcott, who had launched a Republican newspaper, the *Times*, in the Federalist stronghold of Alexandria during the fierce political battles of the late 1790s. Soon after Jefferson's inauguration, Westcott had closed the *Times*, received a government printing contract, and moved his press across the river to Washington. His decision to hire Carpenter and to publish a report of Burr's trial appears to have been a business speculation. By mid-July, Westcott was advertising, for seventy-five cents, the volume of Carpenter's report that would cover the recently completed grand jury stage. At the end of the trial, Westcott, having already spent "about two thousand dollars," began plying his important Republican contacts—including the president, the vice president, and most of the cabinet—for assistance to complete the remaining volumes.[17] The finished work finally appeared in mid-July 1808 as the *Trial of Col. Aaron Burr.*

Midway through the grand jury stage, another well-known Virginia stenographer, David Robertson, began taking notes. A lawyer from Petersburg, Robertson had recorded the debates of the 1788 state convention that ratified the federal Constitution and had reported the 1800 sedition trial of James Callender. Like Hening and Munford, he reported Burr's trial for a newspaper, John Dickson's *Petersburg Intelligencer*, and planned to publish the final report in book form. When his *Reports of the Trials of Colonel Aaron Burr* appeared in August 1808, Robertson explained the relatively thin coverage of the preliminaries by noting that he had not been "prevailed on to undertake" a report until mid-June.[18] Precisely who had prevailed upon him remains unclear; advertising the work, Robertson said only that he had acted "at the earnest request of many respectable gentlemen."[19] Soon after the trial, however, Republican newspapers in Baltimore and New York had warned readers that he had been hired by the defense and that his report would be "cooked to suit the palates of Burr and [Luther] Martin."[20] Recognizing the grave threat that this claim posed to his reputation and sales, Robertson had moved to quash it, sending a denial to the New York newspaper. When the editor failed to print it, he had asked the editors of such leading Republican newspapers as Richmond's *Enquirer* and Washington's *National Intelligencer* to publish it. His published denial included a testimonial in which the prosecution and defense attorneys stated that they believed Robertson to be "incapable of wilful misrepresentation on any subject."[21]

Having a reliable record of Burr's trial seemed so important that, according to one Baltimore editor, if "a correct report" could not be had, it would be better to have "none" at all.[22] Incorrectness could take various forms—incomplete, inaccurate, or biased. Following the trial, Carpenter and Robertson waged a public battle over precisely these

issues. The charge that Robertson had been hired by the defense originated with Carpenter, who told Westcott that Martin had refused to
share the notes for one of his arguments because Burr's supporters "had
been at a very great expense in procuring and employing" Robertson.[23]
In defending his integrity, Robertson shifted the grounds for comparison from impartiality to accuracy. The attorneys who attested to Robertson's honesty also attacked the first volume of Carpenter's work as "a
waste of money to buy, and a waste of time to read."[24] Carpenter quickly
met this attack in a Washington newspaper, attributing any inaccura-
cies to his assigned seat, "which was at a great distance from the bench
and bar," and to "the want of lungs, energy, or something in some of
the speakers." But the greatest difference between the reports regarded
their completeness. Carpenter charged that Robertson had attended
court only fitfully during the "introductory quibblings" and had not
kept notes even on those days—facts that Robertson later acknowledged.[25] But it was in their coverage of the trial's end, not its beginning, that the two reports differed the most. Robertson's two volumes
focused on the treason trial, with an abbreviated account of the misdemeanor trial and no coverage of the committal hearing. Carpenter, in
contrast, devoted the entire third volume to the weeks after the treason
trial. Even if Robertson had not been hired by Burr's friends, his coverage choices suited their interests. His report emphasized the arguments
of the attorneys, while providing little of the testimony against Burr.
Thirty-two men testified after Robertson closed his report. Twenty-six
of them had not appeared in the treason trial and are wholly absent
from Robertson's report, including such key witnesses as John Graham,
Alexander and John Henderson, and James Wilkinson. "A struggle of
wit among acute lawyers," as Charles Francis Adams later remarked,
"seem[ed] the only characteristic of [Robertson's] work."[26]

Neither Robertson's nor Carpenter's report could have served
Jefferson's purposes, simply because neither was available during the
congressional session that began a week after Burr's trial. But the documents that Jefferson sent to Congress in late November 1807 differed
from those reports in significant ways. Robertson and Carpenter provided day-by-day accounts of the activity in the courtroom. Jefferson's
"report" omitted much of what had been said in court, inserted material that had not been heard there, and organized the contents in four

broad categories—official record, witness testimony, supporting documents, and judicial opinions—rather than chronologically. It completely excluded the material that constituted the bulk of Carpenter's and, especially, Robertson's reports—"all the bickerings, misunderstandings, misrepresentations, and sometimes quarrels, of litigating lawyers."[27] It included documents that had not been considered during the trial, including some that Marshall had rejected "as improper to be given as evidence."[28] And, even within its broad categories, only the clerk's record and the judge's opinions appeared in chronological order. All of each witness's testimony was grouped together, even when it had been given in different stages of the trial. Most of the supporting documents simply followed the testimony in which they had been mentioned. The "wretched arrangement and confusion of the printed Documents" led Massachusetts senator John Quincy Adams to suggest that "their title should be the *Anarchiad*."[29] What united Carpenter's, Robertson's, and Jefferson's reports were their claims of accuracy. Jefferson's report included sworn statements from Hening and Munford that the testimony and other evidence was "substantially faithful and correct" and from the *Enquirer* editor Thomas Ritchie that Marshall's opinions had come from the judge's "original manuscript[s] . . . and that the proof sheets [had been] submitted to his inspection and correction."[30]

By the time he sent this report to Congress, Jefferson had been preparing to battle the judiciary over Burr for months. In February 1807, after state and federal judges freed the men that Wilkinson had arrested in New Orleans, Jefferson had worried that the courts seemed "inclined to construe the law too favorably for the accused & too rigidly agt. the Government."[31] For years, he had feared that Federalists would use their life appointments to judicial positions to frustrate the political revolution of his election. Even before he learned of Marshall's 1 April decision that Burr could not yet be charged with treason, Jefferson thought that Federalist judges wanted to bury the evidence to "shield [Burr] from punishment" and avoid exposing his Federalist backers.[32] Marshall's initial opinion only deepened this concern, as did his later ruling that Burr could strike men from the grand jury list. In late May, with the grand jury hearings not even truly begun, Jefferson apprised Hay that he considered it his "duty to provide that full testimony shall be laid before the Legislature, and through them the public." If the grand jury indicted Burr, then the testimony before the petit jury would suffice; if it did not, Hay would need "to have every [witness] privately examined by way of affidavit." Jefferson does not seem to have imagined that, if a grand jury indicted Burr and a petit jury tried him, the "full testimony" still might not appear in court.[33]

As news of Marshall's 31 August ruling spread from Richmond, men and women around the country were astonished. "I have heard with much surprise of Burrs acquital," Elizabeth House Trist wrote Jefferson from New Orleans, remarking that it was only "the finesse of the law" that had "saved him."[34] But it was less the fact than the manner of Burr's acquittal that provoked surprise. "It would satisfy every body," one Richmonder had noted before Marshall ruled, "if the Jury upon a full hearing should say [Burr] was inocent."[35] People had long predicted that Burr would go free but had usually pointed to evidentiary problems—the difficulty of "adducing irrefragable proofs of facts," as one writer put it.[36] As such, Marshall's ruling to end testimony before "the innocent were . . . exculpated" and "the guilty were . . . punished" was stunning.[37] Republican newspapers demanded "a serious investigation" into why "the trial [was] ended ere half the evidence was examined" and why "the most material witnesses [were] suppressed."[38] Even if Marshall's decision was sound, the editor of the *National Intelligencer* reflected, it was still regrettable "that the full disclosure of [Burr's] plot" had been "smothered at the very threshold."[39]

One response to Marshall's ruling was to try to make public evidence that was more extensive and, seemingly, more conclusive than what had been given in court—the testimony that had led the grand jurors to indict Burr and six others. Just fourteen men had testified in the petit jury trial before Marshall suspended the evidence; forty-six had appeared before the grand jury. The fullest record of this testimony belonged to Joseph C. Cabell, the brother of Virginia's governor. After reluctantly loaning his notes to William Wirt, one of the prosecuting attorneys and the governor's brother-in-law, in late June, Cabell had asked Wirt to return them to the governor "to be kept by him confidentially."[40] On the day that Marshall arrested the evidence, the *Enquirer*'s editor asked Cabell to help prevent "this loathsome & most horrible conspiracy" from being "permitted to lurk in Concealment." If the full evidence could not be elicited in court, Ritchie believed that "the Eyes of the public [would] turn towards the Grand Jury." Having heard that Cabell's notes were "beyond all exception the most comprehensive & correct," Ritchie hoped to publish them.[41] This suggestion placed Cabell in a difficult position. He did not want to be partially responsible for keeping the country "in the dark on a subject, in which we all have a vital interest." Nor did he want to be solely responsible for shedding light on the conspiracy since his notes were neither accurate nor complete. "I should infinitely prefer that this important communication should come to the world thro' the channel of a court of Justice," Cabell wrote Ritchie. But, if it did not, he agreed to work with "two or three" other grand jurors to correct his notes before allowing them to be published.[42] As Cabell hoped, the latitude that Marshall gave to the prosecution in the committal hearing made publishing his notes unnecessary.

Marshall's ruling only confirmed Jefferson's fears that the Federalists wanted "not only to clear Burr, but to prevent the evidence from ever going before the world." That, Jefferson insisted to Hay in early September, "must not take place." The ruling made it "more than ever indispensable," in Jefferson's view, "that not a single witness" leave Richmond without his evidence being recorded, either as testimony or deposition. The president also requested copies of the official record and the judge's rulings. "These whole proceedings," he informed Hay, "will be laid before Congress, that they may decide, whether the defect has been in the evidence of guilt, or in the law, or in the application of the law, and that they may provide the proper remedy for the past and the future."[43] The prosecution always saw the committal hearing as the best way of eliciting testimony, not the next step toward convicting Burr. Throughout September, Hay assembled the necessary materials. In early October, Jefferson called Attorney General Caesar A. Rodney to Washington to undertake "the selection and digestion of the documents respecting Burr's treason."[44]

Jefferson left little doubt about the report's purpose in his annual message to Congress of 27 October. He considered it his "duty to lay before [Congress] the proceedings and the evidence publicly exhibited on the arraignment of the principal offenders before the circuit court." With that information, he continued, echoing his letter to Hay, Congress could "judge whether the defect was in the testimony, in the law, or in the administration of the law." "Wherever it shall be found," he concluded, "the Legislature alone can apply or originate the remedy." By "the defect," Jefferson meant whatever failing had allowed "Burr and his associates" to escape punishment for their "enterprises against the public peace." Jefferson's choice of what to include in and omit from his report guided Congress's search for this defect away from "the testimony" and toward either "the law" or "the administration of the law." The report highlighted the gulf between evidence that should have proved Burr's guilt and rulings that had secured his freedom—a gulf that would have been obscured by including the attorneys' arguments. That "the remedy," as Jefferson stated, was something that Congress "alone can apply or originate" further directed its attention away from testimony. It could originate a revision of the laws or an amendment to the Constitution; the only remedy that it "alone" could apply was the impeachment of Marshall.[45]

Jefferson had long hoped that radical change in the judicial branch would result from a battle with it over Burr. Marshall's impeachment would certainly have been a radical change and was ardently desired by some Republicans that fall, but Jefferson viewed the impeachment process as "a farce [that would] not be tried again."[46] He saw an opportunity to achieve something even more sweeping—a constitutional amendment. "This insurrection will probably shew," he had argued in mid-March, "that the fault in our constitution is not that the Executive has too little power, but that the Judiciary either has too much or holds it under too little responsibility."[47] After Marshall's initial ruling that Burr could not be held for treason, Jefferson had informed one confidant: "All this . . . will work well." With "the nation" in a position to "judge both the offender and the judges for themselves," the people would "see . . . and amend the error in our Constitution, which makes any branch independent of the nation." The public's outrage at seeing someone who had plotted treason go unpunished through the courts' interference, Jefferson believed, would carry an amendment through Congress and the states. If the judges' "protection of Burr produces this amendment," he reflected, "it will do more good than his condemnation would have done."[48] By mid-September, Jefferson trusted that Marshall's rulings would "produce an amendment to the Constitution which, keeping the judges independent of the Executive, will not leave them so, of the nation."[49] Jefferson never explained precisely what form the judges' new dependence would take, but he clearly intended something very different from the impeachment process.

The barely veiled criticism of Marshall's handling of Burr's trial in Jefferson's annual message outraged Federalists even before his trial documents went to Congress. After reading the message, one New Englander charged Jefferson with "an abominable slur against the Supreme Judicial authority," while a westerner detected a "blow . . . aimed at the Judiciary System."[50] From Richmond, Cabell reported that "the feds [were] enraged at the President's remark about the administration of the law in Burr's case."[51] In coastal cities and interior towns, Federalist newspapers attacked a message that seemed to instruct Jefferson's legislative followers to impeach Marshall and "his newspaper minions" to write him down.[52] In a widely reprinted piece, Philadelphia's *United States' Gazette* blasted the president for assuming a "right of reviewing and controlling the proceedings of the judiciary." "Perhaps a more atrocious usurpation of power was never attempted in a government of laws," the editor insisted.[53] That Jefferson's attack on the judiciary imperilled the rule of law itself was quickly demonstrated to many Federalists by the events in Baltimore in early November. The "disgraceful proceedings" there seemed to have "been produced by the intemperate and mischevious hint of no other than the president of the United States."[54]

Though "some of the thinking republicans," as Cabell put it, privately regretted the message, most Republicans publicly defended it.[55] Pointing to the president's oath to uphold the Constitution, Republican editors insisted upon the executive's right to call the legislature's attention to the judiciary's actions. Some of the leading Republican newspapers gave Jefferson the benefit of the doubt, accepting that he had truly left it to Congress to decide where "the defect" lay, "without giving his own opinion."[56] Other Republicans read the message in the same way as most Federalists. One newspaper openly advocated the remedies that Jefferson had "strongly hint[ed]" were needed—"some better definition of *treason*" by law or constitutional amendment.[57] Another called for a congressional investigation of Marshall. In late November, the trial report reinforced this view of the message as it, according to one Delaware Republican, "deeply implicate[d] the character of C[hief]

J[ustice] Marshall."[58] Action by congressional Republicans seemed likely; the nature of that action was less clear. After providing the material for the report, Hay worried that, while "intelligent legislators" might make good use of it, "among others it might perhaps do mischief" by undermining "all judicial Systems and law itself."[59]

In the months after Jefferson's message, the search for the defect in Burr's trial fueled activity in three areas—the press, the states, and Congress. In Republican newspapers across the country, essayists and editors used the trial's end and the message's appearance a week later to dissect Marshall's conduct. The most fully developed critiques of the chief justice and the judicial system appeared in three series of essays in leading newspapers. Richmond's *Virginia Argus* published three satirical pieces by "Eubulides." The *Enquirer*'s six-part series of "Cursory Reflections" included four essays on Marshall. In the last, Ritchie concluded that Marshall had "proved that Judges are too independent of the people"; an amendment was needed "to make them more responsible."[60] But the most widely reprinted, and most severe, anti-Marshall essays originated in Philadelphia's *Aurora General Advertiser* over the signature "Lucius." Written as letters to Marshall, the essays tried to demonstrate "that *you have rendered the administration of the law suspected*[;] that you have manifested a *partiality disgraceful to the character of a judge*; and that you have *prostrated the dignity of the chief justice of the United States*."[61] In four essays, "Lucius" scrutinized Marshall's role in the trial from start to finish and concluded by hoping that Marshall would resign or be removed from office.

Before Congress received the documents that were supposed to enable it to identify the defect in Burr's trial, the Ohio and Vermont legislatures decided to propose constitutional amendments along the lines that Jefferson apparently sought. Both states suggested changes to make it easier to remove a federal judge; Ohio also proposed term limits for judicial appointments. Ohio's Edward Tiffin offered his state's proposal to the Senate in early November; Vermont's was not formally presented to Congress until late January. While the proposals never received much attention in Congress, they were taken very seriously by the press and in the states. In New York, the *American Citizen* backed Ohio's proposal as addressing "an evil in the judiciary part of the constitution"; in Virginia, the *Enquirer* praised Ohio and Vermont for their zeal and urged the state legislature to "come boldly forward with [an] amendment."[62] During the congressional session, the Maryland and Massachusetts legislatures adopted resolutions supporting Vermont's proposal, under which the president would remove a judge when directed to do so by a majority of the House of Representatives and two-thirds of the Senate. In late January, Tennessee's legislature submitted a modified proposal, requiring a three-fifths majority in each house. A month later, Pennsylvania's legislature offered an even more radical change, with a judge removable or impeachable on a simple majority vote in both houses. Republicans controlled all of these states' legislatures. Two Federalist-controlled legislatures, Delaware's and Rhode Island's, instructed their senators to vote against Vermont's proposal. Despite evidence of support from six of the sixteen states, Republicans in Congress did not bring any of the proposals to a vote.[63]

If Congress never seriously discussed a constitutional amendment to remedy defects in "the administration of the law," it did consider remedies to defects in "the law" itself. The day after Jefferson's report went to Congress, a House committee asked Attorney General Rodney for suggestions. Rodney replied a month later, proposing three areas for action—a law to "[punish] combinations and conspiracies for the purpose of committing treason," a revision of the neutrality law, and a provision to empower federal officials to require anyone who "was about to commit a crime against the United States" to give security "for his good behaviour."[64] In early March, the committee finally reported a "bill to punish conspiracies to commit treason"; it was never debated. Three weeks earlier, however, Virginia senator William Branch Giles, one of Jefferson's most trusted congressional supporters, had introduced a bill to broaden the definition of "levying war" enough to cover Burr's case. Giles's speech supporting the bill included withering attacks on Marshall's handling of Burr's trial and his grasping for judicial supremacy. Federalists quickly denounced the bill as unconstitutional and the speech as full of "all-unhinging and terrible doctrines."[65] But many Republicans opposed it as well. It passed the Senate, on a party vote, only after being heavily amended and significantly altered. The House never acted upon it. Not until 1867 did Congress pass a law that made conspiring to commit treason a crime.

When the congressional session ended in early May, it was clear that Jefferson's report had failed to serve its immediate purpose. It was not designed to serve any other. It had not been widely distributed, with copies apparently having been printed only for congressmen and some administration supporters. It had never been intended as a complete record of Burr's trial and, thus, was quickly supplanted by Carpenter's and Robertson's reports. Whereas Robertson boasted that his report would "be amusing and interesting to all persons capable of reading and understanding" and "particularly gratifying and useful" "to the lawyer, politician[,] and man of general information," Jefferson's was clearly suited only for Congress.[66] Even in Congress, it was used less for Jefferson's purposes than for the Senate's wrangling over whether or not to seat Ohio's John Smith, given his indictment. In fact, John Quincy Adams's report on this issue was one of the few works to cite it repeatedly. After the session, Jefferson's report appears to have been used rarely.[67] It never became an important source for making sense of the Burr Conspiracy. But, because it was so quickly forgotten, it never became controversial either.

What did become controversial was Jefferson's contact with the prosecution during Burr's trial. The trial reports provided little evidence of these interactions, with Carpenter's including Hay's explicit statement "that he had never received any instruction or communication from [the president]."[68] The extent of Jefferson's involvement first became clear three years after his death, when his grandson included nine letters to Hay about the trial in Jefferson's *Memoir, Correspondence, and Miscellanies* (1829). To many critics, the sheer number suggested the impropriety of Jefferson's involvement in Burr's prosecution. And some passages revealed that Jefferson had been willing to use executive power in a vindictive manner, particularly against the "impudent federal bull-dog," Luther Martin.[69] Within a few years of the letters' publication, the Federalists Timothy Dwight and William Sullivan used them to substantiate old charges of "Jefferson's hostility to an independent judiciary."[70] A mid-century magazine article condemned them as "full of the most ireful and splenetic effusions against" Burr and denounced Jefferson as "arbitrary, vindictive, and unjustifiably bent on shedding [Burr's] blood."[71] And Jefferson's early biographers struggled to handle the letters. In the late 1830s, his first biographer described them as a source of "regret, and even mortification"; twenty years later, a more protective biographer devoted four pages to refuting the charge that Jefferson had "interfered improperly in [Burr's] trials."[72] Biographers and historians have continued to criticize Jefferson's involvement in Burr's trial. While some criticism is certainly justified, a careful reading of Jefferson's letters to Hay—eighteen between 20 May and 11 October 1807—reveals that six were necessitated by the court's request for documents and that two others did not concern the trial. We also need to ask, who but Jefferson could have answered Hay's questions about specific witnesses and documents or even about the general issues of a complex case? Hay exchanged some letters with Rodney regarding the trial, none of which seem to survive. But Rodney largely divorced himself from the trial after the opening stage due to a family emergency. There was no Department of Justice, no bureaucracy between the district attorney and the attorney general, to provide guidance. In Rodney's absence, as Jefferson remarked in mid-June, "the daily correspondence" regarding the trial "of necessity fall[s] upon us."[73] Given these conditions, the letters do not seem as damning as they have been made to appear.

Jefferson's actions after the trial have been criticized as well, though most critics have emphasized the annual message, not the trial report. But Jefferson's report needs to be understood as a deliberate effort on his part to mislead Congress and the public in order to transform the constitutional position of the judicial branch. Burr's trial raised complicated legal issues and exposed interwoven cultural forces. Jefferson's report distilled all of that complexity into one question: had Marshall suppressed clear evidence of treason to protect Burr? But most of Marshall's rulings, especially the most significant and controversial one ending the treason trial, responded less to the witnesses' testimony to which they were so carefully juxtaposed in Jefferson's report, than to the attorneys' arguments that had been equally carefully omitted.

"IN ALL EVENTS MY HONOR CAN & WILL BE DEFENDED"

Wilkinson's final account of the Burr Conspiracy differed from Jefferson's in almost every way. Jefferson produced a single work soon after

Burr's trial; Wilkinson prepared numerous writings across a decade. Jefferson was nearly absent from his account, bolstering its claims to objectivity; Wilkinson was always central to his account, making it easy to connect him to his unsigned writings. Jefferson sought to achieve a public purpose in the present, using the temporary outrage at the chief justice to effect permanent restraints on the judicial branch; Wilkinson wrote to serve private ends, both present and future. "I have sheathed my sword, and drawn my pen," he explained to a fellow officer while writing his memoirs in October 1815, "to fulfil a paramount duty to my contemporaries and to posterity, by recording a faithful narrative of my military life[,] which shall justify the favorable opinion of my friends, and defend my memory against the shafts and detraction of calumny."[74] To Wilkinson, honor and reputation, now and forever, forced him to write about the Burr Conspiracy for nearly a decade. Those concerns shaped the form, frequency, and content of his final accounts. His goal was never in doubt. As a reviewer of Wilkinson's memoirs noted, his "principal object . . . was to remove, as far as possible, the unfavourable impressions which his numerous persecutions were calculated to excite against him."[75]

Wilkinson's most significant publications in this prolonged campaign to clear his name and uphold his honor were two books, *Burr's Conspiracy Exposed* (1811) and *Memoirs of My Own Times* (1816).[76] But they were merely the heaviest weapons in an arsenal that also included private and official correspondence, certificates and testimonials, published essays and letters, handbills, and pamphlets. Few at the time grasped how information moved and how understanding emerged from it better than Wilkinson. As such, few better comprehended how to manipulate information and understanding. Most gentlemen may have known how to use whispers, letters, newspapers, and pamphlets to protect their reputations and to damage their enemies', but Wilkinson knew other tricks, as well. One could write letters to distant friends to publish as objective accounts in their local newspapers. One could dispatch letters and other materials to executive departments, and later request them as official documents. One could solicit depositions, certificates, and testimonials from respected citizens and state, federal, and even foreign officials for use in print or in court. One could even prevent specific newspapers from being sent to places where the lies that they told or the truths that they divulged might pose problems. Wilkinson employed all of these methods, and more, to defend his reputation. In December 1808, he admitted to Secretary of War Henry Dearborn that, in the previous two years, he had spent vast sums "in the support of Witness[e]s, the collecting of Testimony & the pay of printers, to sustain [him]self & vindicate [his] Honor."[77]

Wilkinson's campaign to defend himself against suspicions of participation in Burr's project began long before Burr's trial in Richmond and took various forms. His initial disclosures of the conspiracy to the president in October 1806 certainly composed a part of his effort to protect his honor and position. So did many of his actions in New Orleans between November 1806 and May 1807—sending private letters and official dispatches to the administration, collecting testimonials and depositions, planting favorable items in distant newspapers, intimidating local editors, and, according to some historians, even transporting those who could expose his involvement with Burr to the East for trial. Once in Richmond, Wilkinson counted upon his testimony to clear his name and prove his patriotism. But it was not just his ties to Burr that threatened his reputation. Over the summer of 1806, the *Western World* had revived the story of the Spanish Conspiracy, and others had claimed that he remained connected, even committed, to Spain. Accompanying his initial disclosures to Jefferson had been a letter promising that he could refute such charges "by *living testimony* & *authentic documents*."[78] Even before he left New Orleans, it was believed that he had "commenced the *composition* or *compilation* of a book" that would clear his name.[79] Whether it would address the Burr Conspiracy or the Spanish Conspiracy or both was not said.

In Richmond, Wilkinson wrote about and worked on a book. After the grand jury hearings, he proclaimed his "determin[ation] to give to the world the moment Mr. Burr's fate is descided the full exposition of the transactions in which I have been engaged relative to his sinister projects."[80] By mid-September, when Marshall's rulings threatened to preclude his testimony, he thought that his "only resort [would be] an appeal to the public."[81] He had already asked the president to provide access to the administration's files about the conspiracy. Those papers, he assured Jefferson, would allow him "to vindicate [his] own Character & conduct, to justify that of the Executive in all its relations to [his]

Measures, & to attach the seal of imperishable Infamy to the name of Aaron Burr."[82] Once in possession of the administration's files, he removed twelve of his letters to Jefferson—one of which had recently been the subject of a defense subpoena—placing potentially embarrassing documents under his control. How he might employ such control was well understood at the time. "It is the real genuine letters of W to Mr Jefferson &c that I hope the public See," Thomas Truxton wrote at the time, "not mutilated extracts or New coined letters given in lieu of the real thing."[83] The committal hearing gave him the desired opportunity to defend himself publicly. But, even afterward, rumor still had him "writing [a book] which some say is to ruin not only Burr, but Jefferson, too."[84]

What Wilkinson actually published in late October 1807 was not the expected book. Instead, he limited himself to a brief statement, with a few supporting documents, that appeared in the *Enquirer* as "A Plain Tale" over the signature "A Kentuckian." Wilkinson privately admitted writing this piece, but his authorship was probably never doubted. In style and content, "A Plain Tale" was undeniably his. Though facing widespread suspicions of prior support for Burr's project and lingering criticisms of his actions in New Orleans, Wilkinson addressed events of a decade or more earlier, framing this piece as a defense against specific charges that Burr and his counsel had made "under the tattered banners of the Spanish conspiracy."[85] Wilkinson's focus upon the Spanish Conspiracy, when the defense had hammered upon his actions in New Orleans and alterations to the cipher letter, makes sense in the context of the trial's last weeks. Shortly after Wilkinson testified, two longtime associates with extensive knowledge of his dealings with Spanish officials in the 1790s had arrived in Richmond—Daniel Clark, the delegate to Congress from the Orleans Territory, and Thomas Power, a Spanish subject—having been subpoenaed by Burr. Their presence clearly rattled Wilkinson; it was rumored, he informed Dearborn, "that they are to blow me up."[86] Clark never testified. Power spoke only briefly, revealing a secret correspondence in cipher between Wilkinson and the Spanish governor of Louisiana during the 1790s. Published just ten days later, "A Plain Tale" was a rushed attempt to meet this new threat. Wilkinson dug into his papers for a sworn declaration by Power and a lengthy memorandum from Clark; both proclaimed his innocence of improper involvement with Spain.

As in New Orleans, Wilkinson's labors to restore his honor in Richmond had extended far beyond writing and publishing, highlighted by his sustained effort to bring John Wickham to the dueling ground. Such active means for repairing his reputation continued after he left Richmond. Writing from Baltimore in mid-November, he predicted "a *grave* scene," arising from the fact that his "name & Fame [had] been cruelly wantonly & unjustly assailed."[87] The source of his embarrassment became clear a month later. On Christmas Eve, in Washington, Wilkinson challenged Virginia congressman John Randolph to a duel for having said things months earlier that were "highly injurious to [his] reputation."[88] The next day, Randolph rebuffed the challenge on two grounds—that anything he had said had been "the result of deliberate opinion, founded upon the most authentic evidence," and that he would not "descend to [Wilkinson's] level."[89] Rumors of this exchange quickly circulated among elite Washingtonians. On New Year's Eve morning, the news spread more broadly when Wilkinson had handbills posted around the city declaring that Randolph was "a malicious, scandalous, insolent, prevaricating poltroon."[90] That afternoon, Randolph moved that the House direct the president to order an inquest into the general's conduct, offering evidence from Power that showed that Wilkinson had received over nine thousand dollars from Spanish officials in Louisiana in 1796. Clark then informed the House that he had learned of Wilkinson's Spanish ties as consul in New Orleans and had apprised the administration long ago.

On 1 January 1808, Wilkinson met Randolph's motion by asking Jefferson and Dearborn to call a military court of inquiry so that he could "vindicate [his] aspersed reputation."[91] The administration moved quickly, naming the court's members the next day. Wilkinson sounded confident: "Conscience, Honor, Integrity and Patriotism, with some documents of which [my accusers] have no Idea, will carry me through." But, in retrospect, his request seems quite risky. Evidence that was found in Spanish archives decades later established that he had cooperated with Spanish officials both to promote western secession and to thwart American expansion and that he had received large sums for his efforts. In January 1808, Wilkinson could not have known what evidence had reached the various departments or which witnesses would appear against him, but he must have realized that he was going to be investigated by someone. He chose investigation by a military court, which he could influence, rather than by the House, which he disparaged as Randolph's *"Dunghill."*[92] This gambit worked. Randolph, Clark, and some others briefly continued their attacks in the House. But the military court allowed pro-administration Republicans to prove their concern by supporting the call for an inquest, while preventing a House investigation that would have allowed Randolph and others to use Wilkinson as a "hobby-horse . . . to ride down the present administration."[93] The composition of the military court—colonels Henry Burbeck, Thomas Cushing, and Jonathan Williams—also favored Wilkinson. All were his *"Subalterns,"* as they had to be; Cushing and Williams were among his most loyal supporters.[94] The administration further served Wilkinson by charging the court only with investigating whether he had received money from Spain. His ties to Burr and actions in New Orleans were ignored, though they had been raised in the House. When the court met on 11 January, moreover, it took a limited view of its power to call witnesses—a position that the president endorsed. And it quickly decided that no one could take notes on its proceedings except judge advocate Walter Jones Jr. or Wilkinson.

As a result, an inquiry that many hoped would uncover "the whole truth" turned into a "white wash."[95] The most complete account of the inquest—a deposition that Jones later provided to a congressional committee—suggests that the court relied primarily upon two sources for evidence, the House and Wilkinson. The House sent the documents from Randolph that had precipitated the inquest and a deposition from Clark, but neither man would testify. The House also unanimously adopted a resolution calling on the president to provide anything in the executive archives "touching a combination between the agents of any foreign Government and citizens of the United States . . . or going to show that any officer of the United States has at any time corruptly received money from any foreign Government or its agents."[96] Jefferson answered this resolution with just ten documents. That left Wilkinson as a key source of information. In its first month, the court met once or twice a week, announced that it had no new evidence, and adjourned. In mid-February, Wilkinson began providing witnesses and depositions for these infrequent sessions. Most of his eleven witnesses were used to connect Clark to the Burr Conspiracy or to challenge Clark's deposition. Jones, in contrast, produced just two new depositions. In June, after weeks without a meeting, the court met to "[bring] the case to a conclusion." Wilkinson submitted a written defense and then spoke for two days, "produc[ing] a great number of papers . . . as exhibits" that "had never before been submitted to the court."[97] On 28 June, the military court closed by exonerating Wilkinson, in a measured fashion. "As far as his conduct has been developed by this enquiry," it concluded, "he appears to have discharged the duties of his station with honor to himself and fidelity to his country."[98] Jefferson confirmed the ruling a few days later.

Although the court's "*frigid* sort of *half Acquittal*" did not satisfy Wilkinson, its decision to close its hearings to outsiders gave him a great advantage over his accusers.[99] As it sat, he found ways to publicize what he wanted made public and, usually, to contain what he did not. He provided copies of his opening address—a sarcastic attack on Randolph and Clark that implicated them as "Burrites"—to the *National Intelligencer* and other publications.[100] He also sent unsigned descriptions of court proceedings and witness testimony to the press. There seems to have been little doubt that he was the source of these pieces; Clark even publicly complained that "some person, general Wilkinson I presume," had been "publish[ing] garbled and detached extracts of testimony."[101] After the inquest closed, Wilkinson began preparing the court's "whole proceedings . . . for the press," something that only he or Jones could have done and that only he had any interest in doing. In early October, he promised various confidants that the proceedings would appear within a month in "two octavo volumes."[102] They never appeared, because Wilkinson decided to "wait Clarks motions before" publishing them.[103]

The military inquest neither convinced Wilkinson's accusers of his innocence nor forced them to curtail their attacks. His "corruption," as one critic explained, merely seemed to have "been Carefully covered by a Court of Inquest from which Independence was not to be expected."[104] Clark emerged as the principal figure in the renewed assault, assembling documents and taking depositions in New Orleans. In September 1808, he gave this material to Edward Livingston to translate the Spanish and French documents and write the text. They planned to have the work ready for the next congressional session, but Livingston, who was enmired in the famous batture controversy, delayed. It took nearly a year before Clark's *Proofs of the Corruption of Gen. James Wilkinson* (1809) finally appeared in Philadelphia. Printed, "Clark's pamphlet or rather book" ran to more than one hundred and fifty pages of text, with nearly two hundred pages of appended documents.[105] It sought to prove that Wilkinson had "for years been the pensioner of a foreign power" and that he had received this pay "for the dismemberment and ruin of his country." It also claimed that Wilkinson had "favoured and advised the enterprises of colonel Burr"; "if the plan did not originate with Wilkinson, he was at least one of the chief conspirators." Clark explained that Wilkinson imagined himself as "the founder, the deliverer[,] the Washington of the western country"; both conspiracies, Spanish and Burr, might have realized that vision.[106] The book, according to one writer, "developed a scene of fraud, perfidy and iniquity not surpassed in the annals of the most corrupt and profligate ages."[107]

Clark's book did not provoke Wilkinson to publish the records of the military court, as he had suggested would happen nearly a year earlier, even though discrediting the "Villain" Clark had been central to his defense throughout the inquest.[108] With Clark and Wilkinson together in New Orleans after the general's return in April 1809, some believed that their dispute would be settled with "the aid of a little powder."[109] But the expected explosion never came. Clark awaited the appearance of his book to redeem his reputation. Wilkinson became preoccupied with three other issues—a simmering dispute with John Adair, an intense courtship of Celestine Treadeau, and the daily demands of his troops. It was the last of these issues that caused him the most trouble. In 1809, he lost half of his force of two thousand men to disease or desertion in New Orleans, an encampment at Terre aux Boeufs, and Natchez. Publicly, Wilkinson's response to the arrival of Clark's book seems to have been limited to accepting a testimonial from city officials that condemned the "odious publication" and praised his "calumniated virtue."[110]

The eventual appearance of Clark's book and the shocking depletion of the troops brought Wilkinson a new round of troubles. In late August 1809, after "turn[ing] over a few casual pages" of Clark's book, President James Madison directed his secretary of war to order

Wilkinson back to Washington.[111] When he received this order, Wilkinson asked for a delay of three months in order, as one federal official had learned from the secretary, "to prepare some answer to Clark's book."[112] As he dallied in the West, sentiment turned against him in the East. "Mr Clark has completely put Wilkinson down in this part of the World," one traveller reported from western Virginia in mid-November.[113] Upon returning to Washington in mid-April 1810, Wilkinson faced two congressional investigations. With pro-administration Republicans worried, as one of them informed Madison, that Wilkinson "[hung] like a dead weight upon the administration," the resolutions launching these investigations had passed easily.[114] One committee focused upon the troop deaths. The other addressed the charges in Clark's book about three issues—the Spanish pension, the Spanish Conspiracy, and the Burr Conspiracy. Neither committee completed its inquiries during the session, but each returned a report, with the one concerning the Spanish and Burr conspiracies including over two hundred pages of documents and depositions. It seemed likely that the House would resume these investigations in the fall.

Over the summer of 1810, Wilkinson engaged in a multifront campaign to protect his reputation. In late June, he asked the president to appoint another military inquest; Madison refused. A month later, he launched a failed assault on the citadel of his detractors by asking James Ingersoll, a respected Philadelphia attorney, to provide an opinion on the constitutionality of a congressional enquiry "into the conduct of an executive Officer, who is not liable to impeachment." This "question," Wilkinson insisted, was "pregnant with important consequences to the Nation."[115] Before hearing from Ingersoll, Wilkinson opened another front in his campaign by resuming his writing. An appeal to "the World," he informed Dearborn, "is forced upon me, for *I can obtain no trial Civil or Military.*" Expecting to "be sacrificed to appease Burrs resentment & Clarks villainy," Wilkinson hoped that a full account of his life would undo the damage of Clark's book and the House's investigations.[116] By mid-September, he had engaged John B. Colvin, whose *Colvin's Weekly Register* and *Monitor* had provided friendly coverage, to assist him. In Colvin's view, Wilkinson hoped that his memoirs would "present to the world a picture that will excite its sympathy and sober approbation, if not its clamourous applause." Colvin, a State Department clerk, was charged with writing the volume on *"the Treason of Burr."* Wilkinson provided "numerous original documents," and Colvin conducted research of his own, including asking Jefferson to explain some of his decisions.[117]

The renewal of the House investigations early in the session forced Wilkinson to "suspend" work on the projected four volumes of memoirs with just one finished "in a very rude manner."[118] In late January 1811, he sent printed copies of the nearly completed second volume—Colvin's on the Burr Conspiracy—to some influential figures, including Jefferson, asking that they "be treated with reserve."[119] Still, it seems to have been widely known in Washington that he was "writing a book with the hope of washing away his sins."[120] Instead, he spent much of his time at the committee's sessions, inspecting evidence, examining witnesses, and producing documents. In late February, the committee submitted its report—nearly two hundred documents regarding the Spanish pension and the Burr Conspiracy—without reaching any conclusions. The House sent the report to Madison. The administration conducted its own inquiries and considered its options. On 1 June, Madison ordered a court-martial covering all of the issues of the recent investigations. In late June, the second volume of Wilkinson's memoirs, *Burr's Conspiracy Exposed; and General Wilkinson Vindicated Against the Slanders of His Enemies on that Important Occasion*, finally reached the public.[121]

Burr's Conspiracy Exposed consisted of three parts: a fifteen-page introduction; nearly one hundred pages of text, much of which was probably written by Colvin; and a long appendix of more than one hundred and thirty documents. Wilkinson began by justifying the book's existence. While "a *war of words*" had little appeal, he felt "compelled to resort to the press for the vindication of his character" against Randolph's and Clark's attacks. And his defense had to begin with the Burr Conspiracy because its *"discomfiture [was] the foundation of the hue and cry raised against him."* The language of the introduction rang with Wilkinsonian excess, including a suggestion that the future of "human liberty" in America and beyond hung on his case.[122] That of the text was more measured; "it is owing to my unceasing representations," Colvin informed Jefferson, "that the language of the volume is as temperate as it is."[123] The first sixty pages attempted to "vindicat[e] general Wilkinson *directly*," telling the story of his interactions with Burr in a manner that justified everything from the shared cipher to the Neutral Ground Agreement with Spain. Wilkinson's suspicions of Burr, according to this account, dated to their meeting in St. Louis in September 1805. But they "were not confirmed" until October and November 1806 with the receipt of the cipher letter, the communications of Samuel Swartwout, and other evidence. Though facing "a scheme . . . more artfully contrived" than any in history "to shake the allegiance of an officer to his government," Wilkinson had remained firm and taken crucial steps to defeat Burr's treason. The remaining text then sought "to corroborate [this] vindication *indirectly*, by demonstrating the feebleness and fallacy" of Clark's "proofs of Wilkinson's guilt."[124] Wilkinson probably wrote this section, perhaps in New Orleans after first seeing Clark's book.

Some time in 1811, Wilkinson also prepared a pamphlet to answer the charges about his ties to Spain in Clark's book—"that matchless tissue of impudence, misrepresentation and slander." *A Brief Examination of Testimony, to Vindicate the Character of General James Wilkinson Against the Imputation of a Sinister Connexion with the Spanish Government* differed from *Burr's Conspiracy Exposed* in many ways. It was far less polished and far more vituperative, was much shorter, and had a different publisher. Most importantly, it was unsigned, though anyone who read it must have known its author. What the new pamphlet most resembled in *Burr's Conspiracy Exposed* was the indirect vindication— the attack on Clark—in the last forty pages of the text. The thirty-two-page text of *Brief Examination* unfolded as little more than "concise explanations" of the seventy documents in its appendix. Most of these annotations explained how the associated document undermined some claim or evidence in Clark's book. Others tried to substantiate Wilkinson's charge that Clark's attacks arose from his ties to Burr; Wilkinson's honor had "been stabbed in a thousand places," he insisted, "by the same hands which were raised against the government." The pamphlet was, the author admitted, a "hasty sketch . . . of the testimony most material to correct prejudices [and] rebut fictions and falsehoods."[125]

Brief Examination offers a valuable key for understanding Wilkinson's whole project of defending his reputation in the trying year of 1811. In the "advertisement" for *Burr's Conspiracy Exposed*, he stated that he had intended his memoirs to cover his public life "in regular progression, from his birth to the closing scenes of his persecutions." That plan had been abandoned "to meet the torrent of vilification."[126] As a result, only the first, as-yet-unwritten, volume would provide the chronological story of what Wilkinson called his "horrible life."[127] The other three volumes are better understood as defense pamphlets that addressed specific issues—the Burr Conspiracy (volume 2), the Spanish Conspiracy and pension (volume 3), and the troop deaths at Terre aux Boeufs (volume 4). Even though only one was labelled "memoirs," all three volumes were mobilized to bolster Wilkinson's reputation in 1811. In January, as the congressional committee met, he circulated "an Appendix to the fourth" volume—the supporting documents on the troop deaths—to a select audience "pro bono publico."[128] In June, he published *Burr's Conspiracy Exposed*, the one volume that had been brought, with Colvin's assistance, to a point where he thought that it could appear as a book over his name. And, later that year, during his court-martial, Wilkinson had the rough *Brief Examination* printed as an unsigned, but hardly anonymous, pamphlet.

The court-martial that sat on 4 September in Fredericktown (now Frederick), Maryland, seemed unlikely to produce the same protection of Wilkinson's reputation that the inquest had provided three and a half years earlier. Whereas the inquest had included just three officers, two of whom were closely tied to Wilkinson, the court-martial consisted of a dozen, few of whom came from the general's list. Whereas Jefferson had directed the inquest to investigate only the Spanish pension, Madison provided the court-martial with eight charges, separated into twenty-five specifications: fifteen on the Spanish Conspiracy and pension; three on the Burr Conspiracy; and seven on various acts from 1805 and 1809, including the troop deaths. And, whereas the inquest's meeting site had given Wilkinson easy access to friendly presses in Washington and Baltimore, Fredericktown had only one newspaper that circulated broadly, the hostile *Frederick-Town Herald*. Still, the court-martial sought to protect Wilkinson in various ways. It began by trying to limit its enquiries to events of the previous two years, which would have eliminated all or part of six charges; both the administration and the defendant opposed this maneuver. And it ended by barring the judge advocate from replying to Wilkinson's final statement. Just ten days into the court's sessions, Secretary of War William Eustis warned Madison to be prepared for "a complete and (I should not be surprized to see attached the word) *honorable* acquital of every charge and specification."[129] That is what the court returned on Christmas Day. But Madison still had to confirm the verdict. Doing so required reading the court's full record, including Wilkinson's defense, which Madison described as "6 or 700 pages of the most collossal paper."[130] In mid-February 1812, Madison finally confirmed the court's verdict and restored Wilkinson's sword, even as he noted that both the court and the general had acted in ways that were "evidently and justly objectionable."[131]

Even with a favorable verdict in hand, Wilkinson made no immediate effort to publish the proceedings. By early 1812, long-standing tensions with Great Britain were clearly building toward war. Wilkinson's greatest concern seems to have been to receive a command where he could distinguish himself, but Madison's confirmation of the court's verdict showed that his position remained tenuous. In late February 1812, Wilkinson sent two letters to Madison offering to forbear publishing the court proceedings "at this time" and "to vary or expunge any rank Epithet[s] or acrimonious expression[s]" regarding Eustis, the administration, or the court from his written defense.[132] Even though Wilkinson was "notoriously at War with the Secy. at War, and not loving the President," Eustis and Madison had few options, as long as he did not force their hands by publishing his diatribe.[133] In early April, Wilkinson received orders to return to New Orleans and take command of the southwestern troops. By the time he reached the city two months later, war had been declared by Congress.

Wilkinson did not resume the literary defense of his reputation for three years. In the interim, he suffered various wartime embarrassments, as did most of the army's generals, and faced another court-martial, on charges arising from his wartime service. Though acquitted in mid-April 1815, Wilkinson found that the postwar reorganization of the army left no room for him. He soon took up his memoirs. Their tone was never in doubt. "I shall, beginning with the Chief of the pal-ace, speak of men & measures," he wrote one confidant.[134] The work required extensive research; decades later, a visitor to Wilkinson's Phil-adelphia home remembered finding him "in the midst of his papers, knee deep, all around him on the floor, . . . preparing his *memoirs*, in vindication of himself."[135] To support his labors, Wilkinson sent a circu-lar letter to friends in October 1815, asking them to drum up early sub-scribers and assigning some of them specific territories for their efforts. It would take him another eighteen months to complete his memoirs.

Wilkinson's *Memoirs of My Own Times* finally appeared in what even the author described as "three ponderous Volumes" in April 1817.[136] As in 1811, the result was not what Wilkinson had planned, as the sheer quantity of material had overwhelmed him. "I [had] con-ceived 1500 pages octavo would furnish ample scope for the range I had assigned to my pen," he admitted in the introduction.[137] It had not. The first volume—more than eight hundred and fifty pages, plus appendix—unfolded in two, loosely connected parts. It began with the early years, from Wilkinson's birth through the Revolutionary War. Then, after a couple of discordant chapters on Wilkinson's ser-vice on the southwestern frontier in 1806 and during the Quasi-War in 1799, it shifted to the War of 1812. Throughout, this volume teemed with abuse of Madison and his three secretaries of war. The second volume—nearly six hundred pages, exclusive of appendix—did not simply revise or complete what Wilkinson had called the second vol-ume of his memoirs five years earlier. Instead of an improved *Burr's Conspiracy Exposed*, it provided Wilkinson's long defense from the 1811 court-martial. The court-martial's charges and specifications struc-tured the volume, with just two chapters, totalling about eighty pages, on the Burr Conspiracy. These chapters told the story of Wilkinson's relationship with Burr from late April 1805, when Wilkinson left Washington for St. Louis, to 12 November 1806, when he disclosed his concerns to Jefferson and Claiborne. As he related this chronological tale, Wilkinson addressed any seemingly damaging evidence, supplied numerous supporting documents, and smeared his accusers as parties to Burr's scheme. The final volume—the shortest at less than five hun-dred pages, not counting the appendix—provided the record of the 1815 court-martial.

Within six months of the memoirs' publication, "not a copy remain[ed] for sale," as Wilkinson boasted, "of an Edition of 1500."[138] The work was widely read and widely reviewed, often favorably. But almost all of the attention focused upon the detailed accounts of Revolutionary War battles in the first volume. "Deprived of [the] very interesting matter" in that volume, "there might not be much left for praise," one reader reflected.[139] One review predicted that "few persons [would] be disposed to go through the two last" volumes.[140] Even more than the first, those volumes were "plentifully interspersed" with the "*reflections*, not merely on events, but on characters," that many reviewers found offensive or unnecessary.[141] But that flaw did not prevent at least some readers from drawing the intended lesson—that Wilkinson had "been an ill-requited servant of the publick."[142] The memoirs served Wilkinson's purpose, at least for the present. They raised his reputation higher than it had been in a decade. Many still had doubts about his actions; but they gained greater respect for his character. "I must say," one Pennsylvanian admitted, "that the General's work has improved my estimate both of his heart and his intellects."[143]

This generally positive view of Wilkinson and the memoirs quickly faded, even as he disappeared from public view in first Louisiana and later Mexico. It suffered a serious blow in the summer of 1820 from a lengthy and belated review of the memoirs in the *Literary and Scientific Repository* that, as one reader remarked, "flay[ed Wilkinson] alive."[144] Though unsigned, the review was believed to have come from John Armstrong, one of Madison's secretaries of war. Armstrong did not limit himself to events in which he had played a part—the Revolutionary War and the War of 1812—but addressed as well the Spanish pension and the Burr Conspiracy. And he saw the limits to Wilkinson's recent resurgence. If Wilkinson had "saved his country" "by defeating treason," then why did his claims to "the highest honours of the Commonwealth . . . never fail to excite a smile or a sneer?" Taking apart the story that Wilkinson had crafted in his 1811 defense, Armstrong argued that the general had committed "a double treason." He had "listened to the tempter, and conspired against his country," but had "ultimately weighed the danger, and betrayed his friend and associate."[145] After Wilkinson's death in Mexico in December 1825, the best that could be said of him was that "public opinion [had] long been much divided as to [his] character." Even a friendly death notice admitted that "some parts of his conduct rather appeared inexplicable."[146] In later decades, further research, particularly in Spanish archives, proved many of the charges that Randolph, Clark, and others had made regarding the Spanish Conspiracy and pension. But further research has discovered few new documents about Wilkinson's role in the Burr Conspiracy. With some relatively minor exceptions, what we know is what Wilkinson's contemporaries knew. We have to sort through the same "galimitias of facts and of lies" that they did.[147]

Committed to the idea that, "in all Events my Honor can & will be defended," Wilkinson wrote or compiled thousands of pages of text, testimony, and documents in the decade between "A Plain Tale" and *Memoirs of My Own Times*.[148] His efforts to defend his honor also included submitting material, signed and unsigned, for newspaper publication, arranging public tributes to his service and character, and issuing challenges for duels. The demands seemed interminable and multifarious, arising, as they did, from controversies that spanned a quarter-century of his public life. "To defend the general against all the calumnies by which he has been attacked," Wilkinson asserted in the unsigned *Brief Examination*, "would be a task almost as endless as that of Sisyphus."[149] Central to this project were his efforts to meet the charges of involvement in the Burr Conspiracy, particularly through *Burr's Conspiracy Exposed* and part of the second volume of *Memoirs of My Own Times*. Wilkinson's final accounts of the conspiracy were simultaneously defensive and accusatory, revealing and obfuscating, overwhelming and incomplete. But, despite his hopes, they never seemed definitive and exculpatory to either contemporaries or historians.

"IT WAS HOPED AND EXPECTED . . . THAT FULL LIGHT WOULD HAVE BEEN SHED ON THIS CHAPTER IN OUR COUNTRY'S HISTORY"

Of those whose reputations suffered from either the exposure or the repression of the conspiracy, Burr not only faced the greatest censure, but also lived the longest under it. Joseph Alston and William C. C. Claiborne died in the mid-1810s, Jefferson and Wilkinson in the mid-1820s, Harman Blennerhassett in 1831, and John Marshall in 1835.

Burr lived until September 1836, "drag[ging] out a dishonored existence among a generation which [knew him] only by the history of [his] crimes," as a future secretary of state pityingly wrote in 1831.[150] In the nearly three decades between the Richmond trial and his death, Burr did little to defend or restore his reputation. "He has preserved an unbroken silence," the Kentucky historian Mann Butler remarked in 1834, "for seven and twenty years." Butler foresaw, however, that there might yet be "future disclosures."[151] Three years later, a year after his death, Burr's final account of the conspiracy appeared in the second volume of Matthew Livingston Davis's *Memoirs of Aaron Burr*. Burr's reasons for publishing this account after remaining quiet for so long are almost as difficult to establish as his intentions regarding the conspiracy itself. The book had little prospect of changing anyone's thinking about his actions or his character.

Burr's long "silence" began even before the Richmond trial ended. Burr did little to counter suspicions about his plans and movements during the fall of 1806. He does not seem to have attacked the *Western World*, though friendly local editors would have provided space to do so. After his first trial in Kentucky that November, Burr sent reassuring letters to prominent men in Ohio, Kentucky, and the Indiana Territory. While he may have expected that the letters would be shown to others, they do not appear to have been written for publication. Kentucky's Henry Clay later remarked that, when asked "why he did not contradict in the News papers the accounts that [were] published against him," Burr had replied that "if he should commence the work it would be endless & unavailing."[152] Nor did Burr use the courts to explain himself in ways that protected his reputation. In Kentucky, the Mississippi Territory, and Virginia, most of his comments addressed disputed points of law. Since current legal practice did not permit him to speak in his own defense, he never could offer a comprehensive account of his project. Although he occasionally challenged the prosecution's claims in asserting his innocence, the closest Burr came in court to making sense of his plans and movements for a broader public occurred in his initial examination in Richmond. With Marshall considering whether he should be held for treason, Burr insisted that his "designs were honorable and would have been useful to the United States" and pointed to the supplies on his boats as evidence that his "object was purely peaceable and agricultural." At the same time, he ambiguously remarked that, if "the designs imputed to me ever did exist[,] . . . they were long since abandoned."[153]

In mid-September 1807, Burr found himself in the position that he would occupy for the remainder of his life. His acquittal of treason and misdemeanor could not shake the broadly held opinion that he was guilty of treasonous intent, at least. Over the next nine months, until he departed for Europe in June 1808, Burr's hopes for the future vacillated wildly. At times, he seemed to despair. He spent the winter in Philadelphia, where he rarely entertained company and was even more rarely invited to other homes. "It would not have surprised me," Burr's close friend Charles Biddle later recalled of this period, "to have found he had ended his sufferings with a pistol."[154] At other times, Burr seemed convinced that he could restore his reputation by reviving and bringing to fruition a grand enterprise. During the fall of 1807, Blennerhassett noted several occasions when Burr was working "on reorganizing his projects for action, as if he had never suffered the least interruption."[155] During these months, he did not attempt a public justification of his actions or vindication of his reputation.

When he left for Europe in June 1808, Burr sought not only to distance himself from a hostile press and public, but also to find foreign backing for the kind of military adventure that could restore his reputation, wealth, and influence. Nearly six months earlier, the British consul in Philadelphia had warned his superiors that Burr would probably propose a scheme "to subdue the Floridas[,] conquer Cuba[,] and very probably revolutionize South America."[156] By then, Burr had already sent Samuel Swartwout abroad to revive his old connections to the British government through the Scottish land agent Charles Williamson and the former British minister Anthony Merry. Burr departed New York at a propitious moment. Recent upheavals in Spain, where Napoleon had forced the abdication of the king and installed a Bonaparte on the throne, had turned British policymakers' attention to the Spanish empire. They even sent Williamson to Jamaica, around the time that Burr left New York, to open communications with Cuba. But, if international developments seemed to favor Burr's plans in May and June 1808, they soon dashed his hopes for British support. The emergence of anti-French juntas in Spain offered more direct means for striking at Napoleon, and perhaps opening Spanish colonial markets, than Burr could. Even before Burr reached London in mid-July, British policymakers had decided to support the juntas. British reluctance to provoke a war with the United States also made Burr an unlikely instrument. For ten months, Burr worked diligently to advance his plans. Eventually, the British government grew uncomfortable enough with his presence to demand his departure. "Mr. Jefferson, or the Spanish Juntas, or probably both," Burr reported in April 1809, "have had enough influence to drive me out of this country."[157]

Burr eventually recognized that, if British policymakers saw their interests benefitted by the turmoil in the Spanish empire, Napoleon must see his interests threatened. In February 1810, after eight months in Sweden, Denmark, and the German states, he reached Paris. Within days, he met with Napoleon's foreign minister. During "several interviews" with a subordinate in March, Burr developed his proposals in four memoranda.[158] Their topics included the politics of the United States; the condition of Louisiana; the state of Spain's North American colonies; and the threat of British influence in the Spanish empire. Riddled with unbelievable claims about Burr's influence and access to military and financial backing, these memoranda suggested various ways in which Burr, with French aid, could weaken Great Britain or strengthen France. The options ranged from seizing the Floridas to marching on Mexico, and from establishing a pro-French government in Louisiana to overthrowing that of the United States. While Burr disavowed any plan for "disuniting" the United States, some of his proposals would have been considered tantamount to treason by most Americans; others—particularly "the independence of Florida"—would have been seen as striking at vital interests.[159] By late July 1810, after trying other channels to reach Napoleon, Burr recognized that further overtures would be fruitless. He began trying to arrange a passport to return home; it would take nearly two years for him to complete the journey.

Beginning in June 1812, Burr quickly settled into a quiet life as a New York lawyer, suggesting the devastating impact of a series of blows—the disappointments of London and Paris, the embarrassments of his struggles to return home, and the deaths of his only grandchild in July 1812 and of his beloved daughter six months later. The next decade offered numerous outlets for someone of his interests and ambitions. Americans, in and out of government, grew enthusiastic about revolutionary activity in the Spanish empire. Many wrote or spoke on behalf of the Spanish American patriots in newspapers, magazines, public meetings, and legislative assemblies. Some funded or manned privateering vessels that sailed from American ports to prey on Spanish shipping. Others supported or joined filibustering expeditions that marched from American soil for East Florida and Texas. Burr certainly knew of these activities and had some ties with Spanish American patriots and their allies in New York, but there is no evidence that he took an active role. Whatever hopes and dreams led his old friend, and old nemesis, Wilkinson to revolutionary Mexico in March 1822 had lost their hold over Burr.[160] Burr abandoned his efforts to restore his reputation through deeds, moreover, without taking steps to do so in words.

Eventually, Burr decided to publish an account of his life. Unlike many of the leading statesmen of his day, he had never been much of a writer; his memorandum for the French government on the Spanish colonies, at just over four printed pages, may have been his longest piece. As such, he turned to Davis, a trusted ally from the political battles of the late 1790s and early 1800s, to write his memoirs. Modern genre conventions separate "memoirs" from "biographies" on the basis of authorship. Memoirs are written by the person whose life is being remembered; biographies are written by someone else. In the mid-nineteenth century, this distinction did not exist. That Davis wrote Burr's "memoirs" caused no confusion. The preface to the first volume made clear, moreover, that Burr had engaged Davis, provided his papers, and used his recollections to fill any gaps. One reviewer stated that Davis had "acquitted himself well"—as an "editor," rather than an author—because he had "so connected the materials left by Colonel Burr, as to form a very interesting and satisfactory memoir," while adding "as little matter of his own as possible."[161]

In the preface, Davis explained Burr's decision to break his silence. The precipitating event, according to Davis, was Burr's reading of Jefferson's comments on the election of 1800 in his *Memoir, Correspondence, and Miscellanies* (1829). "From [that] time forward," Davis recalled, Burr "evinced an anxiety that I would prepare his Memoirs." Most historians have accepted this explanation without question. But, if Burr was so anxious in 1830 to have his memoirs written, why did it take until 1836 for the first volume to appear? Davis acknowledged that it was not until "the summer of 1835" that he even began an "examination of [Burr's] letters and papers."[162] Without directly addressing this five-year hiatus, he suggested that a difference of opinion with Burr about how freely the book would attack old foes, particularly George Washington, had fueled delays. What Davis left unsaid was that the two had found more immediate and more subtle ways to attack Jefferson's account of the election. Working with Richard H. Bayard, the son of a key player in the election crisis, Davis and Burr had published a pamphlet in the spring of 1831 with two important depositions on the election; they had managed, moreover, to keep their contribution to this publication hidden.

Though entirely unmentioned by Davis, the spark for renewed work on the memoirs in the summer of 1835 may have been the publication of Samuel L. Knapp's *Life of Aaron Burr* earlier that year. The relationship between Knapp, a former magazine editor and biographer, and Burr is not entirely clear. By January 1834, Burr was working with Knapp to claim a federal pension for his Revolutionary War service. He may have turned to Knapp as his chosen biographer when Davis refused to write the kind of slashing attacks that he wanted. In his preface, however, Knapp suggested that he had considered writing about Burr even before meeting him. Whether the impetus came from Burr or from Knapp, Burr proved a willing subject. "In every inquiry I have made of him," Knapp remarked, "he has given me a manly answer, and, as I firmly believe, such a one as he honestly believed to be true." Knapp left no question about his motives for the book by announcing that it was "time to remove many mountains of prejudice which [had] been heaped upon [Burr]."[163] The few reviews of Knapp's book found little to praise in either style or content. One reviewer denounced the author as "a literary hack" for whom "imagination [was] all-in-all" and the book for "contain[ing] only those incidents" of Burr's life that "were most accessible, and with which, indeed, the whole public were already familiar."[164] Another viewed Knapp's attempt at "a vindication" as a failure since it "amount[ed] to a mere denial" in which "no sort of explanation is attempted, as to the real designs of Burr in his extraordinary movements on our western waters." Much of the coverage of the conspiracy, in fact, took the form of a simple "abridge-ment of the celebrated trial."[165] A comment in Davis's preface suggests that Knapp's book prompted renewed efforts by Burr and Davis. "I am very desirous that a knowledge of Mr. Burr's character and conduct should be derived from his miscellaneous correspondence," Davis re-marked, "and not from what his biographer might write, unsupported by documentary testimony," as was essentially true of Knapp's work. Accordingly, Davis incorporated "many of [Burr's] private letters" and other writings into his book.[166]

Throughout his life, even when he had displayed little other interest in defending his reputation, Burr had been careful about his papers. On the eve of his duel with Alexander Hamilton, he had written a long letter to his daughter explaining how he had organized them and what she should do with them if he died, including "burn[ing] all such as, if by accident made public, would injure any person."[167] Before leaving for Europe four years later, Burr had left her new instructions for caring for his papers. "I never travel," he had further noted, "without giving to my confidential servant or attendant directions for the disposition of my papers, clothes, &c., in case of sudden death."[168] At times, Burr seems to have kept copies of at least some of his outgoing letters and spent time ordering his correspondence, including "burn[ing] or fil[ing] and mark[ing] every paper in his possession" early in his European travels.[169] In late July 1835, as work began in earnest on the memoirs, Burr amended his will to leave his "private papers" to Davis, with in-structions "to destroy or to deliver to the parties interested" any that might injure "individuals against whom I have no complaint"—a far narrower group than that named in the instructions that he had left his daughter thirty years earlier.[170]

But did Burr's papers include anything that Davis could have used to explain Burr's western project? They certainly had once. In mid-January 1807, Burr reportedly exclaimed to officials in the Mississippi Territory, "If I am sacrificed, my Port Folio will prove [Wilkinson] to be a villain."[171] That winter, news of Burr's trunk of "*damning*" docu-ments spread quickly in letters and newspapers; many of these reports placed his "Port Folio in the Hands of his Daughter [Theodosia Burr] Alston."[172] Although Burr quickly denied this claim, he later insisted in Richmond—before the Alstons visited him—that Wilkinson's letters to him were unavailable. When Burr sailed for Europe, moreover, he directed Theodosia to "put all [his] papers and manuscript books into some one box, . . . keeping [herself] the key."[173] There is no clear evidence that she had this box with her when she boarded the *Patriot* in South Carolina on the last day of 1812, but it certainly would have made sense to have taken it on her first visit to her father since his departure for Europe. In his biography, Knapp asserted unequivocally that "a great portion of [Burr's] papers were lost with his daughter."[174] That Burr's papers sank with Theodosia and the *Patriot* remains the accepted explanation for the disappearance of what are assumed to have been revealing documents about his western project.

But Davis clearly had more Burr documents on this subject than Knapp had, or than modern scholars have. Never suggesting that important letters had been lost with Theodosia, Davis claimed, instead, to have worked with "an immense quantity" of Burr's papers, even for the chapters on the conspiracy.[175] Shortly after Burr's death, a New York newspaper even asserted that Davis had received "copies of *all* [Burr's] letters, civil, military and miscellaneous, [and] all the letters which he received for more than sixty years."[176] But Davis did not, in fact, have all of the important documents from this period. When Burr fled the Mississippi Territory in February 1807, he left some of his papers with Harman Blennerhassett and some with Peter Bryan Bruin, an old friend whose Bayou Pierre home had been the meeting point for Burr's boats. Davis knew that Blennerhassett had still possessed a "portmanteau" of Burr's letters as late as October 1812 and tried to acquire them from Margaret Blennerhassett as he worked on the second volume; whether he succeeded—or whether she even had the letters—is not known, though he did receive a copy of at least part of her husband's 1807 prison journal.[177] Davis probably knew nothing of the papers that Burr had left with Bruin, which eventually passed to Mississippi newspaper editor J.F.H. Claiborne. Claiborne seems to have brought them to public attention only in November 1841, promising that they would "be given to the public" in his planned state history; when that book finally appeared nearly forty years later, it merely mentioned Burr's papers without printing them.[178]

The *Memoirs of Aaron Burr*, like all books, embodied a series of decisions by the author—and probably his subject—beyond whether and when to write it. One of the most significant concerned the allocation of space among the different aspects of Burr's life, private and public. The first volume appeared a few months after Burr's death and must have been written during his life. Progressing from Burr's birth to the early stages of the election of 1800, it relies more on his memories and less on his papers than the second volume. It also devotes more space than the second volume to personal matters, such as his childhood, college years, marriage, legal practice, and child-rearing. Still, much of the volume addresses the first great public controversy of Burr's life: his actions in the Revolutionary War. Burr, as Davis noted in the preface, "was far more tenacious of his *military*, than of his professional, political, or moral character"—as the allocation of space reflects.[179] The other three controversies—the election of 1800, the duel with Hamilton, and the conspiracy—were treated in the second volume, which appeared more than a year after Burr's death. Of these, the election received the most extensive coverage, seven of the twenty-one chapters. This issue had provided the initial impetus for the memoirs and probably mattered the most to Davis, whose reputation was implicated in his support for Burr at the time. The duel and its aftermath were covered in two chapters. And the whole period of the conspiracy, from Burr's first tour of the West in 1805 through his departure for Europe three years later, received just over two chapters.

Another significant decision concerned the tone of the book. In the preface and elsewhere throughout the work, Davis asserted his and Burr's shared commitment to honesty and impartiality. Burr, he repeatedly insisted, had "no desire of concealment" and had never "express[ed] . . . a wish to suppress an account of any act of his whole life." He had answered all of Davis's questions "promptly and willingly." Davis, who earned his living writing for newspapers, further claimed that he had performed his part in preparing the memoirs "with the most scrupulous regard to [his] own reputation for correctness." He had tried, as he announced, "to state facts, and the fair deductions from them, without the slightest intermixture of personal feeling."[180] By adopting this tone, Davis and Burr indicated that the memoirs would differ from an argument- and evidence-driven defense pamphlet, such as Wilkinson's *Burr's Conspiracy Exposed*. The two volumes did not always maintain this tone, however. The lengthy discussions of Burr's military service and, especially, of the election of 1800 displayed many characteristics of a defense pamphlet, including the inclusion of sworn statements to bolster specific claims.

Davis reaffirmed the commitment to openness early in his account of the conspiracy. "In his latter days," he reported, "Burr had no longer any motive for concealment[,] nor did he evince the least desire to suppress the facts in relation to any of his acts." While Davis's treatment of the conspiracy did not achieve the promised clarity, it still differed from a defense pamphlet. At least three-quarters of the sixty pages on the conspiracy consisted of documents, with just one-quarter written by Davis. But these documents were not used for a point-by-point refutation of charges against Burr. Instead, they included Burr's letters to his daughter and son-in-law and extracts from his 1805 travel journal and from Blennerhassett's 1807 prison journal. Other than a few already-published items from Adair, Truxton, Jefferson, and others, these documents were new to the public, distinguishing Davis's approach from Knapp's reliance on the published trial records. What was absent from these chapters, however, were letters between Burr and anyone—except his son-in-law—whom the public had linked to his project. Where were the letters that had been written or received on his western travels in 1805 or during his stays in Washington and Philadelphia in early 1806 or while he engaged men, supplies, and boats in the West later that year? Where were Burr's letters to Wilkinson and Blennerhassett? And where were Wilkinson's letters to Burr, especially the never-revealed 13 May 1806 letter that had been mentioned in the cipher letter? Davis noted that Burr's correspondence from just the first eight months of 1806 was "voluminous" but printed none of it, claiming a lack of space. He merely stated that the letters "in no manner develop[ed] any other views than such as relate[d] to land speculations."[181] But, as one reviewer complained, even if they "treat[ed] of speculation in lands only," they seemed "far more important than any of the many letters" that Davis had included.[182]

According to Davis, Burr's travels and other activities in 1805 and 1806 were easily explained. Burr had admitted that "his views were twofold"—"the revolutionizing of Mexico" and "a settlement on what was known as the Bastrop lands." Over time, two separate plans "became in some degree blended" as those who settled the Bastrop grant would have been available to effect Burr's "great object[,] the conquest of Mexico." Davis acknowledged that Burr had encouraged western hostility to Spain and popular expectations of a Spanish war and, "by innuendoes or otherwise, [had] induced some to believe that his arrangements for the invasion of Mexico were with the knowledge, if not the approbation of the government." He named some prominent men who had committed to Burr's plans, including Adair, Clark, and, of course, Wilkinson, whose troops had been "intended as a nucleus, around which the followers of Burr were to form." But Davis insisted that Burr had never considered disunion, a claim that he bolstered with Burr's "deathbed" assurance that he "would as soon have thought of taking possession of the moon." "The charge of treason," Davis concluded, "is so perfectly ridiculous, that one who investigates the subject will be astounded that it ever gained credence." It derived not from anything Burr had done, but from the "corrupt and unprincipled" Wilkinson and the "malignant" Jefferson.[183]

It is not entirely clear what Burr and Davis sought to accomplish with the memoirs. Did they hope to restore Burr's reputation or to damage his enemies'? Did they believe that the people of the mid-1830s, most of whom had come of age since the great controversies of Burr's life, could be led to reassess Burr? Or did they think that the memoirs would have an impact only upon future biographers and historians? Davis never answered these questions. The clearest indication of his purpose may have been the memoirs' epigraph: "I come to bury Caesar, not to praise him."[184] This line from Shakespeare's *Julius Caesar* might be read as an early assertion of the memoirs' impartial tone; one reviewer accepted that Davis's "only aim seems to have been a record of the truth."[185] But, as at least one reviewer noted, the quoted line becomes quite ambiguous in the context of Marc Antony's speech. Antony did not merely wish to "bury Caesar." He also hoped, as Charles Francis Adams explained, to "[use] the body of [his] patron as an instrument by which he might utterly overthrow and destroy" Caesar's enemies.[186]

The *Memoirs of Aaron Burr* sold well, "public curiousity" having been "stimulated . . . by a thousand and one hints of new disclosures and unsuspected revelations."[187] While the volumes were widely read, by both men and women, and widely reviewed, the reviews were often critical. In the *North American Review*, Adams remarked that, while Davis had benefitted from the memoirs' "pretty extensive popularity[,] . . . the reading public" was not "likely to be benefitted at all in the same proportion."[188] "Neither as illustration of history, nor of character," one reviewer lamented, "does [Davis's] work possess the least merit."[189] Another critic believed that the public's disappointment with the work was "in precise proportion to the avidity with which [it] was sought."[190] The responses to the memoirs suggest that there was little chance of changing the public's views of either Burr or the conspiracy in the mid-1830s. The Kentucky historian Mann Butler had suggested as much two years before Burr's death: "Whatever shall be his future disclosures . . . , they will as well have descended to the tomb with their author."[191] While the memoirs were, as one writer recalled two decades later, "for a time a leading topic of conversation and discussion," public interest does not seem to have reflected a willingness to reassess Burr.[192] His reputation had been fixed "by the irreversible decision of public opinion"; the memoirs held little "prospect of resuscitation to the extinguished fame of Aaron Burr." This general perspective extended to the particular case of the conspiracy. "Though acquitted on the technical charge" of treason, according to this reviewer, "a higher tribunal had passed an irreversible judgment on [Burr's] conduct."[193] Another reviewer "presume[d] there can now be but little difference of opinion" about Burr's treason.[194]

Strikingly, this widespread belief that Davis's memoirs could not change readers' opinions of Burr and understandings of the Burr Conspiracy existed alongside diametrically opposed views of whether Burr had intended treason. On this question, each side treated its answer as unassailable and the opposing view as indefensible. This division had also appeared in reviews of Knapp's biography in 1835. The reviewers in the *Literary Gazette* and *New-England Magazine* had generally agreed on Knapp's failures as a writer and historian but had sharply differed in their views of Burr and the conspiracy. The former had dismissed all of "the visions of treasonable designs, unhallowed projects, [and] boundless ambition" that "the name of Burr calls forth" as "absurd and idle vagaries."[195] The latter had considered popular condemnation of Burr "one of the most noble objects in our history, and most striking illustrations of the operation of our institutions."[196] This division reappeared in the reviews of Davis's memoirs. Some readers approached the conspiracy with a seemingly unshakeable confidence of Burr's innocence. They hoped that, now that "the party heat of the day [had] evaporated, . . . the improbability of the story and the weight of the testimony" would convince any doubters of Burr's innocence. As one reviewer noted, Davis had "clearly made out his case" on this issue, "if it indeed needed additional evidence to support it."[197] Another reviewer thought that Davis had "[thrown] no new light upon this transaction," but still saw no reason to question or lament Burr's acquittal.[198] Others sounded equally certain of Burr's treasonable intentions, despite Davis's work. In his widely read piece for the *North American Review*, Adams criticized Davis for deciding "that the charge of treason . . . was not only absurd but ridiculous, without showing wherein the nonsense precisely consist[ed]." He considered it impossible "to believe [Burr's] deathbed declarations" when the evidence of "a double plot" that included a disunionist scheme "seem[ed] hardly deniable."[199]

Only rarely did reviewers express an openness to persuasion on the conspiracy. One of the few who did was the Reverend Francis Lister Hawks in what quickly became a "famous article" in the *New York Review*. In a piece that one reader considered "the most savage cutting up I ever read," Hawks, a former editor of the magazine, expressed not only his uncertainty about Burr's western project, but also a willingness to have been convinced by Davis's memoirs.[200] He had begun the memoirs believing that no one could "say what [Burr's] precise object was" or "answer with certainty" whether he "was guilty of treason or not." The memoirs should have resolved this uncertainty since Davis "enjoyed [Burr's] confidence and possessed his papers"; "it was hoped and expected," Hawks noted, "that full light would have been shed on this chapter in our country's history." It was not. Crucial correspondence had been "withheld," leaving nothing beyond Burr's and Davis's assertions to settle the issue. Ultimately, Hawks found himself voicing the confusion that many Americans had felt at the peak of the crisis thirty years earlier. Burr did not seem "too virtuous to become a traitor" to Hawks, but he was "a man of sense"; it was his "understanding, rather than his heart," that "acquit[ted] him . . . of treason" in Hawks's thinking.[201]

The reception of Davis's memoirs showed that Burr served an important function in mid-nineteenth century American culture—a function that few Americans were willing to surrender despite the efforts of Burr and Davis, or of biographers such as Samuel Knapp and later James Parton. Two years before Burr's death, Butler had highlighted this function, trusting that Burr and Benedict Arnold would forever "be viewed by the virtuous youth of our country, as beacons on the quicksands and rocks of political navigation."[202] The greatest fault of Davis's memoirs, to many, was that they threatened to obscure what seemed so clear. "It is greatly to be wished," Adams insisted, that the effect of Burr's example "upon the aspiring youth of the future, as well as the grown-up gladiators of the present time, may not be weakened or broken by injudicious palliation."[203] Mid-nineteenth century historical and biographical writing often served an explicitly didactic function, offering moral, political, and social lessons for a culture that was experiencing rapid and, often, wrenching change. Both positive and negative examples were required to teach the desired lessons. One review of Davis's memoirs opened with a simple assertion: "There are two classes of men, the study of whose lives is especially profitable"— "the signally good, and the remarkably bad."[204] In the 1830s, few could have wondered in which class to place Burr.

Keeping Burr among the "remarkably"—and, thus, instructively— "bad" required work. A reviewer might claim that the election, the duel, and the treason trial had "secure[d Burr] a place in history, equally conspicuous as a warning and an example."[205] But how secure would that place be if memoirists, biographers, and historians raised real doubts about the commonly accepted story of Burr's actions in these controversies? Over the nineteenth century, novelists and playwrights, short-story authors and schoolbook writers contributed to the cultural project of keeping Burr in his place. Not all of the literally hundreds of novels, plays, magazine articles, and other works that mentioned Burr covered the conspiracy, but many did, including *The Conspiracy; or, The Western Island: A Drama in Five Acts* (1838); James W. Taylor's *The Victim of Intrigue: A Tale of Burr's Conspiracy* (1847); A. E. Dupuy's *The Conspirator* (1850); Emerson Bennett's *The Traitor, or, the Fate of Ambition* (1860); and Edwin Lassetter Bynner's *Zachary*

Phips (1892). Nor did all of the works that included Burr hold to the broadly accepted view of his character and actions. But those who challenged the orthodox perspective made little headway. At the turn of the twentieth century, Charles Felton Pidgin emerged as a leading defender of Burr, particularly regarding the conspiracy. In quick succession, he published *Blennerhassett; or, The Decrees of Fate* (1901), *The Climax; or, What Might Have Been* (1902) "in which Col. Aaron Burr [was] a conspicuous figure," and *Little Burr: The Warwick of America* (1905). He enumerated for his publisher "three points upon which [he had] found more or less unanimity among the reviewers" of *Blennerhassett*. "The first and most important declaration," Pidgin explained, "is that the verdict of history has been rendered in the case of Aaron Burr and that it is useless to present any new evidence or to ask for any modification of the adverse judgments now on record"—as he had tried to do.[206] Long after the Burr Conspiracy, even long after Burr's death, few Americans would relax their certainty about his role in their history.

In the end, Jefferson's, Wilkinson's, and Burr's final accounts of the Burr Conspiracy accomplished relatively little. They could not reverse what each man had seen as the failure of Burr's trial in Richmond. And they did not achieve the particular purposes that each seems to have brought to his work. Jefferson's trial report did not become the grounds for a constitutional amendment limiting judicial power. Wilkinson's numerous writings and other activities did not clean his damaged reputation of the twin stains of the Burr Conspiracy and the Spanish connection. Burr's belated memoirs did not force a revision, or even a serious reconsideration, of his place in American history. But these final accounts also failed to make more sense of Burr's western plans and movements for either contemporaries or later biographers and historians than had key documents from the period of the crisis. Each included serious flaws in the form of obvious biases, omitted documents, and outright lies. That Jefferson's trial report, Wilkinson's various writings, and Burr's memoirs exhibited such flaws did not necessarily make them worse accounts of the conspiracy than Jefferson's 22 January 1807 message to Congress, Burr's and Wilkinson's cipher letter, and William Wirt's "Who is Blennerhassett?" speech—each of which displayed many of the same failings. But those earlier narratives and the understandings that they had shaped, however incomplete and contested, proved almost impossible to dislodge. Even as the nation's hopes and fears changed across the nineteenth century, the old stories continued to shape popular and, increasingly, scholarly thinking about the crisis and the conspiracy.

CONCLUSION

IN THE EARLY 1880S, HENRY ADAMS, THE FIRST GREAT HISTORIAN IN and of the United States, wrote a biography of Aaron Burr that focused upon the Burr Conspiracy. By that time, writing about the conspiracy had become something of a family hobby. Henry's father, Charles Francis Adams, had reviewed Burr's memoirs and European travel journal for the *North American Review* in the late 1830s. Thirty years earlier, Henry's grandfather, John Quincy Adams, had prepared a report for the Senate that called for expelling Ohio's John Smith as a party to the conspiracy. Even Henry's great-grandfather, John Adams, had claimed, in early 1815, that he "could write a volume of biography" about Burr, whom he considered one of "two characters," along with Alexander Hamilton, who had to be "explained" "if American history [was] ever to be understood or related with truth."[1] Henry Adams's Burr biography emerged from his effort to understand and relate, if not the whole of the nation's history, at least the crucial years of the early nineteenth century. He conducted extensive research in European archives, discovering the nature and extent of Burr's overtures to the British and Spanish ministers between 1804 and 1806. After returning from Europe, he worked diligently on the Burr book, completing the manuscript in about two years. He spent the rest of the 1880s trying to decide when and with whom to publish the biography, even as he wrote his magisterial, multivolume *History of the United States during the Administrations of Thomas Jefferson and James Madison* (1889–91). Ultimately, he never published his Burr biography, probably reworking it into the six chapters on the conspiracy in the *History*. But even after all of his research and writing on Burr, even after—according to one historian—"discover[ing] Burr" as a topic for historical study, Adams could still say that "no one ever knew what happened" with "Burr's conspiracy."[2]

That more than a century of additional researching and writing about Aaron Burr, Thomas Jefferson, James Wilkinson, and the other important figures has not provided definitive answers to the old questions about these men's motivations and intentions seems clear. One recent history of the conspiracy opens by stating, "no one has been able to discover what [Burr] really plotted."[3] Any attempt to answer the old questions faces the same evidentiary problems that confronted Adams in the 1880s and many other capable and diligent historians in the decades since. Burr's missing letters and journals—whether lost at sea in 1813 or burned by his biographer in the 1830s or destroyed at some other place and time—have always seemed to present the greatest problem. But, as we have seen, countless other documents have disappeared as well, including some of Jefferson's incoming correspondence, all of Wilkinson's letters to Burr, a collection of depositions from the Ohio Valley, various dispatches from federal officials, and most of John Marshall's personal papers. Much of what does survive from the principal figures seems problematic, moreover. Burr, Jefferson, and Wilkinson may not have been "Rogues," as the Connecticut Federalist Benjamin Ellis concluded by late 1809, but none of them deserve our implicit trust. We can hope, as Ellis did, that, "when Rogues fall out, honest Men get the Truth."[4] But we seem, instead, to face a mass of incomplete, incompatible, and even incredible assertions and explanations in their surviving letters and other writings.

Changing the focus of our questions from the intentions of Burr, Wilkinson, and Jefferson to the crisis that the Burr Conspiracy produced and the ways in which people made sense of swirling rumors, conflicting reports, and differing statements does not eliminate all of the evidentiary problems. But those men's lapses in honesty and accuracy no longer seem so critical when it is not as essential to establish their thinking. And the occasional discoveries of more missing documents—such as the "great number of letters relative to [Burr's] expedition" that the administration never seems to have recovered from their hiding place behind a brick in the chimney of a merchant's house in New Jersey or the sixteen pages that were excised from the letter books of the governor of the Orleans Territory or the letters that cannot be deciphered because the key has been lost—no longer seem so damaging because the facts that they might have contained no longer seem so relevant.[5] Instead, there suddenly seem to be too many letters and diaries, too many newspapers and magazines, too many speeches in assembly halls and arguments in courtrooms, too many pamphlets, too many memoirs, too many novels, too many plays. If we treat these numerous and varied documents simply as repositories of the evidence and facts that we need to settle the timeline, identify the participants, and establish the plot of this great drama, we face evidentiary problems that, while different, were certainly well understood at the time. "The newspapers of the day teem with such a mass of contrasting evidence," one Richmonder complained of a crucial type of source in late April 1807, "that ingenuity is foiled in extracting the truth."[6]

We need to remember, instead, that despite their own evidentiary problems—too little from the desired sources, too much from other sources—most people moved fairly quickly from a state that Thomas Truxton described as "wonderfully perplext" at the height of the Burr crisis to sufficiently certain about Burr's and Wilkinson's and Jefferson's intentions and actions to act themselves.[7] Their certainties, and thus their actions, differed dramatically, with some deciding that Burr was a traitor and others deciding that Wilkinson or Jefferson, or both, was the true villain. They turned vague rumors, conflicting accounts, and incomplete reports into enough certainty to act since they believed that they had to do so. Because they worried about the fragility of both the union and the republic, they looked for crises. And, because their understanding of why events happened emphasized personal agency rather than divine intervention or socioeconomic forces, they looked for conspiracies. Beginning as early as the summer of 1805 and continuing at least through the fall of 1807, many Americans saw dangers that required action, even if their own actions extended no further than supporting or criticizing the actions of those in power. Action required understanding, even if understanding had to be forged from uncertainty.

In trying to comprehend how contemporaries experienced the Burr crisis and made sense of the Burr Conspiracy, in all of its aspects, we discover the richness and complexity of a culture, including assumptions and beliefs that were only rarely or imperfectly articulated. This book has highlighted the great significance of local conditions, the disproportionate power of specific narratives, and the frequent reliance upon preexisting stories for sensemaking. Those factors, stated that broadly, seem likely to play important roles in sensemaking across much of time and space. Using them to understand how contemporaries made sense of this particular crisis and conspiracy has revealed some of the particularities of American culture in the first years of the nineteenth century—the hopes and fears about federal union and republican government; the uncertainty of political authority at the national, regional, state, and local levels; the importance of partisan politics at each of these levels; and the questions about what kinds of people and what kinds of actions might strengthen or threaten still-young institutions.

Investigating the crisis and conspiracy in this manner helps us to understand a period when political structures seemed very fluid and cultural forms offered needed stability. In political terms, those things that held the greatest promise—republican government and federal union—had always failed in the past and seemed unlikely to last far into the future. And the unwelcome emergence of seemingly unbridgeable party divisions at home and of seemingly unlimited warfare abroad multiplied the dangers and accelerated the changes. The countervailing forces often came from a cultural realm that seemed more secure. A broadly shared sense of the importance of honor, reputation, and character played a critical role. It created bonds that allowed men to work together on political issues, helping both to promote and to overcome party divisions. And it underwrote the system by which information was exchanged and evaluated, helping to make any decisions about public affairs possible. Such cultural forms allowed people to make sense of the political world, at a time when that world often threatened to change too much, too quickly, and in too many of the wrong directions.

The cultural forms that enabled people to make sense of and respond to the Burr Conspiracy did not emerge from this crisis unaffected. The old ways—of gentility and deference, of honor and reputation—were already being eroded by the period's political and social transformations. The Burr crisis exposed and accelerated the process in which this older system of moving information, creating understanding, and organizing action was replaced by a newer one that was based on partisanship. The old system relied upon the honor of gentlemen, an honor that was expected to shape what they wrote, what they said, and what they did. Over the course of the Burr crisis, too many gentlemen were shown to or, at least, believed to have acted dishonorably. Perhaps more importantly, they were shown to have counted on the faith that their culture put in the words and actions of gentlemen to hide their manipulations and prevarications. Even as it exposed flaws in the old system, the Burr crisis fueled the partisan divisions that underpinned the emerging system. The new system could move information, create understanding, and organize action as well as the old, as long as one accepted that one's party's truths were the only truths. And it relied most heavily on a medium, the party newspaper, that often seemed to have been designed to ruin men's characters. As a reviewer of an early Burr biography remarked fifty years later, the newspapers of Burr's day were characterized "by a rancor, a personality, and a reckless invention, for which the most discriminating allowance must be made in searching for the facts of character."[8]

Character, reputation, and honor were critical to people's efforts to make sense of the Burr Conspiracy. Assessments of the character of others filled letters and newspapers, assembly halls and courtrooms, and, presumably, homes and taverns because such assessments still underpinned any attempt to make sense. They structured the flow of information, determining who spoke and wrote to whom, what speakers and writers reported and did not report to different audiences, and whether their words were believed, doubted, or rejected. And they established what those whose characters were being assessed might do and could do. That way of making sense survived the Burr crisis, but it was weakened in the process and what would come to replace it was invigorated by the divisions that the crisis fueled.

ACKNOWLEDGMENTS

SOMETIME THIS YEAR, THIS PROJECT WILL REACH ITS TWENTIETH birthday, making it older than many of my students (as they are happy to remind me). I initially thought of writing a book on the Burr Conspiracy as I completed my first book, though the book that I imagined twenty years ago would have looked nothing like this one. From the beginning, I knew that it would be different from most of the history books that I had read, including the one that I had just written. But I could not have said how it would be different, or why it needed to be different, when I first arrived at this topic. The additional reading, teaching, and thinking that happened between my first decision to write on the Burr Conspiracy and its eventual emergence as the focus of my scholarly efforts a few years, and a few projects, later made this book what it is. Inevitably, a project of such duration incurs many debts of many different kinds.

This project has received financial support in various forms. Funds for specific research trips came from a Mellon Research Fellowship from the Virginia Historical Society, an Archie K. Davis Fellowship from the North Caroliniana Society, and numerous Faculty Development Grants and OK-UM Mellon Grants from Kalamazoo College. The most generous support came from two sources. In the early stages of the project, I received an eight-month fellowship from the National Endowment for the Humanities. Throughout the life of the project, I received financial and other assistance from the International Center for Jefferson Studies, which served as a second (at times, a primary) scholarly home for me as I worked on this book. I want to thank the former director Jim Horn and the current director, Andrew O'Shaughnessy, for their long-standing support for this project.

The research for this book carried me to roughly fifty state and local historical societies, college and university special collections departments, history museums, and research centers. While it is impossible to list all of the people who helped me at those places, I want to acknowledge the incredible work that such archives do and the essential roles that they perform in most historical scholarship. I did most of the reading and research for this project in the fast-receding "paper age" at various college and university libraries in Louisiana, Pennsylvania, Delaware, and Michigan. I still have not found one that can rival the incredible holdings for my period and place—in books, journals, and microfilm collections—of the Alderman Library at the University of Virginia. Like all scholars of politics, diplomacy, and public life in the early American republic, I owe an immense debt to the various National Historical Publications and Records Commission–funded papers' projects. I would like to thank, in particular, Barbara Oberg and Jeff Looney and their staffs at the two homes of the Thomas Jefferson Papers and John Stagg, Mary Hackett, David Mattern, and the others at the James Madison Papers for providing access to sources, answers to questions, and words of encouragement.

This project has been enriched by the feedback of a large number of scholars. Most of the individual pieces of this book were first presented in some form: a "brown-bag" lunch at the McNeil Center for Early American Studies; fellows forums at the International Center for Jefferson Studies (four); a faculty study group at Kalamazoo College; the annual conference of the Society for Historians of the Early American Republic (two); the Filson Historical Society's "Secessions" Conference; the Columbia University Seminar on Early American History and Culture; and the Early American Seminar at the University of Virginia (two). I received helpful suggestions from commentators and participants at each of these presentations. An early version of the first part of Chapter 4 appeared in Peter J. Kastor, ed., *The Louisiana Purchase: Emergence of an American Nation* (Washington, D.C.: CQ Press, 2002). I would also like to acknowledge the contribution of some of my students at Kalamazoo College—the (mostly) junior history majors and minors who have read and written on Chapter 8 as part of my research seminar "The Trial in American History" and the senior history majors who have engaged in an epistemological exercise based on the opening vignette of the Third Interlude in the required senior seminar. A number of scholars have read one or more chapters of the book and provided helpful suggestions, including Peter Onuf, Tom Baker, Carolyn Eastman, Peter Kastor, and Ray Swick. I have benefitted immensely from readings of the complete manuscript by Charlene Boyer Lewis (multiple times), Joanne Freeman, Alan Taylor, and Kathleen McDermott. Any and all remaining errors are, of course, my own.

Princeton University Press has been a wonderful home for this project. I want to thank Peter Onuf for bringing my project to the press's attention and the acquisitions editor Eric Crahan for showing such obvious interest in and enthusiasm for it at a time when I was beginning to doubt that I could find a press that saw what I saw in the work. Eric and the press's board have allowed this book to be everything that I wanted it to be; in fact, they have helped it to be more than I had thought possible. At Princeton, I have worked with helpful, friendly people at every stage of the process, including Debbie Tegarden, Hannah Zuckerman, and Gail Schmitt. I also received assistance in the final stages of preparing the manuscript from three people in Kalamazoo—Jax Lee Gardner, Julia Duncan, and Mackenzie Callahan.

A large number of colleagues and friends have supported this project in numerous ways, providing everything from free lodging on research trips to suggestions of primary sources and secondary materials, from prodding questions to relaxing moments. While it is impossible to remember and to name everyone, a list of such contributors has to include Cindy and Mark Aron, John Belohlavek, Seth Cotlar, Greg Dowd, Carolyn Eastman, Rebecca Edwards and Mark Seidel, Mike Foley, Joanne Freeman, Dena Goodman, Tony Iaccarino, Peter Kastor, Jessica McKillip, Greg Midgett, Peter Onuf, Kevin O'Shaughnessy, Rob Parkinson, Leonard Sadosky, Scott and Stacey Starsman, and Alan Taylor. Over the years, my colleagues in the History Department at Kalamazoo College have been wonderfully encouraging and patient. Beyond my own department, I need to thank Jen Einspahr (political theory), Elizabeth Manwell (Latin translations and all things classical), Amy Smith (Shakespeare), and Gail Griffin and Bruce Mills (eighteenth- and nineteenth-century British and American literature, respectively).

If those people have, in general, experienced this project as a source of welcome visits and interesting conversations, I know that there are others, friends and family, who have also experienced it as a cause of postponed or cancelled visits and of prolonged silences. The unflagging support of some of my Kalamazoo friends—Jen Einspahr and Ed Kenny, and Elizabeth Manwell, Matt Shockey, and Thomas Shockey—and of the "Atlanta guys"—Kevin O'Shaughnessy, John Marsh, and Drew Schuler—deserves special recognition. I also want to acknowledge, and to thank, my sister and sisters-in-law—Sara Rabe, Linda Boyer, and Yvonne Boyer—for their love and encouragement. Jim and Anita Lewis, Ann and Robert Fear, and Margareta and Anders Olsson have aided this project and supported me in too many ways to count or to repay.

Even though she is often smarter than I am, Charlene could not have known what I was getting her into when I said that I was thinking of writing on the Burr Conspiracy twenty years ago. She has been an integral part of this project at every step, from my earliest explorations through the research trips, the countless drafts, and the occasional frustrations to the reading of copy edits and page proofs. She has kept me going through those days when I too experienced what Charles Francis Adams called "an insurmountable repugnance to taking up Burr." To acknowledge that this book would not have been the same without her is just a small piece of the far more meaningful acknowledgment that I would not be the same without her.

ABBREVIATIONS

For most repositories, I have used the abbreviations in the Library of Congress's *MARC Code List for Organizations.*

A-Ar	Alabama Department of Archives and History, Montgomery
AHN	America's Historical Newspapers database
Anas	Sawvel, ed., *Complete Anas of Thomas Jefferson*
Annals	Gales, comp., *Debates and Proceedings in the Congress of the United States*
ASP: MA	Lowrie et al., eds., *American State Papers*, Ser. 5, *Military Affairs*
ASP: Misc	Lowrie et al., eds., *American State Papers*, Ser. 10, *Miscellaneous*
BP	Safford, *Blennerhassett Papers*
BwB	Fitch, ed., *Breaking with Burr*
CBHL	Van Horne et al., eds., *Correspondence and Miscellaneous Papers of Benjamin Henry Latrobe*
CLC	Cunningham, ed., *Circular Letters of Congressmen to Their Constituents*
CMPP	Richardson, comp., *Compilation of the Messages and Papers of the Presidents*
CSmH	Henry E. Huntington Library, San Marino, Calif.
CtY	Manuscripts and Archives, Sterling Memorial Library, Yale University, New Haven, Conn.
DeHi	Historical Society of Delaware, Wilmington
DLC	Library of Congress, Washington, D.C.
DNA	National Archives, Washington, D.C.
ECAB	[Hening and Munford], *Examination of Col. Aaron Burr*
GU	Hargrett Rare Book and Manuscript Library, University of Georgia Libraries, Athens
ICHi	Chicago History Museum Research Center, Ill.
ICN	Newberry Library, Chicago, Ill.
ICU	Special Collections Research Center, University of Chicago Library, Ill.
InHi	Indiana Historical Society, Indianapolis
InU	Lilly Library, Indiana University, Bloomington
KyBgW	Library Special Collections, Western Kentucky University, Bowling Green

KyHi   Kentucky Historical Society, Frankfort

KyLoF   Filson Historical Society, Louisville, Ky.

KyU   Special Collections Research Center, Margaret I. King Library, University of Kentucky, Lexington

L-M   Louisiana Historical Center, Louisiana State Museum, New Orleans

LN   New Orleans Public Library, La.

LNHiC   Historic New Orleans Collection, La.

LNT-H   Louisiana Research Collection, Tulane University, New Orleans, La.

LOWJM   [Rives and Fendall, eds.], *Letters and Other Writings of James Madison*

LU   Louisiana and Lower Mississippi Valley Collection, Louisiana State University Libraries, Baton Rouge

M6   Letters Sent by the Secretary of War Relating to Military Affairs

M77   Diplomatic Instructions of the Department of State

M124   Miscellaneous Letters Received by the Secretary of the Navy

M147   Letters Received by the Secretary of the Navy from Commanders

M149   Letters Sent by the Secretary of the Navy to Officers

M179   Miscellaneous Letters of the Department of State

M221   Letters Received by the Secretary of War, Registered Series

M222   Letters Received by the Secretary of War, Unregistered Series

M418   Letters of Application and Recommendation during the Administrations of Thomas Jefferson, 1801–1809

M601   Letters Sent by the Postmaster General

M1136   James Wilkinson Courts Martial, 1811 and 1815

MAB   Davis, *Memoirs of Aaron Burr*

MdHi   H. Furlong Baldwin Library, Maryland Historical Society, Baltimore

MHi   Massachusetts Historical Society, Boston

MiD-B   Burton Historical Collection, Detroit Public Library, Mich.

MiU-C   William L. Clements Library, University of Michigan, Ann Arbor

MoSHi   Missouri History Museum Archives, St. Louis

MoSW   Department of Special Collections, Washington University Libraries, St. Louis, Mo.

Ms-Ar   Mississippi Department of Archives and History, Jackson

NcD   David M. Rubenstein Rare Book and Manuscript Library, Duke University, Durham, N.C.

NcU   Southern Historical Collection, Wilson Library, University of North Carolina, Chapel Hill

NCUN   19th Century U.S. Newspapers database

"NECAB" Joseph C. Cabell, "Notes of Evidence in the Case of Aaron Burr," Cabell Family Papers, Albert and Shirley Small Special Collections Library, University of Virginia, Charlottesville

NjP   Manuscripts Division, Department of Rare Books and Special Collections, Princeton University Library, Princeton, N.J.

NjR   Special Collections and University Archives, Alexander Library, Rutgers University, New Brunswick, N.J.

NHi   New-York Historical Society, N.Y.

NN   New York Public Library, N.Y.

NNC   Butler Library, Columbia University, New York, N.Y.

NNGLI Gilder Lehrman Institute of American History, New York, N.Y.

OCHi   Cincinnati History Library and Archives, Cincinnati Museum Center, Ohio

OClWHi Western Reserve Historical Society, Cleveland, Ohio

OHi   Ohio History Connection, Columbus

OLBWC Rowland, ed., *Official Letter Books of William C. C. Claiborne*

OMC   Dawes Library, Marietta College, Marietta, Ohio

ORCHi Ross County Historical Society, Chillicothe, Ohio

PAB   Kline and Ryan, eds., *Papers of Aaron Burr*

PAG   Prince and Fineman, eds., *Papers of Albert Gallatin*

PAJ   Smith et al., eds., *Papers of Andrew Jackson*

PCAB   Kline and Ryan, eds., *Political Correspondence and Public Papers of Aaron Burr*

PHC   Hopkins et al., eds., *Papers of Henry Clay*

PHi   Historical Society of Pennsylvania, Philadelphia

PJAB-B Bixby, ed., *Private Journal of Aaron Burr*

PJAB-D Davis, ed., *Private Journal of Aaron Burr*

PJMar   Johnson et al., eds., *Papers of John Marshall*

PJM: PS Rutland et al., eds., *Papers of James Madison: Presidential Series*

PJM: SS Brugger et al., eds., *Papers of James Madison: Secretary of State Series*

PPiU-D Darlington Collection, Special Collections Department, University of Pittsburgh, Pa.

Proofs Clark, *Proofs of the Corruption of Gen. James Wilkinson*

PTJ: RS   Looney, ed., *Papers of Thomas Jefferson: Retirement Series*

RASP   Stampp, ed., *Records of Ante-bellum Southern Plantations*

RG21   Record Group 21, U.S. District Court for the Southern District of Ohio

RG28   Record Group 28, Records of the Post Office Department

RG45   Record Group 45, General Records of the Department of the Navy

RG59   Record Group 59, General Records of the Department of State

RG94   Record Group 94, Records of the Adjutant General's Office

RG107   Record Group 107, Records of the Office of the Secretary of War

RTCAB   Robertson, *Reports of the Trials of Colonel Aaron Burr*

ScHi   South Carolina Historical Society, Charleston

ScU   Manuscripts Division, South Caroliniana Library, University of South Carolina, Columbia

T   Tennessee State Library and Archives, Nashville

T265   Records Relating to the Proposed Trials of Aaron Burr and Harman Blennerhassett

TCAB   Carpenter, *Trial of Col. Aaron Burr*

TJC   Ford, ed., *Thomas Jefferson Correspondence*

TPUS   Carter, ed., *Territorial Papers of the United States*

Vi   Library of Virginia, Richmond

View   Daveiss, *A View of the President's Conduct*

ViHi   Virginia Historical Society, Richmond

ViU   Albert and Shirley Small Special Collections Library, University of Virginia, Charlottesville

ViW   Special Collections Research Center, Swem Library, College of William and Mary, Williamsburg, Va.

WHi   Wisconsin Historical Society, Madison

WoTJ   Ford, ed., *Works of Thomas Jefferson*

WPMP   Brown, ed., *William Plumer's Memorandum of Proceedings in the United States Senate*

WrTJ   Lipscomb and Bergh, eds., *Writings of Thomas Jefferson*

WvU   West Virginia and Regional History Center, West Virginia University Libraries, Morgantown

NOTES

INTRODUCTION

1. Thomas Spotswood Hinde to James Madison, 23 July 1829, DLC: James Madison Papers. For biographical material on Hinde, see Harper, *Guide to the Draper Manuscripts*, 120–21. No other history of the Burr Conspiracy mentions him. My use of the term "Burr Conspiracy" (without quotes) should not be taken to mean that I think that Burr actually conspired with others to commit treason or a lesser crime.
2. Madison to Hinde, 17 August 1829, in *LOWJM*, 4:45. The brief account (dated 27 August) is missing from Madison's papers but was later published as "Hinde's Correspondence" (Williams, ed.). For the longer version, see Hinde, "Col Aaron Burrs conspiracy in 1806," 26 September 1829, DLC: Madison Papers. Both versions may have been enclosed in Hinde to Madison, 26 September 1829, ibid.
3. Other than some minor corrections and additions, all of the information in the following history comes from one of the narratives that Hinde prepared for Madison.
4. Hinde, "Col Aaron Burrs conspiracy in 1806," 26 September 1829, DLC: Madison Papers.
5. Ibid.
6. Ibid.
7. Ibid.
8. Ibid. What Hinde described as Wilkinson's "maxim" is that of Satan in John Milton's *Paradise Lost*, 1.262. Hinde adopted the phrase "choice spirits" as a reference to Burr's followers from the cipher letter.
9. Hinde, "Col Aaron Burrs conspiracy in 1806," 26 September 1829, DLC: Madison Papers.
10. Ibid.
11. Ibid.
12. Ibid. In these years, at least two travelling wax figure exhibitions included the Burr-Hamilton duel. See "Burr & Hamilton," *National Intelligencer, and Washington Advertiser* (D.C.), 27 February 1805; "Wax Figures," *Kentucky Gazette and General Advertiser* (Lexington), 9 April 1805; and *Spirit of the Press* (Philadelphia), 1 June 1807.
13. Hinde, "To the Editors," *Daily National Intelligencer* (Washington, D.C.), 12 October 1838. This letter included the 1829 exchange with Madison. For the depositing of material in the State Department, see Hinde, "Col Aaron Burrs conspiracy in 1806," 26 September 1829, DLC: Madison Papers. For the contributions to the *American Pioneer*, a short-lived magazine that published

documents and stories of American history; see Williams, ed., "Hinde's Correspondence"; and Williams, ed., "Autographs." Hinde prepared two other narratives late in his life, one to request congressional compensation for his expenses in exposing the conspiracy and the other—the most extensive and detailed—for publication or preservation; see Hinde, petition to Congress, 20 November 1840, WHi: Draper Manuscript Collection, 6Y183–87; and Hinde, "Notes on Aaron Burrs Conspiracy of 1805–6," 16 June 1845, ibid., 11Y11–41.

14. The same recognition informs a number of works on slave conspiracies and slave conspiracy scares. See, for example, the articles in Gross, ed., "Forum"; Doolen, "Reading and Writing Terror"; Lepore, *New York Burning*; and Rothman, *Flush Times and Fever Dreams*.

15. For other works that study the hotly contested disputes over the meaning of an event more than the seemingly inaccessible reality of the event itself, see Bonomi, *Lord Cornbury Scandal*; Fox, *Trials of Intimacy*; Brewer, *Sentimental Murder*; French, *Rebellious Slave*; Williams, *Death of Captain Cook*; and Hinds, *"Horrid Popish Plot."*

16. In addition to his essays as "The Fredonian" in the *Scioto Gazette* (Ohio) (beginning 9 October 1806) and titled "The Western Expedition" (beginning 19 February 1807) in the *Fredonian* (Ohio), Hinde had prepared a brief history of his work to defeat the conspiracy in March 1808 as a deponent in the case of Ohio senator John Smith; see Hinde, deposition, 17 March 1808, OCHi: Papers in the Defense of John Smith of Ohio.

17. Waller Taylor to William Henry Harrison, 12 January 1807, in Esarey, ed., *Messages and Letters of William Henry Harrison*, 1:201. For early uses of the phrase "enveloped in mystery" (or a close variant), see William Plumer, diary entry, 24 December 1806, in *WPMP*, 540; John Rhea to Jonathan Dayton, 21 January 1807, MiU-C: Jonathan Dayton Papers; John Stokely to Thomas Jefferson, 14 February 1807, DLC: Thomas Jefferson Papers; and Thomas Truxton to Thomas Tingey, 16 February 1807, DLC: Thomas Truxton Papers.

18. Abigail Adams to Mercy Otis Warren, 9 March 1807, in Gelles, ed., *Abigail Adams*, 771. Adams referred to Ann Radcliffe's gothic novel, *The Castle of Udolpho* (1794). For the continued use of "enveloped in mystery," see William A. Burwell, circular letter to constituents, 2 March 1807, in *CLC*, 1:511; Thomas Tudor Tucker to John Page, 5 March 1807, DLC: Thomas Tudor Tucker Papers; and John Randolph to Joseph H. Nicholson, 25 March 1807, DLC: Joseph H. Nicholson Papers.

19. Schultz, *Travels on an Inland Voyage*, 1:165.

20. Robert R. Livingston to Madison, 22 March 1807, DLC: Madison Papers.

21. Jacob Burnet to John Smith, 13 March 1808, OCHi: Papers in the Defense of John Smith of Ohio.

22. Henry Dearborn to James Wilkinson, 21 January 1807, DNA: RG107, M6. See also Tucker to Page, 5 March 1807, DLC: Tucker Papers.

23. Important works on the Burr Conspiracy include McCaleb, *Aaron Burr Conspiracy*; Abernethy, *Burr Conspiracy*; Melton, *Aaron Burr*; and Stewart, *American Emperor*. It is also covered at length in the major biographies of Burr; see, in particular, Wandell and Minnigerode, *Aaron Burr*; Lomask, *Aaron Burr*; and Isenberg, *Fallen Founder*. For historiographical overviews, see Pratt, "Aaron Burr and the Historians"; and Blackwood, "Aaron Burr Conspiracy."

24. Edward Tiffin to Joseph Buell, 20 January 1807, OClWHi: Joseph Buell Papers.

25. Wilkinson, testimony, 20 June 1807, in "NECAB," 67. Explaining to the court why he had burned a letter from Wilkinson during the crisis, John McKee simply stated that he had seen "men arrested for a much less matter than carrying such a letter" (John McKee, testimony, 3 October 1807, in *TCAB*, 3:307).

26. Daveiss, "General John Adair," 231. See also Quisenberry, *Life and Times of Hon. Humphrey Marshall*, 96.

27. Jefferson, special message, 8 April 1808, in *CMPP*, 1:450. For Jefferson's papers, see Julian P. Boyd, "A General View of the Work," in Boyd et al., eds., *Papers of Thomas Jefferson*, 1:x–xviii. For Jefferson's daily log, see Jefferson, "Epistolary Record or Summary Journal of Letters," 1783–1826, DLC: Jefferson Papers. For the polygraph machine, see Malone, *Jefferson and His Time*, 4:419–21.

28. The richest discussion of Jefferson as a letter writer is in Burstein, *Inner Jefferson*. Though old, the two most useful biographies for the public Jefferson are Malone, *Jefferson and His Time*; and Peterson, *Thomas Jefferson and the New Nation*.

29. *Proofs*, 9.

30. Jefferson, "Memorandum on Correspondence with James Wilkinson," enclosed in Jefferson to Ezekial Bacon, 6 March 1811, in *PTJ: RS*, 3:428. Many of these activities are apparent in a single letter from the summer of 1806; see Wilkinson to John Brown, [5 August 1806], CtY: Colonel John Brown and Major General Preston Brown Papers. In July 1807, Lieutenant Edmund P. Gaines informed the president that Wilkinson had altered one of his reports before having it published in a New Orleans newspaper; see Edmund P. Gaines, note on Gaines to Wilkinson, 4 March 1807, enclosed in Gaines to Jefferson, 21 July 1807, DLC: Jefferson Papers. John Randolph, the foreman of the Richmond grand jury, believed that Wilkinson had been active "erasing[,] interlining etc." his papers even beyond the cipher letter (Randolph to Nicholson, 1 September 1808, DLC: Nicholson Papers). The disappearance of the letters to Jefferson was detected, and attributed to Wilkinson, almost immediately; see George Hay to Caesar A. Rodney, 6 December 1807, DeHi: H. Fletcher Brown Collection of Rodney Family Papers. Wilkinson still awaits a scholarly biographer. The best of the popular biographies are Jacobs, *Tarnished Warrior*; and Linklater, *Artist in Treason*.

31. *MAB*, 2:375. For the loss of the Burr papers, see Mary-Jo Kline and Joanne Wood Ryan, "Preface: The History of Burr's Papers" and "Editorial Note: Burr's 'Conspiracy,'" in *PCAB*, 1:xxx–xxxii and 2:918–25.

32. Lord Selkirk, diary entry, 17 March 1804, in White, ed., *Lord Selkirk's Diary*, 257–58. Some Burr letters were stolen from Blennerhassett's descendants by William H. Safford, the editor of *The Blennerhassett Papers* (1864); I discuss the history of the Blennerhassett papers in "'Bring Them *to Light.*'" For a group of Burr letters that Davis gave to Mrs. John Davis in 1839, see Ford, ed., "Some Papers of Aaron Burr." A file of Burr papers that Mississippi newspaper editor and historian J.F.H. Claiborne claimed would "explain much that [had] hitherto been conjectural" was lost when his home burned in 1884 ([J.F.H. Claiborne], "Incidents of the Detention of Aaron Burr by the Civil Authorities of the Mississippi Territory," *Free Trader* [Natchez, Miss.], 17 November 1841, WHi: Draper Manuscript Collection, 26CC28). I discuss the uncertain authorship of the cipher letter and some of the accounts of conversations with Burr in Chapter 5.

33. Plumer, diary entry, 29 November 1806, in *WPMP*, 518.

34. In recent years, a number of historians have experimented with new ways of writing history books. I have found especially inspiring: Davis, *Return of Martin Guerre*; Royster, *Destructive War*; Ayers, *Promise of the New South*; Goodman, *Stories of Scottsboro*; Jordan, *Tumult and Silence at Second Creek*; and Fox, *Trials of Intimacy*.

CHAPTER I. SO MANY STORIES: THE CIRCULATION OF INFORMATION IN THE EARLY REPUBLIC

1. John Randolph to Joseph H. Nicholson, 30 April 1805, DLC: Joseph H. Nicholson Papers. For Wheaton as Burr's landlord, see Joseph Wheaton, deposition, 13 February 1811, in [Bacon], *Report of the Committee*, 203–4.

2. Nicholson to Randolph, 24 May 1805, DLC: Nicholson Papers.

3. "Queries," *United States' Gazette* (Philadelphia), 27 July 1805.

4. [William Duane], *Aurora General Advertiser* (Philadelphia), 30 July 1805. For a similar response, see, for example, [Daniel Bradford], "Col. Burr," *Kentucky Gazette and General Advertiser* (Lexington), 3 September 1805.

5. Henry Dearborn to James Wilkinson, 24 August 1805, ICHi: James Wilkinson Papers; Daniel Clark to Wilkinson, 7 September 1805, in *Proofs*, Appendix, 140, 141. For Burr's stay in New Orleans, see William C. C. Claiborne to James Madison, 6 August 1805, in *TPUS*, 9:489.

6. John Adams to Benjamin Rush, 4 December 1805, in Schutz and Adair, eds., *Spur of Fame*, 45. "Enterprises of great pith" is from Hamlet's "to be or not to be" soliloquy (*Hamlet*, 3.1.85). For the anonymous letters to Jefferson, see "Your Friend" to Thomas Jefferson, [1 December 1805], in McLaughlin, ed., *To His Excellency Thomas Jefferson*, 5; and "A Freind" [*sic*] to Jefferson, [5 December 1805], DLC: Thomas Jefferson Papers.

7. Caesar A. Rodney to Jefferson, 4 January 1807, DLC: Jefferson Papers.

8. Thomas Truxton to Thomas Tingey, 1 June 1807, DLC: Thomas Truxton Papers.
9. General books on this subject include Pred, *Urban Growth and the Circulation*; Brown, *Knowledge is Power*; Warner, *Letters of the Republic*; Ziff, *Writing in the New Nation*; and Gross and Kelley, eds., *Extensive Republic*. For recent work on the postal system, see Kielbowicz, *News in the Mail*; John, *Spreading the News*; and Bergmann, "Delivering a Nation." Narrower studies of particular interest for understanding the Burr Conspiracy include Bretz, "Early Land Communication"; Hecht, "Burr Conspiracy and the Post Office"; and Southerland and Brown, *Federal Road*, 22–31. For the press, see Mott, *American Journalism*; Smith, *Press, Politics, and Patronage*; Leonard, *News for All*; Humphrey, *Press of the Young Republic*; Pasley, *"Tyranny of Printers"*; Brooke, "To Be 'Read by the Whole People'"; and Steffen, "Newspapers for Free." Of particular interest for the Burr Conspiracy is Rayman, "Frontier Journalism in Kentucky." Historians have also addressed the very different, less formal systems that moved information among slaves and Native Americans. See, for example, Sidbury, *Ploughshares into Swords*; Merrell, *Into the American Woods*, 179–224; Nicholls, *Whispers of Rebellion*; and Dowd, *Groundless*.
10. Gideon Granger to [Jefferson], [14/]16 October 1806, in Henshaw, ed., "Burr-Blennerhassett Documents," 10, 12.
11. Jefferson, memorandum, 15 April 1806, in *Anas*, 237. Eaton's meetings with Burr were the subject of Granger's conversation with Ely in mid-October; they are discussed at length in Chapter 5.
12. Duncan Cameron to Walter Alves, 29 June 1807, in *RASP*, Series J, Part 13, Walter Alves Papers.
13. Cuming, *Sketches of a Tour*, 73–74.
14. "From the Register of Monday," *Enquirer* (Richmond, Va.), 11 November 1806, clipped from *Political and Commercial Register* (Philadelphia).
15. In addition to the works about the postal system cited in n. 9 above, see White, *Jeffersonians*, 299–335. Figures for the expansion of post offices and post roads were calculated using the table in ibid., 303. The figure for post-road mileage is somewhat misleading since the same stretch of road might be counted multiple times and some of the expansion relied upon existing roads.
16. Blaize Cenas to Abraham Bradley Jr., 7 January 1807, L-M: Cenas Family Papers. Most of the mail routes that existed at the time of the Burr crisis appear in Bradley, *Map of the United States*; the southernmost route, through Georgia, was added later.
17. Jesse Bledsoe to John Breckinridge, 30 December 1805, in *TPUS*, 13:364.
18. Daniel Smith to Andrew Jackson, 29 December 1806, in *PAJ*, 2:127. See also Leonard Covington to Alexander Covington, 19 December 1806, Ms-Ar: Wailes-Covington Family Papers; and Thomas Worthington to Nathaniel Massie, 24 December 1806, in Massie, *Nathaniel Massie*, 240.

19. Truxton to Charles Biddle, 30 May 1807, in Biddle, *Autobiography of Charles Biddle*, 410. For use of a ship's bag, see Daniel Constable to his parents, 17 March 1807, in Jenkins, *Citizen Daniel*, 106.

20. Thomas Goode to Samuel Johnston, 4 December 1807, NcU: Miscellaneous Letters. Goode foolishly placed his warning in a postscript. For public readings of private letters and various measures to preserve secrecy, see Decker, *Epistolary Practices*; John, *Spreading the News*, 42–44, 156–61; Freeman, *Affairs of Honor*, 114–16; Bannet, *Empire of Letters*; and Henkin, *Postal Age*, 103–6.

21. Wilkinson to Dearborn, 12 November 1806, DNA: RG107, M221, W-209 (3).

22. Granger, circular letter, 18 December 1806, in Hecht, "Burr Conspiracy and the Post Office," 134. This article includes numerous letters from Granger to postmasters and postriders from December 1806 that evince his concerns.

23. William Preston to James Breckinridge, 30 December 1806, ViU: James Breckinridge Papers.

24. Granger to "express courier," 20 December 1806, in Hecht, "Burr Conspiracy and the Post Office," 136.

25. Granger to Robert Strothart, 20 December 1806, in ibid., 135. For Granger, see Hamlin, *Gideon Granger.*

26. William Plumer, diary entry, 21 December 1806, in *WPMP*, 535. In August 1806, the editor of Kentucky's *Palladium* noted that eighty copies of each issue went out either as exchange copies or "to postmasters who act[ed] as agents for" the newspaper ([William Hunter], *Palladium* [Frankfort, Ky.], 28 August 1806).

27. The key resources for early newspapers are Brigham, *History and Bibliography of American Newspapers*; and Brigham, *Additions and Corrections*. I have calculated the figures in this and the following paragraph using Lathem, comp., *Chronological Tables*, 44–75. Some newspapers, particularly short-lived ones, may have been missed in Brigham's and Lathem's lists. For the form and content of early American newspapers and the duties of early American editors, see the general works on the press cited in n. 9 above.

28. The Indiana Territory may have been between newspapers in late 1806 and early 1807, with the *Indiana Gazette* (Vincennes) having folded and the *Western Sun* (Vincennes) not yet having started; see Lathem, comp., *Chronological Tables*, 48. For a thoughtful analysis of newspaper partisanship in the early republic, see Pasley, *"Tyranny of Printers."*

29. Nathaniel Macon to Nicholson, 31 January 1806, DLC: Nicholson Papers.

30. [Ephraim Pentland], *Commonwealth* (Pittsburgh, Pa.), 24 December 1806. For the *Intelligencer*'s relationship with the Jefferson administration, see Smith, *Press, Politics, and Patronage*, 24–38; and Ames, *History of the* National Intelligencer, 37–67. Even the *Intelligencer*, according to one account did "not publish more than one third, or at most, one half of what [was] spoken" in the House of Representatives (George Hoadley to Jeremiah Evarts, 5 February 1807, ViHi: George Hoadley Letter).

31. *Virginia Gazette, and General Advertiser* (Richmond), 6 May 1807, clipped from *Charleston Courier* (S.C.).

32. Thomas Spotswood Hinde, "Notes on Aaron Burrs Conspiracy of 1805–6," 16 June 1845, WHi: Draper Manuscript Collection, 11Y40–41. For the *Morning Chronicle*, see Isenberg, *Fallen Founder*, 247–48. Gardener's newspaper was the *Commentator*, but he later described it as "a federal paper" (J[ames] B. Gardener to Paul Fearing, 30 December 1819, OMC: Samuel P. Hildreth Collection). I discuss Burr's connection to the *Impartial Observer* in Chapter 8.

33. Randolph to Caesar A. Rodney, 28 February [1806], DLC: Rodney Family Papers.

34. "Important," *United States' Gazette*, 31 December 1806.

35. Wilkinson to Jefferson, 21 October 1806, DLC: Burr Conspiracy Collection. For similar concerns, see Edmund P. Gaines to Dearborn, 17 February 1807, DNA: RG107, M221, G-103 (3); and Silas Dinsmore to Dearborn, 23 February 1807, ibid., D-135 (3).

36. Ninian Edwards to William Wirt, [5 January 1807], ICHi: Ninian Edwards Papers. In western Pennsylvania a month earlier, some people had attributed the lack of paper for printing newspapers to Burr's supporters; see "Pennsylvania," *Political Observatory* (Walpole, N.H.), 16 January 1807 (from AHN).

37. Daniel Smith to Andrew Jackson, 19 December 1806, in Bassett, ed., *Correspondence of Andrew Jackson*, 1:157.

38. Granger to Jefferson, 22 February 1814, in *PTJ: RS*, 7:206. Jefferson recalled that Pease "executed [these] trusts to my satisfaction" (Jefferson to Granger, 9 March 1814, in ibid., 236).

39. Granger to Robert Williams, 20 December 1806, Ms-Ar: Territorial Governors' Records, series 488, Administration Papers.

40. Granger to Claiborne, 8 January 1807, DNA: RG28, M601. See Seth Pease to Granger, 19 January 1807, GU: Joseph Wheaton Papers. In late November 1806, after travelling from Kentucky to New Orleans, Nathaniel Cox explained the derangement of the western mails very differently. "Every rider was drunk and behind his engagements," he reported, though "swearing to the most shameful falshoods about the waters" (Nathaniel Cox to Gabriel Lewis, 23 November 1806, L-M: Nathaniel Cox Papers).

41. John Tompkins to Cameron, 30 June 1807, NcU: Cameron Family Papers.

42. For a brilliant examination of the system of information exchange that developed among the elite of seventeenth- and early eighteenth-century England, see Shapin, *Social History of Truth*. For an equally compelling study of letter writing and reading, see Bannet, *Empire of Letters*. For the spread of these practices to colonial America, see Shields, *Civil Tongues and Polite Letters*; Bonomi, *Lord Cornbury Scandal*; and Dierks, *In My Power*. Their continued importance in the early American republic is apparent in Stowe, *Intimacy and Power in the Old South*, 24–30; Perl-Rosenthal, "Private Letters and Public Diplomacy"; and, especially, Freeman, *Affairs of Honor*.

43. William T. Barry to John Barry, 6 December 1806, in Cox, ed., "Letters of William T. Barry," 329; same to same, 2 January 1807, in ibid., 330.

44. Edward Hooker, diary entry, 31 December 1806, in Jameson, ed., "Diary of Edward Hooker," 903.

45. John Quincy Adams to Louisa Catherine Adams, 8 December 1806, MHi: Adams Family Papers. Don Adriano de Armada is the "fantastical Spaniard" in Shakespeare's *Love's Labours Lost*. I discuss the references to Burr as Catiline and to Wilkinson as Leonidas in Chapter 7.

46. Cuming, *Sketches of a Tour*, 74. For conversation and correspondence among gentlemen, see, in addition to the works cited in n. 42 above, Kaplan, *Men of Letters*.

47. Cuming, *Sketches of a Tour*, 71, 72. While the nature, and even existence, of political parties in this era have long been disputed among historians and political scientists, the Quids pose particular problems. One can find Quids in New York politics, in Pennsylvania politics, and in federal politics, but the three groups were distinct from each other. In each case, "quid," or "tertium quid" ("third something"), was more often used with derogatory connotations by the group's political opponents than by its own members or supporters. Fifty years ago, the historian Noble E. Cunningham Jr. made a convincing case that the term is too problematic to use; see Cunningham, "Who Were the Quids?" But it has survived for each of these groups. I use it to refer only to the group of mostly southern Republicans, whether in Congress during the Burr crisis or not, who were linked with Virginia's John Randolph. I acknowledge that by doing so I adopt the usage of Jefferson and his supporters—whom some of Randolph's allies called Quids for drifting toward Federalist principles and policies. When I quote authors who obviously meant another Quid group, I will make that clear in the notes. For the various versions of Quids, see also Risjord, *Old Republicans*, 40–95; Carson, "That Ground Called Quiddism"; and Shankman, "Malcontents and Tertium Quids."

48. John Watkins, speech, 16 March 1807, in *Debate in the House of Representatives of the Territory of Orleans*, 20. For the impact of partisanship on nationalism and on the circulation and evaluation of information, see, in particular, Waldstreicher, *In the Midst of Perpetual Fetes*; Onuf, *Jefferson's Empire*; Pasley, "*Tyranny of Printers*"; and Robertson, "'Look on This Picture.'"

49. [Thomas Ritchie], *Enquirer*, 13 December 1806.

50. James Brown to Benjamin Parke, 5 December 1806, InHi: Albert G. Porter Papers.

51. Jefferson to John Norvell, 14 [*sic*, 11] June 1807, in *WoTJ*, 10:417 [corrected against original in DLC: Jefferson Papers]. Convinced that a newspaper that committed itself to "true facts & sound principles only" could not survive, Jefferson suggested that an editor might commence the process of reform by dividing his newspaper into four parts: "Truths," "Probabilities," "Possibilities," and "Lies." The first of these sections "would be very short,"

while the third and fourth would be "for those readers who would rather have lies for their money than the blank paper they would occupy" (ibid., 417–18).

52. Harry Toulmin to Peter Philip Schuyler, 15 February 1807, ICHi: Wilkinson Papers.

53. William Wirt to Edwards, 2 August 1807, ICHi: Edwards Papers.

54. David Gailard to [Charles] Ellis and [Jonathan] Allen, 7 July 1807, DLC: Ellis & Allan Co. Papers. See also the letters to Ellis and Allan from John Hartwell Cocke of 20 May and 18 and 25 June 1807, ibid. For the merchants' replies, see Ellis and Allan to Cocke, 25 May and 13 July 1807, ViU: John Hartwell Cocke Papers.

55. Thomas Power to Stephen Minor, 6 December 1806, ICN: Everett D. Graff Collection of Western Americana, Thomas Power Letter; Randolph to Nicholson, 1 September 1808, DLC: Nicholson Papers; John F. May to Thomas Ruffin, [16 June 1808], in Hamilton, ed., *Papers of Thomas Ruffin*, 1:120.

56. James Sterrett to Nathaniel Evans, 18 June 1807, LU: Evans (Nathaniel and Family) Papers.

57. John Smith to Jonathan Dayton, 29 December 1807, MiU-C: Jonathan Dayton Papers. At some times and places, government officials did intercept the correspondence of suspected conspirators, though this action does not seem to have been authorized by the administration.

58. Duane to Caesar A. Rodney, 28 January 1807, PHi: Simon Gratz Autograph Collection.

59. Elizabeth House Trist to Mary Gilmer, 15 June 1807, LNHiC: Elizabeth House Trist Letter.

60. Jefferson to Elias Glover, 13 January 1810, DLC: Jefferson Papers.

61. John Rhea to Dayton, 21 January 1807, MiU-C: Dayton Papers.

62. [Stanley Griswold] to Duane, 16 October 1806, in Ford, ed., "Letters of William Duane," 286–87. I attribute this letter to Griswold based on its similarities to Griswold to Elijah Boardman, 10 October 1806, MiD-B: Stanley Griswold Papers.

63. Jefferson to John Smith, 7 May 1807, in *WrTJ*, 11:203.

64. Wyllys Silliman to Albert Gallatin, 12 December 1806, in *PAG*.

65. Benjamin Henry Latrobe, diary entry, 11 December 1806, in Carter, Van Horne, and Formwalt, eds., *Journals of Benjamin Henry Latrobe*, 3:105.

66. William Eaton, testimony, 18 August 1807, in *RTCAB*, 1:484. Eaton quoted the English novelist Samuel Jackson Pratt's *The Pupil of Pleasure, or The New System (Lord Chesterfield's) Illustrated* (1776)—a controversial satire of Chesterfield's famous letters.

67. Truxton to Timothy Pickering, 13 January 1807, MHi: Timothy Pickering Papers.

68. Lewis Kerr to Isaac Briggs, 30 August 1807, MdHi: Briggs-Stabler Papers. For officials' efforts to overcome this view, see Claiborne to Joseph Deville Degoutin

Bellechasse, 7 January 1807, in *OLBWC*, 4:85; and Granger to Rufus Easton, 9 April 1807, in Bay, *Reminiscences of the Bench and Bar of Missouri*, 601–2.

69. James Wilson to Madison, 21 November 1806, DLC: Burr Conspiracy Collection.

70. John Graham to Madison, 22 November 1806, enclosed in same to same, 28 November 1806, ibid. (the italics mark a coded passage that I deciphered).

71. Graham to Alexander Henderson Jr., 12 February 1807, OHi: John Graham Letters.

72. Graham, deposition, 5 February 1807, enclosed in ibid.

73. Graham to Madison, 22 November 1806, enclosed in same to same, 28 November 1806, DLC: Burr Conspiracy Collection. Graham was writing about Alexander's brother John, but the statement applied to both.

74. Truxton to Tingey, 1 June 1807, DLC: Truxton Papers. For a similar opinion, see "Col. Burr," 364.

75. Nicholson to Randolph, 24 May 1805, DLC: Nicholson Papers.

76. Samuel Taggart to John Taylor, 18 February 1807, in "Letters of Samuel Taggart," 212–13.

77. "Extracts of letters from Washington to the Editor of the United States' Gazette," *United States' Gazette*, 26 December 1806.

78. Peter Burr to Worthington, 11 January 1807, OHi: Thomas Worthington Papers.

79. Macon to Nicholson, 30 January 1807, DLC: Nicholson Papers.

80. Claiborne to Wilkinson, 17 January 1807, in *OLBWC*, 4:99–100. See also Caesar A. Rodney to Jefferson, 9 November 1806, DLC: Jefferson Papers; and Daniel Smith to Andrew Jackson, 29 December 1806, in *PAJ*, 2:127.

81. Nathan Williams to Madison, 5 September 1806, DLC: James Madison Papers; Claiborne to Madison, 18 November 1806, in *OLBWC*, 4:36; [Ritchie], "Burr's Conspiracy," *Enquirer*, 22 January 1807.

82. James Taylor to Madison, 13 October 1806, in Padgett, ed., "Letters of James Taylor," 114. For Condit's letter, see John Condit to Silas Condit, 6 January 1807, PHi: Gratz Autograph Collection.

83. [Duane] to Madison, undated [received 5 February 1807], DLC: Jefferson Papers.

84. Elizabeth Wirt to William Wirt, 26 March 1807, MdHi: William Wirt Papers. Gabriel Duvall was the comptroller of the treasury; James Gibbon was the customs collector in Richmond.

85. James Winchester to Andrew Jackson, 6 January 1807, in *PAJ*, 2:138.

86. Nathaniel Saltonstall Jr. to Leverett Saltonstall, 26 June 1807, in Moody, ed., *Saltonstall Papers*, 2:377.

87. Chandler Price to Caesar A. Rodney, 22 July 1807, DeHi: Rodney Collection.

88. "Communication," *Enquirer*, 7 November 1806.

89. [Pentland], *Commonwealth*, 31 December 1806.

90. [John Wood], "The Kentucky Spanish Association, Blount's Conspiracy, and General Miranda's Expedition," *Western World* (Frankfort, Ky.), 7 July 1806.

91. [Stephen C. Carpenter], *People's Friend & Daily Advertiser* (New York), 6 January 1807.

92. [Samuel H. Smith], *National Intelligencer, and Washington Advertiser* (D.C.), 15 August 1806.

93. John G. Jackson to Madison, 26 March 1807, ViU: James Madison Correspondence; *Enquirer*, 19 May 1807; Andrew Jackson to Daniel Smith, 11 February 1807, in *PAJ*, 2:154; Harry Innes to Wilson Cary Nicholas, 7 February 1808, DLC: Wilson Cary Nicholas Papers.

94. Thomas Rodney to Caesar A. Rodney, 30 December 1806, DLC: Rodney Family Papers.

95. John Bigger Jr. to James Findlay, 17 January 1807, in Cox, ed., "Selections from the Torrence Papers," 4:119.

96. Truxton to Jefferson, 23 January 1807, DLC: Jefferson Papers.

97. Edward Tiffin to Worthington, 18 January 1807, OHi: Worthington Papers.

98. John G. Jackson to Dayton, 9 February 1807, PHi: Gratz Autograph Collection.

99. Parke to Brown, 22 January 1807, InHi: Porter Papers.

100. "Extract of a letter from a gentleman of unquestionable character," *American, and Commercial Daily Advertiser* (Baltimore, Md.), 6 March 1807. In this case, the "gentleman" was Wilkinson, and the letter included a number of misleading statements.

101. Bigger to Findlay, 17 January 1807, in Cox, ed., "Selections from the Torrence Papers," 4:118.

102. "Extract of a letter from a gentleman in Erie, Penn., to a member of Congress," *National Intelligencer*, 29 December 1806; Lonson Nash to William Woodbridge, 5 January 1807, MiD-B: William Woodbridge Papers.

103. "Extract of a letter, dated Washington City," *New-York Evening Post*, 20 December 1806. For a similar lesson that was derived from Burr's trial in Richmond, see Randolph to John Marshall, 1 May 1826, in *PJMar*, 10:286–87.

104. Littleton Waller Tazewell to James Monroe, 3 January 1807, DLC: James Monroe Papers.

105. Caesar A. Rodney to Jefferson, 9 November 1806, DLC: Jefferson Papers. Rodney referred to a letter from a Federalist merchant in Pittsburgh to a Federalist senator in Washington; the letter that was mentioned in the *Commonwealth* (see above, n. 89) may have been between the same correspondents.

106. Charles Stewart to Worthington, 21 December 1806, OHi: Worthington Papers.

107. Joseph Bryan to Randolph, 8 March 1807, Vi: Bryan Family Papers.

108. Wilkinson to Jefferson, 1 March 1807, DLC: Burr Conspiracy Collection. See also Claiborne to Madison, 28 February 1807, ibid.

109. On conspiratorial thinking, see, in particular, Bailyn, *Ideological Origins of the American Revolution*; Wood, "Conspiracy and the Paranoid Style"; Hutson, "Origins of 'The Paranoid Style'"; White, "Value of Conspiracy Theory"; and Pfau, *Political Style of Conspiracy*. A common reference point for this issue is Hofstadter, *Paranoid Style in American Politics*. A quick check of various online databases—of newspapers, periodicals, pamphlets, and books—for this period makes clear the relative infrequency of "the Burr Conspiracy" compared with "Burr's Conspiracy." The scholarship on character and reputation in this period is extensive; see, in particular, Adair, "Fame and the Founding Fathers"; Wyatt-Brown, *Southern Honor*; Bushman, *Refinement of America*; Freeman, *Affairs of Honor*; and Trees, *The Founding Fathers and the Politics of Character*.

110. Randolph to Monroe, [5 December 1806], DLC: Monroe Papers. For recent works on the election of 1800, see Horn, Lewis, and Onuf, eds., *Revolution of 1800*; Larson, *Magnificent Catastrophe*; and Sharp, *Deadlocked Election of 1800*. In general, recent works have absolved Burr of the worst of the contemporary charges against him; see also Freeman, *Affairs of Honor*; and Isenberg, *Fallen Founder*. For a different, and quite persuasive, assessment, see Baker, "'Attack Well Directed.'"

111. Plumer, diary entry, 26 December 1806, in *WPMP*, 542.

112. Robert R. Livingston to Madison, 22 March 1807, DLC: Madison Papers.

113. William Creighton to Worthington, 25 January 1807, OHi: Worthington Papers. See also *Enquirer*, 7 November 1806; and John Adams to Rush, 2 February 1807, in Schutz and Adair, eds., *Spur of Fame*, 76.

114. Randolph to Nicholson, 28 June 1807, DLC: Nicholson Papers. Much of the historiography of the Burr Conspiracy divides along the authors' assessments of the character—and reliability—of these three men. The early historiography is discussed, in part, in these terms in Pratt, "Aaron Burr and the Historians." For obvious, recent examples of this phenomenon, see Kennedy, *Burr, Hamilton, and Jefferson*; and Wheelan, *Jefferson's Vendetta*.

115. [Samuel H. Smith], "Aaron Burr," *National Intelligencer*, 12 November 1806.

116. [James Cheetham], "Mr. Burr," *American Citizen* (New York), 8 December 1806.

117. Ellis and Allan to John Heathcock and Co., 10 March 1807, DLC: Ellis & Allan Co. Papers.

118. I discuss the Burr Conspiracy in the context of these fears in Chapters 4 and 7. Important works on rumor and gossip include Allport and Postman, *Psychology of Rumor*; Shibutani, *Improvised News*; Rosnow and Fine, *Rumor and Gossip*; Spacks, *Gossip*; Kapferer, *Rumors*; and Fine, Campion-Vincent, and Heath, eds., *Rumor Mills*. Historians of early America have made good use of these works; see, for example, Shields, *Civil Tongues and Polite Letters*; Bonomi, *Lord Cornbury Scandal*; and Dowd, *Groundless*.

119. Benjamin Henry Latrobe to Philip Mazzei, 19 December 1806, in *CBHL*, 2:333.

120. John G. Jackson to Madison, 26 March 1807, ViU: Madison Correspondence.
121. Joseph Browne to Madison, 17 February 1807, in *TPUS*, 14:98. In December 1806, one Pittsburgh editor had reported that, even as many people around the country were looking to his city for information about the conspiracy, locals were seeking their "information from Kentucky, and the more western points— and while we are staring to the westward, [were often] surprised with budgets [of news] from the east" [Pentland], "Burr's Conspiracy," *Commonwealth*, 24 December 1806.
122. For a similar argument, see Joanne Freeman's discussion of the various forms of written matter that were used in affairs of honor and David Waldstreicher's examination of the coverage of political celebrations in the partisan press in *Affairs of Honor* and *In the Midst of Perpetual Fetes*, respectively.

FIRST INTERLUDE. A CRISIS IN THE CABINET

1. "Extract of a letter from Alexandria in Virginia," 29 October 1806, copied in Jonathan Hamilton to Duncan Cameron, 4 November 1806, NcU: Cameron Family Papers.
2. Ralph Izard Jr. to Alice Izard, 29 October 1806, SCU: Ralph Izard Papers. For Washington at this time, see Young, *Washington Community*; and Green, *Washington*.
3. "Extract of a letter from Alexandria in Virginia," 29 October 1806, copied in Hamilton to Cameron, 4 November 1806, NcU: Cameron Family Papers.
4. "Another letter says," *Enquirer* (Richmond, Va.), 11 November 1806. See also "Extract of a letter from a gentleman at Washington," ibid. The *Enquirer* also included a piece explaining that the ordering of the marines to New Orleans was "not a new measure," but an old policy that had been adopted in response to Spanish activity in the region ("Western Country," ibid.).
5. Thomas Jefferson, memorandum, 22 October 1806, in *Anas*, 246–47. The cases in which the cabinet preferred the district attorney (Kentucky, Tennessee, and the Louisiana Territory) to the governor (Ohio and the Indiana, Mississippi, and Orleans Territories) for these confidential letters are revealing. The district attorney for Kentucky, Joseph Hamilton Daveiss, had been providing the administration with information about Burr for months. The governor of Tennessee, John Sevier, might have seemed unreliable due to his involvement in an earlier separatist scheme. The absent Wilkinson was the governor of the Louisiana Territory. For the origins of Jefferson's "Anas," see Freeman, *Affairs of Honor*, 62–104; and Cogliano, *Thomas Jefferson*, 74–105. These works focus upon the material from the 1790s; the memoranda of Jefferson's cabinet meetings were added to the "Anas" after his death.
6. Jefferson, memorandum, 24 October 1806, in *Anas*, 247–48. Although the reasons for empowering Graham to replace Wilkinson were not recorded, one

consideration was surely the fact that the acting governor was Burr's brother-in-law, the territorial secretary Joseph Browne.

7. Jefferson, memorandum, 25 October 1806, in ibid., 248.

8. Jefferson, memorandum, 22 October 1806, in ibid., 246. I discuss the comparisons of Burr to Catiline in Chapter 7.

9. Henry Dearborn to James Wilkinson, 24 August 1805, ICHi: James Wilkinson Papers. The cabinet was already perturbed at Wilkinson for disregarding an order, which he had received in mid-June in St. Louis, to go first to New Orleans and then to the southwestern frontier to take charge of the troops and defenses; see Jefferson, memorandum, 22 October 1806, in *Anas*, 247.

10. Jefferson, memorandum, 22 October 1806, in *Anas*, 246.

11. Jefferson, special message, 22 January 1807, in *CMPP*, 1:412.

12. Jefferson to Gideon Granger, 9 March 1814, in *PTJ: RS*, 7:236.

13. Jefferson to Katherine Duane Morgan, 26 June 1822, in *WoTJ*, 10:291n. Jefferson had said essentially the same thing to George Morgan fifteen years earlier; see Jefferson to George Morgan, 26 March 1807, in *WrTJ*, 11:174.

14. William Tilghman, "Memorandum," 18 November 1806, ViU: Tracy W. McGregor Autograph Collection. For the surviving letters, see Nathan Williams to James Madison, 5 September 1806, DLC: James Madison Papers; Presley Neville and Samuel Roberts to Madison, 7 October 1806, DLC: Burr Conspiracy Collection; and Granger to [Jefferson], [14/]16 October 1806, in Henshaw, ed., "Burr-Blennerhassett Documents," 10–13. The missing letter from Morgan to Jefferson was dated 29 August and received 15 September; see Jefferson, "Epistolary Record or Summary Journal of Letters," 1783–1826, DLC: Thomas Jefferson Papers. Neville and Roberts did not name Morgan as their source; that he was is clear from George Morgan to Neville, 2 September 1806, ViU: McGregor Autograph Collection. For Morgan's testimony, see George Morgan, testimony, 16 June 1807, in "NECAB," 37; and George Morgan, testimony, 19 August 1807, in *TCAB*, 2:151–56.

15. Jefferson to John Nicholson, 19 September 1806, in *WoTJ*, 10:292n. The missing letter was dated 6 September and received 18 September; see Jefferson, "Epistolary Record," 1783–1826, DLC: Jefferson Papers.

16. Nicholson to Jefferson, 14 October 1806, in *TJC*, 135–36.

17. "Your Friend" to Jefferson, [1 December 1805], in McLaughlin, ed., *To His Excellency Thomas Jefferson*, 5.

18. "A Freind [sic]" to Jefferson, [5 December 1805], DLC: Jefferson Papers.

19. The Daveiss letters, and Jefferson's response to them, are addressed in Chapters 2 and 3. Most were reprinted in *View*. How fully Jefferson shared these letters with his cabinet is unclear, though Madison probably read most of them and Gallatin saw at least the first one; see Albert Gallatin to Jefferson, 12 February 1806, in Adams, ed., *Writings of Albert Gallatin*, 1:290–91. For the correspondence logs, see Jefferson, "Epistolary Record," 1783–1826, DLC: Jefferson Papers.

20. Jefferson, memorandum, 22 October 1806, in *Anas*, 246. For Jefferson's newspaper subscriptions, see Cunningham, *Jeffersonian Republicans in Power*, 254n72.

21. Eaton had met with Jefferson himself about Burr's scheme in the spring of 1806. His accounts of what he said at this meeting varied depending upon his audience. In some contexts, including under oath on two occasions, Eaton stated that he had raised the issue of western separatism with the president and warned that "Burr was a dangerous man" (William Eaton, testimony, 15 June 1807, in "NECAB," 15). But speaking directly with Granger, whom he knew was preparing a report for Jefferson, Eaton said instead that he had "waited upon the President . . . with a design to have gone into a detail[ed] representation" of what he had heard from Burr, but had been dissuaded by Jefferson's hostility to his suggestion to send Burr abroad as a minister (Granger to [Jefferson], [14/]16 October 1806, in Henshaw, ed., "Burr-Blennerhassett Documents," 13). There is no record of the meeting in *Anas*.

22. Nathan Williams to Madison, 5 September 1806, DLC: Madison Papers.

23. Dearborn to Wilkinson, 21 January 1807, DNA: RG107, M6.

24. Jefferson to George Morgan, 19 September 1806, in *WoTJ*, 10:293, 292. For Madison's letter, see Madison to Nathan Williams, 3 November 1806, National Society, Daughters of the American Revolution Archives, Washington, D.C. (photocopy at the Papers of James Madison Project, Charlottesville, Va.). There does not seem to have been a written reply either to Neville and Roberts's 7 October letter or to Granger's [14/]16 October letter.

25. Madison to Robert Williams, 4 November 1806, in *TPUS*, 5:485. Smith's 24 and 25 October letters to Preble and Decatur can be found in DNA: RG45, M149. For the new orders for Wilkinson, see Jefferson, memorandum, 8 November 1806, in *Anas*, 248; and Dearborn to Wilkinson, 8 November 1806, DNA: RG107, M6.

26. Dearborn to Constant Freeman, 27 October 1806, in *TPUS*, 9:684.

27. For Graham's reference to an initial letter from Madison, see John Graham, testimony, 24 September 1807, in *TCAB*, 3:212. Graham related the story of his mission for the court numerous times; on none of these occasions did he remember the timing as anything other than "the latter end of October."

28. Madison to Graham, 31 October 1806, DNA: RG59, entry 7, Miscellaneous Drafts of Instructions.

29. See Graham to Madison, 12 and 28 November 1806, DLC: Burr Conspiracy Collection. Graham sent at least three other reports while on Burr's trail: from Marietta in November, from Lexington in December, and from Nashville in January. There were probably others. The only one that survives in any form is an excerpt of a dispatch from Lexington that Graham included in a letter to Orleans territorial delegate Daniel Clark; see Graham to Daniel Clark, 13 May 1807, in *Proofs*, 99.

30. I discussed the Pease mission in Chapter 1.

31. For ciphers and cipher practices in this period, see Weber, *United States Diplomatic Codes and Ciphers*.
32. Graham to Madison, 12 November 1806, DLC: Burr Conspiracy Collection.
33. Graham to Madison, 28 November 1806, ibid.
34. Blennerhassett's name may have come from the newspapers and been known even at the time of the cabinet meetings. It certainly appeared in a 13 October 1806 letter from army contractor James Taylor, Madison's distant relative, in Kentucky; see Taylor to Madison, 13 October 1806, in Padgett, ed., "Letters of James Taylor," 113–16. Taylor's letter seems to have reached Madison between the last cabinet meeting and Graham's departure for the West, since Graham told Taylor that "the Government was much indebted to [him] for the valuable information [he] had given it in relation of Col. Burr's movements and his partisans" (Taylor, "Autobiography," [ca. 1834], ICU: Reuben T. Durrett Collection, Durrett Codices, 54).
35. Dayton's name had come from Nathan Williams, Smith's from Joseph Hamilton Daveiss; see Nathan Williams to Madison, 5 September 1806, DLC: Madison Papers; and Daveiss to Jefferson, 10 February 1806, in *View*, 12.

CHAPTER 2. LEXINGTON AND FRANKFORT, KENTUCKY: JULY THROUGH DECEMBER 1806

1. For Lexington and Frankfort, in particular, and Kentucky, in general, during this period, see Johnson, *History of Franklin County*; Connelley and Coulter, *History of Kentucky*; Watlington, *Partisan Spirit*; Lancaster, *Vestiges of the Venerable City*; Aron, *How the West Was Lost*; Harrison and Klotter, *New History of Kentucky*; Perkins, *Border Life*; and Friend, *Along the Maysville Road*.
2. Espy, *Memorandums of a Tour*, 8.
3. Visscher, ed., "Memoir of Lexington and Its Vicinity," 41:329. Craig Thompson Friend makes good use of Leavy's recollections of Lexington's human geography in *Along the Maysville Road*, 208–14.
4. Cuming, *Sketches of a Tour*, 183–89.
5. The *Kentucky Journal* had lasted just a few months in late 1795 and early 1796; see Jillson, *Newspapers and Periodicals of Frankfort*.
6. Cuming, *Sketches of a Tour*, 192–93.
7. Robert H. Grayson to James Madison, 1 May 1805, in *PJM: SS*, 9:306. For Olympian Springs, see "Olympian Springs" and "Spas," in Kleber et al., eds., *Kentucky Encyclopedia*, 695–96, 840. Lexington's first stagecoach line, founded in 1803, went to Olympian Springs.
8. "Wax Figures," *Kentucky Gazette and General Advertiser* (Lexington), 12 March 1805.
9. Breathitt, "Commencement of a Journal," 7.

10. "The Fredonian" [Thomas Spotswood Hinde], "The aspect of affairs in the *Western country*, [No. I]," *Scioto Gazette* (Chillicothe, Ohio), 9 October 1806.

11. [Daniel Bradford], *Kentucky Gazette*, 28 May 1805.

12. Ibid., 3 September 1805. For Burr's reception, see also "The Fredonian" [Hinde], "The aspect of affairs in the *Western country*, [No. I]," *Scioto Gazette*, 9 October 1806.

13. Samuel McDowell Jr. to Andrew Reid, 5 November 1805, in Hollingsworth, Williams, and Harris, eds., "Early Kentuckians and the New Nation," 347–48. For Burr's travels in 1805, see Abernethy, *Burr Conspiracy*, 24–37; Lomask, *Aaron Burr*, 2:56–74; Johnson, "Aaron Burr"; and Stewart, *American Emperor*, 97–115.

14. For Wood, see Durey, *Transatlantic Radicals*, 160–63; and, especially, Baker, "John Wood Weighs In." For Street, see Wilson, "General Joseph Monford [*sic*] Street"; and Rayman, "Frontier Journalism in Kentucky." For the controversy over Burr's role in the publication and suppression of Wood's *History*, see Lomask, *Aaron Burr*, 1:314–23; and Mary-Jo Kline and Joanne Wood Ryan, "Editorial Note: The Suppression of John Wood's *History*," in *PCAB*, 2:641–46. A letter from the fall of 1805 makes it clear that Wood and Street left Richmond in September, were in Frankfort by late November, and were still planning to resume their surveying trip in the spring; see John Wood to Thomas Jefferson, 26 November 1805, CSmH: Thomas Jefferson Papers. It is generally accepted that Wood and Street were romantic, as well as business, partners or, at least, that Wood hoped that they would be; see Rayman, "Frontier Journalism in Kentucky," 106–7; and Baker, "John Wood Weighs In" [an earlier draft developed this issue more fully].

15. Joseph Hamilton Daveiss to Jefferson, 10 January 1806, in *View*, 10, 11 [corrected against original in DLC: Thomas Jefferson Papers]. John Wood later claimed that Daveiss had moved against Burr "partly from a sense of neglect" over not having been approached about his project (Harman Blennerhassett, diary entry, 29 August 1807, in *BwB*, 64).

16. Daveiss to Jefferson, 10 February 1806, in *View*, 12. The list follows this letter in DLC: Jefferson Papers. For Daveiss, see Coleman, "Jo Daviess [*sic*], of Kentucky"; and the editorial introduction in Cox and Swineford, eds., *"View of the President's Conduct,"* 53–56. Cox and Swineford included the one letter to Jefferson from this period, of 5 April 1806, that Daveiss omitted; see ibid., 84n73.

17. "Prospectus of a Weekly News-Paper called the *Western World*," *Western World* (Frankfort, Ky.), 26 July 1806. Wood discussed his prior knowledge of Burr's plans and provided some of the history of the *Western World* in his next newspaper, the *Atlantic World*; see [John Wood], "From the Atlantic World," *Virginia Gazette, and General Advertiser* (Richmond), 28 January 1807; and [Wood], "Col. Burr's Conspiracy," *Atlantic World* (Washington, D.C.), 3 February 1807.

18. [Wood], "The Kentucky Spanish Association, Blount's Conspiracy, and Gen. Miranda's Expedition," *Western World*, 7 July 1806. For these conspiracies, see,

in particular, Robertson, *Life of Miranda*; Whitaker, *Spanish American Frontier*; Watlington, *Partisan Spirit*; Ammon, *Genet Mission*; Cayton, "'When Shall We Cease to Have Judases?'"; Melton, *First Impeachment*; Racine, *Francisco de Miranda*; and Stearns, "Borderland Diplomacy."

19. "Communications," *Kentucky Gazette*, 12 July 1806.

20. [William Hunter], *Palladium* (Frankfort, Ky.), 10 July 1806.

21. See *Aurora General Advertiser* (Philadelphia), 28 July 1806; *National Intelligencer, and Washington Advertiser* (D.C.), 15 August 1806; and *Enquirer* (Richmond, Va.), 29 August 1806. The standard reference works list three other Kentucky newspapers in July 1806—Danville's *Informant* and two Louisville newspapers, the *Farmer's Library* and the *Western American*. But it appears that Shelbyville also had a newspaper, the *Emporium*, which carried the "Kentucky Spanish Association" essays; see Samuel G. Hopkins to John Breckinridge, 6 September 1806, DLC: Breckinridge Family Papers. Another Kentucky newspaper, the Russellville *Mirror*, began republishing the series with its first issue in November 1806.

22. [Wood and Joseph M. Street], "Aspect of Domestic Affairs," *Western World*, 12 July 1806.

23. Buckner Thruston to Harry Innes, 18 February 1807, DLC: Harry Innes Papers. See also Matthew Walton to Innes, 10 January 1807, ibid.; John Fowler to Innes, 4 March 1807, ibid.; and Henry Clay to Innes, 16 January 1807, in *PHC*, 1:269–71. For Innes's role in the Spanish Conspiracy, see Whitaker, "Harry Innes and the Spanish Intrigue"; for his response to the *Western World*, see Tachau, *Federal Courts in the Early Republic*, 138–45.

24. John Brown to Jefferson, 25 July 1806, in Padgett, ed., "Letters of Honorable John Brown," 26. Brown also wrote to one of Jefferson's lieutenants, the clerk of the House of Representatives, John Beckley; see John Beckley to John Brown, 8 September 1806, in Gawalt, ed., *Justifying Jefferson*, 278. For connections between leading Kentucky Republicans and the federal government, see Winship, "Kentucky *in* the New Republic."

25. [Hunter], "To Correspondents," *Palladium*, 25 September 1806. For Wood's principal authorship of the "Kentucky Spanish Association" essays, see Rayman, "Frontier Journalism in Kentucky"; and Baker, "John Wood Weighs In," 9. For Coburn's and Marshall's writing of pseudonymous essays, see John Brown to John Coburn, 18 October 1806, KyU: John Brown Papers; and Temple Bodley, "Introduction," in Bodley, ed., *Reprints of Littell's Political Transactions*, xcvi.

26. "The 'Western World,'" *Virginia Argus* (Richmond), 13 September 1806, clipped from *Baltimore Telegraphe* (Md.). This article purports to be an "extract of a letter from a gentleman in St. Louis, to his friend in Baltimore." As he often did, Wilkinson probably wrote it and sent it to Maryland senator Samuel Smith with the expectation that it would be printed in a local newspaper. For clear evidence of Wilkinson planting letters to answer the *Western World*, see Wilkinson to

John Brown, 5 August 1806, CtY: Colonel John Brown and Major General Preston Brown Papers.

27. *Palladium*, 7 August 1806. Littell published *An Epistle from William, Surnamed Littell, to the People of the Realm of Kentucky* that fall, but it said nothing about the Spanish Conspiracy. See "Littell, William," in Kleber et al., eds., *Kentucky Encyclopedia*, 563.

28. Bodley, ed., *Reprints of Littell's Political Transactions*, 3.

29. John Brown to Coburn, 18 October 1806, KyU: Brown Papers.

30. Innes to Jefferson, 25 November 1806, DLC: Jefferson Papers. For the origins of this work, see Bodley, "Introduction," in Bodley, ed., *Reprints of Littell's Political Transactions*, i, xcvi–xcvii.

31. [Street], "Legal Proceedings," *Western World*, 12 July 1806.

32. Street, "Joseph M. Street, & Co. to the People," ibid., 30 August 1806.

33. Wilkinson to John Smith, 4 August 1806, OCHi: Papers in the Defense of John Smith of Ohio. John Brown also considered filing suit very quickly; see Beckley to John Brown, 8 September 1806, in Gawalt, ed., *Justifying Jefferson*, 278.

34. James Morrison to Samuel Smith, 29 September/6 October 1806, DLC: Samuel Smith Family Papers.

35. "The Extract," in [Thomas Ritchie], "'The Western World,'" *Enquirer*, 5 September 1806.

36. Innes to Wilson Cary Nicholas, 10 February 1807, ViHi: Hugh Blair Grigsby Papers. For the Marshall family, see Quisenberry, *Life and Times of Hon. Humphrey Marshall*.

37. John Brown to Coburn, 18 October 1806, KyU: Brown Papers. See also James Brown to Benjamin Sebastian, [8 November 1806], ICHi: Aaron Burr Papers.

38. [Hunter], *Palladium*, 24 July 1806.

39. "Independence" [Thomas Bodley], ibid., 7 August 1806. For Bodley's authorship of "Independence," see his statement to Humphrey Marshall, *Kentucky Gazette*, 13 October 1806. See also two pieces by "A Youth of Frankfort": "John Wood," *Palladium*, 14 August 1806; and "To that Intelligent and Enlightened Political Argus, John Wood," ibid., 21 August 1806.

40. William Littell, "To the People of the Western States," *Palladium*, 14 August 1806.

41. Daveiss to James Madison, 14 August 1806, in *View*, 24.

42. Hopkins to Walter Alves, February 1807, in *RASP*, Series J, Part 13, Walter Alves Papers. For Marshall's defense, see Humphrey Marshall, "To the Independent Citizens of Kentucky," *Palladium*, 2 October 1806.

43. [Hunter], *Palladium*, 4 September 1806.

44. Hopkins, *Western World*, 2 August 1806. See also [Street], "Horrid Attempt at Assassination," ibid., 26 July 1806.

45. "The Extract," in [Ritchie], "'The Western World,'" *Enquirer*, 5 September 1806.

46. "Remarks Addressed to the Citizens of Kentucky, by an Inhabitant of Tennessee," *Impartial Review, and Cumberland Repository* (Nashville, Tenn.), 13 September 1806.
47. "Phocion," *Palladium*, 21 August 1806.
48. Littell, "To the People of the Western Country," ibid.
49. "Candidus," ibid. See also "A Citizen of Frankfort," ibid.; and "A Youth of Frankfort," "To that Intelligent and Enlightened Political Argus, John Wood," ibid. Surprisingly, little use seems to have been made, at least in print, of Wood's and Street's romantic relationship (see above, n. 14). "Phocion" did include within Wood's catalog of sins "an eccentricity of morals" that had "[led] him into crimes too infamous to be mentioned" and described him as "an outcast of nature" ("Phocion," ibid.).
50. [Bodley], "Independence," ibid., 4 September 1806.
51. "Communications," *Kentucky Gazette*, 25 August 1806.
52. "A Citizen of Frankfort," *Palladium*, 21 August 1806.
53. Ibid.
54. [Street], "A Congratulatory Epistle to the Dupes of Innes, Todd and Brown—and an Appeal to a Court of Ladies," *Western World*, 7 November 1806.
55. "Law Intelligence," *Palladium*, 13 November 1806. For Street's problems in November and December, see Rayman, "Frontier Journalism in Kentucky," 108–9.
56. "The Extract," in [Ritchie], "'The Western World,'" *Enquirer*, 5 September 1806. See also Hopkins to Breckinridge, 6 September 1806, DLC: Breckinridge Family Papers.
57. Wilkinson to John Smith, 4 August 1806, OCHi: Papers in the Defense of John Smith of Ohio.
58. "Communications," *Kentucky Gazette*, 18 August 1806. See also "The Extract," in [Ritchie], "'The Western World,'" *Enquirer*, 5 September 1806.
59. Bodley, statement, 16 July 1806, in James M. Bradford to Hunter, *Palladium*, 24 July 1806.
60. James M. Bradford to Hopkins, 18 July 1806, ibid. Bradford had to pick his words carefully in order not to impugn Hopkins by suggesting that he was willing to act as a second for someone who was not a gentleman. Street offered a somewhat different account of these events in *Western World*, 19 and 26 July 1806.
61. [Street], "Horrid Attempt at Assassination," *Western World*, 26 July 1806. For Adams's different, and more favorable, accounts, see George Adams to Hunter, *Palladium*, 31 July 1806; and the letters and statements of Bodley, W. Akin, and Adams in ibid., 7 August 1806. According to an account by a Street descendant, the wound was nearly fatal; see Wilson, "General Joseph Monford [*sic*] Street," 24.
62. Adams, "To the Editor of the Palladium," *Palladium*, 7 August 1806. For the Adams-Street affair, see Rayman, "Frontier Journalism in Kentucky," 103–5. Even after this incident, Adams continued his rise to prominence in Kentucky

and later in Mississippi; see Rowland, *Mississippi*, 1:28; Johnson, *History of Franklin County*, 69; and Connelley and Coulter, *History of Kentucky*, 1:458.

63. [Street], "Indictments," *Western World*, 4 October 1806; [Street], "To Thomas Bodley," ibid., 18 October 1806. See also [Street], "More Challenges," ibid., 7 November 1806.

64. John Brown to Jefferson, 25 July 1806, in Padgett, ed., "Letters of Honorable John Brown," 24.

65. Hopkins to Alves, February 1807, in *RASP*, Series J, Part 13, Alves Papers.

66. [Wood and Street], "No Federalism! No Burrism!," *Western World*, 12 July 1806.

67. "The Western World," ibid., 2 August 1806, clipped from *Ohio Herald* (Chillicothe). For the first reference to Burr in the "Kentucky Spanish Association" essays, see *Western World*, 26 July 1806. I discussed the "Queries," which originally appeared in the *United States' Gazette* in June 1805, in Chapter 1. Even these brief mentions of Burr were noted by the editor of one New England newspaper; see [Joseph Cushing], "The Western World," *Farmer's Cabinet* (Amherst, N.H.), 19 August 1806 (from AHN).

68. Benjamin Henry Latrobe to Albert Gallatin, 19 November 1806, in *CBHL*, 2:291. The *Aurora* began reprinting the *Western World* essays on 28 July; Burr's name appeared the next day in the "No Federalism! No Burrism!" essay.

69. [Wood and Street], "Colonel Aaron Burr," *Western World*, 15 September 1806. In fact, Burr was barely mentioned in that day's "Kentucky Spanish Association" essay, and only as connected to Edmond Charles Genet a decade earlier.

70. [?] Ficklen to Abraham Bradley Jr., 19 October [1806], ICHi: James Wilkinson Papers.

71. [Wood and Street], "Colonel Aaron Burr," *Western World*, 15 September 1806.

72. For Burr's movements during these months, see Abernethy, *Burr Conspiracy*, 63–79; Lomask, *Aaron Burr*, 2:123–41; Johnson, "Aaron Burr"; and Stewart, *American Emperor*, 151–58. For Bastrop and the Bastrop grant, see Mitchell and Calhoun, "Marquis de Maison Rouge"; and Bacarisse, "Baron de Bastrop."

73. "Extract of a letter from a gentleman in Shelbyville (Ken.) to his friend," *Enquirer*, 5 December 1806. For Burr's activities in Lexington, see the letters, notes, and editorial comments in *PCAB*, 2:994–1001. Despite his two federal positions, John Jordan does not seem to have provided information about his lodger's activities to either Secretary of the Navy Robert Smith or Postmaster General Gideon Granger.

74. [Daniel Bradford], *Kentucky Gazette*, 30 October 1806.

75. "An Observer" [Humphrey Marshall], *Western World*, 18 October 1806.

76. "One of the People" [Humphrey Marshall], ibid., 7 November 1806. "One of the People" may have been written by Daveiss rather than Marshall.

77. [Cushing], "The Western World," ibid., 27 September 1806, clipped from *Farmer's Cabinet*. The first "Fredonian" appeared in the *Western World*'s 1 November issue.

78. Hinde, "Col Aaron Burrs conspiracy in 1806," 26 September 1829, DLC: James Madison Papers.
79. Hinde to John S. Williams, 16 May 1843, in Williams, ed., "Autographs," *American Pioneer*, 419. See also [Hinde], "John Wood and His World," *Fredonian* (Chillicothe, Ohio), 7 March 1807. For similar assessments, see Samuel Taggart to John Taylor, 19 January 1807, in "Letters of Samuel Taggart," 207; Benjamin Parke to James Brown, 22 January 1807, InHi: Albert G. Porter Papers; and Samuel L. Mitchill to Catherine Mitchill, 13 February 1807, in "Dr. Mitchill's Letters from Washington," 751.
80. Wood to Hunter, 22 June 1807, DLC: Innes Papers.
81. Wood to Clay, 9 October 1806, in *PHC*, 1:244–45. For Wood's change of heart, see also Baker, "John Wood Weighs In," 12–13.
82. Daveiss to James Madison, 16 November 1806, in *View*, 27.
83. "Communication," *Palladium*, 13 November 1806. Burr's first trial in Kentucky is thoroughly covered in Beard, "Colonel Burr's First Brush with the Law." See also Abernethy, *Burr Conspiracy*, 95–97; Lomask, *Aaron Burr*, 2:142–45; Tachau, *Federal Courts in the Early Republic*, 140–42; and Stewart, *American Emperor*, 170–72. For the court record, see Wilson, ed., "Court Proceedings of 1806 in Kentucky."
84. "Regulus" [Clay], [9 July 1808], in *PHC*, 1:366.
85. "Communication," *Palladium*, 13 November 1806.
86. Matthew Backus to James Backus, 25 November 1806, OHi: Backus-Woodbridge Collection.
87. [Hunter], *Palladium*, 13 November 1806.
88. Aaron Burr to Edward Tupper, [18 November 1806], in *PCAB*, 2:1002.
89. For Burr's intentions and movements, see the letters, notes, and editorial comments in ibid., 998–1006, as well as Burr to Latrobe, 26 October 1806, in *CBHL*, 2:277.
90. Innes to Nicholas, 10 February 1807, ViHi: Grigsby Papers.
91. William T. Barry to John Barry, 6 December 1806, in Cox, ed., "Letters of William T. Barry," 328. Barry further noted that Innes had given his testimony "with much reluctance[:] he cried like a child, was attacked with a Vertigo that night, and was under the necessity of being bled twice." Within days of his resignation, Sebastian asked the Spanish minister to have his pension reinstated; see Sebastian to Marquis de Yrujo, 1 December 1806, InHi: Benjamin Sebastian Papers.
92. [Hunter], *Palladium*, 4 December 1806. For the committee hearings, see Bodley, "Introduction," in Bodley, ed., *Reprints of Littell's Political Transactions*, c–cix; and Warren, "Benjamin Sebastian and the Spanish Conspiracy."
93. Burr to William Henry Harrison, 27 November 1806, in *PCAB*, 2:1005.
94. Burr to Clay, 1 December 1806, in *PHC*, 1:257. See also Burr to Clay, 27 November 1806, in ibid., 256. For Clay's doubts, see Plumer, diary entry, 29

December 1806, in *WPMP*, 547. For Clay's relationship with and work for Burr, see Mayo, *Henry Clay*, 240–57.

95. Clay, argument, 2 December 1806, in Wood, *Full Statement of the Trial and Acquittal*, 10. For Burr's second trial in Kentucky, see Beard, "Colonel Burr's First Brush with the Law"; Jillson, "Aaron Burr's 'Trial' for Treason"; Abernethy, *Burr Conspiracy*, 97–99; Lomask, *Aaron Burr*, 145–49; and Tachau, *Federal Courts in the Early Republic*, 142–44.

96. *View*, 30.

97. Wood to Clay, 4 December 1806, in *PHC*, 1:259–60. Wood may have been trying to secure payment—a loan from Clay or agent's fees from Burr—for the service that he was to render the next day in court. Clay and Wood could have discussed in advance what Wood would say, but Wood later insisted that he had not spoken with Burr since 1802; see Wood to Hunter, 22 June 1807, DLC: Innes Papers.

98. Wood, testimony, 5 December 1806, in Wood, *Full Statement of the Trial and Acquittal*, 35.

99. Abraham Hite et al., grand jury report, 5 December 1806, in Wilson, ed., "Court Proceedings of 1806 in Kentucky," 40.

100. Clay to Richard Pindell, 15 October 1829, in *PHC*, 7:501.

101. *National Intelligencer*, 29 December 1806.

102. William T. Barry to John Barry, 8 December 1806, ViU: William T. Barry Letters. See also Ninian Edwards to William Wirt, [5 January 1807], ICHi: Ninian Edwards Papers.

103. James Taylor, "Autobiography," ICU: Reuben T. Durrett Collection, Durrett Codices, 56. See also "Regulus" [Clay], [9 July 1808], in *PHC*, 1:367.

104. Marshall, *History of Kentucky*, 2:411.

105. Daveiss to James Taylor, 22 July 1808, KyHi: Joseph H. Daviess [*sic*] Papers.

106. James Taylor, "Autobiography," ICU: Durrett Codices, 56.

107. [Street], "Col. Burr Before the Federal Court," *Western World*, 18 December 1806.

108. "Frankfort," *Enquirer*, 6 January 1807, clipped from [Hunter], *Palladium*.

109. "Resolution," 3 December 1806, in Kentucky, *Journal of the House of Representatives*, 118.

110. "Extract of a letter from Winchester (K.)," *National Intelligencer*, 2 February 1807. Wood's *Full Statement of the Trial and Acquittal of Aaron Burr* was published in Alexandria, D.C. A prospectus for the *Atlantic World* appeared in the *Intelligencer* as early as 9 January 1807. The army contractor James Taylor later recalled that Graham had sent him to Frankfort to tell Daveiss to hold Burr because Graham "had abundant evidence in his possession to convict Burr of treason," but Taylor had arrived a day or two after the trial (James Taylor, "Autobiography," ICU: Durrett Codices, 55). For the official actions, see Abernethy, *Burr Conspiracy*, 109–10.

111. John Monroe to James Madison, 29 January 1807, DNA: RG59, M418, filed under "Monroe, John."

112. "Extract of a letter from a Gentleman in Lexington (K) to the Editor of the Enquirer," *Enquirer*, 17 March 1807.

113. Sebastian to Innes, 12 April 1808, DLC: Innes Papers. For the Wood-Street clash, see Baker, "John Wood Weighs In," 19. For Clay's newspaper battles, see the essays, notes, and editorial comments in *PHC*, 1:328–43, 346–53, and 358–67. For the investigation of Innes, see Tachau, *Federal Courts in the Early Republic*, 45–52.

114. James Taylor to Dolley Payne Madison, 2 January 1831, in Mattern and Shulman, eds., *Selected Letters of Dolley Payne Madison*, 289. The Taylor-Daveiss affair had its origins in Daveiss's "counter party" on the night of the Burr ball in Frankfort; see Daveiss to James Taylor, 22 and 23 July 1808, KyHi: Daviess [*sic*] Papers; James Taylor to Daveiss, 22 July 1808, KyHi: Gen. James Taylor Papers; James Taylor to Louis Marshall, 22 July 1808, ibid.; James Taylor to James Madison, 13 November 1808, in Padgett, ed., "Letters of James Taylor," 127; and James Taylor, "Autobiography," ICU: Durrett Codices, 58–60. For the Clay-Marshall duel, see Quisenberry, *Life and Times of Hon. Humphrey Marshall*, 100–103. The two men exchanged three rounds, with both leaving slightly injured; see Clay to James Clark, 19 January 1809, in *PHC*, 1:400. For the case of Innes v. Street, see Rayman, "Frontier Journalism in Kentucky," 111.

115. For the Clay biography and Marshall pamphlet, see Prentice, *Biography of Henry Clay*, 28–42; and Marshall, *Biography of Henry Clay*. For the later books, see Butler, *History of the Commonwealth of Kentucky*; Brown, *Political Beginnings of Kentucky*; Green, *Spanish Conspiracy*; Quisenberry, *Life and Times of Hon. Humphrey Marshall*; and Bodley, "Introduction," in Bodley, ed., *Reprints of Littell's Political Transactions*. For a historiographical overview of the Spanish Conspiracy, see Watlington, *Partisan Spirit*, 253–60.

116. [Street], *Western World*, 18 December 1806.

117. Joseph Crockett to Jefferson, 9 January 1807, DLC: Jefferson Papers.

118. William T. Barry to John Barry, 24 February 1807, ViU: Barry Letters.

CHAPTER 3. GUILT BEYOND QUESTION: THE NARRATIVE OF THOMAS JEFFERSON

1. "Extracts of letters from Washington," *New-York Commercial Advertiser*, 17 January 1807 (from AHN).

2. K. K. Van Rensselaer to Jonathan Dayton, 6 January 1807, MiU-C: Jonathan Dayton Papers.

3. George Clinton to Edmond Charles Genet, 24 January 1807, NHi: AHMC—Edmond Charles Genet Papers.

4. Thomas Jefferson, special message, 22 January 1807, in *CMPP*, 1:412.

5. Jefferson to William C. C. Claiborne, 3 February 1807, in *WrTJ*, 11:151.
6. Jefferson, Sixth Annual Message, 2 December 1806, in *CMPP*, 1:406.
7. Jefferson, Proclamation, 27 November 1806, in ibid., 404.
8. Jefferson, Sixth Annual Message, 2 December 1806, in ibid., 407. Over the past two centuries, numerous biographers and historians have examined the administration's response to the Burr crisis in the fall of 1806. Some have seen it as too much; others have viewed it as too little; and a few have treated it as just right. See, in particular, Abernethy, *Burr Conspiracy*; Adams, "Jefferson's Military Policy"; Peterson, *Thomas Jefferson and the New Nation*; Malone, *Jefferson and His Time*, vol. 5; Lomask, *Aaron Burr*, vol. 2; Onuf, *Jefferson's Empire*; Isenberg, *Fallen Founder*; and Stewart, *American Emperor*. These judgments have frequently depended on the author's assessments of Burr's intentions—how great a threat did he pose?—and Jefferson's character—would he exploit popular fears to crush, or have killed, a political rival?
9. Daniel Clark to Edward Livingston, 8 December 1806, NjP: Edward Livingston Papers.
10. [Stephen C. Carpenter], *People's Friend & Daily Advertiser* (New York), 30 December 1806.
11. "Clinton-Jeffersonianus," "A Speck of War: or, The Good Sense of the People of the Western Country," *New-York Evening Post*, 7 January 1807. The phrase "a speck of war" came from the annual message. Jefferson defended his decision not to expand the army and navy in a time of domestic and, especially, foreign tensions on the grounds that "Were armies to be raised whenever a speck of war is visible in our horizon, we never should have been without them" (Jefferson, Sixth Annual Message, 2 December 1806, in *CMPP*, 1:410). For Jefferson and the press, see Mumper, "Jeffersonian Image in the Federalist Mind"; and Knudson, *Jefferson and the Press*.
12. [William Coleman], "President's Message," *New-York Evening Post*, 11 December 1806. See also Fisher Ames to Josiah Quincy, 11 December 1806, in Allen, ed., *Works of Fisher Ames*, 2:1535; and James Ross to Dayton, 6 January 1807, MiU-C: Dayton Papers.
13. Jefferson, note on James Madison to Jefferson, [30 October 1806], in Smith, ed., *Republic of Letters*, 3:1454. For Madison's role in the administration response, see Brant, *James Madison*, 344–59.
14. Jefferson to William Duane, 24 November 1806, DLC: Thomas Jefferson Papers. See also Jefferson to Thomas Mann Randolph, 3 November 1806, in *WrTJ*, 18:250. For the debate over a "common law of crimes" in the early republic, see Henderson, *Congress, Courts, and Criminals*; Palmer, "Federal Common Law of Crimes"; Presser, "Supra-Constitution"; and Preyer, "Jurisdiction to Punish."
15. Clark to Livingston, 8 December 1806, NjP: Livingston Papers.
16. John Quincy Adams to Louisa Catherine Adams, 2 December 1806, MHi: Adams Family Papers.

17. Burwell Bassett to Joseph Prentis, 24 December 1806, ViU: Webb-Prentis Family Papers. See also Leonard Covington to Alexander Covington, 19 December 1806, Ms-Ar: Wailes-Covington Family Papers; and Jeremiah Morrow to James Findlay, 24 December 1806, in Cox, ed., "Selections from the Torrence Papers," 4:117.

18. "Communication," *People's Friend*, 10 January 1807.

19. John Randolph to George Hay, 3 January 1806 [*sic*, 1807], DLC: John Randolph of Roanoke Papers. See also Randolph to Edward Dillon, 11 January 1807, NcU: Dillon-Polk Family Papers. For Federalist complaints, see, for example, Van Rensselaer to Dayton, 6 January 1807, MiU-C: Dayton Papers; and Samuel White to Dayton, 17 January 1807, ibid.

20. Nathaniel Macon to Joseph H. Nicholson, 6 January 1807, DLC: Joseph H. Nicholson Papers. See also Richard Stanford to Duncan Cameron, 29 December 1806, NcU: Cameron Family Papers; John Quincy Adams to Louisa Catherine Adams, 7 January 1807, MHi: Adams Family Papers; James Hillhouse to Simeon Baldwin, 8 January 1807, in Baldwin, ed., *Life and Letters of Simeon Baldwin*, 453; and James M. Garnett to James Hunter, 17 January 1807, Vi: Garnett-Mercer-Hunter Family Papers.

21. Samuel Latham Mitchill to Catharine Mitchill, 7 January 1807, in "Dr. Mitchill's Letters from Washington," 750.

22. William Plumer, diary entry, 27 December 1806, in *WPMP*, 543. See also Thomas Worthington to Nathaniel Massie, 30 November 1806, in Massie, *Nathaniel Massie*, 238–39.

23. Samuel Smith to Wilson Cary Nicholas, 31 December 1806, ViU: Papers of the Randolph Family of Edgehill and Wilson Cary Nicholas.

24. John Randolph, speech, 16 January 1807, in *Annals*, 9th Cong., 2nd sess., 334, 336.

25. White to Dayton, 17 January 1807, MiU-C: Dayton Papers; Joseph Winston to William Lenoir, 5 January 1807, NcU: Lenoir Family Papers. As recorded, Randolph's speech does not seem nearly as explosive as contemporary comments suggest. But it was this speech, among others, that led one Connecticut Federalist to mention that, in reporting congressional debates, the editor of the *Intelligencer* "omit[ted] or soften[ed] many expresions which bear hard on the ruling powers" (George Hoadley to Jeremiah Evarts, 5 February 1807, ViHi: George Hoadley Letter).

26. John Randolph, speech, 16 January 1807, in *Annals*, 9th Cong., 2nd sess., 336.

27. Garnett to Hunter, 17 January 1807, Vi: Garnett-Mercer-Hunter Family Papers.

28. Samuel Taggart to John Taylor, 19 January 1807, in "Letters of Samuel Taggart," 207. For the congressional debate, see *Annals*, 9th Cong., 2nd sess., 334–59. The vote on the call for information was 109 to 14; that on the amended request for a statement of administration measures was 67 to 52 (ibid., 357, 358).

29. Van Rensselaer to Dayton, 6 January 1807, MiU-C: Dayton Papers. See also unknown correspondent to John Rhea, [17 January 1807], copied in Rhea to Dayton, 21 January 1807, ibid.
30. [Enos Bronson], *United States' Gazette* (Philadelphia), 15 January 1807.
31. Abigail Adams to John Quincy Adams, [16 January 1807], MHi: Adams Family Papers. Adams clearly meant Ariadne, who, in Greek mythology, gave Theseus the ball of string that enabled him to find his way out of the labyrinth after killing the minotaur.
32. Taggart to Taylor, 19 January 1807, in "Letters of Samuel Taggart," 207.
33. "The following is a sketch of the substance of the *Message* delivered in congress by the president relative to Burr's conspiracy," *American, and Commercial Daily Advertiser* (Baltimore, Md.), 24 January 1807.
34. Samuel Latham Mitchill to Catharine Mitchill, 22 January 1807, in "Dr. Mitchill's Letters from Washington," 751.
35. Jefferson, special message, 22 January 1807, in *CMPP*, 1:412.
36. Ibid., 414.
37. Ibid., 413–16. I examine Jefferson's discussion of Burr's followers in Chapter 10.
38. Ibid., 412–13.
39. Ibid., 414–15. I discuss the administration's actions in November and December at greater length and from a somewhat different perspective in "'Strongest Government on Earth.'" For the executive branch under Jefferson, see also Bowers, *Jefferson in Power*; McDonald, *Presidency of Thomas Jefferson*; Cunningham, *Process of Government under Jefferson*; Johnstone, *Jefferson and the Presidency*; and Balogh, *Government Out of Sight*.
40. Worthington to Massie, 30 November 1806, in Massie, *Nathaniel Massie*, 238–39.
41. Plumer, diary entry, 27 December 1806, in *WPMP*, 543–44.
42. Worthington to unknown correspondent, 12 January 1807, ORCHi: Early Statehood Papers.
43. Plumer, diary entry, 16 January 1807, in *WPMP*, 577.
44. Worthington to unknown correspondent, 12 January 1807, ORCHi: Early Statehood Papers.
45. Plumer, diary entry, 16 January 1807, in *WPMP*, 577.
46. Jefferson, special message, 22 January 1807, in *CMPP*, 1:412.
47. Ibid.
48. When Congress failed to act quickly on this suggestion from his annual message, Jefferson secretly prepared a draft bill and sent it to a congressional ally, requesting that he "copy the within & burn [the] original." The president wanted to hide his role because he was "very unwilling to meddle personally with the details of the proceedings of the legislature" (Jefferson to John Dawson, 19 December 1806, DLC: Jefferson Papers). The House of Representatives eventually passed a wide-ranging bill on this issue, but Senate amendments narrowed the final act to a mere authorization for the president to use the armed forces in cases

of domestic insurrection; see *Annals*, 9th Cong., 2nd sess., 217–18, 328, 673, 1286.

49. William A. Burwell, memorandum, [ca. late 1808], in Gawalt, ed., "'Strict Truth,'" 126.

50. Robert Smith to Jefferson, 22 December 1806, DLC: Jefferson Papers. For Smith, see Armstrong, *Politics, Diplomacy and Intrigue*. I consider Jefferson's apparent resistance to Smith's pressure more fully in "'Strongest Government on Earth.'"

51. Burwell, memorandum, [ca. late 1808], in Gawalt, ed., "'Strict Truth,'" 126. Robert Smith's brother, Maryland senator Samuel Smith, shared these concerns, criticizing Jefferson for remaining "perfectly tranquil" when "any other Man" would have pursued "decisive measures" (Samuel Smith to Nicholas, 31 December 1806, ViU: Papers of the Randolph Family of Edgehill and Wilson Cary Nicholas).

52. Jefferson to Robert Smith, 23 December 1806, in *WoTJ*, 10:331. The previous day, Jefferson had suggested that he still considered it possible that "we shall be obliged to make a great national armament" to suppress the conspiracy, though it seemed more likely that "the Western States" would accomplish the task (Jefferson to John Langdon, 22 December 1806, in *WrTJ*, 19:158).

53. Jefferson, First Inaugural Address, 4 March 1801, in *CMPP*, 1:322.

54. Burwell, memorandum, [ca. late 1808], in Gawalt, ed., "'Strict Truth,'" 126.

55. Plumer, diary entry, 27 December 1806, in *WPMP*, 544. Tennessee senator Daniel Smith similarly reported that the administration, having received the reports from Ohio, "now consider the danger as nearly passed over" (Daniel Smith to Andrew Jackson, 29 December 1806, in *PAJ*, 2:127).

56. Jefferson to Charles Clay, 11 January 1807, in *WrTJ*, 11:133.

57. "Letter from Washington," *Columbian Centinel* (Boston), 31 January 1807.

58. John Beckley to John Brown, 23 January 1807, in Gawalt, ed., *Justifying Jefferson*, 280.

59. Burwell, memorandum, [ca. late 1808], in Gawalt, ed., "'Strict Truth,'" 127. For the spread of the message, see *New-York Evening Post*, 26 January 1807; *Enquirer* (Richmond, Va.), 27 January 1807; *Columbian Centinel*, 31 January 1807; *Charleston Courier* (S.C.), 4 February 1807; *Commonwealth* (Pittsburgh, Pa.), 4 February 1807; *Kentucky Gazette and General Advertiser* (Lexington), 14 February 1807; *Impartial Review, and Cumberland Repository* (Nashville, Tenn.), 21 February 1807; *Mississippi Herald & Natchez Gazette*, 25 February 1807; and Claiborne to Madison, 28 February 1807, DLC: Burr Conspiracy Collection.

60. Duane to Caesar A. Rodney, 28 January 1807, PHi: Simon Gratz Autograph Collection.

61. "The Crisis," *People's Friend*, 9 February 1807, clipped from *Frederick-Town Herald* (Md.).

62. Henry Clay to Thomas Todd, 24 January 1807, in *PHC*, 1:272.

63. Bassett to Prentis, 27 January 1807, ViU: Webb-Prentis Family Papers.

64. George Washington Campbell, circular letter to constituents, 25 February 1807, in *CLC*, 1:495; Marmaduke Williams, circular letter to constituents, 26 February 1807, in ibid., 503.
65. Burwell, circular letter to constituents, 2 March 1807, in ibid., 511.
66. [Elijah Pentland], *Commonwealth*, 4 February 1807.
67. [Thomas Ritchie], "Burr's Conspiracy," *Enquirer*, 13 February 1807; Williams, circular letter to constituents, 26 February 1807, in *CLC*, 1:503; George Washington Campbell, circular letter to constituents, 25 February 1807, in ibid., 495; Henry Clay to [Thomas Hart], 1 February 1807, in *PHC*, 1:273.
68. Bassett, circular letter to constituents, [February 1807], in *CLC*, 1:509.
69. Williams, circular letter to constituents, 26 February 1807, in ibid., 503. See also [Ritchie], "A Glance at Congress," *Enquirer*, 27 January 1807.
70. George Washington Campbell, circular letter to constituents, 25 February 1807, in *CLC*, 1:496.
71. Ibid., 495 (emphasis added).
72. "A Citizen," *Impartial Review*, 21 February 1807. See also William Branch Giles to Jefferson, 6 April 1807, DLC: Jefferson Papers; and John Lithgow to Jefferson, May [1807], ibid.
73. John Quincy Adams to Abigail Adams, [3 February 1807], MHi: Adams Family Papers.
74. [Carpenter], *People's Friend*, 28 January 1807.
75. George Izard to Henry Izard, 13 February 1807, ScU: Ralph Izard Papers. "The many headed Monster" was the people.
76. "Letter from Washington," *Columbian Centinel*, 31 January 1807.
77. John Adams to Benjamin Rush, 2 February 1807, in Schutz and Adair, eds., *Spur of Fame*, 76.
78. Beverley Tucker to John Randolph, 28 January 1806 [*sic*, 1807], ViW: Tucker-Coleman Papers. In the late sixteenth century, St. Omers had been founded across the English Channel as a Jesuit college for English Catholics.
79. James Hillhouse to Rebecca Hillhouse, 23 January 1807, CtY: Hillhouse Family Papers. See also Timothy Pickering to John Pickering, 25 January 1807, MHi: Timothy Pickering Papers; and White to Dayton, MiU-C: Dayton Papers.
80. Thomas Boylston Adams to John Quincy Adams, 8 February 1807, MHi: Adams Family Papers. Adams quoted John Wood, who had repeatedly declared his belief in Burr's innocence since the December 1806 grand jury hearing in Kentucky.
81. "Letter from Washington," *Columbian Centinel*, 31 January 1807.
82. John Adams to Rush, 2 February 1807, in Schutz and Adair, eds., *Spur of Fame*, 76.
83. "Letter from Washington," *Columbian Centinel*, 31 January 1807.
84. Tucker to John Randolph, 28 January 1806 [*sic*, 1807], ViW: Tucker-Coleman Papers.
85. Tucker to John Randolph, 31 January 1807, ibid.

86. Rhea to Dayton, 28 January 1807, MiU-C: Dayton Papers.

87. [Carpenter], *People's Friend*, 28 January 1807.

88. Tucker to John Randolph, 28 January 1806 [*sic*, 1807], ViW: Tucker-Coleman Papers. Tucker believed that Napoleonic France—"whose uniform object is conquest, & whose favorite maxim is *dividé & impera*"—was behind Burr's plans, though other Quids suggested British involvement. Federalists usually pointed to France or Spain. See Charles Carroll to Charles Carroll Jr., 26 January 1807, MdHi: Charles Carroll Papers; and Timothy Pickering to Rebecca Pickering, 25 January 1807, MHi: Pickering Papers.

89. [Carpenter], *People's Friend*, 28 January 1807; "A Sentinel," *Washington Federalist* (Georgetown, D.C.), 14 February 1807. "A Sentinel" may have been Kentucky Federalist Humphrey Marshall, who was in Washington at the time, knew of Joseph Hamilton Daveiss's January 1806 letter to Jefferson, and shared that knowledge with other Federalists in the capital; see Plumer, diary entry, 22 February 1807, in *WPMP*, 621.

90. [Carpenter], *People's Friend*, 4 February 1807.

91. "A Sentinel," *Washington Federalist*, 14 February 1807. See also [Carpenter], *People's Friend*, 16 February 1807.

92. Thomas Boylston Adams to John Quincy Adams, 8 February 1807, MHi: Adams Family Papers.

93. Plumer, diary entry, 26 January 1807, in *WPMP*, 591, 592.

94. Silas Brown to Ephraim Brown, 7 March 1807, in [Harter, ed.], *Aaron Burr Expedition*, 9.

95. Jefferson, special message, 22 January 1807, in *CMPP*, 1:415.

96. Thomas Truxton to Timothy Pickering, 6 January 1807, MHi: Pickering Papers. See also same to same, 13 and 20 January and 22 February 1807, ibid.; and Truxton to Thomas Tingey, 13 and 19 January 1807, DLC: Thomas Truxton Papers.

97. Joseph Alston to Charles Pinckney, [February 1807], enclosed in Pinckney to Jefferson, 16 February 1807, DLC: Jefferson Papers. A printed copy of the public letter was enclosed in Alston to Jefferson, 11 February 1807, ibid.

98. "Copy of a letter from the Honorable Joseph Alston to His Excellency Charles Pinckney," *Georgetown Gazette, and Commercial Advertiser* (S.C.), 11 February 1807.

99. Silas Brown to Ephraim Brown, 7 March 1807, in [Harter, ed.], *Aaron Burr Expedition*, 9.

100. Jefferson to Justus Erich Bollman, 25 January 1807, DLC: Jefferson Papers. For Madison's account, see [Madison], "Substance of a communication made on the 23 of Jany, 1807, by Doctor Bollman to the President," [23 (*sic*, 24) January 1807], in *LOWJM*, 2:393–401. On most points, Madison's memorandum is similar to Bollman's written communication; see Bollman to Jefferson, 26 January 1807, DLC: Jefferson Papers. But it also indicates at least some of the questions that were asked.

101. Bollman to Jefferson, 26 January 1807, DLC: Jefferson Papers.
102. [Madison], "Substance of a communication," [23 (*sic*, 24) January 1807], in *LOWJM*, 2:396.
103. Bollman to Jefferson, 26 January 1807, DLC: Jefferson Papers.
104. [Madison], "Substance of a communication," [23 (*sic*, 24) January 1807], in *LOWJM*, 2:396.
105. Bollman to Jefferson, 26 January 1807, DLC: Jefferson Papers. See also [Madison], "Substance of a communication," [23 (*sic*, 24) January 1807], in *LOWJM*, 2:398–400. Merry, in fact, had reported to his superiors in London that Burr's goal was western separatism; see his letters between August 1804 and November 1805 in *PCAB*, 2:891–92, 927–30, 932–33, and 943–48. See also Wright, *Britain and the American Frontier*, 140–50; and Lester, *Anthony Merry* Redivivus, 98–112.
106. [Madison], "Substance of a communication," [23 (*sic*, 24) January 1807], in *LOWJM*, 2:396–97. Jefferson later stated that Bollman had not requested any assurances that his disclosures would not be used against him; see Jefferson to Hay, 20 May 1807, in *WrTJ*, 11:205.
107. Bollman to Jefferson, 26 January 1807, DLC: Jefferson Papers.
108. [Madison], "Substance of a communication," [23 (*sic*, 24) January 1807], in *LOWJM*, 2:400–401. Bollman's revelations did convince the administration that Burr had "*intrigued*" with both the British and Spanish ministers (Madison to Monroe, 30 January 1807, DNA: RG59, M77 [the italics mark a coded word that I deciphered using cipher "WE028" in Weber, *United States Diplomatic Codes and Ciphers*, 478–89]).
109. Rhea to Dayton, 28 January 1807, MiU-C: Dayton Papers. See also White to Dayton, 25 January 1807, ibid.; Duane to Rodney, 28 January 1807, PHi: Gratz Autograph Collection; John Quincy Adams to Louisa Catherine Adams, 4 February 1807, MHi: Adams Family Papers; and "Extract of a Letter from a Member of Congress to His Friend in this Place," *Palladium* (Frankfort, Ky.), 5 March 1807.
110. Jefferson to Hay, 20 May 1807, in *WrTJ*, 11:205. In a widely reprinted letter, Bollman publicly criticized Jefferson and Hay—who allowed Wilkinson to read the memorandum—for spreading and misrepresenting his communication; see Bollman, "To the Editor of the Aurora," *Aurora General Advertiser* (Philadelphia), 16 July 1807.
111. Bollman, testimony, 15 June 1807, in "NECAB," 20, 22. Bollman also changed his story about the letter that he had delivered to Wilkinson, which was definitely from Burr in January, but only allegedly from Burr by June; see ibid., 24.
112. John Rowan to Joseph Hamilton Daveiss, undated, KyLoF: Joseph Hamilton Daveiss Papers. For defense pamphlets, see, in particular, Goodman, "Hume-Rousseau Affair"; and Freeman, *Affairs of Honor*, 99–113.
113. *View*, [3]. By mid-June, Daveiss had learned that his removal from office "was not owing to any part of [his] conduct with regard to Burr." Instead, Kentucky's

John Pope informed him, Jefferson had removed Daveiss after learning of disparaging remarks that he had made about the administration—"that it was milk & water &c."—in a tavern room "on the evening of Burr's ball" in Frankfort in early December 1806. "That & other communications of the like nature," Pope explained, "excited old Tom's wrath & produced your removal" (John Pope to Daveiss, 15 June 1807, KyLoF: Daveiss Papers). This new knowledge did not appear in Daveiss's pamphlet, however.

114. Rowan to Daveiss, 18 April 1807, KyLoF: Daveiss Papers.

115. *View*, [3], 33.

116. Ibid., 96, 88, 110, 119.

117. Ibid., 119, 121–24, 126. Though focused upon the 22 January message, Daveiss's satire incorporated a number of the president's public documents, including his first inaugural address. "It was a time that tried horses souls," however, played upon Tom Paine's 1776 essay "The Crisis."

118. David B. Ogden to William Meredith, 10 December 1807, PHi: Meredith Family Papers.

119. [Jonathan S. Findlay], *Washington Federalist*, 11 November 1807. See also "New Pamphlet," *New-York Evening Post*, 12 October 1807.

120. Harman Blennerhassett, diary entry, 18 November 1807, in *BwB*, 168–69.

121. James Morrison to James Wilkinson, 9 September 1807, ICU: Reuben T. Durrett Collection, Miscellaneous Manuscripts. For Jefferson's ownership of the pamphlet, see Sowerby, comp., *Catalogue of the Library of Thomas Jefferson*, 3:360.

122. [Robert D. Richardson], *Fredonian* (Chillicothe, Ohio), 11 September 1807.

123. [Timothy Terrell and Samuel Terrell], *Mississippi Messenger* (Natchez), 10 December 1807.

124. William Wirt to Ninian Edwards, 26 December 1807, ICHi: Ninian Edwards Papers.

125. Ibid.

126. [Terrell and Terrell], *Mississippi Messenger*, 10 December 1807.

127. *View*, 42.

128. Among Jefferson's defenders, see, for example, Tucker, *Life of Thomas Jefferson*; and Randall, *Life of Thomas Jefferson*. Among his critics, see, for example, Danvers, *Picture of a Republican Magistrate*; [Sullivan], *Familiar Letters on Public Characters*; and Dwight, *Character of Thomas Jefferson*.

129. Henry Dearborn to Wilkinson, 3 February 1807, DNA: RG107, M6. For the administration's blanket pardon of suspected officers, see Jefferson to Dearborn, 29 March 1807, in *WrTJ*, 11:179–80; and Dearborn to Henry Burbeck, 30 March 1807, ICHi: Henry Dearborn Papers. Samuel Watson of the United States Military Academy generously provided me with a list of sixteen army officers, beyond Wilkinson, who were implicated in some form. See also Skelton, *American Profession of Arms*, 80–82.

130. For Jefferson's meeting with Burr, see Jefferson, memorandum, 15 April 1806, in *Anas*, 237–38.

131. Jefferson, special message, 22 January 1807, in *CMPP*, 1:412.
132. Plumer, diary entry, 8 January 1807, in *WPMP*, 561. See also Jefferson's letters to: George Morgan, 26 March 1807, in *WrTJ*, 11:174; Giles, 20 April 1807, in ibid., 187–91; and the Marquis de Lafayette, 26 May 1807, in *WoTJ*, 10:409.
133. Jefferson to James Bowdoin, 2 April 1807, in *WrTJ*, 11:185–86.
134. Dearborn to Wilkinson, 21 January 1807, DNA: RG107, M6. It may not have been possible for Jefferson's message to address Eaton's disclosures about a planned coup. Eaton apparently had not mentioned this danger in either his conversation with Postmaster General Gideon Granger in mid-October 1806 or his interview with a Boston newspaper a month later; I discuss those disclosures at greater length in the First Interlude and Chapter 5. On 22 January, the day of the message, the Indiana territorial delegate Benjamin Parke reported that Eaton's latest disclosure had not been "known till within two or three days" (Benjamin Parke to James Brown, 22 January 1807, InHi: Albert G. Porter Papers). But it would have taken several days for Jefferson to write the message and additional time to recopy it in a better hand. Two days earlier, Isaac Coles, Jefferson's secretary, had noted in his diary: "writing the whole day for the President papers relating to Burrs conspiracy" (Isaac Coles, diary entry, 20 January 1807, DLC: Isaac Coles Diary).
135. Curiously, Jefferson continued to assert that the first hints had reached him in September, long after the publication of Daveiss's pamphlet. See his letters to: Gideon Granger, 19 March 1814, in *WrTJ*, 14:114; and Katherine Duane Morgan, 26 June 1822, in *WoTJ*, 10:291n. Such assertions may be difficult to explain, but they are impossible to believe.
136. Jefferson, special message, 22 January 1807, in *CMPP*, 1:416.
137. Plumer, diary entry, 21 December 1806, in *WPMP*, 536; Plumer, diary entry, 27 December 1806, in ibid., 543.
138. Jefferson, special message, 22 January 1807, in *CMPP*, 1:415.
139. Plumer, diary entry, 8 January 1807, in *WPMP*, 562–63.
140. Jefferson to Edward Tiffin, 2 February 1807, in *WrTJ*, 11:147. Tiffin had this letter published in the *Scioto Gazette*, from which it was reprinted in the *Intelligencer*; see "From the Scioto Gazette," *National Intelligencer, and Washington Advertiser* (D.C.), 23 March 1807. For similar statements of the lessons of the Burr Conspiracy, see Jefferson's letters to: the Marquis de Lafayette, 26 May 1807, in *WoTJ*, 10:410; Isaac Weaver Jr., 7 June 1807, in *WrTJ*, 11:220–21; and James [*sic*, Samuel] Brown, 27 October 1808, in ibid., 12:184. It also appeared in the draft of a message that Jefferson seems to have considered sending to Congress late in the session; see Jefferson, draft message, [20 September (*sic*, early March) 1807], DLC: Jefferson Papers.
141. Simkins, *Oration*, 28. See also [Ritchie], "Burr's Conspiracy," *Enquirer*, 13 February 1807; William Findley to John Hemphill, February 1807, NcD: Hemphill Family Papers; "The Conspiracy, [II]," *National Intelligencer*, 16 March 1807;

and John Campbell to David Campbell, 3 April 1807, NcD: Campbell Family Papers.

142. [John B. Colvin], *Republican Advocate* (Fredericktown, Md.), 7 November 1807 (from AHN).

143. [Bronson], *United States' Gazette*, 19 August 1807.

CHAPTER 4. THE THREAT TO THE UNION

1. Abernethy, *Burr Conspiracy*, 274. See also Kennedy, *Burr, Hamilton, and Jefferson*; Melton, *Aaron Burr*; Wheelan, *Jefferson's Vendetta*; Isenberg, *Fallen Founder*; Hoffer, *Treason Trials of Aaron Burr*; Stewart, *American Emperor*; and Newmyer, *Treason Trial of Aaron Burr*. Of the recent popular and scholarly works, only David O. Stewart's suggests that Burr might have considered dividing the union.

2. George Washington, Farewell Address, 17 September 1796, in *CMPP*, 1:215.

3. Jeremiah Morrow to James Findlay, 24 December 1806, in Cox, ed., "Selections from the Torrence Papers," 4:118.

4. For early American thinking about regions and sections, see Onuf, "Federalism, Republicanism, and the Origins of American Sectionalism."

5. Samuel Tenney to Winthrop Sargent, 19 February 1804, MHi: Winthrop Sargent Papers. New England Federalists imagined disunion in two forms— the West separating from the East and New England separating from the South and West. For the latter, see Gannon, "Escaping 'Mr. Jefferson's Plan of Destruction.'"

6. Benjamin Tallmadge, quoted in Sparks, *Memories of Fifty Years*, 199.

7. Uriah Tracy to James McHenry, 19 October 1803, in Steiner, *Life and Correspondence of James McHenry*, 522.

8. Espy, *Memorandums of a Tour*, 25.

9. Adams, *American Principles*, 38.

10. John Quincy Adams to William Plumer, 16 August 1809, in Ford, ed., *Writings of John Quincy Adams*, 3:340.

11. [Thomas Ritchie], *Enquirer* (Richmond, Va.), 4 November 1806.

12. Washington to Henry Knox, 5 December 1784, quoted in Onuf, *Statehood and Union*, 4; Thomas Jefferson to James Monroe, 9 July 1786, in Boyd et al., eds., *Papers of Thomas Jefferson*, 10:112–13.

13. For western separatism, see Watlington, *Partisan Spirit*; Slaughter, *Whiskey Rebellion*; Onuf, *Statehood and Union*; Cayton, "'When Shall We Cease to Have Judases?'"; Kastor, "'Equitable Rights and Privileges'"; Melton, *First Impeachment*; and Barksdale, *Lost State of Franklin*.

14. Manasseh Cutler to Ephraim Cutler, 21 March 1801, in Cutler and Cutler, *Life, Journals and Correspondence*, 2:44.

15. [Joseph Cushing], "Western World," *Farmer's Cabinet* (Amherst, N.H.), 19 August 1806 (from AHN).

16. B[enjamin] Walker to Thomas Law, 25 October 1806, MdHi: Thomas Law Family Papers.
17. "Extract of a letter from Alexandria in Virginia," 29 October 1806, enclosed in Jonathan Hamilton to Duncan Cameron, 4 November 1806, NcU: Cameron Family Papers. See also Ralph Izard Jr. to Alice Izard, 29 October 1806, ScU: Ralph Izard Papers.
18. [Ritchie], "Sleep Not!," *Enquirer*, 7 October 1806.
19. James Taylor to James Madison, 13 October 1806, in Padgett, ed., "Letters of James Taylor," 115.
20. John H. Nicholson to Jefferson, 14 October 1806, in *TJC*, 136. See also John McClean to Thomas Worthington, 6 February 1807, OHi: Thomas Worthington Papers.
21. Fisher Ames to Josiah Quincy, 1 January 1807, in Allen, ed., *Works of Fisher Ames*, 2:1545.
22. Plumer to Jedidiah Morse, 17 January 1807, DLC: William Plumer Papers. See also John Adams to Benjamin Rush, 2 February 1807, in Schutz and Adair, eds., *Spur of Fame*, 76.
23. [Ritchie], *Enquirer*, 4 November 1806.
24. George Washington Campbell to Andrew Jackson, 6 February 1807, in *PAJ*, 2:151; John Bigger Jr. to Findlay, 17 January 1807, in Cox, ed., "Selections from the Torrence Papers," 4:120; Worthington to Nathaniel Massie, 29 January 1807, in Massie, *Nathaniel Massie*, 241.
25. Jackson to Henry Dearborn, 17 March 1807, in *PAJ*, 2:158. The formula with which Jackson began this passage—suggesting that only ignorance, or lunacy, could lead someone to expect widespread western support for disunion—was common. Usually, it was applied to Burr and his supporters, either to exonerate them or to assert their misunderstanding of western conditions. See, for example, [William Hunter], *Palladium* (Frankfort, Ky.), 13 November 1806; and [Ritchie], *Enquirer*, 4 November 1806. But Jackson was applying it to Dearborn, who had seemed to impugn Jackson's fidelity to the union. Jackson probably did not mail this letter.
26. Philip Van Cortlandt to Pierre Van Cortlandt Jr., 30 December 1804, in Judd, ed., *Van Cortlandt Family Papers*, 3:183.
27. [Hunter], *Palladium*, 10 July 1806.
28. Benjamin Parke to James Brown, 22 January 1807, InHi: Albert G. Porter Papers. See also Bigger to Findlay, 17 January 1807, in Cox, ed., "Selections from the Torrence Papers," 4:120. According to the historian George Rogers Taylor, 1805 and 1806 were "boom years" in the Ohio Valley (Taylor, "Agrarian Discontent in the Mississippi Valley," 472).
29. [William Duane], *Aurora General Advertiser* (Philadelphia), 5 November 1806.
30. [Samuel H. Smith], *National Intelligencer, and Washington Advertiser* (D.C.), 1 December 1806.
31. Nick Warfield Jr. to John Payne, 14 January 1807, DLC: John Payne Papers.

32. Samuel Johnston to unknown correspondent, 18 March 1803, NcU: Hayes Collection. For the Mississippi Crisis, see Onuf, "Expanding Union"; and Lewis, *Louisiana Purchase*.

33. Rufus King to Madison, 29 March 1801, in *PJM: SS*, 1:55. Similar fears were expressed by the ministers in Paris and Madrid; see, for example, Robert R. Livingston to Madison, 14 March 1802, in ibid., 3:26; and Charles Pinckney to Madison, 20 March 1802, in ibid., 54.

34. Madison to Livingston and Monroe, 2 March 1803, in ibid., 4:366.

35. William T. Barry to John Barry, 9 May 1803, in "Letters of William T. Barry," 13:108. See also David Holmes to James Allen, 12 January 1803, ViHi: Allen Family Papers.

36. William T. Barry to John Barry, 2 January 1807, in Cox, ed., "Letters of William T. Barry," 329.

37. Wilson Cary Nicholas to Thomas Mann Randolph, 25 January 1807, ViU: Papers of the Randolph Family of Edgehill and Wilson Cary Nicholas.

38. [Ritchie], "Cursory Reflections—No. I, Portrait of Aaron Burr," *Enquirer*, 30 October 1807.

39. Charles Carroll to Charles Carroll Jr., 23 January 1807, in Rowland, *Life of Charles Carroll of Carrollton*, 275–76.

40. Thomas Truxton to Timothy Pickering, 20 January 1807, MHi: Timothy Pickering Papers. See also Augustus John Foster to Lady Elizabeth Foster, 29 December 1806, DLC: Augustus John Foster Papers; and Littleton Waller Tazewell to Monroe, 3 January 1807, DLC: James Monroe Papers.

41. Joseph Hamilton Daveiss to Madison, 14 August 1806, in *View*, 24.

42. John Graham, deposition, 5 February 1807, enclosed in Graham to Alexander Henderson Jr., 12 February 1807, OHi: John Graham Letters.

43. Campbell, circular letter to constituents, 25 February 1807, in *CLC*, 1:495.

44. Jefferson to Charles Clay, 11 January 1807, in *WrTJ*, 11:133. See also Jefferson's letters to DuPont de Nemours and the Marquis de Lafayette, 14 July 1807, in ibid., 276 and 279.

45. Benjamin Henry Latrobe to Christian Ignatius Latrobe, 2 April 1807, in *CBHL*, 2:402. For the commander's estimate, see James Wilkinson to Samuel Smith, 14 November 1806, PPiU-D: James Wilkinson Papers. Historians generally accept the smaller figure. See, for example, Abernethy, *Burr Conspiracy*, 165; and Crackel, *Mr. Jefferson's Army*, 150.

46. Benjamin Hawkins to Dearborn, 18 February 1807, in Grant, ed., *Letters, Journals, and Writings of Benjamin Hawkins*, 2:512. For the other reports, see Jackson to Dearborn, [4 January 1807], in *PAJ*, 2:136; James Finley to Worthington, 31 January 1807, OHi: Worthington Papers; and Edward Tiffin to Worthington, 9 January 1807, ibid.

47. Thomas Freeman to Peter Hagner, 30 December 1806, NcU: Peter Hagner Papers. Peter Hagner was an assistant accountant in the War Department.

48. Frederick Bates to Augustus B. Woodward, 3 December 1806, in Marshall, ed., *Life and Papers of Frederick Bates*, 1:87.

49. "Cincinnati," *National Intelligencer*, 16 January 1807.

50. Samuel Smith to unknown correspondent, 28 February 1806 [*sic*, 1807], ViU: Carter-Smith Papers. Smith's comments were precipitated by the appointment of William Clark, a lieutenant in the artillery who had recently returned from the expedition to the Pacific Ocean, as lieutenant colonel in an infantry regiment "*Over the heads of all the Officers of that Corps.*" "No Man of feeling Could Stand this Insult," in Smith's view.

51. [Ritchie], "Western World," *Enquirer*, 5 September 1806.

52. "Extract of a letter from Alexandria in Virginia," 29 October 1806, enclosed in Hamilton to Cameron, 4 November 1806, NcU: Cameron Family Papers.

53. William Martin to Daniel Smith, 16 January 1807, in Bassett, ed., *Correspondence of Andrew Jackson*, 1:164n1.

54. Jackson to [William Preston Anderson], [3 January 1807], in *PAJ*, 2:134.

55. Thomas Rodney to R[ichard] Claiborne, 5 January 1806 [*sic*, 1807], DLC: Rodney Family Papers. For similar concerns, see William T. Barry to John Barry, 2 January 1807, in Cox, ed., "Letters of William T. Barry," 329; and *Faithful Picture of the Political Situation*, 11.

56. [Ritchie], "Burr's Expedition," *Enquirer*, 27 December 1806.

57. Thomas Rodney to Caesar A. Rodney, 21 November 1806, in Gratz, ed., "Thomas Rodney," 44:292. See also "Extracts from letters to a member of Assembly," *Enquirer*, 15 January 1807.

58. [Stephen C. Carpenter], *People's Friend & Daily Advertiser* (New York), 6 January 1807.

59. John Randolph to George Hay, 3 January 1806 [*sic*, 1807], DLC: John Randolph of Roanoke Papers. For similar views, see also Robert Mackay to Eliza Anne Mackay, 10 January 1807, in Hartridge, ed., *Letters of Robert Mackay*, 56; and Samuel Taggart to John Taylor, 19 January 1807, in "Letters of Samuel Taggart," 205.

60. Joseph Winston to William Lenoir, 5 January 1807, NcU: Lenoir Family Papers. See also William T. Barry to John Barry, 2 January 1807, in Cox, ed., "Letters of William T. Barry," 329.

61. [William Davis], *Norfolk Gazette and Publick Ledger* (Va.), 6 August 1806.

62. John Stokely to Jefferson, 14 February 1807, DLC: Thomas Jefferson Papers. See also Jackson to William C. C. Claiborne, 12 November 1806, in *PAJ*, 2:116; and Silas Dinsmore to Tench Coxe, 4 January 1807, enclosed in Coxe to Dearborn, [10 February 1807], DNA: RG107, M221, C-238 (3).

63. Daveiss to Madison, 14 August 1806, in *View*, 24.

64. Wilkinson to Dearborn, 12 November 1806, DNA: RG107, M221, W-209 (3). See also Wilkinson to Samuel Smith, 14 November and 10 December 1806, PPiU-D: Wilkinson Papers.

65. William C. C. Claiborne to Madison, 5 December 1806, in *OLBWC*, 4:42. For the full range of concerns about the local populace in New Orleans in the first years after the Purchase, see Dargo, *Jefferson's Louisiana*; Kastor, *Nation's Crucible*; and Vernet, *Strangers on Their Native Soil*.

66. John Randolph to Joseph H. Nicholson, 20 February 1807, DLC: Joseph H. Nicholson Papers.

67. "Extracts from letters to a member of Assembly," *Enquirer*, 15 January 1807. "White or black caps" suggests a body of men united across racial lines by class.

68. Francis J. Dallam to Richard Dallam, 1 February 1807, MdHi: Dallam Papers.

69. John A. Davidson to Cowles Mead, 20 January 1807, in Rowland, *Third Annual Report*, 68. Conversely, the "few negroes" that militia colonel William Wooldridge found among Burr's men at Bayou Pierre do not seem to have caused any panic (W[illiam] H. Wooldridge to Mead, 14 January 1807, in ibid., 54).

70. Dinsmore to John McKee, 7 January 1807, in Owens, ed., "Burr's Conspiracy," 169. Dinsmore had recently become a slave-owning planter himself; see Kennedy, *Burr, Hamilton, and Jefferson*, 318. From New Orleans in early December, Robert Sterry insisted that the city was not in danger from anyone, "unless it is the Negroes—and very little from them" (Robert Sterry to Stephen Bradley, 10 December 1806, GU: Joseph Wheaton Papers). For the dangers of racial or servile rebellion in the Orleans Territory in the first years after the purchase, see, in particular, Rodriguez, "Ripe for Revolt," 56–86.

71. Wilkinson to Dearborn, 26 December 1806, DNA: RG107, M221, W-221 (3); Wilkinson to William C. C. Claiborne, 6 December 1806, in *OLBWC*, 4:47. See also Wilkinson's letters to: Thomas Cushing, 7 November 1806, in Wilkinson, *Memoirs of My Own Times*, 2:Appendix 99; Jefferson, 9 December 1806, PHi: Daniel Parker Papers; Daniel Clark, [10 December 1806], PHi: Gilpin Family Papers; and Vicente Folch and Juan Ventura Morales, 6 January 1807, quoted in McCaleb, *New Light on Aaron Burr*, 52. For Burr's slaveowning, see Aaron Burr to Theodosia Burr Alston, 10 July 1804, in *MAB*, 2:322. Roger Kennedy made the strongest claim that Burr's antislavery activities in New York during the 1790s and plans for what Kennedy called a "possibly abolitionist colony" on the Bastrop grant in 1806 alarmed slaveholders in the Southwest and Washington (Kennedy, *Burr, Hamilton, and Jefferson*, 242–53, quote at 252). But the evidence that he adduced is very thin, incorrectly applied, and often carelessly cited. After the crisis had ended, as he defended his actions in New Orleans, Wilkinson occasionally suggested that his fears had been much greater than the evidence from the time suggests. Before the Richmond grand jury, he testified that Judge James Workman, whom he suspected of favoring Burr's plans, could have "raise[d] a corps of 500 mulattos" through his "connect[ion] with a first-rate mulatto woman" (Wilkinson, testimony, 22 June 1807, in "NECAB," 72). Similarly, in his 1811 defense pamphlet, he claimed that Burr "could have used the slaves at his discretion" (Wilkinson, *Burr's Conspiracy*

Exposed, 38). But he had held "the very opposite impression" during the crisis (Wilkinson to Jefferson, 19 April 1807, DLC: Burr Conspiracy Collection).

72. Wilkinson to Samuel Smith, 14 November 1806, PPiU-D: Wilkinson Papers. These concerns were widely shared in New Orleans; see James Workman to William C. C. Claiborne, 5 January 1807, in [Workman], *Letter to the Respectable Citizens*, 3; and John Watkins, speech, 16 March 1807, in *Debate in the House of Representatives of the Territory of Orleans*, 17–18. In early December, Governor Claiborne directed the militia to "maintain a strict guard among the Slaves" (William C. C. Claiborne to "the Colonels, Majors, and Captains of the Regiments," 9 December 1806, in Rowland, *Third Annual Report*, 121). Six weeks later, he reiterated the need for nightly militia patrols for that purpose; see William C. C. Claiborne to Wilkinson, 19 January 1807, in *OLBWC*, 4:102.

73. Wilkinson to William C. C. Claiborne, 3 January 1807, LNT-H: James Wilkinson Collection. Wilkinson did want "the aid of the whole Militia of the Coast below this City and its precincts." But those parishes included fewer slaves; see "A General return of the Census of the Territory of Orleans taken for the year 1806," 31 December 1806, in *TPUS*, 9:702. For evidence that Claiborne and Wilkinson used these census figures to decide which parishes to draw upon for militia support, see William C. C. Claiborne to Wilkinson, 4 January 1807, in *OLBWC*, 4:80. In early January 1807, Wilkinson even expressed the wish that he had the "power to organize the people of color," which would have provided him with an additional "Six Hundred hardy fellows in arms" (Wilkinson to Dearborn, 8/9 January 1807, DNA: RG107, M222, W-1807).

74. Jackson to Daniel Smith, 12 November 1806, in *PAJ*, 2:118.

75. Richard Neale, testimony, 24 September 1807, in *TCAB*, 3:210.

76. "Carthage," *Impartial Review, and Cumberland Repository* (Nashville, Tenn.), 24 January 1807. The phrase "imagined community" is drawn from Benedict Anderson's classic study of nationalism, *Imagined Communities*.

77. "The address of captains Kilgore and Appleton, to the Volunteers of Robertson county (Tennessee)," *Impartial Review*, 24 January 1807. See also "Resolution of Citizens of the Territory," 13 February 1807, in *TPUS*, 14:99. For concerns about "posterity," see Royster, *Revolutionary People at War*. For conflicting views of loyalty within the United States in this period, see Tsiang, *Question of Expatriation*; Kettner, *Development of American Citizenship*, 173–209, 248–86; Smith, *Civic Ideals*, 137–96; and Bradburn, *Citizenship Revolution*, 101–38. Differing American and European ideas of loyalty contributed to the dispute between the United States and Great Britain over impressment—a dispute that raged for two decades and helped to bring about war in 1812; see Perkins, *Prologue to War*.

78. Coxe to Madison, 2 March 1807, DLC: James Madison Papers.

79. "Resolutions by the Legislative Assembly," [20 February 1807], in *TPUS*, 9:707. See also "Resolution," 3 December 1806, in Kentucky, *Journal of the House of Representatives*, 118; Abraham Shepherd and Thomas Kirker to Jefferson, 6 December 1806, DLC: Jefferson Papers; and "Resolutions by the Territorial

Legislature," [27 January 1807], in *TPUS*, 5:507. Abraham Shepherd and Thomas Kirker forwarded a resolution from the Ohio state assembly.

80. Benjamin Field to Jefferson, 9 February 1807, DLC: Jefferson Papers. For other resolutions from public meetings and militia musters, see *Impartial Review*, 3, 17, and 24 January 1807; "Wilkinson County," *Mississippi Messenger* (Natchez), 27 January 1807; *National Intelligencer*, 16 and 28 January 1807; and "Communication," *Palladium*, 19 March 1807.

81. "Extract of a letter from a Gentleman in Lexington (K) to the Editor of the Enquirer," *Enquirer*, 17 March 1807. For similar letters, see also *National Intelligencer*, 7 and 21 January and 11 March 1807; Joseph Crockett to Jefferson, 9 January 1807, DLC: Jefferson Papers; and James Robertson to Daniel Smith, 2 February 1807, in Bassett, ed., *Correspondence of Andrew Jackson*, 1:164n.

82. *Impartial Review*, 11 July 1807. See also "Fourth of July," ibid., 23 July 1807; and *Palladium*, 15 July and 13 August 1807. For western responses to the Burr Conspiracy, see, in addition to general histories, Henshaw, "Aaron Burr Conspiracy in the Ohio Valley"; Cox, "Western Reaction to the Burr Conspiracy"; and Dunbar, "Burr 'Conspiracy' and the Old Northwest." For the tensions in early American nationalism, particularly as apparent in festive culture and the press, see Waldstreicher, *In the Midst of Perpetual Fetes*.

83. Field to Jefferson, 9 February 1807, DLC: Jefferson Papers.

84. James Taylor to Madison, 13 October 1806, in Padgett, ed., "Letters of James Taylor," 115; Wyllys Silliman to Worthington, 20 January 1807, OHi: Worthington Papers. For similar fears expressed by a Kentuckian about the loyalty of Tennesseeans, see William T. Barry to John Barry, 27 January 1807, ViU: William T. Barry Letters.

85. Resolutions, enclosed in William W. Cooke to Madison, 14 April 1807, DNA: RG59, M179.

86. Henry Clay to [John Bradford], [1 February 1807], in *PHC*, 1:276.

87. [Hunter], *Palladium*, 27 November 1806. For the political work that was done by honor in the early republic, see Freeman, *Affairs of Honor*.

88. *Faithful Picture of the Political Situation*, [4]; [Thomas Eastin], *Impartial Review*, 3 January 1807; Jackson to Bissell, 9 January 1807, in *PAJ*, 2:142.

89. "Lexington," *National Intelligencer*, 2 February 1807; [Eastin], *Impartial Review*, 3 January 1807.

90. Field to Jefferson, 9 February 1807, DLC: Jefferson Papers.

91. Watkins, speech, 16 March 1807, in *Debate in the House of Representatives of the Territory of Orleans*, 17.

92. William Creighton to Worthington, 25 January 1807, OHi: Worthington Papers.

93. [Eastin], *Impartial Review*, 3 January 1807.

94. Shepherd and Kirker to Jefferson, 6 December 1806, DLC: Jefferson Papers.

95. [Eastin], *Impartial Review*, 17 January 1807.

96. Resolutions, enclosed in Cooke to Madison, 14 April 1807, DNA: RG59, M179.

97. "The following is an extract of a letter received from a gentleman of the highest respectability residing in west Tennesee," *National Intelligencer*, 7 January 1807.

98. John Nicholson to Jefferson, 14 October 1806, in *TJC*, 136; Creighton to Worthington, 25 January 1807, OHi: Worthington Papers.

99. James Taylor, "Autobiography," ICU: Reuben T. Durrett Collection, Durrett Codices, 54.

100. "Querist" [Harman Blennerhassett], "[No. I]," *Western Spy* (Cincinnati, Ohio), 7 October 1806, clipped from *Ohio Gazette* (Marietta). The most convenient place to find the four "Querist" essays is *Alexandria Daily Advertiser* (D.C.), 13–15 November 1806 (from AHN).

101. Jonathan Dayton to Jacob Burnet, 10 July 1807, OCHi: Jacob Burnet Papers. Writing to his superiors in Madrid, the Marquis de Yrujo similarly argued that, if a separatist movement began in the West, easterners would be unwilling "to fight against their fellow-citizens, who, according to the principles laid down in the declaration of the independence of this country, have the same right to separate themselves, which these colonies had to sever the political bands which united them to England" (Marquis de Yrujo to Don Pedro Cevallos, 18 December 1806, in *Proofs*, Appendix, 191).

102. The anti-"Querist" writers in the West in the fall of 1806 included Thomas Spotswood Hinde, who provided five "Fredonian" essays for the *Scioto Gazette* (beginning 9 October); Humphrey Marshall, who wrote as both "An Observer" and "One of the People" for the *Western World* (on 18 October and 7 November, respectively); and Matthew Nimmo, who published seven essays titled "Conspiracy" and signed "Regulus" in the *Western Spy* (beginning 21 October). The *Western Spy* also printed at least two essays by "Sidney" (beginning 14 October), a piece by "An American" (on 21 October), and three fables by "Myself" (beginning 25 November). At least four essays titled "Union" appeared in the *Scioto Gazette* (the second of which ran on 25 December). The *Ohio Herald* printed at least one anti-"Querist" editorial; see "From the Ohio Herald," *Alexandria Daily Advertiser*, 11 November 1806 (from AHN). During the same months, eastern newspapers also discussed union and disunion. The most extensive defense of union could be found in a series of at least six essays under the title "Advantages of Union, with an Inquiry into the Compatibility of Republican Government with an Extensive Territory," which appeared in the *National Intelligencer* (beginning 6 October 1806).

103. "An American," *Western Spy*, 21 October 1806. See also "The Fredonian" [Thomas Spotswood Hinde], "The aspect of affairs in the Western Country, and Col. Burr's late visit, [No. II]," *Enquirer*, 25 November 1806, clipped from *Scioto Gazette* (Chillicothe, Ohio).

104. "Regulus" [Matthew Nimmo], "Conspiracy, No. I," *Western Spy*, 21 October 1806; "Regulus" [Nimmo], "Conspiracy, No. II," ibid., 28 October 1806. For Nimmo's authorship of the "Regulus" essays, see Abraham Baldwin to Jefferson, 20 January 1807, DNA: RG59, M418, filed under "Nimmo, Matthew or John?";

and Daniel Symmes to Samuel Huntington, 21 June 1807, OCHi: Daniel Symmes Letter. Nimmo posited that Burr had written the "Querist" essays and Blennerhassett had merely delivered them to the *Ohio Gazette* (see "Regulus" [Nimmo], "Conspiracy, No. VI [*sic*, IV]," *Western Spy*, 18 November 1806).

105. "Querist" [Blennerhassett], "[No. IV]," *Western Spy*, 4 November 1806, clipped from *Ohio Gazette*.

106. "Querist" [Blennerhassett], "[No. I]," ibid., 7 October 1806.

107. "Regulus" [Nimmo], "Conspiracy, No. I," ibid., 21 October 1806. For land sales, see "Regulus" [Nimmo], "Conspiracy, No. VI [*sic*, IV]," ibid., 18 November 1806.

108. For unionist thinking in the 1780s and beyond, see Nagel, *One Nation Indivisible*; Stampp, "Concept of a Perpetual Union"; Onuf, *Origins of the Federal Republic*; Matson and Onuf, *Union of Interests*; Knupfer, *Union as It Is*; Lewis, *American Union and the Problem of Neighborhood*; Hendrickson, *Peace Pact*; Kersh, *Dreams of a More Perfect Union*; and LaCroix, *Ideological Origins of American Federalism*.

109. "Regulus" [Nimmo], "Conspiracy, No. II," *Western Spy*, 28 October 1806.

110. [McClean], "To the Public," *Western Star* (Lebanon, Ohio), 13 February 1807.

111. "An Observer" [Humphrey Marshall], *Western World* (Frankfort, Ky.), 18 October 1806.

112. Ibid.

113. "Sydney," "No. II," *Western Spy*, 21 October 1806.

114. "Querist" [Blennerhassett], "To the Printer of the Ohio Gazette [No. IV]," *Alexandria Daily Advertiser*, 15 November 1806 (from AHN). During the Richmond trial, Blennerhassett boastfully recorded in his diary that Burr's attorney, Luther Martin, considered the fourth "Querist" a powerful "piece of argumentation . . . on the merits of the question respecting a severance of the union" (Blennerhassett, diary entry, 27 September 1807, in *BwB*, 108).

115. "Regulus" [Nimmo], "Conspiracy, No. III," *Western Spy*, 4 November 1806.

116. "One of the People" [Marshall], *Western World*, 7 November 1806; Worthington to unknown correspondent, 12 January 1807, ORCHi: Early Statehood Papers. See also "Myself," "[No. III]," *Western Spy*, 9 December 1806.

117. "An Observer" [Marshall], *Western World*, 18 October 1806.

118. "Regulus" [Nimmo], "Conspiracy, No. VII," *Western Spy*, 30 December 1806.

119. "An Observer" [Marshall], *Western World*, 18 October 1806.

120. William C. C. Claiborne, "Speech to Assembly," 13 January 1807, in *OLBWC*, 4:89.

121. "Sydney," "No. I," *Western Spy*, 14 October 1806. For a versification of the Farewell Address, see "The Fredonian" [Hinde], "Aspect of the Affairs in the Western Country and the *emissaries* of Col. Burr, No. V," *Scioto Gazette*, 20 November 1806.

122. Jared Mansfield to Jefferson, 31 October 1806, in *TPUS*, 14:23. See also "Regulus" [Nimmo], "Conspiracy, No. II," *Western Spy*, 28 October 1806.

123. Robertson to Daniel Smith, 2 February 1807, in Bassett, ed., *Correspondence of Andrew Jackson*, 1:164n.

124. William A. Burwell, circular letter to constituents, 2 March 1807, in *CLC*, 3:516. See also Worthington to unknown correspondent, 12 January 1807, ORCHi: Early Statehood Papers; Marmaduke Williams, circular letter to constituents, 26 February 1807, in *CLC*, 3:503; and John W. Gurley, speech, 16 March 1807, in *Debate in the House of Representatives of the Territory of Orleans*, 33.

125. Richard Peters to Pickering, 24 February 1807, MHi: Pickering Papers. See also Jefferson to Lafayette, 26 May 1807, in *WoTJ*, 10:411.

126. Ames to Quincy, 20 December 1806, in Allen, ed., *Works of Fisher Ames*, 2:1538.

127. Ames to Pickering, 22 December 1806, in ibid., 1539–40. Ames—the archest of arch-Federalists—quoted Jefferson's first inaugural address; see Jefferson, First Inaugural Address, 4 March 1801, in *CMPP*, 1:321.

128. Beverley Tucker to John Randolph, 31 January 1807, ViW: Tucker-Coleman Papers.

129. Henry Clay to Langdon Cheves, 5 March 1821, in *PHC*, 3:58. I discuss western separatism between 1819 and 1821 in *American Union and the Problem of Neighborhood*, 126–54.

130. Thomas Sidney Jesup to Jackson, 18 August 1816, DLC: Thomas Sidney Jesup Papers; Jesup to Monroe, 8 September 1816, ibid. In September 1808, Governor Claiborne reported that someone "at Natches" hoped that Cuba would fall "into the hands of Great Britain, which will give her the Command of the Mississippi and of course the Western commerce, and [might] induce the Western Citizens to pursue their best Interest, which was to form a separate Government, bounded Eastwardly by the Alegany Mountains" (William C. C. Claiborne to Madison, 7 September 1808, in *OLBWC*, 4:213). Although Claiborne omitted the person's name, he may have been referring to Harman Blennerhassett. Blennerhassett may or may not have understood this form of disunionism in 1806 or 1808, but he certainly understood it by 1818. In a memorandum for Lord Dalhousie, the British lieutenant-governor of Nova Scotia, Blennerhassett, writing "as a British subject, and a lover of my country," urged him, in the event of war with the United States, to seize Florida and use it to "annihilate the trade of New Orleans." "The destruction of their Commerce," he predicted, would "induce [westerners] to assume a seperate, & distinct interest, & Government from their Atlantic Neighbours upon the least encouragement & support from the British Government" (Blennerhassett to Lord Dalhousie, [20 May 1818], OHi: Blennerhassett Family Papers at Campus Martius Museum).

131. See, for example, Turner, *Rise of the New West*; and Philbrick, *Rise of the West*.

132. Brackenridge, *Recollections of Persons and Places*, 104. See also Hall, *Letters from the West*, 101–3. For Brackenridge, see Keller, *Nation's Advocate*.

SECOND INTERLUDE. THE CRIME ON
BLENNERHASSETT ISLAND

1. The interpretation and all of the information in this column come from the prosecution's case in Burr's treason trial in Richmond, including the indictment, the grand jury testimony of six eyewitnesses, and the prosecution's opening argument. See [George Hay], indictment, [ca. 22 May 1807], in *ASP: Misc*, 1:486–87; Peter Taylor, Jacob Allbright, Simeon Poole, Dudley Woodbridge Jr., Edmund Dana, and John Monholland, testimony, 16, 18, and 23 June 1807, in "NECAB," 27–28, 41, 44–46, 82–83; and Hay, argument, 17 August 1807, in *RTCAB*, 1:446–50. A second, otherwise identical, indictment named 11 December as the date of the treason; it must have quickly become clear that the men and boats had left by then. The format of this opening was inspired by chapter 20 of John Barth's novel *The Floating Opera* (1956).

2. The interpretation and most of the information in this column come from documents in Margaret Blennerhassett's 1842 petition to Congress. See Margaret Blennerhassett, petition, 7 March 1842, in Senate Committee of Claims, *Report on the Memorial of Margaret Blennerhasset*, 5–6; Morgan Neville and William Robinson Jr., statement, [late January 1807], in ibid., 8; and Dudley Woodbridge Jr. to William Woodbridge, 2 April 1842, in ibid., 13–14. The volunteers' pursuit of the boats along the river is mentioned in John Stokely to Thomas Jefferson, 14 February 1807, DLC: Thomas Jefferson Papers. Neville had earlier described some of these events in a widely reprinted newspaper piece; see [Neville], "A Letter from One of the Young Gentlemen who Lately Left this Town," *Pittsburgh Gazette* (Pa.), 13 January 1807. But a comparison of this letter—which is replete with literary allusions—with his later sworn statement suggests that Neville exaggerated and invented events (some of which have been repeated by historians) for satirical purposes. For Neville's literary career, see Flanagan, "Morgan Neville."

3. Margaret Blennerhassett to Harman Blennerhassett, 26 August 1807, in *BP*, 284.

4. See Harman Blennerhassett, "Brief on behalf of Harman Blennerhassett, confined in the Penitentiary at Richmond, Va., under an indictment for high treason," [7–23 August 1807], in *BwB*, 190–91; and Julian Depestre, affidavit, 1 October 1807, in *TCAB*, 3:316. Burr's slave Harry was almost certainly with him, though neither Depestre nor Blennerhassett mentioned him. Burr's German secretary, Charles Willie, was not, having gone ahead to Chillicothe; see examination of Charles Willie, 9 April 1807, enclosed in Harry Toulmin to Jefferson, 5/13 April 1807, DLC: Edmond Charles Genet Papers. A number of historians place Burr on the island for a much longer time. See, for example, Abernethy, *Burr Conspiracy*, 67; Lomask, *Aaron Burr*, 2:129; and Swick, *Island Called Eden*, 41. They rely on vague and often contradictory testimony, whereas

Blennerhassett's and Depestre's recollections were precise and consistent. Burr also remembered staying on the island one night, but remembered it as 31 August; see Aaron Burr, remarks, 19 August 1807, in *RTCAB*, 1:512.

5. Bernard, *Retrospections of America*, 188.

6. Thomas Rodney, diary entry, 24 September 1803, in Smith and Swick, eds., *Journey through the West*, 70, 72. In general, the most reliable histories of the Blennerhassetts and the island are those of Ray Swick, the former director of Blennerhassett Island State Historical Park; see, in particular, his "Harman Blennerhassett"; "Aaron Burr's Visit to Blennerhassett Island"; and *Island Called Eden*. Also useful are Wood, *None Called Him Neighbor*; and Turner, "Harman Blennerhassett."

7. Harman Blennerhassett to Burr, 21 December 1806, in *BP*, 118. See also Harman Blennerhassett, "Brief," [7–23 August 1807], in *BwB*, 188–89; Harman Blennerhassett to John Devereux, 15 December 1805, in *BP*, 112–15; and Burr to Harman Blennerhassett, 15 April, 17 May, and 24 July 1806, in ibid., 119–21, 121–22, and 122–23. Unfortunately, Burr's first letter to Blennerhassett was among those stolen by William H. Safford and never published; I discuss this theft in "'Bring Them *to Light*.'"

8. "Querist" [Harman Blennerhassett], "[No. I]," *Western Spy* (Cincinnati, Ohio), 7 October 1806.

9. "Querist" [Harman Blennerhassett], "[No. II]," September 1806, in *BP*, 139. For the travails of the *Ohio Gazette*, see Matthew Backus to James Backus, 25 November 1806, OHi: Backus-Woodbridge Collection. I have been unable to find copies of the *Ohio Gazette*. An extensive outline for the series in Blennerhassett's papers suggests that he projected far more than the four essays that were published; see [Harman Blennerhassett], "Condition of the Country in General," DLC: Harman Blennerhassett Papers.

10. Matthew Backus to James Backus, 17 September 1806, OHi: Backus-Woodbridge Collection.

11. James Taylor to James Madison, 13 October 1806, in Padgett, ed., "Letters of James Taylor," 113–14. For the first public identification of Blennerhassett, see "An American," *Western Spy*, 21 October 1806. See also Morris [*sic*, Maurice] Belknap to Timothy E. Danielson, 11 October 1806, excerpted in William Eaton to Madison, 27 October 1806, DLC: Burr Conspiracy Collection; "The Fredonian" [Thomas Spotswood Hinde], "The Fredonian—No. IV," *Scioto Gazette* (Chillicothe, Ohio), 6 November 1806; and "Regulus" [Matthew Nimmo], "Conspiracy, No. VI [*sic*, IV]," *Western Spy*, 18 November 1806.

12. "Resolutions," *Enquirer* (Richmond, Va.), 14 November 1806. The *Ohio Gazette* was still without paper, but the resolutions were printed in the *Monongalia Gazette* (Morgantown, Va.) and widely reprinted in other newspapers.

13. Belknap to Danielson, 11 October 1806, excerpted in Eaton to Madison, 27 October 1806, DLC: Burr Conspiracy Collection.

14. James Wilson to Madison, 21 November 1806, ibid. The precise timing and relative importance of these events is not clear. For Blennerhassett's trip, see also Harman Blennerhassett, "Brief," [7–23 August 1807], in *BwB*, 197.

15. Harman Blennerhassett, "Brief," [7–23 August 1807], in *BwB*, 197, 199, 201, 202. Phelps provided a similar account of this meeting to the Richmond grand jury; see Hugh Phelps, testimony, 19 June 1807, in "NECAB," 52–53. Taylor's testimony explains why it took so long for Harman to respond to his wife's anxious note. Since Margaret did not know where her husband was, Taylor went to Chillicothe and Cincinnati before finally finding him in Lexington; see Peter Taylor, testimony, 18 August 1807, in *RTCAB*, 1:492.

16. Harman Blennerhassett, "Brief," [7–23 August 1807], in *BwB*, 205.

17. John Graham, testimony, 24 September 1807, in *TCAB*, 3:213–14.

18. Graham, testimony, 16 and 17 June 1807, in "NECAB," 33.

19. Wilson to Madison, 21 November 1806, DLC: Burr Conspiracy Collection.

20. Graham to Madison, 22 November 1806, excerpted in same to same, 28 November 1806, ibid. (the italics mark coded passages that I deciphered). I discuss this document in the First Interlude. The original of this letter has not survived.

21. Wilson to Madison, 21 November 1806, ibid.

22. Graham to Madison, 28 November 1806, ibid.

23. Edward Tiffin to Thomas Worthington, 18 December 1806, OHi: Thomas Worthington Papers.

24. William Constable, diary entry, 8 December 1806, in Jenkins, *Citizen Daniel*, 89.

25. Different accounts place the arrival of the proclamation on 12 or 13 December, see Griffin Greene to Albert Gallatin, 17 December 1806, DNA: RG45, M124; and "Extract of a letter from Return J. Meigs," *National Intelligencer, and Washington Advertiser* (D.C.), 29 December 1806. According to one of the president's correspondents, the proclamation served as a "Blank Prosses, to be filled with any name or names according to the Passions of those in whose hands it might happen to fall" (Stokely to Jefferson, 14 February 1807, DLC: Jefferson Papers). With this license, local militia companies committed illegal and destructive acts at a number of sites along the Ohio; see, for example, James Ross to James McHenry, 12 January 1807, NjP: Fuller Collection of Aaron Burr.

26. Harman Blennerhassett, diary entry, 8 August 1807, in *BwB*, 12.

27. Dudley Woodbridge Jr. to Harman Blennerhassett, 8 June 1807, in *BP*, 249.

28. Thomas Neale to Harman Blennerhassett, 30 July 1807, OMC: Samuel P. Hildreth Collection.

29. William Skinner to Archibald Woods, 12 March 1807, ViW: Archibald Woods Papers. For Parson and Jim, see Harman Blennerhassett to Dudley Woodbridge Jr., 23 February 1807, OHi: Backus-Woodbridge Collection; Margaret Blennerhassett to Harman Blennerhassett, 26 August 1807, in *BP*, 284; and Edward W. Tupper, deposition, 8 September 1807, in Henshaw, ed., "Burr-Blennerhassett

Documents," 23. Skinner also mentioned the attachment of one slave family, and Harman Blennerhassett noted that "Ransom" (he did not acknowledge his slave's last name) had been sold (Harman Blennerhassett, diary entry, 13 August 1807, in *BwB*, 20).

30. Neale to Harman Blennerhassett, 30 July 1807, OMC: Hildreth Collection.

31. Neale to Harman Blennerhassett, 11 March 1807, ibid.; Dudley Woodbridge Jr. to Harman Blennerhassett, 8 June 1807, in *BP*, 250. After speaking with Woodbridge and former neighbor Edmund Dana in Richmond in August, Blennerhassett described his slaves as "vagrant and *latitant* [in hiding]" (Harman Blennerhassett to Margaret Blennerhasset, 4–7 August 1807, in ibid., 277). The secondary literature has little to say about the Blennerhassett slaves, but Ray Swick includes a brief discussion, with a partial list of names, in *Island Called Eden*, 22–23. For slaves in Ohio in this period, see Pocock, "Slavery and Freedom in the Early Republic"; and Owens, "Law and Disorder North of the Ohio."

32. Harman Blennerhassett, diary entry, [24 January 1807], in *BwB*, 186. For the request to prepare an inventory, see Harman Blennerhassett to Wilson, 10 December 1806, WvU: Harman Blennerhassett Papers.

33. Harman Blennerhassett to Dudley Woodbridge Jr., 17 April 1807, KyLoF: Harman Blennerhassett Papers.

34. Harman Blennerhassett to Dudley Woodbridge Jr., 23 February 1807, OHi: Backus-Woodbridge Collection.

35. Harman Blennerhassett to Wilson, 11 March 1807, WvU: Blennerhassett Papers. He also hoped to recover his scientific apparatus and chemicals, which he believed he could sell in Natchez; see Harman Blennerhassett to David Wallace, 11 March 1807, PPiU-D: James Wilkinson Papers.

36. Harman Blennerhassett to Dudley Woodbridge Jr., 23 February 1807, OHi: Backus-Woodbridge Collection.

37. Harman Blennerhassett to Dudley Woodbridge Jr., 17 April 1807, KyLoF: Blennerhassett Papers. Blennerhassett was discharged without trial.

38. Henry Clay to Harman Blennerhassett, 22 July 1807, in *BP*, 271. See also Lewis Sanders to William Woodbridge, 15 and 17 July and 18 November 1807, MiD-B: William Woodbridge Papers.

39. Harman Blennerhassett to Margaret Blennerhassett, 18 July 1807, in *BP*, 263.

40. William Constable, diary entry, 22 November 1806, in Jenkins, *Citizen Daniel*, 80. Constable's brother recorded seeing the men engaged in "a military parade," though a "great part [had] no other arms than bats or poles" (Daniel Constable, diary entry, 20 October 1806, in ibid., 77).

41. Hay, argument, 17 September 1807, in *TCAB*, 3:127. That courts in Kentucky and the Mississippi Territory had already freed Burr might have militated against those options. Most secondary works either ignore these decisions—as decisions—or attribute them to information that seems only to have been known after they were made. See, for example, Melton, *Aaron Burr*, 164–65; Hoffer, *Treason Trials of Aaron Burr*; and Newmyer, *Treason Trial of Aaron Burr*.

42. Hay, argument, 17 September 1807, in *TCAB*, 3:127. For the cabinet meeting that redirected Burr's captors to Richmond, see Jefferson's docket on Egbert Benson to Jefferson, 25 March 1807, DLC: Burr Conspiracy Collection.

43. John Marshall, comment, 17 September 1807, in *TCAB*, 3:129.

44. William Plumer, diary entry, 4 March 1807, in *WPMP*, 641. More than two months earlier, Plumer had recorded another meeting in which Jefferson had asserted that the government had "full evidence to convict [Blennerhassett] of being engaged in the conspiracy" (Plumer, diary entry, 27 December 1806, in ibid., 543).

45. [Thomas Ritchie], *Enquirer*, 27 March 1807. See also "Extract of a letter from a correspondent, dated Fredericksburgh," *New-York Evening Post*, 30 March 1807.

46. Caesar A. Rodney, "Interrogatories," [ca. 6 April 1807], DLC: Burr Conspiracy Collection. For the dating of this document, see John G. Jackson to George Jackson Jr., 18 April 1807, OHi: John G. Jackson Letters. For the arrival of this material, see Hay, comment, 1 June 1807, in *RTCAB*, 1:106. This presumably rich source of information was considered inadmissable and has disappeared. Collector Brian Hardison has found what seems to be a deposition in response to Rodney's request, or perhaps the original notes for the submitted deposition; see Hardison and Swick, "Recruit for Aaron Burr." He generously allowed me to look through his collection of Burr material in October 2007.

47. Allbright, testimony, 19 August 1807, in *RTCAB*, 1:509.

48. Tiffin to Henry Dearborn, 14 December 1806, excerpted in "Western News," *Alexandria Daily Advertiser* (D.C.), 1 January 1807 (from AHN).

49. Allbright, testimony, 19 August 1807, in *RTCAB*, 1:512.

50. Burr, cross-examination of William Love, 19 August 1807, in ibid., 517.

51. Dudley Woodbridge Jr., testimony, 19 August 1807, in ibid., 526. In early September 1807, Tupper provided a lengthy deposition about these events that flatly denied Allbright's story of the levelling of guns. This deposition does not seem to have been entered into the trial record; see Tupper, deposition, 8 September 1807, in Henshaw, ed., "Burr-Blennerhassett Documents," 13–27. The prosecution and defense ultimately agreed that, even if muskets had been levelled at Tupper, it would not have constituted levying war against the United States since Tupper was a militia general, rather than an army officer, and could not exercise even that authority outside of Ohio; see Benjamin Botts, argument, 25 August 1807, in *RTCAB*, 2:124.

52. Burr, cross-examination of Dudley Woodbridge Jr., 19 August 1807, in *RTCAB*, 1:526; Dudley Woodbridge Jr., testimony, 19 August 1807, in ibid.

53. George Hay to Jefferson, 1 September 1807, DLC: Jefferson Papers.

54. John Marshall, opinion, 31 August 1807, in *PJMar*, 7:114.

55. Hay to Caesar A. Rodney, 2 November 1807, DeHi: H. Fletcher Brown Collection of Rodney Family Papers.

56. Harman Blennerhassett to Margaret Blennerhassett, 4–7 August 1807, in *BP*, 277.

57. Harman Blennerhassett, diary entry, 10 October 1807, in *BwB*, 126. For the prospect of recovering some of his auctioned property, see Neale to Harman Blennerhassett, 30 July 1807, OMC: Hildreth Collection; and Harman Blennerhassett, diary entry, 13 August 1807, in *BwB*, 20.

58. Harman Blennerhassett to Margaret Blennerhassett, 7 October 1807, in *BP*, 291.

59. Harman Blennerhassett to Wilson, 11 March 1807, WvU: Blennerhassett Papers.

60. Harman Blennerhassett to Margaret Blennerhassett, 21–24 October 1807, in *BP*, 301. See also same to same, 17 November 1807, in ibid., 514.

61. Harman Blennerhassett to Margaret Blennerhassett, 17 December 1807, in ibid., 519.

62. Robert Miller to Paul Fearing, 11 February 1808, OMC: Hildreth Collection. Miller was furious about this development. He had wanted his agent in Marietta to attach the slaves, though he had recognized the difficulty of doing so. How "you will make them property on that side is to me an inegima," Miller had remarked (Miller to Fearing, 25 October 1807, ibid.). Miller's February 1808 letter also reported that Blennerhassett had purchased additional slave families around Marietta.

63. Harman Blennerhassett to David Putnam, 8 August 1807 [*sic*, 1810?], OHi: Putnam Family Papers. Although this letter is not easily dated, it was sent from La Cache, which Blennerhassett purchased in February 1810; see Boswell, "La Cache," 314.

64. Harman Blennerhassett to Putnam, 15 July 1808, OMC: Hildreth Collection. Dudley Woodbridge Jr. eventually cleared his debt to Blennerhassett by sending him slaves from Virginia; see Gruenwald, *River of Enterprise*, 77.

65. Harman Blennerhassett to Putnam, 8 August 1807 [*sic*, 1810?], OHi: Putnam Family Papers.

66. See "Conflagration," *Western Spectator* (Marietta, Ohio), 12 March 1811.

67. Margaret Blennerhassett, petition, 7 March 1842, in Senate Committee of Claims, *Report on the Memorial of Margaret Blennerhasset*, 5–6. See also Robert Emmett to Clay, 15 February 1842, in ibid., 7; and Margaret Blennerhassett to Clay, mid-March 1842, in *PHC*, 9:680. Margaret had also written about the flight from the island and destruction of her home in poetry; see "A Lady" [Margaret Blennerhassett], *Widow of the Rock*.

68. Clay, remarks, 14 March 1842, in *Congressional Globe*, 27th Cong., 2nd sess., 315.

69. [William Woodbridge], report, 5 August 1842, in Senate Committee of Claims, *Report on the Memorial of Margaret Blennerhasset*, 2–3.

70. Ibid., 4.

71. These efforts seem to have begun within a few years of Margaret Blennerhassett's death; see Harman Blennerhassett Jr.'s letters to Isaac N. Coffin and A. Flesher, 13 January 1845 and 20 February 1846, DLC: Blennerhassett Papers. For the

later reports, see Senate Committee of Claims, *Report on the Memorial of Harman Blennerhassett and Joseph Lewis Blennerhassett*; and Senate Committee of Claims, *Report on the Memorial of the Heirs of Herman Blennerhassett*. Joseph Lewis Blennerhassett was still pursuing this claim as late as 1857; see his letter to Theresa Blennerhassett, 1 July 1857, DLC: Blennerhassett Papers.

72. Green, "Blennerhassetts," 410. See also [Wallace], "Biographical Sketch of Harman Blennerhassett," 138; Clark, "Blennerhassett and Aaron Burr"; and "Blennerhassett Island," *Cleveland Daily Herald* (Ohio), 19 August 1874 (from NCUN).

73. "Blennerhassett's Slave," *Richmond Whig* (Va.), 25 November 1853 (from AHN).

74. Thomas, *Emigrant*, 45. For the island's appearance in maps, see Smith, *Mapping of Ohio*; and Stephenson and McKee, eds., *Virginia in Maps*. The earliest map to include the island was completed in October 1806; see Swick, "Harman Blennerhassett," 244n2.

75. Abbey, "Blennerhassett Papers," 468. In August 2004, the park's director, Ray Swick, graciously showed me around the house and site.

CHAPTER 5. THE ENTERPRISE COMMENCED: THE CIPHER LETTER AS NARRATIVE

1. See Aaron Burr's reassuring letters to: Edward W. Tupper, [18 November 1806], in *PCAB*, 2:1002; William Henry Harrison, 27 November 1806, in ibid., 1005; and Henry Clay, 1 December 1806, in *PHC*, 1:256–57.

2. Charles Biddle to Nicholas Biddle, 2 June [*sic*, July] 1807, PHi: Charles Biddle Papers. For Jefferson's message to Congress, see Chapter 3.

3. "The following is a sketch of the substance of the documents delivered to congress by the president relative to Burr's conspiracy," *American, and Commercial Daily Advertiser* (Baltimore, Md.), 24 January 1807.

4. William Plumer, diary entry, 22 January 1807, in *WPMP*, 584. Every scholar who writes on Burr or the conspiracy has discussed the cipher letter; for an especially thorough account, see Mary-Jo Kline and Joanne Wood Ryan, "Editorial Note: The 'Cipher Letter' to Wilkinson," in *PCAB*, 2:973–86. I discuss Kline and Ryan's reading of the letter below.

5. Thomas Jefferson, special message, 22 January 1807, in *CMPP*, 1:413.

6. James Wilkinson, affidavit, [18 December 1806], in *ASP: Misc*, 1:471. For Wilkinson's second affidavit, see Wilkinson, affidavit, 26 December 1806, in ibid., 472–73. For Jefferson's follow-up message, see Jefferson, special message, 26 January 1807, in *CMPP*, 1:417.

7. "Cyphers," *Enquirer* (Richmond, Va.), 3 November 1807. For Swartwout's story, see his grand jury testimony: Samuel Swartwout, testimony, 16 June 1807, in "NECAB," 30; and Swartwout, deposition, [16 June 1807], in Henshaw, ed., "Burr-Blennerhassett Documents," 53 (though labelled a deposition, this

document is a different record of the same testimony). For Bollman's role, see James Madison, "Substance of a communication made on the 23 of Jany, 1807, by Doctor Bollman to the President," [23 (*sic*, 24) January 1807], in *LOWJM*, 2:394, 396; Justus Erich Bollman to Jefferson, 26 January 1807, DLC: Thomas Jefferson Papers; and Bollman, testimony, 15 June 1807, in "NECAB," 24.

8. Wilkinson, testimony, [19 June 1807], in Henshaw, ed., "Burr-Blennerhassett Documents," 47. Wilkinson treated the Dayton letter even more delicately than the Burr letter, waiting an additional two months before sending the president a copy. His failure to disclose Dayton's role in a more timely manner nearly led to his indictment for misprision of treason in Richmond in June 1807. For the letter, see Jonathan Dayton to Wilkinson, 24 July 1806, in Wilkinson, *Burr's Conspiracy Exposed*, Appendix, 15. A copy was enclosed in Wilkinson to Jefferson, 17 February 1807, DLC: Burr Conspiracy Collection. Wilkinson also enclosed a letter to Dayton that Jefferson could forward, if he chose, that offered not to use the letters if Dayton would "come forward whenever a trial may ensue" to testify against Burr (Wilkinson to Dayton, 17 February 1807, in Wilkinson, *Burr's Conspiracy Exposed*, Appendix, 101). I discuss the near-indictment of Wilkinson below. The Stephens letter seems to have disappeared.

9. The timing of Swartwout's arrival and departure mattered to Wilkinson because he later had to justify his delay in conveying the information to the administration. Testifying in Richmond, Wilkinson stated that Swartwout had reached Natchitoches on 8 October and departed ten days later; see Wilkinson, testimony, 26 September 1807, in *TCAB*, 3:236, 239. Before the Richmond grand jury, Swartwout claimed both an earlier arrival and a shorter stay; see Swartwout, deposition [*sic*, testimony], [16 June 1807], in Henshaw, ed., "Burr-Blennerhassett Documents," 54. Cushing supported Wilkinson, placing Swartwout's arrival "on or about the 8th October" (Thomas Cushing, deposition, 15 November 1806, in Wilkinson, *Memoirs of My Own Times*, 2:Appendix 92).

10. Wilkinson to Jefferson, 21 October 1806, DLC: Burr Conspiracy Collection.

11. Wilkinson to Jefferson, 21 October 1806 ["Confidential"], ibid.

12. [Wilkinson] to [Jefferson], 20 October 1806, ibid. The editors of the Burr papers state that Wilkinson "pretended to have received" this document (Kline and Ryan, "Editorial Note: The 'Cipher Letter' to Wilkinson," in *PCAB*, 2:976). I do not see anything to justify that statement. Rather than trying to disguise his authorship of the unsigned document, Wilkinson may merely have sought to provide Jefferson with something to show to cabinet members and others that gave no indication of its source. Wilkinson included it in his 1811 defense pamphlet and his 1816 memoirs, identifying himself as the author and Jefferson as the addressee.

13. Thomas A. Smith, deposition, [ca. 1811], in Wilkinson, *Memoirs of My Own Times*, 2:Appendix 94. See also Wilkinson to [Jefferson], 6 December 1806, DLC: Burr Conspiracy Collection. For Wilkinson's letter to the War Department, see Wilkinson to Henry Dearborn, 21 October 1806, DNA: RG107, M221, W-196

(3). Only a fragment of the letter to Samuel Smith seems to have survived; see Wilkinson to Samuel Smith, 23 October 1806, excerpted in Samuel Smith to Jefferson, 13 January 1807, DLC: Jefferson Papers. For Lieutenant Smith, see Steward, *Frontier Swashbuckler*, 78–80.

14. Wilkinson to Jefferson, 12 November 1806, ViHi: Wickham Family Papers. Wilkinson removed the original of this letter, and perhaps the enclosure, from the government's files during Burr's trial in Richmond (see Introduction). The available copies include only those parts of the letter that Jefferson provided to the court. Jefferson's note on this copy acknowledges that the original included "some passages entirely confidential . . . which my duties & the public interest forbid me to make public" (Jefferson, note, 7 September 1807, on ibid.). For the Neutral Ground Agreement, see, in particular, Cox, "Louisiana-Texas Frontier during the Burr Conspiracy"; Haggard, "Neutral Ground"; and Holmes, "Showdown on the Sabine." For Dayton's second coded letter, see Dayton to [Wilkinson], 16 July 1807 [*sic*, 1806], in Wilkinson, *Burr's Conspiracy Exposed*, Appendix, 15–16.

15. Wilkinson to Dearborn, 12 November 1806, DNA: RG107, M221, W-209 (3). An earlier letter had almost entirely concerned Wilkinson's negotiation of the Neutral Ground Agreement; see Wilkinson to Dearborn, 4 November 1806, ibid., W-211 (3).

16. Wilkinson to William C. C. Claiborne, 12 November 1806, in *OLBWC*, 4:55. For Briggs's role, see Isaac Briggs, "Statement," 2 January 1807, DLC: Jefferson Papers; and Briggs, deposition, 6 January 1811, in Wilkinson, *Memoirs of My Own Times*, 2:Appendix 59. Briggs also carried a letter to Senator Smith. While it did not mention the cipher letter, it included numerous quotes from something that Wilkinson described as "an indubitable source"—most of which paraphrase passages in the cipher letter (Wilkinson to Samuel Smith, 14 November 1806, PPiU-D: James Wilkinson Papers).

17. Wilkinson, affidavit, [18 December 1806], in *ASP: Misc*, 1:471. For Wilkinson's use of the cipher letter, see Claiborne and John Shaw, statement, 3 December 1806, in *OLBWC*, 4:38–40; and Wilkinson to [Jefferson], 6 December 1806, DLC: Burr Conspiracy Collection. For Wilkinson's dispatch, see Wilkinson to Jefferson, 9 December 1806, PHi: Daniel Parker Papers. Wilkinson's New Orleans opponents later claimed that he had read the cipher letter to a meeting of the city's merchants on 9 December. But there is little evidence to support that claim, and Claiborne insisted upon its falsity; see Claiborne's marginal notes on Jefferson's copy of *Debate in the House of Representatives of the Territory of Orleans*, 5, at the Library of Congress.

18. Wilkinson, affidavit, 26 December 1806, in *ASP: Misc*, 1:472.

19. Jefferson to Wilkinson, 3 January 1807, in *WrTJ*, 11:130. For Jefferson's receipt of the dispatches through Lieutenant Smith, see Jefferson, memorandum, 25 November 1806, in *Anas*, 249. Jefferson also had Briggs prepare a written account that included as much as he could recall of the cipher letter and of the

second encoded letter from Dayton to Wilkinson; see Briggs, "Statement," 2 January 1807, DLC: Jefferson Papers. For Briggs's failed effort to acquire the dictionary, see Benjamin Johnson to Briggs, 21 January 1807, ibid. When James Lowry Donaldson arrived in Washington on 12 January bearing Wilkinson's 9 December dispatch, he could have described the cipher letter's contents since Wilkinson had shown it to him in New Orleans; see Dearborn to Wilkinson, 21 January 1807, DNA: RG107, M6; and James L. Donaldson, deposition, 26 January 1807, in *TCAB*, 3:379.

20. Wilkinson to Jefferson, 13 February 1807, DLC: Burr Conspiracy Collection.
21. Wilkinson to Jefferson, 26 February 1807, ibid. See also Wilkinson to Jefferson, 17 February 1807, ibid.
22. Wilkinson to Jefferson, 15 April 1807, ibid. In mid-March, Wilkinson had chosen Seth Pease, whom Jefferson and Postmaster General Gideon Granger had sent to remove Burrites from the postal service in December, to carry other confidential papers to the president, but Wilkinson still withheld the cipher letter; see Wilkinson to Jefferson, 12 March 1807, ibid.
23. [Burr] to [Wilkinson], 29 July 1806, as rendered in Wilkinson, affidavit, [18 December 1806], in *ASP: Misc*, 1:471.
24. Ibid.
25. For congressmen writing to their constituents and others, see Benjamin Parke to James Brown, 22 January 1807, InHi: Albert G. Porter Papers; George Washington Campbell, circular letter to constituents, 25 February 1807, in *CLC*, 1:495; and William A. Burwell, circular letter to constituents, 2 March 1807, in ibid., 511–12.
26. John Marshall, opinion, 21 February 1807, in *PJMar*, 6:490. For the proceedings in this case, see Haskins and Johnson, *Foundations of Power*, 255–61; Brunson, *Adventures of Samuel Swartwout*, 15–28; Hoffer, *Treason Trials of Aaron Burr*, 95–122; and Newmyer, *Treason Trial of Aaron Burr*, 47–65.
27. Marshall, opinion, 21 February 1807, in *PJMar*, 6:492–95.
28. I discussed the doubts about Jefferson's honesty as part of the response to his 22 January 1807 message in Chapter 3.
29. [Thomas Ritchie], "'The Western World,'" *Enquirer*, 5 September 1806. Works that cover all or most of these incidents include Shreve, *Finished Scoundrel*; Wilkinson, *Wilkinson, Soldier and Pioneer*; Hay, "Some Reflections"; Jacobs, *Tarnished Warrior*; Hay and Werner, *Admirable Trumpeter*; Duty, "James Wilkinson"; Posey, "Rascality Revisited"; Risjord, *Representative Americans*, 260–83; and Linklater, *Artist in Treason*. For Wilkinson's involvement in the Spanish Conspiracy and continuing connection with Spain, see also Shepherd, "Wilkinson and the Beginnings"; Cox, "General Wilkinson and His Later Intrigues"; Whitaker, *Spanish American Frontier*; Watlington, *Partisan Spirit*; and Narrett, "Geopolitics and Intrigue." For his clash with Wayne, see also Wensorski, "Wilkinson Conspiracy." For Jeffersonians' suspicions of Wilkinson and the army, see also Crackel, *Mr. Jefferson's Army*. For Wilkinson's governorship of the Louisiana

Territory, see also Carter, "Burr-Wilkinson Intrigue in St. Louis"; and Foley, "James A. Wilkinson."

30. Andrew Jackson to Campbell, 15 January 1807, in *PAJ*, 2:147.

31. James Sterrett to Nathaniel Evans, 19 December [1806], LU: Evans (Nathaniel and Family) Papers.

32. Thomas Rodney to Caesar A. Rodney, 17 December 1806, DLC: Rodney Family Papers. See also Cowles Mead to Claiborne, 14 December 1806, in *OLBWC*, 4:66; Jackson to [William Preston Anderson], [3 January 1807], in *PAJ*, 2:134; and Ninian Edwards to William Wirt, [5 January 1807], ICHi: Ninian Edwards Papers.

33. William Plumer, diary entry, 12 January 1807, in *WPMP*, 569. Both Samuel Latham Mitchill, a senator from New York, and Andrew Gregg, a representative from backcountry Pennsylvania, however, readily accepted Wilkinson's innocence of any prior knowledge of or involvement in Burr's plans; see Samuel Latham Mitchill to Catharine Mitchill, 7 January 1807, in "Dr. Mitchill's Letters from Washington," 751; and Andrew Gregg to James Potter, 16 January 1807, WHi: Draper Manuscript Collection, PP144–45. Both men clearly had inside information about the cipher letter from either Jefferson or Samuel Smith.

34. Littleton Waller Tazewell to James Monroe, 3/4 January 1807, DLC: James Monroe Papers.

35. [Stephen C. Carpenter], *People's Friend & Daily Advertiser* (New York), 14 January 1807.

36. Jefferson, special message, 22 January 1807, in *CMPP*, 1:413.

37. Charles Geirs to Jefferson, 24 February 1807, in McLaughlin, ed., *To His Excellency Thomas Jefferson*, 9.

38. "A Citizen," *Impartial Review, and Cumberland Repository* (Nashville, Tenn.), 21 February 1807. This view was explicitly challenged a week later; see "A Whig of '76," ibid., 28 February 1807. But South Carolina's Henry Middleton Rutledge found the same sentiment as "A Citizen" when he visited Nashville a month later; see Henry Middleton Rutledge to Henry Izard, 25 March 1807, ScHi: Henry Middleton Rutledge Letter.

39. Thomas Worthington to Albert Gallatin, 19 March 1807, in *PAG*. Opinion in Ohio is also suggested by "A.," "For the Fredonian," *Fredonian* (Chillicothe, Ohio), 7 March 1807. For views in Lexington, Pittsburgh, and New Orleans, see, respectively, "Extract of a letter from a Gentleman in Lexington (K) to the Editor of the Enquirer," *Enquirer*, 17 March 1807; Ross to McHenry, 27 February 1807, NjP: Fuller Collection of Aaron Burr; and P. T. Schenck to James Findlay, 8 May 1807, in Cox, ed., "Selections from the Torrence Papers," 4:126.

40. Timothy Pickering to John Pickering, 9 [*sic*, 19] February 1807, MHi: Timothy Pickering Papers. "If really a party in the project," Pickering continued, Wilkinson "must be deemed worse: for even robbers pay some regard to *honour towards one another*." A similar idea appeared in a brief poem in the pro-Burr *Atlantic*

World, which included the couplet: "A traitor to traitors stands traitor the first: / For a thief among thieves is of all thieves the worst" ([John Wood], "No Particular Reference," *Atlantic World* [Washington, D.C.], 3 February 1807).

41. John Rhea to Dayton, 28 January 1807, MiU C: Jonathan Dayton Papers. See also [Carpenter], *People's Friend*, 7 February 1807; Thomas Truxton to Timothy Pickering, 12 February 1807, MHi: Pickering Papers; and "Concerning Col. Burr's Western Prospects," *Virginia Gazette, and General Advertiser* (Richmond), 4 April 1807. For the views of a Virginia Quid, see Beverley Tucker to John Randolph, 28 January 1806 [*sic*, 1807] and 31 January 1807, ViW: Tucker-Coleman Papers.

42. Wirt to Edwards, 2 February 1807, ICHi: Edwards Papers. See also [Ritchie], "Wilkinson & Burr," *Enquirer*, 3 March 1807.

43. William Plumer, diary entry, 22 January 1807, in *WPMP*, 584.

44. Samuel White to Dayton, 25 January 1807, MiU-C: Dayton Papers.

45. "Hector," "For the People's Friend," *People's Friend*, 26 February 1807. "Hector" was clearly an intimate of Swartwout's and may have been Swartwout himself.

46. "A Whig of '76," *Impartial Review*, 28 February 1807.

47. Marshall, opinion, 1 April 1807, in *PJMar*, 7:15–16.

48. William Plumer, diary entry, 22 January 1807, in *WPMP*, 584. Two of Richmond's newspapers—one Republican, one Federalist—read Marshall's opinion as implicating Wilkinson in Burr's plans, however; see [Samuel Pleasants Jr.], *Virginia Argus* (Richmond), 14 April 1807; and [Augustine Davis], "Col. Burr's Commitment," *Virginia Gazette*, 4 April 1807.

49. Rhea to Dayton, 28 January 1807, MiU-C: Dayton Papers. See also "Union, No. 4," *Scioto Gazette* (Chillicothe, Ohio), 12 February 1807; "Hector," "For the People's Friend," *People's Friend*, 26 February 1807; "A.," "For the Fredonian," *Fredonian*, 7 March 1807; and "Gen. Wilkinson," *Newburyport Herald* (Mass.), 14 April 1807 (from AHN).

50. [Pleasants], *Virginia Argus*, 17 April 1807. Samuel Pleasants assumed, contra Marshall, that Swartwout had delivered the cipher key along with the letter; see ibid., 14 April 1807. An Ohio essayist similarly concluded that either Swartwout had provided the key or Wilkinson had managed to decipher the letter without it; see "Justice," *Scioto Gazette*, 5 March 1807.

51. Thomas Boylston Adams to John Quincy Adams, 8 February 1807, MHi: Adams Family Papers. See also Beverley Tucker to Randolph, 31 January 1807, ViW: Tucker-Coleman Papers.

52. William Plumer to William Plumer Jr., 24 January 1807, DLC: William Plumer Papers.

53. Thomas Rodney to Caesar A. Rodney, 20 January 1807, DLC: Rodney Family Papers; same to same, 26 January 1807, ibid. Eight days earlier, Burr had accused Wilkinson of "vile fabrications" in a letter to Governor Mead, but had not specified the cipher letter (Burr to Mead, 12 January 1807, in *PCAB*, 2:1009). Most secondary accounts state that the cipher letter was published in New

Orleans in December and seen by Burr in the 6 January edition of Natchez's *Mississippi Messenger* at Bayou Pierre on 10 January. Seeing the cipher letter in the newspaper allegedly caused him to abandon his plans and seek an accommodation with local authorities. The story seems to have originated with historian Henry Adams; perhaps the only contemporary source that offers any support for it is Jacob Dunbaugh, testimony, 21 September 1807, in *TCAB*, 3:179. While the loss of some issues of the four New Orleans newspapers and two Natchez newspapers for this period makes it hard to be certain, it seems unlikely that Burr actually saw the deciphered letter on 10 January. The New Orleans newspapers did report Wilkinson's 18 December appearance in court and mention the cipher letter. But the surviving issues of the New Orleans and Natchez newspapers do not include the letter itself. The 6 January edition of the *Messenger* did not even mention the letter. The only thing that could have alarmed Burr in that issue was an official proclamation from Mead; see Mead, "Proclamation," *Mississippi Messenger* (Natchez), 6 January 1807. Burr later suggested that it was this item, not anything about the cipher letter, that had altered his plans; see Burr, remarks, 31 March 1807, in *ECAB*, 24. It is not clear how or when he first saw Wilkinson's version of the letter.

54. *Western World* (Frankfort, Ky.), 12 February 1807. This letter places Burr's denial as early as 16 January. The news seems to have reached New Orleans in one of two letters, both of which are now missing, from Mead to Claiborne; see Wilkinson to Dearborn, 29 and 30 January 1807, DNA: RG107, M221, W-247 (3) and W-248 (3).

55. "Extract of a letter, dated Washington, Mississippi Territory," *National Intelligencer, and Washington Advertiser* (D.C.), 23 February 1807.

56. "Extract of a letter from a gentleman of unquestionable character, dated New-Orleans," *American*, 16 March 1807. For the original letter, see Wilkinson to Samuel Smith, 17 February 1807, PPiU-D: Wilkinson Papers. Despite Smith's alterations, "the internal evidence of the author," as one New Orleanian noted of a number of these letters, was "irresistible" ("Extract of a letter from New Orleans," *Morning Chronicle* [New York], 28 May 1807). Wilkinson continued these attacks in official and private letters; see, for example, his letters to: Dearborn, 13 February 1807, DNA: RG107, M221, W-243 (3); and Jonathan Williams, 2 April 1807, InU: Jonathan Williams Manuscripts.

57. Burr, remarks, 31 March 1807, in *ECAB*, 24. The record of Burr's comments before the Mississippi territorial court is incomplete and garbled, making it imposible to know whether he had denied writing the cipher letter there; see Thomas Rodney, notes, 3 February 1807, printed in Hamilton, *Anglo-American Law on the Frontier*, 261.

58. Burr to Charles Biddle, 18 April 1807, in *PCAB*, 2:1030. Burr's 4 April letter to Biddle is missing, but Biddle's 16 April response suggests that it included a denial of authorship of the cipher letter; see Charles Biddle to Burr, [ca. 16 April 1807], PHi: Biddle Papers. Truxton's 30 March letter to Burr is also missing,

but the commodore mentioned it in another letter while he awaited Burr's response; see Truxton to Thomas Tingey, 9 April 1807, DLC: Thomas Truxton Papers. For Burr's later assurances, see Truxton's letters to: Charles Biddle, 11 July 1807, in Biddle, *Autobiography of Charles Biddle*, 411; Tingey, 15 July 1806, DLC: Truxton Papers; and Jefferson, 23 July 1807, DLC: Jefferson Papers. For the *Observer's* coverage, see, in particular, [Samuel Brooks], *Impartial Observer* (Richmond, Va.), 25 April 1807. I discuss Burr's use of this newspaper in Chapter 8.

59. Joseph H. Nicholson to Monroe, [12 April 1807], DLC: Monroe Papers. Nicholson presided over the Maryland court that freed John Adair and Peter V. Ogden (who had travelled with Swartwout and the cipher letter from Pittsburgh as far as Natchez) in mid-February. Ogden may have known of the variance between the original and the deciphered version, but precisely how is unclear. For Truxton's doubts, see "Extract of a letter from Commodore Truxton to the honorable Joseph Alston," *Georgetown Gazette, and Commercial Advertiser* (S.C.), 28 March 1807.

60. "Extract of a letter, dated New-Orleans," *Morning Chronicle*, 3 June 1807. Since it seems unlikely that Wilkinson had read the cipher letter to the merchants (see above, n. 17), the discrepancies may actually have been noticed by someone who had been shown the letter by Wilkinson but did not want to expose himself by admitting that.

61. "Col. Burr's Trial," *Norfolk Gazette and Publick Ledger* (Va.), 5 June 1807. For rumors that the key had been lost, see, for example, James Taylor to Madison, 13 July 1807, in Padgett, ed., "Letters of James Taylor," 120.

62. [Burr] to Wilkinson, [22–29 July 1807], in *PCAB*, 2:987 (I have standardized the font). Biographical information about these men can be found in standard reference sources. See also: for Latrobe, Hamlin, *Benjamin Henry Latrobe*; for Morgan, Savelle, *George Morgan*; and for Truxton, Ferguson, *Truxton of the Constellation*. Some of Andrew Jackson's firsthand information about Burr's project reached the administration, but only indirectly through Governor Claiborne and Tennessee senator George Washington Campbell, who defied Jackson by showing the president a confidential letter; see editorial note on Jackson to Campbell, 15 January 1807, in *PAJ*, 2:150n11. For Jackson's dealings with Burr, see Ranck, "Andrew Jackson and the Burr Conspiracy"; and Remini, *Andrew Jackson and the Course of American Empire*.

63. Morgan's letters of 29 August and 21 October 1806 to the president have disappeared, but Jefferson clearly viewed them as both explicit and important; I discussed these letters in the First Interlude. I consider Eaton's disclosures at length below. Truxton prepared a plan to counteract Burr's movements in August but did not send it to Jefferson until early December; see Truxton to Jefferson, 4 December 1806, DLC: Jefferson Papers. He later stated that he had first provided his information about Burr's plans to the administration in a letter of 28 November to Dearborn after "[becoming] alarmed" at the reports in *"Western*

Newspapers" (Truxton to Jefferson, 23 July 1807, ibid.); if so, it is now missing. Latrobe prepared a memorandum about his meetings with Burr a week before the proclamation but did not send it to Secretary of the Treasury Albert Gallatin until after its publication; see Benjamin Henry Latrobe to Gallatin, 19/28 November 1806, in *CBHL*, 2:290–96. Bollman requested a meeting with the president soon after the publication of Jefferson's message and Wilkinson's affidavit; I discussed his disclosures in Chapter 3. Alston responded to the inclusion of his name in the printed cipher letter by publishing a letter to South Carolina's governor and forwarding it to Jefferson; see "Copy of a letter from the Honorable Joseph Alston to His Excellency Charles Pinckney," *Georgetown Gazette*, 11 February 1807; and Joseph Alston to Jefferson, 11 February 1807, DLC: Jefferson Papers. Truxton's private campaign to clear his name expanded after the publication of the cipher letter. In late February, he reacted to Alston's public letter by printing a letter of his own; see "Extract of a letter from Commodore Truxton to the honorable Joseph Alston," *Georgetown Gazette*, 28 March 1807. In late March, at Jefferson's request, Truxton provided a formal deposition concerning his meetings with Burr; see Truxton, affidavit, 27 March 1807, CSmH: Huntington Manuscripts Collection. Stoddert's name began appearing in letters and newspapers in late January as someone who knew Burr's plans; see, for example, Nathaniel Macon to Nicholson, 30 January 1807, DLC: Joseph H. Nicholson Papers. He provided a statement to the federal district attorney Walter Jones Jr. in February for the Bollman and Swartwout cases. But Stoddert did not go public with any information until late March, when he published a brief piece in the *National Intelligencer* that was widely reprinted; see Benjamin Stoddert to Samuel H. Smith, *National Intelligencer*, 20 March 1807. I discuss Adair's semipublic and public statements in Chapter 6.

64. "Copy of a letter from the Honorable Joseph Alston to His Excellency Charles Pinckney," *Georgetown Gazette*, 11 February 1807.

65. William Tilghman, "Memorandum," 10 November 1806, ViU: Tracy W. McGregor Autograph Collection. Tilghman, the chief justice of Pennsylvania, recorded what Morgan and his sons had told him nearly two months earlier about their conversations with Burr in late August. For Latrobe, see Latrobe to Gallatin, 19/28 November 1806, in *CBHL*, 2:290–96.

66. "Extract of a letter from Commodore Truxton to the honorable Joseph Alston," *Georgetown Gazette*, 28 March 1807. For Adair's similar statement, see Adair, "For the National Intelligencer," *National Intelligencer*, 4 March 1807.

67. Stoddert to Samuel H. Smith, *National Intelligencer*, 20 March 1807. Stoddert's published letter sought less to dissociate himself from Burr than to refute the "dishonourable" implications of a recent report in Philadelphia's *Aurora General Advertiser* that he had disclosed Burr's plans to the administration. The *Aurora* had effectively suggested, Stoddert believed, that, "after allowing myself to be the depository of [Burr's] secrets[,] I had the treachery to betray him." But Stoddert acknowledged that, during the Bollman and Swartwout proceedings, he

had provided a written statement, but not a formal deposition, to the district attorney in Washington "at his request."

68. Stoddert, deposition, 9 October 1807, in Henshaw, ed., "Burr-Blennerhassett Documents," 8. Stoddert's written statement of February has disappeared. Its contents were probably similar to his testimony before the Richmond grand jury in June and the deposition that he prepared in October. Both disavowed any knowledge of "treason or misdemeanor, committed or intended to be committed, by Burr" (Stoddert, testimony, 13 June 1807, in "NECAB," 5).

69. For Eaton's activities before his involvement with Burr, see Rodd, *General William Eaton*; and the often-unreliable Edwards, *Barbary General*. Eaton's contacts with Burr and his testimony in various conspiracy-related trials are covered in Wright and Macleod, "William Eaton's Relations with Aaron Burr."

70. William Plumer, diary entry, 22 January 1807, in *WPMP*, 583. I discussed Eaton's various accounts of his meeting with Jefferson above, First Interlude, n. 21. In mid-October, Eaton's information was first revealed to Granger by Massachusetts representative William Ely and later confirmed by Eaton; see Granger to [Jefferson], [14/]16 October 1806, in Henshaw, ed., "Burr-Blennerhassett Documents," 10–13. For the disclosure to Madison, see Eaton to Madison, 27 October 1806, DLC: Burr Conspiracy Collection. Reports of Eaton's meetings with Burr began appearing in newspapers in early November; see, for example, "Extract of a letter from a gentleman of respectability in Hampshire County, Mass. to his friend in this vicinity," *Enquirer*, 7 November 1806; [Isaiah Thomas Jr.], "The EX VICE PRESIDENT Turned TRAITOR," *Massachusetts Spy* (Worcester), 12 November 1806 (from AHN); and [Benjamin Russell], "Ex Vice-President Burr," *Columbian Centinel* (Boston), 19 November 1806. For Eaton's first published account, see [John Park], "Some Further Particulars of Col. Burr's Treason," *Repertory* (Boston), 25 November 1806 (from AHN).

71. Eaton, deposition, 26 January 1807, in [Prentiss], *Life of the Late Gen. William Eaton*, 396–99.

72. Ibid., 399–400, 402.

73. ["The Conspiracy, I"], *National Intelligencer*, 13 March 1807. This essay was the first in a four-part series, the naming of which began with the second installment. See also "The Conspiracy, [II]," ibid., 16 March 1807. That the administration took Eaton's disclosures seriously is clear from the "Interrogatories" that the attorney general prepared to help build the case against Burr. He directed that potential witnesses be asked whether, to their knowledge, Burr's plans extended "so far, as ultimately to contemplate a complete and total revolution by force" and if he had said "that with five hundred men he either could or would send the President of the United States to Monticello, or assassinate him, intimidate Congress to pass the government of the United States into his own hands, and effect by force the destruction of the federal constitution" (Caesar A. Rodney, "Interrogatories," [ca. 6 April 1807], DLC: Burr Conspiracy Collection).

74. [Carpenter], *People's Friend*, 4 February 1807. For the comments of a leading Republican editor, see [William Duane], "The Conspiracy," *Aurora General Advertiser* (Philadelphia), 4 December 1806.

75. [William Coleman], "President's Message," *New-York Evening Post*, 11 December 1806. See also [Carpenter], *People's Friend*, 16 January and 7 February 1807.

76. "Communication," *Washington Federalist* (Georgetown, D.C.), 28 February 1807.

77. [Wood], "Col. Burr's Conspiracy, [II]," *Atlantic World*, 10 February 1807. I discussed the possibility that Wood set up the *Atlantic World* at Burr's request and with Burr's funds in Chapter 2. Eaton later came under attack in the Burr-funded *Impartial Observer*.

78. Matthew Livingston Davis to William P. Van Ness, 11 February 1807, NHi: Matthew Livingston Davis Papers. See also Edwards to Wirt, [5 January 1807], ICHi: Edwards Papers; Tench Coxe to Madison, [11 January 1807], DLC: James Madison Papers; Worthington to an unknown correspondent, 12 January 1807, ORCHi: Early Statehood Papers; Truxton to Tingey, 19 January 1807, DLC: Truxton Papers; and Parke to Brown, 22 January 1807, InHi: Porter Papers.

79. John T. Bowdoin to Joseph Prentis Jr., 6 February 1807, ViU: Webb-Prentis Family Papers; Rutledge to Izard, 25 March 1807, ScHi: Rutledge Letter.

80. William Plumer, diary entry, 28 November 1806, in *WPMP*, 516.

81. Joseph Bryan to Randolph, 8 March 1807, Vi: Bryan Family Papers.

82. Louisa Catherine Adams to John Quincy Adams, 19 December 1806, MHi: Adams Family Papers.

83. Thomas Tudor Tucker to John Page, 26 January 1807, DLC: Thomas Tudor Tucker Papers. Some criticized the mode and timing of Eaton's revelations without expressing doubts about the information; see, for example, John Quincy Adams to Louisa Catherine Adams, 8 December 1806, MHi: Adams Family Papers; Parke to Brown, 22 January 1807, InHi: Porter Papers; and "Communication," *Washington Federalist*, 28 February 1807.

84. Timothy Pickering to Henry Pickering, 28 December 1806, in Pickering and Upham, eds., *Life of Timothy Pickering*, 4:111.

85. Timothy Pickering to John Pickering, 25 January 1807, MHi: Pickering Papers.

86. [Duane], "An Outlaw Emperor," *Aurora*, 14 March 1807. See also Macon to Nicholson, 30 January 1807, DLC: Nicholson Papers; and Caesar A. Rodney to Thomas Rodney, 26 February 1807, DeHi: H. Fletcher Brown Collection of Rodney Family Papers.

87. [Ritchie], *Enquirer*, 21 April 1807.

88. Truxton to Timothy Pickering, 22 February 1807, MHi: Pickering Papers.

89. Eaton, deposition, 26 January 1807, in [Prentiss], *Life of the Late Gen. William Eaton*, 398; [Burr] to Wilkinson, [22–29 July 1807], in *PCAB*, 2:986 (I have standardized the font).

90. Jefferson to William B. Giles, 20 April 1807, in *WrTJ*, 11:188. The two men that Jefferson did not name may have been George Morgan and Alexander Henderson, whose disclosures about Harman Blennerhassett and events on the Ohio River had been made to John Graham five months earlier.

91. William Plumer, diary entry, 26 December 1806, in *WPMP*, 542.

92. John Hartwell Cocke to [Charles] Ellis and [Jonathan] Allan, 18 June 1807, DLC: Ellis & Allan Co. Papers.

93. Wilkinson, testimony, 19 June 1807, in "NECAB," 58. Wilkinson had recently tried to get a copy of his first warning letter from Secretary of the Navy Robert Smith only to be informed that Smith made it an "invariable practice to destroy all private letters" soon after receiving them (Robert Smith to Wilkinson, 22 June 1807, ICU: Reuben T. Durrett Collection, Miscellaneous Manuscripts).

94. For Wilkinson's testimony, as for everyone else's who appeared before the grand jury, the most complete record is that of Joseph C. Cabell; see Wilkinson, testimony, 19, 20, 22, and 23 June 1807, in "NECAB," 53–76 and 87. Another version of Wilkinson's testimony appears in Henshaw, ed., "Burr-Blennerhassett Documents." It is unclear how a record of Wilkinson's (and Swartwout's) grand jury testimony made it into the papers of Ohio militia general John Stites Gano. A third version of part of Wilkinson's testimony can be found in the Burr Family Papers at Yale University's Sterling Memorial Library and is included in the microfilm edition of the Burr papers. Following the archivists at Yale, the editors of the Burr papers have mislabelled this document as "David Robertson's notes on the testimony of Wilkinson and Littleton Waller Tazewell"; see *PAB*. Instead, it is part of Tazewell's notes on the grand jury proceedings, which were referred to by Tazewell late in the trial; see Tazewell, testimony, 1 [*sic*, 2] October 1807, in *TCAB*, 3:290. How the document came into Burr's (or the Burr family's) possession is a mystery. But, according to Harman Blennerhassett, Burr possessed "a complete file of all the Depositions made before the Gr. Jury," something "that few other men in his circumstances could have procured" (Harman Blennerhassett, diary entry, 2 September 1807, in *BwB*, 100). See also [Duane], "From Richmond," *Aurora*, 15 August 1807; and St. George Tucker to Cabell, 20 September 1807, ViU: Bryan Family Papers.

95. [Burr] to [Wilkinson], 29 July 1806, as rendered in Wilkinson, affidavit, [18 December 1806], in *ASP: Misc*, 1:471; [Burr] to [Wilkinson], 22 July 1806, as rendered in "NECAB," 73.

96. [Burr] to [Wilkinson], 22 July 1806, as rendered in "NECAB," 73.

97. Cabell, notes on Wilkinson's testimony, 22 June 1807, in ibid., 75.

98. Cabell, notes on Wilkinson's testimony, 23 June 1807, in ibid., 87.

99. Robert B. Taylor, deposition, [ca. February 1811], in [Bacon], *Report of the Committee*, 299.

100. Randolph to Nicholson, 28 June 1807, DLC: Nicholson Papers.

101. Burr, comment, 25 June 1807, in *RTCAB*, 1:328.

102. Hay to Jefferson, 25 June 1807, DLC: Jefferson Papers.

103. Alexander McRae, comment, 25 June 1807, in *RTCAB*, 1:329. The letters in Burr's possession, Wilkinson claimed, could "expose me for many follies & indiscretions—but no wickedness or dishonor" (Wilkinson to Samuel Smith, 24 [*sic*, 25] June 1807, PPiU-D: Wilkinson Papers).

104. [Wilkinson], "Drowning Men catch at Straws," *Enquirer*, 1 July 1807. This anonymous "communication" closely followed the language that Wilkinson had used three days earlier in a letter to John Smith; see Wilkinson to John Smith, 28 June 1807, OCHi: Papers in the Defense of John Smith of Ohio. For the original charge, see *Virginia Gazette*, 27 June 1807.

105. John Tompkins to Duncan Cameron, 30 June 1807, NcU: Cameron Family Papers. For a defense of Wilkinson in the Republican press, see *Virginia Argus*, 1 July 1807.

106. William Daniel to Augustine Davis, *Enquirer*, 28 July 1807, clipped from *Virginia Gazette*. Daniel had been a grand juror. The juror John Brockenbrough also identified these three issues but insisted that no vote had been taken on the question of treason; see John Brockenbrough, "From the Virginia Gazette," *Virginia Argus*, 18 July 1807. Cabell did not include this discussion in his grand jury notes. For the newspaper battle, see also "Recriminator," *Virginia Herald* (Fredericksburg), 30 June 1807; Beverley, "From the Herald," *Virginia Argus*, 18 July 1807; and Beverley to Augustine Davis, *Virginia Gazette*, 12 August 1807.

107. Dudley Woodbridge Jr. to William Woodbridge, 21/23 June 1807, MiD-B: William Woodbridge Papers.

108. Truxton to Charles Biddle, 25 June 1807, in Biddle, *Autobiography of Charles Biddle*, 410. In this letter, Truxton made clear that he had not seen the original letter or the grand jury's rendering of it but did not say who had told him its contents.

109. Cabell, "Questions intended to be propounded to Genl. Wilkinson," 10 July 1807, ViU: Cabell Family Papers. This document is in two parts, the eight questions and a concluding paragraph explaining their origins. That final paragraph seems to have been written years later but is not dated. For Randolph's disclosures, see Randolph to Nicholson, 28 June 1807, DLC: Nicholson Papers. For Cabell's reluctant decision to loan his notes to Wirt, see Cabell to Wirt, 27 June 1807, ViU: Cabell Family Papers. It is not known if the prosecuting attorneys ever posed these questions to Wilkinson.

110. Cabell to Isaac Coles, 23 July 1807, ViU: Cabell Family Papers.

111. Chandler Price to Caesar A. Rodney, 22 July 1807, DeHi: Rodney Collection.

112. Harman Blennerhassett, diary entry, 27 August 1807, in *BwB*, 59; [William Pechin], *American*, 2 September 1807. For another early newspaper account, see *New-York Commercial Advertiser*, 1 September 1807 (from AHN). None of the Richmond newspapers mentioned this incident, perhaps because it quickly became common knowledge there. The poison was administered by Duncan's slave, Frank, who confessed that he had been offered seven hundred dollars, a horse, and his freedom by James Kinney, another government witness; see

[Duane], *Aurora*, 1 September 1807. Frank ultimately went free and, because a slave could not testify against a white person under Virginia law, Kinney was never tried; see Miles Selden, affidavit, 3 October 1807, *Enquirer*, 20 October 1807.

113. [Swartwout], "Extract of a letter from a gentleman of veracity and honour, to his friend in this city, dated Richmond," *New-York Gazette & General Advertiser*, 24 September 1807 (from AHN).

114. [Enos Bronson], *United States' Gazette* (Philadelphia), 25 September 1807. For the other pieces, see "Man of Feeling" [Williams], "To the Printers of the New-York Gazette," *New-York Gazette*, 28 September 1807 (from AHN); "Democraticus," "For the Evening Post," *Baltimore Evening Post* (Md.), 29 September 1807; and *Democrat* (Boston), 3 October 1807. Wilkinson identified Williams as "Man of Feeling"; see Wilkinson to Williams, 2 October 1807, NjP: Fuller Collection.

115. Luther Martin, "For the Virginia Gazette," *Virginia Gazette*, 6 November 1807. Wilkinson's friend Jonathan Thompson had pressured the *New-York Gazette*'s editor into revealing Swartwout; see "Extract of a letter from Jonathan Thompson to his friend in this city, dated New-York," *Enquirer*, 20 October 1807. In late October, Wilkinson asked another New York ally to plant Thompson's letter, with supporting certificates and a brief statement of his own, in the New York press; see Wilkinson to Williams, 22 October 1807, NjP: Fuller Collection. Duncan's deposition appeared in the *Enquirer* on 7 October.

116. *Democrat*, 3 October 1807.

117. Blennerhassett, diary entry, 22 September 1807, in *BwB*, 101.

118. John Wickham, argument, 29 September 1807, in *TCAB*, 3:257. See Wilkinson, testimony, 26 and 29 September and 1, 2, and 3 October 1807, in ibid., 236–96. Over the course of his testimony, Wilkinson introduced four depositions, nineteen letters, and the cipher keys. Most of the depositions were read as part of his testimony; *TCAB* includes one deposition, the letters, and the keys as appendices.

119. John Baker, argument, 29 September 1807, in ibid., 257–58.

120. Abner Duncan, deposition, 5 September 1807, in ibid., 243–44.

121. Wilkinson, testimony, 29 September 1807, in ibid., 249, 250.

122. Wilkinson, testimony, 26 September 1807, in ibid., 245. Wilkinson, in fact, had sworn only that the deciphered version in the affidavits was "substantially as fair an interpretation as [he had] heretofore been able to make" (Wilkinson, affidavit, [18 December 1806], in *ASP: Misc*, 1:471).

123. Wilkinson, testimony, 29 September 1807, in *TCAB*, 3:250. Letters of 14 and 18 December 1806 are among the many of his letters to the president that Wilkinson apparently removed from the official record while it was in his possession in the fall of 1807; see Introduction. One of Jefferson's own letters makes clear, however, that it was Wilkinson's 14 December 1806 letter that provided his first copy of the cipher letter; see Jefferson to Charles Pinckney, 20 January 1807, in *WrTJ*, 11:142.

124. Wickham, cross-examination of Wilkinson, 29 September 1807, in *TCAB*, 3:253.
125. Wilkinson, testimony, 29 September 1807, in ibid., 252.
126. Tazewell, testimony, 1 [*sic*, 2] October 1807, in ibid., 291.
127. Baker, argument, 29 September 1807, in ibid., 252.
128. Wilkinson, testimony, 3 October 1807, in ibid., 295.
129. Wilkinson, testimony, 1 October 1807, in ibid., 268.
130. Thomas Rodney to Caesar A. Rodney, 12 November 1807, in Gratz, ed., "Thomas Rodney," 45:53. The published Burr papers include eight letters from Burr to Wilkinson during the latter's governorship of the Louisiana Territory, all of which survive only as presented to Congress or the public by Wilkinson beginning in 1811. Wilkinson showed Cabell five Burr letters from this period at the time of the grand jury hearings, including two that are not in the published Burr papers; see Cabell, "List of Letters shewn me by Genl. Wilkinson," ViU: Cabell Family Papers. In his deposition, Duncan reported that, after his arrival in Richmond in mid-August, Wilkinson had asked him and James L. Donaldson to read "four or five letters," in cipher, from Burr that Wilkinson said he had not looked at since leaving St. Louis—presumably including those that he had shown Cabell a few weeks earlier. Duncan accepted Wilkinson's claim that he did not remember "their particular contents" and even asserted that, based on the general's responses when "certain passages" were read to him, "he had but partially decyphered them" (Duncan, deposition, 5 September 1807, in *TCAB*, 3:244).
131. "Hector," "For the People's Friend," *People's Friend*, 28 February 1807. Only if it had been delivered with the cipher letter would a recently devised key not have implicated Wilkinson in Burr's plans.
132. Wilkinson to Jefferson, 13 February 1807, DLC: Burr Conspiracy Collection.
133. Wickham, argument, 1 October 1807, in *TCAB*, 3:272. For Wilkinson's account, see Wilkinson, testimony, 26 September 1807, in ibid., 246.
134. Tazewell, testimony, 1 [*sic*, 2] October 1807, in ibid., 291. Tazewell also testified that, before the grand jury, Wilkinson had initially said that Smith had prepared the cipher in 1804, 1805, or 1806. On being reminded that Smith was already dead then, Wilkinson had pushed the date back to 1794. Tazewell also informed the court that, in the months since he had first seen the sheet of paper with the cipher keys on it, the date 1801 had been added.
135. Wilkinson, testimony, 1 October 1807, in ibid., 272.
136. Blennerhassett, diary entry, 15 October 1807, in *BwB*, 133. See also Cabell to Coles, 6 November 1807, ViU: Cabell Family Papers; and John F. May to Thomas Ruffin, 13 December 1807, in Hamilton, ed., *Papers of Thomas Ruffin*, 1:115.
137. Randolph to Nicholson, 8 November 1807, DLC: Nicholson Papers.
138. Hay to Jefferson, 15 October 1807, DLC: Jefferson Papers. For Wirt, see Wirt to Edwards, 12 March 1808, ICHi: Edwards Papers.

139. [Ritchie], "Cursory Reflections—No. I, Portrait of Aaron Burr," *Enquirer*, 30 October 1807. For the other items in the series, see ibid., 3, 6, 10, 17, and 24 November 1807.

140. "Cyphers," ibid., 3 November 1807.

141. [Samuel Pleasants Jr.], *Virginia Argus*, 27 October 1807.

142. Ibid., 30 October 1807.

143. "Mr. O'Conner," *North American, and Mercantile Daily Advertiser* (Baltimore, Md.), 3 March 1808, clipped from *Norfolk Herald* (Va.).

144. Marshall, opinion, 20 October 1807, in *PJMar*, 7:159.

145. McCaleb, *Aaron Burr Conspiracy*, 68–69; Wandell and Minnigerode, *Aaron Burr*, 2:79; Schachner, *Aaron Burr*, 322 (all three books use this phrase). Even Matthew Livingston Davis and James Parton—Burr's staunchest defenders among his early biographers—presented the cipher letter in this manner; see *MAB*, 2:384, 400; and Parton, *Life and Times of Aaron Burr*, 413. Surveying the historiography in 1945, Julius Pratt did not note any questions about Burr's authorship of the cipher letter; see Pratt, "Aaron Burr and the Historians," 457–58. Works from the next thirty-five years also treated this issue as settled; see Abernethy, *Burr Conspiracy*, 59; Parmet and Hecht, *Aaron Burr*, 251–52; Daniels, *Ordeal of Ambition*, 334; and Geissler, *Jonathan Edwards to Aaron Burr, Jr.*, 220–21.

146. Adams, *History of the United States of America*, 1:777. Thomas Perkins Abernethy similarly viewed the cipher letter as "the most concrete evidence" of Burr's thinking (Abernethy, *Burr Conspiracy*, 59).

147. [Coleman], "Wilkinson," *New-York Evening Post*, 29 October 1807.

148. The different stages in the dissolution of Wilkinson's reputation are covered, and sometimes challenged, in the secondary literature on Wilkinson (see above, n. 29). I examine the investigations of Wilkinson and his efforts to defend his reputation in Chapter 11. There were rumors about the purpose of Burling's mission to Mexico City as early as the spring of 1807 and more solid information was available by the late 1810s, but Davis published the first concrete evidence; see "Extract of a Letter dated New-Orleans," *People's Friend*, 5 June 1807; *MAB*, 2:400–404; and Parton, *Life and Times of Aaron Burr*, 430–31n. For Gayarré's revelations, see Gayarré, *History of Louisiana*. The material found in Spanish and Spanish colonial archives concerned various issues. For Wilkinson's role in the Burr Conspiracy, see Adams, *History of the United States of America*, 1:783–86; and "Interview of Governor Folch with General Wilkinson." For the Burling mission, see McCaleb, *Aaron Burr Conspiracy*, 143–46; and Shepherd, ed., "Letter of General James Wilkinson." For Wilkinson's later Spanish connections, see Cox, "General Wilkinson and His Later Intrigues."

149. Wickham, argument, 17 October 1807, in *TCAB*, 3:390.

150. Marquis de Yrujo to Pedro Cevallos Guerra, 28 January 1807, printed in Adams, *History of the United States of America*, 1:838–39.

151. Wilkinson to John Adair, 28 September 1806, excerpted in Adair to James Bradford, *People's Friend*, 31 July 1807, clipped from *Orleans Gazette and Commercial Advertiser* (New Orleans), 16 June 1807.

152. Wilkinson to Walter Burling, 15 November 1806, DLC: Burr Conspiracy Collection. Wilkinson later billed the government $1,750 for Burling's mission. See Wilkinson to Jefferson, 16 July 1808, DNA: RG107, M222, W-1808; and Wilkinson to Dearborn, 19 July 1808, ibid.

153. Wilkinson to Jefferson, 21 October 1806 ["Confidential"], DLC: Burr Conspiracy Collection. See also Wilkinson to Dearborn, 16 and 22 January and 27 February 1807, DNA: RG107, M221, W-235 (3) enclosure, W-239 (3), and W-255 (3). For Wilkinson's earlier reports on military conditions in Mexico, see, for example, Wilkinson to Dearborn, 8 September 1805, ICU: Durrett Collection, Miscellaneous Manuscripts.

154. Wilkinson to Samuel Smith, 10 December 1806, PPiU-D: Wilkinson Papers. For Wilkinson's interest in Spanish Mexico, see, in particular, Narrett, "Geopolitics and Intrigue."

155. Wilkinson, *Burr's Conspiracy Exposed*, 67, 69, 72 (emphasis added). The point-by-point format responded to the discussion in Daniel Clark's *Proofs of the Corruption of Gen. James Wilkinson* (1809).

156. Kline and Ryan, "Editorial Note: The 'Cipher Letter' to Wilkinson," in *PCAB*, 2:973, 985, 986.

157. Lomask, *Aaron Burr*, 2:118.

158. Isenberg, *Fallen Founder*, 363. Other recent works that largely accept Kline and Ryan's argument include Melton, *Aaron Burr*, 120, 179; Wheelan, *Jefferson's Vendetta*, 137–38, 145; Hoffer, *Treason Trials of Aaron Burr*, 48; and Newmyer, *Treason Trial of Aaron Burr*, 7–8, 30. For a rare dissent, see Stewart, *American Emperor*, 160–61, 309–12.

159. Kline and Ryan, "Editorial Note: The 'Cipher Letter' to Wilkinson," in *PCAB*, 2:984–86. In a letter to his and Burr's confidant Charles Biddle, Wilkinson suggested an inversion of Kline and Ryan's hypothesis. After Dayton insisted that he had written only one letter in cipher to the general, Wilkinson posited that the other "Dayton" letters that he had received in Natchitoches and New Orleans had been forged by Burr, "as he [had] done in other Cases" (Wilkinson to Charles Biddle, 20 July 1807, PHi: Biddle Family Papers).

160. In a mid-August letter to her half-brother, Burr's daughter placed her expected departure for "the new Settlement . . . about the 15 Octr" (Theodosia Burr Alston to A[ugustine] J[ames] Frederic Prevost, 18 August 1806, MoSW: Burr-Purkett Family Papers). For skeptical views, see Slaughter, "Conspiratorial Politics," 77–78; Stagg, "Enigma of Aaron Burr," 381; Crackel, *Mr. Jefferson's Army*, 214–15n22; and Stewart, *American Emperor*, 309–12.

161. Kline and Ryan, "Editorial Note: The 'Cipher Letter' to Wilkinson," in *PCAB*, 2:984.

162. Rufus Easton to Jefferson, undated, DLC: Burr Conspiracy Collection. Dayton may have possessed his own copies of the alphabet and hieroglyphic ciphers as he employed them, as well as another cipher based on the key word "France," in letters to Wilkinson; see "NECAB," 17. He may also have used Burr's copies.

163. William Plumer, diary entry, 20 February 1807, in *WPMP*, 616. Plumer recorded what he had learned that day from Bollman, who had been informed of the discrepancy by Swartwout.

164. Bollman to Jefferson, 26 January 1807, DLC: Jefferson Papers. See also Madison, "Substance of a communication," [23 (*sic*, 24) January 1807], in *LOWJM*, 2:394.

165. Bollman, testimony, 15 June 1807, in "NECAB," 24. Alexander sailed to New Orleans with Bollman. He allegedly recruited men on Burr's behalf and was arrested by Wilkinson in December; see Abernethy, *Burr Conspiracy*, 172–73.

166. Swartwout, testimony, 16 June 1807, in "NECAB," 30. For his testimony at the end of the trial, see Swartwout, testimony, 19 October 1807, in *TCAB*, 3:406.

167. Burr to Theodosia Burr Alston, 28 September 1807, in *MAB*, 2:411.

168. [Burr] to Wilkinson, [22–29 July 1807], in *PCAB*, 2:986 (I have standardized the font). The other "names" that might have been altered are place names—Ohio, England, Jamaica, Mississippi, Natchez, and B[aton] R[ouge]. But it seems very unlikely that Burr meant any of those.

169. One of the published letters from New Orleans in June 1807 claimed that Wilkinson had replaced "Dayton" with "Alston" when he sent the deciphered letter to the president; but the only reference to Alston in the original letter appeared in plain text as "the Husband" ([Burr] to Wilkinson, [22–29 July 1807], in *PCAB*, 2:987). Replacing Dayton with Truxton would have fit with Wilkinson's other efforts to hide Dayton's involvement. But the symbols for "d," "a," and "y" are straight lines, whereas the symbols for "t," "r," and "u" are curved lines. For Decatur, see Allison, *Stephen Decatur*; and Tucker, *Stephen Decatur*. Neither book mentions Decatur's possible involvement with Burr. For Truxton's and Wilkinson's concerns, see Truxton to Tingey, 9 April and 20 June 1807, DLC: Truxton Papers; and Truxton to Charles Biddle, 11 July 1807, in Biddle, *Autobiography of Charles Biddle*, 414.

170. *MAB*, 400, 384.

171. [Armstrong], *"Memoirs of my own times,"* 20n.a.

CHAPTER 6. NEW ORLEANS, ORLEANS TERRITORY: NOVEMBER 1806 THROUGH MAY 1807

1. The literature on eighteenth- and early nineteenth-century New Orleans is immense. For this section, I have relied upon Brown, *Constitutional History of the Louisiana Purchase*; Clark, *New Orleans*; Dargo, *Jefferson's Louisiana*; Hanger,

Bounded Lives; Kukla, *Wilderness So Immense*; Bradley, ed., *Interim Appointment*; Vernet, *Strangers on Their Native Soil*; and Faber, *Building the Land of Dreams*.

2. Schultz, *Travels on an Inland Voyage*, 2:191.

3. John G. Stuart, diary entry, 3 June 1806, in Stuart, "Journal Remarks or Observations," 21.

4. Daniel Constable to his parents, 17 March 1807, in Jenkins, *Citizen Daniel*, 104.

5. William C. C. Claiborne to James Madison, 16 May 1805, in *OLBWC*, 3:299. Five decades later, Vincent Nolte recalled that in 1806 three-fifths of the whites were French, one-fifth were Spanish, and the remaining fifth were "Americans, among whom were some Germans" (Nolte, *Fifty Years in Both Hemispheres*, 86). For a thoughtful discussion of national identity in New Orleans in this period, see Kastor, "'They Are All Frenchmen.'"

6. Schultz, *Travels on an Inland Voyage*, 2:193–96. "Even at the ball Room," according to one immigrant from Kentucky, the Americans generally went as "Spectators . . . to see the french boys & girls dance as you would visit a theatre to see the Actors perform" (Nathaniel Cox to Gabriel Lewis, 17 September 1807, L-M: Nathaniel Cox Papers).

7. Robin, *Voyage to Louisiana*, 263n. The Americans preferred salted meats and unleavened biscuits with "whiskey, tafia, and rum," while the French wanted "fresh meat for their stews," leavened bread, and wine (ibid., 262n).

8. Stuart, diary entry, 4 June 1806, in Stuart, "Journal Remarks or Observations," 21. On that day, "an American was stab'd . . . by a Spaniard."

9. Robin, *Voyage to Louisiana*, 264. For the politics of the city's newspapers, see Claiborne to Robert Smith, 18 November 1809, in *OLBWC*, 5:14–17; and Kendall, "Early New Orleans Newspapers."

10. R[egin] D. Shepherd to Thomas Worthington, 8 October 1806, OHi: Thomas Worthington Papers.

11. Claiborne to Madison, 16 May 1805, in *OLBWC*, 3:299–300.

12. James Brown to Benjamin Parke, 6 August 1805, InHi: Albert G. Porter Papers. See also Jonathan S. Findlay to James Findlay, 6 February 1806, in Cox, ed., "Selections from the Torrence Papers," 4:115; and Shepherd to Worthington, 8 October 1806, OHi: Worthington Papers. Despite numerous reports of Claiborne's "want of talents and weight of Character," Jefferson and Madison stood behind him (Madison to Thomas Jefferson, 17 March 1805, in *PJM: SS*, 9:140). For Claiborne as territorial governor, see Prichard, "Selecting a Governor"; Hatfield, *William Claiborne*; Kastor, *Nation's Crucible*; and Couch, "William Charles Cole Claiborne."

13. James Sterrett to Nathaniel Evans, 25 February 1805, LU: Evans (Nathaniel and Family) Papers. Sterrett identified the principals in three affairs of honor; in two of these affairs, one principal was considered a supporter of the governor (Richard Raynal Keene and John W. Gurley) and the other was seen as an opponent (James Alexander and Edward Livingston). In the third affair, Abraham Ellery appears to have been at odds with the governor, but I have not been able

to discover the politics of the other principal, Arthur Morgan. For the politics of these men, see Shepherd to Worthington, 8 October 1806, OHi: Worthington Papers; and Bradley, ed., *Interim Appointment*. For the death of Claiborne's brother-in-law, see Kendall, "According to the Code."

14. [James Bradford], *Orleans Gazette and Commercial Advertiser* (New Orleans), 28 June 1805 (from AHN). See also Claiborne to Madison, 26 June 1805, in *OLBWC*, 3:105; and *Louisiana Gazette* (New Orleans), 28 June 1805. According to the standard reference materials, there are no extant copies of the *Moniteur* or *Télégraphe* for 1805.

15. Aaron Burr, journal entry, [ca. 25 June-10 July 1805], in *MAB*, 2:371.

16. Ibid. For Burr's meetings with Clark and Morales and snubbing of Casa Calvo, see Marqués de Casa Calvo to James Wilkinson, 15 July 1805, ICHi: James Wilkinson Papers; and *Proofs*, 94. Most secondary works say that Burr met with the "Mexican Association" or "Mexican Society" while in New Orleans; see McCaleb, *Aaron Burr Conspiracy*, 32–34; Abernethy, *Burr Conspiracy*, 28–29; Dargo, *Jefferson's Louisiana*, 55–56; Isenberg, *Fallen Founder*, 296–97; and Faber, *Building the Land of Dreams*, 231. The best history of the association in this period finds no link to Burr; see Bradley, ed., *Interim Appointment*, 596–603.

17. Claiborne to Madison, 6 August 1805, in *TPUS*, 9:489. Burr may have dined with Claiborne, as well; see *Proofs*, 94.

18. Shepherd to Worthington, 8 October 1806, OHi: Worthington Papers.

19. John Graham to Madison, 2 January 1805 [*sic*, 1806], in *TPUS*, 9:554 [the italicized passages were originally encoded]. See also Claiborne's letters to Jefferson, Madison, and Henry Dearborn between November 1805 and October 1806 in *OLBWC*.

20. Claiborne to Jefferson, 9 July 1806, in *TPUS*, 9:670. For Claiborne's obvious dismay at this development, see also his letter to Madison, 22 May 1806, in *OLBWC*, 3:305–6. For Daniel Clark, see Wohl, "Man in the Shadow"; Wohl, "Not Yet Saint nor Sinner"; and Alexander, "Daniel Clark."

21. *Louisiana Gazette*, 25 November 1806. The engineers arrived on 19 November; the infantry returned to the city two days later.

22. Wilkinson to Claiborne, 12 November 1806, in *OLBWC*, 4:55. Claiborne received the letter five days later; see Claiborne to Wilkinson, 17 November 1806, in ibid., 44.

23. Claiborne to Madison, 18 November 1806, in ibid., 37. See also Claiborne to Cowles Mead, 18 November 1806, in ibid., 35–36.

24. Wilkinson to Claiborne, 12 November 1806, in ibid., 56.

25. Cox to Alexander Henderson, 5 April 1807, WvU: Henderson-Tomlinson Family Papers.

26. For the crisis in New Orleans, see McCaleb, *Aaron Burr Conspiracy*, 170–202; McCaleb, *New Light on Aaron Burr*, 45–62; Shreve, *Finished Scoundrel*; Hay and Werner, *Admirable Trumpeter*, 234–69; Abernethy, *Burr Conspiracy*, 165–82; Dargo, *Jefferson's Louisiana*, 51–73; Hatfield, *William Claiborne*, 211–36; Vernet,

Strangers on Their Native Soil, 116–34; Linklater, *Artist in Treason*, 256–63; and Stewart, *American Emperor*, 186–92. Of these works, Thomas Perkins Abernethy's *Burr Conspiracy* made the strongest claims about the existence of "a powerful Burr clique" in New Orleans (167).

27. "Extract of a letter from a correspondent at New-Orleans, to the Editor dated Nov. 28, 1806," *Impartial Review, and Cumberland Repository* (Nashville, Tenn.), 27 December 1806. For Wilkinson's arrival, see *Louisiana Gazette*, 28 November 1806.

28. Thomas Power to Stephen Minor, 6 December 1806, ICN: Everett D. Graff Collection of Western Americana, Thomas Power Letter.

29. James Brown to Parke, 5 December 1806, InHi: Porter Papers.

30. John Shaw to Robert Smith, 9 December 1806, DNA: RG45, M147.

31. Claiborne to Madison, 9 December 1806, in *OLBWC*, 4:52.

32. *Louisiana Gazette*, 9 December 1806. The details about Burr's numbers and schedule did not appear in the *Gazette* until the next issue but had probably circulated orally before that time; see *Louisiana Gazette*, 12 December 1806. For the orders that imposed the embargo, see Claiborne's letters to: Shaw, 9 December 1806, in *OLBWC*, 4:67; and William Brown, 10 December 1806, in ibid., 67–68. For the Battalion of Orleans Volunteers, see Gelpi, "Mr. Jefferson's Creoles."

33. "Extract of a Letter, dated New-Orleans, Dec. 9, 1806," *National Intelligencer, and Washington Advertiser* (D.C.), 16 January 1807.

34. [John Mowry], *Louisiana Gazette*, 12 December 1806.

35. "Extract of a letter from a gentlemen at New-Orleans, to his friend in this place, dated December 11th. 1806," *Impartial Review*, 3 January 1807.

36. *Louisiana Gazette*, 12 December 1806.

37. Wilkinson, return, *Louisiana Gazette*, 19 December 1806. The return was delivered in court on 18 December. According to one account, Wilkinson also denounced two Claiborne supporters—James Workman, the judge of the Orleans County court, and Richard Raynal Keene—before the court on 18 December; see Oliver H. Spencer to Evans, 19 November [*sic*, December] 1806, LU: Evans Papers.

38. Spencer to Evans, 19 November [*sic*, December] 1806, LU: Evans Papers.

39. Claiborne, proclamation, 16 December 1806, in *TPUS*, 9:694.

40. Spencer to Evans, 19 November [*sic*, December] 1806, LU: Evans Papers. For Claiborne's efforts regarding the militia and navy, see Claiborne to Paul Lanusse and Benjamin Morgan, 16 December 1806, in *OLBWC*, 4:62; and Henry Hopkins, general orders, 16 December 1806, in *TPUS*, 9:713. For the departure of the naval vessels, see Jacob Jones to Edward Preble, 10 February 1807, DLC: Edward Preble Papers.

41. Sterrett to Evans, 19 December 1806, LU: Evans Papers; [Edward Livingston], "Memorial: To the Honorable the Senate and House of Representatives of the United States, in Congress assembled," in *Debate in the House of Representatives*

of the Territory of Orleans, 7. For rumors of martial law, see also Alexander Macomb to Jonathan Williams, 8 January 1807, InU: Jonathan Williams Manuscripts; and "New-Orleans in an Uproar!," *People's Friend & Daily Advertiser* (New York), 13 January 1807. The source of this newspaper account had left New Orleans on 10 December. For Livingston's authorship of the memorial, see below, n. 143. The memorial mentioned only Alexander; that Ogden suffered similar treatment is clear from Edward Livingston, "To the Public," *Louisiana Gazette*, 30 December 1806.

42. Sterrett to Evans, 19 December 1806, LU: Evans Papers. Another letter of the same date was more sympathetic to the general but still reported a sense of "great alarm" in the city ("We have been favored with the following extract of a letter from a gentleman of correct political information," *Mississippi Herald & Natchez Gazette*, 30 December 1806).

43. *Louisiana Gazette*, 23 December 1806.

44. "Extract of a letter, dated New-Orleans, Jan. 5," *Morning Chronicle* (New York), 19 February 1807. For the continuing efforts to organize the militia, see Hopkins, general orders, 24 December 1806, in *TPUS*, 9:713–14. For Wilkinson's investigations, see Claiborne to Wilkinson, 29 December 1806, in *OLBWC*, 4:73. For Livingston's efforts, see Hatcher, *Edward Livingston*, 132–33.

45. Edward Livingston, "To the Public," *Louisiana Gazette*, 30 December 1806.

46. "Extract of a letter from a gentleman of talents in New-Orleans, to the Editor of the Review, dated January 1st, 1807," *Impartial Review*, 24 January 1807.

47. Ibid.

48. John Watkins to Wilkinson, 4 January 1807, ICHi: Wilkinson Papers. A request from Wilkinson prompted these measures; see Kastor, *Nation's Crucible*, 138.

49. Shaw to Robert Smith, 12 January 1807, DNA: RG45, M147.

50. "Extract of a letter, dated New-Orleans, Jan. 5," *Morning Chronicle*, 19 February 1807. For Mead's and Jefferson's proclamations, see *Louisiana Gazette*, 2 and 6 January 1807, respectively. The 6 January issue also included William Eaton's first public disclosures of Burr's proposals to him; I discussed Eaton's disclosures in Chapter 5.

51. Claiborne, "Circular to the Inhabitants Farmers," 6 January 1807, in *OLBWC*, 4:84.

52. Hopkins, general orders, 9 January 1807, in *TPUS*, 9:717. See also Hopkins's general orders of the previous two days in ibid., 716–17. For military service by free blacks in New Orleans, see Everett, "Emigres and Militiamen"; and McConnell, *Negro Troops of Antebellum Louisiana*.

53. Wilkinson, notice, [6 January 1807], as "Postscript," *Louisiana Gazette*, 6 January 1807. For the federalizing of the volunteers, see ibid., 9 January 1807. For the sailing of the *Revenge*, see Shaw to Robert Smith, 12 January 1807, DNA: RG45, M147. The intercepted letter was not presented as evidence against Burr, not published, and not found by the editors of the Burr papers. It probably did

542 | NOTES TO PAGES 220–222

not exist. Shaw mentioned this letter, dating it to 30 November and describing it in terms that fit with Wilkinson's coffeehouse posting, but it is not clear that he had actually seen it; see Shaw to Robert Smith, 24 December 1806, ibid.

54. "New-York," *Columbian Centinel* (Boston), 11 February 1807.

55. Wilkinson to Dearborn, 8/9 January 1807, DNA: RG107, M222, W-1807.

56. Claiborne, "Speech to the two Houses of the Assembly," 13 January 1807, in *OLBWC*, 4:88–89. The indictment of Kerr and Workman is printed in ibid., 170–71. Claiborne sat in the assembly chamber without speaking while a clerk read his address in French; see "House of Representatives, Monday, January 12, 1807," *Louisiana Gazette*, 16 January 1807.

57. "New-Orleans, January 15," *Pittsburgh Gazette* (Pa.), 10 March 1807, clipped from *Orleans Gazette*, 15 January 1807. For the legislature's closed-door sessions, see *Louisiana Gazette*, 20 January 1807.

58. Richard Relf to Daniel W. Coxe, 16 January 1807, PHi: Daniel W. Coxe Papers. One resident who supported Adair's arrest believed that "more was to be feared from his military talents and popularity than from Burr himself" ("Extract of a letter from a young gentleman in New-Orleans, to his relation in Peacham," *North Star* [Danville, Vt.], 24 March 1807 [from AHN]). For the arrests and the response, see also Claiborne to Madison, 15 January 1807, in *OLBWC*, 4:95–97; Wilkinson to Dearborn, 15 January 1807, DNA: RG107, M221, W-234 (3); Shaw to Robert Smith, 16 January 1807, DNA: RG45, M147; Sterrett to Evans, 16 January 1807, LU: Evans Papers; and "Extract, Dated Orleans, 16th Jan. 1807," *Public Advertiser* (New York), 24 February 1807 (from AHN).

59. Claiborne to Several Members of Congress, 15 January 1807, in *OLBWC*, 4:98.

60. Robert Smith to Shaw, 20 December 1806, *Louisiana Gazette*, 16 January 1807. For the legislature, see ibid., 20 January 1807.

61. John Pintard to S[tephen] C. Carpenter, 21 January 1807, in "More Liberty!!!," *People's Friend*, 25 February 1807.

62. [Bradford], *Mississippi Herald*, 27 January 1807, clipped from *Orleans Gazette*, 21 January 1807. Unfortunately, no issues of the *Orleans Gazette* seem to have survived from late October 1806 to early February 1807. For Claiborne's new orders, see Relf to Coxe, 16 January 1807, PHi: Coxe Papers. The governor presented a 20 December 1806 letter from Secretary Dearborn to the legislature on 19 January; see Claiborne, message, 19 January 1807, in *OLBWC*, 4:116.

63. "From the Coffee House Books, Jan. 21," *Louisiana Gazette*, 23 January 1807.

64. Julien Poydras, "Answer of the Legislative Council of this Territory to the Governor's Speech," *Orleans Gazette*, 5 February 1807 (from AHN).

65. "Sketch of the Proceedings of the House of Representatives," 23 January 1807, ibid. "Flagrant abuses of power" comes from a paragraph in the draft of the House's response to Claiborne's message that was removed by the full house, ten to six. For the milder substitute, see Watkins and Eligius Fromentin to Claiborne, 26 January 1807, in *OLBWC*, 4:113.

66. Andrew Jackson to Daniel Smith, 11 February 1807, in *PAJ*, 2:154. Jackson admitted that "the last part of this [report was] not well authenticated." See also "Extract of a letter to a gentleman in this place, dated Natchez, January 26, 1807," *Pittsburgh Gazette*, 3 March 1807.

67. *Louisiana Gazette*, 27 January 1807.

68. "Natchez, Jan. 27," *Orleans Gazette*, 5 February 1807 (from AHN). The "treaty" between Burr and Mead appeared in one of the New Orleans newspapers on 29 or 30 January (Edward Livingston to Robert R. Livingston, 30 January 1807, NHi: Robert R. Livingston and Livingston Family Papers).

69. Edward Livingston to Robert R. Livingston, 30 January 1807, NHi: Livingston and Livingston Family Papers. See also Cox to Henderson, 5 April 1807, WvU: Henderson-Tomlinson Family Papers. The embargo had been lifted at the end of December; see Claiborne to Shaw, 31 December 1806, in *OLBWC*, 4:74.

70. James Johnson to Henry Clay, 5 February 1807, in *PHC*, 1:277.

71. "Sketch of the Proceedings of the House of Representatives," 27 January 1807, *Orleans Gazette*, 5 February 1807 (from AHN).

72. "Extract from the Journal of the House of Representatives of this Territory," *Louisiana Gazette*, 3 February 1807.

73. "New-Orleans, January 15," *Pittsburgh Gazette*, 20 March 1807, clipped from *Orleans Gazette*, 29 January 1807.

74. Cox to Henderson, 5 April 1807, WvU: Henderson-Tomlinson Family Papers.

75. For Claiborne's secret message, see Claiborne, message, 10 February 1807, in *OLBWC*, 4:118. That it was secret is apparent from Watkins to Claiborne, 18 February 1807, in ibid., 122–23. The *Orleans Gazette* quickly leaked it to the public; see "New-Orleans, Feb. 20," *Enquirer* (Richmond, Va.), 7 April 1807, clipped from *Orleans Gazette*, 20 February 1807. For news of Burr's arrest, see Claiborne to Madison, 3 March 1807, in Owens, ed., "Burr's Conspiracy," 172–73; and "Extract of a letter from E. P. Gaines, post master at Fort Stoddert, to the post master of this place," *Louisiana Gazette*, 3 March 1807. For the dismissal of the volunteers, see T[homas] Cushing, general orders, 7 March 1807, *Louisiana Gazette*, 13 March 1807; and Wilkinson to Dearborn, 13 March 1807, DNA: RG107, M221, W-260 (3). For Wilkinson's departure, see *Louisiana Gazette*, 22 May 1807.

76. [Brown], "Annals of Europe and America," 98. The author was almost certainly the novelist Charles Brockden Brown, who edited the *American Register, or General Repository of History, Politics, and Science*, which appeared in two long volumes each year during its short life. For Brown's thinking about history, see Kamrath, "Charles Brockden Brown."

77. Edward Livingston to Robert R. Livingston, 30 January 1807, NHi: Livingston and Livingston Family Papers; Claiborne to Jackson, 27 March 1807, in *PAJ*, 2:159. Claiborne mentioned, in particular, the territorial legislature's memorial to Congress.

78. Wilkinson to John Smith, 14 November 1806, OCHi: Papers in the Defense of John Smith of Ohio. Wilkinson probably sent this letter by express to the national capital, expecting the senator to attend the congressional session. See also Claiborne to Madison, 5 December 1806, in *OLBWC*, 4:48.

79. Edward Livingston to Robert R. Livingston, 30 January 1807, NHi: Livingston and Livingston Family Papers. While there is no evidence that Burr's agents intercepted the mails, it seems certain that Wilkinson's did, though he refused to answer questions on this issue on the stand in Richmond; see Wilkinson, testimony, 29 September 1807, in *TCAB*, 3:258.

80. Cox to Henderson, 5 April 1807, WvU: Henderson-Tomlinson Family Papers.

81. James Brown to Clay, 1 September 1808, in *PHC*, 1:376. The available sources from New Orleans provide no evidence of editors or essayists filling local newspapers with pieces in Burr's defense, of groups or individuals holding dinners in his honor, or of gentlemen committing their reputations on his behalf.

82. Francis Du Suan de la Croix, affidavit, 8 March 1809, in *Proofs*, Appendix, 143. De la Croix was a member of the territorial legislature.

83. Joseph Deville Degoutin Bellechasse, affidavit, 20 March 1807, in ibid., Appendix, 148. Bellechasse commanded the first regiment of the New Orleans militia. Bellechasse's and de la Croix's depositions, as well as those of Dominique Bouligny and Peter Derbigny, were recorded two years after the crisis during a fierce dispute between Clark and Wilkinson, which I examine in Chapter 11. See also Dominique Bouligny, affidavit, 8 May [*sic*, March] 1809, in ibid., Appendix, 143–45; and Peter Derbigny, affidavit, 28 February 1809, in ibid., Appendix, 149–50. Wilkinson knew of Clark's conversation with Bellechasse in early December 1806; see Wilkinson to Daniel Clark, 10 December 1806, in ibid., Appendix, 150.

84. Claiborne to Jefferson, 3 May 1807, in *TPUS*, 9:731. Claiborne blamed "the Intrigues of Burr and his Partisans," rather than Wilkinson's investigations and denunciations.

85. Cowles Mead to Claiborne, 23 November 1806, in *OLBWC*, 4:83. Both Jackson and Wilkinson had written on 12 November; see their letters in ibid., 53–54 and 55–56, respectively.

86. Claiborne to Madison, 8 December 1806, in Rowland, *Third Annual Report*, 121.

87. Claiborne to Cowles Mead, [ca. January 1807], in *OLBWC*, 4:105. Even at this late date, Claiborne, who insisted that he thought the general "was faithful to his Country," could calculate that, "if indeed General Wilkinson should be disposed ultimately to betray his Country, I had not force sufficient to counteract his views" (ibid., 105–6). In this letter, Claiborne placed his decision on 4 January. Other evidence points to a few days later; see Wilkinson to Dearborn, 8/9 January 1807, DNA: RG107, M222, W-1807.

88. Timothy Pickering to John Pickering, 25 January 1807, MHi: Timothy Pickering Papers. Numerous scholars argue that such calculations best explain the

arrest and deportation of Bollman, Swartwout, Alexander, Ogden, and Adair since they could have revealed Wilkinson's role in the conspiracy.

89. Cowles Mead to Claiborne, 14 December 1806, in *OLBWC*, 4:66.

90. Claiborne, among others, thought that Wilkinson honestly feared Burr's force. Among scholarly works, this idea has been most effectively argued in Crackel, *Mr. Jefferson's Army*, 149–57. Many of Wilkinson's contemporaries believed that he manufactured a crisis to restore his reputation—the position that Burr's counsel took in Richmond. Scholars have echoed this view and tied it to the arrests and deportations; see, in particular, Abernethy, *Burr Conspiracy*, 165–82; Mary-Jo Kline and Joanne Wood Ryan, "Editorial Note: The 'Cipher Letter' to Wilkinson," in *PCAB*, 2:980–82; and Stewart, *American Emperor*, 186–92. For the idea that Wilkinson wanted to delay a final decision, see Thomas Rodney to Caesar A. Rodney, 17 December 1806, DLC: Rodney Family Papers; and Ninian Edwards to William Wirt, [5 January 1807], ICHi: Ninian Edwards Papers. For an account that addresses a number of factors, include the poor health of Wilkinson's wife, see Linklater, *Artist in Treason*, 258–60.

91. Wilkinson to Dearborn, 9 January 1807, DNA: RG107, M221, W-225 (3). See also Claiborne to Madison, 15 January 1807, in *OLBWC*, 4:96. The embargo effectively prevented the departures of commercial vessels that would have provided a safer and cheaper way to communicate with Washington. Wilkinson's official letters to Dearborn were filed in two collections at the Department of War—the Registered Series and the Unregistered Series. Copies of two other letters can be found in ICHi: Wilkinson Papers. Most of Claiborne's official letters can be found in *OLBWC*. Three of his official letters to Madison survive only in DLC: Burr Conspiracy Collection. Two other letters can be found in Rowland, *Third Annual Report*, 120–21; and Owens, ed., "Burr's Conspiracy," 172–73. Both men's duties led them to write official letters to other department heads on occasion. Six of Shaw's letters were written in New Orleans; the other two were sent from Natchez. All of them can be found in the records of the Department of the Navy. Other men in New Orleans could have sent official letters to the administration, including the federal district attorney, the postmaster, the customs officer, and the naval agent, but I have found no evidence of any of them writing in an official capacity.

92. For Claiborne's enclosures, see his letters to Madison of 15 January 1807, in *OLBWC*, 4:95; and 23 and 27 March 1807, in *TPUS*, 9:722, 723. For Wilkinson's depositions, see his letters to Dearborn of 10 and 11 January 1807, DNA: RG107, M222, W-1807; and 15, 16, and 22 January and 6 and 13 February 1807, DNA: RG107, M221, W-234 (3), W-235 (3), W-239 (3), W-249 (3), and W-243 (3). That Wilkinson assembled more depositions, memoranda of conversations, and letters during the crisis than he sent to Washington in these weeks seems clear.

93. Wilkinson to Claiborne, 3 January 1807, LNT-H: James Wilkinson Collection. Wilkinson seems to have lived and been headquartered at the home of Bernard

Marigny along the river, east of the Vieux Carré; see "New-Orleans," *National Intelligencer*, 6 April 1807. Twenty-six letters between Claiborne and Wilkinson and seven letters between Claiborne and Shaw from December 1806 and January 1807 can be found in *OLBWC*; a few additional letters to or from Claiborne are housed in other collections. There is one letter from Wilkinson to Shaw, before Shaw's departure from New Orleans, in DNA: RG45, M147.

94. Claiborne and Shaw, statement, 3 December 1806, in *OLBWC*, 4:40.

95. Claiborne to Wilkinson, 25 December 1806, in ibid., 69. Claiborne also secured a signed statement from Shaw, who had heard his conversation with Wilkinson on this issue; see Shaw, statement, 26 December 1806, in ibid., 69–70. For the earlier exchange, see Wilkinson to Claiborne, 15 December 1806, in ibid., 58–60; and Claiborne to Wilkinson, 17 December 1806, in ibid., 62–65. That they dined together between these letters is clear from Wilkinson to Claiborne, 16 December 1806, in ibid., 62. On another occasion, Claiborne tried to force Wilkinson to put into writing a request that he had already made verbally; see Claiborne to Wilkinson, 2 January 1807, in ibid., 77.

96. Claiborne to Wilkinson, 19 January 1807, in ibid., 102.

97. Shaw to Robert Smith, 4 December 1806, DNA: RG45, M147. See also, for example, Claiborne to Madison, 8 December 1806, in Rowland, *Third Annual Report*, 120; and Wilkinson to Dearborn, 8/9 January 1807, DNA: RG107, M222, W-1807.

98. Claiborne to Several Members of Congress, 15 January 1807, in *OLBWC*, 4:97. Most of Claiborne's unofficial letters to Madison are in DLC: Burr Conspiracy Collection; one was copied into his official letter books.

99. Dearborn to Wilkinson, 23 January 1807, DNA: RG107, M6. For a reference to Wilkinson's private correspondence with Dearborn, see Wilkinson to Dearborn, 25 December 1806, DNA: RG107, M221, W-217 (3). Some of his correspondence from New Orleans with Samuel Smith can be found in PPiU-D: James Wilkinson Papers. Dearborn's 23 January letter refers to his perusal of a now-missing unofficial letter from Wilkinson to Robert Smith. A later letter to the secretary of the navy survives in LN: James Wilkinson Letter. That Samuel Smith shared at least some of the private letters that he received from Wilkinson with the president is clear from Samuel Smith to Jefferson, 13 January 1807, DLC: Thomas Jefferson Papers.

100. Jefferson to Claiborne, 27 April 1806, DLC: Jefferson Papers. As I mentioned in the Introduction, many of Wilkinson's letters to Jefferson from these months survive only as appendixes to the general's published memoirs; see Wilkinson, *Burr's Conspiracy Exposed*, Appendixes 73–81, 83, and 85–90. The original of one letter can be found in PHi: Daniel Parker Papers. The recipient's copies of four more of the letters in Wilkinson's memoirs can be found in DLC: Burr Conspiracy Collection. Another seven letters exist only in that collection. An 1811 letter from Jefferson to the chair of the congressional committee investigating Wilkinson mentioned three additional letters that Wilkinson had sent to

the committee and that were not among Jefferson's papers and that did not appear in Wilkinson's memoirs; see Jefferson to Ezekial Bacon, 6 March 1811, in *PTJ: RS*, 3:428–29. Claiborne's letters to the president were published in *OLBWC* and *TPUS*.

101. Claiborne to Madison, 25 November 1806, in *OLBWC*, 4:37. Even Claiborne's official letter books were far from an automatic and, thus, neutral record of his outgoing official letters. Even though it is not clear that anyone in Washington ever saw them, they were carefully managed. Some incoming letters were inserted. Some items were entered out of chronological order, suggesting that Claiborne may have waited to decide whether he wanted to consider them official. And, most interestingly, some items were excised, including a twelve-page section from January 1807; see ibid., 115.

102. Wilkinson to Dearborn, 8/9 January 1807, DNA: RG107, M222, W-1807. Contrary to Wilkinson's request, the letter landed in the files of the War Department, though in the Unregistered Series rather than the more formal Registered Series. A mid-February letter from Wilkinson to Dearborn similarly began as an official dispatch, drifted into the general's "private concerns," and closed with a request to treat the letter as "private," but it still ended up in the official files (Wilkinson to Dearborn, 17 February 1807, DNA: RG107, M221, W-244 [3]).

103. Claiborne to Madison, 6 February 1807, DLC: Burr Conspiracy Collection; Claiborne to Jefferson, 3 May 1807, in *TPUS*, 9:730.

104. Claiborne to Wilkinson, 4 January 1807, in *OLBWC*, 4:82.

105. Wilkinson to Robert Smith, [ca. 9 January 1807], LN: Wilkinson Letter; Wilkinson to Samuel Smith, 10 December 1806, PPiU-D: Wilkinson Papers.

106. Wilkinson to Jefferson, 18 December 1806, in Wilkinson, *Burr's Conspiracy Exposed*, Appendix, 88.

107. James Brown to Clay, 10 April 1807, in *PHC*, 1:289.

108. Lewis Kerr, deposition, 8 September 1807, in Henshaw, ed., "Burr-Blennerhassett Documents," 34.

109. *Faithful Picture of the Political Situation*, 28. I discuss the authorship of this pamphlet below.

110. Clark, comment, 24 December 1806, in *Annals*, 9th Cong., 2nd sess., 215.

111. "Extract of a letter from Washington City," *New-York Evening Post*, 30 December 1806. The author admitted that his information was "second hand." The version of Clark's comments in the *Louisiana Gazette* was longer than and somewhat different from the one in the *National Intelligencer*. It rendered "another corps" as "black corps" and had Clark suggesting that Orleanians' willingness to mobilize against Burr was conditional on the replacement of the governor; see *Louisiana Gazette*, 13 February 1807.

112. William Plumer, diary entry, 20 February 1807, in *WPMP*, 614–15. Henry Clay seems to have shown the letter to Plumer, a New Hampshire senator, on the day that he received it. Published descriptions of the letter's contents, often

including brief quotes, appeared in countless newspapers. See, for example, *National Intelligencer*, 23 February 1807; *Republican Advocate* (Fredericktown, Md.), 27 February 1807 (from AHN); and "Z," "More Great Conspirators!," *Repertory* (Boston), 6 March 1807 (from AHN). For perhaps the most widely reprinted version, see "Washington, Saturday morning, Feb. 21," *United States' Gazette* (Philadelphia), 25 February 1807. The actual letter does not seem to have been published. Shortly after arriving in Washington, James Alexander visited congressmen at their boardinghouses to recount his tale; see Joseph Hopkinson to William Meredith, 7 February 1807, PHi: Meredith Family Papers.

113. Clark, statement, *National Intelligencer*, 21 January 1807. Clark had been named by the editor William Duane more than a week earlier.

114. James Alexander, "From the Baltimore Federal Gazette," *New-York Evening Post*, 18 February 1807. For Adair's public letter, see Adair, "For the National Intelligencer," *National Intelligencer*, 4 March 1807. For Mead's letter, see W. C. Mead, "From the Baltimore Daily Advertiser," *Morning Chronicle*, 21 February 1807. Mead had taken Swartwout to Washington. Certificates that accompanied Mead's published statement reported that Workman had told him of an expedition against Mexico that was approved by the administration and directed by Wilkinson and Burr.

115. "Extract of a letter from a young gentleman in New-Orleans, to his relation in Peacham," *North Star*, 24 March 1807 (from AHN).

116. "Extract of a letter from a gentleman of talents in New-Orleans, to the Editor of the Review, dated January 1st, 1807," *Impartial Review*, 24 January 1807. For more or less neutral reports on events in New Orleans, see "We have been favored with the following extract of a letter from a gentleman of correct political information," *Mississippi Herald*, 30 December 1806; "Extract of a letter, dated New-Orleans, Jan. 5," *Morning Chronicle*, 9 February 1807; and "Extract of a letter from a gentleman at New-Orleans, dated March 6, 1807," *Kentucky Gazette and General Advertiser* (Lexington), 31 March 1807.

117. [Andrew Marschalk], remarks on "Eliza," "Female Parliament," *Mississippi Herald*, 11 March 1807.

118. "Eliza," "Female Parliament," ibid.

119. "Eliza" to Marschalk, ibid. Both pieces were rich with sexual innuendo, with the second reporting that the women were "busy at our *breast-works*" and that "in a few days our *covert-way* will be impregnable."

120. J. W. [*sic*, B.] Prevost to Samuel H. Smith, 6 January 1807, *National Intelligencer*, 18 March 1807.

121. [Carpenter], *People's Friend*, 1 May 1807. Workman and Carpenter had been friends in Charleston; see Bradley, ed., *Interim Appointment*, 394–95. At least four New York City newspapers (*Commercial Advertiser*, *Evening Post*, *Gazette*, and *Herald*) published all or part of Livingston's appeal beginning in early February. Whether he sent it directly to their editors or to his brother Robert is unclear. In a late-January letter to Robert, though, Edward mentioned "several"

recent letters that he assumed had been intercepted due to his "reflections on the Conduct of the petty tyrant and the fools who now administer the government here"; without these letters, we cannot determine whether Edward directed Robert to have the appeal or other writings published (Edward Livingston to Robert R. Livingston, 30 January 1807, NHi: Livingston and Livingston Family Papers).

122. "Aurelius," *People's Friend*, 28 May 1807. For the first letter, see ibid., 24 April 1807; it was addressed to the editor and dated "New-Orleans, March 26, 1807." The second letter enclosed documents from New Orleans from as late as 23 April.

123. "The Best Answer," *Aurora General Advertiser* (Philadelphia), 2 July 1807.

124. [William Duane], *Louisiana Gazette*, 13 March 1807, clipped from *Aurora*. For Wilkinson's signed letters, see Wilkinson, "For the Public," *National Intelligencer*, 6 May 1807; and Wilkinson, "To the Printer of the American," *American, and Commercial Daily Advertiser* (Baltimore, Md.), 19 May 1807.

125. "Extract of a letter from New-Orleans," *American*, 28 February 1807. A brief introductory paragraph dated "Baltimore, Feb. 28," asked the editor "to give publicity to the following statement." For evidence of Smith's handiwork with a different letter, compare an original letter (Wilkinson to Samuel Smith, 17 February 1807, PPiU-D: Wilkinson Papers) to the printed version ("Extract of a letter from a gentleman of unquestionable character, dated New-Orleans, 17th February, 1807," *American*, 16 March 1807). For new pieces that seem to have been based upon Wilkinson's letters, see "Communication," ibid., 13 and 27 February 1807.

126. An incomplete run of the biweekly *Moniteur* for the period of the Burr crisis includes a few official documents from the territorial government, but almost no local news or commentary. There do not seem to be any surviving issues of the *Télégraphe* from Wilkinson's six months in New Orleans. For Wilkinson's use of that newspaper to respond to Adair, see Wilkinson, "To the Printer of the American," *American*, 19 May 1807. The same material appeared in the *Intelligencer* three days later; since that version does not include the cover letter, I assume that Wilkinson sent it directly to the *Intelligencer*'s editor. That "Veritas" was Wilkinson seems unlikely; a writer in another New Orleans newspaper disparaged the author as the general's "bog Trotter" ("From the Orleans Gazette," *Tennessee Gazette, and Mero District Advertiser* [Nashville], 25 April 1807).

127. [Bradford], *Mississippi Herald*, 27 January 1807, clipped from *Orleans Gazette*, 21 January 1807.

128. *Faithful Picture of the Political Situation*, 26–27.

129. Bradford, "Remarks on the Above," *Mississippi Herald*, 18 March 1807, clipped from *Orleans Gazette*, 26 February 1807.

130. "Centurio," "To the Editor of the Louisiana Gazette," *Louisiana Gazette*, 8 May 1807. The strong similarities between this essay and the above pamphlet suggest either one author or plagiarism.

131. "Orleans Legislature," *Orleans Gazette*, 5 February 1807 (from AHN). The *Louisiana Gazette* included some of the same material.
132. "New-Orleans, January 15," *Pittsburgh Gazette*, 10 March 1807, clipped from *Orleans Gazette*, 29 January 1807.
133. Wilkinson to Jefferson, 20 March 1807, DLC: Burr Conspiracy Collection.
134. Schenck to James Findlay, 8 May 1807, in Cox, ed., "Selections from the Torrence Papers," 4:126. "The Lawyers and the Printers," Claiborne later remarked, were "the most restless, turbulent members of this Society" (Claiborne to Madison, 17 July 1807, DLC: James Madison Papers).
135. Alexander, "Extracts of a letter from Mr. Alexander, to his correspondent in this city," *Louisiana Gazette*, 31 March 1807.
136. "From the Baltimore American," ibid., 31 March 1807.
137. "Centurio," "To the Editor of the Louisiana Gazette," ibid., 8 May 1807.
138. Review of *A Letter to the Respectable Citizens*, 229. For the outcomes of the two trials, see *Louisiana Gazette*, 6 March 1807.
139. Edward Livingston, argument, 10 February 1807, in [Davezac], *Trials of the Honb. James Workman*, 32, 33. Davezac found various ways to justify omitting the arguments of prosecuting attorneys John W. Gurley ("his indisposition . . . prevented him from correcting our notes, which were taken in a manner too imperfect for publication") and Abner L. Duncan (no explanation), as well as district attorney James Brown ("the impatience manifested by the public to obtain the report of the trial") (ibid., 144, 173). It is not clear when the pamphlet became available. Davezac registered the title on 5 March, and the pamphlet was mentioned in the *Louisiana Gazette* the next day, but a document on the last page is dated 22 May.
140. William Duer, argument, 10 February 1807, in ibid., 68, 46. Kerr lost most of his defense team in the February trial to illness, which forced him to act as his own attorney and allowed him to say things that he could not have said as a defendant.
141. *Debate in the House of Representatives of the Territory of Orleans*, title page. The resolution seems to have been adopted on 22 January 1807, perhaps the first day of real business of the session; see "Orleans Legislature," *Orleans Gazette*, 5 February 1807.
142. Joseph Parrot, comments, 16 March 1807, in *Debate in the House of Representatives of the Territory of Orleans*, 9.
143. When the *Enquirer* printed the memorial in early May, it reported that it was "said to be the production of the celebrated Edward Livingston" ("General Wilkinson," *Enquirer*, 1 May 1807). Claiborne heard that Livingston was the author from one of Livingston's confidants; see Claiborne's marginal note on p. 3 of the copy that he sent to Jefferson, at the Library of Congress. It seems likely that Bradford first published the memorial and debate in the *Orleans Gazette* within days of the discussion, but no issues of his newspaper survive for March or early April 1807. The memorial and debate were being reprinted as early as

mid-April in Nashville; see editors' note, *PAJ*, 2:160n3. Other newspapers published the memorial alone, though their source is rarely apparent. The copy that appeared in New York's *People's Friend* in early May had been sent by the author of the "Aurelius" essays in late March; see "To the Editor of the People's Friend," *People's Friend*, 24 April 1807; and "Memorial," ibid., 1 May 1807. It is unclear when the pamphlet was printed, but Claiborne sent a copy to Jefferson in mid-May; see Claiborne to Jefferson, 19 May 1807, in *TPUS*, 9:734. For a full discussion of the history of and debate over the memorial, see Bradley, ed., *Interim Appointment*, 350–62. At Wilkinson's request, Vicente Folch, the governor of Spanish West Florida, used his influence in the legislature to defeat the memorial; see Vicente Folch to the Marqués de Someruelos, 25 June 1807, in "Interview of Governor Folch with General Wilkinson," 839.

144. [Edward Livingston], "Memorial," in *Debate in the House of Representatives of the Territory of Orleans*, 5–6.

145. William Donaldson, comments, 16 January 1807, in ibid., 9.

146. Parrot, comments, 16 March 1807, in ibid., 11. For Watkins's expanded history of the crisis, see Watkins, comments, 16 March 1807, in ibid., 15–28.

147. [James Workman], *Letter to the Respectable Citizens*, xiii. This pamphlet was probably the first of the three to become available at Bradford's print shop. It was advertised on 27 March, though Workman's introduction was dated the next day; see *Louisiana Gazette*, 27 March 1807. The introduction to Workman's *Letter* was reprinted in some eastern newspapers, including New York's *People's Friend*.

148. Workman to Claiborne, 5 January 1807, in [Workman], *Letter to the Respectable Citizens*, 2.

149. Workman to Claiborne, 11 February 1807, in ibid., 24. For the availability of Workman's and Davezac's pamphlets in New York, see the advertisement in *New-York Commercial Advertiser*, 25 July 1807 (from AHN). For the review, see Review of *A Letter to the Respectable Citizens*.

150. Edward Livingston to Robert R. Livingston, 30 January 1807, NHi: Livingston and Livingston Family Papers.

151. [Mowry], *Louisiana Gazette*, 10 March 1807. See also "Aurelius," "To the Editor of the People's Friend," *People's Friend*, 28 May 1807. George Dargo attributed the pamphlet, which he called "a position paper for the Watkins-Workman group," to Livingston and claimed that it was written following the defeat of the memorial (Dargo, *Jefferson's Louisiana*, 203n49). Livingston's biographer, Edward Hatcher, did not mention the pamphlet; see Hatcher, *Edward Livingston*.

152. [Workman], *Letter to the Respectable Citizens*, iv. The editor of a scholarly reprint of *A Faithful Picture* considered Workman the more likely author; see Winston, ed., *"Faithful Picture of the Political Situation,"* 360. The best biography of Workman does not mention the pamphlet; see Bradley, ed., *Interim Appointment*, 389–414.

153. Watkins, comments, 16 March 1807, in *Debate in the House of Representatives of the Territory of Orleans*, 15. Watkins's biographers do not link him to the pamphlet; see Johnson, "Dr. John Watkins"; and Bradley, ed., *Interim Appointment*, 299–371.

154. *Faithful Picture of the Political Situation*, 3. Other pamphlets about the Burr crisis in New Orleans originated elsewhere in the spring and summer of 1807. A widely read anti-Wilkinson diatribe, *A Short Review of the Late Proceedings at New Orleans*, first appeared in South Carolina and was reprinted in Richmond. Signed "Agrestis," it was generally considered the work of Burr's son-in-law, Joseph Alston, though others ascribed it to Burr's daughter, Theodosia Burr Alston; neither had been in New Orleans during the crisis. A pro-Wilkinson, anti-Claiborne poem, "The Invitation," appeared from a Natchez press in August. Signed "A Louisianian" and often attributed to a French Louisianian, it was written by New Orleanian James Johnston, who had been in the city during the Burr crisis but travelled to Natchez to publish his poem to protect his anonymity; see James Johnston to Wilkinson, 10 and 17 August 1807, ICHi: Wilkinson Papers.

155. *Faithful Picture of the Political Situation*, 3, 4, 25, 16, 20, 28, 39, 46, 48.

156. Ibid., 46.

157. Richard Stites et al. to Wilkinson, 7 February 1807, in "Tribute of Applause," *Enquirer*, 10 April 1807. It is not clear whether the shipmasters' statement first appeared in a New Orleans newspaper.

158. Poydras et al. to Wilkinson, [23 March 1807], in "Addresses," *Louisiana Gazette*, 27 March 1807. For the announcement, see "Communication," ibid., 20 March 1807.

159. Poydras to Claiborne, [23 March 1807], in "Addresses," ibid., 27 March 1807.

160. [Mowry], "Addresses," ibid. Ninety-two men signed both addresses, while thirty-six signed just the address to Wilkinson and twenty signed just the address to Claiborne. For Claiborne's and Wilkinson's use of these documents, see Claiborne to Madison, 27 March 1807, in *TPUS*, 9:723; Claiborne to Jackson, 27 March 1807, in *PAJ*, 2:159; "General Wilkinson," *Enquirer*, 1 May 1807; and "Memorial to General Wilkinson," *National Intelligencer*, 4 May 1807. The *Enquirer* and *Intelligencer* may simply have reprinted this material from the *Louisiana Gazette*, but the fact that both included only the address to Wilkinson leads me to suspect his direct involvement.

161. "Extract of a letter from New Orleans, dated April 20, 1807," *Morning Chronicle*, 28 May 1807. The author also reported that "about two thirds of" the shipmasters who had signed the earlier address had been "afloat on the ocean during the" crisis.

162. "Extract of a letter from New-Orleans, dated June 18," *Impartial Review*, 4 July 1807.

163. [Bradford], *Orleans Gazette*, 25 June 1807.

164. *Faithful Picture of the Political Situation*, 46–48.

165. Clark to Claiborne, 28 May 1807, filed with Claiborne to Jefferson, 12 June 1807, DLC: Jefferson Papers. The full exchange of letters was sent by Claiborne to Jefferson in early September but has been filed with the governor's first post-duel letter to the president of mid-June; see Claiborne to Jefferson, 1 September 1807, ibid. For Wilkinson's departure and Clark's arrival, see *Louisiana Gazette*, 22 May 1807.

166. Claiborne to Jefferson, 17 June 1807, in *TPUS*, 9:743. For the governor's injuries and recovery, see also his letters to Jefferson of 12 June 1807, DLC: Jefferson Papers; and 28 June 1807, in *TPUS*, 9:745. Nine months later, Gurley was killed in a duel by Philip Jones, a Livingston ally. While "the dispute was of a private nature," Claiborne believed that "party politicks [had] promoted this unfortunate affair" (Claiborne to Jefferson, 5 March 1808, DLC: Jefferson Papers).

167. Richard Raynal Keene to Clark, 12 June 1807, PHi: Coxe Papers. See also Relf to Clark, 12 June 1807, ibid. A more neutral source reported that it was "universally agreed" that both men had "beheaved as well on the occasion as possible" (Elizabeth House Trist to Mary Gilmer, 15 June 1807, LNHiC: Elizabeth House Trist Letter).

168. Chandler Price to Caesar A. Rodney, 22 July 1807, DeHi: Rodney Collection. Price had lived in New Orleans and was well-informed of opinion there. See also Samuel Hodgdon to Winthrop Sargent, 18 July 1807, MHi: Winthrop Sargent Papers.

169. Claiborne to Jefferson, 1 September 1807, DLC: Jefferson Papers.

170. Claiborne to Jefferson, 28 June 1807, in *TPUS*, 9:745. See also Claiborne to Dearborn, 13 December 1807, in ibid., 768–69. For Claiborne's appointments in these months, see Thomas B. Robertson, "Return of Civil Appointments, Pardons &c from the 1st of July, to the 31st Decr. 1807 inclusive," [January 1808], in *OLBWC*, 4:146–47.

171. For Claiborne's use of "Burrites," see, for example, his letters to: Madison, 17 March 1808 and 1 January 1809, in *OLBWC*, 4:167 and 284; Jefferson, 1 September 1808, in ibid., 208; and Robert Smith, 31 December 1809, in ibid., 5:63.

172. James Brown to Parke, 24 November 1807, InHi: Porter Papers.

173. Schenck to James Findlay, 8 May 1807, in Cox, ed., "Selections from the Torrence Papers," 4:124.

CHAPTER 7. THE THREAT TO THE REPUBLIC

1. W. Heath to John Adams, [28 December 1807], MHi: Adams Family Papers.
2. John Quincy Adams to Thomas Boylston Adams, [10 February 1807], ibid.
3. Jesse Higgins to Jonathan and Matthew Roberts, 8 May 1807, PHi: Jonathan Roberts Papers.
4. Henry Guest to Thomas Jefferson, 10 December 1806, DLC: Thomas Jefferson Papers.

5. John Badollet to Albert Gallatin, 14 January 1807, in Thornbrough, ed., "Correspondence of John Badollet," 72. See also William Eustis to Thomas Law, 1 January 1807, MdHi: Thomas Law Family Papers; Thomas Rodney to R[ichard] Claiborne, 5 January 1806 [sic, 1807], DLC: Rodney Family Papers; and John Cameron to Duncan Cameron, 3 February 1807, NcU: Cameron Family Papers.

6. James Workman to William C. C. Claiborne, 25 January 1807, in [Workman], *Letter to the Respectable Citizens*, 19.

7. "The Fredonian" [Thomas Spotswood Hinde], "The aspect of the affairs in the Western Country and the *emissaries* of Col. Burr, No. V," *Scioto Gazette* (Chillicothe, Ohio), 20 November 1806.

8. [Thomas Ritchie], "A parallel, drawn from Antiquity," *Enquirer* (Richmond, Va.), 3 January 1807.

9. "Regulus" [Matthew Nimmo], "Conspiracy, No. I," *Western Spy* (Cincinnati, Ohio), 21 October 1806.

10. [Joseph M. Street], "Colonel Aaron Burr, Late Vice President of the United States," *Western World* (Frankfort, Ky.), 13 September 1806.

11. Workman, comments, 13 February 1807, in [Davezac], *Trials of the Honb. James Workman*, 165.

12. Goldsmith, *Goldsmith's Roman History*, 171–74. This work was the most recent American edition of a much-reprinted 1772 history for use in schools. Its author, Oliver Goldsmith, was an English poet, novelist (*The Vicar of Wakefield* [1766]), and dramatist (*She Stoops to Conquer* [1773]). A similar volume that was "designed for the use of young Ladies and Gentlemen" was published in Philadelphia in 1809; it also covered Catiline's conspiracy at length (*New Roman History*). For more recent histories of Catiline, see Kaplan, *Catiline*; and Hutchinson, *Conspiracy of Catiline*. For knowledge of and thinking about Greek and Roman history in revolutionary and early republican America, see Reinhold, *Classick Pages*; Richard, *Founders and the Classics*; Winterer, *Culture of Classicism*; Winterer, *Mirror of Antiquity*; and Shalev, *Rome Reborn on Western Shores*.

13. Alexander Hamilton to James A. Bayard, 6 August 1800, in Syrett and Cooke, eds., *Papers of Alexander Hamilton*, 25:58; Moses Hopkins to Calvin Jones, 19 July 1804, T: Jones Family Papers. Hamilton returned to this analogy in various letters at the height of the electoral crisis. See also [James Cheetham], "Mr. Burr," *Republican Watch-Tower* (New York), 19 September 1804 (from AHN).

14. [Street], "Colonel Aaron Burr, Late Vice President of the United States," *Western World*, 13 September 1806.

15. "Regulus" [Nimmo], "Conspiracy, No. V," *Western Spy*, 2 December 1806. I discuss Burr's followers in Chapter 10.

16. [Ritchie], "A parallel, drawn from Antiquity," *Enquirer*, 3 January 1807. For other references to Burr as Catiline in the *Enquirer*, see [Ritchie], "Aaron Burr," ibid., 28 November 1806; [Ritchie], "American Cataline," ibid., 30 December

1806; "Burr's Conspiracy," ibid., 13 February 1807; and [Ritchie], "Cursory Reflections—Portrait of Aaron Burr, No. II," ibid., 3 November 1807.

17. Jefferson, memorandum, 22 October 1806, in *Anas*, 246. He returned to this analogy six weeks later but did not find it entirely apt; see Jefferson to Caesar A. Rodney, 5 December 1806, in *WoTJ*, 10:322.

18. Joseph Hamilton Daveiss to James Madison, 16 November 1806, in *View*, 28.

19. Wyllys Silliman to Thomas Worthington, 6 January 1807, OHi: Thomas Worthington Papers; Daniel Mulford, diary entry, 12 September 1807, DLC: Daniel Mulford Papers; John Campbell to David Campbell, 3 April 1807, NcD: Campbell Family Papers; Caesar A. Rodney to Jefferson, 4 January 1807, DLC: Jefferson Papers (each of the four misspelled "Catiline").

20. Thomas Truxton to Timothy Pickering, 13 January 1807, MHi: Timothy Pickering Papers. See also "A Sentinel," *Washington Federalist* (Georgetown, D.C.), 14 February 1807.

21. Thomas Leiper to Jefferson, 11 January 1807, DLC: Jefferson Papers.

22. Silliman to Gallatin, 12 December 1806, in *PAG*. Hamilton had described Burr as "an embryo-Cæsar" as early as 1792 (Hamilton to an unknown correspondent, 26 September 1792, in Syrett and Cooke, eds., *Papers of Alexander Hamilton*, 12:480).

23. Philip Reed to Joseph H. Nicholson, 29 December 1806, DLC: Joseph H. Nicholson Papers. See also [Stephen C. Carpenter], *People's Friend & Daily Advertiser* (New York), 14 January 1807.

24. William Wirt to Ninian Edwards, 2 February 1807, ICHi: Ninian Edwards Papers. Sylla (or Sulla) was a Roman general who marched on Rome and became dictator in the last decades of the Roman republic; Augustus was the first ruler of the Roman empire. Orlando Furioso, the hero of Ludovico Ariosto's epic poem of the same name, and Don Quixote were fictional characters. For Eaton's account of Burr's comments, see William Eaton, testimony, 26 September 1807, in *TCAB*, 3:234.

25. Eaton, deposition, 26 January 1807, in [Prentiss], *Life of the Late Gen. William Eaton*, 399–400. See also Eaton, testimony, 26 September 1807, in *TCAB*, 3:233. The firsthand accounts of Benjamin Stoddert, George Morgan, and John Henderson included similar stories, but, as grand jury testimony, never became widely known. See their testimony of 13, 16, and 18 June 1807 (respectively), in "NECAB," 5–6, 37, and 48. Of these men, only Morgan discussed a possible coup in open court and only briefly; see George Morgan, testimony, 19 August 1807, in *RTCAB*, 1:502.

26. ["The Conspiracy, I"], *National Intelligencer, and Washington Advertiser* (D.C.), 13 March 1807. This essay was the first in a four-part series, the naming of which began with the second installment.

27. Worthington to Nathaniel Massie, 19 January 1807, in Massie, *Nathaniel Massie*, 240.

28. Wirt to Edwards, 2 February 1807, ICHi: Edwards Papers.

29. Nick Warfield Jr. to John Payne, 14 January 1807, DLC: John Payne Papers.

30. Rufus Easton to Gideon Granger, 18 July 1807, MoSHi: Rufus Easton Papers.

31. "A Virginian," *Virginia Argus* (Richmond), 24 March 1807. See also John Page to [St. George Tucker], 4 February 1807, ViW: Tucker-Coleman Papers.

32. Jefferson to William B. Giles, 20 April 1807, in *WrTJ*, 11:187.

33. Tench Coxe to Madison, 2 March 1807, DLC: James Madison Papers.

34. "Federal Facts and Arguments," *Virginia Argus*, 27 March 1807.

35. [William Duane], "Cogitations," *Aurora General Advertiser* (Philadelphia), 1 December 1806.

36. Robert Troup to Charles Williamson, [ca. April-May 1807], ICN: Edward A. Ayer Manuscript Collection, Charles Williamson Papers. See also Robert Gamble to Thomas Massie, 26 January 1807, ViHi: Massie Family Papers.

37. [Ritchie], "Communication," *Enquirer*, 3 February 1807.

38. Madison, "Substance of a communication made on the 23 of Jany, 1807, by Doctor Bollman to the President," [23 (*sic*, 24) January 1807], in *LOWJM*, 2:397.

39. Alexander Macomb to Jonathan Williams, 8 January 1807, InU: Jonathan Williams Manuscripts.

40. "Union, No. 2," *Scioto Gazette*, 25 December 1806.

41. Caesar A. Rodney, "Interrogatories," [ca. 6 April 1807], DLC: Burr Conspiracy Collection. See also Eaton, testimony, 15 June 1807, in "NECAB," 8.

42. Warfield to Payne, 14 January 1807, DLC: Payne Papers.

43. [Coxe to Madison], 1 March 1807, DLC: Madison Papers. See also "Extract of a letter, dated Nashville," *National Intelligencer*, 26 January 1807.

44. William Plumer, diary entry, 28 November 1806, in *WPMP*, 515. Plumer may have considered Mexico to be in South America.

45. "Union, No. 2," *Scioto Gazette*, 25 December 1806.

46. Coxe to Madison, [11 January 1807], DLC: Madison Papers. See also Jefferson to the Marquis de Lafayette, 14 July 1807, in *WrTJ*, 11:277. I discussed this thinking from a different angle in Chapter 4.

47. ["The Conspiracy, I"], *National Intelligencer*, 13 March 1807.

48. Cowles Mead, proclamation, 23 December 1806, in Rowland, *Third Annual Report*, 42. See also Thomas Rodney to Jefferson, 21 November 1806, in Gratz, ed., "Thomas Rodney," 44:296; John Clopton, circular letter to constituents, 20 February 1807, in *CLC*, 1:491; and "Who are Conspirators?," *Fredonian* (Chillicothe, Ohio), 4 April 1807. For American ideas about conspiracy in this period, see Knox, *Conspiracy in American Politics*; and the works cited above, Chapter 1, n. 109.

49. James Finley to Worthington, 31 July 1807, OHi: Worthington Papers.

50. Harry Toulmin to Jefferson, 5 April 1807, DLC: Edmond Charles Genet Papers. See also Taylor, *Victim of Intrigue*, 107.

51. William Findley to John Hemphill, February 1807, NcD: Hemphill Family Papers. For the search for a Cicero, see [Street], "Colonel Aaron Burr, Late Vice President of the United States," *Western World*, 13 September 1806; and "The

Fredonian" [Hinde], "The aspect of affairs in the Western Country, and Col. Burr's late visit, [No. II]," *Enquirer*, 25 November 1806, clipped from *Scioto Gazette*.

52. Simkins, *Oration*, 27–28.

53. John Campbell to David Campbell, 3 April 1807, NcD: Campbell Family Papers. Washington Academy later became Washington and Lee University. See also John Henry Purviance to James Monroe, 7 April 1807, NN: James Monroe Papers; and Charles Minifie, "Parody on the Song of Plato," enclosed in Minifie to Jefferson, 17 October 1807, DLC: Jefferson Papers. According to Minifie, his piece had been sung in Washington on the Fourth of July.

54. "Burr's Conspiracy," *Enquirer*, 13 February 1807.

55. [Ritchie], "Cursory Reflections—Portrait of Aaron Burr, No. II," ibid., 3 November 1807.

56. Robert Emory and Thomas Wright to Jefferson, 18 March 1809, in *PTJ: RS*, 1:62.

57. Thompson, *Compendious View*, 4.

58. Kennedy, *Memoirs of the Life of William Wirt*, 1:150. The only modern author to take this possibility seriously is David O. Stewart, and even he largely consigns it to an endnote; see Stewart, *American Emperor*, 125, 350n9.

59. Hall, *Letters from the West*, 109. See also Parton, *Life and Times of Aaron Burr*, 408–9.

60. Butler, *History of the Commonwealth of Kentucky*, 320.

61. John Quincy Adams to Abigail Adams, [3 February 1807], MHi: Adams Family Papers.

62. Littleton Waller Tazewell to Monroe, 3 January 1807, DLC: James Monroe Papers.

63. Thomas Rodney to Caesar A. Rodney, [ca. 11/]12 February 1807, in Gratz, ed., "Thomas Rodney," 44:300. See also Thomas Rodney, "Note," 10 February [1807], printed in Hamilton, *Anglo-American Law on the Frontier*, 265.

64. "The Crisis," *People's Friend*, 9 February 1807, clipped from *Frederick-Town Herald* (Md.). See also "Gen. Wilkinson," *Newburyport Herald* (Mass.), 14 April 1807 (from AHN).

65. Philander Smith to Jedidiah Smith, April 1807, NNGLI: Gilder Lehrman Collection. See also Thomas Rodney to Caesar A. Rodney, 12 January and 23 February 1807, DLC: Rodney Family Papers; and "Communication," *Mississippi Messenger* (Natchez), 20 January 1807, in Rowland, *Third Annual Report*, 99. For concerns about the stoppages on the Ohio River, see Tazewell to Monroe, 3 January 1807, DLC: Monroe Papers; James Ross to James McHenry, 12 January 1807, NjP: Fuller Collection of Aaron Burr; [Morgan Neville], "A Letter from One of the Young Gentlemen who Lately Left this Town," *Pittsburgh Gazette* (Pa.), 13 January 1807; Henry Weaver Sr. to Jefferson, 11 February 1807, in McLaughlin, ed., *To His Excellency Thomas Jefferson*, 6–8; and Matthew Backus to James Backus, 30 March 1807, OHi: Backus-Woodbridge Collection.

66. "Extract of a letter from New Orleans," *Morning Chronicle* (New York), 28 May 1807. I discussed most of these acts in Chapter 6. For habeas corpus in the United States, see Halliday, *Habeas Corpus*; and Wert, *Habeas Corpus in America*.

67. The best contemporary account of the Senate debate over the suspension bill is William Plumer, diary entry, 23 February 1807, in *WPMP*, 585–89. Whether it was adopted without a vote, unanimously, with one opposing vote (Delaware's James A. Bayard), or with three opposing votes (Bayard, another Federalist, and a Republican) is unclear. See, respectively, John Quincy Adams to Abigail Adams, [3 February 1807], MHi: Adams Family Papers; Samuel Smith, notes for speech, [ca. 1826], DLC: Samuel Smith Family Papers; John Quincy Adams to John Adams, 27 January 1807, in Ford, ed., *Writings of John Quincy Adams*, 3:158; and Garnett to Hunter, 8 February 1807, Vi: Garnett-Mercer-Hunter Family Papers. For the House debate, see *Annals*, 9th Cong., 2nd sess., 402–25. For the idea that the suspension bill was principally intended to cover Wilkinson's arrests, see William Ellery to William Stedman, 19 February 1807, NNGLI: Gilder Lehrman Collection; Beverley Tucker to John Randolph, 12 February 1807, ViW: Tucker-Coleman Papers; "From the Baltimore Federal Gazette of February 19," *New-York Evening Post*, 23 February 1807; and William A. Burwell, circular letter to constituents, 2 March 1807, in *CLC*, 1:512.

68. Samuel Taggart to John Taylor, 18 February 1807, in "Letters of Samuel Taggart," 212. See also Samuel Smith to John Spear Smith, 18 February 1807, DLC: Smith Family Papers; "Extracts of Letters to the Editor of the United States' Gazette," *United States' Gazette* (Philadelphia), 23 February 1807; and "Extract of a letter from a member of congress to his friend in this place," *Impartial Review, and Cumberland Repository* (Nashville, Tenn.), 4 April 1807.

69. "Extracts of Letters to the Editor of this Gazette," *United States' Gazette*, 24 February 1807. According to the quoted letter, the measure lost only because some of its supporters were caught offguard by the vote and were absent from the House. For the debate and vote, see *Annals*, 9th Cong., 2nd sess., 501–90. A few Republicans must have voted against postponement.

70. Whether Jefferson was, in fact, behind the suspension bill is unclear. William A. Burwell, a Virginia representative who had formerly served as Jefferson's private secretary, recalled that, on the night that the suspension bill passed the Senate, Jefferson had assured him that it had not been sought by the administration, "add[ing that] it would give him great pain, that his presidency should furnish such a precedent" (Burwell, memorandum, [ca. late 1808], in Gawalt, ed., "'Strict Truth,'" 127). But, nearly two decades after proposing the suspension, Giles remembered that he had received "the first suggestion . . . of that measure" from Vice President George Clinton, who said that he had "consulted the Administration upon the subject" (Giles to Samuel Smith, 18 March 1826, DLC: Smith Family Papers).

71. Jefferson to James Wilkinson, 3 February 1807, in *WrTJ*, 11:149. This letter "lifted from [Wilkinson's] breast a load of anxiety" (Wilkinson to Jefferson, 20 March 1807, DLC: Burr Conspiracy Collection). For the administration's early support for Wilkinson, see also Henry Dearborn to Wilkinson, 21 and 23 January and 3 February 1807, DNA: RG107, M6; and Jefferson to William C. C. Claiborne, 3 February 1807, in *WrTJ*, 11:151.

72. *View*, 35. For Wilkinson's efforts to use Jefferson's message and letter and Dearborn's instructions to strengthen his position, see "Aurelius," *People's Friend*, 24 April 1807.

73. [Rufus King], undated essay, in King, ed., *Life and Correspondence of Rufus King*, 4:547. In time, Jefferson would come under attack as well for what seemed to some critics to be a willingness to disregard republican principles in his effort to have Burr convicted of treason; see Chapter 11.

74. "Liberty. No Tyranny," *New-York Evening Post*, 27 March 1807, clipped from *Norfolk Gazette and Public Ledger* (Va.). In Congress, according to one report, Virginia Quid John Randolph similarly charged that Wilkinson's conduct was "the most daring usurpation that ever did, will, or can exist, in this or any country" ("From Washington," *People's Friend*, 27 February 1807).

75. "Col. Burr," 363.

76. *Faithful Picture of the Political Situation*, 26; "Agrestis," *Short Review of the Late Proceedings*, 31.

77. [Carpenter], *People's Friend*, 24 April 1807.

78. Wilkinson to Dearborn, 12 November 1806, DNA: RG107, M221, W-209 (3). Isaac Briggs, the federal surveyor who had carried Wilkinson's November 1806 dispatches to Washington, also recalled the general using this analogy; see Isaac Briggs, deposition, 6 January 1811, in Wilkinson, *Memoirs of My Own Times*, 2:Appendix 59. An article in defense of Wilkinson in Baltimore's *American* employed the same analogy; see "Communication," *American, and Commercial Daily Advertiser* (Baltimore, Md.), 13 February 1807.

79. Wilkinson to John Smith, 14 November 1806, OCHi: Papers in the Defense of John Smith of Ohio.

80. Wilkinson to José de Iturrigaray, 17 November 1806, in Shepherd, ed., "Letter of General James Wilkinson," 536. Years later, Richard Raynal Keene, who had been denounced as a Burr supporter by Wilkinson in New Orleans in December 1806, began investigating Walter Burling's 1806 mission to Mexico City, perhaps in preparation for writing his sweeping defense pamphlet, *A Letter of Vindication to His Excellency Colonel Monroe* (1824). While in Madrid as a colonel in the Spanish army, Keene learned some of the details from Iturrigaray, who recalled that Wilkinson had "likened himself to *Leonidas in the pass of Thermopylæ*" (Richard Raynal Keene to Patrick Mangan, 21 July 1821, in *MAB*, 2:403). Iturrigaray's widow also provided her recollections of the mission. In 1821, Keene sent her statement to Patrick Mangan, the priest who had translated for Burling, requesting his account. Mangan confirmed what Keene had learned

from the former viceroy and his widow and added his own memories, including Wilkinson's use of the Leonidas image; see Mangan to Keene, 23 July 1821, in ibid., 403–4. The fruits of Keene's research appeared in the second volume of Matthew Livingston Davis's biography of Aaron Burr in 1837.

81. "Agrestis," *Short Review of the Late Proceedings*, 36. For Ireland, England, and France, respectively, see ibid., 6, 31, and 34.

82. "Col. Burr," 364.

83. "Agrestis," *Short Review of the Late Proceedings*, 6; Edward Livingston to Robert R. Livingston, 30 January 1807, NHi: Robert R. Livingston and Livingston Family Papers. "Agrestis" likened Wilkinson to England's Charles I and France's Louis XIV.

84. [Carpenter], *People's Friend*, 18 March 1807; Truxton to Pickering, 12 February 1807, MHi: Pickering Papers.

85. Danvers, *Picture of a Republican Magistrate*, 21. For the Popish Plot, see Kenyon, *Popish Plot*; and Hinds, *"Horrid Popish Plot."*

86. [John Scull], comments on [Neville], "A Letter from One of the Young Gentlemen who Lately Left this Town," *Pittsburgh Gazette*, 13 January 1807. See also Gabriel Shaw to William Meredith, 17 February 1807, PHi: Meredith Family Papers.

87. "From WASHINGTON," *Columbian Centinel* (Boston), 11 February 1807.

88. "From the Baltimore Federal Gazette of February 19," *New-York Evening Post*, 23 February 1807. For other comparisons of Wilkinson to Bonaparte, see Workman to William C. C. Claiborne, 25 January 1807, in [Workman], *Letter to the Respectable Citizens*, 19; and Watkins, speech, 16 March 1807, in *Debate in the House of Representatives of the Territory of Orleans*, 19.

89. [Scull], comments on [Neville], "A Letter from One of the Young Gentlemen who Lately Left this Town," *Pittsburgh Gazette*, 13 January 1807.

90. [Carpenter], *People's Friend*, 21 February 1807. For similar views expressed by Republicans, see Andrew Jackson to Daniel Smith, 11 February 1807, in *PAJ*, 2:155; and [Benjamin Bradford], "How long will Tyrants reign?," *Tennessee Gazette, and Mero District Advertiser* (Nashville), 25 April 1807.

91. [John Wood], "Colonel Burr," *Atlantic World* (Washington, D.C.), 31 March 1807. See also [Peter Marchant and Aaron Willington], *Charleston Courier* (S.C.), 17 April 1807.

92. "From the Augusta Herald," *People's Friend*, 13 April 1807. This piece also appeared in the *Louisiana Gazette* (New Orleans), 15 May 1807. For a similar charge by a Burrite newspaper, see [Samuel Brooks], *Impartial Observer* (Richmond, Va.), 18 April 1807.

93. Julien Poydras, "Answer of the Legislative Council of this Territory to the Governor's Speech," *Orleans Gazette and General Advertiser* (New Orleans), 5 February 1807.

94. [Workman], *Letter to the Respectable Citizens*, iii. The author—a judge in the city's court—still insisted, however, that the extraordinary situation of Wilkinson's

NOTES TO PAGES 262–264 | 561

tyrannies remained preferable to ordinary conditions under Spain's rule; see ibid., xiv.

95. Edward Livingston to Robert R. Livingston, 30 January 1807, NHi: Livingston and Livingston Family Papers; James Brown to Henry Clay, 10 April 1807, in *PHC*, 1:289; Joseph A. Parrott to James M. Bradford, *Orleans Gazette*, 18 June 1807.

96. [Edward Livingston], "Memorial: To the Honorable the Senate and House of Representatives of the United States, in Congress assembled," in *Debate in the House of Representatives of the Territory of Orleans*, 9.

97. Livingston, "To the Public," *Louisiana Gazette*, 30 December 1806.

98. *Faithful Picture of the Political Situation*, 46. See also "Aurelius," *People's Friend*, 24 April 1807.

99. Brown to Clay, 1 September 1808, in *PHC*, 1:375.

100. "H.E.," *Mississippi Herald & Natchez Gazette*, 27 January 1807. While the politics of the *Mississippi Herald* are not entirely clear, its principal editor, Andrew Marschalk, was often considered a Federalist; see Haynes, *Mississippi Territory and the Southwest Frontier*, 63.

101. Robert Williams to Jefferson, 14 March 1807, in *TPUS*, 5:529. Williams, the territorial governor, did not approve the bill; Wilkinson County can still be found in the southwestern corner of Mississippi.

102. [Thomas Eastin], *Impartial Review*, 14 February 1807; [Benjamin Bradford], "How long will Tyrants reign?," *Tennessee Gazette*, 25 April 1807.

103. "Guzman," "For the Fredonian," *Fredonian*, 14 March 1807. For such views in the private letters of westerners, see John Steele to Winthrop Sargent, 21 January 1807, MHi: Winthrop Sargent Papers; William T. Barry to John Barry, 27 January 1807, ViU: William T. Barry Letters; and Thomas Rodney to Caesar A. Rodney, 23 February 1807, DLC: Rodney Family Papers.

104. [Hinde], "Burr & Wilkinson," *Fredonian*, 4 April 1807.

105. [Eastin], *Impartial Review*, 14 February 1807.

106. Jackson to Daniel Smith, 11 February 1807, in *PAJ*, 2:155.

107. Henry Middleton Rutledge to Henry Izard, 25 March 1807, ScHi: Henry Middleton Rutledge Letter.

108. Mead to Madison, 13 April 1807, in *TPUS*, 5:545. Mead's tenure as acting governor ended when Robert Williams returned to Natchez in January. See also Matthew Lyon to Jefferson, 22 February 1807, DLC: Jefferson Papers; and John Lithgow to Jefferson, May 1807, ibid.

109. Taggart to Taylor, 8 February 1807, in "Letters of Samuel Taggart," 211. See also John Wickham, argument, 31 March 1807, in *ECAB*, 16.

110. William Plumer to William Plumer Jr., 23 February 1807, in Mevers et al., eds., *William Plumer Papers*; same to same, 25 February 1807, in ibid.

111. [Brooks], *Impartial Observer*, 18 April 1807; Garnett to Hunter, 8 February 1807, Vi: Garnett-Mercer-Hunter Family Papers. For evidence that Brooks's *Observer* was in Burr's employ in the spring of 1807, see Chapter 8.

112. "General Wilkinson again," *Mississippi Herald*, 3 April 1807, clipped from *Frederick-Town Herald*. See also [Carpenter], *People's Friend*, 21 and 24 February 1807; and "Liberty. No Tyranny," *New-York Evening Post*, 27 March 1807, clipped from *Norfolk Gazette*.

113. [William Pechin], *American*, 7 February 1807. Later in the month, the newspaper ran a two-part series that was very forceful in the general's defense; see "Communication," ibid., 13 and 27 February 1807. I discussed Samuel Smith's influence over the *American* in Chapter 6.

114. [Samuel Pleasants Jr.], *Virginia Argus*, 14 April 1807; [Duane], *Troy Gazette* (Troy, N.Y.), 24 February 1807, clipped from *Aurora* (from AHN).

115. "A Virginian," *Virginia Argus*, 24 March 1807. The most important administration newspaper, the *National Intelligencer*, was more guarded, repeatedly stating in the spring of 1807 that it was too early to judge Wilkinson's actions; see "The Conspiracy, [IV]," *National Intelligencer*, 20 March 1807; and [Samuel H. Smith], ibid., 30 March 1807. Such restraint did not prevent a Federalist newspaper from quoting a few carefully selected lines from the *Intelligencer* as evidence that it was "spinning out endless columns *in vindication* of" the general; see [Marchant and Willington], *People's Friend*, 6 May 1807, clipped from *Charleston Courier*.

116. [Marchant and Willington], *Charleston Courier*, 17 April 1807. The author named the *Aurora, Enquirer, Intelligencer,* and *Virginia Argus* in this group.

117. [Wood], "Colonel Burr," *Atlantic World*, 31 March 1807.

118. [Carpenter], *People's Friend*, 24 March 1807. See also Brooks to Jefferson, 16 May 1807, *Impartial Observer*, 23 May 1807.

119. "Another Letter—Same Date," *Columbian Centinel*, 11 February 1807. William Plumer, a New Hampshire Federalist who had voted for the suspension bill in the Senate, later berated himself for doing so and "rejoice[d]" that it "did not pass into a law" (William Plumer, diary entry, 21 February 1807, in *WPMP*, 619). The Burrite "Agrestis" devoted more than half of his or her pamphlet to the suspension bill; see "Agrestis," *Short Review of the Late Proceedings*, 19–42.

120. Garnett to Hunter, 8 February 1807, Vi: Garnett-Mercer-Hunter Family Papers. The New York Federalist Rufus King offered a similar criticism, also mentioning the Bastille and alluding to lettres de cachet through a reference "to the Mysterious Man in the Iron Mask" ([King], undated essay, in King, ed., *Life and Correspondence of Rufus King*, 4:547).

121. John McDonagh [Sr.] to John McDonagh [Jr.], 18 March 1807, in LNT-H: John McDonagh Papers. See also "Federal Facts and Arguments," *Trenton True American* (N.J.), 16 March 1807 (from AHN); *National Intelligencer*, 25 March 1807; and [Duane], "Warm Federalism," *Pittsfield Sun* (Mass.), clipped from *Aurora* (from AHN).

122. Burwell, circular letter to constituents, 2 March 1807, in *CLC*, 1:512.

123. John Campbell to David Campbell, 3 April 1807, NcD: Campbell Family Papers. Even the *American* and the *Argus* shied away from supporting the suspension bill; see *American*, 7 February 1807; and "General Wilkinson," *Louisiana Gazette*, 15 May 1807, clipped from *Virginia Argus*.

124. Due to the embargo in New Orleans and the delays in the western mails, most people east of the Appalachians learned of Wilkinson's arrests by reading Jefferson's 22 January message to Congress or an account of the message in a letter from Washington. News of the arrests arrived first in Charleston, South Carolina, in early January in the ship that carried Bollman to Washington. Brief reports from Charleston ran in other eastern newspapers over the next few weeks; see, for example, *New-England Palladium* (Boston), 20 January 1807 (from AHN). But more thorough accounts came later. For example, Edward Livingston's late December address "To the Public"—which sparked criticism of Wilkinson in many western newspapers—did not appear in any eastern newspaper that I have seen until after Jefferson's message. The *New-York Evening Post* seems to have reprinted it first, on 2 February; Jefferson's message had appeared in New York newspapers at least as early as 27 January.

125. Samuel White to Jonathan Dayton, 15 February 1807, MiU-C: Jonathan Dayton Papers. White was a senator from Delaware. See also unknown writer to unknown recipient, 17 February 1807, NcU: Peter Hagner Papers. It seems clear that the author was a Quid congressman. For evidence that Republican congressmen in Washington expected the president to punish Wilkinson, see Lyon to Jefferson, 22 February 1807, DLC: Jefferson Papers; and William Plumer, diary entry, 21 February 1807, in *WPMP*, 618–19. Plumer recorded the views of Jefferson's son-in-law, Thomas Mann Randolph, a Virginia congressman.

126. Benjamin Parke to Brown, 2 January 1808, InHi: Albert G. Porter Papers. Parke was the delegate from the Indiana Territory.

127. For the link between necessity and self-preservation in the Burr crisis, see Guest to Jefferson, 10 December 1806, DLC: Jefferson Papers; "The Conspiracy, [III]," *National Intelligencer*, 18 March 1807; and "A Jurisconsult," "Communication," *Virginia Argus*, 20 May 1807, clipped from *Liberty Hall* (Cincinnati, Ohio). For Wilkinson's reliance upon the doctrine of necessity in his interactions with Claiborne, see his letters of 6 December 1806, in *OLBWC*, 4:46–47; and 3 January 1807, LNT-H: James Wilkinson Collection. For his employment of the doctrine in letters to Washington, see Wilkinson to Dearborn, 4 November 1806, DNA: RG107, M221, W-211 (3); Wilkinson to Jefferson, 12 November 1806, in Wilkinson, *Memoirs of My Own Times*, 2:Appendix 100; and Wilkinson to Jefferson, 9 December 1806, PHi: Daniel Parker Papers. For his public use of this doctrine, see Livingston, "To the Public," *Louisiana Gazette*, 30 December 1806. By the time he left New Orleans, though, Wilkinson insisted that he had "never attempted to justify the infractions of the law which were forced on [him] . . . by an impending great calamity" (Wilkinson to Daniel Clark, 24 May 1807, in *Proofs*, Appendix, 153).

128. Dearborn to Wilkinson, 3 February 1807, DNA: RG107, M6. See also Jefferson to: Wilkinson, 3 February 1807, in *WrTJ*, 11:149–50; and William C. C. Claiborne, 3 February 1807, in ibid., 151.

129. "Communication," *American*, 27 February 1807.

130. [Ritchie], "General Wilkinson," *Enquirer*, 1 May 1807. See also [Pechin], *American*, 7 February 1807; "Communication," ibid., 13 February 1807; "The Conspiracy, [III and IV]," *National Intelligencer*, 18 and 20 March 1807; [Pleasants], *Virginia Argus*, 14 and 21 April 1807; and [John Dickson], *Petersburg Intelligencer* (Va.), 25 September 1807. Some western Republicans challenged the necessity of Wilkinson's measures. See, for example, Brown to Parke, 28 March 1808, InHi: Porter Papers.

131. [Brooks], *Impartial Observer*, 18 April 1807; "Agrestis," *Short Review of the Late Proceedings*, 30. See also Workman to William C. C. Claiborne, 25 January 1807, in [Workman], *Letter to the Respectable Citizens*, 18–19; and "Liberty. No Tyranny," *New-York Evening Post*, 27 March 1807, clipped from *Norfolk Gazette*.

132. Workman to William C. C. Claiborne, 11 February 1807, in [Workman], *Letter to the Respectable Citizens*, 27. See also William Plumer, diary entry, 26 January 1807, in *WPMP*, 592; and "Political Sketches, and Admonitions, Suitable to the Present Time," *Impartial Observer*, 12 June 1807.

133. Watkins, speech, 16 March 1807, in *Debate in the House of Representatives of the Territory of Orleans*, 26. See also James Elliot, speech, 18 February 1807, in *Annals*, 9th Cong., 2nd sess., 532–33; [Marchant and Willington], *Charleston Courier*, 17 April 1807; and "Agrestis," *Short Review of the Late Proceedings*, 6–8, 30–31, and 37–38. "Agrestis" seemed willing to accept the doctrine of necessity in other cases; see ibid., 11–12.

134. [Pleasants], *Virginia Argus*, 14 April 1807. See also "General Wilkinson," *Louisiana Gazette*, 15 May 1807, clipped from *Virginia Argus*.

135. Parke to Brown, 2 January 1808, InHi: Porter Papers. Parke had been in Washington during the Burr crisis and had backed Wilkinson, "probably to my shame," at that time.

136. "Communication," *American*, 27 February 1807.

137. [Pleasants], *Virginia Argus*, 21 April 1807.

138. "The Conspiracy, [III]," *National Intelligencer*, 18 March 1807.

139. John B. Colvin to Jefferson, 14 September 1810, in *PTJ: RS*, 3:78. Colvin asked Jefferson to address the question, "Are there not periods when, in free governments, it is necessary for officers in responsible stations to exercise an authority beyond the law—and, was not the time of Burr's treason such a period?" (ibid., 79).

140. Jefferson to Colvin, 20 September 1810, in ibid., 99–101. Colvin informed Jefferson that he had incorporated this letter into the manuscript with few changes; see Colvin to Jefferson, 4 February 1811, in ibid., 359–60. The editors of the retirement series of Jefferson's papers have helpfully identified all of

Colvin's and Wilkinson's alterations in the notes to Jefferson's letter. For the passage in Wilkinson's memoirs, see Wilkinson, *Burr's Conspiracy Exposed*, 49–57. Jefferson's letter has received the attention of political scientists. Two of the best recent discussions are by Jeremy D. Bailey; see his "Executive Prerogative and the 'Good Officer'" and *Thomas Jefferson and Executive Power*, 225–57.

141. Jefferson to William C. C. Claiborne, 3 February 1807, in *WrTJ*, 11:151; Jefferson, [draft message], [20 September (*sic*, early March) 1807], DLC: Jefferson Papers; Jefferson to Wilkinson, 3 February 1807, in *WrTJ*, 11:149.

142. Martha Jefferson Randolph to Elizabeth House Trist, [ca. September 1807], ViHi: Elizabeth (House) Trist Papers.

143. Magruder, *Letter from Allan B. Magruder*, 22; Brown to Parke, 28 March 1808, InHi: Porter Papers.

144. See, respectively, Thompson, *Compendious View*, 21–22; Danvers, *Picture of a Republican Magistrate*, 24–26; and [Brown], "Annals of Europe and America," 98–102.

145. Madison to Hinde, 17 August 1829, in *LOWJM*, 4:45.

146. For the role of conspiracy thinking in American political culture, see, in addition to previously cited works, Critchlow, Korasick, and Sherman, eds., *Political Conspiracies in America*. At least four encyclopedias of conspiracies have been published in recent years: Knight, *Conspiracy Theories in American History*; Jeffers, *History's Greatest Conspiracies*; Burnett, ed., *Conspiracy Encyclopedia*; and Newton, *Encyclopedia of Conspiracies and Conspiracy Theories*. Jeffers ranks the Burr Conspiracy fifty-ninth of his one hundred conspiracies, seven spots behind Benedict Arnold; Knight discusses Burr at some length. Neither Burnett nor Newton include the Burr Conspiracy.

147. John Campbell to David Campbell, 3 April 1807, NcD: Campbell Family Papers.

148. Anthony Butler to Jackson, 17 May 1827, in *PAJ*, 6:320–21.

149. James Buchanan, "Speech on the Question of Establishing a Board of Exchequer," 29 December 1841, in Moore, ed., *Works of James Buchanan*, 5:87. See also Rosalie Stier Calvert to H. J. Stier, June 1812, in Callcott, ed., *Mistress of Riversdale*, 252; and John Adams to Jefferson, 21 December 1819, in Cappon, ed., *Adams-Jefferson Letters*, 2:551.

150. Meriwether Lewis to William Eustis, 18 August 1809, in *TPUS*, 14:291.

151. Andrew Erwin to Patrick C. Darby, [ca. 20 November 1822], in McLean, ed., *Papers Concerning Robertson's Colony in Texas*, 1:516.

THIRD INTERLUDE. THE ARREST OF AARON BURR

1. Nicholas Perkins to Caesar A. Rodney, [ca. late March–early April 1807], in Stumpf, ed., "Arrest of Aaron Burr," 118. Stuart Stumpf dates this document "prior to the Burr trial which opened in August 1807" (ibid., 117). But Rodney

probably asked Perkins to prepare it when both were in Richmond for the first phase of Burr's trial.

2. Ibid., 119.

3. Perkins, testimony, 30 March 1807, in *ECAB*, 4.

4. Perkins to Rodney, [ca. late March–early April 1807], in Stumpf, ed., "Arrest of Aaron Burr," 119–21. For Gaines's role, see Silver, *Edmund Pendleton Gaines*, 14–18.

5. Perkins to Rodney, [ca. late March–early April 1807], in Stumpf, ed., "Arrest of Aaron Burr," 122.

6. Everything in this vignette, through the incident in South Carolina, comes from one of Perkins's three recorded accounts: the memorandum that he prepared for Attorney General Caesar A. Rodney, probably in late March or early April 1807; his 30 March 1807 testimony at Burr's initial examination; and an article in the Richmond *Enquirer* that seems to have been based upon an interview with him. The first two accounts are cited above, nn. 1 and 3; for the third, see [Thomas Ritchie], "Arrest of Aaron Burr," *Enquirer* (Richmond, Va.), 31 March 1807. Perkins appeared before the grand jury, but not in the public phases of Burr's trial. The unpublished notes on his grand jury testimony include just a few sentences, suggesting that what he said was very close to his comments during the examination; see Perkins, testimony, 16 June 1807, in "NECAB," 40–41. For the messenger from the administration and the arrival in Richmond, see James Madison to Lewis Ford, 23 March 1807, in "Capture of Aaron Burr"; Henry Dearborn to "Officer who has charge of Col. Burr," DNA: RG107, M6; [Thomas Jefferson], undated notes on verso of Egbert Benson to Jefferson, 25 March 1807, DLC: Burr Conspiracy Collection; "Col. Burr," *Virginia Herald* (Fredericksburg), 27 March 1807; and "Aaron Burr," *Virginia Gazette, and General Advertiser* (Richmond), 28 March 1807.

The date of Burr's departure from Fort Stoddert is not clear from Perkins's accounts. All of the historians who include a date, including the most recent, place it much too late. Following Albert James Pickett's *History of Alabama* (1851), they have Burr and his escort leaving either Fort Stoddert or a smaller fort fifteen miles away at Tensaw on 5 March. Contemporary sources suggest that Gaines, Burr, and a group of soldiers left Fort Stoddert on 23 February (four days after the arrest) for Tensaw; there, they met Perkins and the other civilians, who took charge of Burr and began the trip east the next day. By 5 March, the party was roughly three hundred miles from Fort Stoddert near present-day Macon, Georgia. See Aaron Burr to Robert Ashley, 23 February [1807], in *PAB*; "Extract of a letter from E. P. Gaines, post master at Fort Stoddert, to the post master at this place," *Louisiana Gazette* (New Orleans), 3 March 1807; "Aaron Burr," *Farmer's Gazette* (Sparta, Ga.), 7 March 1807 (from AHN); Benjamin Hawkins to William R. Boote, 7 March 1807, in Grant, ed., *Letters, Journals, and Writings of Benjamin Hawkins*, 2:515; "Extract of a letter from a gentleman of respectability in Cowetah (Creek Nation)," *National Intelligencer*, *and Washington Advertiser* (D.C.), 23 March 1807; and Perkins, "acct. with Edmund P. Gaines," 24 January 1810, T: Tennessee Historical Society, Miscellaneous Files, Nicholas Perkins Papers. The escort seems to have used a new federal mail route to reach Georgia; see Southerland and Brown, *Federal Road*.

7. [Ritchie], *Enquirer*, 27 March 1807. Ritchie's source was probably Lewis Ford, the messenger whom the administration had sent to redirect Burr's escort.

8. Here, I paraphrase an assertion that influences this whole book: "The ways in which what happened and that which is said to have happened are and are not the same may itself be historical" (Trouillot, *Silencing the Past*, 4).

9. Few people would have heard Perkins's testimony on 30 March, but it was published within two weeks in the *Examination of Col. Aaron Burr* and republished in 1808 in David Robertson's *Report of the Trials of Col. Aaron Burr*. The *Enquirer* piece that was almost certainly based upon an interview with Perkins would have been widely read in that newspaper and others. But the most thorough of Perkins's accounts—the memorandum that he prepared for Rodney—did not become widely available until 1896; see "Capture of Aaron Burr." A more accurate transcription appears in Stumpf, ed., "Arrest of Aaron Burr," 117–23. Both published versions rely upon a draft or copy in T: Perkins Papers; Rodney's copy has been lost.

10. For Burr, see Burr, comments, 31 March 1807, in *ECAB*, 23–24. For Gaines's reports, see Edmund P. Gaines to James Wilkinson, 19 February 1807, in "Capture of Aaron Burr," 146–47 (the same letter was sent to Robert Williams); Gaines to Dearborn, 22 February 1807, DNA: RG107, M221, G-107 (3); and Gaines to Wilkinson, 4 March 1807, enclosed in Wilkinson to Dearborn, 12 March 1807, ibid., W-262 (3). For published versions of the latter two letters, see *National Intelligencer*, 8 April 1807; and "Extract of a letter from Fort Stoddert," *Louisiana Gazette*, 13 March 1807. For Ashley's comments, see Ashley, "To the Printers of the Georgetown S.C. Gazette," *National Intelligencer*, 20 April 1807. Pickett interviewed Malone and Mrs. Hinson (by then Mrs. Sturdevant) in the late 1840s. For the Malone interview, see Albert James Pickett, "Notes taken from the lips of Mr Thos Malone of Washington County Ala in relation to the arrest of Aaron Burr in 1807," A-Ar: Albert J. Pickett Papers. The notes from Pickett's interview with Mrs. Sturdevant have disappeared. I discuss most of these accounts below.

11. Burr's destination after leaving Natchez, for example, was a point of contention in both the court and the press. See, for example, John Wickham, argument, 31 March 1807, in *ECAB*, 16; [Ritchie], "Arrest of Aaron Burr," *Enquirer*, 31 March 1807; *Virginia Gazette*, 18 April 1807, clipped from *Augusta Herald* (Ga.); Ashley, "To the Printers of the Georgetown S.C. Gazette," *National Intelligencer*, 20 April 1807; and Thompson, *Compendious View*, 46–47.

12. Rodney to Jefferson, 27 March 1807, DLC: Thomas Jefferson Papers; "Extract of a letter from George Kennedy, esq., post-master at Chester Court-House, in

this state, to the Editors of this paper," *City Gazette and Daily Advertiser* (Charleston, S.C.), 23 March 1807.

13. The most recent work on the Burr Conspiracy dismisses, in an endnote, the whole issue of Burr's disguise as "not material" (Stewart, *American Emperor*, 371n24).

14. Rodney to Jefferson, 26 March 1807, DLC: Jefferson Papers. Thomas Spotswood Hinde explicitly compared himself and his young associates to André's captors in some of his accounts; see, for example, Hinde, "To the Editors," *Daily National Intelligencer* (Washington, D.C.), 12 October 1838. The public memory of André and his captors in the early republic is brilliantly examined in Cray, "Major John André and the Three Captors." See also Reynolds, "Patriots and Criminals"; and Trees, "Benedict Arnold."

15. Jefferson to James Bowdoin, 2 April 1807, in *WrTJ*, 11:186.

16. [Samuel H. Smith], *National Intelligencer*, 30 March 1807. Perkins did not mention the reward in any of his three recorded accounts of the arrest. But he knew of it before Burr's arrival in Wakefield from the letter, which he did mention, that had informed him of Burr's flight; see Lemuel Henry to Perkins, 9 February 1807, in "Capture of Aaron Burr," 141. Some authors have suggested, or more, that Perkins was motivated by what one called "the possibility of profitable patriotism" (Kennedy, *Burr, Hamilton, and Jefferson*, 335). If so, his expectations were long delayed, if not entirely disappointed. Sometime on the day of Burr's arrest, Perkins and Gaines agreed to split the reward, but they still had not received it nearly three years later; see Gaines to Perkins, 9 [*sic*, 19] February 1807, in "Capture of Aaron Burr," 149; and Perkins, "acct. with Edmund P. Gaines," 24 January 1810, T: Perkins Papers.

17. Gaines to Dearborn, 22 February 1807, RG107: M221, G-107 (3). See also Gaines to Perkins, 9 [*sic*, 19] February 1807, in "Capture of Aaron Burr," 148.

18. Perkins, T[homas] Malone, John Mills, Samuel McCormack, John Jay Henry, and H. B. Slade, pledge, 23 February 1807, T: Perkins Papers. The published version of this document omits Malone; see "Capture of Aaron Burr," 149.

19. Perkins to unknown correspondent, 29 March 1807, in "Capture of Aaron Burr," 153. At the time, there was considerable confusion about the size of Burr's escort, with numbers ranging from seven to ten. See, for example, "To the Editor of the Aurora," *Sun* (Pittsfield, Mass.), 2 May 1807 (from AHN) (seven); [Ritchie], *Enquirer*, 27 March 1807 (seven and eight); and "Extract of a letter from a gentleman of respectability in Cowetah (Creek Nation)," *National Intelligencer*, 23 March 1807 (ten). This confusion has carried over into historical works. It may have arisen, in part, because the original escort—Perkins, five civilians, and two soldiers—was joined by others for the final leg of the trip; see Boote to Dearborn, 20 March 1807, DNA: RG107, M221, B-206 (3).

20. [Ritchie], *Enquirer*, 27 March 1807; [Ritchie], "Arrest of Aaron Burr," ibid., 31 March 1807.

21. [Ritchie], ibid., 17 April 1807.

22. [Samuel Pleasants Jr.], *Virginia Argus* (Richmond), 31 March 1807.
23. George Hay, argument, 31 March 1807, in *ECAB*, 10; Wickham, argument, 31 March 1807, in ibid., 16. The record of Perkins's testimony does not include a description of Burr's appearance or even an assertion that he was in disguise, but Hay referred "to Perkins's evidence" for that claim. See also Rodney to Jefferson, 30 March 1807, DLC: Jefferson Papers.
24. Tucker, *Blackstone's Commentaries*, book IV, sec. 387.
25. Hay, argument, 31 March 1807, in *ECAB*, 10.
26. Burr, comments, 31 March 1807, in ibid., 24. For Burr's trial in the Mississippi Territory and its aftermath, see Abernethy, *Burr Conspiracy*, 215–21.
27. Thompson, *Compendious View*, 47. Burr's attempts "to escape," according to Thompson, "were evidences of a disregard to his own reputation" (49n). Burr had fled prosecution for dueling or murder after killing Alexander Hamilton in July 1804. Within a week, he had placed himself beyond legal peril by going to Philadelphia. He had then travelled to coastal Georgia. In both places, and on the road between them, he had been discreet. But, while returning to Washington beginning in October, he had made numerous public appearances in Republican cities and towns. In the capital, he had resumed his duties as vice president. During these months, divisions over whether Burr could be treated as a gentleman generally followed party lines. For Burr's actions in the aftermath of the duel, see Lomask, *Aaron Burr*, 1:357–62; Fleming, *Duel*, 347–60; Isenberg, *Fallen Founder*, 268–69; and Stewart, *American Emperor*, 39–51.
28. Harman Blennerhassett, diary entry, 8 August 1807, in *BwB*, 12. Blennerhassett was referring to how the Republican press in Richmond treated him following his own journey under guard from Lexington, Kentucky. But there is considerable evidence that gentlemen viewed such treatment as inherently damaging to their own or each other's status. See, for example, G[eorge] P[oindexter], opinion, 21 January 1807, Ms-Ar: J.F.H. Claiborne Collection; [Ritchie], *Enquirer*, 7 April 1807; Nathaniel Beverley Tucker to [St. George Tucker], 12 April 1807, ViW: Tucker-Coleman Papers; and James Morrison to Wilkinson, 9 September 1807, ICU: Reuben T. Durrett Collection, Miscellaneous Manuscripts.
29. "Aaron Burr," *Democrat* (Boston), 8 April 1807. For the wearing of costumes, masks, and disguises by gentlemen, see especially Greenberg, *Honor and Slavery*, 25–31. Greenberg focuses upon one of the most famous cases of a gentleman allegedly discovered in disguise in American history—that of the former president of the Confederacy, Jefferson Davis. Perhaps the most famous case of discovery in disguise prior to Burr's arrest concerned the failed attempt of King Louis XVI to escape revolutionary France; see Tackett, *When the King Took Flight*.
30. "Extract of a letter from a correspondent, dated Fredericksburgh," *New-York Evening Post*, 30 March 1807; [William Coleman], comments on ibid.
31. "Extract of a letter from a gentleman of respectability to his friend in this city," *Charleston Courier* (S.C.), 23 March 1807.

32. William Tatham to Jefferson, 27 March 1807, in McPherson, ed., "Letters of William Tatham," 191 [corrected against original in DLC: Jefferson Papers].
33. Pickett, "Notes taken from the lips of Mr Thos Malone," A-Ar: Pickett Papers. George Strother Gaines, who was staying with his brother at Fort Stoddert, also remembered Burr's overcoat, hat, pants, and boots, though in less detail; see Pickett, "Conversation with George S. Gaines," 1847, in Pate, ed., *Reminiscences of George Strother Gaines*, 143.
34. John Randolph to Joseph H. Nicholson, 25 March 1807, DLC: Joseph H. Nicholson Papers.
35. Wilkinson to Jefferson, 20 March 1807, DLC: Burr Conspiracy Collection.
36. Rodney to Jefferson, 27 March 1807, DLC: Jefferson Papers.
37. Unidentified letter from Fort Stoddert, ca. mid- to late March 1807, quoted in Claiborne, *Mississippi, as a Province, Territory and State*, 1:289.
38. "Burr Taken," *Newburyport Herald* (Mass.), 10 April 1807 (from AHN).
39. John McDonogh [Sr.] to John McDonogh [Jr.], 30 March 1807, LNT-H: John McDonogh Papers.
40. [George Adams], "Portrait of Burr," *Kentucky Gazette and General Advertiser* (Lexington), 17 September 1805, clipped from *Palladium* (Frankfort, Ky.). A Philadelphia magazine reprinted this description in May 1807; see "Miscellany." The key work on gentility and respectability in the late eighteenth and early nineteenth centuries is Bushman, *Refinement of America*. For the clothing appropriate to various occupations and classes, see Copeland, *Working Dress*; Warwick, Pitz, and Wyckoff, *Early American Dress*; and Wass and Fandrich, *Clothing through American History*. For the meaning of dress, see also Calvert, "Function of Fashion in Eighteenth-Century America"; and Baumgarten, *What Clothes Reveal*.
41. Wilkinson to Dearborn, 12 March 1807, DNA: RG107, M221, W-262 (3). That Ashley had been with Burr since Natchez is clear; see Harry Toulmin to Gaines, undated, enclosed in Gaines to Dearborn, 17 February 1807, ibid., G-103 (3); and "Extract of a letter dated town of Washington, near Natchez," *National Intelligencer*, 20 March 1807.
42. Toulmin to [Gaines], 18 May 1807, enclosed in Gaines to unknown correspondent, 22 June 1807, PPiU-D: Darlington Autograph Collection.
43. Gaines to Wilkinson, 4 March 1807, enclosed in Wilkinson to Dearborn, 13 March 1807, DNA: RG107, M221, W-262 (3). How and when Ashley escaped is unclear. In a May 1807 deposition, Callier (often rendered as "Caller" by modern historians) stated that Ashley had "continued in custody three or four days, and then escaped" (John Callier, deposition, 9 May 1807, *National Intelligencer*, 10 August 1807). Four decades later, Malone recalled that Ashley had escaped the night of his arrest. A letter from Ashley to Burr indicates that he was still in custody in Wakefield on 22 February, two days after his arrest. In it, Ashley stated that he had been given "the liberty of riding to fort Stoddert tomorrow by giving Security for my return the next day" (Ashley to Burr, [22

February 1807], enclosed in Boote to Dearborn, 20 March 1807, DNA: RG107, M221, B-206 [3]). If Ashley rode to Fort Stoddert on 23 February, he did not find Burr there. That day, Burr wrote Ashley a brief note from Tensaw, about fifteen miles away, urging him to "follow and join me as soon as possible" if he was "under no legal restraints" (Burr to Ashley, 23 February [1807], in *PAB*). Ashley may never have received this note. It is possible that Ashley surrendered his security in order to follow Burr and that no one who had given him "the liberty" of leaving Wakefield wanted to admit their part in his escape.

44. Ashley, "To the Printers of the Georgetown S.C. Gazette," *National Intelligencer*, 20 April 1807. Ashley seems to have begun working to correct misperceptions about Burr's actions, though not appearance, even earlier, having spoken to an editor in Georgia before crossing into South Carolina; see *Virginia Gazette*, 18 April 1807, clipped from *Augusta Herald*. I have not found the piece that prompted Ashley's letter. But, if his letter originally appeared in the 4 April issue of the *Georgetown Gazette*, as seems likely, it could not have been an answer to even the earliest account from Richmond.

45. Rodney to Jefferson, 27 March 1807, DLC: Jefferson Papers. Charles Willie and Harry, Burr's slave, became lost crossing the Mississippi Territory, striking the Tombigbee more than one hundred miles north of their destination. On arriving at Fort St. Stephens, Willie was arrested by John Callier. After being freed, he was arrested a second time, taken to Fort Stoddert, and examined by Judge Harry Toulmin. See Thomas Maury to Wilkinson, 29 March 1807, DLC: Burr Conspiracy Collection; examination of Charles Willie, 9 April 1807, enclosed in Toulmin to Jefferson, 5/13 April 1807, DLC: Edmond Charles Genet Papers; and Blennerhassett, diary entry, 21 August 1807, in *BwB*, 44.

46. Gaines to Dearborn, 22 February 1807, DNA: RG107, M221, G-107 (3).

47. Robert Gamble to Thomas Massie, 30 March 1807, ViHi: Massie Family Papers.

48. William H. Cabell to Joseph C. Cabell, 2 April 1807, ViU: Cabell Family Papers.

49. Randolph to Joseph Scott, 23 August 1807, ViU: John Randolph Papers Microfilm.

50. [Ritchie], "Arrest of Aaron Burr," *Enquirer*, 31 March 1807. "If he is not a gentleman," Perkins recalled telling Gaines, "we will not regard his displeasure."

51. [Smith], *National Intelligencer*, 1 April 1807.

52. "To the Editor of the Aurora," *Sun*, 2 May 1807 (from AHN). See also the unidentified letter from Fort Stoddert, ca. mid- to late March 1807, quoted in Claiborne, *Mississippi, as a Province, Territory and State*, 1:289. The author of this letter had arrived at Fort Stoddert weeks after Burr and Perkins had left and had based his account on others' reports.

53. Thompson, *Compendious View*, 47–48. A decade before the flood of new accounts that began in the late 1840s, the Ohio historian Caleb Atwater had Perkins recognize the disguised Burr from "his brilliant eye, which shone like a diamond,

beneath an old, broad-brimmed, flapped hat" (Atwater, *History of the State of Ohio*, 181).

54. Pickett, *History of Alabama*, 2:223.

55. Victor, *History of American Conspiracies*, 309.

56. Pickett, *History of Alabama*, 2:216.

57. Clark, "Blennerhassett and Aaron Burr," 107.

58. Parton, *Life and Times of Aaron Burr*, 444–45.

59. Review of *The Life of Harman Blennerhassett*, 317. For an interesting discussion of changing ideas about physical appearance and character in the late eighteenth and early nineteenth century, see Lukasik, *Discerning Characters*.

60. Pickett, *History of Alabama*, 2:218, 220n. Pickett, Safford, Clark, Parton, and Victor each used the verb "to fascinate" in describing Burr's relations with his captors; I discuss fascination at length in Chapter 10.

61. Parton, *Life and Times of Aaron Burr*, 445.

62. Gaines to Dearborn, 22 February 1807, DNA: RG107, M221, G-107 (3).

63. Gaines to Perkins, 9 [*sic*, 19] February 1807, in "Capture of Aaron Burr," 148.

64. Clark, "Blennerhassett and Aaron Burr," 108.

65. Pickett, *History of Alabama*, 2:222–23.

66. Parton, *Life and Times of Aaron Burr*, 449.

67. "Aaron Burr," *Farmer's Gazette*, 7 March 1807 (from AHN). This piece also described a similar incident on the same day, involving "an honest old farmer." In this second encounter, according to the author, "Burr made no reply— remembering, no doubt, the repartee he had received" from the innkeeper. Perkins did not mention these possibly apocryphal incidents.

68. Pickett, *History of Alabama*, 2:226. See also Safford, *Life of Harman Blennerhassett*, 148–49; and Parton, *Life and Times of Aaron Burr*, 451.

69. See Safford's *Life of Harman Blennerhassett*, 152, and *Blennerhassett Papers*, 226n. A bibliographic record in A-Ar: Pickett Papers states that Pickett's material appeared first as an undated pamphlet, *Arrest of Aaron Burr in Alabama in 1807*, and then as an extra edition of the *Weekly Flag & Advertiser* (Montgomery, Ala.). For other early newspaper versions, see *Alabama Journal* (Montgomery), 18 January 1849; and *Alabama Beacon* (Greensboro), 3 February 1849.

70. Parton, *Life and Times of Aaron Burr*, 449n.

71. Victor, *History of American Conspiracies*, 309.

72. Gaines to Pickett, 17 August 1847, A-Ar: Pickett Papers. While he insisted that he was "blessed with a good memory," Gaines would not answer Pickett's questions about past events for publication without checking his recollections against the "public documents" (Gaines to Pickett, 21 September 1847, ibid.). The Pickett Papers include no evidence that Gaines ever provided information about Burr's arrest. For Pickett's written and oral sources, see Pickett, *History of Alabama*, 2:229–30n. For his effort to contact Perkins, see F. Stith to Pickett, 16 February 1848, A-Ar: Pickett Papers. For Pickett as a historian, see Owsley, "Albert J. Pickett"; and O'Brien, *Conjectures of Order*, 2:631–36.

73. Pickett, "Conversation with George S. Gaines," 1847, in Pate, ed., *Reminiscences of George Strother Gaines*, 143.

74. Ibid., 143–45. For Malone's errors, see Pickett, "Notes taken from the lips of Mr Thos Malone," A-Ar: Pickett Papers. For my dating of Burr's departure from Fort Stoddert, see above n. 6.

75. Pickett, "Notes taken from the lips of Mr Thos Malone," A-Ar: Pickett Papers.

76. Pickett, "Conversation with George S. Gaines," 1847, in Pate, ed., *Reminiscences of George Strother Gaines*, 143. That Gaines and Pickett emphasized the incongruity of Burr's boots is striking—that was what had famously undone Major John André's disguise.

77. "Pickett's History of Alabama," 193. It made even less sense for Safford to include long chapters on Burr's arrest in *The Life of Harman Blennerhassett* and *The Blennerhassett Papers* since his subject was far from the scene.

78. [Pickett], *Arrest of Aaron Burr in Alabama*, 5, 6. Pickett did acknowledge that Burr's faults "in regard to females [were] despicable and highly to be condemned" (ibid., 6). Pickett was an Alabama planter, a Jacksonian Democrat, an advocate of (and participant in) Indian removal, and an opponent of abolition; see Owsley, "Albert J. Pickett."

79. For the backward-looking dimension of Romanticism, see Kenney and Workman, "Ruins, Romance, and Reality"; Girouard, *Return to Camelot*; and Blanning, *Romantic Revolution*, 121–34. For elite Southerners' identification with medieval Europe in this period, see Taylor, *Cavalier and Yankee*; Wyatt-Brown, *Southern Honor*; and Boyer Lewis, *Ladies and Gentlemen on Display*, 201–6.

80. [Pickett], *Arrest of Aaron Burr in Alabama*, 6. The literature on nineteenth-century culture and cultural change is extensive. See, in particular, Halttunen, *Confidence Men and Painted Women*; Blumin, *Emergence of the Middle Class*; and Bushman, *Refinement of America*.

81. [Smith], *National Intelligencer*, 1 April 1807.

CHAPTER 8. RICHMOND, VIRGINIA:
MARCH THROUGH OCTOBER 1807

1. Jonathan Mason, diary entry, 13 January 1805, in Ellis, ed., "Diary of the Hon. Jonathan Mason," 19; Alexander Dick, diary entry, 29 April 1808, ViU: Alexander Dick Journal.

2. John Tyler, "Richmond and Its Memories," November 1858, in Tyler, *Letters and Times of the Tylers*, 1:219. Tyler had moved to Richmond in 1808 when his father became governor. The material on eighteenth- and early nineteenth-century Richmond in this section comes from Christian, *Richmond*; Stanard, *Richmond*; Scott, *Old Richmond Neighborhoods*; Reps, *Tidewater Towns*, 267–81; Click, *Spirit of the Times*, 9–20; and Sidbury, *Ploughshares into Swords*, 151–83.

3. "Memoranda Made by Thomas R. Joynes," 147.

4. William Martin, diary entry, 14 May 1809, in Elmore, ed., *Journal of William D. Martin*, 17.

5. Tyler, "Richmond and Its Memories," November 1858, in Tyler, *Letters and Times of the Tylers*, 1:219. Tyler quoted, incorrectly, Ovid's description in *Metamorphoses* (1.7) of the matter from which the Earth was created.

6. Mason, diary entry, 17 January 1805, in Ellis, ed., "Diary of the Hon. Jonathan Mason," 20; Merritt M. Robinson to William Short, 5 June 1805, DLC: William Short Papers.

7. [Thomas Manson], comments on "From the Farmer's Cabinet," *Impartial Observer* (Richmond, Va.), 2 December 1806. For the prospectus, see Samuel Brooks, "To the Public," ibid., 10 May 1806.

8. John Page, testimonial, 16 January 1807, ibid., 19 January 1807.

9. [Manson], comments on "From the Farmer's Cabinet," ibid., 2 December 1806. I discuss the history of the *Observer* after it resumed publication in mid-April 1807 below.

10. Mason, diary entry, 13 January 1805, in Ellis, ed., "Diary of the Hon. Jonathan Mason," 19. For Richmond's Federalists, see Risjord, "Virginia Federalists," 507.

11. John Randolph to James Monroe, 30 May 1807, DLC: James Monroe Papers. See also Horatio Turpin to Thomas Jefferson, 1 June 1807, in *TJC*, 145; and David Watson to George Watson, 19 June 1807, ViHi: Watson Family Papers.

12. [Thomas Ritchie], *Enquirer* (Richmond, Va.), 27 March 1807.

13. George Read to Caesar A. Rodney, 24 June 1807, DeHi: Rodney Collection; Luther Martin to unknown correspondent, 13 July 1807, PPiU-D: Darlington Autograph Collection.

14. Caesar A. Rodney to Jefferson, 10 May 1807, DNA: RG21, T265.

15. Martin to unknown correspondent, 13 July 1807, PPiU-D: Darlington Autograph Collection.

16. This approach is common in works that focus on Burr's trial, such as Beirne, *Shout Treason*; Faulkner, "John Marshall and the Burr Trial"; Hoffer, *Treason Trials of Aaron Burr*; and Newmyer, *Treason Trial of Aaron Burr*. It is not surprising in such histories of the judicial system, biographies of the chief justice, and discussions of treason law as Beveridge, *Life of John Marshall*, 3:343–545; Chapin, *American Law of Treason*, 98–113; Haskins and Johnson, *Foundations of Power*, 246–91; Smith, *John Marshall*, 348–74; Newmyer, *John Marshall and the Heroic Age*, 179–202; and Carso, *"Whom Can We Trust Now?,"* 96–128. But it also informs many biographies of Burr and general accounts of the conspiracy; see, for example, Wandell and Minnigerode, *Aaron Burr*, 2:175–221; Abernethy, *Burr Conspiracy*, 227–49; McCaleb, *Aaron Burr Conspiracy*, 258–300; Lomask, *Aaron Burr*, 2:222–98; Melton, *Aaron Burr*, 101–219; and Stewart, *American Emperor*, 226–70.

17. *Virginia Argus* (Richmond), 31 March 1807; Caesar A. Rodney to Jefferson, 21 [*sic*, 31] March 1807, DLC: James Madison Papers.

18. For the arguments, testimony, and opinion in this stage, see *ECAB*; and *RTCAB*, 1:1–20.

19. James Innes to Francis Jerdone, 22 May 1807, ViW: Jerdone Family Papers.

20. Andrew Jackson to [William Preston Anderson], 16 June 1807, in *PAJ*, 2:168; John Tompkins to Duncan Cameron, 23 May 1807, NcU: Cameron Family Papers. For other predictions, see Philip Slaughter to Thomas Towles, 16 May 1807, KyLoF: Thomas Towles Papers; Earl Sproat to Soloman Sibley, 18 May 1807, MiD-B: Soloman Sibley Papers; Abner S. Barton to Lewis Sanders, 27 May 1807, KyLoF: Sanders Family Papers; Christopher Anthony to Frederick Bates, 28 May 1807, in Marshall, ed., *Life and Papers of Frederick Bates*, 130; Randolph to Monroe, 30 May 1807, DLC: Monroe Papers; and *People's Friend & Daily Advertiser* (New York), 9 June 1807.

21. The district court judge Cyrus Griffin sat with Marshall on the Burr trial but seems to have had very little impact. Early on, district attorney Hay referred to a "decision of the Judges" in a letter but immediately corrected himself by adding, parenthetically, "or rather of *the Judge*" (George Hay to Jefferson, 31 May 1807, DLC: Thomas Jefferson Papers). For the proceedings in open court during this phase, see *RTCAB*; and *TCAB*. The best source for the grand jury hearings is "NECAB." For other, incomplete, versions, see Chapter 5, n. 94.

22. Joseph Scott to Joseph C. Cabell, 2 April 1807, ViU: Cabell Family Papers. The Republican William Thompson later described the grand jury as "composed of men whose talents elevate their judgment above suspicion" (Thompson, *Compendious View*, 69n). For a similar assessment from a Federalist newspaper, see [William Davis], *Norfolk Gazette and Public Ledger* (Va.), 12 June 1807.

23. Benjamin Stoddert to John Rutledge, 4 June 1807, NcU: John Rutledge Papers.

24. Jefferson to John W. Eppes, 28 May 1807, in *WoTJ*, 10:412.

25. Tompkins to Duncan Cameron, 23 May 1807, NcU: Cameron Family Papers. For a similar analysis by a prosecuting attorney, see William Wirt to Ninian Edwards, 2 August 1807, ICHi: Ninian Edwards Papers. Jefferson, Rodney, and Wirt initially questioned Marshall's decision to allow Burr to challenge jurors, though Rodney eventually admitted that, by "exploring the recesses of a bottomless pit, the common law," he had found justification (Caesar A. Rodney to Madison, 31 May 1807, DLC: Madison Papers). See also Jefferson to Hay, 16 May 1807, in *WrTJ*, 11:209. For a scholarly discussion of this issue, see Tartar and Holt, "Apparent Political Selection."

26. Samuel Irvine to Samuel Rose, 21 June 1807, KyLoF: Samuel Rose Papers.

27. Dudley Woodbridge Jr. to William Woodbridge, 21 June 1807, MiD-B: William Woodbridge Papers.

28. Marshall, comments, 10 June 1807, in *RTCAB*, 1:148.

29. Jefferson to Hay, 12 June 1807, in *WrTJ*, 11:229.

30. Jefferson to Hay, 17 June 1807, in ibid., 232. For Jefferson's response to the subpoena, see, in addition to the works cited in n. 16 above, Malone, *Jefferson and His Time*, 5:320–28; and Yoo, "First Claim."

31. Washington Irving to James Kirke Paulding, 22 June 1807, in Aderman, Klein-field, and Banks, eds., *Washington Irving*, 1:239. Irving did not hear Wilkinson testify before the grand jury but was in the courtroom. For his interest in the Burr trial, see Williams, *Life of Washington Irving*, 1:96–99; and Burstein, *Original Knickerbocker*, 56–61.

32. Tompkins to Duncan Cameron, 25 June 1807, NcU: Cameron Family Papers. See also Hay to Jefferson, 17 June 1807, DLC: Jefferson Papers.

33. Joseph Bryan to Randolph, 20 July 1807, Vi: Bryan Family Papers. Predictions from the final week before the grand jury handed down indictments include David Watson to George Watson, 19 June 1807, ViHi: Watson Family Papers; John D. Blair to Patrick Gibson, 23 June 1807, Vi: Gibson Family Papers; and Robert Gamble to Thomas Massie, 23 June 1807, ViHi: Massie Family Papers.

34. Hay to Jefferson, 14 June 1807, DLC: Jefferson Papers. These comments were made shortly after the grand jury hearings began in earnest following Wilkinson's arrival. Ten days later, Hay confessed to Jefferson that he did not have the "patience" to "[wade] thro' this abyss of human depravity" (Hay to Jefferson, 25 June 1807, ibid.).

35. Marshall to William Cushing, 29 June 1807, in *PJMar*, 7:60. In this letter, Marshall mentioned a letter to Justice Bushrod Washington that probably raised the same questions. Many of Marshall's personal papers were destroyed or lost; see Charles F. Hobson et al., "The Plan of the Volume and Editorial Policy," in ibid., xxi.

36. Wirt to Peachy R. Gilmer, 18 July 1807, DLC: William Wirt Papers. See also Hay to Jefferson, 24 June 1807, DLC: Jefferson Papers.

37. John Wickham to Jonathan Dayton, 24 July 1807, MiU-C: Jonathan Dayton Papers.

38. William Eaton to Stephen Pynchon, 3 August 1807, Ms-Ar: Ventress (James Alexander) and Family Papers. The treason trial is fully documented in *TCAB*; and *RTCAB*.

39. Elias Glover to Ethan A. Brown, 17 August 1807, OHi: Ethan Allen Brown Papers.

40. Tompkins to Duncan Cameron, 25 August 1807, NcU: Cameron Family Papers.

41. Marshall, opinion, 31 August 1807, in *PJMar*, 7:74. For other appraisals of these arguments, see Dudley Woodbridge Jr. to William Woodbridge, 23 August 1807, MiD-B: Woodbridge Papers; Harman Blennerhassett, diary entries, 25 and 30 August 1807, in *BwB*, 53, 66; and Hay to Jefferson, 1 September 1807, DLC: Jefferson Papers. Wirt's 25 August speech is discussed at length in Chapter 9.

42. Marshall, opinion, 31 August 1807, in *PJMar*, 7:74, 114. Marshall insisted that he had not overturned the earlier Supreme Court ruling but merely stated its "sound and true legal construction" (Marshall, opinion, 18 September 1807, in

ibid., 146). This ruling is discussed at length in legal histories of the trial; see the works cited above, n. 16.

43. John Graham to Nathaniel Massie, 30 August 1807, in Massie, *Nathaniel Massie*, 247.

44. Wirt to Dabney Carr, 1 September 1807, in Kennedy, *Memoirs of the Life of William Wirt*, 1:203. Even among those who knew of the defense motion, there was still an expectation that Burr would hang or, as one observer put it, be made to "dance upon nothing" (William Cameron to Duncan Cameron, 27 August 1807, NcU: Cameron Family Papers). Another of Duncan Cameron's Virginia correspondents similarly believed that the trial would "end with an exibition on the tight rope" (Tompkins to Duncan Cameron, 25 August 1807, ibid.).

45. Hay to Jefferson, 11 August 1807, DLC: Jefferson Papers. The attorney general insisted to the end that it was "impossible" that the defense would "overturn" the Bollman and Swartwout ruling (Caesar A. Rodney to Jefferson, 31 August 1807, ibid.).

46. Hay to Jefferson, 5 September 1807, ibid. No one seems to have discussed the other option: pursuing the other six treason indictments.

47. Edward Bates to Richard Bates, 18 September 1807, ViHi: Edward Bates Papers. I discuss Jefferson's use of the later stages of the trial to elicit testimony in Chapter 11.

48. Wirt to Carr, 14 September 1807, in Kennedy, *Memoirs of the Life of William Wirt*, 1:205. For the full proceedings of this stage, see *TCAB*.

49. Thomas Todd to Harry Innes, 23 September 1807, DLC: Harry Innes Papers.

50. Though David Robertson apparently attended and took notes on the committal hearing, he did not include it in *RTCAB*; the only full source for this stage is *TCAB*. For Marshall's early uncertainty, see Marshall to Cushing, 29 June 1807, in *PJMar*, 7:61.

51. Marshall, opinion, 18 September 1807, in *PJMar*, 7:145. The Fifth Amendment protection against double jeopardy applies only to capital offenses, not to misdemeanors.

52. Aaron Burr to Theodosia Burr Alston, 28 September 1807, in *MAB*, 2:411. See also Harman Blennerhassett, diary entry, 21 September 1807, in *BwB*, 99.

53. Edward Bates to Richard Bates, 18 September 1807, ViHi: Bates Papers.

54. Nicholas Biddle to Monroe, 31 October 1807, DLC: Monroe Papers.

55. "Price Current—Richmond Market," *Virginia Argus*, 24 June 1807. "Accounts of particular trials commonly derive their interest," a reviewer in a Philadelphia periodical wrote, "not so much from the points of law which are involved in them, as from the notoriety of the persons or the singularity of the events which give rise to them" ([Brown], "Sketch of American Literature," 177).

56. Edward Bates to Richard Bates, 18 September 1807, ViHi: Bates Papers; Tompkins to Duncan Cameron, 25 August 1807, NcU: Cameron Family Papers.

57. Graham to Madison, 30 August 1807, DLC: Madison Papers.

58. Thomas Truxton to Thomas Tingey, 20 June 1807, DLC: Thomas Truxton Papers.

59. "James Wilkinson and Suite," *Enquirer*, 13 June 1807. For similar views, see Jesse Higgins to Jonathan and Matthew Roberts, 8 May 1807, PHi: Jonathan Roberts Papers; [Samuel Pleasants Jr.], *Virginia Argus*, 16 May 1807; Return J. Meigs Jr. to Sophia Meigs, 11 August 1807, InU: Meigs Manuscripts; and Tompkins to Duncan Cameron, 25 August 1807, NcU: Cameron Family Papers.

60. Irving to Mary Fairlie, 13 May 1807, in Aderman, Kleinfield, and Banks, eds., *Washington Irving*, 1:236. See also Higgins to Jonathan and Matthew Roberts, 8 May 1807, PHi: Roberts Papers; Stoddert to Rutledge, 4 June 1807, NcU: Rutledge Papers; and Charles Williamson to Lord Melville, 9 February 1808, ICN: Edward A. Ayer Manuscript Collection, Charles Williamson Papers. "Character" meant not a unique, and perhaps bizarre, personality, but the estimation of a person's qualities; see *OED Online*, December 2016 ed., s.v. "character," n. 13. In other words, a "character" was something you *had*—something that was assigned to you by those who knew, and knew of, you—rather than something you *were*. For recent discussions of the trial that pay more attention to collisions of character than to technicalities of law, see Ferguson, *Trial in American Life*, 79–116; and Isenberg, *Fallen Founder*, 323–65.

61. Jackson to Thomas Monteagle Bayly, 27 June 1807, in *PAJ*, 2:169; Burr to Alston, 22 June 1807, in *MAB*, 2:408. See also Truxton to Charles Biddle, 30 May 1807, in Biddle, *Autobiography of Charles Biddle*, 410; and "Candor," "Richmond," *Virginia Gazette, and General Advertiser* (Richmond), 24 October 1807. The elite regularly appeared in court in civil cases. There had been two celebrated criminal trials of gentlemen in Virginia in the previous fifteen years. In 1793, Richard Randolph had been tried in Cumberland County for the murder of his sister-in-law's infant child; see Doyle, "Randolph Scandal"; and Kierner, *Scandal at Bizarre*. And, in 1806, George Swinney had been tried in Richmond for the murder of his granduncle (and Jefferson's former law tutor) George Wythe; see Boyd, "Murder of George Wythe"; and Chadwick, *I Am Murdered*.

62. Truxton to Thomas Tingey, 9 May 1807, DLC: Truxton Papers.

63. "Burr's Trial," *New-York Evening Post*, 8 June 1807.

64. Burr to Jonathan Rhea, 25 July 1807, in *PCAB*, 2:1037. Burr seemed less concerned with the testimony of Thomas Morgan, but he was "a lad of 18 or 19."

65. Burr to Alston, 18 June 1807, in *MAB*, 2:407.

66. [Prentiss], *Life of the Late Gen. William Eaton*, 435. The attacks on Eaton had begun in February in John Wood's *Atlantic World*. In early June, the *Observer* reprinted one of these pieces, along with new material from Wood and new strictures of its own; see *Impartial Observer*, 5 June 1807. Later attacks included a series of eight essays in the *Gazette*—signed "Investigator" and written by Luther Martin—that appeared between 24 June and 7 October. For Martin's authorship, see Harman Blennerhassett, diary entry, 26 September 1807, in

BwB, 105. For Burr's pledge to degrade Eaton's character, see Harman Blenner-hassett, diary entry, 22 September 1807, in ibid., 100–101; Burr, remarks, 25 September 1807, in *TCAB*, 3:232; and *Enquirer*, 30 October 1807.

67. Eaton to Pynchon, 5 October 1807, Ms-Ar: Ventress and Family Papers.

68. Eaton to Pynchon, 12 October 1807, DLC: William Eaton Papers. Eaton also injured his reputation with his activities outside of the courtroom—heavy drinking, betting on the trial, and swaggering about Richmond in a turban and with a cutlass; see *Columbian Centinel* (Boston), 6 June 1807; and [Prentiss], *Life of the Late Gen. William Eaton*, 408, 435–36. Eaton's behavior in Richmond is covered in Wright and Macleod, "William Eaton's Relations with Aaron Burr"; and Edwards, *Barbary General*, 253–57. In contrast, Thomas Truxton used his appearance at the trial to redress the damage that had followed the linking of his name to Burr's project. He considered it part of his "duty as a Man of honor" to testify (Truxton to Caesar A. Rodney, 9 May 1807, CSmH: Huntington Manuscripts Collection). But others needed to know that he had testified. After his testimony, he delivered a written statement to the grand jury that had nothing to do with Burr's plans and everything to do with the rumors that still clung to his own name; see Truxton to Randolph and the Grand Jury, 23 June 1807, enclosed in Truxton to Jefferson, 25 June 1807, DLC: Jefferson Papers. Truxton then forwarded copies of this statement to friends whom he could trust to circulate it; see his letters to: Charles Biddle, 11 July 1807, in Biddle, *Autobiography of Charles Biddle*, 411–14; and Timothy Pickering, 22 November 1807, MHi: Timothy Pickering Papers. For Truxton's involvement in Burr's trial, see Ferguson, *Truxton of the Constellation*, 246–49; and Geissler, "Commodore Goes to Court."

69. John Hook to Bowker Preston, 12 June 1807, Vi: John Hook Records. In later decades, "tag rag" was inverted to "rag tag"; the phrase "tag rag and bobtail" was very old and referred to the despicable part of the community; see *OED Online*, December 2016 ed., s.v. "tag rag."

70. Anthony to Frederick Bates, 28 May 1807, in Marshall, ed., *Life and Papers of Frederick Bates*, 130. The Blennerhassetts were clearly unsettled by the prospect. Harman's prison journal includes numerous attacks on Allbright and Taylor; see, for example, Harman Blennerhassett, diary entries, 12 and 19 August 1807, in *BwB*, 19–20 and 39. Margaret attributed her husband's confinement to "the perjury of a wretch [Taylor] not many degrees from a brute," reflecting, "it is in vain, I am convinced more and more every day, to expect principle without some refinement" (Margaret Blennerhassett to Harman Blennerhassett, 26 August 1807, in *BP*, 283–84).

71. Benjamin Botts, argument, 25 August 1807, in *RTCAB*, 2:134.

72. "Trial of Mr. Burr," *Columbian Centinel*, 24 June 1807. The *Centinel*'s use of "Mr." for Eaton (and Burr, in the article title) rather than a military rank was surely deliberate. Six weeks later, Blennerhassett noted that Richmond's Republican newspapers "dropp[ed] the Mister" before his name in reporting his arrival in the city (Harman Blennerhassett, diary entry, 8 August 1807, in *BwB*, 12).

73. Edmund Dana, testimony, 18 June 1807, in "NECAB," 46.
74. Stoddert to Rutledge, 4 June 1807, NcU: Rutledge Papers.
75. "Caution!," *Impartial Observer*, 1 June 1807. See also Martin, argument, 28 August 1807, in *RTCAB*, 2:263. Fairlamb's plans, as presented by the *Observer*, included strong echoes of Gabriel's Conspiracy of seven years earlier. The *Argus* printed a mild challenge to the *Observer*'s claims; see "Frederick-Town, (Mar.)," *Virginia Argus*, 17 June 1807.
76. Caesar A. Rodney to Jefferson, 10 August 1807, DLC: Jefferson Papers. Allbright and Taylor first testified early in the grand jury stage when the prosecution tried to persuade Marshall that Burr should be tried for treason, but their testimony was not recorded; see *RTCAB*, 1:96.
77. Caesar A. Rodney to James Taylor, 2 July 1807, DeHi: H. Fletcher Brown Collection of Rodney Family Papers. After visiting western Virginia and southern Ohio, the Kentucky army contractor James Taylor reported that he had found "abundance of proof of the fair character of both Taylor & Albright" (James Taylor to Madison, 4 August 1807, ibid.).
78. Burr, argument, 19 August 1807, in *TCAB*, 2:161.
79. Hay, argument, 19 August 1807, in ibid., 162; Burr, argument, 19 August 1807, in ibid. Robertson's version of this exchange does not include the suggestion of prosecutorial misconduct; see *RTCAB*, 1:511.
80. [Ritchie], *Enquirer*, 14 January 1808. See also John Quincy Adams, notes for speech in Senate, [8 April 1808], MHi: Adams Family Papers.
81. Wirt to Edwards, 2 August 1807, ICHi: Edwards Papers.
82. Caesar A. Rodney to Jefferson, 1 October 1807, DLC: Jefferson Papers.
83. Botts, argument, 26 August 1807, in *RTCAB*, 2:176; ibid., 177; Marshall, comment, in ibid.
84. Harman Blennerhassett, diary entry, 8 October 1807, in *BwB*, 124.
85. Hay to Jefferson, 11 June 1807, DLC: Jefferson Papers.
86. Hay to Jefferson, 14 June 1807, ibid.
87. Harman Blennerhassett, diary entry, 27 September 1807, in *BwB*, 108.
88. Glover to Ethan A. Brown, 29 May 1807, OHi: Brown Papers; Nathaniel Saltonstall Jr. to Leverett Saltonstall, 12 June 1807, in Moody, ed., *Saltonstall Papers*, 2:375. Assessments of most of the trial's attorneys were scattered through Wilkinson's letters and Blennerhassett's journal.
89. William H. Cabell to Joseph C. Cabell, 12 April 1807, ViU: Cabell Family Papers. "Without form, and void" is from the first chapter of Genesis (King James Version) and refers to the chaos from which everything was created.
90. Glover to Ethan A. Brown, 29 May 1807, OHi: Brown Papers.
91. "Extract of a letter from a gentleman in Richmond to his friend in the country," *Enquirer*, 20 June 1807. See also Wirt to Edwards, 2 August 1807, ICHi: Edwards Papers; and George Poindexter to Thomas Rodney, 31 October 1807, PHi: Simon Gratz Autograph Collection. The administration tried to find evidence

that Martin had conspired with Burr; see Caesar A. Rodney to Samuel Smith, 22 June 1807, PHi: Ferdinand J. Dreer Collection.

92. Harman Blennerhassett, diary entry, 30 August 1807, in *BwB*, 67–68.

93. Thompson, *Compendious View*, 73n. For Martin's involvement, see Clarkson and Jett, *Luther Martin of Maryland*, 245–73.

94. [Ritchie], "Cursory Reflections—No. I, Portrait of Aaron Burr," *Enquirer*, 30 October 1807. The "portrait" of Wilkinson was never published. For sensibility and the body, see Bushman, *Refinement of America*; Fliegelman, *Declaring Independence*; and Lukasik, *Discerning Characters*.

95. Truxton to Thomas Tingey, 9 May 1807, DLC: Truxton Papers.

96. Irving to Paulding, 22 June 1807, in Aderman, Kleinfield, and Banks, eds., *Washington Irving*, 1:239. See also "Extract of a letter from Richmond," *Middlesex Gazette* (Middletown, Conn.), 26 June 1807 (from AHN); and Justus Erich Bollman to Alston, 27 July 1807, PHi: Gratz Autograph Collection.

97. "Greatness," *Virginia Argus*, 16 September 1807.

98. Nathaniel Saltonstall Jr. to Leverett Saltonstall, 4/12 June 1807, in Moody, ed., *Saltonstall Papers*, 2:376. See also Truxton to Thomas Tingey, 1 June 1807, DLC: Truxton Papers; Hay to Jefferson, 9 June 1807, DLC: Jefferson Papers; and Return J. Meigs Jr. to Sophia Meigs, 11 August 1807, InU: Meigs Manuscripts.

99. Scott, *Memoirs of Lieut.-General Scott*, 1:13. Antonio Canova was a Venetian sculptor in the late eighteenth and early nineteenth centuries who was renowned for his nudes.

100. Harman Blennerhassett, diary entry, 19 August 1807, in *BwB*, 39.

101. Burr to Alston, 15 May 1807, in *MAB*, 2:406.

102. "The Pig got loose and killed the Butcher," *New-York Evening Post*, 9 September 1807.

103. Tompkins to Duncan Cameron, 25 August 1807, NcU: Cameron Family Papers. See also "For the Argus," *Virginia Argus*, 7 October 1807. Both Hay and Wirt questioned Burr's legal talents and viewed his reliance on legal technicalities to prevent exposure as dishonorable; see Hay to Jefferson, 31 May and 9 June 1807, DLC: Jefferson Papers; and Wirt to Gilmer, 18 July 1807, DLC: Wirt Papers.

104. "Extract from a letter written by a resident of Richmond Hill," *Enquirer*, 23 June 1807. "Rude undigested mass" is a translation of Ovid's description of matter before creation (see above, n. 5).

105. [Pleasants], *Virginia Argus*, 10 June 1807. See also William Branch Giles to Jefferson, 6 April 1807, DLC: Jefferson Papers; and Truxton to Thomas Tingey, 1 June 1807, DLC: Truxton Papers.

106. James Wilkinson to Henry Dearborn, 17 June 1807, DNA: RG107, M222, W-1807. See also Wilkinson's letters to: Jefferson, 17 June 1807, DLC: Burr Conspiracy Collection; and Samuel Smith, 19 June 1807, PPiU-D: James Wilkinson Papers.

107. I discussed the grand jury's handling of Wilkinson, and the newspaper battle it sparked, in Chapter 5.

108. Hay to Jefferson, 14 June 1807, DLC: Jefferson Papers.
109. Truxton to Jefferson, 23 July 1807, ibid. Similarly, Blennerhassett later complained of Wilkinson's "bloated arrogance" (Harman Blennerhassett, diary entry, 23 September 1807, in *BwB*, 101).
110. Harman Blennerhassett, diary entry, 26 September 1807, in *BwB*, 105.
111. Harman Blennerhassett, diary entry, 29 September 1807, in ibid., 111. Wilkinson, however, insisted that Burr's "several feeble attacks on my Integrity & veracity" had all "recoiled on Himself" (Wilkinson to Jonathan Williams, 4 October 1807, InU: Jonathan Williams Manuscripts).
112. Edward Bates to Richard Bates, 18 September 1807, ViHi: Bates Papers. Bates reported popular sentiment, which he shared to some degree. But he also noted that he was "not ready to say that any opinion" of Marshall's was "an unconsciencious one."
113. Stoddert to Rutledge, 4 June 1807, NcU: Rutledge Papers. Stoddert trusted that Marshall would "not err at all."
114. [Pleasants], *Virginia Argus*, 17 April 1807.
115. Read to Caesar A. Rodney, 24 June 1807, DeHi: Rodney Collection.
116. Hay to Jefferson, 11 August 1807, DLC: Jefferson Papers. Writing just a few days earlier, Wirt, in contrast, rejected the idea that Marshall was "warped by [his] prejudices." "Never did I know a man who was more solicitous to cast every bias from his mind & decide every proposition on its abstract merits," Wirt confided to a friend (Wirt to Edwards, 2 August 1807, ICHi: Edwards Papers).
117. Gamble to Thomas Massie, 1 September 1807, ViHi: Massie Family Papers; Edward Tupper to Thomas Worthington, 1 September 1807, ORCHi: Early Statehood Papers. Tupper was a Republican but was unhappy with what he saw as the prosecution's excesses.
118. Marshall, opinion, 31 August 1807, in *PJMar*, 7:115.
119. Wirt to Edwards, 2 August 1807, ICHi: Edwards Papers.
120. "Extract from a Handbill," *People's Friend*, 2 July 1807.
121. Bollman to Alston, 27 July 1807, PHi: Gratz Autograph Collection. For a similar description, see John F. May to Thomas Ruffin, 9 September 1807, in Hamilton, ed., *Papers of Thomas Ruffin*, 1:111. Even fifty years later, Burr's biographer James Parton considered it necessary to state that Burr had been "utterly unmoved" by the indictment and to suggest that press reports to the contrary merely pandered to public wishes (Parton, *Life and Times of Aaron Burr*, 476).
122. Wirt to Edwards, 2 August 1807, ICHi: Edwards Papers. Hay likewise reported that Marshall "gazed at [Burr], for a long time, without appearing conscious that he was doing so, with an expression of sympathy & Sorrow, as Strong, as the human countenance can exhibit without *palpable* emotion" (Hay to Jefferson, 11 August 1807, DLC: Jefferson Papers). In Chapter 5, I discussed another moment when character issues shaped the legal battles—when the grand jury asked

Marshall to have Burr turn over the Wilkinson letter that was mentioned in the cipher letter.

123. Irving to Paulding, 22 June 1807, in Aderman, Kleinfield, and Banks, eds., *Washington Irving*, 1:239–40. For the widespread anticipation of this "interview," see also James Sterrett to Nathaniel Evans, 8 May 1807, LU: Evans (Nathaniel and Family) Papers; Truxton to Thomas Tingey, 9 May 1807, DLC: Truxton Papers; Charles Biddle to Nicholas Biddle, 2 June [*sic*, July] 1807, PHi: Charles Biddle Papers; and Thompson, *Compendious View*, 85n.

124. "Extract from a letter written by a resident of Richmond Hill," *Enquirer*, 23 June 1807. The quote is from the "to be or not to be" soliloquy in Shakespeare's *Hamlet*, 3.1.86.

125. Wilkinson to Jefferson, 17 June 1807, DLC: Burr Conspiracy Collection. A newspaper account condensed the entire incident into just three sentences but still described Burr's "countenance [as] marked by a haughty contempt" and Wilkinson as "calm, dignified and commanding" (*Petersburg Intelligencer* [Va.], 19 June 1807).

126. Wirt to Edwards, 2 August 1807, ICHi: Edwards Papers. "Protervity" means "stubbornness" or "impudence" (*OED Online*, December 2016 ed., s.v. "protervity," n. 1). My colleague Max Cherem discerned this word in Wirt's script, after it had eluded me and many others for years.

127. Irving to Paulding, 22 June 1807, in Aderman, Kleinfield, and Banks, eds., *Washington Irving*, 1:240. For Irving's expectation that a letter to Paulding would see publication, see Aderman and Kime, *Advocate for America*, 28–51.

128. Wilkinson to Jefferson, 17 June 1807, DLC: Burr Conspiracy Collection. Wilkinson's phrasing suggests a struggle between body and self, with his eyes flashing "indignation" at Burr "in spite of myself."

129. "Dramatic Intelligence," *Virginia Argus*, 17 June 1807. See also "Dramatic Intelligence," ibid., 24 June 1807. For a response that continued the theater metaphor, see [Brooks], *Impartial Observer*, 20 June 1807.

130. "The following sketch is communicated by one of our correspondents, a great ANATEUR of the Drama," *Virginia Argus*, 14 October 1807. "Anateur" referred to someone who wrote about the stage. A writer in the *Gazette* countered that the recent amusements should be called "*'King Tom's Puppet shew,*' or *'Much a do about Nothing'*" ("Comus," *Virginia Gazette*, 17 October 1807). Volpone, Italian for "sly fox," was the lead character in a Ben Jonson play from 1606.

131. "Extract from a letter written by a resident of Richmond Hill," *Enquirer*, 28 April 1807.

132. Gamble to Thomas Massie, 3 August 1807, ViHi: Massie Family Papers.

133. *RTCAB*, 1:3. See also Gamble to Thomas Massie, 30 March 1807, ViHi: Massie Family Papers.

134. [Pleasants], *Virginia Argus*, 23 May 1807.

135. Tompkins to Duncan Cameron, 23 May 1807, NcU: Cameron Family Papers. See also James Innes to Jerdone, 22 May 1807, ViW: Jerdone Family Papers.

136. Return J. Meigs Jr. to Sophia Meigs, 11 August 1807, InU: Meigs Manuscripts. For the disappearance of the crowds, at least in the courtroom, see Harman Blennerhassett, diary entry, 8 October 1807, in *BwB*, 124.

137. [Pleasants], *Virginia Argus*, 23 May 1807.

138. "Extract of a letter from Richmond," *Morning Chronicle* (New York), 4 June 1807.

139. Wilkinson to Samuel Smith, 20 June 1807, PPiU-D: Wilkinson Papers. Wilkinson believed that these men, particularly Ashley, would, in "the dernier resort[,] . . . assassinate me."

140. John Pryor, advertisement, *Virginia Gazette*, 29 July 1807.

141. For Saint-Mémin, see Norfleet, *Saint-Mémin in Virginia*; and Miles, *Saint-Mémin*. Saint-Mémin developed the physiognotrace to prepare the initial silhouette. The pantograph reduced the profile to fit into a small circle on a copper plate. The graver and roulette were then used to engrave the interior details on the plate. For twenty-five dollars, Saint-Mémin's sitters received a chalk likeness, twelve engraved impressions, and a copper plate from which more images could be struck. Other artists who advertised in Richmond newspapers during Burr's trial included J. B. Anderson, E. Dean, and John McConachy & L. Remouit; see [Catterall], *Richmond Portraits*, 241–43.

142. Mordecai, *Virginia, Especially Richmond, in By-gone Days*, 251.

143. Truxton to Thomas Tingey, 1 June 1807, DLC: Truxton Papers. About the same time, Truxton recorded his daily schedule: "up at 6[,] go to Court at 10, adjourn at 3," "dine every day at 1/2 past 4, rise at 8 from dinner[,] . . . at an evening party at 1/2 past 8, and in bed at 12" (Truxton to Charles Biddle, 30 May 1807, in Biddle, *Autobiography of Charles Biddle*, 409).

144. Irving to [Fairlie?], 7 July 1807, in Aderman, Kleinfield, and Banks, eds., *Washington Irving*, 1:244; Irving to Gouverneur Kemble, 1 July 1807, in ibid., 242.

145. Graham to Madison, 14 August 1807, DLC: Madison Papers. For the Virginia Springs, see Boyer Lewis, *Ladies and Gentlemen on Display*.

146. William H. Cabell to Joseph C. Cabell, 9 April 1807, ViU: Cabell Family Papers.

147. Hook to Preston, 12 June 1807, Vi: Hook Records. See also Slaughter to Towles, 16 May 1807, KyLoF: Towles Papers; and Randolph to Monroe, 30 May 1807, DLC: Monroe Papers. For Virginia's Quids, see Cunningham, "Who Were the Quids?"; Risjord, *Old Republicans*; and Carson, "That Ground Called Quiddism." For the presidential election, see also Ammon, "James Monroe and the Election of 1808."

148. [Pleasants], *Virginia Argus*, 31 March 1807. See also [Ritchie], *Enquirer*, 7 April 1807. For Ritchie's activities during the trial, see Ambler, *Thomas Ritchie*, 37–41.

149. [Augustine Davis], *Virginia Gazette*, 4 April 1807.

150. [Pleasants], *Virginia Argus*, 16 May 1807. Hay, Marshall, Martin, and Wilkinson each used Richmond's newspapers, in one way or another, during the trial.

151. Wilkinson to John Smith, 28 June 1807, OCHi: Papers in the Defense of John Smith of Ohio. For Brooks's denial that he had been bought by Burr, see [Brooks], *Impartial Observer,* 25 April and 9 May 1807.

152. Harman Blennerhassett, diary entry, 29 September 1807, in *BwB,* 112. Even though Augustine Davis was providing space for Martin in the *Gazette,* the newspaper was considered inadequate because it "had no circulation" and lacked the kind of editor that Burr wanted (ibid.). For Brooks's efforts to save his newspaper, see [Brooks], "To Our Readers," *Impartial Observer,* 5 June 1807.

153. [Brooks], *Impartial Observer,* 18 April 1807.

154. Ibid., 25 April 1807.

155. Brooks to Jefferson, ibid., 16 May 1807. Brooks advertised the pamphlet in his last issue; see "Just Published," ibid., 2 July 1807. It had originally appeared in Georgetown, South Carolina—the Alstons' home—just a few weeks earlier; see *Georgetown Gazette, and Commercial Advertiser* (S.C.), 20 June 1807. Burr probably arranged for its republication. Later, during his European travels, he gave a copy to the editor of the important *Edinburgh Review;* see Burr, diary entry, 9 January 1809, in *PJAB-B,* 1:52.

156. "*It is a bad wind that blows nobody good,*'" *People's Friend,* 9 June 1807.

157. David Watson to George Watson, 5 August 1807, ViHi: Watson Family Papers. See also Nathaniel Macon to Nicholson, 12 July 1807, DLC: Joseph H. Nicholson Papers; Charles Ellis and Jonathan Allan to John Hartwell Cocke, 13 July 1807, ViU: John Hartwell Cocke Papers; and Charles Carter to St. George Tucker, 16 September 1807, ViW: Tucker-Coleman Papers. For the arrival of the news of the *Chesapeake* Affair in Richmond, see Randolph to Nicholson, 25 June 1807, DLC: Nicholson Papers. A fourth crew member soon died of his wounds.

158. Tompkins to Duncan Cameron, 30 June 1807, NcU: Cameron Family Papers. See also Alexander McRae to Jefferson, 27 June 1807, DLC: Jefferson Papers; Wilkinson to Samuel Smith, 29 June 1807, PPiU-D: Wilkinson Papers; and William Duane to Monroe, undated, interlined within Jonathan M. Taylor to Monroe, 25 July 1807, NN: James Monroe Papers.

159. Samuel Mordecai to Rachel Mordecai, 16 July 1807, NcU: Mordecai Family Papers. See also Return J. Meigs Jr. to Sophia Meigs, 11 August 1807, InU: Meigs Manuscripts. According to one account, "even the ladies . . . [were] forming themselves into volunteer corps," with plans to meet the troops outside of the city and "escort them" ("Extract of a letter received at N.Y. dated Richmond," *Candid Review* [Bairdstown, Ky.], 8 September 1807). For another account of women's support, see Wirt to Carr, 19 July 1807, in Kennedy, *Memoirs of the Life of William Wirt,* 1:297. For the *Chesapeake* Affair and the ensuing response, see Gaines, "*Chesapeake* Affair"; and Tucker and Reuter, *Injured Honor.*

160. Macon to Nicholson, 3 August 1807, DLC: Nicholson Papers. The *Argus* continued to publish material criticizing "the leading federal and Burr partisans" despite their strong stand in the crisis ("'Look Out for Breakers,'" *Virginia*

Argus, 29 July 1807, clipped from *Aurora General Advertiser* [Philadelphia]). It was on this issue, far more than the trial, that differences appeared between Richmond's Republican editors, as the *Enquirer*'s Ritchie sought "a general union of all parties, and applaud[ed] those, who have shewn by their example, that union is also their creed" ([Ritchie], *Enquirer*, 24 July 1807).

161. Duncan Cameron to Walter Alves, 29 June 1807, in *RASP*, Series J, Part 13, Walter Alves Papers. See also [Pleasants], *Virginia Argus*, 23 May 1807; and Irvine to Rose, 21 June 1807, KyLoF: Rose Papers.

162. Randolph to Monroe, 30 May 1807, DLC: Monroe Papers.

163. William H. Cabell to Joseph C. Cabell, 9 April 1807, ViU: Cabell Family Papers. See also Randolph to Nicholson, 25 June 1807, DLC: Nicholson Papers; and Gamble to Thomas Massie, 3 August 1807, ViHi: Massie Family Papers. The literature on the political battles of the 1790s is extensive. Two early works to recognize their social dimension are Smelser, "Federalist Period as an Age of Passion"; and Howe, "Republican Thought and the Political Violence."

164. [Davis], "Par Nobile Fratrum," *Virginia Gazette*, 20 May 1807. For visiting and other forms of hospitality, see Wyatt-Brown, *Southern Honor*, 331–39; Carson, *Ambitious Appetites*; and Hemphill, *Bowing to Necessities*.

165. Truxton to Caesar A. Rodney, 9 May 1807, CSmH: Huntington Manuscripts Collection. In this letter, Truxton spelled out three reasons for not socializing with Burr that were peculiar to his situation. Other letters make clear that he was not only thinking of himself. Months earlier, for example, he had called for Burr to be "give[n] up as an Outcast" (Truxton to Pickering, 13 January 1807, MHi: Pickering Papers).

166. [Stephen C. Carpenter], *People's Friend*, 13 April 1807. For the Republican view, see William Eustis to Thomas Law, 26 April 1807, MdHi: Thomas Law Family Papers.

167. Bollman to Alston, 27 July 1807, PHi: Gratz Autograph Collection.

168. Irving to Kemble, 1 July 1807, in Aderman, Kleinfield, and Banks, eds., *Washington Irving*, 1:242. See also "Virginia Bastiles!," *Pittsburgh Gazette* (Pa.), 28 July 1807. For Burr's stay at the Swan Tavern, see *Enquirer*, 7 April 1807. Burr left Richmond on 28 April and returned on 14 May; see ibid., 1 May 1807; and *Virginia Argus*, 16 May 1807.

169. Botts, remarks, 26 June 1807, in *RTCAB*, 1:350.

170. The proceedings in court are fully covered in ibid., 350–59. Moving Burr to the penitentiary required special permission from the governor since Virginia, as John Randolph explained, had "no state prison except for convicts" and Burr had not been convicted (Randolph to Nicholson, 25 June 1807, DLC: Nicholson Papers). Confining Burr in Martin's rented home was an expensive arrangement. Even after paying for modifications to secure the room, it required seven men to guard Burr—at a cost of seven dollars per day; see Scott to Gallatin, 8 August 1807, in *PAG*. It was also controversial; see, for example, Jefferson to Hay, 20 August 1807, in *WrTJ*, 11:341. For Burr's final Richmond lodgings, see

Burr to Alston, 30 July 1807, in *MAB*, 2:410; and Harman Blennerhassett, diary entry, 7 September 1807, in *BwB*, 82.

171. Albert James Pickett, "Notes taken from the lips of Mr Thos Malone of Washington County Ala in relation to the arrest of Aaron Burr in 1807," A-Ar: Albert J. Pickett Papers.

172. Gamble to Thomas Massie, 30 March 1807, ViHi: Massie Family Papers. Gamble considered these low numbers, noting that "*only* 4. or 5" visitors had seen Burr since his arrival late on 26 March (emphasis added).

173. "To the Editor of the Aurora," *Sun* (Pittsfield, Mass.), 2 May 1807 (from AHN). See also "Communication," *Virginia Argus*, 17 April 1807.

174. [Davis], "Col. Burr's Commitment," *Virginia Gazette*, 4 April 1807.

175. [Davis], "Par Nobile Fratrum," ibid., 20 May 1807.

176. "Extract from a letter written by a resident of Richmond Hill," *Enquirer*, 28 April 1807; "Feast of Treason," *Democratic Press* (Philadelphia), 22 April 1807, clipped from *Republican* (Petersburg, Va.) (from AHN).

177. "Communication," *Virginia Argus*, 7 April 1807. See also "Communication," ibid., 10 April 1807. The italicized "*unfortunate gentleman*" should probably be read as sarcasm. Fifty years later, the historian George Tucker reported, based on "direct information from Mr. Wickham" and his "own personal knowledge," that Marshall had accepted the invitation without knowing that Burr would be a guest, had been informed of the fact before the dinner, but had decided to attend anyway rather than "seem[ing] to cast censure on his friend." Still, according to Tucker, Marshall "had no intercourse whatever with Burr, sat at the opposite end of a long table, and withdrew from the company immediately after dinner" (Tucker, *History of the United States*, 2:295–96). Curiously, almost no one seems to have criticized Marshall for dining with Wickham, who had already been retained as Burr's attorney. There is evidence, moreover, that, even during the most intense days of the treason trial, Marshall played chess with Wickham and discussed the trial as they played; see Harman Blennerhassett, diary entry, 23 August 1807, in *BwB*, 49.

178. "A Stranger from the Country" [Benjamin Watkins Leigh], *Enquirer*, 10 April 1807. Various well-placed Republicans identified Leigh, a Petersburg attorney, as the author; see William H. Cabell to Joseph C. Cabell, 12 April 1807, ViU: Cabell Family Papers; and May to Ruffin, 9 September 1807, in Hamilton, ed., *Papers of Thomas Ruffin*, 1:111. Oddly, Leigh, who became a prominent Whig, later married first Marshall's niece and then Wickham's daughter; see Robert B. Tunstall, "Leigh, Benjamin Watkins," in *Dictionary of American Biography*, 11:152–53. Marshall's attendance at Wickham's dinner long remained controversial. A half-century later, John Lewis still believed that Marshall had "acted very imprudent" in "din[ing] with the man he was to try for treason at *John Wickham's*" (John Lewis, interview with John Dabney Shane, 3 September 1855, WHi: Draper Manuscript Collection, 15CC14). See also "A True Madisonian" to Madison, 10 October 1812, in *PJM: PS*, 5:385.

179. Hay to Caesar A. Rodney, 15 April 1807, PHi: Gratz Autograph Collection. For the impact of the published attacks, see also William H. Cabell to Joseph C. Cabell, 12 April 1807, ViU: Cabell Family Papers; and Caesar A. Rodney to Jefferson, 6 May 1807, DLC: Jefferson Papers.

180. Irving to [Fairlie?], 7 July 1807, in Aderman, Kleinfield, and Banks, eds., *Washington Irving*, 1:244. Writing in late June, Luther Martin insisted, in contrast, that Burr had "many warm friends here at this time, who are not, and have not been, deterred from proving their attachment to him" (Martin to Alston, 26 June 1807, in Ford, ed., "Some Papers of Aaron Burr," 124). And, decades later, John Barney, who had been Burr's amanuensis in Richmond, recalled a dinner with Burr at Martin's house that included "twenty ladies and gentlemen of rank, fortune, and fashion" (John Barney, unpublished memoirs, quoted in Parton, *Life and Times of Aaron Burr*, 481).

181. Harman Blennerhassett, diary entry, 28 September 1807, in *BwB*, 110.

182. "Latest from Richmond," *New-York Evening Post*, 1 July 1807. The prison referred to was the city jail, not the state penitentiary. No Richmond source reported this incident. John Barney recalled that, whenever he visited Burr at the penitentiary, his carriage "was freighted with cake, confectionery, [and] flowers" (Barney, unpublished memoirs, quoted in Parton, *Life and Times of Aaron Burr*, 482).

183. Burr to Alston, 24 July 1807, in *MAB*, 2:410.

184. Burr to Alston, 3 July 1807, in ibid., 409.

185. Burr to Alston, 6 July 1807, in ibid., 410.

186. Burr to Alston, 30 July 1807, in ibid.

187. Alston to [Margaret] Blennerhassett, 5 August 1807, in Ford, ed., "Some Papers of Aaron Burr," 125. For descriptions of Burr's lodgings other than those in his or his daughter's letters, see Ellis and Allan to Cocke, 13 July 1807, ViU: Cocke Papers; and Harman Blennerhassett to Margaret Blennerhassett, 4 August 1807, in *BP*, 274.

188. Harman Blennerhassett to Margaret Blennerhassett, 4 August 1807, in *BP*, 274.

189. Harman Blennerhassett, diary entry, 30 August 1807, in *BwB*, 65. For Blennerhassett's day without visitors, see his diary entry, 15 August 1807, in ibid., 26–27.

190. Harman Blennerhassett, diary entry, 12 August 1807, in ibid., 19.

191. Harman Blennerhassett, diary entry, 4 August 1807, in ibid., 4; Harman Blennerhassett, diary entry, 20 August 1807, in ibid., 40.

192. Harman Blennerhassett to Margaret Blennerhassett, 4 August 1807, in *BP*, 275.

193. Harman Blennerhassett, diary entry, 5 August 1807, in *BwB*, 5, 7. For the very different lifestyle of the ordinary inmates, see Harman Blennerhassett, diary entry, 14 August 1807, in ibid., 22–23. Republicans had criticized Marshal Joseph Scott for allowing Burr "to eat & drink such good things as his money would purchase or his friends bestow upon him" (Randolph to Scott, 23 August

1807, ViU: John Randolph Papers Microfilm). See also Page to Jefferson, 11 July 1807, DLC: Jefferson Papers.

194. Harman Blennerhassett, diary entry, 13 August 1807, in *BwB*, 22.

195. Thomas Tudor Tucker to Page, 13 August 1807, DLC: Thomas Tudor Tucker Papers. See also William H. Cabell to Joseph C. Cabell, 9 April 1807, ViU: Cabell Family Papers; and Hook to Preston, 12 June 1807, Vi: Hook Records.

196. Harman Blennerhassett, diary entry, 14 August 1807, in *BwB*, 25.

197. "Extract from Richmond," *National Aegis* (Worcester, Mass.), 16 September 1807 (from AHN); Harman Blennerhassett, diary entry, 5 September 1807, in *BwB*, 78. Burr's letters after his release do not refer to any socializing; local newspapers no longer discussed his social life. In his journal, Blennerhassett mentioned one dinner at Burr's lodgings, but the small party included no Richmonders; see Harman Blennerhassett, diary entry, 16 September 1807, in ibid., 91. Evidence of Blennerhassett's far more active social life is scattered throughout his journal for September and October; for the most part, his socializing was limited to a small group of families, some Federalist and some foreign-born.

198. Return J. Meigs Jr. to Sophia Meigs, 11 August 1807, InU: Meigs Manuscripts; Tupper to Worthington, 1 September 1807, ORCHi: Early Statehood Papers.

199. "VIRGINIA, Richmond," *Columbian Centinel*, 27 June 1807. Other guests included Thomas Truxton, William Eaton, and John Graham; see "Extract of a letter from Richmond," *National Intelligencer, and Washington Advertiser* (D.C.), 19 June 1807. Surprisingly, none of the Richmond newspapers commented upon this event. The only other accounts of it that I have found are Truxton's, which are discussed below.

200. "From Richmond," *Public Advertiser* (New York), 20 June 1807 (from AHN).

201. Truxton to Charles Biddle, 30 May 1807, in Biddle, *Autobiography of Charles Biddle*, 409. For Gibbon's invitation, which Truxton reluctantly accepted, see Truxton to Thomas Tingey, 1 June 1807, DLC: Truxton Papers.

202. Thomas Tingey to Margaret Tingey, 21 July 1807, DLC: Thomas Tingey Papers. Thomas Tingey, a naval commodore, described "the wild Miss M____ M____n" as "fool-hardy (a kind of sea phrase) if not worse." Her coterie may have included Bollman, Swartwout, and Ogden, whom Truxton saw "very frequently in society" in Richmond (Truxton to Thomas Tingey, 20 June 1807, DLC: Truxton Papers). Six years earlier, she had been heavily involved in a family scandal involving the elopement of her barely fifteen-year-old sister Eleonora with Richard Raynal Keene, her father's law student; see Clarkson and Jett, *Luther Martin of Maryland*.

203. Jefferson to Page, 17 July 1807, DLC: Jefferson Papers.

204. Page to Jefferson, 11 July 1807, ibid. Gibbon also sent an explanation to Gabriel Duvall, who was both comptroller of the Treasury Department and his brother-in-law; see Hay to Jefferson, 13 July 1807, ibid. Jefferson's response to Page would not have been entirely reassuring. It laid out his normal principles regarding Federalist office-holding before stating: "Nothing which I have *yet* heard of

Major Gibbons places him in danger from these principles" (Jefferson to Page, 17 July 1807, ibid. [emphasis added]).

205. Page to Jefferson, 25 July 1807, ibid. Mary and Betsy Gibbon were sent to stay with their father's sister, Jane Duvall; see Thomas Tingey to Margaret Tingey, 21 July 1807, DLC: Tingey Papers. Truxton received two letters from Gibbon by 27 July, the second of which made clear that he could not stay at the Gibbon home and that "the girls [were] to be at Washington . . . during the pending trial" (Truxton to Thomas Tingey, 27 July 1807, DLC: Truxton Papers).

206. Samuel Mordecai to Rachel Mordecai, 16 July 1807, NcU: Mordecai Family Papers; Wilkinson to Williams, 22 October 1807, NjP: Fuller Collection of Aaron Burr. While Burr informed his daughter that women could visit him in the penitentiary, it is not clear that any, other than her, did; see Burr to Alston, 6 July 1807, in *MAB*, 2:410. Fifty years later, however, Richard Bayard reported that Burr, "whilst he was imprisoned in Richmond," had "seduced the daughter of a gentleman," one of the many "ladies of the place, who [had] visited him & brought him various luxuries" (Sidney George Fisher, diary entry, 23 October 1857, in Wainwright, ed., *Philadelphia Perspective*, 282).

207. Irving to [Fairlie?], 7 July 1807, in Aderman, Kleinfield, and Banks, eds., *Washington Irving*, 1:244. "Not a lady . . . in Richmond, whatever may be her husbands sentiments on the subject," Irving believed, would not "rejoice on seeing Col Burr at liberty" (ibid., 244–45). See also Bollman to Alston, 27 July 1807, PHi: Gratz Autograph Collection.

208. Harman Blennerhassett, diary entry, 18 October 1807, in *BwB*, 134. For Catherine Gamble, see Harman Blennerhassett, diary entry, 20 September 1807, in ibid., 97. Jefferson had removed Mary (Randolph) Randolph's husband, David Meade Randolph, from the office of federal marshal early in his presidency; see Malone, *Jefferson and His Time*, 4:208.

209. *Virginia Argus*, 24 June 1807. The "daggers and stilettos" were metaphorical, a part of the *Argus*'s satirical commentary on the trial as a play. For similar predictions in private letters, see Hook to Preston, 12 June 1807, Vi: Hook Records; and Harman Blennerhassett to Margaret Blennerhassett, 6 [*sic*, 5] July 1807, in *BP*, 248.

210. *Columbian Centinel*, 30 May 1807. Neither Adair nor Claiborne attended the trial.

211. "Rumour," *Georgetown Gazette*, 20 June 1807. See also "Extract of a letter from New-Orleans," *Impartial Review, and Cumberland Repository* (Nashville, Tenn.), 20 June 1807; and "Extract of a letter from Richmond," *Middlesex Gazette*, 26 June 1807 (from AHN). The scholarly literature on the duel is extensive; see, in particular, Wyatt-Brown, *Southern Honor*; and Freeman, *Affairs of Honor*.

212. Wilkinson to Charles Biddle, 20 July 1807, PHi: Biddle Family Papers.

213. Wilkinson to Samuel Smith, 20 June 1807, PPiU-D: Wilkinson Papers; Wilkinson to Samuel Smith, 10 May 1807, ibid.

214. Wilkinson to Dearborn, 17 June 1807, DNA: RG107, M222, W-1807.
215. Truxton to Jonathan Dayton, 5 August 1808, PHi: Gratz Autograph Collection. By the time that he wrote this letter, more than a year after the incident, Truxton intended to "Spit in his face" if Wilkinson "should Again offer his hand." Neither Truxton nor Wilkinson used the word "cutting" to describe this incident, though it was used in that way at the time.
216. Wilkinson to Charles Biddle, 24 June 1807, PHi: Biddle Family Papers. Similarly, Truxton turned to nautical metaphors—watching for "*Side Winds*," trusting "the Needle of [his] Compass" to "[point] out [his] Course," arriving safely in "port"—to relate his behavior in this incident (Truxton to Jefferson, 23 July 1807, DLC: Jefferson Papers).
217. Biddle, *Autobiography of Charles Biddle*, 316. Ann Biddle, Wilkinson's recently deceased wife of nearly thirty years, was Charles Biddle's cousin. For Truxton's most important letter to Biddle on this subject, see Truxton to Charles Biddle, 11 July 1807, in ibid., 411–14; for Wilkinson's letter to Biddle, see above, n. 212. In addition to his letters to Dayton and Jefferson (cited above, nn. 215 and 216), Truxton also wrote at length about this incident to Tingey; see Truxton to Thomas Tingey, 20 June 1807, DLC: Truxton Papers.
218. Jackson to Andrew Hamilton, 2 July 1807, in *PAJ*, 2:170, 171.
219. William P. Tebbs to Jackson, 10 July 1807, in ibid., 171. For Jackson's final remarks to Hamilton, see ibid., 172n2.
220. Dudley Woodbridge Jr. to William Woodbridge, 21/23 June 1807, MiD-B: Woodbridge Papers.
221. Hay to Wickham, 16 September 1807, ViHi: Wickham Family Papers. For the precipitating comments, see Wickham, argument, 12 September 1807, in *TCAB*, 3:92. "Much warm, confusing, and serious conversation occurred between" Hay and Wickham in court the day after Hay's letter (ibid., 129). Having found no other correspondence concerning this affair, I suspect that it was resolved through either a single letter from Wickham to Hay or an unrecorded apology in court. I mentioned the Wirt-Botts clash above and discuss the Swartwout-Wilkinson and Wilkinson-Wickham affairs below.
222. Charles Biddle to Burr, undated, PHi: Charles Biddle Papers. At the top of the same page of Biddle's letter book is a note reading: "Aug. 10. 1807. wrote Gl. Wilkinson bout his having an affair with Coll B. or D[ayto]n."
223. Wilkinson to Charles Biddle, 25 August 1807, PHi: Biddle Family Papers. Biddle apparently tried again, responding to this letter with what Wilkinson referred to as an "admonitory Letter" about dueling (Wilkinson to Charles Biddle, 19 September 1807, ibid.). The tenor of Smith's letters to Wilkinson is clear in the latter's replies; see Wilkinson to Samuel Smith, 19 and 20 June 1807, PPiU-D: Wilkinson Papers.
224. *Pittsburgh Gazette*, 16 June 1807. The quoted letter was dated 27 May. It is not clear whether the insult or insults had occurred in court or elsewhere.

225. Harman Blennerhassett to Margaret Blennerhassett, 6 [*sic*, 5] July 1807, in *BP*, 248. Blennerhassett was in Nashville when he wrote this letter; his predictions were based on letters that had arrived there from Richmond.

226. Wilkinson to Samuel Smith, 20 June 1807, PPiU-D: Wilkinson Papers. Even after the treason and misdemeanor stages, Wilkinson thought that he had to wait until the end of the committal hearings to issue any challenges; see Wilkinson to Charles Biddle, 19 September 1807, PHi: Biddle Family Papers.

227. Wilkinson to Samuel Smith, 10 June 1807, PPiU-D: Wilkinson Papers. Many histories of the trial claim that Randolph ordered Wilkinson stripped of his sword before he entered the grand jury room. I have found no contemporary evidence of that incident. The story can be traced back to James Alston Cabell's *Trial of Aaron Burr* (1900) and no further. Cabell neither provided a citation for his account, which includes a direct quote, nor claimed special knowledge through his family connections. Wilkinson was stripped of his sword at his 1811 court-martial; see Linklater, *Artist in Treason*, 292. For Wilkinson's changed view of Randolph, see his letters to Smith, 19 and 24 June 1807, PPiU-D: Wilkinson Papers. For his late December challenge, see Chapter 11.

228. Eaton to Pynchon, 15 October 1807, Ms-Ar: Ventress and Family Papers. Eaton, according to this letter, had "declared in public circles that *[he] would fight Burr*, and only him, of all his associates." Even six weeks earlier, Eaton had expected to "appear as [a] principal" in one of the "trials in the Court of Chivalry" that he assumed would follow the court proceedings (Eaton to Pynchon, 1 September 1807, in "Letter of William Eaton on Burr's Trial," 285).

229. Eaton to Pynchon, 19 October 1807, Ms-Ar: Ventress and Family Papers.

230. [Brooks], *Impartial Observer*, 5 June 1807.

231. Wilkinson to Samuel Smith, 20 June 1807, PPiU-D: Wilkinson Papers.

232. Wilkinson to Williams, 4 October 1807, InU: Williams Manuscripts; Harman Blennerhassett, diary entry, 3 October 1807, in *BwB*, 117.

233. Silas Dinsmore, certificate, *Virginia Gazette*, 24 October 1807. Smith, who had been indicted for treason, recognized that Wilkinson's sentiments applied to him, as well; see T. H. Cushing and John Fowler, certificate, ibid.

234. Samuel Swartwout, "To his Excellency Brigadier General James Wilkinson," ibid. The same "advertisement"—Swartwout's letter and the certificates of Dinsmore and Cushing and Fowler—appeared in numerous newspapers. See, for example, *Baltimore Evening Post* (Md.), 26 October 1807; and *Impartial Review*, 26 November 1807. Swartwout had first tried to challenge Wilkinson the previous day; see Harman Blennerhassett, diary entry, 19 October 1807, in *BwB*, 136; and Swartwout, "To his Excellency Brigadier General James Wilkinson," *Virginia Gazette*, 24 October 1807.

235. [Pleasants], *Virginia Argus*, 30 October 1807.

236. *Petersburg Intelligencer*, 23 October 1807. See also *American, and Commercial Daily Advertiser* (Baltimore, Md.), 27 October 1807.

237. Wilkinson to Williams, 27 October 1807, InU: Williams Manuscripts. For Wilkinson's efforts to have the posting published, see Wilkinson to Williams, 21 October 1807, NjP: Fuller Collection. Wilkinson's 27 October letter is the only source that I have found for the alleged nose-pulling incident. Nose pulling (or tweaking) was considered one of the greatest possible insults and, thus, one of the surest ways to force a duel; see Greenberg, "Nose, the Lie, and the Duel"; and Freeman, *Affairs of Honor*, 172.

238. Wilkinson to Dearborn, 14 November 1807, DNA: RG107, M222, W-1807. According to Wilkinson, on the day of the posting, Swartwout had "pretended" to act as a gentleman should by "hunting for [Wilkinson] to chastise [him]." "Yet," Wilkinson informed Williams, "I was frequently on the street & he knew my lodgings" (Wilkinson to Williams, 21 October 1807, NjP: Fuller Collection).

239. Wilkinson to Wickham, 20 October 1807, ViHi: Wickham Family Papers, #1. The letters in this sequence were numbered in order, probably by an archivist. For the legislative assembly as a protected space, see Stowe, *Intimacy and Power in the Old South*, 70. Affairs of honor and even duels did result from things said in Congress in the first fifty years of the federal government, including the Lyon-Griswold affair of 1798, the Campbell-Gardenier duel of 1808, the Clay-Randolph duel of 1826, and the Cilley-Graves duel of 1838. Joanne Freeman's forthcoming work will provide new insight into violence in Congress before the Civil War.

240. Miles Selden, affidavit, 6 October 1807, ViHi: Wickham Family Papers, #2. This incident must have occurred on 27 May. Selden's account suggests that there was an immediate awareness, even among the attorneys, that Wickham's comments were grounds for a challenge.

241. Wickham to William Upshaw, 21 October 1807, ibid., #3.

242. Wickham to Wilkinson, [ca. 23 October 1807], ibid., #5.

243. Wilkinson to Williams, 4 October 1807, InU: Williams Manuscripts.

244. Harman Blennerhassett, diary entry, 29 September 1807, in *BwB*, 111. Joseph C. Cabell, one of the grand jurors, similarly reported that Wilkinson had "lost ground" in terms of "public opinion, or rather *republican* opinion," near the end of the trial (Joseph C. Cabell to Isaac Coles, 6 November 1807, ViU: Cabell Family Papers). For Wilkinson's belief that Wickham would not duel, see Wilkinson to Williams, 21 October 1807, NjP: Fuller Collection.

245. Wilkinson to Wickham, 24 October 1807, ViHi: Wickham Family Papers, #6.

246. Upshaw to Wickham, 24 October 1807, ibid., #7.

247. Wilkinson to Williams, 27 October 1807, InU: Williams Manuscripts. For a less confident prediction from the same day, see Wilkinson to Dearborn, 27 October 1807, DNA: RG107, M222, W-1807.

248. Wickham to Upshaw, 29 October 1807, ViHi: Wickham Family Papers, #9.

249. Upshaw to Wickham, 29 October 1807, ibid., #10.
250. George Poindexter to Thomas Rodney, 31 October 1807, PHi: Gratz Autograph Collection. Poindexter alluded to Shakespeare's *Macbeth*, in which Lady Macbeth urges her husband to "screw [his] courage to the sticking-place" (*Macbeth*, 1.7.59). For Wickham's delay, see Wickham to Upshaw, 30 October [1807], ViHi: Wickham Family Papers, #11. For Upshaw's final letter, see Upshaw to Wickham, 30 October 1807, ibid., #12.
251. Wickham, "Memorandum of John Wickham," 31 October 1807, ViHi: Wickham Family Papers, #15. Unfortunately, much of this letter is illegible. Wickham had said essentially the same thing in court on the last day of Wilkinson's testimony; see Wickham, argument, 3 October 1807, in *TCAB*, 3:296.
252. Wilkinson to Wickham, 24 October 1807, ViHi: Wickham Family Papers, #6.
253. *United States' Gazette* (Philadelphia), 2 November 1807. It is not clear who could have written this letter. The affair may not have been well known even in Richmond. The only contemporary references to it that I have found have been in letters of men who learned about it directly from the principals or seconds; see Poindexter to Thomas Rodney, 31 October 1807, PHi: Gratz Autograph Collection; and Joseph C. Cabell to Coles, 6 November 1807, ViU: Cabell Family Papers.
254. Wilkinson to William MacPherson, 7 November 1807, PHi: W. M. Horner Collection in MacPherson Family Papers.
255. *United States' Gazette*, 10 November 1807. The same day, MacPherson assured Wilkinson that he had "stopt the US. G. being sent to Richmond"—how is not known—and promised to send a bill once he "settle[d] the expence" (MacPherson to Wilkinson, 10 November 1807, ICHi: James Wilkinson Papers).
256. Marshall to Richard Peters, 23 November 1807, in *PJMar*, 7:165. For Swartwout's departure (24 October), see Wilkinson to Williams, 27 October 1807, InU: Williams Manuscripts. For Blennerhassett and Martin's (25 October), see Harman Blennerhassett, diary entry, 27 October 1807, in *BwB*, 139. Burr seems to have followed a day later. Wilkinson did not leave until early November.
257. [Ritchie], "Cursory Reflections—No. I, Portrait of Aaron Burr," *Enquirer*, 30 October 1807. For the rest of this series, see ibid., 3, 6, 10, 17, and 24 November. The *Gazette*'s limited post-trial coverage can be found on 24 October 1807 (Swartwout's posting and a letter to the editor signed "Candor," possibly by Martin) and 6 November 1807 (a letter from Martin to the editor). The *Argus*'s much more extensive coverage appeared in a number of issues in the month after the trial. I discuss the "Lucius" essays in Chapter 11; they appeared in the *Enquirer* on 1, 4, 8, and 11 December.
258. Marshall to Peters, 23 November 1807, in *PJMar*, 7:165.
259. Marshall to Cushing, 29 June 1807, in ibid., 60.
260. Botts, argument, 26 August 1807, in *RTCAB*, 2:135.

CHAPTER 9. WHO IS BLENNERHASSETT?
THE NARRATIVE OF WILLIAM WIRT

1. [Pidgin], "Opening Address," 8 See also Charles Felton Pidgin to William K. Bixby, 30 August 1902, MoSHi: Aaron Burr Papers. It seems likely that the Legion met just once, in July 1903; see Wandell, *Aaron Burr in Literature*, 170.

2. Jesse Higgins to Jonathan and Matthew Roberts, 8 May 1807, PHi: Jonathan Roberts Papers.

3. James Sterrett to Nathaniel Evans, 21 August 1807, LU: Evans (Nathaniel and Family) Papers. Elbridge Gerry urged that "the political wound" that had been exposed by the grand jury "be probed to the bottom" (Elbridge Gerry to James Madison, 5 July 1807, DLC: James Madison Papers).

4. [Samuel H. Smith], *National Intelligencer, and Washington Advertiser* (D.C.), 29 June 1807.

5. William Wirt, argument, 17 August 1807, in *RTCAB*, 1:454, 457. In recent decades, lawyers and legal scholars have examined the use of narrative in the courtroom; see, for example, the essays in Bennett and Feldman, eds., *Reconstructing Reality in the Courtroom*; Brooks and Gewirtz, eds., *Law's Stories*; and Sarat and Kearns, eds., *Rhetoric of Law*. Of particular interest are Robert A. Ferguson's case studies of narrative in this period's trials; see his "Untold Stories in the Law," in Brooks and Gewirtz, eds., *Law's Stories*, 84–98; "Becoming American: High Treason and Low Invective in the Republic of Laws," in Sarat and Kearns, eds., *Rhetoric of Law*, 103–33; and *Trial in American Life*. "Becoming American" and chapter 3 of *Trial in American Life* discuss Wirt's "Who is Blennerhassett?" speech.

6. Elias Glover to Ethan A. Brown, 17 August 1807, OHi: Ethan Allen Brown Papers. For the remarks, see George Hay, argument, 17 August 1807, in *RTCAB*, 1:446–50.

7. John Marshall, opinion, 18 August 1807, in *PJMar*, 7:73.

8. John Wickham, argument, 20 August 1807, in *RTCAB*, 1:566.

9. Wirt, argument, 25 August 1807, in [Wirt], *Two Principal Arguments*, 61–62, 65–66. Of the published versions, Wirt preferred this one, which he considered "a pretty faithful statement" (Wirt to Ninian Edwards, 26 December 1807, ICHi: Ninian Edwards Papers). The "Who is Blennerhassett?" passage comprises less than three of the sixty-eight pages of Wirt's argument as it appears in *RTCAB*.

10. Wirt, argument, 25 August 1807, in [Wirt], *Two Principal Arguments*, 62–64. William Shenstone (1714–63) was an English poet and landscape gardener. Though Wirt could not have known it, the great irony of his Adam and Eve metaphor is that Harman and Margaret Blennerhassett had fled to their island Eden because they had already "fallen" in the view of their Irish and English friends and families. Margaret was Harman's niece, the child of his sister and brother-in-law. While rumors of their incestuous marriage had circulated

earlier, it was not until 1901, when Therese Blennerhassett-Adams, a distant relative, published "The True Story of Harman Blennerhassett," that the full story was known.

11. Wirt, argument, 25 August 1807, in [Wirt], *Two Principal Arguments*, 61–65. For solidly researched, historical accounts of the incidents described by Wirt, see Ray Swick's "Aaron Burr's Visit to Blennerhassett Island" and *Island Called Eden*. See also Lowther, *Blennerhassett Island in Romance and Tragedy*; Wood, *None Called Him Neighbor*; and Turner, "Harman Blennerhassett."

12. Dudley Woodbridge Jr. to William Woodbridge, 23/25 August 1807, MiD-B: William Woodbridge Papers.

13. Marshall, opinion, 31 August 1807, in *PJMar*, 7:74.

14. Kennedy, *Memoirs of the Life of William Wirt*, 1:131. There is no modern biography of Wirt. For nineteenth-century biographies, see [Peter Hoffman Cruse], "Biographical Sketch of William Wirt," in Wirt, *Letters of the British Spy*, 9–91; and Kennedy, *Memoirs of the Life of William Wirt*.

15. Bishop James Madison to Joseph C. Cabell, 31 May 1807, ViU: Cabell Family Papers. Wirt would have been willing to work for Burr if Burr's messenger had found him first; see Wirt to Edwards, 2 August 1807, ICHi: Edwards Papers.

16. William H. Cabell to Joseph C. Cabell, 2 April 1807, ViU: Cabell Family Papers. Wirt and William Cabell were brothers-in-law.

17. Wirt to Peachy R. Gilmer, 18 July 1807, DLC: William Wirt Papers. A year earlier, writing to Peachy Gilmer's brother Francis, Wirt had made clear the alternative to rising "to the heights of public notice": "think of being buried all your life in obscurity—confounded with the gross and ignorant herd around you—crawling in the kennel of filth and trash with the mass of human maggots and reptiles all your life" (Wirt to Francis Walker Gilmer, 9 October 1806, ViU: Francis Walker Gilmer Correspondence).

18. Nathaniel Saltonstall Jr. to Leverett Saltonstall, 12 June 1807, in Moody, ed., *Saltonstall Papers*, 2:375; James Wilkinson to Samuel Smith, 24 June 1807, PPiU-D: James Wilkinson Papers.

19. [Cruse], "Biographical Sketch of William Wirt," in Wirt, *Letters of the British Spy*, 56.

20. William H. Cabell to Joseph C. Cabell, 21 October 1807, ViU: Cabell Family Papers. For this argument, see Wirt, argument, 17/19 October 1807, in [Wirt], *Two Principal Arguments*, 104–208.

21. *Virginia Argus* (Richmond), 26 August 1807.

22. Return J. Meigs Jr. to Sophia Meigs, 11 August 1807, InU: Meigs Manuscripts.

23. Wirt, argument, 25 August 1807, in [Wirt], *Two Principal Arguments*, 61, 63.

24. Burr, cross-examination, 19 August 1807, in *RTCAB*, 1:521. One rejected juror from Wood County had said that he thought that Burr "had seduced Blennerhasset into some acts that were not right" (Thomas Creel, comments, 10 August 1807, in ibid., 372).

25. Dudley Woodbridge Jr., testimony, 19 August 1807, in ibid., 521, 523.

26. Harris, *Journal of a Tour*, 125.
27. [Morgan Neville], "A letter from one of the young gentlemen who lately left this town," *Pittsburgh Gazette* (Pa.), 13 January 1807. Blennerhassett's own description of the island was very similar to Wirt's. In December 1805, Blennerhassett had described his home and lands for John Devereux, an Irish exile in Baltimore whom he hoped would show his letter to potential buyers; see Harman Blennerhassett to John Devereux, 15 December 1805, in *BP*, 112–15. There is no evidence that Wirt saw this description.
28. [Cruse], "Biographical Sketch of William Wirt," in Wirt, *Letters of the British Spy*, 86. For Rodney's questions, see Caesar A. Rodney, "Interrogatories," [ca. 6 April 1807], DLC: Burr Conspiracy Collection.
29. Wirt, argument, 25 August 1807, in [Wirt], *Two Principal Arguments*, 62. In his journal, Blennerhassett recorded only two visits to the courtroom before 25 August, and Wirt may not have been there for one of them; see Blennerhassett, diary entries, 10 and 22 August 1807, in *BwB*, 16, 44–45. In 1800, legal matters and business affairs had brought Blennerhassett to Richmond, but Wirt did not live in the capital at that time, and there is no reason to think that they met.
30. Dudley Woodbridge Jr. to William Woodbridge, 23/25 August 1807, MiD-B: Woodbridge Papers.
31. Kennedy, *Memoirs of the Life of William Wirt*, 1:186.
32. Charles Fenton Mercer, deposition, 21 September 1807, in *ASP: Misc*, 1:596–97. Mercer found no evidence that Blennerhassett had been tempted away from this life "to carry fire and sword to the peaceful habitations of men who [had] never done him wrong."
33. John F. May to Thomas Ruffin, 13 December 1807, in Hamilton, ed., *Papers of Thomas Ruffin*, 1:115. May and Ruffin had been law students together in the office of David Robertson, one of the stenographers at Burr's trial; see Scott, *Memoirs of Lieut.-General Scott*, 1:11n. Burr's son-in-law, Joseph Alston, was not impressed. According to Blennerhassett, Alston "found Wirt . . . monotonous, with bad or no action" (Blennerhassett, diary entry, 26 August 1807, in *BwB*, 59).
34. Review of *A Discourse on the Life and Character of Wm. Wirt*, 17. General Winfield Scott, a young lawyer in 1807, remembered Wirt's speech more than fifty years later; see Scott, *Memoirs of Lieut.-General Scott*, 1:14–15.
35. For the initial publication, see *Enquirer* (Richmond, Va.), 26 September 1807; and *Petersburg Intelligencer* (Va.), 29 September 1807. For the spread of the "Who is Blennerhassett?" passage, see, for example, *New-York Evening Post*, 3 October 1807; *Raleigh Register and North Carolina State Gazette*, 8 October 1807; *Commonwealth* (Pittsburgh, Pa.), 4 November 1807; *Mississippi Messenger* (Natchez), 12 November 1807; and *Louisiana Gazette* (New Orleans), 20 November 1807.
36. "Advertisement," in [Wirt], *Two Principal Arguments*, [iii]. For the other 1808 versions, see *TCAB*, 2:283–86; and *RTCAB*, 2:96–98.

37. Coombs, *Trial of Aaron Burr for High Treason*, iii. For Wirt's speech, see ibid., 249–51.

38. "Oratory—Once More," *Daily National Intelligencer* (Washington, D.C.), 6 November 1838 (from NCUN). For just seventy-five cents, one could have been entertained by both a "stupendous Giraffe" in the afternoon and Bronson's recitation in the evening. For collections that included Wirt's speech, see Cooke, *American Orator*, 258–62; Carpenter, *Select American Speeches*, 2:279–357; Williston, comp., *Eloquence of the United States*, 4:394–417; Moore, ed., *American Eloquence*, 2:461–69; Brewer, ed., *World's Best Orations*, 10:3908–10; McClure and Andrews, eds., *Famous American Statesmen and Orators*, 2:278–307; and Reed, ed., *Political Oratory*, 5:2135–40. Richard Beale Davis mentioned the William Wirt societies in *Intellectual Life in Jefferson's Virginia*, 385, 475n86.

39. Taylor, *Victim of Intrigue*, 70.

40. "Story of Blannerhassett," 461. For similar comments, see the brief biographies of Luther Martin and William Wirt by Ashley Mulgrave Gould and John Handy Hall, respectively, in Lewis, ed., *Great American Lawyers*, 2:27 and 284.

41. Todd, "Blennerhassett and His Island," 236. The muckraker Ida Tarbell had said essentially the same thing five years earlier in "The Trial of Aaron Burr," 410. At the Eaton Family and Day School's annual exhibition in South Norridgewock, Maine, in 1870, for example, Charles H. Lowe declaimed "Blennerhassett's Temptations" ("Letter from South Norridgewock," *Bangor Daily Whig & Courier* [Maine], 28 June 1870 [from NCUN]).

42. [Cruse], "Biographical Sketch of Wirt," in Wirt, *Letters of the British Spy*, 56. See Kennedy, *Memoirs of the Life of William Wirt*, 1:177–80.

43. "Intemperance," *Essex Register* (Salem, Mass.), 25 January 1827, clipped from *Providence Literary Cadet* (R.I.) (from AHN).

44. Charles Willson Peale, diary entry, 15 December 1818, in Miller, ed., *Selected Papers of Charles Willson Peale and His Family*, 3:640. For Watterston's work, see [Watterston], *Letters from Washington*, 63–65. In a similar book from 1834, William Sullivan included a long extract as an example of Wirt's eloquence; see [Sullivan], *Familiar Letters on Public Characters*, 197–98.

45. Blennerhassett, diary entries, 26 August, 30 September, and 3 October 1807, in *BwB*, 58, 114, 120. Another handwritten copy of the "Who is Blennerhassett?" passage can be found on loose sheets among Blennerhassett's papers; see DLC: Harman Blennerhassett Papers.

46. Blennerhassett, diary entries, 29 August, 30 September, 4 October, and 18 November 1807, in *BwB*, 65, 114, 121, 168. For other early descriptions of Burr, see Blennerhassett, diary entries, 6 and 23 August 1807, in ibid., 9, 48.

47. Blennerhassett, diary entries, 18 and 25 August, 10 November, and 10 October 1807, in ibid., 36, 55, 54, 159, 126. Blennerhassett did not actually believe that Alston was the author of the pamphlet, considering it far more likely that his wife, Theodosia, had written it. "To suppose Alston the author wd. be preposterous," he remarked. "Obscurity may consistently veil the parentage of Hercules;

but it wd. be ridiculous to suppose him the offspring of a Dwarf" (Blennerhassett, diary entry, 17 August 1807, in ibid., 34). Blennerhassett viewed himself as equally cunning in his handling of the Philadelphia newspaper editor William Duane; see Blennerhassett, diary entries, 23 August and 12 November 1807, in ibid., 51–52, 163–64.

48. Blennerhassett, diary entries, 29 August, 12 November, and 27 August 1807, in ibid., 63, 165, 60–61. Blennerhassett recorded this exchange with Alston on 27 August but described it as having taken place earlier. In 1811, he informed Alston that he was willing to meet him on the dueling ground; see Blennerhassett to Joseph Alston, 2 March 1811, in BP, 537. In 1817, he brought a dispute with New Orleans merchant Vincent Nolte to the verge of a duel by calling him "an impertinent Puppy, Cheat, and Liar" and naming a place where they could meet (Blennerhassett to Vincent Nolte, 21 July 1817, DLC: Blennerhassett Papers). And, the next year, Blennerhassett and his oldest son were charged with assault with intent to kill for beating a neighbor in Port Gibson, Mississippi; see Boswell, "La Cache," 320–23.

49. Blennerhassett, diary entries, 4 October and 30 September 1807, in BwB, 121, 114. The diary's editor suggests the St. George analogy; see Raymond E. Fitch, "Introduction: 'The Fascination of this Serpent,'" in ibid., xlix.

50. Blennerhassett, diary entries, 27 October and 10 November 1807, in ibid., 141, 160.

51. Blennerhassett, diary entries, 7, 13, 14, and 23 August 1807, in ibid., 11, 21–22, 24–25, 50. On 23 August, Blennerhassett noted: "I have again laid by my brief which I shall not probably soon resume" (Blennerhassett, diary entry, 23 August 1807, in ibid., 52). He does not appear to have added much after that date. Burr's reply was not quite as unfeeling as Blennerhassett's paraphrasing suggests; see Aaron Burr to Blennerhassett, 14 August 1807, in BP, 281.

52. Blennerhassett, "Brief on behalf of Harman Blennerhassett, confined in the Penitentiary at Richmond, Va., under an indictment for high treason," [7–23 August 1807], in ibid., 188–94.

53. Ibid., 189, 195, 197.

54. Blennerhassett to Joseph Alston, 2 March 1811, in BP, 536. See also Blennerhassett to Burr, 16 April 1813, in ibid., 551. For the Alstons' view of this maneuver, see Theodosia Burr Alston to Burr, 10 May 1811, in PJAB-D, 2:161. Blennerhassett seems to have attempted to use his knowledge of the Burr Conspiracy, and possibly his papers, to leverage funds out of Andrew Jackson, as well; see Jonathan Thompson to Andrew Jackson, 3 July 1812, in PAJ, 2:309.

55. Blennerhassett to E. S. Thomas, 19 November 1814, in Thomas, Reminiscences of the Last Sixty-Five Years, 2:72. Thomas, the editor of a Charleston newspaper, had been charged with libel by Alston.

56. For Davis's use of the journal, see MAB, 2:393–99. Harman Blennerhassett Jr. worked with William Wallace to publish the brief and some letters in August 1845 as "Biographical Sketch of Harman Blennerhassett." In 1850, William H.

Safford reprinted that material in his *Life of Harman Blennerhassett*. In the late 1850s, Safford began working with Joseph Lewis Blennerhassett (the youngest of Harman and Margaret's sons) and Theresa M. Blennerhassett (the widow of Joseph's cousin) to make public more complete versions of the correspondence and journal, as well as the brief, in *The Blennerhassett Papers* (1864). During these decades, Harman Jr., Joseph Lewis, and Theresa wrote separate manuscripts, based upon the papers, none of which was published. Ultimately, the papers, buttressed by various letters and manuscripts from Harman's family and descendants, were sold to the Library of Congress in 1900. I discuss the post-1807 history of the papers in "'Bring Them *to Light*.'"

57. "Burr and Blennerhassett," *Daily National Intelligencer*, 14 April 1845 (from NCUN). See also "'Who then is Blennerhasset,'" *Watch-Tower* (Cooperstown, N.Y.), 3 May 1830 (from AHN).

58. "Island Paradise," 222. See also Thomas, *Emigrant*, 45; and Lossing, "Burr's Conspiracy," 71.

59. [Warren Isham], "Letters from the Senior Editor, No. 23," *Ohio Observer* (Hudson), 16 November 1833 (from NCUN); Green, "Blennerhassetts," 410. Wirt did not use the phrase "in an evil hour," but it certainly fit his imagery. An old idiom, it was perhaps most famously used by John Milton in *Paradise Lost* (1667) to describe the moment when Eve bit into the apple: "So saying, her rash hand in evil hour / Forth reaching to the Fruit, she pluck'd, she eat" (9.780–81). The association of this phrase with Blennerhassett Island probably began, at least in print, with Melish, *Travels in the United States of America*, 2:110.

60. *Daily Atlas* (Boston), 23 June 1842, clipped from *Newark Daily Advertiser* (N.J.) (from NCUN).

61. "Obituary," *Daily National Intelligencer*, 20 January 1853 (from NCUN).

62. "An Aged Woman Gone," *Salt Lake Semi-Weekly Tribune* (Utah), 18 November 1898 (from NCUN). While a prominent Burrite in terms of New York politics, John Swartwout had rarely been linked to the conspiracy.

63. "Blennerhassett Island," *Cleveland Daily Herald* (Ohio), 19 August 1874, clipped from *Cincinnati Commercial* (Ohio) (from NCUN).

64. "Blennerhassett's Island," *North American and United States Gazette* (Philadelphia), 24 July 1871, clipped from *Cincinnati Commercial* (from NCUN); "Blanherhasset," *Richmond Enquirer* (Va.), 5 December 1833 (from AHN); [Isham], "Letters from the Senior Editor, No. 23," *Ohio Observer*, 16 November 1833 (from NCUN).

65. *Essex Register*, 25 January 1827 (from AHN).

66. Steele, *Summer Journey in the West*, 253.

67. Horace Holley to Mary Austin Holley, 21 May 1818, MiU-C: Horace Holley Papers.

68. Hall, *Letters from the West*, 106–7.

69. Lambert, *Travels*, 3:204–5.

70. Bennett, *Traitor*, 11, 15, 13. See also "Citizen," *Conspiracy*.

71. Bynner, *Zachary Phips*, 59.
72. Pidgin, *Blennerhassett*, iii, 67. For scholarly discussions of the dramatic and literary works about Burr and Blennerhassett, see Lowther, *Blennerhassett Island in Romance and Tragedy*; Nolan, *Aaron Burr and the American Literary Imagination*; and Hamilton, "Villains and Cultural Change," 231–93. For a recent literary reading of the Burr phenomenon, see Drexler and White, *Traumatic Colonel*.
73. Hildreth, *History of the United States of America*, 2:597, 596.
74. Victor, *History of American Conspiracies*, 276.
75. Adams, *History of the United States of America*, 1:779.
76. [Hildreth], "Biographical Sketch of Herman Blennerhassett," 374. Hildreth revised this article in his 1852 book *Biographical and Historical Memoirs*, 491–528. Some of the fruits of his research into the Blennerhassetts can be found in OHi: Samuel P. Hildreth Papers. For Safford's quotations from Wirt, see *Life of Harman Blennerhassett*, 67–70; and *BP*, 126–27.
77. Randall, "Blennerhassett," 144, 146.
78. Brackenridge, *Recollections of Persons and Places*, 181–82. Thirty years later, the publication of the Blennerhassett papers confirmed that the couple wanted to leave the island and saw Burr as a way to do so; see Blennerhassett to Devereux, 15 December 1805, in *BP*, 112–15. See also Blennerhassett to Dudley Woodbridge Jr., 23 December 1805, OHi: Backus-Woodbridge Collection.
79. Taylor, *Victim of Intrigue*, 70.
80. [Pickett], *Arrest of Aaron Burr in Alabama*, 6. See also Pickett, *History of Alabama*, 2:231.
81. "Story of Blannerhassett," 461. Other mid-century articles with long extracts from Wirt include Clark, "Blennerhassett and Aaron Burr," 68; and Watkins, "Blennerhassett's Island," 97–99.
82. Indictment, 17 August 1807, in *RTCAB*, 1:430. This phraseology had entered American courts from English legal proceedings. It was not peculiar to this case.
83. Edward Bates to Richard Bates, 18 September 1807, ViHi: Edward Bates Papers.
84. Elizabeth Drinker, diary entry, 7 September 1807, in Crane, ed., *Diary of Elizabeth Drinker*, 3:2073.
85. Wirt, argument, 25 August 1807, in [Wirt], *Two Principal Arguments*, 62. For the cultural significance of the "vine and fig tree" image, see Brown, "Eighteenth-Century Virginia Plantation Gardens"; and Dreisbach, "'Vine and Fig Tree' in George Washington's Letters." The roots of this cultural construct reach back to republican Greece and Rome. For its use in literature that would have been familiar to part of Wirt's audience, see Williams, *Country and the City*. See also Ackerman, *Villa*; Thornton, *Cultivating Gentlemen*; Schulz, *Paradise Preserved*; and Girouard, *Life in the English Country House*. The literary critic John Seelye suggests that the Blennerhassetts were inspired by Gilbert Imlay's *The Emigrants* (1793); see Seelye, *Beautiful Machine*, 187–90. Imlay's novel presented the

American frontier as the ideal place for a life of romantic sentiment; see, in particular, Cayton, *Love in the Time of Revolution*.

86. Thomas Rodney to Caesar A. Rodney, 30 December 1806, DLC: Rodney Family Papers. For Judge Rodney's encounter with the "wild and excentric" Blennerhassett and his "inchanted island," see Thomas Rodney, diary entry, 24 September 1803, in Smith and Swick, eds., *Journey through the West*, 72.

87. St. George Tucker to Joseph C. Cabell, 13 August 1807, ViU: Bryan Family Papers.

88. Mercer, deposition, 21 September 1807, in *ASP: Misc*, 1:597. Wirt's account was malleable enough that, as the cultural power of the republican idyll faded over the nineteenth century, his image of Blennerhassett Island could be recast. Some late nineteenth-century writers likened the Blennerhassetts' home to an exotic locale, whether an aristocrat's "magnificent mansion," "an American Alhambra," or "one of the fabled palaces of Aladdin" (Randall, "Blennerhassett," 131; Abbey, "Blennerhassett Papers," 530; [Abbott], "'And Who Was Blennerhasset?,'" 352). Such terms suggested a similar refinement and retirement for a new era.

89. Royall Tyler, *Contrast*, in Kierner, *Contrast*, 60, 66. For Brother Jonathan, see Morgan, *American Icon*. As Morgan and others have shown, Tyler's Jonathan was based upon an existing character type.

90. [Hildreth], "Biographical Sketch of Herman Blennerhassett," 368. See also [Wallace], "Biographical Sketch of Harman Blennerhassett," 133–34; Safford, *Blennerhassett Papers*, 19–28; and [Abbott], "'And Who Was Blennerhasset?,'" 347. For Irish reformism and radicalism in the 1790s, see Curtin, *United Irishmen*. Blennerhassett's most careful biographer, Ray Swick, could find little evidence of his involvement with the United Irishmen but says that he "held its tenets close to his heart" (Swick, "Harman Blennerhassett," 33). David A. Wilson calls Blennerhassett "another leading United Irishmen" but says nothing about his role (Wilson, *United Irishmen, United States*, 61). Blennerhassett's name appeared on three of six surviving lists of United Irishmen that an informer provided in the early 1790s; see McDowell, "Personnel of the Dublin Society," 21. Most scholarly works on the United Irishmen do not mention him at all; none that I have seen reveal anything beyond his presence on the informer's lists.

91. [Abbott], "'And Who Was Blennerhasset?,'" 352. Novelist Eliza Ann Dupuy had her Margaret Blennerhassett character reading *Paradise Lost* when her husband announces that he is going to join the Burr character in *The Conspirator* (1850); see Nolan, *Aaron Burr and the American Literary Imagination*, 128.

92. Wirt, argument, 25 August 1807, in [Wirt], *Two Principal Arguments*, 65. At least two of the Blennerhassetts' neighbors—the Virginian Thomas Creel and the Ohioan Dudley Woodbridge Jr.—believed, however, that Burr had "misled" Harman "through the medium of [Margaret]" (Creel, comments, 10 August 1807, in *RTCAB*, 1:372). See also Dudley Woodbridge Jr. to William Woodbridge, 23/25 August 1807, MiD-B: Woodbridge Papers.

93. Hildreth, ed., "History of a Voyage," 93. See also Bay, *Reminiscences of the Bench and Bar of Missouri*, 82; [Abbott], "'And Who Was Blennerhasset?,'" 356–57; and [Edward Mansfield], "Mrs. Blennerhassett," *Toledo Blade* (Ohio), 20 August 1850, clipped from *Cincinnati Chronicle* (Ohio).

94. See Safford, *Life of Harman Blennerhassett*, 61; Parton, *Life and Times of Aaron Burr*, 389; Adams, *History of the United States of America*, 1:755; and Abernethy, *Burr Conspiracy*, 27. For similar discussions, see also Bradley, "Harman Blennerhassett," 103; Rice, "Burr's Western Expedition," 732; and Gibbens, *Historic Blennerhassett Island Home*, 20. Burr's reputation as a womanizer fueled another intriguing factual error in accounts of his first visit to the island. His travelling companion, Gabriel Shaw, was frequently described as a woman. This error probably derived from a simple transcription mistake ("Mrs." for "Mr.") in the initial publication of Blennerhassett's brief. It was repeated again and again, even though it conflicted with the earlier account in *MAB*.

95. Hildreth, *History of the United States of America*, 2:596–97.

96. D. C. Wallace to Hildreth, 31 August 1846, OHi: Hildreth Papers. An 1850 newspaper article described Margaret as "at best but an 'accomplished courtezan'" and asserted that she was "indebted to [Wirt's speech] for much of the romance, and all the purity of her character" ([Mansfield], "Mrs. Blennerhassett," *Toledo Blade*, 20 August 1850, clipped from *Cincinnati Chronicle*). For Mansfield's authorship of this piece, see "Mrs. Blennerhassett," 166. This piece was widely circulated and quickly disputed; see William H. Safford to Hildreth, 8 October 1850, OMC: Samuel P. Hildreth Collection. Curiously, in his later published memoirs, Edward Mansfield had only positive things to say about Margaret; see Edward Mansfield, *Personal Memories*, 8. Another round of assailing and defending Margaret's reputation in the press followed in 1859; see Swick, "Harman Blennerhassett," 293–94.

97. Benjamin Botts, argument, 25 August 1807, in *RTCAB*, 2:123–24.

98. [Pidgin], "Opening Address," 8. That this allegation made it into literary accounts is clear from *Amorous Intrigues and Adventures of Aaron Burr*, 97–100.

99. Blennerhassett-Adams, "True Story of Harman Blennerhassett," 354. "The bowers of Eden" is Blennerhassett-Adams's condensation and reordering of Wirt's "such was the state of Eden, when the serpent entered its bowers."

100. *OED Online*, December 2016 ed., s.v. "bower," nn. 3 and 2b.

101. Cooke, *American Orator*, 20, 22. For an earlier manual, see *Forum Orator*. For oratorical education, see Wallace, ed., *History of Speech Education*; and Clark and Halloran, eds., *Oratorical Culture in Nineteenth-Century America*. In recent years, literary critics, rhetoricians, and historians have analyzed the cultural power of oratorical performance and the spoken word in the early republic at length; see, in particular, Gustafson, *Eloquence Is Power*; Warren, *Culture of Eloquence*; Fliegelman, *Declaring Independence*; Cmiel, *Democratic Eloquence*; and Eastman, *Nation of Speechifiers*.

102. Wirt, *Letters of the British Spy*, 132–33.

103. "Y" [Wirt], "The Rainbow, Series 2d., No. II—On Forensic Eloquence," *Enquirer*, 10 November 1804. Whether Wirt wrote all of the "Rainbow" essays is unclear, but he certainly contributed this one. For a thorough discussion of Wirt's writings on oratory, see Hample, "William Wirt's Familiar Essays."

104. Gilmer, *Sketches of American Orators*, 36.

105. Southard, *Discourse on the Professional Character and Virtues*, 28–29.

106. May to Ruffin, 13 December 1807, in Hamilton, ed., *Papers of Thomas Ruffin*, 1:115.

107. Wirt to Edwards, 26 December 1807, ICHi: Edwards Papers.

108. Wirt to Edwards, 2 February 1807, ibid.

109. Wirt to Edwards, 26 December 1807, ibid.

110. "Burr's Case," *New-York Evening Post*, 3 October 1807. One Richmond newspaper assigned most of the attorneys in Burr's trial the names of leading British orators, including Curran for Wirt; see "The following sketch is communicated by one of our correspondents, a great ANATEUR of the Drama," *Virginia Argus*, 14 October 1807. For nationalist concerns about American cultural contributions, see, among other works, Ellis, *After the Revolution*; Robert A. Ferguson, "The American Enlightenment, 1750–1820," and Michael T. Gilmore, "The Literature of the Revolutionary and Early National Periods," in Bercovitch and Patell, eds., *Cambridge History of American Literature*, 1:345–537 and 539–693; and Haynes, *Unfinished Revolution*, 51–76.

111. Glover to Brown, 29/30 May 1807, OHi: Brown Papers. See also William H. Cabell to Joseph C. Cabell, 12 April 1807, ViU: Cabell Family Papers.

112. Moore, "William Wirt," 31–32; "Thomas Jefferson," 372.

113. Review of *The Life of Harman Blennerhassett*, 321.

114. Mann Butler, "Fifth Lecture," [1844], ICU: Reuben T. Durrett Collection, Mann Butler Papers.

115. Hall, *Letters from the West*, 95.

CHAPTER 10. THE CONFLICT OVER BURR'S FOLLOWERS

1. Caesar A. Rodney to James Madison, [4 April 1809], in *PJM: PS*, 1:99.

2. James Wilkinson to Thomas Jefferson, 12 November 1806, in Wilkinson, *Memoirs of My Own Times*, 2:Appendix 100.

3. Brief biographies of most of these men can be gleaned from the major works on the conspiracy and on Burr; see, in particular, McCaleb, *Aaron Burr Conspiracy*; Abernethy, *Burr Conspiracy*; Lomask, *Aaron Burr*; Isenberg, *Fallen Founder*; and Stewart, *American Emperor*.

4. Estimates of the size and composition of Burr's force at Bayou Pierre varied widely, even from those who visited the encampment. One officer counted "about fifty five or sixt men[,] some women & children[,] & a few negroes"; another source reported a force that did "not exceed 100 men and they [were] not

all armed"; and militia colonel Ferdinand L. Claiborne saw "about 150 well armed men" (W. H. Wooldridge to Cowles Mead, 14 January 1807, in Rowland, *Third Annual Report*, 54; Thomas Fitzpatrick to Mead, 15 January 1807, in ibid., 61; Ferdinand L. Claiborne to Mead, 16 January 1807, in ibid., 62). The numbers elsewhere are even harder to estimate. But, at Beaver, Pennsylvania, alone, the Irish surveyor Daniel Constable saw "5 or 6 hundred" men under Comfort Tyler and Israel Smith; only a few dozen of them made it to Bayou Pierre (Daniel Constable, diary entry, 20 October 1806, in Jenkins, *Citizen Daniel*, 77). For published names, see, for example, the lists in "Extract of a letter from a gentleman in Meadville, Pennsylvania, to a member of Congress," *National Intelligencer, and Washington Advertiser* (D.C.), 22 December 1806; and [Ephraim Pentland], "Burr's Conspiracy," *Commonwealth* (Pittsburgh, Pa.), 24 December 1806.

5. [William Davis], *Norfolk Gazette and Public Ledger* (Va.), 29 December 1806. I discussed events in Kentucky in Chapter 2.

6. "From Washington," *Columbian Centinel* (Boston), 4 March 1807.

7. "Extract of a Letter," ibid., 23 February 1807.

8. [Stephen C. Carpenter], *People's Friend & Daily Advertiser* (New York), 16 January 1807.

9. [Pentland], "Burr's Conspiracy," *Commonwealth*, 24 December 1806. A Pittsburgh Republican explained the limited local reaction to Burr's preparations by noting that "the aristocrats [had] a majority in this town" ("Extract of a letter, dated, Pittsburgh," *Enquirer* [Richmond, Va.], 15 January 1807).

10. "Extract of a letter from a gentleman in Pittsburgh, Pen., to a member of Congress," *National Intelligencer*, 22 December 1806.

11. "Extract of a letter from a gentleman in Meadville, Pennsylvania, to a member of Congress," ibid., 22 December 1806. For Duane's charges, see, for example, [William Duane], "The Conspiracy," *Aurora General Advertiser* (Philadelphia), 3 December 1806; and ibid., 4 December 1806.

12. [Aaron Burr] to Wilkinson, [22–29 July 1806], in *PCAB*, 2:986–87 (I have standardized the font).

13. Alexander Hamilton, "Constitutional Convention. Remarks on the Ineligibility of Members of the House of Representatives for Other Offices," [22 June 1787], in Syrett and Cooke, eds., *Papers of Alexander Hamilton*, 4:216.

14. See Shakespeare's *1 Henry VI*, 5.3.3, and *Julius Caesar*, 3.1.163. For American thinking about Caesar and his assassins, see Richard, *Founders and the Classics*, 90–93.

15. Thomas Truxton, testimony, 18 August 1807, in *RTCAB*, 1:487.

16. Benjamin Stoddert, deposition, 9 October 1807, in Henshaw, ed., "Burr-Blennerhassett Documents," 8.

17. [John Park], "Some Further Particulars of Col. Burr's Treason," *Repertory* (Boston), 25 November 1806 (from AHN). See also William Eaton, deposition, 26 January 1807, in [Prentiss], *Life of the Late Gen. William Eaton*, 399. Burr seems

to have used similar terms in conversations that only became public much later, describing his followers as "young men of talents" and as "gentlemen of the first respectability" (Andrew Jackson to George Washington Campbell, 15 January 1807, in *PAJ*, 2:149; Biddle, *Autobiography of Charles Biddle*, 313).

18. Elias Glover, testimony, undated, in Henshaw, ed., "Burr-Blennerhassett Documents," 59; Glover, testimony, 18 June 1807, in "NECAB," 43.

19. Charles Fenton Mercer, deposition, 21 September 1807, in *TCAB*, 3:314.

20. "Ex Vice-President Burr," *Columbian Centinel*, 19 November 1806. "Much pith and moment" is from some versions of Shakespeare's *Hamlet*, 3.1.88.

21. "A Friend of the Union and of Truth," "Colonel Aaron Burr," *Enquirer*, 14 November 1806.

22. Eaton, testimony, 15 June 1807, in "NECAB," 13.

23. [Thomas Ritchie], *Enquirer*, 4 November 1806. At the time, the editor was looking for evidence to exonerate Burr and Kentucky Republicans from the *Western World*'s charges.

24. Jackson to James Winchester, 4 October 1806, in *PAJ*, 2:111.

25. Burr to Benjamin Henry Latrobe, 26 October 1806, in *CBHL*, 2:276. Eighteen months earlier, before he purchased a claim in the Bastrop grant, Burr had tried to interest Latrobe with an offer to direct the construction of a canal around the falls of the Ohio River; see Hamlin, *Benjamin Henry Latrobe*, 220–25; and Sprague, "Louisville Canal." Comfort Tyler had employed some of the same inducements with Daniel Constable, an Irish surveyor who was travelling in the United States; see Jenkins, *Citizen Daniel*, 72–80.

26. Jefferson, special message, 22 January 1807, in *CMPP*, 1:414.

27. Jefferson to Dupont de Nemours, 14 July 1807, in *WrTJ*, 11:276; Jefferson to Wilkinson, 3 February 1807, in ibid., 149.

28. Wilkinson to Jefferson, 21 October 1806, DLC: Burr Conspiracy Collection; Wilkinson to Jefferson, 9 December 1806, PHi: Daniel Parker Papers.

29. "Extract of a letter from a public character in Warren, Trumbull county and state of Ohio," *National Intelligencer*, 15 December 1806; "Pennsylvania," *Political Observatory* (Walpole, N.H.), 16 January 1807 (from AHN). According to the latter, a report from Beaver, Burr's men terrorized the local innkeepers, "danc[ing] on Tables, Bureaus, &c." "in the Rage of Intoxication."

30. Henry Dearborn to Jackson, 19 December 1806, in *PAJ*, 2:125. See also Dearborn to Constant Freeman, 20 December 1806, DNA: RG107, M6.

31. William Findley to John Hemphill, February 1807, NcD: Hemphill Family Papers; Campbell, circular letter to constituents, 25 February 1807, in *CLC*, 1:494.

32. Abraham Verdon and Lucas Hooghkerk to Jefferson, 21 February 1807, DLC: Thomas Jefferson Papers. At a similar meeting one month earlier (too early to have received Jefferson's message) and one county to the west, the Republicans of Herkimer, New York, had called Burr and his followers "daring and unprincipled spirits" (Westel Willoughby Jr. and John Nicholson to Jefferson, 26 January 1807, ibid.).

33. "Communication," *Enquirer*, 3 February 1807.
34. William Plumer, diary entry, 26 January 1807, in *WPMP*, 591. For another Federalist's use of this language, see James Hillhouse to Rebecca Hillhouse, 23 January 1807, CtY: Hillhouse Family Papers.
35. Jefferson, special message, 22 January 1807, in *CMPP*, 1:414.
36. [Thomas] Power to Stephen Minor, 6 February 1807, LU: Minor Family Papers. See also Augustus John Foster to Lady Elizabeth Foster, 31 March 1807, DLC: Augustus John Foster Papers.
37. [Ritchie], *Enquirer*, 4 November 1806.
38. "An Inhabitant of the I[ndiana] Territory," *Virginia Argus* (Richmond), 17 November 1807.
39. "One of the People" [Humphrey Marshall], *Western World* (Frankfort, Ky.), 7 November 1806.
40. "Extract of a letter from a gentleman in Meadville, Pennsylvania, to a member of Congress," *National Intelligencer*, 22 December 1806. See also Campbell, circular letter to constituents, 25 February 1807, in *CLC*, 1:494.
41. "A Jurisconsult," "Wilkinson and Burr," *Enquirer*, 15 May 1807; Jefferson to the Marquis de Lafayette, 26 May 1807, in *WoTJ*, 10:410.
42. "Union, No. 2," *Scioto Gazette* (Chillicothe, Ohio), 25 December 1806. Joseph Hamilton Daveiss similarly explained that Burr's followers were "men without fortune or expectation save from some revolution" (Joseph Hamilton Daveiss to Madison, 16 November 1806, in *View*, 28). For Wilkinson's fears, see Wilkinson to [Jefferson], 6 December 1806, DLC: Burr Conspiracy Collection.
43. Jefferson, special message, 22 January 1807, in *CMPP*, 1:414.
44. Jefferson, Proclamation, 27 November 1806, in ibid., 404. Cowles Mead, the acting governor of the Mississippi Territory, issued his own proclamation on the same grounds; see Mead, proclamation, 23 December 1806, in Rowland, *Third Annual Report*, 42. Both Jefferson and Mead believed that this tactic had succeeded in reducing Burr's support; see Jefferson to de Nemours, 14 July 1807, in *WrTJ*, 11:275–76; and Mead to Dearborn, 26 January 1807, in Rowland, *Third Annual Report*, 71. For the story of one self-acknowledged dupe, Pittsburgh's George Woolfrey, see [Thomas Spotswood Hinde], "The Western Expedition, No. III," *Fredonian* (Chillicothe, Ohio), 7 March 1807.
45. Martin D. Hardin to Mark Hardin, 2 January 1806 [*sic*, 1807], ICHi: Hardin Collection. See also "Extract of a letter from the Hon. Wm. Dickson, to a gentleman in the county," *Impartial Review, and Cumberland Repository* (Nashville, Tenn.), 17 January 1807.
46. Mead to Dearborn, 19 January 1807, in Rowland, *Third Annual Report*, 66.
47. William A. Burwell, circular letter to constituents, 2 March 1807, in *CLC*, 1:512.
48. Jefferson, special message, 22 January 1807, in *CMPP*, 1:414.
49. Jefferson to George Hay, 5 June 1807, in *WrTJ*, 11:218. See also Thomas Acheson to Samuel Smith, 13 February 1807, DNA: RG59, M418, filed under "Baird,

George"; Thomas T. Davis to Dearborn, 29 July 1807, DNA: RG107, M222, D-1807; and Walter Taylor to Jefferson, 16 September 1807, in "Correspondence of Thomas Jefferson," 100–101.

50. William Henry Harrison to Robert Williams, 3 April 1807, DLC: Jefferson Papers. Harrison was well positioned to comment upon this issue since Burr had tried to convince him that his plans had "been communicated to several of the principal officers of our Government," including "one high in the confidence of the administration" (Burr to Harrison, 27 November 1806, in *PCAB*, 2:1005); see also same to same, 24 October 1806, in ibid., 996.

51. Robert Williams to Madison, 23 February 1807, DLC: Burr Conspiracy Collection.

52. James McHenry to John Rhea, 5 November 1807, CtY: Burr Family Papers. See also Benjamin Henry Latrobe to Erick Bollmann [*sic*, Justus Erich Bollman], 23 August 1812, in *CBHL*, 3:368.

53. Plumer, diary entry, 29 November 1806, in *WPMP*, 517.

54. John Lewis to Gabriel Lewis, 9 December 1806, KyBgW: Lewis-Starling Collection; Timothy Pickering to Rebecca Pickering, 25 January 1807, MHi: Timothy Pickering Papers. For "address," see also William Fleming, diary entry, 17 September 1806, ViHi: Stanard Family Papers; and Augustus John Foster to Lady Elizabeth Foster, 29 December 1806, DLC: Foster Papers.

55. For the evolving definition of "fascinate," see *OED Online*, December 2016 ed.

56. Contemporary thinking about fascination and the fascinating power of rattlesnakes is discussed at length in Leventhal, *In the Shadow of the Enlightenment*, 137–67. See also Hutchins, "Rattlesnakes in the Garden." For Barton's critique, see his *Memoir Concerning the Fascinating Faculty which has been Ascribed to the Rattle-Snake*. Fifty years after Barton, belief in the power of fascination remained strong enough for John B. Newman to publish *Fascination* (1848).

57. John Quincy Adams to Thomas Boylston Adams, [1 April 1805], MHi: Adams Family Papers.

58. [George Adams], "Portrait of Burr," *Kentucky Gazette and General Advertiser* (Lexington), 17 September 1805, clipped from *Palladium* (Frankfort, Ky.). This intriguing document was reprinted in May 1807 in a popular Philadelphia magazine; see "Miscellany." When the archivist Dunbar Rowland reprinted it again in the early twentieth century, Burr's eyes glowed with "veneal" rather than "venereal" fire, though whether as the result of a simple transcription error or changed moral standards is unclear (George Adams, "Sketch of Aaron Burr," in Rowland, *Third Annual Report*, 170). For the importance of movement, deportment, and conversation to gentility, see Annas, "Elegant Art of Movement"; and Bushman, *Refinement of America*.

59. John Quincy Adams to Thomas Boylston Adams, [1 April 1805], MHi: Adams Family Papers. "Whether the original seducer of mankind has embodied himself in the person of the little *ex-vice*," Adams further noted, "I am not competent to pronounce."

60. "The Fredonian" [Hinde], "The aspect of affairs in the *Western country*, [No. I]," *Scioto Gazette*, 9 October 1806; [John Wood], "Colonel Aaron Burr," *Western World*, 13 September 1806.

61. [Wood], "Colonel Aaron Burr," *Western World*, 13 September 1806. "Enchant" and "charm" also carried implications of supernatural powers.

62. Taylor, *Victim of Intrigue*, 35; Bynner, *Zachary Phips*, 52; [Wallace], "Biographical Sketch of Harman Blennerhassett," 149.

63. [Wallace], "Biographical Sketch of Harman Blennerhassett," 149.

64. James Taylor, "Autobiography," ICU: Reuben T. Durrett Collection, Durrett Codices, 53. The abolitionist William Lloyd Garrison, who met the aged Burr in the early 1830s, recalled more than a quarter century later: "he had a remarkable eye, more penetrating, more fascinating than any I had ever seen" (William Lloyd Garrison, editorial, 8 January 1858, in Garrison and Garrison, *William Lloyd Garrison*, 276). For later discussions of Burr's powers of fascination, see Hamilton, "Villains and Cultural Change," 149–51, 215, and 258–61.

65. Benjamin Henry Latrobe to Jonathan Williams, 1 April 1807, in Jeffrey, ed., *Microfiche Edition of the Papers of Benjamin Henry Latrobe*.

66. Benjamin Henry Latrobe to Albert Gallatin, 19/28 November 1806, in *CBHL*, 2:294.

67. Benjamin Henry Latrobe to Jonathan Williams, 1 April 1807, in Jeffrey, ed., *Microfiche Edition of the Papers of Benjamin Henry Latrobe*.

68. George Clinton to DeWitt Clinton, 28 December 1806, NNC: DeWitt Clinton Papers. Clinton referred to New York state's version of "quiddism"—the supporters of Governor Morgan Lewis.

69. ["The Conspiracy, I"], *National Intelligencer*, 13 March 1807.

70. [Rodney], "Interrogatories," [ca. 6 April 1807], DLC: Burr Conspiracy Collection.

71. Daveiss to Madison, 16 November 1806, in *View*, 28.

72. "Extract of a letter from a gentleman in Pittsburgh, Pen., to a member of Congress," *National Intelligencer*, 22 December 1806; "Important Communication!," *Enquirer*, 7 October 1806.

73. Mead to Dearborn, 19 January 1807, in Rowland, *Third Annual Report*, 65.

74. *Tennessee Gazette, and Mero District Advertiser* (Nashville), 28 March 1807.

75. See Wiebe, *Opening of American Society*, 143–67. The "revolution in choices" shook established sources of religious, legal, familial, and cultural, as well as political, authority. See, for example, Ellis, *Jeffersonian Crisis*; Hatch, *Democratization of American Christianity*; Wood, *Radicalism of the American Revolution*; Cmiel, *Democratic Eloquence*, 23–93; and Boyer Lewis, *Elizabeth Patterson Bonaparte*, 192–220. In 1800, the median age was just over sixteen. For the frustrations experienced by young men in this era, see Kett, *Rites of Passage*, 11–61; and Rotundo, *American Manhood*, 56–74.

76. "The Western Country," *Charleston Courier* (S.C.), 28 October 1806. Mark Kann discusses bachelors and "other disorderly men" in this period in *Republic of Men*,

52–78. But his definition of bachelor encompasses far more than contemporaries would have. See also Chudacoff, *Age of the Bachelor*, 21–44; and McCurdy, *Citizen Bachelors*. For women's roles, see, in particular, Lewis, "Republican Wife."

77. Benjamin Henry Latrobe to Christian Ignatius Latrobe, 5 January 1807, in *CBHL*, 2:352.

78. [Wood], "Col. Burr's Conspiracy," *Atlantic World* (Washington, D.C.), 3 February 1807. Wood claimed to be reporting a conversation between Burr and Charles Lynch, who had sold Burr the stake in the Bastrop grant.

79. Benjamin Henry Latrobe to Gallatin, 19 November 1806, in *CBHL*, 2:292.

80. For class divisions in the early republic, see, among other works, Bushman, *Refinement of America*; Burke, *Conundrum of Class*, 1–52; and Huston, "American Revolutionaries." For the "few" and the "many," see, especially, the writings of the Massachusetts farmer William Manning in Merrill and Wilentz, eds., *Key of Liberty*. Political fears of mobs and aristocrats are discussed in Fischer, *Revolution of American Conservatism*; Kerber, *Federalists in Dissent*, 173–215; Appleby, *Capitalism and a New Social Order*, 70–78; Wood, *Radicalism of the American Revolution*; and Murrin, "Escaping Perfidious Albion."

81. [Carpenter], *People's Friend*, 14 January 1807. For private comments, see, for example, Thomas Boylston Adams to John Quincy Adams, 10 November 1802, quoted in Kerber, *Federalists in Dissent*, 177; and Jacob Bigelow Jr. to Jacob Bigelow, 16 April 1807, quoted in Fischer, *Revolution of American Conservatism*, 156.

82. "The Observer" [Marshall], *Western World*, 15 October 1806.

83. "Extract of a Letter," *Columbian Centinel*, 23 February 1807.

84. Wilkinson to Jefferson, 13 September 1807, DLC: Jefferson Papers. For the similar views of James Brown, another longtime Kentuckian who had recently moved to New Orleans, see Wilkinson to [Jefferson], 6 December 1806, DLC: Burr Conspiracy Collection.

85. A[nthony] Butler to Thomas Sumter, 14 August 1807, DLC: Thomas Sumter Papers.

86. Ninian Edwards to William Wirt, [5 January 1807], ICHi: Ninian Edwards Papers. For class-based political and social tensions in the trans-Appalachian West, see, for example, Cayton, *Frontier Republic*; Slaughter, *Whiskey Rebellion*; and Aron, *How the West Was Lost*.

87. Plumer, diary entry, 29 November 1806, in *WPMP*, 516.

88. Frederick Bates to Augustus B. Woodward, 3 December 1806, in Marshall, ed., *Life and Papers of Frederick Bates*, 1:87; "Tyler's Creek, Ken.," *Enquirer*, 27 December 1806.

89. [Pentland], "Burr's Conspiracy," *Commonwealth*, 24 December 1806.

90. Daniel Bissell to Dearborn, 13 January 1807, DNA: RG107, M221, B-190 (3). A published letter from western Virginia described one group of Burr's followers as "a number of young lawyers, physicians, etc." ("Extracts of letters from Wood

Court House, Virginia," *American, and Commercial Daily Advertiser* [Baltimore, Md.], 26 January 1807).

91. William Love, testimony, 19 August 1807, in *RTCAB*, 1:517; Hay, cross-examination of Love, 19 August 1807, in ibid.

92. Truxton to Thomas Tingey, 13 January 1807, DLC: Thomas Truxton Papers.

93. Thomas Morgan, testimony, 19 August 1807, in *RTCAB*, 1:506.

94. William Eaton, testimony, 15 June 1807, in "NECAB," 13. See also Truxton to Timothy Pickering, 13 January 1807, MHi: Pickering Papers; and Eaton, testimony, 26 September 1807, in *TCAB*, 3:233.

95. Stoddert, deposition, 9 October 1807, in Henshaw, ed., "Burr-Blennerhassett Documents," 8.

96. Benjamin Henry Latrobe to Philip Mazzei, 19 December 1806, in *CBHL*, 2:330–33.

97. *New Roman History*, 83–84.

98. Wilkinson to Dearborn, 17 February 1807, DNA: RG107, M221, W-244 (3).

99. Edmund P. Gaines to Jefferson, 21 July 1807, DLC: Jefferson Papers.

100. [John Binns], "Burr's Conspiracy," *Democratic Press* (Philadelphia), 27 March 1807 (from AHN).

101. [William Pechin], *American*, 1 September 1807.

102. [Duane], *Politics for American Farmers*, 25–27, 95, 86.

103. See, among many examples, *American*, 17 October and 9 November 1807; *Baltimore Evening Post* (Md.), 29 September, 24 October, and 30 November 1807; and *Virginia Argus*, 14 October 1807.

104. John Page to Jefferson, 25 July 1807, DLC: Jefferson Papers.

105. Wirt to Dabney Carr, 19 July 1807, in Kennedy, *Memoirs of the Life of William Wirt*, 1:198. For Blennerhassett, see Harman Blennerhassett, diary entry, 17 November 1807, in *BwB*, 167.

106. [Baptist Irvine], *Whig, or Political Telescope* (Baltimore, Md.), 17 November 1807. To a lesser extent, the same process occurred with "best blood" and "dull pursuits of civil life." See, for example, William T. Barry to John Barry, 27 January 1807, ViU: William T. Barry Letters; Freeman to unknown correspondent, 5 March 1807, DLC: Burr Conspiracy Collection; and John Sloane to Thomas Worthington, 6 August 1808, OHi: Thomas Worthington Papers.

107. For deference, see, in particular, Beeman, "Varieties of Deference."

108. [Ritchie], "Aaron Burr," *Enquirer*, 28 November 1807.

109. [Ritchie], "A parallel, drawn from Antiquity," ibid., 3 January 1807. Ritchie quoted book II of Sallust's *Conspiracy of Catiline*.

110. *MAB*, 2:56. For a recent, scholarly discussion, see Nancy Isenberg's "'Little Emperor'" and *Fallen Founder*.

111. "Important Communication!," *Western Spy* (Cincinnati, Ohio), 18 November 1806, clipped from *Farmer's Monitor* (Herkimer, N.Y.).

112. Henry Baldwin to unknown correspondent, 18 February 1808, DLC: Burr Conspiracy Collection. Though Baldwin was addressing reports of a renewal of

Burr's project, he explicitly stated that these recruitment practices echoed those of eighteen months earlier.

113. Silas Brown Jr. to Ephraim Brown, 26 October 1807, in [Harter, ed.], *Aaron Burr Expedition*, 15–20. By the summer of 1811, Brown was the chief clerk of the Bank of Mississippi in Natchez.

114. Marquis de Yrujo to Pedro Cevallos Guerra, 1 January 1806, printed in Adams, *History of the United States of America*, 1:767.

115. John Quincy Adams, "Notes on the cases of Aaron Burr and John Smith, with some other intrusive notes," [ca. December 1807], MHi: Adams Family Papers. Adams quoted *1 Henry IV*, 4.2.30. For Adams's own frustrations as a young lawyer, see East, *John Quincy Adams*.

116. John Adams to Jefferson, 21 December 1819, in Cappon, ed., *Adams-Jefferson Letters*, 2:551.

117. Hinde, "To the Editors," *Daily National Intelligencer* (Washington, D.C.), 12 October 1838. For Marshall, see Marshall, *History of Kentucky*, 2:372.

118. Hall, *Letters from the West*, 103–4.

119. [J.F.H. Claiborne], "Incidents of the Detention of Aaron Burr by the Civil Authorities of the Mississippi Territory," *Free Trader* (Natchez, Miss.), 17 November 1841, WHi: Draper Manuscript Collection, 26CC27. Claiborne quoted the testimony of George Poindexter, the territory's attorney general, from the final stage of Burr's trial in Richmond; see George Poindexter, testimony, 2 October 1807, in *RTCAB*, 3:289. Claiborne repeated this statement nearly forty years later in his *Mississippi, as a Province, Territory and State*, 1:282. For other mid-century descriptions, see Brackenridge, *Recollections of Persons and Places*, 103; and Safford, *Life of Harman Blennerhassett*, 110.

120. Hale, *Man without a Country*, 23–25.

121. Ibid., 23.

122. Hale, "Author's Note to Edition of 1897," in *Man without a Country*, 13. Robert A. Ferguson discusses the link between Hale's story and Burr at some length in *Trial in American Life*, 100–106. For Hale, see Holloway, *Edward Everett Hale*.

FOURTH INTERLUDE. A "RISING" IN BALTIMORE

1. Harman Blennerhassett, diary entry, 2 November 1807, in *BwB*, 148. For the men's residences, see Harman Blennerhassett, diary entry, 1 November 1807, in ibid., 147; "Grand Titularies," *Baltimore Evening Post* (Md.), 2 November 1807; and *American, and Commercial Daily Advertiser* (Baltimore, Md.), 3 November 1807. For the locations of Martin's home and William Evans's inn, see M'Henry, *Baltimore Directory*, 44, 82.

2. Luther Martin, "To the Citizens of Maryland," *Federal Gazette & Baltimore Daily Advertiser* (Md.), 2 November 1807.

3. Harman Blennerhassett, diary entries, 1 and 2 November 1807, in *BwB*, 147, 148. Tyler was not present, but two other "Burrites" were—John Cummins and C. F. Luckett. See also "Extract of a letter from a gentleman in Baltimore, to his friend in this City, dated November 4th, 1807," *Virginia Gazette, and General Advertiser* (Richmond), 13 November 1807.

4. "'Verbum Set,'" "An Earnest Proposal," *Whig, or Political Telescope* (Baltimore, Md.), 3 November 1807. The *Whig*'s editor later insisted that Martin was not included, but it is difficult to read it any other way; see [Baptist Irvine], "From the Whig," *Virginia Argus* (Richmond), 10 November 1807, clipped from *Whig*, 5 November 1807.

5. "Awful!!!," [3 November 1807], *Aurora General Advertiser* (Philadelphia), 7 November 1807. "Quid" probably referred to New York or Pennsylvania state politics.

6. Harman Blennerhassett, diary entry, 3 November 1807, in *BwB*, 150–52. Blennerhassett dined at his lodgings until mid-afternoon, before moving to safer quarters in the garret of his inn. For Martin's return to his home the next morning, see Harman Blennerhassett, diary entry, 4 November 1807, in ibid., 153. For the sequence of these events, see James Biays et al., "Report," *American*, 19 November 1807. The roles of Mayor Smith, other civil officials, and local militia officers in calling out the cavalry companies later emerged as an important and, thus, disputed issue. My account relies on Blennerhassett's diary and [John Hewes], "The Empire of the Laws!," *Federal Gazette*, 3 November 1807.

7. "VIVAT REPUBLICA" [Irvine], "Reward of Merit," *Virginia Argus*, 10 November 1807, clipped from *Whig*, 4 November 1807.

8. Ibid.; Harman Blennerhassett to Margaret Blennerhassett, 3 November 1807, in *BP*, 510.

9. Harman Blennerhassett, diary entry, 3 November 1807, in *BwB*, 152.

10. "Extract of a letter from Baltimore, Nov. 3 [*sic*, 4]," *New-York Gazette & General Advertiser*, 9 November 1807, clipped from *Political and Commercial Register* (Philadelphia) (from AHN). The letter's date is clearly erroneous; it refers to the burning of the effigies as having happened "yesterday."

11. "VIVAT REPUBLICA" [Irvine], "Reward of Merit," *Virginia Argus*, 10 November 1807, clipped from *Whig*, 4 November 1807. In addition to the quoted sources, I have drawn details in this paragraph from "Extract of a letter, addressed to the editor, dated Baltimore, November 4, 1807," *Washington Federalist* (Georgetown, D.C.), 7 November 1807; Nathaniel Saltonstall Jr. to Leverett Saltonstall, 8 November 1807, in Moody, ed., *Saltonstall Papers*, 2:406; and "Extract of a letter from a gentleman in Baltimore, to his friend in this City, dated November 4th, 1807," *Virginia Gazette*, 13 November 1807. The most thorough secondary account can be found in Steffen, *Mechanics of Baltimore*, 232–39. For the various forms of crowd action in this period, see Slaughter, "Crowds in Eighteenth-Century America"; Gilje, *Rioting in America*; and Gilje, "Crowd in American History."

12. Morris [*sic*, Maurice] B. Belknap to Timothy E. Danielson, 11 October 1806, excerpted in William Eaton to James Madison, 27 October 1806, DLC: Burr Conspiracy Collection.

13. Francis J. Dallam to Richard Dallam, 1 February 1807, MdHi: Dallam Papers. Three months earlier, Nashville's citizens had given Burr "a splendid Dinner" (Francis J. Dallam, diary entry, 27 September 1806, ibid.). Dallam's diary also provides the date of Burr's departure and describes the burning of his effigy; see 23 and 30 December 1806, ibid.

14. *Mirror* (Russellville, Ky.), 9 January 1807.

15. *National Intelligencer, and Washington Advertiser* (D.C.), 23 January 1807. In addition to the piece in the *Mirror* cited above, see also items in *Federal Gazette*, 28 January 1807; *Morning Chronicle* (New York), 29 January 1807; *City Gazette and Daily Advertiser* (Charleston, S.C.), 2 February 1807; *Enquirer* (Richmond, Va.), 3 February 1807; *Connecticut Courant* (Hartford), 11 February 1807 (from AHN); and *Farmer's Gazette* (Sparta, Ga.), 7 March 1807 (from AHN). For the original account, see "Communication," *Impartial Review, and Cumberland Repository* (Nashville, Tenn.), 3 January 1807. It was reprinted in *Enquirer*, 27 January 1807; and *Sun* (Pittsfield, Mass.), 14 February 1807 (from AHN).

16. [Elijah Pentland], *Commonwealth* (Pittsburgh, Pa.), 4 February 1807.

17. "The new Judiciary System," *Portland Gazette and Maine Advertiser* (Mass.), 9 February 1807 (from AHN).

18. Harman Blennerhassett, diary entry, 3 November 1807, in *BwB*, 153. For the treatment of Burr and his associates in Richmond, see Chapter 8. For Burr's stay in the District of Columbia, see Isaac A. Coles to William H. Cabell, undated, ViU: Cabell Family Papers; and *National Intelligencer*, 4 November 1807. For Blennerhassett and Martin's time there, see Harman Blennnerhassett, diary entry, 27 October 1807, in *BwB*, 139. The president, however, asked the attorney general if Burr, Blennerhassett, Swartwout, and Martin could be arrested while in the city; see Thomas Jefferson to Caesar A. Rodney, 28 October 1807, CSmH: Thomas Jefferson Papers. For Blennerhassett's untroubled stay in Philadelphia, see Harman Blennerhassett to Margaret Blennerhassett, 17 November 1807, in *BP*, 512.

19. John McDonogh [Sr.] to John McDonogh [Jr.], 30 March 1807, LNT-H: John McDonogh Papers.

20. William D. Martin, diary entry, 18 May 1809, in Elmore, ed., *Journal of William D. Martin*, 25.

21. "The Fast Day," *Kline's Weekly Carlisle Gazette* (Pa.), 7 August 1812, clipped from *Democratic Press* (Philadelphia) (from AHN). For politics and society in early national Baltimore, see Cassell, "Structure of Baltimore's Politics"; Ridgway, *Community Leadership in Maryland*, 71–95; Browne, *Baltimore in the Nation*, 17–60; Steffen, *Mechanics of Baltimore*; and Rockman, *Scraping By*. For the events of 1812, see Cassell, "Great Baltimore Riot"; Hickey, "Darker Side of Democracy"; Gilje, "Baltimore Riots of 1812"; and Gilje, "'Le Menu Peuple' in America." For

incidents after 1812 that sustained Baltimore's reputation as "mobtown," see Melton, *Hanging Henry Gambrill*; and Shalhope, *Baltimore Bank Riot*.

22. Harman Blennerhassett, diary entry, 3 November 1807, in *BwB*, 153. For the Whig Club's sponsorship, see "Prospectus of THE WHIG," *Whig*, 3 November 1807. Irvine would later emerge as a prominent advocate of Spanish American revolution and would be sent as a special agent to Venezuela in 1818; see Hanke, "Baptis Irvine's Reports," 360–63.

23. I have not been able to find copies of the *Weekly Register of Politics and News*, but part of its second issue was reprinted in the *Republican Watch-Tower* (New York), 8 December 1807. Its successor began in mid-January. In its first issue, Colvin stated that he had published three issues of the periodical; see [Colvin], editorial, 16. A fifth newspaper, the *Baltimore Weekly Price-Current*, confined itself to commercial matters.

24. Harman Blennerhassett, diary entry, 3 November 1807, in *BwB*, 150–53. See also Harman Blennerhassett to Margaret Blennerhassett, 3 November 1807, in *BP*, 510. Even though this incident preceded by just two days the greatest annual occasion for "riot" in Anglo-American political culture, Guy Fawkes Day, I have seen no evidence that anyone connected the two events or that Baltimoreans usually commemorated that day.

25. Harman Blennerhassett to Margaret Blennerhassett, 17 November 1807, in *BP*, 512.

26. [William Pechin], *American*, 4 November 1807.

27. "VIVAT REPUBLICA" [Irvine], "Reward of Merit," *Virginia Argus*, 10 November 1807, clipped from *Whig*, 4 November 1807. Unfortunately, I have found no issues of the *Whig* between 4 and 8 November. But the few pieces that were reprinted elsewhere suggest the tone of Irvine's discussions in the missing issues.

28. [Hewes], "The Empire of the Laws!," *Federal Gazette*, 3 November 1807.

29. Luther Martin to Hewes, ibid., 4 November 1807.

30. Hewes, comments on ibid. For the Federalist letters, see "Extract of a letter, addressed to the editor, dated Baltimore, November 4, 1807," *Washington Federalist*, 7 November 1807; "Extract of a letter from Baltimore, Nov. 3 [*sic*, 4]," *New-York Gazette*, 9 November 1807, clipped from *Political and Commercial Register* (from AHN); and "Extract of a letter from a gentleman in Baltimore, to his friend in this City, dated November 4th, 1807," *Virginia Gazette*, 13 November 1807. For the account in the *Evening Post*, see [Hezekiah Niles and Leonard Frailey], *Baltimore Evening Post*, 4 November 1807.

31. [Hewes], comments on Luther Martin to Hewes, *Federal Gazette*, 4 November 1807.

32. "Extract of a letter from a gentleman in Baltimore, to his friend in this City, November 4th, 1807," *Virginia Gazette*, 13 November 1807.

33. "VIVAT REPUBLICA" [Irvine], "Reward of Merit," *Virginia Argus*, 10 November 1807, clipped from *Whig*, 4 November 1807. According to one Federalist

account, those hostile to the procession had "hoot[ed] and hiss[ed]" as it passed ("Extract of a letter from a gentleman in Baltimore, to his friend in this City, November 4th, 1807," *Virginia Gazette*, 13 November 1807).

34. [Irvine], "From the Whig," *Virginia Argus*, 10 November 1807, clipped from *Whig*, 5 November 1807. The *Evening Post* agreed that the burning of the effigies had been applauded by "a great multitude of people," without trying to say who they were ([Niles and Frailey], *Baltimore Evening Post*, 4 November 1807).

35. Nathaniel Saltonstall Jr. to Leverett Saltonstall, 8 November 1807, in Moody, ed., *Saltonstall Papers*, 2:406. For the residences of six of the men, see M'Henry, *Baltimore Directory*, 19, 62, 76, 91, 95, 98. Neither Irvine nor William Conklin appeared in the directory, but Irvine probably lived near the *Whig* office on Gay Street, and Conklin was a member of a Fell's Point volunteer company; see Steffen, *Mechanics of Baltimore*, 237.

36. [Harry Croswell], "Mobbing," *Balance, and Columbian Repository* (Hudson, N.Y.), 24 November 1807.

37. "Extract of a letter from a gentleman in Baltimore, to his friend in this City, November 4th, 1807," *Virginia Gazette*, 13 November 1807.

38. Luther Martin to Hewes, *Federal Gazette*, 4 November 1807.

39. "VIVAT REPUBLICA" [Irvine], "Reward of Merit," *Virginia Argus*, 10 November 1807, clipped from *Whig*, 4 November 1807. Similarly, the handbill that announced the executions had invoked "the unanimous voice of every honest man in the community" ("Awful!!!," [3 November 1807], *Aurora*, 7 November 1807).

40. [Niles and Frailey], *Baltimore Evening Post*, 4 November 1807. Using the passive voice also made it unnecessary to identify the active agents: "after being paraded through the principal streets," the effigies "were hung, and afterwards burnt."

41. "Communication," *Impartial Review*, 3 January 1807; Francis J. Dallam to Richard Dallam, 1 February 1807, MdHi: Dallam Papers. In contrast, the Federalist Maurice B. Belknap separated the "mad rabble" who had threatened to mob Alston and tar and feather Burr in Marietta from "the steady part of the community" who "would soon put a stop to such proceedings" (Belknap to Danielson, 11 October 1806, excerpted in Eaton to Madison, 27 October 1806, DLC: Burr Conspiracy Collection).

42. [Hewes], "The Empire of the Laws!," *Federal Gazette*, 3 November 1807.

43. Luther Martin to Hewes, ibid., 4 November 1807.

44. "Extract of a letter, addressed to the editor, dated Baltimore, November 4, 1807," *Washington Federalist*, 7 November 1807.

45. "Extract of a letter from Baltimore, Nov. 3 [*sic*, 4]," *New-York Gazette*, 9 November 1807, clipped from *Political and Commercial Register* (from AHN).

46. [Niles and Frailey], *Baltimore Evening Post*, 4 November 1807.

47. [Pechin], *American*, 4 November 1807.

48. "VIVAT REPUBLICA" [Irvine], "Reward of Merit," *Virginia Argus*, 10 November 1807, clipped from *Whig*, 4 November 1807.

49. [Irvine], "From the Whig," *Public Advertiser* (New York), 6 November 1807, clipped from *Whig*, 4 November 1807 (from AHN).

50. [William Coleman], "Riot in Baltimore," *New-York Evening Post*, 7 November 1807; [Enos Bronson], "Baltimore Riot," *United States' Gazette*, 11 November 1807. For "mob," see, for example, [Coleman], "Baltimore Mob," *New York Herald*, 11 November 1807 (from AHN); [Croswell], "The Judiciary," *Balance*, 17 November 1807; and [Benjamin Russell], "The Odds," *Columbian Centinel* (Boston), 18 November 1807.

51. *New-York Commercial Advertiser*, 9 November 1807 (from AHN); *New-York Evening Post*, 13 November 1807; *Newburyport Herald* (Mass.), 24 November 1807 (from AHN).

52. [Zachariah Lewis], *New-York Spectator*, 11 November 1807 (from AHN); [Coleman], "Riot in Baltimore," *New-York Evening Post*, 7 November 1807.

53. [Coleman], "Baltimore Mob," *New-York Evening Post*, 9 November 1807.

54. [Jonathan S. Findlay], *Washington Federalist*, 7 November 1807. See also [Lewis], *New-York Spectator*, 11 November 1807 (from AHN).

55. [James Cheetham], *American Citizen* (New York), 9 November 1807. For another Republican newspaper that was willing to use the word "mob" for this incident, see *Political Observatory* (Walpole, N.H.), 16 November 1807 (from AHN).

56. [Bronson], "Baltimore Riot," *United States' Gazette*, 11 November 1807; [Croswell], *Balance*, 17 November 1807. See also [Hewes], *Federal Gazette*, 12 November 1807.

57. [Benjamin Parks], *Democrat* (Boston), 14 November 1807. For the *Intelligencer's* earliest reference to the incident in Baltimore, see *National Intelligencer*, 23 November 1807. For its coverage of Burr's reception elsewhere, see ibid., 4 November 1807; and "Extract of a letter dated Philadelphia," ibid., 18 November 1807. In its 10 November issue, the *Virginia Argus* published four pieces from Baltimore; the *Enquirer* reprinted the same pieces in the same order three days later. From the *Federal Gazette*, the Richmond newspapers reprinted "The Empire of the Laws" from 3 November and Martin's letter to Hewes, with Hewes's brief comments, from the next day. From the *Whig*, they took "Reward of Merit" from 4 November and Irvine's refutation of Hewes's comments on Martin's letter from the next day. While the pieces were published in the order in which they had appeared, doing so effectively allowed Irvine's two pieces to serve as correctives to Hewes's. For Republican newspapers that reprinted the *Evening Post's* account, see *Public Advertiser*, 7 November 1807 (from AHN); and *Phenix* (Providence, R.I.), 14 November 1807 (from AHN).

58. [Croswell], *Balance*, 17 November 1807.

59. [Charles Holt], "Proceedings at Baltimore," *Bee* (Hudson, N.Y.), 17 November 1807 (from AHN). See also [John Barker], *Albany Register* (N.Y.), 24 November 1807 (from AHN).

60. [William Duane], *Aurora*, 7 November 1807.

61. [Parks], "Mobs! Mobs! Mobs!," *Democrat*, 21 November 1807.

62. "At a Meeting," *American*, 7 November 1807. For Dorsey's warrant, see Biays et al., "Report," ibid., 19 November 1807.

63. Luther Martin to Hewes, 5 November 1807, *Federal Gazette*, 6 November 1807.

64. [Irvine], "Brief Chronicles," *Albany Register*, 1 December 1807, clipped from *Whig*, 9 November 1807 (from AHN). For Biays and O'Reilly, see, respectively, Biays, communication, *American*, 10 November 1807; and Joseph C. O'Reilly, "To the Public," *Whig*, 10 November 1807.

65. Zebulon M. Pike to Rodney, 12 [*sic*, 8] November 1807, ICHi: Zebulon Pike Papers; Nathaniel Saltonstall Jr. to Leverett Saltonstall, 8 November 1807, in Moody, ed., *Saltonstall Papers*, 2:407.

66. "Democratic Meeting," *American*, 9 November 1807.

67. "The following address was yesterday presented to General JAMES WILKINSON by the officers of the 27th Reg. Maryland Militia," *Baltimore Evening Post*, 9 November 1807. For Wilkinson's arrival in Baltimore, see *American*, 9 November 1807.

68. [Irvine], *Whig*, 17 November 1807.

69. Pike to Rodney, 12 [*sic*, 8] November 1807, ICHi: Pike Papers.

70. [Jacob Frank], *Public Advertiser*, 14 November 1807 (from AHN).

71. [Hewes], "The Times," *Federal Gazette*, 10 November 1807; ibid., 9 November 1807. For the growing importance of party, see [Hewes], "'Democratic Meeting,'" ibid.

72. "Senex," "To All Honest Men," ibid., 10 November 1807.

73. [Irvine], "Brief Chronicles," *Albany Register*, 1 December 1807, clipped from *Whig*, 9 November 1807 (from AHN).

74. [Irvine], "Pitiful Falsehood," *Whig*, 13 November 1807. For the personal attacks, see, for example, ibid., 11 November 1807.

75. [Irvine], "Review of the Rioters," ibid., 16 November 1807. The warrant declared that the "assemblage" that had marched through the city and burned the effigies was "unlawful" because it "tend[ed] to endanger the public peace" (Walter Dorsey, warrant, 5 November 1807, in "Choice Document," ibid., 16 November 1807).

76. [Hewes], "The Times," *Federal Gazette*, 10 November 1807.

77. [Irvine], "The 'friends of order,' in disorder!," *Whig*, 10 November 1807.

78. [Hewes], "The Times," *Federal Gazette*, 10 November 1807; [Irvine], *Whig*, 11 November 1807. The previous day, Irvine had said that the crowd at Dorsey's was composed "of about two hundred persons (*black* and white)" ([Irvine], "The 'friends of order,' in disorder!," ibid., 10 November 1807).

79. [Irvine], "The 'friends of order,' in disorder!," *Whig*, 10 November 1807. Irvine may have been correct. In an essay that had been in Hewes's hands before Monday's *Federal Gazette* was printed and, thus, before Monday evening's rumors, "Senex" warned of something very similar to the rumored plan; see *Federal*

Gazette, 9 November 1807; and "Senex," "To All Honest Men," ibid., 10 November 1807.

80. "A Republican," "Communication," *Federal Gazette*, 11 November 1807.

81. [Irvine], "Adjourned Meeting," *Whig*, 14 November 1807. Irvine made clear that "all but democratic republicans [would] be compelled to retire" from the hall.

82. Biays et al., "Report," *American*, 19 November 1807. In addition to Biays and Frailey, the committee included Theodorick Bland (attorney), James L. Donaldson (attorney and federal officeholder), William Lowry (federal officeholder), John McKim Jr. (merchant), John Patterson (storeowner), and William Stewart (doctor). Of these men, only Bland and Donaldson are missing from M'Henry's *Baltimore Directory* (1807). As attorneys, neither are likely to have lived in Fell's Point; Bland certainly had not in 1804. Donaldson, a federal land officer in the Louisiana Territory, had only returned to Baltimore temporarily.

83. "Democratic Meeting," *American*, 9 November 1807.

84. Biays et al., "Report," ibid., 19 November 1807.

85. [Pechin], ibid., 19 November 1807.

86. [Colvin], "The Effigies," *Republican Watch-Tower*, 8 December 1807, clipped from *Weekly Register of Politics and News* 1 (ca. 5 December 1807). Colvin doubted that "'mobs,' properly speaking," could exist in the United States because the urban population was "not sufficiently numerous" and the people "enjoy[ed] too much liberty to be guilty of actions that are violent in any extraordinary degree." Colvin's moderation is clear from Cheetham's approving introduction.

87. [Hewes], "New Projects," *Federal Gazette*, 21 November 1807.

88. "A Republican," "For the FEDERAL GAZETTE," ibid., 14 December 1807.

89. Biays, "To the Citizens of the City of Baltimore," *American*, 30 November 1807.

90. "To the Honorable the General Assembly of Maryland," ibid. Those who supported the petition often argued that they merely wanted to restore to Baltimoreans the political equality that they had enjoyed before the Federalist-dominated state legislature established the corporation in 1794; see, for example, "Tammany," "The Charter," *Whig*, 7 December 1807; and "Tammany," "Hints and Queries," ibid., 12 January 1808. The committee also presented a memorial to the general assembly asking for "an enquiry into the Judicial misconduct of Judge Dorsey" ("Pantheonic Committee," *North American, and Mercantile Daily Advertiser* [Baltimore, Md.], 29 January 1808). That memorial was rejected, forty-three to sixteen; see Maryland, *Votes and Proceedings*, 120.

91. For the legislative history of the petition and bill, see Maryland, *Votes and Proceedings*, 78, 101, 111, 112, 124. For the reform efforts, see Steffen, *Mechanics of Baltimore*, 204–8.

92. "Tammany," "The Charter," *Whig*, 5 December 1807. For other pieces by "Tammany," see ibid., 7 and 12 December 1807 and 9, 12, 21, and 25 January 1808.

93. [Irvine], "The New Paper," ibid., 12 December 1807.

94. "Tammany," "A Passing Glance," ibid., 25 January 1808. For the earlier criticisms, see [Irvine], "Insult upon Injury," ibid., 9 January 1808; and "Tammany," "Hints and Queries," ibid., 12 January 1808.

95. "Tammany," ibid., 21 January 1808. For other exhortations to vote, see "A Child of '76," "To the Citizens of Baltimore," ibid., 30 January 1808; and "A Democratic Republican," "Fellow-Citizens of Baltimore," ibid. On 30 January, the *Whig* listed the pro-reform candidates under the heading "Republican Ticket." "A Democratic Republican" labelled the opposition candidates "the British ticket."

96. "A Republican," "For the North American," *North American*, 29 January 1808. For the final vote, see "Result of the Election," ibid., 2 February 1808.

97. [Irvine], "Review of the Rioters," *Whig*, 16 November 1807. "Tammany" referred to earlier petitions to reform the charter in a number of essays; see, for example, "Tammany," "The Charter," ibid., 7 December 1807.

98. "Sicilias," "To the People of Maryland," *American*, 20 November 1807.

99. [Colvin], "The Effigies," *Republican Watch-Tower*, 8 December 1807, clipped from *Weekly Register of Politics and News* 1 (ca. 5 December 1807).

CHAPTER 11. FINAL ACCOUNTS OF THE BURR CONSPIRACY

1. Charles Francis Adams, diary entry, 20 December 1838, in Donald et al., eds., *Diary of Charles Francis Adams*, 8:158. See also Adams's diary entries for 12, 16, and 22 November 1838, in ibid., 138, 142, and 144.

2. Charles Francis Adams, diary entry, 30 January 1839, in ibid., 182.

3. Charles Francis Adams, diary entry, 5 February 1839, in ibid., 184.

4. Charles Francis Adams, diary entry, 15 March 1839, in ibid., 202. For the final reading, see Charles Francis Adams, diary entry, 10 May 1839, in ibid., 233. For the review, see [Adams], review of *Memoirs [and] Private Journal of Aaron Burr*.

5. Charles Francis Adams, diary entry, 13 February 1839, in Donald et al., eds., *Diary of Charles Francis Adams*, 8:188.

6. Charles Francis Adams, diary entry, 14 February 1839, in ibid., 189. The editorial notes identify the Athenæum's relevant holdings. The library seems to have bound Jefferson's collection of trial documents with congressional documents from an investigation of Wilkinson into three volumes as *Trial of Burr including the Arguments during the Examination and Trial of Gen. Wilkinson*; see ibid., n1. As the library's records show him taking out two volumes, Adams probably chose Robertson's version. Those records also show that he borrowed only the second volume of Wilkinson's memoirs, probably meaning *Burr's Conspiracy Exposed* (1811) rather than the second volume of the 1816 memoirs. I appreciate the assistance of Carolle R. Morini, the Caroline D. Bain Archivist and research librarian at the Athenæum, in tracking down this information.

7. [Adams], review of *Memoirs [and] Private Journal of Aaron Burr*, 192.

8. John Graham to James Brown, 8 September 1807, DLC: James Brown Papers.

9. Nathaniel Macon to Joseph H. Nicholson, 30 January 1807, DLC: Joseph H. Nicholson Papers. The reporters of Burr's trial could have chosen from a number of shorthand systems. For early nineteenth-century trial reports, see Cohen, *Pillars of Salt*, 167–94.

10. *RTCAB*, 2:177. The exchange, between Benjamin Botts and William Wirt, may have been tangential, as stenographer David Robertson suggested, but it was hardly insignificant since Wirt thought that his honesty and, thus, his honor had been assailed; I mentioned this dispute in Chapter 8. Robertson acknowledged that he had "considerably condensed" the arguments on minor points to reduce the volumes' cost ("Preface," in ibid., 1:[iii]).

11. William Wirt to Peachy R. Gilmer, 18 July 1807, DLC: William Wirt Papers.

12. William Eaton to Stephen Pynchon, 21 August 1807, Ms-Ar: Ventress (James Alexander) and Family Papers. During the trial, the court reporters were most scrupulous about the judge's opinions, relying upon Marshall's manuscripts rather than their own notes; see Charles F. Hobson et al., "Editorial Note: United States v. Burr," in *PJMar*, 7:11. That they also worked with the attorneys is clear from "Advertisement," in [Wirt], *Two Principal Arguments*, [ii]. For an attempt to correct the record of a witness's testimony before publication, see *Enquirer* (Richmond, Va.), 14 October 1807.

13. [William W. Hening and William Munford], "Trial of Aaron Burr," *Virginia Argus* (Richmond), 26 August 1807.

14. William Sampson to Grace Sampson, 6 February 1807, DLC: William Sampson Papers. For Sampson, an Irish radical and attorney, see Wilson, *United Irishmen, United States*. The other early account of the trial, William Thompson's *A Compendious View of the Trial of Aaron Burr*, was a narrative. While it could not have served Jefferson's purposes in the fall of 1807 in part because of its form, it met with his approval. Jefferson saw a large portion of it that summer and wrote supportively to Thompson; see William Thomson [*sic*, Thompson] to Thomas Jefferson, 10 July 1807, in *TJC*, 145–46; and Jefferson to Thomson [*sic*, Thompson], 26 September 1807, in *WoTJ*, 10:501–2.

15. [Samuel Pleasants Jr.], "Burr's Trial," *Virginia Argus*, 20 May 1807. Pleasants invited "all other editors of new-papers" to copy his coverage. The examination ended on 1 April, with the pamphlet advertised as available in Richmond on 11 April; see *Virginia Argus*, 10 April 1807.

16. George Hay to Jefferson, 15 October 1807, DLC: Thomas Jefferson Papers. See also David Robertson to Littleton Waller Tazewell, 29 October 1807, CtY: Burr Family Papers. In late May, Jefferson had authorized Hay to have the testimony "taken as verbatim as possible" and to "go into any expense necessary for this purpose" (Jefferson to Hay, 26 May 1807, in *WrTJ*, 11:209–10).

17. George Clinton to DeWitt Clinton, 15 November 1807, NNC: DeWitt Clinton Papers. For the hiring of Carpenter, see "Trial of Col. Aaron Burr," *National Intelligencer, and Washington Advertiser* (D.C.), 22 May 1807. For Carpenter, see

the testimonials in "This day is Published," *Washington Expositor, and Weekly Register* (D.C.), 16 July 1808. According to the historian Culver H. Smith, Carpenter had also recorded congressional debates for the *Intelligencer*; see Smith, *Press, Politics, and Patronage*, 27. For Westcott, see also Pasley, *"Tyranny of Printers,"* 139–40. Alexandria, formerly and presently a part of Virginia, was within the District of Columbia. For the advertisement, see "In the Press," *National Intelligencer*, 15 July 1807. For Westcott's patrons and the publication of the completed work, see "This day is Published," *Washington Expositor*, 16 July 1808.

18. "Preface," in *RTCAB*, 1:[iii]. Robertson was courting subscribers while the misdemeanor trial was still in process; see *Enquirer*, 9 September 1807.

19. "Proposals, for Publishing by Subscription, a Report of the Trial of Col. Aaron Burr," *Virginia Argus*, 16 September 1807.

20. [James Cheetham], "Burr's Trial," *Republican Watch-Tower* (New York), 23 December 1807. See also [Baptis Irvine], "Caution," *Whig, or Political Telescope* (Baltimore, Md.), 20 November 1807. Concern that Burr would have a trial report prepared to his purposes had arisen before the grand jury phase when Virginia newspapers reported that John Wood, who had published a report of Burr's trials in Kentucky and edited the pro-Burr *Atlantic World* in Washington, had hired "one of the first Stenographers in the United States" to help him report the trial ("The Contemplated Trial of Col. Burr," *Impartial Observer* [Richmond, Va.], 9 May 1807).

21. Hay, Wirt, Benjamin Botts, and Edmund Randolph, statement, 23 February 1808, *Enquirer*, 18 March 1808. John Wickham and Alexander McRae provided separate, equally positive, statements. See also *Aurora General Advertiser* (Philadelphia), 19 March 1808; and *National Intelligencer*, 21 March 1808. After seeing the published report, Wirt's opinion was more critical; see Wirt to Ninian Edwards, 26 November 1808, ICHi: Ninian Edwards Papers.

22. [Irvine], *Whig*, 3 December 1807. In the 1860s, when he prepared a one-volume report of the trial, J. J. Coombs incorporated material from both Carpenter and Robertson, drawing primarily from the latter "as the most accurate and reliable" (Coombs, *Trial of Aaron Burr for High Treason*, iii). He did not explain how he made that determination.

23. [Thomas Carpenter], deposition, 4 November 1807, *Washington Expositor*, 26 March 1808. Defying an agreement with Carpenter, Westcott showed this deposition to Republican officials, including Vice President George Clinton, and editors, including those who exposed Robertson. The spread of Carpenter's charge can be traced in George Clinton to DeWitt Clinton, 15 November 1807, NNC: Clinton Papers; [Irvine], "Caution," *Whig*, 20 November 1807; [Cheetham], "Burr's Trial," *Republican Watch-Tower*, 23 December 1807; and [Carpenter], "To the Editors of the Washington Expositor," *Washington Expositor*, 26 March 1808.

24. Hay, Wirt, Botts, and Edmund Randolph, statement, 23 February 1808, *Enquirer*, 18 March 1808. Wickham likewise described the few passages of

Carpenter's first volume that he had read as "extremely incorrect" (John Wickham, statement, ibid.).

25. [Carpenter], "To the Editors of the Washington Expositor," *Washington Expositor*, 26 March 1808.

26. Charles Francis Adams, diary entry, 15 February 1839, in Donald et al., eds., *Diary of Charles Francis Adams*, 8:189. Robertson continued to attend the trial and to take notes during the committal hearing; see Harman Blennerhassett, diary entries, 27 September and 6 October 1807, in *BwB*, 108, 123.

27. [Carpenter], "To the Editors of the Washington Expositor," *Washington Expositor*, 26 March 1808. By including all of the testimony from the committal hearing, Carpenter's report certainly suited Jefferson better than Robertson's. It is noteworthy that, when Jefferson donated his personal library to Congress after the War of 1812, it included Carpenter's report, but not Robertson's; see Sowerby, comp., *Catalogue of the Library of Thomas Jefferson*, 2:300–302.

28. Harman Blennerhassett, diary entry, 3 October 1807, in *BwB*, 116. Some of the added material was on behalf of either Burr or Blennerhassett.

29. John Quincy Adams, "Notes on the cases of Aaron Burr and John Smith, with some other intrusive notes," [ca. December 1807], MHi: Adams Family Papers. Adams was using Jefferson's collection of documents to prepare a report on John Smith for the Senate.

30. Hening and Munford, statement, 21 October 1807, in *ASP: Misc*, 1:491; William Richardson, statement, 21 October 1807, in ibid., 611.

31. William Plumer, diary entry, 4 March 1807, in *WPMP*, 641. See also Plumer, diary entry, 27 February 1809, DLC: William Plumer Papers.

32. Jefferson to James Bowdoin, 2 April 1807, in *WrTJ*, 11:186. For Jefferson's concerns before he learned of Marshall's 1 April decision, see also his letters to: [Joseph C.] Cabell, 18 March 1807, ViU: Thomas Jefferson Papers; and G[eorge] Morgan, 26 March 1807, in *WrTJ*, 11:174.

33. Jefferson to Hay, 26 May 1807, in *WrTJ*, 11:209. For Hay's response, see Hay to Jefferson, 31 May 1807, DLC: Jefferson Papers. For Jefferson's thinking in the period between Marshall's rulings of 1 April and 31 August, see also Jefferson to William B. Giles, 20 April 1807, in *WrTJ*, 11:187–91.

34. Elizabeth House Trist to [Jefferson], 27 October 1807, NcU: Nicholas P. Trist Papers. See also William Eaton to Stephen Pynchon, 1 September 1807, in "Letter of William Eaton on Burr's Trial," 285; "C. D.," "Communication," *New-York Evening Post*, 1 September 1807; George Watson to David Watson, 22 October 1807, ViHi: Watson Family Papers; "Investigator," "To John Marshall, Esq. Chief Justice of the United States," *American, and Commercial Daily Advertiser* (Baltimore, Md.), 18 November 1807; and Walter Leake to [Wilson Cary Nicholas], 15 December 1807, in Jordan, ed., "Partisan Politics in Territorial Mississippi," 237.

35. John Tompkins to Duncan Cameron, 25 August 1807, NcU: Cameron Family Papers.

36. Thomas Tudor Tucker to John Page, 16 June 1807, DLC: Thomas Tudor Tucker Papers. See also [Ritchie], "Treason," *Enquirer*, 27 January 1807; Thomas Acheson to Samuel Smith, 13 February 1807, DNA: RG59, M418, filed under "Baird, George"; and Charles Willson Peale to John Isaac Hawkins, 3 March 1807, in Miller, ed., *Selected Papers of Charles Willson Peale and His Family*, 2:1005.

37. Samuel Brown to Jefferson, 3 June 1808, in Padgett, ed., "Letters of Doctor Samuel Brown," 106. See also Edward Tupper to Thomas Worthington, 1 September 1807, ORCHi: Early Statehood Papers; [Charles Holt], *Bee* (Hudson, N.Y.), 15 September 1807 (from AHN); Thomas Todd to Harry Innes, 27 September 1807, DLC: Harry Innes Papers; and Jenkins Whiteside to George Washington Campbell, 20 December 1807, T: George Washington Campbell Correspondence.

38. "Communication," *Public Advertiser* (New York), 8 September 1807 (from AHN). See also "The Judiciary," *Tickler* (Philadelphia), 4 November 1807.

39. [Samuel H. Smith], *National Intelligencer*, 7 September 1807.

40. Joseph C. Cabell to William Wirt, 27 June 1807, ViU: Cabell Family Papers.

41. Ritchie to Joseph C. Cabell, 31 August [1807], ibid.

42. Joseph C. Cabell to Ritchie, 10 September 1807, ibid. Cabell did not send the letter in exactly this form; a note on the verso states that "another *more conditional*" was sent in its place. Ritchie had already seen the notes, which Cabell knew; see [William H. Cabell] to [Joseph C. Cabell], [ca. 31 August 1807], ibid. For the other records of grand jury testimony, see above Chapter 5, n. 94.

43. Jefferson to Hay, 4 September 1807, in *WrTJ*, 11:360.

44. Jefferson to Robert Smith [*sic*, Caesar A. Rodney], 8 October 1807, in ibid., 11:377. See also Jefferson to Hay, 11 October 1807, in ibid., 19:162; and Hay to Jefferson, 15 and 21 October 1807, DLC: Jefferson Papers. For the committal hearing as a way to elicit testimony, see Ritchie to Joseph C. Cabell, 31 August 1807, ViU: Cabell Family Papers; Graham to James Brown, 8 September 1807, DLC: Brown Papers; James Wilkinson to Jefferson, 13 September 1807, DLC: Jefferson Papers; and "Treason Developed!," *Petersburg Intelligencer* (Va.), 25 September 1807. Hay's 21 October letter to Jefferson makes clear that he was also corresponding directly with Rodney, though those letters do not seem to have survived. Jefferson initially intended to include some evidence "which was not publicly heard," presumably from his own files (Jefferson, first draft of Seventh Annual Message, [ca. October 1807], in *WoTJ*, 11:523).

45. Jefferson, Seventh Annual Message, 27 October 1807, in *CMPP*, 1:429. Two drafts of this section of the message are reprinted, in parallel columns, in *WoTJ*, 11:522–24. The attorney general suggested omitting all that I have quoted above on the grounds that Burr had been committed "for further trial" in Ohio (Rodney to Jefferson, [ca. 23 October 1807], in ibid., 510n). Obviously, Jefferson did not follow that advice. But the drafts included far more explosive language than the final message. Originally, Jefferson had suggested that there was "a radical defect in the administration of the law," contrasted "the pliability of the law as

construed in the case of Fries" against "it's wonderful refractoriness as construed in that of Burr," and noted that "the right of the jury too to decide law as well as fact seems nugatory without the evidence pertinent to their sense of the law" (Jefferson, first draft of Seventh Annual Message, [ca. October 1807], in ibid., 524). For the report, see [Jefferson], *Message from the President of the United States.*

46. Jefferson to Giles, 20 April 1807, in *WrTJ*, 11:191.

47. Jefferson to [Joseph C.] Cabell, 18 March 1807, ViU: Jefferson Papers. Jefferson seems to have developed these ideas even earlier in the draft of a message to Congress. While the archivists have filed it in mid-September 1807, it seems designed to address a situation that never happened—the freeing of Burr by some court on a writ of habeas corpus. As such, it may have been written in response to the Supreme Court's freeing of Justus Erich Bollman and Samuel Swartwout in late February; it was probably not delivered because the congressional session was scheduled to end a few days later. "If such be the law, the legislature will consider whether it shd. not be amended," Jefferson had suggested; "if it not be the law, they alone can take measures for ensuring a more correct administration of it in future" (Jefferson, draft message, [20 September (*sic*, early March) 1807], DLC: Jefferson Papers).

48. Jefferson to Giles, 20 April 1807, in *WrTJ*, 11:190–91. See also Jefferson's letters to: John W. Eppes, 28 May 1807, in *WoTJ*, 10:412–13; and Rodney, 19 August 1807, DLC: Jefferson Papers.

49. Jefferson to Wilkinson, 20 September 1807, in *WrTJ*, 11:375. For similar sentiments, see Thomas Tudor Tucker to Page, 24 September 1807, DLC: Tucker Papers; *Aurora*, 24 October 1807; and Isaac A. Coles to Joseph C. Cabell, 18 November 1807, ViU: Cabell Family Papers [Coles was Jefferson's private secretary]. For earlier Republican attempts to amend the constitutional process for removing judges, see Ames, "Proposed Amendments"; and Ellis, *Jeffersonian Crisis.*

50. Leverett Saltonstall, diary entry, 2 November 1807, in Moody, ed., *Saltonstall Papers*, 2:400–401; Richard L. Savin to James Hamilton, 25 December 1807, PHi: James Hamilton Collection.

51. Joseph C. Cabell to Coles, 6 November 1807, ViU: Cabell Family Papers.

52. "A Republican," *Federal Gazette & Baltimore Daily Advertiser* (Md.), 30 November 1807, clipped from *Frederick-Town Herald* (Md.).

53. [Enos Bronson], *United States' Gazette* (Philadelphia), 30 October 1807. For other Federalist attacks on this section of the message, see "The Message," *Washington Federalist* (Georgetown, D.C.), 31 October 1807; "Mr. Editor," ibid., 11 November 1807; "The Judiciary," *Balance, and Columbian Repository* (Hudson, N.Y.), 17 November 1807; "One of the Jury," *Virginia Gazette, and General Advertiser* (Richmond), 17 November 1807; and "President's Message (Concluded)," *New-York Evening Post*, 9 December 1807.

54. [William Jackson], comment on "Extract of a letter from Baltimore," *New-York Gazette & General Advertiser*, 9 November 1807, clipped from *Political and*

Commercial Register (Philadelphia) (from AHN); "A Republican," *Federal Gazette*, 30 November 1807, clipped from *Frederick-Town Herald*. See also *Boston Repertory*, 17 November 1807 (from AHN).

55. Joseph C. Cabell to Coles, 6 November 1807, ViU: Cabell Family Papers. See also Benjamin Parke to James Brown, 2 January 1808, InHi: Albert G. Porter Papers.

56. [Pleasants], *Virginia Argus*, 3 November 1807. See also [Samuel H. Smith], *National Intelligencer*, 13 November 1807.

57. [Hezekiah Niles and Leonard Frailey], *Baltimore Evening Post* (Md.), 28 October 1807.

58. George Read to Rodney, 29 November 1807, DeHi: Rodney Collection. For calls for a congressional investigation, see [Irvine], "'It Started!—like a Guilty thing,'" *Whig*, 25 November 1807. Irvine's title quoted Horatio's description of the ghost's response to the cock's crow in the opening scene of *Hamlet*, 1.1.148.

59. Hay to Jefferson, 15 October 1807, DLC: Jefferson Papers.

60. [Ritchie], "Cursory Reflections—Portrait of the Chief Justice, No. VI," *Enquirer*, 24 November 1807. For the other "Cursory Reflections" on Marshall, see ibid., 6, 10, and 17 November 1807. For "Eubulides," see *Virginia Argus*, 3, 6, and 13 November 1807. The first and second "Eubulides" essays were dated 1 September, probably for effect.

61. "Lucius" [John Lewis], "Letter the First," *Aurora*, 21 November 1807. For the other letters, see ibid., 25 and 28 November and 1 December 1807. The authorship of the "Lucius" essays was a great mystery. Everyone from Tom Paine to the *Aurora* editor William Duane and from the attorneys William Wirt and George Hay to author William Thompson (see above, n. 14) was proposed as the author at one time or another. Historians and biographers have followed these erroneous suppositions in identifying "Lucius"; see, for example, Beveridge, *Life of John Marshall*, 3:533–35; Malone, *Jefferson and His Time*, 5:355; Wheelan, *Jefferson's Vendetta*, 256; and Newmyer, *Treason Trial of Aaron Burr*, 156, 175. Speaking with the historian John Dabney Shane nearly fifty years later in Kentucky, John Lewis admitted that he had written them; see John Lewis, interview with John Dabney Shane, [3 September 1855], WHi: Draper Manuscript Collection, 15CC13–16.

62. [Cheetham], "Mr. Tiffin's resolution," *American Citizen* (New York), 11 November 1807; [Ritchie], "Cursory Reflections—Portrait of the Chief Justice, No. VI," *Enquirer*, 24 November 1807. In Virginia, the lower house supported its amendment by a wide margin, but the upper house rejected it, thirteen to six; see "The following are the Amendments to the Federal Constitution, which have been adopted by the House of Delegates," *Enquirer*, 16 January 1808; and *National Intelligencer*, 29 January 1808. Though Ohio's proposal required the same majority in each house as the existing constitutional language, it did not require the full impeachment process.

63. The best discussion of the amendment effort is in Ames, "Proposed Amendments," 149–50, 327–28. For Maryland, see Maryland, *Votes and Proceedings*, 103.

64. Rodney to John Randolph, 2 December 1807, in *ASP: Misc*, 1:717, 718. Only one member of the committee was a Federalist; see *Annals*, 10th Cong., 1st sess., 795. For the proposed bill, see ibid., 1717–18.

65. Joseph Story to P. P. Fay, 13 February 1808, in Story, ed., *Life and Letters of Joseph Story*, 1:159. See also Rufus King to Timothy Pickering, 16 February 1808, in King, ed., *Life and Correspondence of Rufus King*, 5:73–74; and Richard Peters to Pickering, 16 February 1808, MHi: Timothy Pickering Papers. For the Giles bill, see Anderson, *William Branch Giles*, 116–21; Malone, *Jefferson and His Time*, 5:368–70; and Currie, *Constitution in Congress*, 138–42. According to these authors, the final form of the bill does not survive. That it had been seriously altered is clear from John Quincy Adams's diary: "The bill which was originally the Treason bill, now changed into a bill for the punishment of certain crimes, [has] finally passed" (John Quincy Adams, diary entry, 6 April 1808, in Adams, ed., *Memoirs of John Quincy Adams*, 1:527). Massachusetts senator Timothy Pickering described the Giles bill as "a *Presidential* measure," but I have seen no evidence that Jefferson was responsible for it (Pickering to King, 24 February 1808, in King, ed., *Life and Correspondence of Rufus King*, 5:75).

66. "Preface," in *RTCAB*, 1:[iv].

67. For Adams's report, see "Report on Senator John Smith," 31 December 1807, in *ASP: Misc*, 1:701–3. For Smith's connections to Burr and near-expulsion from the Senate, see Pitcher, "John Smith"; Wilhelmy, "Senator John Smith"; and Cayton, "Senator John Smith." Other early works that used Jefferson's report include *Proofs*; and Wilkinson, *Burr's Conspiracy Exposed*. It became more easily accessible decades later with the publication of *Annals of Congress* and *American State Papers*; see *Annals*, 10th Cong., 1st sess., Appendix, 386–778; and *ASP: Misc*, 1:486–645.

68. Hay, argument, 17 September 1807, in *TCAB*, 3:128. The defense had complained of presidential interference on numerous occasions; see, for example, Botts, argument, 26 August 1807, in *RTCAB*, 2:169.

69. Jefferson to Hay, 19 June 1807, in *WrTJ*, 11:235. For the original publication of the letters to Hay, see Randolph, ed., *Memoir, Correspondence, and Miscellanies*, 4:75–103 (quote at 102).

70. Dwight, *Character of Thomas Jefferson*, 67. See also [Sullivan], *Familiar Letters on Public Characters*, 189–96.

71. "Thomas Jefferson," 371, 372.

72. Tucker, *Life of Thomas Jefferson*, 2:254; Randall, *Life of Thomas Jefferson*, 3:217.

73. Jefferson to Rodney, 19 June 1807, DLC: Jefferson Papers. Rodney's eldest son was ill; see Rodney to Jefferson, 16 June 1807, ibid.; and Jefferson to Hay, 5 June 1807, in *WrTJ*, 11:219. In the late 1850s, Henry S. Randall noted that many of the letters could not have been avoided and that Rodney's absence left no one

between Hay and Jefferson; see Randall, *Life of Thomas Jefferson*, 3:218–20. For Jefferson's image in his lifetime and beyond, see Peterson, *Jefferson Image in the American Mind*; and McDonald, *Confounding Father*.

74. Wilkinson to David Brearley, October 1815, ICHi: James Wilkinson Papers. See also Wilkinson to unknown correspondent, 15 April 1817, NN: James Wilkinson Papers.

75. Review of *Memoirs of My Own Times. By General JAMES WILKINSON*, 40.

76. I explain below why *Burr's Conspiracy Exposed* was labelled the second volume of Wilkinson's memoirs when it was published in 1811 and why it was different from the actual second volume of *Memoirs of My Own Times* when that work appeared five years later.

77. Wilkinson to Henry Dearborn, 26 December 1808, DNA: RG107, M222, W-1808. For gentlemen's knowledge of the weapons of "paper war," see Freeman, *Affairs of Honor*. Examples of Wilkinson's use of most of these tactics have appeared in earlier chapters. For a failed attempt to plant exculpatory material in the official record to answer a congressional request, see Wilkinson to Jefferson, 22 January 1808, DLC: Jefferson Papers; and Jefferson to Wilkinson, 24 January 1808, ibid. Wilkinson responded to this setback by having the document published in a local periodical; see [Colvin], "General Wilkinson."

78. Wilkinson to Jefferson, 21 October 1806, DLC: Burr Conspiracy Collection. I discussed these dispatches in Chapter 5.

79. "Extract of a letter from New-Orleans," *Charleston Courier* (S.C.), 27 June 1807.

80. Wilkinson to John Smith, 28 June 1807, OCHi: Papers in the Defense of John Smith of Ohio. See also Wilkinson to Samuel Smith, 20 June 1807, PPiU-D: James Wilkinson Papers.

81. Wilkinson to Charles Biddle, 19 September 1807, PHi: Biddle Family Papers.

82. Wilkinson to Jefferson, 13 September 1807, DLC: Jefferson Papers. Jefferson did as asked but had Hay reserve all letters that were marked or written as confidential; see Jefferson to Hay, 20 September 1807, in *WrTJ*, 11:374.

83. Thomas Truxton to Dayton, 12 September 1807, PHi: Simon Gratz Autograph Collection. "*Ws Offer of a Copy leads me to this remark*," Truxton continued. Jefferson had returned the subpoenaed letter, of 12 November 1806, to Hay just before Wilkinson's initial request for access to the papers; see Jefferson to Hay, 7 September 1807, in *WrTJ*, 11:365. Under investigation by a congressional committee in early 1811, Wilkinson turned over copies of nineteen letters to Jefferson from "exactly the period of Burr's conspiracy." Asked by the committee chair to verify the letters, Jefferson found that he was "not in possession of a single original" and pointed the committee to the material that he had given to Rodney in the spring of 1807 (Jefferson to Ezekial Bacon, 6 March 1811, in *PTJ: RS*, 3:430). Only six of the seventeen letters are in the Burr Conspiracy Collection at the Library of Congress; one more is at the Historical Society of Pennsylvania among the papers taken from the War Department by the clerk Daniel Parker.

The remaining letters survive only in the form presented to the committee by Wilkinson.

84. Harman Blennerhassett, diary entry, 17 October 1807, in *BwB*, 134. See also *Democratic Press* (Philadelphia), 4 November 1807 (from AHN).

85. "A Kentuckian" [Wilkinson], "A Plain Tale," *Enquirer*, 27 October 1807. For Wilkinson's admission of authorship, see Wilkinson to Jonathan Williams, 27 October 1807, InU: Jonathan Williams Manuscripts. Apparently on his own initiative, Jonathan Williams published a pamphlet version in New York a few weeks later. The pamphlet added documents from the same issue of the *Enquirer* that had appeared over the pseudonym "Justitia," including two letters from Burr to Indiana territorial governor William Henry Harrison; they were the only Burr Conspiracy material in the pamphlet. That Wilkinson was "Justitia" seems clear; he had explicitly mentioned "Burrs Letters to Governor Harrison" in requesting access to the administration's files (Wilkinson to Jefferson, 15 September 1807, DLC: Jefferson Papers).

86. Wilkinson to Dearborn, 11 October 1807, DNA: RG107, M222, W-1807. For Power's testimony, see Thomas Power, testimony, 17 October 1807, in *TCAB*, 3:389–94.

87. Wilkinson to Thomas Biddle, 17 November 1807, DLC: James Wilkinson Papers.

88. Wilkinson to John Randolph, 24 December 1807, in [Wilkinson, comp.], *[Correspondence between Wilkinson & Randolph]*, [1]. This unsigned and untitled pamphlet appeared in early 1808; see "Extract of a letter from a member of Congress to a gentleman in this city," *Enquirer*, 9 January 1808. It includes Wilkinson's challenge, Randolph's reply, and the documents that Randolph presented to the House on 31 December. The attribution to Wilkinson seems to have come from an archivist (as did the handwritten title) and is almost certainly incorrect. Wilkinson would hardly have published something so embarrassing without adding a statement or document to turn it to his advantage. He met this unwelcome publication by sending the press his response to Randolph's rebuff; see "In compliance with our promise, we copy the last letter of Gen. W. to Mr. R.," ibid., 12 January 1808.

89. John Randolph to Wilkinson, 25 December 1807, in [Wilkinson, comp.], *[Correspondence between Wilkinson & Randolph]*, [2].

90. Wilkinson, "Hector Unmasked," *Democratic Press*, 4 January 1808 (from AHN). This handbill appeared in newspapers across the country. For events in the House, see *Annals*, 10th Cong., 1st sess., 1257–69; Samuel Taggart to John Taylor, 2 January 1808, in "Letters of Samuel Taggart," 298; "Extract of a letter to the Editor," *Whig*, 3 January 1808; and Wilkinson to Jacob Kingsbury, 11 January 1808, MiD-B: Jacob Kingsbury Papers.

91. Wilkinson to Dearborn, 1 January 1807 [*sic*, 1808], DNA: RG107, M221, W-422 (3). Wilkinson had informed Hay of his intention to request an inquiry in mid-October; see Hay to Jefferson, 15 October 1807, DLC: Jefferson Papers.

92. Wilkinson to Kingsbury, 11 January 1808, MiD-B: Kingsbury Papers. See also Wilkinson to Solomon Van Renssalaer, 14 September [*sic*, 10 or 12 January] 1808, KyLoF: James Wilkinson Miscellaneous Papers; and Wilkinson to John Brown, 22 January 1808, InHi: Northwest Territory Collection. Even after Wilkinson's request was accepted, rumor around Washington had the general planning to cane Randolph and Randolph "intend[ing] to send for one of his negro drivers to horsewhip the General" ("From Washington," *Columbian Centinel* [Boston], 13 January 1808). For the court of inquiry and the House debates, see Abernethy, *Burr Conspiracy*, 264–75. Wilkinson's activities after 1807 are covered most fully in Jacobs, *Tarnished Warrior*; and Linklater, *Artist in Treason*.

93. John Pope to Edwards, 9 January 1808, in Washburne, ed., *Edwards Papers*, 1:35. For the delicate position in which pro-administration Republicans found themselves on this issue, see John Nicholas to Wilson Cary Nicholas, 27 January 1808, ViU: Carter-Smith Papers; Richard M. Johnson, circular letter to constituents, 10 April 1808, in *CLC*, 2:554; and Benjamin Howard, circular letter to constituents, 20 April 1808, in ibid., 576. For the passage of the resolution asking Jefferson to institute an inquiry (72 to 49) and the defeat of proposals creating a House committee with the powers to subpoena testimony (38 to 72) and documents (46 to 59) to investigate Wilkinson, see, respectively, 13, 5, and 21 January 1808, in *Annals*, 10th Cong., 1st sess., 1458–59, 1322–23, and 1487–88. The best discussion of the House's role can be found in Chalou, "James Wilkinson."

94. James M. Garnett to James Hunter, 24 January 1808, Vi: Garnett-Mercer-Hunter Family Papers. During the Burr crisis, Cushing had been Wilkinson's most trusted officer on the southwestern frontier. Williams, who was related to the general by marriage, had been his preferred second in the affair of honor with Wickham and had had "A Plain Tale" printed as a pamphlet. For the court's limited powers, see Walter Jones Jr. to James Monroe, 18 January 1808, DLC: James Monroe Papers. For Jefferson's endorsement of those limits, see Jefferson, special message, 20 January 1808, in *CMPP*, 1:437–38. For the restrictions on note-taking, see [Samuel H. Smith], "Court of Inquiry in the case of Gen. Wilkinson," *National Intelligencer*, 15 January 1808.

95. Johnson, circular letter to constituents, 10 April 1808, in *CLC*, 2:554; Garnett to Hunter, 24 January 1808, Vi: Garnett-Mercer-Hunter Family Papers. See also *Mississippi Messenger* (Natchez), 11 February 1808. For early doubts that the court would reveal anything against Wilkinson, see Joseph Hopkinson to Pickering, 13 January 1808, MHi: Pickering Papers; William Ely to Plumer, 24 January 1808, in Mevers et al., eds., *William Plumer Papers*; and "Correspondence from Washington," *Newburyport Herald* (Mass.), 29 January 1808 (from AHN).

96. Resolution, in *Annals*, 10th Cong., 1st sess., 1460. Clark's deposition was published in pamphlet form, but it also appeared in newspapers beginning in

mid-January; see Clark, *Deposition of Daniel Clark*. It can also be found in *Proofs*, Appendix, 105–9; and *ASP: Misc*, 1:704–5.

97. Walter Jones Jr., deposition, 1 May 1810, in *ASP: Misc*, 2:125. Jefferson provided the House with two sets of documents; see ibid., 1:706–12 and 712–13. In mid-March, the House approved a bill expanding the court's powers to call witnesses; see *Annals*, 10th Cong., 1st sess., 1827–28. The Senate returned an amended version of the bill to the House a month later; it was never passed into law.

98. H[enry] Burbeck, T[homas] H. Cushing, and Jona[than] Williams, verdict, *National Intelligencer*, 4 July 1808.

99. Wilkinson to Jonathan Williams, 3 October 1808, InU: Williams Manuscripts. Wilkinson moved quickly to make the most of this acquittal, arranging a public tribute in Washington and having the supporting address and his reply published in the *Intelligencer*; see Cornelius Coningham to Wilkinson, 14 July 1808, *National Intelligencer*, 20 July 1808; and Wilkinson to Coningham, 15 July 1808, ibid. An item exposing and attacking Wilkinson's role in this tribute appeared in the next issue; see "Washington," ibid., 22 July 1808.

100. [Samuel H. Smith], "Court of Enquiry in the Case of General Wilkinson," *National Intelligencer*, 20 January 1808. During this period, the magazine and newspaper editor John B. Colvin emerged as one of Wilkinson's most reliable supporters in *Colvin's Weekly Register* and, beginning in May, the *Monitor* (his third publishing venture in six months). See, for example, [Colvin], "Commander in Chief"; and Colvin's editorials in *Monitor* (Washington, D.C.), 21 and 25 June and 2 July 1808 (from AHN).

101. Clark, "To the Public," *National Intelligencer*, 25 April 1808. See also "More Evidence Against General Wilkinson," *North American, and Mercantile Daily Advertiser* (Baltimore, Md.), 18 July 1808. For some of Wilkinson's unsigned squibs, see "Gen. Wilkinson," *National Intelligencer*, 13 January and 24 February 1808. One of Wilkinson's own witnesses publicly denied the accounts of his testimony that appeared in the press; see Robert T. Spence, "For the National Intelligencer," ibid., 4 March 1808.

102. Wilkinson to Charles Biddle, 6 October 1808, PHi: Biddle Family Papers. Wilkinson claimed to have been working on his defense for "six weeks" (Wilkinson to John Law, 6 October 1808, MdHi: Law Papers). See also Wilkinson to Jonathan Williams, 3 October 1808, InU: Williams Manuscripts. In April 1810, the House committee that was investigating Wilkinson discovered that he had taken from the War Department the documents that had been collected by the military court; see *ASP: Misc*, 2:80, 126. They were returned by Wilkinson that November; see [Bacon], *Report of the Committee*, 5–6.

103. Wilkinson to Law, 9 October 1808, MdHi: Law Papers. Wilkinson looked to the sword, as well as the pen, to redeem his honor. During the inquest, it had become clear that Maryland's Robert Goodloe Harper had driven many of the recent attacks; see "Mr. R. G. Harper's Examination," in *Proofs*, Appendix,

122–23. Wilkinson had responded by denouncing Harper as a Burrite, among other things; see "Gen. Wilkinson," *Monitor*, 21 June 1808 (from AHN). After the inquest, Wilkinson and Harper waged a paper war through the Washington *Monitor* and the Baltimore *North American*, which gained intensity when Wilkinson, having failed to force Harper to duel, posted him as a coward; see Robert Goodloe Harper to Wilkinson, 27 October 1808, *North American*, 27 October 1808; and "Harper Posted!," *Monitor*, 1 November 1808 (from AHN).

104. James Brown to Henry Clay, 1 September 1808, in *PHC*, 1:375.

105. James Sterrett to Nathaniel Evans, 9 September 1809, LU: Evans (Nathaniel and Family) Papers. For the cooperation between Clark and Livingston, see Clark to Daniel W. Coxe, 2 July 1809, PHi: Daniel W. Coxe Papers; and Clark to Edward Livingston, 22 July 1809, NjP: Edward Livingston Papers. For the batture controversy, see Hatcher, *Edward Livingston*, 139–89; Dargo, *Jefferson's Louisiana*, 74–101; and Kelman, *River and Its City*, 19–59. Daniel W. Coxe filed the copyright in Philadelphia on 13 July 1809; see *Proofs*, [ii]. While Livingston tried to maintain the fiction of Clark's sole authorship by dating both the body of the text and a postscript as written in New Orleans, his role was known, at least in some circles; see William C. C. Claiborne to James Madison, 7 September 1808, in *OLBWC*, 4:211; and Plumer, diary entry, 21 October 1809, DLC: Plumer Papers.

106. *Proofs*, 4, 6, 115, 49. Clark also responded at length to Wilkinson's charge that he was connected to Burr's schemes; see ibid., 92–114. Clark's understanding of Wilkinson's expansive view is close to that in Narrett, "Geopolitics and Intrigue."

107. [Jacob Wagner and Alexander Contee Hanson Jr.], "Mr. Clarke's Pamphlet," *Federal Republican, & Commercial Gazette* (Baltimore, Md.), 31 August 1809. Over the next eighteen issues, the newspaper excerpted much of the book. For the Clark-Wilkinson clash, see, in particular, Hay, "Some Reflections"; and Wohl, "Man in the Shadow," 169–89.

108. Wilkinson to Van Renssalaer, 14 September [*sic*, 10 or 12 January] 1808, KyLoF: Wilkinson Miscellaneous Papers. See also Wilkinson to John Brown, 22 January 1808, InHi: Northwest Territory Collection.

109. John Barclay to John Holker, 10 June 1808, MiU-C: John Holker Papers. For Wilkinson's return to New Orleans, see Clark to Livingston, 19 April 1809, NjP: Livingston Papers.

110. Thomas Porée and William Bourgiois to Wilkinson, 4 October 1809, [Wilkinson], *Brief Examination*, 4. The testimonial was probably arranged, and possibly written, by Wilkinson. For Wilkinson's dispute with Adair, see Nathaniel Williams to Law, 24 April 1809, MdHi: Thomas Law Family Papers; Wilkinson to Samuel Smith, 2 May 1809, PPiU-D: Wilkinson Papers; and "General Wilkinson," *Ordeal*. For the courtship of Treadeau, see Sterrett to Evans, 10 June 1809 and 10 March 1810, LU: Evans Papers. For the soldiers under Wilkinson's

command, see Jacobs, *Tarnished Warrior*, 247–60; and Linklater, *Artist in Treason*, 284–88.

111. James Madison to Graham, 2 September 1809, in *PJM: PS*, 1:349. Madison received Clark's book at Montpelier just a day or two before writing Secretary of War William Eustis; see Madison's letters to: Graham, 29 August 1809, in ibid., 344; and William Eustis, 30 August 1809, in ibid., 345.

112. James Taylor to James Findlay, undated, in Cox, ed., "Selections from the Torrence Papers," 4:129n.

113. Daniel C. Holliday to Evans, 14 November 1809, LU: Evans Papers. See also Plumer, diary entry, 21 October 1809, DLC: Plumer Papers.

114. John Wayles Eppes to James Madison, 18 January 1810, in *PJM: PS*, 2:189. North Carolina congressman Joseph Pearson, who moved the formation of the second committee, alluded to Clark's book; see Joseph Pearson, speech, 21 March 1810, in *Annals*, 11th Cong., 2nd sess., 1748. For the votes, see 13 March and 4 April 1810, in ibid., 1533, 1755–56. For the reports, see *ASP: MA*, 1:268–95; and *ASP: Misc*, 2:79–127. The report on the Spanish and Burr conspiracies was published as [Butler], *Report of the Committee, Appointed to Inquire into the Conduct of Brigadier Gen. J. Wilkinson*.

115. Wilkinson to James Ingersoll, 22 July 1810, LNHiC: James Wilkinson Letters. Wilkinson submitted four questions about the constitutionality of the House's actions. Five months later, when he accepted the committee's invitation to attend its meetings, Wilkinson explicitly questioned the constitutionality of its proceedings; see Wilkinson to Ezekiel Bacon, 23 December 1810, in [Bacon], *Report of the Committee*, 8. For Wilkinson's request and Madison's refusal, see Wilkinson to Eustis, 24 June 1810, in Wilkinson, *Memoirs of My Own Times*, 2:Appendix 129; and Eustis to Wilkinson, 28 June 1810, in ibid.

116. Wilkinson to Dearborn, 3 July 1810, NHi: AHMC—James Wilkinson Papers. See also Wilkinson to Jefferson, 21 January 1811, in *PTJ: RS*, 3:323–24.

117. John B. Colvin to Jefferson, 14 September 1810, in *PTJ: RS*, 3:78. I discussed Jefferson's reply regarding the powers of executive officers in Chapter 7.

118. Wilkinson to Jefferson, 21 January 1811, in ibid., 324.

119. Wilkinson to [Samuel Lathem] Mitchill, 30 January 1811, LNT-H: Aaron Burr Papers.

120. Willie Blount to Andrew Jackson, 26 February 1811, in *PAJ*, 2:259. See also Benjamin Henry Latrobe to Justus Erich Bollman, [29 March 1811], in Jeffrey, ed., *Microfiche Edition of the Papers of Benjamin Henry Latrobe*.

121. For the report, see [Bacon], *Report of the Committee*. A new committee had been appointed to investigate the troop deaths; it did not issue a new report. An exchange of letters with Jefferson in early April suggests that Madison may have been trying to learn how deeply invested the former president remained in protecting Wilkinson; see James Madison to Jefferson, 1 April 1811, in *PJM: PS*, 3:239–40; and Jefferson to James Madison, 7 April 1811, in ibid., 249–51. For the administration's inquiries, see also the editorial notes to William O. Allen to

James Madison, 4 April 1811, in ibid., 246. For the court-martial, see the letters between Wilkinson and Eustis in Wilkinson, *Memoirs of My Own Times*, 2:Appendixes 131 and 132. *Burr's Conspiracy Exposed* was advertised as available for purchase in the *National Intelligencer*, 25 June 1811.

122. Wilkinson, *Burr's Conspiracy Exposed*, Introduction, 8–9, 11, 4. The three sections of the book are separately paginated.

123. Colvin to Jefferson, 4 February 1811, in *PTJ: RS*, 3:359.

124. Wilkinson, *Burr's Conspiracy Exposed*, 59, 4, 15. The direct vindication concluded with the material that Colvin had received from Jefferson (ibid., 56–59). The indirect vindication that follows consists of enumerated points (which are entirely absent in the first section) and relevant documents.

125. [Wilkinson], *Brief Examination*, 3, 5, 30, 29. At the beginning of *Burr's Conspiracy Exposed*, Wilkinson had promised that "an ample exposition of the imputed Spanish conspiracy" would soon appear (Wilkinson, *Burr's Conspiracy Exposed*, [iii]). I do not see any reason to doubt Wilkinson's authorship of *Brief Examination*; James Ripley Jacobs and Andro Linklater—Wilkinson's most scholarly biographers—seem to have missed it entirely.

126. Wilkinson, *Burr's Conspiracy Exposed*, [iii].

127. Wilkinson to Dearborn, 3 July 1810, NHi: Wilkinson Papers.

128. Wilkinson, *Burr's Conspiracy Exposed*, [iii]; Wilkinson to Mitchill, 30 January 1811, LNT-H: Burr Papers. Wilkinson had sent this material to Jefferson at the same time, along with the appendix to the first volume; see Wilkinson to Jefferson, 21 January 1811, in *PTJ: RS*, 3:324; and Sowerby, comp., *Catalogue of the Library of Thomas Jefferson*, 2:416–18. He described the fourth volume as "nearly ready for the press" in late April (Wilkinson to James Madison, 20 April 1811, in *PJM: PS*, 3:276).

129. Eustis to James Madison, 14 September 1811, in *PJM: PS*, 3:463. According to Henry Lee, Wilkinson was "seriously alarmed" by the choice of Fredericktown (Henry Lee to James Madison, 19 July 1811, in ibid., 386). For the two-year rule, see Eustis to James Madison, 11 September 1811, in ibid., 454. For the court-martial, see Jacobs, *Tarnished Warrior*, 267–75; and Linklater, *Artist in Treason*, 289–97.

130. James Madison to Jefferson, 7 February 1812, in *PJM: PS*, 4:169. For the record of the court-martial, see DNA: RG94, M1136.

131. James Madison, addendum, 14 February 1812, in "General Wilkinson," *National Intelligencer*, 25 February 1812.

132. Wilkinson to James Madison, 27 February 1812, in *PJM: PS*, 4:214.

133. Benjamin Henry Latrobe to Henry S. B. Latrobe, 20 May 1812, in *CBHL*, 3:299. See also J[ohn] M[oncure] Daniel to Dennis Claude, 14 February 1812, LU: Wilkinson (James) Letters.

134. Wilkinson to Law, 1 December 1816, MdHi: Law Papers. See also Wilkinson to Van Rensselaer, 7 November 1816, MoSHi: James Wilkinson Papers. For

Wilkinson's wartime service and final court-martial, see Jacobs, *Tarnished Warrior*, 276–314; and Linklater, *Artist in Treason*, 297–317.

135. D. C. Humphreys, interview with Shane, WHi: Draper Manuscript Collection, 16CC293. The circular is enclosed in Wilkinson to Brearley, [October 1815], ICHi: Wilkinson Papers.

136. Wilkinson to Thomas Aspinwall, 26 September 1817, NHi: Wilkinson Papers. A fourth volume consisted of maps of various encampments and battlegrounds that had been discussed in the previous volumes.

137. Wilkinson, *Memoirs of My Own Times*, 1:vi.

138. Wilkinson to Aspinwall, 26 September 1817, NHi: Wilkinson Papers.

139. Alexander Graydon to John Lardner, 5 May 1817, PHi: Society Collection—Graydon, Alexander.

140. Review of *Memoirs of my own times. By General James Wilkinson*, 84.

141. Review of *Memoirs of my own times*: by General James Wilkinson, 40.

142. "Wilkinson's Memoirs," 324. See also Benjamin H. Latrobe to Henry S. B. Latrobe, 7 August 1817, in *CBHL*, 3:925. For the difficulty of determining the reactions of readers other than reviewers to literary works in this period, see Jackson, "Reader Retailored."

143. Graydon to Lardner, 5 May 1817, PHi: Society Collection—Graydon. But Graydon also mentioned Wilkinson's "vanities, his ambition, and love of splendour, his heretofore faulty politicks and management to stand well with the ruling power."

144. John Pintard to Eliza Noel Pintard Davidson, 2 December 1820, in [Barck, ed.], *Letters from John Pintard*, 1:351. For the last decade of Wilkinson's life, see, especially, Hay, "General James Wilkinson."

145. [Armstrong], *"Memoirs of my own times,"* 15.

146. "General Wilkinson," *Niles' Weekly Register*, 18.

147. Hale, "Author's Note to Edition of 1897," in *Man without a Country*, 11. Hale was referring, in particular, to Wilkinson's memoirs, which he described as "preposterous," but the same statement could be made about the whole corpus of evidence regarding Wilkinson and the Burr Conspiracy (ibid., 13).

148. Wilkinson to Law, 6 October 1808, MdHi: Law Papers. Including their appendixes, "A Plain Tale," *Burr's Conspiracy Exposed*, *Brief Examination*, and the memoirs total well over three thousand printed pages.

149. [Wilkinson], *Brief Examination*, 3. During these years, Wilkinson had promised additional writings that never appeared, including a response to Joseph Hamilton Daveiss's *A View of the President's Conduct* in early 1808, a record of the inquest that fall, and three more volumes of memoirs; see Wilkinson to John Brown, 22 January 1808, InHi: Northwest Territory Collection; and Wilkinson, *Memoirs of My Own Times*, 1:vii.

150. William H. Seward to unknown correspondent, [January 1831], in Seward, *Autobiography of William H. Seward*, 170.

151. Butler, *History of the Commonwealth of Kentucky*, 319. Just a handful of the men and women whose reputations were damaged by the conspiracy outlived Burr, including John Adair (d. 1840), Margaret Blennerhassett (d. 1842), Andrew Jackson (d. 1845), and Samuel Swartwout (d. 1856).

152. Plumer, diary entry, 29 December 1806, in *WPMP*, 549. In the memoirs, Davis stated that Burr had taken this approach for all controversies, which he called "a great error" (*MAB*, 1:418). See Burr's letters to: Edward W. Tupper, [18 November 1806], in *PCAB*, 2:1002; William Henry Harrison, 27 November 1806, in ibid., 1005; and Clay, 1 December 1806, in *PHC*, 1:256–57.

153. Burr, comments, 31 March 1807, in *ECAB*, 23. For the proceedings in Kentucky, see Wood, *Full Statement of the Trial and Acquittal*. The best record of the hearings in the Mississippi Territory is Judge Thomas Rodney's notes in Hamilton, *Anglo-American Law on the Frontier*, 260–63. Burr's comments during the Richmond trial are scattered throughout Carpenter's and Robertson's reports.

154. Biddle, *Autobiography of Charles Biddle*, 323.

155. Blennerhassett, diary entry, 13 September 1807, in *BwB*, 87. See also the diary entries of 20 September, 4 and 11 October, and 10 November 1807, in ibid., 97–98, 120, 127–28, and 159. In December, Burr spent an "afternoon & evening" with the family of Princeton University president Samuel Stanhope Smith; Smith's daughter reported that she had "never [seen] him in better spirits" (Susan F. Smith to William Hamilton, 8 December 1807, NcU: William S. Hamilton Papers).

156. Phineas Bond to George Canning, 30 December 1807, as quoted in Mary-Jo Kline and Joanne Wood Ryan, "Editorial Note: The Road to Exile," in *PCAB*, 2:1045.

157. Burr to Mrs.——, 25 April 1809, in *PJAB-D*, 1:212. Burr's prospects also suffered because Williamson died in September. For this initial phase of Burr's European travels, see, in particular, Lomask, *Aaron Burr*, 2:293–317; Kline and Ryan, "Editorial Note: The Road to Exile," in *PCAB*, 2:1040–46; Isenberg, *Fallen Founder*, 369–80; and Stewart, *American Emperor*, 273–83. Also valuable for these issues are Cox, "Hispanic-American Phases"; and Hay, "Charles Williamson and the Burr Conspiracy."

158. Burr, diary entry, 28 March 1810, in *PJAB-B*, 1:430.

159. [Burr], "The United States," [1–13 March 1810], in *PCAB*, 2:1105; Louis Roux to the Duc de Cadore, 13 March 1810, in ibid., 1119. Translations of the four memoranda are grouped as "Documents Delivered to the Ministry of Foreign Affairs," in ibid., 1103–15. For their creation and delivery, see Kline and Ryan, "Editorial Note: Aaron Burr and Napoleon's Court," in ibid., 1099–1102. Burr's memorandum on the United States was "not at all clear," according to a description prepared for the emperor. But the foreign ministry surmised that Burr was proposing "to overthrow the Republican government" using the thousands of sailors left unemployed by the Embargo (unknown author, [summary of (Burr), "The United States"], undated, in ibid., 1105n). For Burr's time in Paris and

struggles to return to the United States, see also Lomask, *Aaron Burr*, 2:331–58; Kline and Ryan, "Editorial Note: Escape from the Empire" and "Editorial Note: Burr's Return to America," in *PCAB*, 2:1131–34 and 1145–48; Isenberg, *Fallen Founder*, 386–93; Stewart, *American Emperor*, 286–88; and Merrill and Endicott, *Aaron Burr in Exile*.

160. The literature on American interest in and support for the Spanish American revolutions in the 1810s and early 1820s is extensive. The surviving evidence suggests that Burr's interest grew only after independence had been achieved and investment opportunities had emerged; see Kline and Ryan, "Editorial Note: Burr and Latin American Independence," in *PCAB*, 2:1169–71.

161. Review of *Memoirs of Aaron Burr*, *New-York Mirror*, 215. For Davis, see Mushkat, "Matthew Livingston Davis"; and Pasley, "Matthew Livingston Davis's Notes." For memoir and autobiography in this period, see Freeman, *Rewriting the Self*; Arch, *After Franklin*; and Yagoda, *Memoir*. The bibliography in Casper, *Constructing American Lives*, includes numerous "memoirs" that were written by someone other than the subject.

162. *MAB*, 1:iii–iv. Joanne Freeman provides the most thorough discussion of Burr's efforts to defend himself against charges arising from the election of 1800; see Freeman, *Affairs of Honor*, 199–261. Burr had long collected exonerating evidence on this issue, including initiating the fraudulent lawsuit that forced senators James A. Bayard and Samuel Smith to provide depositions in 1805 and 1806. Before departing for Europe in 1808, Burr had directed his daughter to make use of the depositions "without any reserve" (Burr to Theodosia Burr Alston, [May 1808], in *PJAB-D*, 1:12). Davis printed some of the 1830 correspondence among Burr, Richard Bayard, and himself; see *MAB*, 2:100–111. But he seems to have been much clearer about his and Burr's roles in a conversation with Kentucky's James Taylor in Washington in late 1830 or early 1831; see James Taylor to Dolley Madison, 2 January 1831, in Mattern and Shulman, eds., *Selected Letters of Dolley Payne Madison*, 288–89.

163. Knapp, *Life of Aaron Burr*, vii, ix. It is not clear when this book was published, but a review appeared in early May 1835. For Knapp, see George Harvey Genzmer, "Knapp, Samuel Lorenzo," in *Dictionary of American Biography*, 10:452. For Knapp's consultations with Burr on the pension, see Burr's letters to Nelson Chase of 5 January 1834, in *PAB*; and 21 January 1834, in *PCAB*, 2:1219. Most recent biographies of Burr do not mention Knapp or Knapp's book.

164. Review of *The Life of Aaron Burr*, 143. "Such common, every-day matters as facts," the reviewer complained, Knapp "passes by, to reach after some gaudy butterfly, whose wings have brushed over his mind."

165. Review of *Life of Col. Aaron Burr*, 14–15.

166. *MAB*, 1:v. Davis also remarked that Burr was concerned "that '*kind friends*,'" a label that could easily have covered Knapp, "by attempts at explanation, might unintentionally misrepresent acts which they did not understand" (ibid., iv).

167. Burr to Theodosia Burr Alston, 10 July 1804, in ibid., 2:322.

168. Burr to Theodosia Burr Alston, [ca. April-May 1808], in *PJAB-D*, 1:13.
169. Burr to Jeremy Bentham, 2 February 1809, in ibid., 155. Burr referred to his outgoing letters, including "letter-press copies," in his 1804 instructions to Theodosia (Burr to Theodosia Burr Alston, 10 July 1804, in *MAB*, 2:323).
170. Burr, codicil, 26 July 1835, in *PCAB*, 1:xxx.
171. George Poindexter, testimony, 1 October 1807, in *TCAB*, 3:273. Poindexter, the federal district attorney for the Mississippi Territory, had heard Burr make this statement.
172. Buckner Thruston to Innes, 18 February 1807, DLC: Innes Papers. Letters reporting the existence of Burr's "Port Folio" flowed to the south, north, and east within days of his surrender. The news reached Wilkinson in New Orleans within two weeks; see Wilkinson to Dearborn, 29 January 1807, DNA: RG107, M221, W-247 (3). It arrived in central Kentucky within a month; see "Extract of a letter to the editor of the Palladium," *Enquirer*, 17 March 1807; and *Western World* (Frankfort, Ky.), 12 February 1807. And it reached the nation's capital a few days later, spreading first in congressional circles and then through Republican newspapers. See Taggart to Taylor, 18 February 1807, in "Letters of Samuel Taggart," 213; John Randolph to Edward Dillon, 21 February [1807], NcU: Dillon-Polk Family Papers; "Extract of a letter," *National Intelligencer*, 23 February 1807; and "Rumors," *Enquirer*, 24 February 1807.
173. Burr to Theodosia Burr Alston, [late May 1808], in *PJAB-D*, 1:20. A piece denying that there were "any papers of colonel Burr's in the possession of Mrs. Alston" appeared in early April in the same South Carolina newspaper that Joseph Alston had used two months earlier to deny any involvement in Burr's western project; see "Georgetown, S.C.," *National Intelligencer*, 20 April 1807, clipped from *Georgetown Gazette, and Commercial Advertiser* (S.C.). For Burr's insistence that he did not have Wilkinson's letters in Richmond, see Burr, comments, 25 June 1807, in *RTCAB*, 1:329.
174. Knapp, *Life of Aaron Burr*, viii. Recalling a conversation with the aging Burr from decades earlier, Benjamin Silliman described the contents of the box that may have been lost with Theodosia (he could not recall whether Burr had said that or he had heard it elsewhere) as documents that Burr had transcribed in the 1790s for a planned history of the Revolution; see Benjamin D. Silliman to Edward F. de Lancey, 22 January 1876, printed in Jones, *History of New York*, 1:609. (Nancy Isenberg's *Fallen Founder*, 398, led me to this letter.) In early 1813, it was thought that the *Patriot* had gone down in a storm. By 1820, however, new reports suggested that the former privateer had been seized by pirates, stripped of its valuables, and scuttled with its passengers and crew onboard. Further, but still inconclusive, support for this explanation appeared occasionally throughout the nineteenth century. For Theodosia's death, see Lomask, *Aaron Burr*, 2:361–63; Swick, "Theodosia Burr Alston"; and Côté, *Theodosia Burr Alston*, 259–327.
175. *MAB*, 1:iv.

176. "Late Col. Burr," 84. This piece had been clipped from the *New-York Gazette*.
177. Harman Blennerhassett to Burr, 4 October 1812, in *MAB*, 2:399. For Davis's efforts to recover Burr's papers, see Matthew Livingston Davis to Margaret Blennerhassett, 24 April 1837, DLC: Harman Blennerhassett Papers. According to published reports, Burr had left papers with his secretary, Charles Willie, that were examined by federal officials when Willie was detained in March; see "Burr's Papers Seized," *Enquirer*, 19 May 1807, clipped from *Orleans Gazette and Commercial Advertiser* (New Orleans). While this report from New Orleans was widely reprinted, the occasional editor who doubted it seems to have been justified in doing so. Judge Harry Toulmin's surviving letters about his questioning of Willie say nothing about Burr's papers; see Harry Toulmin to Jefferson, 5/13 April 1807, DLC: Edmond Charles Genet Papers; and Toulmin to James Madison, 14 April 1807, DLC: James Madison Papers. Nor were such papers produced during Burr's trial.
178. [J.F.H. Claiborne], "Incidents of the Detention of Aaron Burr by the Civil Authorities of the Mississippi Territory," *Free Trader* (Natchez, Miss.), 17 November 1841, WHi: Draper Manuscript Collection, 26CC28. For the history, see Claiborne, *Mississippi, as a Province, Territory and State*. Four years later, a fire destroyed Claiborne's "house and papers" (H. S. Halbert to Claiborne, 21 March 1884, DLC: John F. H. Claiborne Papers). Claiborne died barely two months afterward.
179. *MAB*, 1:iii.
180. Ibid., iv–v.
181. Ibid., 2:378, 375–76. Davis probably paid to use Blennerhassett's journal; he assured Margaret Blennerhassett that, "at the close of his life, [Burr] sought no concealment" (Davis to Margaret Blennerhassett, 24 April 1837, DLC: Blennerhassett Papers).
182. [Hawks], "*Memoirs of Aaron Burr*," 208n. For Hawks's authorship of this review, see below, n. 200. For another reviewer who considered Davis's claims of impartiality misleading, see Review of *Memoirs of Aaron Burr*, *American Quarterly Review*, 21:78.
183. *MAB*, 2:378–80, 383. Burr made the "deathbed" statement to Davis in June 1835, fifteen months before his death; see ibid., 378–79n.
184. Ibid., 1:[i]. Davis quoted Shakespeare's *Julius Caesar*, 3.2.76.
185. "Aaron Burr," *American Monthly Magazine*, 172.
186. [Adams], review of *Memoirs [and] Private Journal of Aaron Burr*, 157. Adams explicitly denied any "insinuat[ion] that Mr. Davis had the sense of the whole speech in his mind, when he took the extract from it to adorn his title-page." For a similar comment on the epigraph, see Review of *Memoirs of Aaron Burr*, *American Quarterly Review*, 21:74–75.
187. Review of *Memoirs of Aaron Burr*, *American Quarterly Review*, 21:74. For a widely read article that would have helped to fuel interest in the memoirs, see "Late Col. Burr."

188. [Adams], review of *Memoirs [and] Private Journal of Aaron Burr*, 158. Charles Francis Adams's father read the memoirs in the fall of 1837, including at least one evening when he read aloud from the first volume "to the ladies" of the household (John Quincy Adams, diary entry, 16 November 1837, in Adams, ed., *Memoirs of John Quincy Adams*, 9:429). A Virginia woman also reported reading aloud, "rather laboriously," from the memoirs (Anna C. Shirley to Charles [Campbell], undated, ViW: Charles Campbell Papers).

189. "Aaron Burr," *United States Magazine and Democratic Review*, 245.

190. Review of *Memoirs of Aaron Burr*, *American Quarterly Review*, 21:74. For a rare exception, see "Aaron Burr," *American Monthly Magazine*. The greatest criticism of Davis arose not from his treatment of any of Burr's public controversies, but from his admission that Burr had retained numerous letters that "indicat[ed] no very strict morality in some of his female correspondents." Davis claimed to have received many pleas for these letters once it was known that he would inherit Burr's papers, but he said that he had "committed [them] to the fire" "with [his] own hands" (*MAB*, 1:v–vi). The brief discussion of these letters suggested to readers and reviewers some combination of Burr's immorality, Davis's disloyalty, and even Davis's duplicity. This issue was revived two decades later with the publication of James Parton's *Life and Times of Aaron Burr* (1858), which, by denying that any of the letters had been "of the gross and abominable Kind that Mr. Davis would have us believe," fueled a new round of comments on Burr's morals and Davis's memoirs (James Parton to Samuel Osgood, 27 January 1858, NHi: AHMC—James Parton Papers).

191. Butler, *History of the Commonwealth of Kentucky*, 319. Others had hoped that Burr would write something so that his knowledge of the past "should not perish with [him]" (John Randolph to Jackson, 6 December 1832, in Bassett, ed., *Correspondence of Andrew Jackson*, 4:497).

192. "Aaron Burr," *New Englander and Yale Review*, 292.

193. "Aaron Burr," *United States Magazine*, 221, 248–49. For a similar opinion, see "Thomas Jefferson," *Globe* (Washington, D.C.), 22 November 1837 (from NCUN).

194. Review of *Memoirs of Aaron Burr*, *American Quarterly Review*, 22:380.

195. Review of *Life of Col. Aaron Burr*, 14.

196. Review of *The Life of Aaron Burr*, 143.

197. Review of *Memoirs of Aaron Burr*, *American Quarterly Review*, 22:380. See also "Aaron Burr," *National Atlas and Tuesday Morning Mail*, 380.

198. "Aaron Burr," *United States Magazine*, 245.

199. [Adams], review of *Memoirs [and] Private Journal of Aaron Burr*, 192–94.

200. George Templeton Strong, diary entry, 11 January 1838, in Nevins and Thomas, eds., *Diary of George Templeton Strong*, 1:81–82. Strong identified Hawks as the author and viewed Burr, not Davis, as Hawks's victim. For Hawks, see J. G. DeR. Hamilton, "Hawks, Francis Lister," in *Dictionary of American Biography*, 8:416–17.

201. [Hawks], *"Memoirs of Aaron Burr,"* 207, 209–10.

202. Butler, *History of the Commonwealth of Kentucky*, 319. Parton's *Life and Times of Aaron Burr* sold even better than Davis's memoirs, going through more than a dozen editions in the quarter century after its initial publication. Like Davis's memoirs, Parton's biography was widely reviewed, and, like Davis, Parton met with widespread criticism for his defense of Burr. For Parton, see, especially, Flower, *James Parton*, 41–46; and Casper, *Constructing American Lives*, 225–31.

203. [Adams], review of *Memoirs [and] Private Journal of Aaron Burr*, 159. For a similar statement of Burr's cultural role twenty years later, see "Aaron Burr," *New Englander*, 311.

204. [Hawks], *"Memoirs of Aaron Burr,"* 175. For nineteenth-century biography, see, especially, Casper, *Constructing American Lives*. The most valuable discussion of the cultural work performed by Burr's villainy, and of the extensive effort required to maintain a villainous Burr, is Hamilton, "Villains and Cultural Change." See also Kline, "Aaron Burr as a Symbol of Corruption"; and Drexler and White, *Traumatic Colonel*.

205. "Aaron Burr," *United States Magazine*, 249.

206. Charles Felton Pidgin to C. M. Clark Pub. Co., [ca. 1901–2], NjR: Charles Felton Pidgin Collection. Pidgin was active in the formation of the Aaron Burr Legion, which was founded in February 1902. He continued to mine the same vein with his 1907 book, *Theodosia, the First Gentlewoman of Her Time*. For Burr's place in nineteenth-century novels, plays, and short stories, see Wandell, *Aaron Burr in Literature*; Nolan, *Aaron Burr and the American Literary Imagination*; and Hamilton, "Villains and Cultural Change." Hamilton also examines the presentation of Burr in schoolbooks.

CONCLUSION

1. John Adams to James Lloyd, 14 February 1815, in Adams, ed., *Works of John Adams*, 10:122. I discussed Charles Francis Adams's review in Chapter 11. For John Quincy Adams's report, see "Report on Senator John Smith," 31 December 1807, in *ASP: Misc*, 1:701–3.

2. Ford, ed., "Some Papers of Aaron Burr," 48; Henry Adams to Samuel Eliot Morison, 28 November 1913, in Levenson et al., eds., *Letters of Henry Adams*, 6:624. For Adams's Burr biography, see Samuels, *Henry Adams*, 204–13.

3. Melton, *Aaron Burr*, 1.

4. Benjamin Ellis to Jacob Kingsbury, 30 November 1809, MiD-B: Jacob Kingsbury Papers. Ellis later ranked Burr, Wilkinson, and Jefferson with Benedict Arnold; see Ellis to Kingsbury, 15 February 1810, ibid.

5. Henry Baldwin to unknown correspondent, 18 February 1808, DLC: Burr Conspiracy Collection. The administration considered sending "a special agent" to obtain the papers from their hiding place but does not seem to have done so

(Albert Gallatin to Thomas Jefferson, 10 March 1808, DLC: Thomas Jefferson Papers). For the excised letter-book pages, see *OLBWC*, 4:33, 83, 115. Undecipherable letters include [Aaron Burr] to "Henry Windbourne," undated, DLC: Burr Conspiracy Collection; and John Graham to James Madison, 28 November 1806, ibid. For Burr's authorship of the letter to "Windbourne," see the examination of Charles Willie, Burr's personal secretary, in Harry Toulmin to Jefferson, 5/13 April 1807, DLC: Edmond Charles Genet Papers.

6. "Extract from a letter written by a resident of Richmond Hill, to his friend in the country," *Enquirer* (Richmond, Va.), 28 April 1807.

7. Thomas Truxton to Thomas Tingey, 13 January 1807, DLC: Thomas Truxton Papers.

8. "Aaron Burr," *Southern Literary Messenger*, 326.

PRIMARY SOURCE
BIBLIOGRAPHY

MANUSCRIPTS

Alabama

Alabama Department of Archives and History, Montgomery (A-Ar)

    Albert J. Pickett Papers

California

Henry E. Huntington Library, San Marino (CSmH)

    Huntington Manuscripts Collection
    Thomas Jefferson Papers (microfilm ed.)

Connecticut

Manuscripts and Archives, Sterling Memorial Library, Yale University, New Haven (CtY)

    Colonel John Brown and Major General Preston Brown Papers
    Burr Family Papers
    Hillhouse Family Papers

Delaware

Historical Society of Delaware, Wilmington (DeHi)

    H. Fletcher Brown Collection of Rodney Family Papers
    Duff Family Papers
    Fisher Papers
    Rodney Collection

District of Columbia

Library of Congress (DLC)

    Charles Bancker Papers
    Harman Blennerhassett Papers (microfilm ed.)
    Breckinridge Family Papers

Isaac Briggs Papers
James Brown Papers
Burr Conspiracy Collection (microfilm ed.)
George Washington Campbell Papers
John F. H. Claiborne Papers
Isaac Coles Diary
William Eaton Papers
Ellis & Allan Co. Papers
William Eustis Papers
Augustus John Foster Papers
Edmond Charles Genet Papers (microfilm ed.)
Francis and Gideon Granger Papers
Harry Innes Papers
Thomas Jefferson Papers (online ed.)
Thomas Sidney Jesup Papers
James Madison Papers (microfilm ed.)
John McKee Papers
James Monroe Papers (microfilm ed.)
Gouverneur Morris Papers (microfilm ed.)
Daniel Mulford Papers
Wilson Cary Nicholas Papers
Joseph H. Nicholson Papers
John Payne Papers
William Plumer Papers (microfilm ed.)
Edward Preble Papers
John Randolph of Roanoke Papers
Rodney Family Papers, 1770–1907
William Sampson Papers (microfilm ed.)
William Short Papers (microfilm ed.)
John Smith (ca. 1735–ca. 1824) Papers
Samuel Smith Family Papers (microfilm ed.)
Thomas Sumter Papers
Benjamin Tappan Papers (microfilm ed.)
Thomas Tingey Papers
Thomas Truxton Papers, 1795–1820
Thomas Tudor Tucker Papers (microfilm ed.)
James Wilkinson Papers
William Wirt Papers (microfilm ed.)

National Archives (DNA)

Record Group 21, Records of the U.S. District Court for the Southern
District of Ohio

Records Relating to the Proposed Trials of Aaron Burr and Harman Blennerhassett (T265)

Record Group 28, Records of the Post Office Department

Letters Sent by the Postmaster General, 1789–1826 (M601)

Record Group 45, General Records of the Department of the Navy

Letters Received by the Secretary of the Navy from Commanders (M147)

Letters Sent by the Secretary of the Navy to Officers, 1798–1868 (M149)

Miscellaneous Letters Received by the Secretary of the Navy, 1801–1884 (M124)

Miscellaneous Letters Sent by the Secretary of the Navy, 1798–1886 ("General Letter Books") (M209)

Record Group 49, Records of the Bureau of Land Management

Letters Received by the Surveyor General of the Territory Northwest of the River Ohio, 1797–1856 (M479)

Record Group 56, General Records of the Department of the Treasury

Letters Sent by the Secretary of the Treasury Relating to Public Lands ("N" Series), 1801–1878 (M733)

Record Group 59, General Records of the Department of State

Diplomatic Instructions of the Department of State, 1801–1906 (M77)

Domestic Letters of the Department of State, 1784–1906 (M40)

Letters of Application and Recommendation during the Administrations of Thomas Jefferson, 1801–1809 (M418)

Miscellaneous Drafts of Instructions, 1806–1870 (entry 7)

Miscellaneous Letters of the Department of State, 1789–1906 (M179)

Territorial Papers: Orleans (T260)

Record Group 94, Records of the Adjutant General's Office, 1780s–1917

James Wilkinson Courts Martial, 1811 and 1815 (M1136)

Record Group 107, Records of the Office of the Secretary of War

Letters Received by the Secretary of War, Registered Series, 1801–1870 (M221)

Letters Received by the Secretary of War, Unregistered Series, 1801–1870 (M222)

Letters Sent by the Secretary of War Relating to Military Affairs (M6)

Georgia

Hargrett Rare Book and Manuscript Library, University of Georgia Libraries, Athens (GU)

Joseph Wheaton Papers (microfilm ed.)

Illinois

Chicago History Museum Research Center (ICHi)

Aaron Burr Papers
Henry Dearborn Papers
Ninian Edwards Papers
Hardin Collection
Zebulon Pike Papers
Uriah Tracy Papers
James Wilkinson Papers (microfilm ed.)
William Woodbridge Papers

Newberry Library, Chicago (ICN)

Edward E. Ayer Manuscript Collection

Charles Williamson Papers

Everett D. Graff Collection of Western Americana

Aaron Burr Letters
Agreement between Aaron Burr and Cowles Mead
Julian Depestre Affidavit
Jacob Dunbaugh Letter
John McKee Letters
Thomas Power Letter

Special Collections Research Center, University of Chicago Library (ICU)

Reuben T. Durrett Collection

Mann Butler Papers
Durrett Codices
Miscellaneous Manuscripts

Indiana

Lilly Library, Indiana University, Bloomington (InU)

Meigs Manuscripts
Jonathan Williams Manuscripts

Indiana Historical Society, Indianapolis (InHi)

> Northwest Territory Collection
> Albert G. Porter Papers
> Benjamin Sebastian Papers

Kentucky

Library Special Collections, Western Kentucky University, Bowling Green (KyBgW)

> Lewis-Starling Collection

Kentucky Historical Society, Frankfort (KyHi)

> Joseph H. Daviess [sic] Papers
> Gen. James Taylor Papers

Special Collections Research Center, Margaret I. King Library, University of Kentucky, Lexington (KyU)

> Thomas Bodley Papers
> John Brown Papers
> James Wilkinson Papers

Filson Historical Society, Louisville (KyLoF)

> George Mortimer Bibb Papers
> Harman Blennerhassett Papers
> Orlando Brown Papers
> Joseph Hamilton Daveiss Papers
> Samuel Rose Papers
> Sanders Family Papers
> Charles Wilkins Short Papers
> Thomas Towles Papers
> James Wilkinson Miscellaneous Papers

Louisiana

Louisiana and Lower Mississippi Valley Collection, Louisiana State University Libraries, Baton Rouge (LU)

> Butler (Richard) Papers
> Claiborne (William C. C.) Letters and Depositions
> Evans (Nathaniel and Family) Papers
> Minor Family Papers
> Wilkinson (James) Letters

Historic New Orleans Collection (LNHiC)

    Elizabeth House Trist Letter
    James Wilkinson Letters
    Wilkinson-Stark Papers

Louisiana Research Collection, Tulane University, New Orleans (LNT-H)

    Aaron Burr Papers
    Grima Family Papers
    John McDonogh Papers
    James Wilkinson Collection

Louisiana Historical Center, Louisiana State Museum, New Orleans (L-M)

    Cenas Family Papers
    Nathaniel Cox Papers
    Record Group 68

New Orleans Public Library (LN)

    James Wilkinson Letter

Maryland

H. Furlong Baldwin Library, Maryland Historical Society, Baltimore (MdHi)

    Briggs-Stabler Papers
    Charles Carroll Papers (microfilm ed.)
    Dallam Papers
    Robert Goodloe Harper Papers (microfilm ed.)
    Thomas Law Family Papers
    Law Papers
    William Wirt Papers (microfilm ed.)

Massachusetts

Massachusetts Historical Society, Boston (MHi)

    Adams Family Papers (microfilm ed.)
    Thomas Jefferson Papers (Coolidge Collection) (online ed.)
    Timothy Pickering Papers (microfilm ed.)
    Winthrop Sargent Papers (microfilm ed.)

Michigan

William L. Clements Library, University of Michigan, Ann Arbor (MiU-C)

    Jonathan Dayton Papers
    John Holker Papers

Horace Holley Papers
Thomas Jefferson Papers
Miscellaneous Manuscripts
Samuel Latham Mitchill Papers
Southwest Territory Papers

Burton Historical Collection, Detroit Public Library (MiD-B)

Lewis Cass Papers
Stanley Griswold Papers
Jacob Kingsbury Papers
Soloman Sibley Papers
H. E. Watkins Papers
William Woodbridge Papers
Augustus Woodward Papers

Mississippi

Mississippi Department of Archives and History, Jackson (Ms-Ar)

J. F. H. Claiborne Collection
Territorial Governors' Records, series 488, Administrative Papers
Ventress (James Alexander) and Family Papers
Wailes-Covington Family Papers

Missouri

Missouri History Museum Archives, St. Louis (MoSHi)

Daniel Bissell Papers
Aaron Burr Papers
William C. Carr Papers
Chouteau Collection
Clark Family Collection
Rufus Easton Papers
John Baptiste Charles Lucas Papers
James Wilkinson Papers

Department of Special Collections, Washington University Libraries, St. Louis (MoSW)

Burr-Purkett Family Papers

New Jersey

Special Collections and University Archives, Alexander Library, Rutgers University, New Brunswick (NjR)

Charles Felton Pidgin Collection

Manuscripts Division, Department of Rare Books and Special Collections, Princeton University Library, Princeton (NjP)

> Aaron Burr Collection
> Fuller Collection of Aaron Burr
> Edward Livingston Papers

New York

Butler Library, Columbia University, New York (NNC)

> DeWitt Clinton Papers (microfilm ed.)

Gilder Lehrman Institute of American History, New York (NNGLI)

> Gilder Lehrman Collection (online ed.)

New-York Historical Society (NHi)

> AHMC—Edmond Charles Genet Papers
> AHMC—James Parton Papers
> AHMC—James Wilkinson Papers
> BV—Rufus King Papers
> Matthew Livingston Davis Papers
> Jacob Kingsbury and Kingsbury Family Papers
> Robert R. Livingston and Livingston Family Papers (microfilm ed.)
> William P. Van Ness Papers

New York Public Library (NN)

> James Monroe Papers (microfilm ed.)
> William Peter Van Ness Papers
> James Wilkinson Papers

North Carolina

Southern Historical Collection, Wilson Library, University of North Carolina, Chapel Hill (NcU)

> Cameron Family Papers
> Dillon-Polk Family Papers
> Peter Hagner Papers
> William S. Hamilton Papers
> Hayes Collection
> Lenoir Family Papers
> Miscellaneous Letters
> Mordecai Family Papers

Thomas Ruffin Papers
John Rutledge Papers
Nicholas P. Trist Papers

David M. Rubenstein Rare Book and Manuscript Library, Duke University, Durham (NcD)

Campbell Family Papers
Hemphill Family Papers

Ohio

Ross County Historical Society, Chillicothe (ORCHi)

Early Statehood Papers

Cincinnati History Library and Archives, Cincinnati Museum Center (OCHi)

Jacob Burnet Papers
Charles E. Cist Papers
Papers in the Defense of John Smith of Ohio (microfilm ed.)
William Prince Papers
Daniel Symmes Letter

Western Reserve Historical Society, Cleveland (OClWHi)

Joseph Buell Papers (microfilm ed.)
Samuel Huntington Papers
George Tod Papers

Ohio History Connection, Columbus (OHi)

Backus-Woodbridge Collection (microfilm ed.)
Blennerhassett Family Papers at Campus Martius Museum (microfilm ed.)
Ethan Allen Brown Papers (microfilm ed.)
John Graham Letters
Samuel P. Hildreth Papers
John G. Jackson Letters
Nathaniel Massie Papers (microfilm ed.)
Putnam Family Papers
Caleb Thorniley Letter
Edward Tiffin Papers (microfilm ed.)
Isaac Van Horne Papers
Thomas Worthington Papers (microfilm ed.)

Dawes Memorial Library, Marietta College (OMC)

Samuel P. Hildreth Collection

Pennsylvania

Historical Society of Pennsylvania, Philadelphia (PHi)

> Biddle Family Papers (microfilm ed.)
> Charles Biddle Papers
> Nicholas Biddle Letters
> Pierce Butler Letterbooks (microfilm ed.)
> Daniel W. Coxe Papers
> Ferdinand J. Dreer Collection
> Gilpin Family Papers
> Simon Gratz Autograph Collection
> James Hamilton Collection
> W. M. Horner Collection in MacPherson Family Papers
> Meredith Family Papers
> Daniel Parker Papers
> Jonathan Roberts Papers
> Society Collection—Graydon, Alexander
> Truxton-Biddle Letters

Darlington Collection, Special Collections Department, University of Pittsburgh (PPiU-D)

> Darlington Autograph Collection
> James Wilkinson Papers

South Carolina

South Carolina Historical Society, Charleston (ScHi)

> Henry Middleton Rutledge Letter

Manuscripts Division, South Caroliniana Library, University of South Carolina, Columbia (ScU)

> Samuel Green Papers
> Ralph Izard Papers
> John McFarlane Letter

Tennessee

Tennessee State Library and Archives, Nashville (T)

> George Washington Campbell Correspondence
> Jones Family Papers
> Sneed Family Papers
> Tennessee Historical Society, Miscellaneous Files
>
> > Nicholas Perkins Papers

Virginia

Albert and Shirley Small Special Collections Library, University of Virginia, Charlottesville (ViU)

> William T. Barry Letters
> James Breckinridge Papers
> Bryan Family Papers
> Cabell Family Papers (microfilm ed.)
> Carter-Smith Papers
> John Hartwell Cocke Papers
> Alexander Dick Journal
> Francis Walker Gilmer Correspondence
> Thomas Jefferson Papers (microfilm ed.)
> James Madison Correspondence
> Tracy W. McGregor Autograph Collection
> John Randolph Papers Microfilm
> Papers of the Randolph Family of Edgehill and Wilson Cary Nicholas
> John Smith Letter
> Webb-Prentis Family Papers
> James Wilkinson Letter

Library of Virginia, Richmond (Vi)

> Bryan Family Papers (microfilm ed.)
> Garnett-Mercer-Hunter Family Papers
> Gibson Family Papers
> John Hook Records
> Tazewell Family Papers

Virginia Historical Society, Richmond (ViHi)

> Allen Family Papers
> Edward Bates Papers
> Bemiss Family Papers
> Peachy Ridgway Gilmer Papers
> Graham Family Papers
> Hugh Blair Grigsby Papers
> George Hoadley Letter
> Massie Family Papers
> Stanard Family Papers
> Elizabeth (House) Trist Papers
> U.S. Circuit Court (7th Circuit), Ohio District, Papers
> Watson Family Papers
> Wickham Family Papers

Special Collections Research Center, Swem Library, College of William and Mary, Williamsburg (ViW)

> Charles Campbell Papers
> Jerdone Family Papers
> Tucker-Coleman Papers (microfilm ed.)
> Archibald Woods Papers

West Virginia

West Virginia and Regional History Center, West Virginia University Libraries, Morgantown (WvU)

> Harman Blennerhassett Papers
> Henderson-Tomlinson Family Papers

Wisconsin

Wisconsin Historical Society, Madison (WHi)

> Draper Manuscript Collection (microfilm ed.)

NEWSPAPERS

District of Columbia

(Georgetown) *Washington Federalist*
(Washington) *Atlantic World*
National Intelligencer, and Washington Advertiser
Washington Expositor, and Weekly Register

Georgia

(Savannah) *The Southern Patriot and Commercial Advertiser*

Kentucky

(Bairdstown) *Candid Review*
(Frankfort) *The Palladium*
(Frankfort) *The Western World*
(Lexington) *Kentucky Gazette and General Advertiser*
(Louisville) *The Western American*
(Russellville) *The Mirror*

Maryland

(Baltimore) *American, and Commercial Daily Advertiser*
Baltimore Evening Post

Federal Gazette & Baltimore Daily Advertiser
(Baltimore) *Federal Republican, & Commercial Gazette*
(Baltimore) *The North American, and Mercantile Daily Advertiser*
(Baltimore) *Whig, or Political Telescope*

Massachusetts

(Boston) *Columbian Centinel*
(Boston) *The Democrat*

Mississippi Territory

Mississippi Herald & Natchez Gazette
(Natchez) *Mississippi Messenger*

New York

(Hudson) *The Balance, and Columbian Repository*
(New York) *American Citizen*
(New York) *Morning Chronicle*
New-York Evening Post
(New York) *People's Friend & Daily Advertiser*
(New York) *Republican Watch-Tower*

North Carolina

Raleigh Register and North Carolina State Gazette

Ohio

(Chillicothe) *The Fredonian*
(Chillicothe) *The Scioto Gazette*
(Cincinnati) *Western Spy*
(Lebanon) *Western Star*

Orleans Territory

(New Orleans) *The Louisiana Gazette*
(New Orleans) *Moniteur de la Louisiane*
(New Orleans) *The Orleans Gazette and Commercial Advertiser*

Pennsylvania

(Philadelphia) *Aurora General Advertiser*
(Philadelphia) *The Spirit of the Press*
(Philadelphia) *The Tickler*
(Philadelphia) *United States' Gazette*
(Pittsburgh) *The Commonwealth*
Pittsburgh Gazette

South Carolina

Charleston Courier
(Charleston) *City Gazette and Daily Advertiser*
(Charleston) *L'Oracle*
Georgetown Gazette, and Commercial Advertiser

Tennessee

(Nashville) *Impartial Review, and Cumberland Repository*
(Nashville) *Tennessee Gazette, and Mero District Advertiser*

Virginia

(Fredericksburg) *Virginia Herald*
Norfolk Gazette and Public Ledger
Petersburg Intelligencer
(Richmond) *Enquirer*
(Richmond) *Impartial Observer*
(Richmond) *Virginia Argus*
(Richmond) *Virginia Gazette, and General Advertiser*

Newspaper databases

America's Historical Newspapers, NewsBank (AHN)
19th Century U.S. Newspapers, Gale Group (NCUN)

BOOKS AND ARTICLES

"Aaron Burr." *American Monthly Magazine*, n.s., 3 (February 1837): 172–80.
"Aaron Burr." *National Atlas and Tuesday Morning Mail* 1 (10 January 1837): 379–80.
"Aaron Burr." *New Englander and Yale Review* 16 (May 1858): 291–311.
"Aaron Burr." *Southern Literary Messenger* 26 (May 1858): 321–39.
"Aaron Burr." *United States Magazine and Democratic Review* 1 (January 1838): 221–49.
Abbey, R. "Blennerhassett Papers." *Home Circle* 6 (1860): 468–70, 528–31, 738–43.
[Abbott, John S. C.]. "And Who Was Blennerhasset?" *Harper's New Monthly Magazine* 54 (February 1877): 347–57.
Adams, Charles Francis, ed. *Memoirs of John Quincy Adams: Comprising Portions of His Diary from 1795 to 1848*. 12 vols. Philadelphia: J. B. Lippincott & Co., 1874–77.
[———]. Review of *Memoirs [and] Private Journal of Aaron Burr*. *North American Review* 49 (July 1839): 155–206.

————, ed. *The Works of John Adams, Second President of the United States: With a Life of the Author, Notes and Illustrations*. 10 vols. Boston: Little, Brown and Company, 1856.

Adams, Henry, ed. *The Writings of Albert Gallatin*. 3 vols. Philadelphia: J. B. Lippincott & Co., 1879.

Adams, John Quincy. *American Principles: A Review of Works of Fisher Ames, Compiled by a Number of His Friends*. Boston: Everett and Munroe, 1809.

Aderman, Ralph M., Herbert L. Kleinfield, and Jenifer S. Banks, eds. *Washington Irving: Letters*. 4 vols. Boston: Twayne Publishers, 1978–82.

Agrestis [pseud.]. *A Short Review of the Late Proceedings at New Orleans; And Some Remarks upon the Bill for Suspending the Privilege of the Writ of Habeas Corpus, which Passed the Senate of the United States During the Last Session of Congress. In Two Letters to the Printer, by Agrestis*. Georgetown, S.C.: n.p., 1807. Reprint, Richmond, Va.: Office of the *Impartial Observer*, 1807.

Allen, W. B., ed. *Works of Fisher Ames*. 2 vols. Indianapolis, Ind.: Liberty Classics, 1983.

The Amorous Intrigues and Adventures of Aaron Burr. New York: n.p., ca. 1861.

[Armstrong, John]. "*Memoirs of my own times. By General James Wilkinson.*" *Literary and Scientific Repository* 1 (1820): 1–24, 441–71.

Atwater, Caleb. *A History of the State of Ohio: Natural and Civil*. Cincinnati, Ohio: Glezen & Shepard, 1838.

[Bacon, Ezekial]. *Report of the Committee Appointed to Inquire into the Conduct of General Wilkinson, February 26, 1811*. Washington, D.C.: A. and G. Way, 1811.

Baldwin, Simeon E., ed. *Life and Letters of Simeon Baldwin*. New Haven, Conn.: Tuttle, Morehouse, and Taylor Co., 1919.

[Barck, Dorothy C., ed.]. *Letters from John Pintard to His Daughter, Eliza Noel Pintard Davidson, 1816–1833*. 4 vols. New York: New-York Historical Society Collections, 1940–41.

Barton, Benjamin Smith. *A Memoir Concerning the Fascinating Faculty which has been Ascribed to the Rattle-Snake and Other American Serpents*. Philadelphia: Henry Sweitzer, 1796.

Bassett, John Spencer, ed. *Correspondence of Andrew Jackson*. 7 vols. Washington, D.C.: Carnegie Institution of Washington, 1926–35.

Bay, W.V.N. *Reminiscences of the Bench and Bar of Missouri: With an Appendix Containing Biographical Sketches of Nearly All of the Judges and Lawyers Who Have Passed Away, Together with Many Interesting and Valuable Letters Never Before Published of Washington, Jefferson, Burr, Granger, Clinton, and Others, Some of Which Throw Additional Light upon the Famous Burr Conspiracy*. St. Louis, Mo.: F. H. Thomas and Company, 1878.

Bennett, Emerson. *The Traitor; or, The Fate of Ambition*. Cincinnati, Ohio: Stratton & Barnard, 1850. Reprint, Cincinnati, Ohio: U. P. James, 1860.

Bernard, John. *Retrospections of America, 1797–1811*. Edited by Mrs. Bayle Bernard. New York: Harper & Brothers, 1887.

Biddle, Charles. *Autobiography of Charles Biddle: Vice-President of the Supreme Executive Council of Pennsylvania, 1745–1821.* Philadelphia: E. Claxton and Company, 1883.

Bixby, William K., ed. *The Private Journal of Aaron Burr: Reprinted in Full from the Original Manuscript in the Library of Mr. William K. Bixby, of St. Louis, Mo.* 2 vols. Rochester, N.Y.: Genesee Press, 1903.

Blennerhassett-Adams, Therese. "The True Story of Harman Blennerhassett." *Century Illustrated Magazine*, n.s., 62 (July 1901): 351–56.

Bodley, Temple, ed. *Reprints of Littell's Political Transactions in and Concerning Kentucky and Letter of George Nicholas to his Friend in Virginia, also General Wilkinson's Memorial.* Louisville, Ky.: John P. Morton & Company, 1926.

Boyd, Julian P., et al., eds. *The Papers of Thomas Jefferson.* 42 vols. to date. Princeton, N.J.: Princeton University Press, 1950–.

Brackenridge, Henry M. *Recollections of Persons and Places in the West.* Philadelphia: J. Kay, Jun., and Brother, 1834.

Bradley, Abraham, Jr. *Map of the United States, Exhibiting the Post-roads, the Situations, Connexions & Distances of the Post-Offices, State Roads, Counties, & Principal Rivers.* Engraved by Francis Shallus. [Philadelphia: F. Shallus, 1804].

Bradley, Arthur Granville. "Harman Blennerhassett." *Macmillan's Magazine* 43 (June 1880): 97–108.

Bradley, Jared William, ed. *Interim Appointment: W. C. C. Claiborne Letter Book, 1804–1805.* Baton Rouge: Louisiana State University Press, 2001.

Breathitt, John. "Commencement of a Journal from Kentucky to the State of Pennsylvania—&c March 28th 1805." *Register of the Kentucky Historical Society* 52 (January 1954): 5–24.

Brewer, David J., ed. *The World's Best Orations: From the Earliest Period to the Present Time.* 10 vols. St. Louis, Mo.: Ferd P. Kaiser, 1900.

[Brown, Charles Brockden]. "Annals of Europe and America for 1807." *American Register, or General Repository of History, Politics, and Science, for 1807* 2 (1807): 1–22, 25–104.

[———]. "A Sketch of American Literature, for 1806–7." *American Register, or General Repository of History, Politics, and Science, for 1807* 1 (1807): 173–93.

Brown, Everett Somerville, ed. *William Plumer's Memorandum of Proceedings in the United States Senate, 1803–1807.* New York: Macmillan Company, 1923.

Brown, John Mason. *The Political Beginnings of Kentucky: A Narrative of Public Events Bearing on the History of that State up to the time of Its Admission into the American Union.* Louisville, Ky.: John P. Morton and Company, 1889.

Brugger, Robert J., et al., eds. *The Papers of James Madison: Secretary of State Series.* 10 vols. to date. Charlottesville: University Press of Virginia, 1986–.

Butler, Mann. *A History of the Commonwealth of Kentucky.* Louisville, Ky.: Wilcox, Dickerman & Co., 1834.

[Butler, William]. *Report of the Committee, Appointed to Inquire into the Conduct of Brigadier Gen. J. Wilkinson, May 1st, 1810.* Washington, D.C.: Roger C. Weightman, 1810.

Bynner, Edwin Lassetter. *Zachary Phips.* Boston: Houghton, Mifflin and Company, 1892.

Callcott, Margaret Law, ed. *Mistress of Riversdale: The Plantation Letters of Rosalie Stier Calvert, 1795–1821.* Baltimore, Md.: Johns Hopkins University Press, 1991.

Cappon, Lester J., ed. *The Adams-Jefferson Letters: The Complete Correspondence between Thomas Jefferson and Abigail and John Adams.* 2 vols. Chapel Hill: University of North Carolina Press, 1959.

"The Capture of Aaron Burr." *American Historical Magazine* 1 (April 1896): 140–53.

Carpenter, S. C. *Select American Speeches, Forensic and Parliamentary, with Prefatory Remarks: Being a Sequel to Dr. Chapman's 'Select Speeches'.* 2 vols. Philadelphia: J. W. Campbell, 1815.

Carpenter, T[homas]. *The Trial of Col. Aaron Burr, on an Indictment for Treason, Before the Circuit Court of the United States, Held in Richmond, (Virginia), May Term, 1807: Including the Arguments and Decisions on All the Motions Made during the Examination and Trial, and on the Motion for an Attachment against Gen. Wilkinson.* 3 vols. Washington, D.C.: Westcott & Co., 1807–8.

Carter, Clarence Edwin, et al., eds. *The Territorial Papers of the United States.* 28 vols. Washington, D.C.: United States Government Printing Office, 1934–76.

Carter, Edward C., II, John C. Van Horne, and Lee Formwalt, eds. *The Journals of Benjamin Henry Latrobe.* 3 vols. New Haven, Conn.: Yale University Press, 1977–80.

Citizen [pseud.]. *The Conspiracy; or, The Western Island, A Drama, in Five Acts.* New York: Henry Spear, 1838.

Claiborne, J.F.H. *Mississippi, as a Province, Territory and State with Biographical Notices of Eminent Citizens.* Vol. 1. Jackson, Miss.: Power & Barksdale, 1880.

Clark, D. W. "Blennerhassett and Aaron Burr." *Ladies' Repository* 14 (1854): 66–69, 107–11.

Clark, Daniel. *Deposition of Daniel Clark, the Delegate in the House of Representatives of the United States, from the Territory of Orleans, in Relation to the Conduct of General James Wilkinson.* Washington: A. & G. Way, 1808.

———. *Proofs of the Corruption of Gen. James Wilkinson, and of His Connexion with Aaron Burr.* Philadelphia: Wm. Hall, jun., and George W. Pierie, 1809. Reprint, New York: Arno Press, 1971.

"Col. Burr." *Observer* 1 (6 June 1807): 363–64.

Coleman, R. T. "Jo Daviess [*sic*], of Kentucky." *Harper's New Monthly Magazine* 21 (August 1860): 341–57.

[Colvin, John B.]. Editorial. *Colvin's Weekly Register* 1 (16 January 1808): 16.

[———]. "The Commander in Chief." *Colvin's Weekly Register* 1 (1808): 6–12, 19–27, 37–39.

[————]. "General Wilkinson." *Colvin's Weekly Register* 1 (20 February 1808): 81–83.

Cooke, Increase. *The American Orator: Or, Elegant Extracts in Prose and Poetry; Comprehending a Diversity of Oratorical Specimens, of the Eloquence of Popular Assemblies, of the Bar, of the Pulpit, &c. Principally Intended for the Use of Schools and Academies. To Which are prefixed, a Dissertation on Oratorical Delivery and the Outline of Gestures.* New Haven, Conn.: Sydney's Press, 1811.

Coombs, J. J. *The Trial of Aaron Burr for High Treason, in the Circuit Court of the United States for the District of Virginia, Summer Term, 1807.* Washington, D.C.: W. H. & C. H. Morrison, Publishers, 1864. Reprint, New York: Notable Trials Library, 1992.

"Correspondence of Thomas Jefferson, 1788–1826." *Glimpses of the Past* 3 (April–June 1936): 77–133.

Cox, Isaac J., ed. "Letters of William T. Barry, 1806–1810, 1829–1831." *American Historical Review* 16 (January 1911): 327–36.

————, ed. "Selections from the Torrence Papers." *Quarterly Publications of the Historical and Philosophical Society of Ohio* 1 (July–September 1906): 63–96; 2 (1907): 5–36, 93–120; 3 (July–September 1908): 65–102; 4 (July–September 1909): 93–138; 6 (January–March 1911): 1–44; 13 (April–June 1918): 79–130.

————, and Helen A. Swineford, eds. *"View of the President's Conduct Concerning the Conspiracy of 1806,* by J. H. Daveiss: A Reprint." *Quarterly Publications of the Historical and Philosophical Society of Ohio* 12 (April–June/July–September 1917): 49–154.

Crane, Elaine Forman, ed. *The Diary of Elizabeth Drinker.* 3 vols. Boston: Northeastern University Press, 1991.

Cuming, Fortescue. *Sketches of a Tour to the Western Country, through the States of Ohio and Kentucky; A Voyage down the Ohio and Mississippi Rivers, and a Trip through the Mississippi Territory, and Part of West Florida.* Pittsburgh, Pa.: Cramer, Spear & Eichbaum, 1810. Reprint, Cleveland, Ohio: Arthur H. Clark Company, 1904.

Cunningham, Noble E., Jr., ed. *Circular Letters of Congressmen to Their Constituents, 1789–1829.* 3 vols. Chapel Hill: University of North Carolina Press, 1978.

Cutler, William Parker, and Julia Perkins Cutler. *Life, Journals and Correspondence of Rev. Manasseh Cutler, LL.D.* 2 vols. Cincinnati, Ohio: Robert Clarke & Co., 1888.

Danvers, Jonathan Thierry. *A Picture of a Republican Magistrate of the New School: Being a Full Length Likeness of His Excellency Thomas Jefferson, President of the United States: To Which is Added a Short Criticism on the Characters and Pretensions of Mr. Madison, Mr. Clinton, and Mr. Pinckney.* New York: E. Sargeant, 1808.

Daveiss, J[oseph] H[amilton]. *A View of the President's Conduct, Concerning the Conspiracy of 1806.* Frankfort, Ky.: Joseph M. Street, 1807.

Daveiss, Mrs. M. T. "General John Adair." *American Historical Register and Monthly Gazette of the Patriotic-Hereditary Societies of the United States of America* 3 (October 1895): 228–34.

[Davezac, Auguste]. *The Trials of the Honb. James Workman, and Col. Lewis Kerr, Before the United States' Court, for the Orleans District, on a Charge of High Misdemeanor, in Planning and Setting on Foot, Within the United States, an Expedition for the Conquest and Emancipation of Mexico*. New Orleans, Orleans Territory: Bradford & Anderson, 1807.

Davis, Matthew L. *Memoirs of Aaron Burr: With Miscellaneous Selections from His Correspondence*. 2 vols. New York: Harper & Brothers, 1836–37. Reprint, Freeport, N.Y.: Books for Libraries Press, 1970.

————, ed. *The Private Journal of Aaron Burr, during His Residence of Four Years in Europe; With Selections from His Correspondence*. 2 vols. New York: Harper & Brothers, 1838.

Debate in the House of Representatives of the Territory of Orleans, on a Memorial to Congress, Respecting the Illegal Conduct of General Wilkinson. New Orleans, Orleans Territory: Bradford & Anderson, 1807.

Donald, Aïda DiPage, et al., eds. *Diary of Charles Francis Adams*. 8 vols. to date. Cambridge, Mass.: Belknap Press of Harvard University Press, 1964–.

"Dr. Mitchill's Letters from Washington, 1801–1813." *Harper's New Monthly Magazine* 48 (April 1879): 740–55.

[Duane, William]. *Politics for American Farmers: Being a Series of Tracts, Exhibiting the Blessings of Free Government, As It Is Administered in the United States, Compared with the Boasted Stupendous Fabric of British Monarchy*. Washington, D.C.: R. C. Weightman, 1807.

Dwight, Theodore. *The Character of Thomas Jefferson, as Exhibited in His Own Writings*. Boston: Weeks, Jordan & Company, 1839.

Ellis, George E., ed. "Diary of the Hon. Jonathan Mason." *Proceedings of the Massachusetts Historical Society*, 2nd ser., 2 (March 1885): 5–34.

Elmore, Anna D., ed. *The Journal of William D. Martin: A Journey from South Carolina to Connecticut in the Year 1809*. Charlotte, N.C.: Heritage House, 1959.

Esarey, Logan, ed. *Messages and Letters of William Henry Harrison*. 2 vols. Indianapolis: Indiana Historical Society, 1922.

Espy, Josiah Murdoch. *Memorandums of a Tour Made by Josiah Espy in the States of Ohio and Kentucky and Indiana Territory in 1805*. Cincinnati, Ohio: Robert Clarke & Co., 1870.

A Faithful Picture of the Political Situation of New Orleans, at the Close of the Last and the Beginning of the Present Year, 1807. New Orleans, Orleans Territory: n.p., 1807. Reprint, Boston: n.p., 1808.

Fitch, Raymond E., ed. *Breaking with Burr: Harman Blennerhassett's Journal, 1807*. Athens: Ohio University Press, 1988.

Ford, Paul Leicester, ed. *The Works of Thomas Jefferson* [Federal Edition]. 12 vols. New York: G. P. Putnam's Sons, 1904–5.

Ford, Worthington Chauncey, ed. "Letters of William Duane." *Proceedings of the Massachusetts Historical Society*, 2nd ser., 20 (May 1906): 257–394.

————, ed. "Some Papers of Aaron Burr." *Proceedings of the American Antiquarian Society*, n.s., 29 (1919): 43–128.

————, ed. *Thomas Jefferson Correspondence: Printed from the Originals in the Collections of William K. Bixby.* Boston: Plimpton Press, 1916.

————, ed. *Writings of John Quincy Adams.* 7 vols. New York: Macmillan Company, 1913–17.

The Forum Orator, Or the American Public Speaker: Consisting of Examples and Models of Eloquence, Both that of the Bar and Popular Assembly, of Orations and Speeches in the British Parliament and American Congress, and the Pleadings of Distinguished Advocates in Both Countries. Boston: David Carlisle, 1804.

Gales, Joseph, comp. *The Debates and Proceedings in the Congress of the United States.* 42 vols. Washington, D.C.: Gales and Seaton, 1834–56.

Garrison, Wendell Phillips, and Frances Jackson Garrison. *William Lloyd Garrison, 1805–1879: The Story of His Life Told by His Children.* 4 vols. New York: Century Co., 1885.

Gawalt, Gerard W., ed. *Justifying Jefferson: The Political Writings of John James Beckley.* Washington, D.C.: Library of Congress, 1995.

————, ed. "'Strict Truth': The Narrative of William Armistead Burwell." *Virginia Magazine of History and Biography* 101 (January 1993): 103–32.

Gayarré, Charles. *History of Louisiana: The Spanish Domination.* New York: William J. Widdleton, Publisher, 1866.

Gelles, Edith, ed. *Abigail Adams: Letters.* New York: Library of America, 2016.

"General Wilkinson." *Niles' Weekly Register* 30 (11 March 1826): 18.

"General Wilkinson." *Ordeal* 1 (10 June 1809): 360–62.

Gibbens, Alvaro F. *Historic Blennerhassett Island Home, Near Parkersburg, W. Va.: Expedition against Spain.* Parkersburg, W.Va.: Globe Printing and Binding Co., 1899.

Gilmer, Francis Walker. *Sketches of American Orators.* Baltimore, Md.: Fielding Lucas Jr., 1816.

Goldsmith, Oliver. *Goldsmith's Roman History: Abridged by Himself for the Use of Schools.* 4th Amer. ed. Wilmington, Del.: Rev. William Pryce, 1806.

Grant, C. L., ed. *Letters, Journals, and Writings of Benjamin Hawkins.* 2 vols. Savannah, Ga.: Beehive Press, 1980.

Gratz, Simon, ed. "Thomas Rodney." *Pennsylvania Magazine of History and Biography* 43 (1919): 1–23, 117–42, 208–27, 332–67; 44 (1920): 47–72, 170–89, 270–84, 289–308; 45 (1921): 34–65, 180–203.

Green, J. H. "The Blennerhassetts." *Emerson Bennett's Dollar Monthly* 1 (September 1860): 408–10.

Green, Thomas Marshall. *The Spanish Conspiracy: A Review of Early Spanish Movements in the South-west: Containing Proofs of the Intrigues of James Wilkinson and John Brown; of the Complicity Therewith of Judges Sebastian, Wallace, and Innes; The Early Struggles of Kentucky for Autonomy; The Intrigues of Sebastian in 1795–7, and the Legislative Investigation of His Corruption.* Cincinnati, Ohio: R. Clarke & Co., 1891.

Hale, Edward Everett. *The Man without a Country and Other Stories.* Boston: Little, Brown, and Company, 1898.

Hall, [James]. *Letters from the West: Containing Sketches of Scenery, Manners, and Customs and Anecdotes Connected with the First Settlements of the Western Sections of the United States.* London: Henry Colburn, 1828.

Hamilton, J. G. de Roulhac, ed. *The Papers of Thomas Ruffin.* 4 vols. Publications of the North Carolina Historical Society. Raleigh, N.C.: Edwards & Broughton Printing Co., 1918–20.

Harris, Thaddeus Mason. *The Journal of a Tour into the Territory Northwest of the Alleghany Mountains: Made in the Spring of the Year 1803, with a Geographical and Historical Account of the State of Ohio.* Boston: Manning and Loring, 1805. Reprint, Cleveland, Ohio: Arthur H. Clark Company, 1904.

[Harter, Mrs. Michael D., ed.]. *The Aaron Burr Expedition: Letters to Ephraim Brown from Silas Brown, 1805–1815.* [Mansfield, Ohio]: privately printed, ca. 1915.

Hartridge, Walter Charlton, ed. *The Letters of Robert Mackay to His Wife: Written from Ports in America and England, 1795–1816.* Athens: University of Georgia Press, 1949.

[Hawks, Francis Lister]. "Memoirs of Aaron Burr." *New York Review* 2 (January 1838): 175–213.

Hecht, Arthur, ed. "The Burr Conspiracy and the Post Office Department." *Missouri Historical Society Bulletin* 12 (January 1956): 128–45.

[Hening, William W., and William Munford]. *The Examination of Col. Aaron Burr before the Chief Justice of the United States, upon the Charge of a High Misdemeanor, and of Treason against the United States.* Richmond, Va.: S. Grantland, 1807.

Henshaw, Lesley, ed. "Burr-Blennerhassett Documents." *Quarterly Publications of the Historical and Philosophical Society of Ohio* 9 (January–April 1914): 3–60.

Hildreth, Richard. *The History of the United States of America: From the Adoption of the Federal Constitution to the End of the Sixteenth Congress.* Rev. ed. 3 vols. New York: Harper & Brothers, Publishers, 1851.

Hildreth, Samuel P. *Biographical and Historical Memoirs of the Early Pioneer Settlers of Ohio, with Narratives of Incidents and Occurrences in 1775.* Cincinnati, Ohio: H. W. Derby & Co., Publishers, 1852.

[————]. "Biographical Sketch of Herman Blennerhassett, and Mrs. Margaret Blennerhassett." *American Review: A Whig Journal Devoted to Politics and Literature* 1 (April 1848): 368–83.

————, ed. "History of a Voyage from Marietta to New Orleans, in 1805." *American Pioneer* 1 (1842): 89–105, 128–45.

Hollingsworth, Lynne, Kenneth H. Williams, and James Russell Harris, eds. "Early Kentuckians and the New Nation: The Samuel McDowell Family Letters." *Register of the Kentucky Historical Society* 100 (Summer 2002): 329–48.

Hopkins, James F., et al., eds. *The Papers of Henry Clay.* 10 vols. and Supplement. Lexington: University Press of Kentucky, 1959–92.

"An Interview of Governor Folch with General Wilkinson." *American Historical Review* 10 (July 1905): 832–40.

"The Island Paradise." *Yale Literary Magazine* 20 (April 1855): 220–24.

Jameson, J. Franklin, ed. "Diary of Edward Hooker, 1805–1808." In *Annual Report of the American Historical Association for the Year 1896.* Washington, D.C.: Government Printing Office, 1897.

[Jefferson, Thomas]. *Message from the President of the United States, Transmitting a Copy of the Proceedings and of the Evidence Exhibited on the Arraignment of Aaron Burr, and Others, Before the Circuit Court of the United States, Held in Virginia, in the Year 1807.* Washington, D.C.: A. & G. Way, Printers, 1807.

Jeffrey, Thomas E., ed. *The Microfiche Edition of the Papers of Benjamin Henry Latrobe.* Microfiche ed. Clifton, N.J.: James T. White & Co., 1976.

Jenkins, J. Brian. *Citizen Daniel (1775–1835) and the Call of America: Early Correspondence of the Constables of Horley.* Hartford, Conn.: Aardvark Editorial Services, 2000.

Johnson, Herbert A., et al., eds. *The Papers of John Marshall.* 12 vols. Chapel Hill: University of North Carolina Press, 1974–2006.

Jones, Thomas. *History of New York during the Revolutionary War, and of the Leading Events in the Other Colonies at That Period.* Edited by Edward Floyd deLancey. Vol. 1. New York: New York Historical Society, 1879.

Jordan, Daniel P., ed. "Partisan Politics in Territorial Mississippi: A Staunch Republican's Direct Report, December, 1807." *Journal of Mississippi History* 41 (August 1979): 231–40.

Judd, Jacob, ed. *Van Cortlandt Family Papers.* 4 vols. Tarrytown, N.Y.: Sleepy Hollow Press, 1976–81.

Keene, Richard Raynal. *A Letter of Vindication to His Excellency Colonel Monroe, President of the United States.* Philadelphia: n.p., 1824.

Kennedy, John P. *Memoirs of the Life of William Wirt, Attorney-General of the United States.* Rev. ed. 2 vols. Philadelphia: Lea and Blanchard, 1850.

Kentuckian [James Wilkinson]. *A Plain Tale, Supported by Authentic Documents, Justifying the Character of General Wilkinson.* Edited by Jonathan Williams. New York: n.p., 1807.

Kentucky House of Representatives. *Journal of the House of Representatives of the Commonwealth of Kentucky: Begun and Held at the Capitol, in the Town of Frankfort, on Monday the Third of November, in the Year of Our Lord One Thousand, Eight Hundred and Six, and of the Commonwealth the Fifteenth.* Frankfort, Ky.: William Hunter, 1806.

Kierner, Cynthia A. *The Contrast: Manners, Morals, and Authority in the Early American Republic.* New York: New York University Press, 2007.

King, Charles R., ed. *The Life and Correspondence of Rufus King: Comprising His Letters, Private and Official, His Public Documents and His Speeches.* 6 vols. New York: G. P. Putnam's Sons, 1894–1900.

Kline, Mary-Jo, and Joanne Wood Ryan, eds. *The Papers of Aaron Burr, 1756–1836*. Microfilm ed. Glen Rock, N.J.: Microfilming Corporation of America, 1978.
————, eds. *Political Correspondence and Public Papers of Aaron Burr*. 2 vols. Princeton, N.J.: Princeton University Press, 1983.
Knapp, Samuel Lorenzo. *The Life of Aaron Burr*. New York: Wiley & Long, 1835.
Lady [Margaret Blennerhassett]. *The Widow of the Rock and Other Poems*. Montreal: E. V. Sparhawk, 1824.
Lambert, John. *Travels through Lower Canada and the United States of North America, in the Years 1806, 1807, and 1808: To Which are Added, Biographical Notices and Anecdotes of Some of the Leading Characters in the United States, and of Those who have, at Various Periods, Borne a Conspicuous Part in the Politics of that Country*. 3 vols. London: Richard Phillips, 1810.
"The Late Col. Burr." *Niles' Weekly Register* 10 (8 October 1836): 83–84.
"Letter of William Eaton on Burr's Trial." *Historical Magazine, and Notes and Queries Concerning the Antiquities, History and Biography of America* 7 (September 1863): 285.
"Letters of Samuel Taggart, 1803–1814." *Proceedings of the American Antiquarian Society*, n.s., 33 (1923): 113–226, 297–438.
"Letters of William T. Barry." *William and Mary Quarterly* 13 (1904): 107–16, 236–44; 14 (1905): 19–23, (1906): 230–41.
Levenson, J. C., et al., eds. *The Letters of Henry Adams*. 6 vols. Cambridge, Mass.: Belknap Press of Harvard University Press, 1982–88.
Lipscomb, Andrew A., and Albert Ellery Bergh, eds. *The Writings of Thomas Jefferson*. Definitive ed. 20 vols. Washington, D.C.: Thomas Jefferson Memorial Association, 1905-7.
Looney, J. Jefferson, ed. *The Papers of Thomas Jefferson: Retirement Series*. 11 vols. to date. Princeton, N.J.: Princeton University Press, 2004–.
Lossing, Benson J. "Burr's Conspiracy." *Harper's New Monthly Magazine* 25 (June 1862): 69–77.
Louisianian [James Johnston]. *The Invitation, A Poem Addressed to General Wilkinson, Commander in Chief of the United States Army*. Natchez, Mississippi Territory: Andrew Marschalk, [1807].
Lowrie, Walter, et al., eds. *American State Papers: Documents, Legislative and Executive, of the Congress of the United States*. 38 vols. in 10 series. Washington, D.C.: Gales and Seaton, 1832–61.
Magruder, Allan B. *A Letter from Allan B. Magruder, Esq. of Opelousas, to His Correspondent in the State of Virginia, Dated 20th Nov. 1807*. New Orleans, Orleans Territory: Bradford & Anderson, 1808.
Mansfield, Edward D. *Personal Memories: Social, Political, and Literary, with Sketches of Many Noted People, 1803–1843*. Cincinnati, Ohio: R. Clarke, 1879.
Marshall, Humphrey. *Biography of Henry Clay—By Geo. D. Prentice: Reviewed and Revised by Humphrey Marshall in Relation to Himself and the Late Col. J. H. Daviess*. Maysville, Ky.: *Monitor* Office, 1832.

————. *The History of Kentucky, Exhibiting an Account of the Modern Discovery; Settlement; Progressive Improvement; Civil and Military Transactions; and the Present State of the Country.* 2 vols. Frankfort, Ky.: Geo. S. Robinson, 1824.

Marshall, Thomas Maitland, ed. *The Life and Papers of Frederick Bates.* 2 vols. St. Louis: Missouri Historical Society, 1926.

Maryland House of Delegates. *Votes and Proceedings of the House of Delegates: November Session 1807.* Early State Records Online. Archives of Maryland Online. Accessed 30 April 2011. http://aomol.msa.maryland.gov/megafile/msa /speccol/sc4800/sc4872/html/index.html.

Massie, David Meade. *Nathaniel Massie, a Pioneer of Ohio: A Sketch of His Life and Selections from His Correspondence.* Cincinnati, Ohio: Robert Clarke Company, 1896.

Mattern, David B., and Holly Shulman, eds. *Selected Letters of Dolley Payne Madison.* Charlottesville: University of Virginia Press, 2003.

McClure, Alexander K., and Byron Andrews, eds. *Famous American Statesmen and Orators, Past and Present: With Biographical Sketches and Their Famous Orations.* 6 vols. New York: F. F. Lovell, 1902.

McLaughlin, Jack, ed. *To His Excellency Thomas Jefferson: Letters to a President.* New York: W. W. Norton & Company, 1991.

McLean, Malcolm D., comp. and ed. *Papers Concerning Robertson's Colony in Texas.* Vol. 1, *1788–1822, The Texas Association.* Fort Worth: Texas Christian University Press, 1974.

McPherson, Elizabeth Gregory, ed. "Letters of William Tatham." *William and Mary Quarterly*, 2nd ser., 16 (1936): 162–91, 362–98.

Melish, John. *Travels in the United States of America, in the Years 1806 & 1807, and 1809, 1810, & 1811; Including an Account of Passage betwixt America and Britain, and Travels through Various Parts of Great Britain, Ireland, and Canada.* 2 vols. Philadelphia: Thomas & George Palmer, 1812.

"Memoranda Made by Thomas R. Joynes on a Journey to the States of Ohio and Kentucky, 1810." *William and Mary Quarterly* 10 (1902): 145–58, 221–32.

Merrill, Michael, and Sean Wilentz, eds. *The Key of Liberty: The Life and Democratic Writings of William Manning, "A Laborer," 1747–1814.* Cambridge, Mass.: Harvard University Press, 1993.

Mevers, Frank C., et al., eds. *The William Plumer Papers, 1778–1854: William Plumer, 1759–1850, and William Plumer, Jr., 1789–1854.* Microfilm ed. New York: Microfilming Corporation of America, 1982.

M'Henry, James. *Baltimore Directory, and Citizens' Register, for 1807.* Baltimore, Md.: Warner & Hanna, 1807.

Miller, Lillian B., et al., eds. *The Selected Papers of Charles Willson Peale and His Family.* 5 vols. New Haven, Conn.: Yale University Press, 1983–2000.

"Miscellany." *Port-Folio* 3 (16 May 1807): 314–15.

Moody, Robert E., ed. *The Saltonstall Papers, 1607–1815: Selected and Edited and with Biographies of Ten Members of the Saltonstall Family in Six Generations.* 2 vols. Boston: Massachusetts Historical Society, 1973–74.

Moore, Frank, ed. *American Eloquence: A Collection of Speeches and Addresses, by the Most Eminent Orators of America; with Biographical Sketches and Illustrative Notes*. 2 vols. New York: D. Appleton and Company, 1857.

Moore, John Bassett, ed. *The Works of James Buchanan: Comprising His Speeches, State Papers, and Private Correspondence*. 12 vols. Philadelphia: J. B. Lippincott Company, 1908–11. Reprint, New York: Antiquarian Press Ltd., 1960.

Moore, W. "William Wirt." *Literary Scrap Book and Monthly Family Magazine* 1 (April 1855): 30–32.

Mordecai, Samuel. *Virginia, Especially Richmond, in By-gone Days; With a Glance at the Present: Being Reminiscences and Last Words of An Old Citizen*. 2nd ed. Richmond, Va.: West & Johnson, Publishers, 1860. Reprint, Richmond, Va.: Dietz Press, 1946.

"Mrs. Blennerhassett." *Supplement to the Courant* 15 (19 October 1850): 166.

Nevins, Allan, and Milton Halsey Thomas, eds. *The Diary of George Templeton Strong*. 4 vols. New York: Macmillan, 1952.

A New Roman History: From the Foundation of Rome, to the End of the Commonwealth. Philadelphia: Mathew Carey, 1809.

Newman, John B. *Fascination, or The Philosophy of Charming: Illustrating the Principles of Life in Connection with Spirit and Matter*. New York: Fowler and Wells, 1848.

Nolte, Vincent Otto. *Fifty Years in Both Hemispheres; Or, Reminiscences of the Life of a Former Merchant*. New York: Redfield, 1854.

Owens, Thomas McAdory, ed. "Burr's Conspiracy." *Transactions of the Alabama Historical Society* 3 (1888–89): 167–77.

Padgett, James A., ed. "The Letters of Doctor Samuel Brown to President Jefferson and James Brown." *Register of the Kentucky State Historical Society* 35 (April 1937): 99–130.

———, ed. "The Letters of Honorable John Brown to the Presidents of the United States." *Register of the Kentucky State Historical Society* 35 (January 1937): 1–28.

———, ed. "The Letters of James Taylor to the Presidents of the United States." *Register of the Kentucky State Historical Society* 34 (April 1936): 103–36.

Parton, J[ames]. *The Life and Times of Aaron Burr, Lieutenant-Colonel in the Army of the Revolution, United States Senator, Vice-President of the United States, etc.* New York: Mason Brothers, 1858.

Pate, James P., ed. *The Reminiscences of George Strother Gaines: Pioneer and Statesman of Early Alabama and Mississippi, 1805–1843*. Tuscaloosa: University of Alabama Press, 1998.

Pickering, Octavius, and Charles W. Upham, eds. *The Life of Timothy Pickering*. 4 vols. Boston: Little, Brown, 1867–73.

[Pickett, Albert James]. *Arrest of Aaron Burr in Alabama in 1807*. N.p.: n.p., ca. 1850.

———. *History of Alabama*. 2 vols. Charleston, S.C.: Walker & Jones, 1851.

"Pickett's History of Alabama." *Southern Quarterly Review* 21 (January 1852): 182–209.

Pidgin, Charles Felton. *Blennerhassett; Or, The Irony of Fate: A Dramatic Romance in a Prologue and Four Acts Founded upon Incidents in the Life of Harman Blennerhassett, His Wife Margaret, Aaron Burr, His Daughter Theodosia, and Alexander Hamilton*. Boston: C. M. Clark Publishing Co., 1901.

[———]. "Opening Address of the Councilor-in-Chief at the Aaron Burr Memorial Meeting." In *The Aaron Burr Memorial: Prepared and Edited by the Grand Camp of the Aaron Burr Legion in Commemoration of the 147th Anniversary of the Birthday of Colonel Aaron Burr*, edited by [Charles Felton Pidgin], 3–9. Boston: Mount Vernon Book and Music Co., 1905.

Prentice, George D. *Biography of Henry Clay*. Hartford, Conn.: Samuel Hammer, Jr., and John Jay Phelps, Publishers, 1831.

[Prentiss, Charles]. *The Life of the Late Gen. William Eaton: Several Years an Officer in the United States' Army, Consul at the Regency of Tunis on the Coast of Barbary, and Commander of the Christian and Other Forces that Marched from Egypt Through the Desert of Barca, in 1805, and Conquered the City of Derne, which Led to the Treaty of Peace between the United States and the Regency of Tripoli: Principally Collected from His Correspondence and Other Manuscripts*. Brookfield, Mass.: E. Merriam & Co., 1813.

Prince, Carl E., and Helene H. Fineman, eds. *The Papers of Albert Gallatin*. Microfilm ed. Philadelphia: Rhistoric Publications, 1970.

Randall, Henry S. *The Life of Thomas Jefferson*. 3 vols. New York: Derby & Jackson, 1858.

Randolph, Thomas Jefferson, ed. *Memoir, Correspondence, and Miscellanies: From the Papers of Thomas Jefferson*. 4 vols. Charlottesville, Va.: F. Carr and Co., 1829.

Reed, Thomas B., ed. *Political Oratory*. 5 vols. Philadelphia: Dorian and Company, 1903.

Review of *A Discourse on the Life and Character of Wm. Wirt*, by John P. Kennedy. *Southern Literary Messenger* 1 (August 1834): 16–18.

Review of *A Letter to the Respectable Citizens, Inhabitants of the County of Orleans*. *Monthly Register, Magazine, and Review of the United States* 3 (September 1807): 228–30.

Review of *The Life of Aaron Burr*. *New-England Magazine* 9 (August 1835): 143.

Review of *Life of Col. Aaron Burr*. *Literary Gazette* 2 (1 May 1835): 14–15.

Review of *The Life of Harman Blennerhassett*. *North American Review* 79 (October 1854): 297–326.

Review of *Memoirs of Aaron Burr*. *American Quarterly Review* 21 (March 1837): 74–112; 22 (December 1837): 350–87.

Review of *Memoirs of Aaron Burr*. *New-York Mirror* 14 (31 December 1836): 215.

Review of *Memoirs of my own times*: by General James Wilkinson. *American Monthly Magazine and Critical Review* 1 (May 1817): 40–44.

Review of *Memoirs of my own times. By General James Wilkinson*. *North American Review and Miscellaneous Journal* 6 (November 1817): 78–109.

Review of *Memoirs of my own Times. By General JAMES WILKINSON. Portico* 4 (July 1817): 28–41.

Rice, Harvey. "Burr's Western Expedition." *Magazine of Western History* 5 (April 1887): 730–46.

Richardson, James D., comp. *A Compilation of the Messages and Papers of the Presidents, 1789–1897.* 10 vols. Washington, D.C.: U.S. Government Printing Office, 1897–99.

[Rives, William C., and Philip R. Fendall, eds.]. *Letters and Other Writings of James Madison, Fourth President of the United States.* 4 vols. Philadelphia: J. B. Lippincott & Co., 1865.

Robertson, David. *Reports of the Trials of Colonel Aaron Burr, (Late Vice President of the United States,) for Treason, and for a Misdemeanor, in Preparing the Means of a Military Expedition against Mexico, a Territory of the King of Spain, with whom the United States were at Peace. In the Circuit Court of the United States, Held at the City of Richmond, in the District of Virginia, in the Summer Term of the Year 1807.* 2 vols. Philadelphia: Hopkins and Earle, 1808. Reprint, New York: Da Capo Press, 1969.

Robin, C. C. *Voyage to Louisiana.* Edited and translated by Stuart O. Landry, Jr. New Orleans, La.: Pelican Publishing Company, 1966.

Rowland, Dunbar, ed. *Official Letter Books of William C. C. Claiborne, 1801–1816.* 6 vols. Jackson, Miss.: State Department of Archives and History, 1917.

———. *Third Annual Report of the Director of the Department of Archives and History of the State of Mississippi, from October 1, 1903, to October 1, 1904, with Accompanying Historical Documents Concerning the Aaron Burr Conspiracy.* Nashville, Tenn.: Brandon Printing Company, 1905.

Rowland, Kate Mason. *The Life of Charles Carroll of Carrollton, 1737–1832, with His Correspondence and Public Papers.* 2 vols. New York: G. P. Putnam's Sons, 1898.

Rutland, Robert A., et al., eds. *The Papers of James Madison: Presidential Series.* 8 vols. to date. Charlottesville: University Press of Virginia, 1984–.

Safford, William H. *The Blennerhassett Papers, Embodying the Private Journal of Harman Blennerhassett, and the Hitherto Unpublished Correspondence of Burr, Alston, Comfort Tyler, Devereaux, Dayton, Adair, Miro, Emmett, Theodosia Burr Alston, Mrs. Blennerhassett, and Others, Their Contemporaries; Developing the Purposes and Aims of those Engaged in the Attempted Wilkinson and Burr Revolution.* Cincinnati, Ohio: Moore, Wilstach & Baldwin, 1864.

———. *The Life of Harman Blennerhassett: Comprising an Authentic Narrative of the Burr Expedition: and Containing Many Additional Facts Not Heretofore Published.* Cincinnati, Ohio: Ely, Allen & Looker, 1850. Reprint, Cincinnati, Ohio: Moore, Anderson, Wilstach & Keys, 1853.

Sawvel, Franklin B., ed. *The Complete Anas of Thomas Jefferson.* New York: Round Table Press, 1903.

Schultz, Christian, Jr. *Travels on an Inland Voyage through the States of New-York, Pennsylvania, Virginia, Ohio, Kentucky, and Tennessee, and through the Territories of*

Indiana, Louisiana, Mississippi, and New-Orleans. 2 vols. New York: Isaac Riley, 1810. Reprint, Ridgewood, N.J.: Gregg Press, 1968.

Schutz, John A., and Douglass Adair, eds. *The Spur of Fame: Dialogues of John Adams and Richard Rush, 1805–1813.* San Marino, Calif.: Huntington Library Press, 1923.

Scott, Winfield. *Memoirs of Lieut.-General Scott, Ll.D.* 2 vols. New York: Sheldon & Company, Publishers, 1864.

Seward, Frederick W. *Autobiography of William H. Seward, from 1801 to 1834: With a Memoir of His Life, and Selections from His Letters from 1831 to 1846.* New York: D. Appleton and Company, 1877.

Shepherd, William R., ed. "A Letter of General James Wilkinson, 1806." *American Historical Review* 9 (April 1904): 533–37.

Simkins, Eldred. *An Oration, in Commemoration of the Anniversary of American Independence, Delivered at Edgefield Court-House, on the Fourth of July 1807.* Augusta, Ga.: *Chronicle* Office, 1807.

Smith, Dwight L., and Ray Swick, eds. *A Journey through the West: Thomas Rodney's 1803 Journal from Delaware to the Mississippi Territory.* Athens: Ohio University Press, 1997.

Smith, James Morton, ed. *The Republic of Letters: The Correspondence between Thomas Jefferson and James Madison, 1776–1826.* 3 vols. New York: W. W. Norton & Company, 1995.

Smith, Sam B., et al., eds. *The Papers of Andrew Jackson.* 10 vols. to date. Knoxville: University of Tennessee Press, 1980–.

Southard, S. L. *A Discourse on the Professional Character and Virtues of the Late William Wirt.* Washington, D.C.: Gales and Seaton, 1834.

Sowerby, E. Millicent, comp. *Catalogue of the Library of Thomas Jefferson.* 5 vols. Washington, D.C.: Library of Congress, 1953. Reprint, Charlottesville: University Press of Virginia, 1983.

Sparks, William H. *The Memories of Fifty Years.* Philadelphia: Claxton, Remsen, & Haffelinger, 1872.

Stampp, Kenneth, ed. *Records of Ante-bellum Southern Plantations: From the Revolution through the Civil War.* Microfilm ed. Bethesda, Md.: CIS, 1985–.

Steele, [Eliza R.]. *A Summer Journey in the West.* New York: John S. Taylor, 1841.

Steiner, Bernard C. *The Life and Correspondence of James McHenry: Secretary of War under Washington and Adams.* Cleveland, Ohio: Burrow Brothers Company, 1907.

"The Story of Blannerhassett." *Southern Literary Messenger* 27 (December 1858): 458–68.

Story, William W., ed. *Life and Letters of Joseph Story, Associate Justice of the Supreme Court of the United States.* 2 vols. Boston: Charles C. Little and James Brown, 1851.

Stuart, John G. "A Journal Remarks or Observations in a Voyage down the Kentucky, Ohio, Mississippi Rivers, &c." *Register of the Kentucky Historical Society* 50 (January 1952): 5–25.

Stumpf, Stuart O., ed. "The Arrest of Aaron Burr: A Documentary Record."
Alabama Historical Quarterly 42 (Fall–Winter 1980): 113–23.

[Sullivan, William]. *Familiar Letters on Public Characters, and Public Events, from the
Peace of 1783, to the Peace of 1815.* 2nd ed. Boston: Russell, Odiorne and Metcalf,
1834.

Syrett, Harold C., and Jacob E. Cooke, eds. *The Papers of Alexander Hamilton.* 27
vols. New York: Columbia University Press, 1961–87.

Tarbell, Ida M. "The Trial of Aaron Burr." *McClure's Magazine* 18 (March 1902):
403–13.

Taylor, James W. *The Victim of Intrigue: A Tale of Burr's Conspiracy.* Cincinnati, Ohio:
Robinson & Jones, 1847.

"Thomas Jefferson: Part III, The Trial of Burr." *American Whig Review* 12 (October
1850): 367–75.

Thomas, E. S. *Reminiscences of the Last Sixty-Five Years.* Hartford, Conn.: Case,
Tiffany, and Burnham, 1840.

Thomas, Frederick W. *The Emigrant; Or, Reflections While Descending the Ohio: A
Poem.* Rev. ed. Cincinnati, Ohio: J. Drake, 1872.

Thompson, William. *A Compendious View of the Trial of Aaron Burr (Late Vice
President of the United States) Charged with High-Treason: Together with Biographical Sketches of Several Eminent Characters.* Petersburg, Va.: Somerville and Conrad,
1808.

Thornbrough, Gayle, ed. *The Correspondence of John Badollet and Albert Gallatin,
1804–1836.* Indianapolis: Indiana Historical Society, 1963.

Tucker, George. *The History of the United States, from Their Colonization to the End of
the Twenty-sixth Congress, in 1841.* 4 vols. Philadelphia: J. B. Lippincott & Co.,
1857.

——. *The Life of Thomas Jefferson, Third President of the United States: With Parts of
His Correspondence Never Before Published, and Notices of His Opinions on Questions
of Civil Government, National Policy, and Constitutional Law.* 2 vols. London:
Charles Knight and Co., 1837.

Tucker, St. George. *Blackstone's Commentaries: With Notes of Reference, to the Constitution and Laws, of the Federal Government of the United States; and of the Commonwealth of Virginia.* 5 vols. Philadelphia: William Young Birch and Abraham
Small, 1803.

Tyler, Lyon G. *The Letters and Times of the Tylers.* 3 vols. Richmond, Va.: Whittet &
Shepperson, 1884–85; Williamsburg, Va.: n.p., 1896.

U.S. Congress. Senate. Committee of Claims. *Report on the Memorial of Harman
Blennerhassett and Joseph Lewis Blennerhassett*, 31st Cong., 2nd sess., doc. 258,
1851.

——. *Report on the Memorial of Margaret Blennerhasset*, 27th Cong., 2nd sess., doc.
394, 1842.

——. *Report on the Memorial of the Heirs of Herman Blennerhassett.* 32nd Cong., 1st
sess., doc. 334, 1852.

Van Horne, John C., et al., eds. *The Correspondence and Miscellaneous Papers of Benjamin Henry Latrobe.* 3 vols. New Haven, Conn.: Yale University Press, 1984–88.

Victor, Orville J. *History of American Conspiracies: A Record of Treason, Insurrection, Rebellion, &c., in the United States of America, from 1760 to 1860.* New York: James D. Torrey, Publisher, 1863. Reprint, New York: Arno Press, 1969.

Visscher, Nina, ed. "Memoir of Lexington and Its Vicinity: With Some Notice of Many Prominent Citizens and Its Institutions of Education and Religion." *Register of the Kentucky State Historical Society* 40 (1942): 107–31, 253–67, 353–75; 41 (1943): 44–62, 107–37, 250–60, 310–46; 42 (January 1944): 26–53.

Wainwright, Nicholas B., ed. *A Philadelphia Perspective: The Diary of Sidney George Fisher Covering the Years 1834–1871.* Philadelphia: Historical Society of Pennsylvania, 1967.

[Wallace, William]. "Biographical Sketch of Harman Blennerhassett." *American Review: A Whig Journal of Politics, Literature, Art and Science* 2 (August 1845): 133–49.

Washburne, E. B., ed. *The Edwards Papers: Being a Portion of the Collection of the Letters, Papers, and Manuscripts of Ninian Edwards.* 2 vols. Chicago: Chicago Historical Society, 1884–85.

Watkins, W. B. "Blennerhassett's Island." *Ladies' Repository* 19 (February 1859): 97–99.

[Watterston, George]. *Letters from Washington, on the Constitution and Laws; with Sketches of Some of the Prominent Public Characters of the United States.* Washington, D.C.: Jacob Gideon, Junr., 1818.

White, Patrick C. T., ed. *Lord Selkirk's Diary, 1803–1804: A Journal of His Travels in British North America and the Northeastern United States.* Toronto: Champlain Society, 1958.

[Wilkinson, James]. *A Brief Examination of Testimony, to Vindicate the Character of General James Wilkinson Against the Imputation of a Sinister Connection with the Spanish Government, for Purposes Hostile to His Own Country; With a Glance at Several Topics of Minor Import.* Washington, D.C.: W. Cooper, 1811.

———. *Burr's Conspiracy Exposed; and General Wilkinson Vindicated Against the Slanders of His Enemies on that Important Occasion.* Washington, D.C.: privately printed, 1811.

[———, comp.]. *[Correspondence between Wilkinson & Randolph].* N.p.: n.p., 1808.

———. *Memoirs of My Own Times.* 4 vols. Philadelphia: Abraham Small, 1816.

"Wilkinson's Memoirs." *Portico* 3 (April 1817): 323–24.

Williams, John S., ed. "Autographs." *American Pioneer* 2 (September 1843): 416–21.

———, ed. "Hinde's Correspondence." *American Pioneer* 2 (August 1843): 363–68.

Williston, E. B., comp. *Eloquence of the United States.* 5 vols. Middletown, Conn.: E. & H. Clark, 1827.

Wilson, Samuel M., ed. "The Court Proceedings of 1806 in Kentucky against Aaron Burr and John Adair." *Filson Club Historical Quarterly* 10 (January 1936): 31–40.

Winston, James E., ed. *"A Faithful Picture of the Political Situation of New Orleans at the Close of the Last and the Beginning of the Present Year, 1807."* Louisiana Historical Quarterly 11 (July 1928): 359–433.

Wirt, William. *The Letters of the British Spy*, 10th ed. With an introduction by Richard Beale Davis. New York: J. & J. Harper, 1832. Reprint, Chapel Hill: University of North Carolina Press, 1970.

[————]. *The Two Principal Arguments of William Wirt, Esquire, on the Trial of Aaron Burr, for High Treason, and on the Motion to Commit Aaron Burr and Others, for Trial in Kentucky.* Richmond, Va.: Samuel Pleasants, Jun., 1808.

Wood, John. *A Full Statement of the Trial and Acquittal of Aaron Burr, Esq.: Containing, All the Proceedings and Debates that Took Place before the Federal Court at Frankfort, Kentucky, November 25, 1806.* Alexandria, D.C.: Cottom and Stewart, 1807.

[Workman, James]. *A Letter to the Respectable Citizens, Inhabitants of the County of Orleans: Together with Several Letters to his Excellency Governor Claiborne, and Other Documents Relative to the Extraordinary Measures Lately Pursued in this Territory.* New Orleans, Orleans Territory: Bradford & Anderson, 1807.

SECONDARY SOURCE
BIBLIOGRAPHY

PUBLISHED

Abernethy, Thomas Perkins. *The Burr Conspiracy*. New York: Oxford University Press, 1954.

Ackerman, James A. *The Villa: Form and Ideology of Country Houses*. Princeton, N.J.: Princeton University Press, 1990.

Adair, Douglass. "Fame and the Founding Fathers." In *Fame and the Founding Fathers: Essays by Douglass Adair*, edited by Trevor Colbourn, 3–26. New York: W. W. Norton & Company, 1974.

Adams, Henry. *History of the United States of America during the Administrations of Thomas Jefferson and James Madison*. 9 vols. New York: Charles Scribner's Sons, 1889–91. Reprint, 2 vols. New York: Library of America, 1986.

Aderman, Ralph M., and Wayne R. Kime. *Advocate for America: The Life of James Kirke Paulding*. Selinsgrove, Pa.: Susquehanna University Press, 2003.

Alexander, Elizabeth Urban. "Daniel Clark: Merchant Prince of New Orleans." In *Nexus of Empire: Negotiating Loyalty and Identity in the Revolutionary Borderlands, 1760s–1820s*, edited by Gene Allen Smith and Sylvia L. Hilton, 241–67. Gainesville: University of Florida Press, 2010.

Allison, Robert J. *Stephen Decatur: American Naval Hero, 1779–1820*. Amherst: University of Massachusetts Press, 2005.

Allport, Gordon W., and Leo Postman. *The Psychology of Rumor*. New York: Holt, Rinehart and Winston, 1947.

Ambler, Charles Henry. *Thomas Ritchie: A Study in Virginia Politics*. Richmond, Va.: Bell Book & Stationary Co., 1913.

Ames, Herman V. "The Proposed Amendments to the Constitution of the United States during the First Century of Its History." In *Annual Report of the American Historical Association for the Year 1896*. Vol. 2. Washington, D.C.: U.S. Government Printing Office, 1897.

Ames, William E. *A History of the* National Intelligencer. Chapel Hill: University of North Carolina Press, 1972.

Ammon, Harry. *The Genet Mission*. New York: W. W. Norton & Company, 1973.

———. "James Monroe and the Election of 1808 in Virginia." *William and Mary Quarterly*, 3rd ser., 20 (January 1963): 33–56.

Anderson, Benedict. *Imagined Communities: Reflections on the Origin and Spread of Nationalism*. Rev. ed. London: Verso, 2006.

Anderson, Dice Robins. *William Branch Giles: A Study in the Politics of Virginia and the Nation from 1790 to 1830*. Menasha, Wisc.: George Banta Publishing Co., 1914.

Annas, Alicia M. "The Elegant Art of Movement." In *An Elegant Art: Fashion and Fantasy in the Eighteenth Century*, edited by Edward Maeder, 35–58. New York: Harry N. Abrams, 1983.

Appleby, Joyce. *Capitalism and a New Social Order: The Republican Vision of the 1790s*. New York: New York University Press, 1984.

Arch, Stephen Carl. *After Franklin: The Emergence of Autobiography in Post-Revolutionary America, 1780–1830*. Hanover, N.H.: University Press of New England, 2001.

Armstrong, Thom M. *Politics, Diplomacy and Intrigue in the Early Republic: The Cabinet Career of Robert Smith, 1801–1811*. Dubuque, Iowa: Kendall-Hunt Publishing Company, 1991.

Aron, Stephen. *How the West Was Lost: The Transformation of Kentucky from Daniel Boone to Henry Clay*. Baltimore, Md.: Johns Hopkins University Press, 1996.

Ayers, Edward L. *The Promise of the New South: Life after Reconstruction*. New York: Oxford University Press, 1992.

Bacarisse, Charles A. "Baron de Bastrop." *Southwestern Historical Quarterly* 58 (January 1955): 319–30.

Bailey, Jeremy David. "Executive Prerogative and the 'Good Officer' in Thomas Jefferson's Letter to John B. Colvin." *Presidential Studies Quarterly* 34 (December 2004): 732–54.

———. *Thomas Jefferson and Executive Power*. Cambridge: Cambridge University Press, 2007.

Bailyn, Bernard. *The Ideological Origins of the American Revolution*. Cambridge, Mass.: Belknap Press of Harvard University Press, 1967.

Baker, Thomas N. "'An Attack Well Directed': Aaron Burr Intrigues for the Presidency." *Journal of the Early Republic* 31 (Winter 2011): 553–98.

———. "John Wood Weighs In: Making Sense of the Burr Conspiracy in the Western World." *Ohio Valley History* 14 (Winter 2014): 3–22.

Balogh, Brian. *A Government Out of Sight: National Authority in Nineteenth-Century America*. Cambridge: Cambridge University Press, 2009.

Bannet, Eve Tavor. *Empire of Letters: Letter Manuals and Transatlantic Correspondence, 1688–1820*. Cambridge: Cambridge University Press, 2005.

Barksdale, Kevin T. *The Lost State of Franklin: America's First Secession*. Lexington: University Press of Kentucky, 2009.

Baumgarten, Linda. *What Clothes Reveal: The Language of Clothing in Colonial and Federal America*. New Haven, Conn.: Yale University Press, 2002.

Beard, W. E. "Colonel Burr's First Brush with the Law: An Account of the Proceedings against Him in Kentucky." *Tennessee Historical Magazine* 1 (March 1915): 3–20.

Beeman, Richard R. "The Varieties of Deference in Eighteenth-Century America." *Early American Studies* 3 (Fall 2005): 311–40.

Beirne, Francis F. *Shout Treason: The Trial of Aaron Burr.* New York: Hastings House, 1959.

Bennett, W. Lance, and Martha S. Feldman. *Reconstructing Reality in the Courtroom: Justice and Judgment in American Culture.* New Brunswick, N.J.: Rutgers University Press, 1981.

Bercovitch, Sacvan, and Cyrus R. K. Patell, eds. *The Cambridge History of American Literature.* Vol. 1, *1590–1820.* Cambridge: Cambridge University Press, 1994.

Bergmann, William H. "Delivering a Nation through the Mail: The Post Office in the Ohio Valley, 1789–1815." *Ohio Valley History* 8 (Fall 2008): 1–18.

Beveridge, Albert J. *The Life of John Marshall.* 4 vols. Boston: Houghton Mifflin Co., 1916–19.

Blanning, Tim. *The Romantic Revolution: A History.* New York: Modern Library, 2011.

Blumin, Stuart. *The Emergence of the Middle Class: Social Experience in the American City, 1760–1900.* Cambridge: Cambridge University Press, 1989.

Bonomi, Patricia U. *The Lord Cornbury Scandal.* Chapel Hill: University of North Carolina Press, 1998.

Boswell, Ira M. "La Cache." *Publications of the Mississippi Historical Society* 7 (1903): 313–23.

Bowers, Claude G. *Jefferson in Power: The Death Struggle of the Federalists.* Boston: Houghton Mifflin Company, 1936.

Boyd, Julian P. "The Murder of George Wythe." *William and Mary Quarterly,* 3rd ser., 12 (October 1955): 513–42.

Boyer Lewis, Charlene. *Elizabeth Patterson Bonaparte: An American Aristocrat in the Early Republic.* Philadelphia: University of Pennsylvania Press, 2012.

———. *Ladies and Gentlemen on Display: Planter Society at the Virginia Springs, 1790–1860.* Charlottesville: University Press of Virginia, 2001.

Bradburn, Douglas. *The Citizenship Revolution: Politics and the Creation of the American Union, 1774–1804.* Charlottesville: University of Virginia Press, 2009.

Brant, Irving. *James Madison.* Vol. 4, *James Madison: Secretary of State, 1800–1809.* Indianapolis, Ind.: Bobbs-Merrill Company, 1953.

Bretz, Julian P. "Early Land Communication with the Lower Mississippi Valley." *Mississippi Valley Historical Review* 13 (June 1926): 3–29.

Brewer, John. *A Sentimental Murder: Love and Madness in the Eighteenth Century.* New York: Farrar, Straus and Giroux, 2004.

Brigham, Clarence S. *Additions and Corrections to History and Bibliography of American Newspapers, 1690–1820.* Worcester, Mass.: American Antiquarian Society, 1961.

———. *History and Bibliography of American Newspapers, 1690–1820.* 2 vols. Worcester, Mass.: American Antiquarian Society, 1947.

Brooke, John L. "To Be 'Read by the Whole People': Press, Party, and Public Sphere in the United States, 1790–1840." *Proceedings of the American Antiquarian Society* 110 (April 2000): 41–118.

Brooks, Peter, and Paul Gewirtz, eds. *Law's Stories: Narrative and Rhetoric in the Law.* New Haven, Conn.: Yale University Press, 1996.

Brown, C. Allan. "Eighteenth-Century Virginia Plantation Gardens: Translating an Ancient Idyll." In *Regional Garden Design in the United States*, edited by Therese O'Malley and Marc Treib, 125–62. Washington, D.C.: Dumbarton Oaks Research Library and Collection, 1995.

Brown, Everett S. *The Constitutional History of the Louisiana Purchase, 1803–1812.* Berkeley: University of California Press, 1920.

Brown, Richard D. *Knowledge is Power: The Diffusion of Information in Early America, 1700–1865.* New York: Oxford University Press, 1989.

Browne, Gary Lawson. *Baltimore in the Nation, 1789–1861.* Chapel Hill: University of North Carolina Press, 1980.

Brunson, B. R. *The Adventures of Samuel Swartwout in the Age of Jefferson and Jackson.* Lewiston, N.Y.: Edwin Mellen Press, 1989.

Burke, Martin J. *The Conundrum of Class: Public Discourse on the Social Order in America.* Chicago: University of Chicago Press, 1995.

Burnett, Thom, ed. *Conspiracy Encyclopedia: The Encyclopedia of Conspiracy Theories.* New York: Chamberlain Bros., 2005.

Burstein, Andrew. *The Inner Jefferson: Portrait of a Grieving Optimist.* Charlottesville: University Press of Virginia, 1995.

———. *The Original Knickerbocker: The Life of Washington Irving.* New York: Basic Books, 2007.

Bushman, Richard L. *The Refinement of America: Persons, Houses, Cities.* New York: Alfred A. Knopf, 1992.

Cabell, James Alston. *The Trial of Aaron Burr.* Albany, N.Y.: Argus Company, 1900.

Calvert, Karin. "The Function of Fashion in Eighteenth-Century America." In *Of Consuming Interests: The Style of Life in the Eighteenth Century*, edited by Cary Carson, Ronald Hoffman, and Peter J. Albert, 252–83. Charlottesville: University Press of Virginia, 1994.

Carso, Brian F., Jr. *"Whom Can We Trust Now?": The Meaning of Treason in the United States, from the Revolution through the Civil War.* Lanham, Md.: Lexington Books, 2006.

Carson, Barbara G. *Ambitious Appetites: Dining, Behavior, and Patterns of Consumption in Federal Washington.* Washington, D.C.: American Institute of Architects Press, 1990.

Carson, David A. "That Ground Called Quiddism: John Randolph's War with the Jefferson Administration." *Journal of American Studies* 20 (April 1986): 71–92.

Carter, Clarence E. "The Burr-Wilkinson Intrigue in St. Louis." *Missouri Historical Society Bulletin* 10 (July 1954): 447–64.

Casper, Scott E. *Constructing American Lives: Biography and Culture in Nineteenth-Century America*. Chapel Hill: University of North Carolina Press, 1999.

Cassell, Frank A. "The Great Baltimore Riot of 1812." *Maryland Historical Magazine* 70 (Fall 1975): 241–59.

———. "The Structure of Baltimore's Politics in the Age of Jefferson, 1795–1812." In *Law, Society, and Politics in Early Maryland*, edited by Aubrey C. Land, Lois Green Carr, and Edward C. Papenfuse, 277–96. Baltimore, Md.: Johns Hopkins University Press, 1977.

[Catterall, Louise F.]. *Richmond Portraits: In an Exhibition of Makers of Richmond, 1737–1860*. Richmond, Va.: Valentine Museum, 1949.

Cayton, Andrew R. L. *The Frontier Republic: Ideology and Politics in the Ohio Country, 1780–1825*. Kent, Ohio: Kent State University Press, 1986.

———. *Love in the Time of Revolution: Transatlantic Literary Radicalism and Historical Change, 1793–1818*. Chapel Hill: University of North Carolina Press, 2013.

———. "Senator John Smith: The Rise and Fall of a Frontier Entrepreneur." In *The Human Tradition in Antebellum America*, edited by Michael A. Morrison, 67–81. Wilmington, Del.: Scholarly Resources Inc., 2000.

———. "'When Shall We Cease to Have Judases?': The Blount Conspiracy and the Limits of the 'Extended Republic.'" In *Launching the "Extended Republic": The Federalist Era*, edited by Ronald Hoffman and Peter J. Albert, 156–89. Charlottesville: University Press of Virginia, 1996.

Chadwick, Bruce. *I Am Murdered: George Wythe, Thomas Jefferson, and the Killing That Shocked a New Nation*. Hoboken, N.J.: John Wiley & Sons, 2009.

Chalou, George C. "James Wilkinson—The Spanish Connection, 1810." In *Congress Investigates: A Documented History, 1792–1974*, edited by Arthur M. Schlesinger Jr. and Roger Bruns, 1:105–20. 5 vols. New York: Chelsea House Publishers, 1975.

Chapin, Bradley. *The American Law of Treason: Revolutionary and Early National Origins*. Seattle: University of Washington Press, 1964.

Christian, W. Ashbury. *Richmond: Her Past and Present*. Richmond, Va.: L. H. Jenkins, 1912.

Chudacoff, Howard P. *The Age of the Bachelor: Creating an American Subculture*. Princeton, N.J.: Princeton University Press, 1999.

Clark, Gregory, and S. Michael Halloran, eds. *Oratorical Culture in Nineteenth-Century America: Transformations in the Theory and Practice of Rhetoric*. Carbondale: Southern Illinois University Press, 1993.

Clark, John G. *New Orleans, 1718–1812: An Economic History*. Baton Rouge: Louisiana State University Press, 1970.

Clarkson, Paul S., and R. Samuel Jett. *Luther Martin of Maryland*. Baltimore, Md.: Johns Hopkins Press, 1970.

Click, Patricia C. *The Spirit of the Times: Amusements in Nineteenth-Century Baltimore, Norfolk, and Richmond*. Charlottesville: University Press of Virginia, 1989.

Cmiel, Kenneth. *Democratic Eloquence: The Fight over Popular Speech in Nineteenth-Century America.* New York: William Morrow and Company, 1990.

Cogliano, Francis D. *Thomas Jefferson: Reputation and Legacy.* Charlottesville: University of Virginia Press, 2006.

Cohen, Daniel A. *Pillars of Salt, Monuments of Grace: New England Crime Literature and the Origins of American Popular Culture, 1674–1860.* New York: Oxford University Press, 1993.

Connelley, William Elsey, and E. M. Coulter. *History of Kentucky.* 5 vols. Chicago: American Historical Society, 1922.

Copeland, Peter F. *Working Dress in Colonial and Revolutionary America.* Westport, Conn.: Greenwood Press, 1977.

Côté, Richard N. *Theodosia Burr Alston: Portrait of a Prodigy.* Mount Pleasant, S.C.: Corinthian Books, 2003.

Couch, R. Randall. "William Charles Cole Claiborne: An Historiographical Review." *Louisiana History* 36 (Fall 1995): 453–65.

Cox, Isaac Joslin. "General Wilkinson and His Later Intrigues with the Spaniards." *American Historical Review* 19 (July 1914): 794–812.

———. "Hispanic-American Phases of the Burr Conspiracy." *Hispanic American Historical Review* 12 (May 1932): 145–75.

———. "The Louisiana-Texas Frontier during the Burr Conspiracy." *Mississippi Valley Historical Review* 10 (December 1923): 274–84.

———. "Western Reaction to the Burr Conspiracy." *Transactions of the Illinois State Historical Society* 35 (1928): 73–87.

Crackel, Theodore J. *Mr. Jefferson's Army: Political and Social Reform of the Military Establishment, 1801–1809.* New York: New York University Press, 1987.

Cray, Robert E., Jr. "Major John André and the Three Captors: Class Dynamics and Revolutionary Memory Wars in the Early Republic, 1780–1831." *Journal of the Early Republic* 17 (Fall 1997): 371–97.

Critchlow, Donald T., John Korasick, and Matthew C. Sherman, eds. *Political Conspiracies in America: A Reader.* Bloomington: Indiana University Press, 2008.

Cunningham, Noble E., Jr. *The Jeffersonian Republicans in Power: Party Operations, 1801–1809.* Chapel Hill: University of North Carolina Press, 1963.

———. *The Process of Government under Jefferson.* Princeton, N.J.: Princeton University Press, 1978.

———. "Who Were the Quids?" *Mississippi Valley Historical Review* 50 (September 1963): 252–63.

Currie, David P. *The Constitution in Congress: The Jeffersonians, 1801–1829.* Chicago: University of Chicago Press, 2001.

Curtin, Nancy. *United Irishmen: Popular Politics in Ulster and Dublin, 1791–1798.* Oxford, U.K.: Clarendon Press, 1998.

Daniels, Jonathan. *Ordeal of Ambition: Jefferson, Hamilton, Burr.* Garden City, N.Y.: Doubleday, 1970.

Dargo, George. *Jefferson's Louisiana: Politics and the Clash of Legal Traditions.* Cambridge, Mass.: Harvard University Press, 1975.

Davis, Natalie Zemon. *The Return of Martin Guerre.* Cambridge, Mass.: Harvard University Press, 1983.

Davis, Richard Beale. *Intellectual Life in Jefferson's Virginia, 1790–1830.* Chapel Hill: University of North Carolina Press, 1964.

Decker, William Merrill. *Epistolary Practices: Letter Writing in America before Telecommunications.* Chapel Hill: University of North Carolina Press, 1998.

Dierks, Konstantin. *In My Power: Letter Writing and Communications in Early America.* Philadelphia: University of Pennsylvania Press, 2009.

Doolen, Andy. "Reading and Writing Terror: The New York Conspiracy Trials of 1741." *American Literary History* 16 (Fall 2004): 377–406.

Dowd, Gregory Evans. *Groundless: Rumors, Legends, and Hoaxes on the Early American Frontier.* Baltimore, Md.: Johns Hopkins University Press, 2015.

Doyle, Christopher L. "The Randolph Scandal in Early National Virginia, 1792–1815." *Journal of Southern History* 69 (May 2003): 283–318.

Dreisbach, Daniel L. "The 'Vine and Fig Tree' in George Washington's Letters: Reflections on a Biblical Motif in the Literature of the American Founding Era." *Anglican and Episcopal History* 76 (September 2007): 299–326.

Drexler, Michael J., and Ed White. *The Traumatic Colonel: The Founding Fathers, Slavery, and the Phantasmatic Aaron Burr.* New York: New York University Press, 2014.

Dunbar, Willis F. "The Burr 'Conspiracy' and the Old Northwest." *Michigan History Magazine* 16 (Spring 1932): 143–73.

Durey, Michael. *Transatlantic Radicals and the Early American Republic.* Lawrence: University Press of Kansas, 1997.

Duty, Tony E. "James Wilkinson (1757–1825)." *Texana* 9, no. 4 (1971): 291–355.

East, Robert A. *John Quincy Adams: The Critical Years, 1785–1794.* New York: Bookman Associates, 1962.

Eastman, Carolyn. *A Nation of Speechifiers: Making an American Public after the Revolution.* Chicago: University of Chicago Press, 2009.

Edwards, Samuel. *Barbary General: The Life of William H. Eaton.* Englewood Cliffs, N.J.: Prentice-Hall, 1968.

Ellis, Joseph J. *After the Revolution: Profiles of Early American Culture.* New York: W. W. Norton & Company, 1979.

Ellis, Richard E. *The Jeffersonian Crisis: Courts and Politics in the Young Republic.* New York: Oxford University Press, 1971.

Everett, Donald E. "Emigres and Militiamen: Free Persons of Color in New Orleans, 1803–1815." *Journal of Negro History* 38 (October 1953): 377–402.

Faber, Eberhard L. *Building the Land of Dreams: New Orleans and the Transformation of Early America.* Princeton, N.J.: Princeton University Press, 2016.

Faulkner, Robert K. "John Marshall and the Burr Trial." *Journal of American History* 53 (September 1966): 247–58.

Ferguson, Eugene S. *Truxton of the* Constellation: *The Life of Commodore Thomas Truxton, U.S. Navy, 1755–1822.* Baltimore, Md.: Johns Hopkins Press, 1956.

Ferguson, Robert A. *The Trial in American Life.* Chicago: University of Chicago Press, 2007.

Fine, Gary Alan, Véronique Campion-Vincent, and Chip Heath, eds. *Rumor Mills: The Social Impact of Rumor and Legend.* New Brunswick, N.J.: Aldine Transaction, 2005.

Fischer, David Hackett. *The Revolution of American Conservatism: The Federalist Party in the Era of Jeffersonian Democracy.* New York: Harper & Row, 1965.

Flanagan, John T. "Morgan Neville, Early Western Chronicler." *Western Pennsylvania Historical Magazine* 21 (December 1938): 255–66.

Fleming, Thomas. *The Duel: Alexander Hamilton, Aaron Burr, and the Future of America.* New York: Basic Books, 2000.

Fliegelman, Jay. *Declaring Independence: Jefferson, Natural Language, and the Culture of Performance.* Stanford, Calif.: Stanford University Press, 1993.

Flower, Milton E. *James Parton: The Father of Modern Biography.* Durham, N.C.: Duke University Press, 1951.

Foley, William E. *The Genesis of Missouri: From Wilderness Outpost to Statehood.* Columbia: University of Missouri Press, 1989.

———. "James A. Wilkinson: Territorial Governor." *Missouri Historical Society Bulletin* 25 (October 1968): 3–17.

Fox, Richard Wightman. *Trials of Intimacy: Love and Loss in the Beecher-Tilton Scandal.* Chicago: University of Chicago Press, 1999.

Freeman, Joanne B. *Affairs of Honor: National Politics in the New Republic.* New Haven, Conn.: Yale University Press, 2001.

Freeman, Mark. *Rewriting the Self: History, Memory, Narrative.* New York: Routledge, 1993.

French, Scot. *The Rebellious Slave: Nat Turner in American Memory.* Boston: Houghton Mifflin Company, 2004.

Friend, Craig Thompson. *Along the Maysville Road: The Early Republic in the Trans-Appalachian West.* Knoxville: University of Tennessee Press, 2005.

Gaines, Edwin M. "The *Chesapeake* Affair: Virginians Mobilize to Defend National Honor." *Virginia Magazine of History and Biography* 64 (April 1956): 131–42.

Gannon, Kevin M. "Escaping 'Mr. Jefferson's Plan of Destruction': New England Federalists and the Idea of a Northern Confederacy, 1803–1804." *Journal of the Early Republic* 21 (Fall 2001): 413–44.

Geissler, Suzanne B. "The Commodore Goes to Court." *Naval History* 11 (March–April 1997): 31–36.

———. *Jonathan Edwards to Aaron Burr, Jr.: From the Great Awakening to Democratic Politics.* New York: Edwin Mellen Press, 1981.

Gelpi, Paul D., Jr. "Mr. Jefferson's Creoles: The Battalion d'Orléans and the Americanization of Creole Louisiana, 1803–1815." *Louisiana History* 48 (Summer 2007): 295–316.

Gilje, Paul A. "The Baltimore Riots of 1812 and the Breakdown of the Anglo-American Mob Tradition." *Journal of Social History* 13 (Summer 1980): 547–64.

———. "The Crowd in American History." *ATQ: The American Transcendental Quarterly* 17 (September 2003). 135–59.

———. "'Le Menu Peuple' in America: Identifying the Mob in the Baltimore Riots of 1812." *Maryland Historical Magazine* 81 (Spring 1986): 50–66.

———. *Rioting in America.* Bloomington: Indiana University Press, 1996.

Girouard, Mark. *Life in the English Country House: A Social and Architectural History.* New Haven, Conn.: Yale University Press, 1978.

———. *The Return to Camelot: Chivalry and the English Gentleman.* New Haven, Conn.: Yale University Press, 1981.

Goodman, Dena. "The Hume-Rousseau Affair: From Private *Querelle* to Public *Procès.*" *Eighteenth-Century Studies* 25 (Winter 1991–92): 171–201.

Goodman, James. *Stories of Scottsboro.* New York: Pantheon Books, 1994.

Green, Constance McLaughlin. *Washington: Village and Capital, 1800–1878.* Princeton, N.J.: Princeton University Press, 1962.

Greenberg, Kenneth S. *Honor and Slavery: Lies, Duels, Noses, Masks, Dressing as a Woman, Gifts, Strangers, Humanitarianism, Death, Slave Rebellions, the Proslavery Argument, Baseball, Hunting and Gambling in the Old South.* Princeton, N.J.: Princeton University Press, 1996.

———. "The Nose, the Lie, and the Duel in the Antebellum South." *American Historical Review* 95 (February 1990): 57–74.

Gross, Robert A., ed. "Forum: The Making of a Slave Conspiracy, Part[s] 1 [and 2]." *William and Mary Quarterly* 58 (October 2001): 913–76; 59 (January 2002): 135–202.

———, and Mary Kelley, eds. *An Extensive Republic: Print, Culture, and Society in the New Nation, 1790–1840.* Chapel Hill: University of North Carolina Press, 2010.

Gruenwald, Kim M. *River of Enterprise: The Commercial Origins of Regional Identity in the Ohio Valley, 1790–1850.* Bloomington: Indiana University Press, 2002.

Gustafson, Sandra M. *Eloquence is Power: Oratory and Performance in Early America.* Chapel Hill: University of North Carolina Press, 2000.

Haggard, J. Villasana. "The Neutral Ground between Louisiana and Texas, 1806–1821." *Louisiana Historical Quarterly* 28 (October 1945): 1001–1128.

Halliday, Paul D. *Habeas Corpus: From England to Empire.* Cambridge, Mass.: Belknap Press of Harvard University Press, 2010.

Halttunen, Karen. *Confidence Men and Painted Women: A Study of Middle-Class Culture in America, 1830–1870.* New Haven, Conn.: Yale University Press, 1982.

Hamilton, William Baskerville. *Anglo-American Law on the Frontier: Thomas Rodney and His Territorial Cases.* Durham, N.C.: Duke University Press, 1953.

Hamlin, Arthur S. *Gideon Granger.* Canandaigua, N.Y.: Granger Homestead Society, 1982.

Hamlin, Talbot. *Benjamin Henry Latrobe.* New York: Oxford University Press, 1955.

Hample, Judy. "William Wirt's Familiar Essays: Criticism of Virginia Oratory." *Southern Speech Communication Journal* 44 (Fall 1978): 25–41.

Hanger, Kimberly S. *Bounded Lives, Bounded Places: Free Black Society in Colonial New Orleans, 1769–1803*. Durham, N.C.: Duke University Press, 1997.

Hanke, Lewis. "Baptis Irvine's Reports on Simón Bolívar." *Hispanic American Historical Review* 16 (August 1936): 360–73.

Hardison, Brian D., and Ray Swick. "A Recruit for Aaron Burr: Lewis Wetzel and the Burr 'Conspiracy.'" *West Virginia History*, n.s., 3 (Fall 2009): 75–86.

Harper, Josephine. *Guide to the Draper Manuscripts*. Madison: State Historical Society of Wisconsin, 1983.

Harrison, Lowell H., and James C. Klotter. *A New History of Kentucky*. Lexington: University Press of Kentucky, 1997.

Haskins, George Lee, and Herbert A. Johnson. *Foundations of Power: John Marshall, 1801–15*. New York: Macmillan Publishing Co., 1981.

Hatch, Nathan O. *The Democratization of American Christianity*. New Haven, Conn.: Yale University Press, 1989.

Hatcher, William B. *Edward Livingston: Jeffersonian Republican and Jacksonian Democrat*. Baton Rouge: Louisiana State University Press, 1940.

Hatfield, Joseph T. *William Claiborne: Jeffersonian Centurion in the American Southwest*. Lafayette: University of Southwestern Louisiana Press, 1976.

Hay, Thomas Robson. "Charles Williamson and the Burr Conspiracy." *Journal of Southern History* 2 (May 1936): 175–210.

———. "General James Wilkinson—The Last Phase." *Louisiana Historical Quarterly* 19 (April 1936): 407–35.

———. "Some Reflections on the Career of General James Wilkinson." *Mississippi Valley Historical Review* 21 (March 1935): 471–94.

———, and M. R. Werner. *The Admirable Trumpeter: A Biography of General James Wilkinson*. Garden City, N.Y.: Doubleday, 1941.

Haynes, Robert V. *The Mississippi Territory and the Southwest Frontier, 1795–1817*. Lexington: University Press of Kentucky, 2010.

Haynes, Sam W. *Unfinished Revolution: The Early American Republic in a British World*. Charlottesville: University of Virginia Press, 2010.

Hemphill, C. Dallett. *Bowing to Necessities: A History of Manners in America, 1620–1860*. New York: Oxford University Press, 1999.

Henderson, Dwight F. *Congress, Courts, and Criminals: The Development of Federal Criminal Law, 1801–1829*. Westport, Conn.: Greenwood Press, 1985.

Hendrickson, David C. *Peace Pact: The Lost World of the American Founding*. Lawrence: University Press of Kansas, 2003.

Henkin, David M. *The Postal Age: The Emergence of Modern Communications in Nineteenth-Century America*. Chicago: University of Chicago Press, 2006.

Henshaw, Leslie. "The Aaron Burr Conspiracy in the Ohio Valley." *Ohio Archaeological and Historical Society Publications* 24 (April 1915): 121–37.

Hickey, Donald R. "The Darker Side of Democracy: The Baltimore Riots of 1812." *Maryland Historian* 7 (Fall 1976): 1–20.

Hinds, Peter. *"The Horrid Popish Plot": Roger L'Estrange and the Circulation of Political Discourse in Late Seventeenth-Century London.* New York: Oxford University Press, 2010.

Hoffer, Peter Charles. *The Treason Trials of Aaron Burr.* Lawrence: University Press of Kansas, 2008.

Hofstadter, Richard. *The Paranoid Style in American Politics and Other Essays.* New York: Alfred A. Knopf, 1965.

Holloway, Jean. *Edward Everett Hale: A Biography.* Austin: University of Texas Press, 1956.

Holmes, Jack D. L. "Showdown on the Sabine: General James Wilkinson vs. Lieutenant-Colonel Simón de Herrera." *Louisiana Studies* 3 (Spring 1964): 46–76.

Horn, James, Jan Ellen Lewis, and Peter S. Onuf, eds. *The Revolution of 1800: Democracy, Race, and the New Republic.* Charlottesville: University of Virginia Press, 2002.

Howe, John R., Jr. "Republican Thought and the Political Violence of the 1790s." *American Quarterly* 19 (Summer 1967): 147–65.

Humphrey, Carol Sue. *The Press of the Young Republic, 1783–1833.* Westport, Conn.: Greenwood Press, 1996.

Huston, James L. "The American Revolutionaries, the Political Economy of Aristocracy, and the American Conception of the Distribution of Wealth, 1765–1900." *American Historical Review* 98 (October 1993): 1079–1105.

Hutchins, Zachary McLeod. "Rattlesnakes in the Garden: The Fascinating Serpents of the Early Edenic Republic." *Early American Studies* 9 (Fall 2011): 677–715.

Hutchinson, Lester. *The Conspiracy of Catiline.* New York: Barnes and Noble, 1967.

Hutson, James H. "The Origins of 'The Paranoid Style in American Politics': Public Jealousy from the Age of Walpole to the Age of Jackson." In *Saints and Revolutionaries: Essays in Early American History*, edited by David D. Hall, John M. Murrin, and Thad W. Tate, 342–72. New York: W. W. Norton & Company, 1984.

Isenberg, Nancy. *Fallen Founder: The Life of Aaron Burr.* New York: Viking, 2007.

———. "The 'Little Emperor': Aaron Burr, Dandyism, and the Sexual Politics of Treason." In *Beyond the Founders: New Approaches to the Political History of the Early American Republic*, edited by Jeffrey L. Pasley, Andrew W. Robertson, and David Waldstreicher, 129–58. Chapel Hill: University of North Carolina Press, 2004.

Jackson, Leon. "The Reader Retailored: Thomas Carlyle, His American Audiences, and the Politics of Evidence." In *Reading Acts: U.S. Readers' Interactions with Literature, 1800–1950*, edited by Barbara Ryan and Amy M. Thomas, 79–106. Knoxville: University of Tennessee Press, 2002.

Jacobs, James R. *Tarnished Warrior: Major-General James Wilkinson*. New York: Macmillan Co., 1938.

Jeffers, H. Paul. *History's Greatest Conspiracies: One Hundred Plots, Real and Suspected, That Have Shocked, Fascinated, and Sometimes Changed the World*. Guilford, Conn.: Lyons Press, 2004.

Jillson, Willard Rouse. "Aaron Burr's 'Trial' for Treason, at Frankfort, Kentucky, 1806." *Filson Club Historical Quarterly* 17 (October 1943): 202–29.

———. *The Newspapers and Periodicals of Frankfort, Kentucky, 1795–1945*. Frankfort: Kentucky State Historical Society, 1945.

John, Richard R. *Spreading the News: The American Postal System from Franklin to Morse*. Cambridge, Mass.: Harvard University Press, 1995.

Johnson, Jerah. "Dr. John Watkins: New Orleans' Lost Mayor." *Louisiana History* 36 (Spring 1995): 187–96.

Johnson, L. F. *The History of Franklin County, Ky.* Frankfort, Ky.: Roberts Printing Co., 1912. Reprint, Frankfort, Ky.: Historic Frankfort Press, 1975.

Johnson, Leland R. "Aaron Burr: Treason in Kentucky?" *Filson Club Historical Quarterly* 75 (Winter 2001): 1–32.

Johnstone, Robert M., Jr. *Jefferson and the Presidency: Leadership in the Young Republic*. Ithaca, N.Y.: Cornell University Press, 1978.

Jordan, Winthrop D. *Tumult and Silence at Second Creek: An Inquiry into a Civil War Slave Conspiracy*. Rev. ed. Baton Rouge: Louisiana State University Press, 1995.

Kamrath, Mark L. "Charles Brockden Brown and the 'Art of the Historian': An Essay Concerning (Post)modern Historical Understanding." *Journal of the Early Republic* 21 (Summer 2001): 231–60.

Kann, Mark E. *A Republic of Men: The American Founders, Gendered Language, and Patriarchal Politics*. New York: New York University Press, 1998.

Kapferer, Jean-Noël. *Rumors: Uses, Interpretations, and Images*. Translated by Bruce Fink. New Brunswick, N.J.: Transaction Publishers, 1990.

Kaplan, Arthur. *Catiline: The Man and His Role in the Roman Revolution*. New York: Exposition Press, 1968.

Kaplan, Catherine O'Donnell. *Men of Letters in the Early Republic: Cultivating Forums of Citizenship*. Chapel Hill: University of North Carolina Press, 2008.

Kastor, Peter J. "'Equitable Rights and Privileges': The Divided Loyalties in Washington County, Virginia, during the Franklin Separatist Crisis." *Virginia Magazine of History and Biography* 105 (Spring 1997): 193–226.

———, ed. *The Louisiana Purchase: Emergence of an American Nation*. Washington, D.C.: CQ Press, 2002.

———. *The Nation's Crucible: The Louisiana Purchase and the Creation of America*. New Haven, Conn.: Yale University Press, 2004.

———. "'They Are All Frenchmen': Background and Nation in an Age of Transformation." In *Empires of the Imagination: Transatlantic Histories of the Louisiana Purchase*, edited by Peter J. Kastor and François Weil, 239–67. Charlottesville: University of Virginia Press, 2009.

Keller, William F. *The Nation's Advocate: Henry Marie Brackenridge and Young America*. Pittsburgh, Pa.: University of Pittsburgh Press, 1956.

Kelman, Ari. *A River and Its City: The Nature of Landscape in New Orleans*. Berkeley: University of California Press, 2003.

Kendall, John S. "According to the Code." *Louisiana Historical Quarterly* 23 (January 1940): 141–61.

———. "Early New Orleans Newspapers." *Louisiana Historical Quarterly* 10 (July 1927): 383–401.

Kennedy, Roger G. *Burr, Hamilton, and Jefferson: A Study in Character*. New York: Oxford University Press, 1999.

Kenney, Alice P., and Leslie J. Workman. "Ruins, Romance, and Reality: Medievalism in Anglo-American Imagination and Taste, 1750–1840." *Winterthur Portfolio* 10 (1975): 131–63.

Kenyon, John. *The Popish Plot*. London: William Heinemann Ltd., 1972.

Kerber, Linda K. *Federalists in Dissent: Imagery and Ideology in Jeffersonian America*. Ithaca, N.Y.: Cornell University Press, 1970.

Kersh, Rogan. *Dreams of a More Perfect Union*. Ithaca, N.Y.: Cornell University Press, 2001.

Kett, Joseph F. *Rites of Passage: Adolescence in America, 1790 to the Present*. New York: Basic Books, 1977.

Kettner, James H. *The Development of American Citizenship, 1608–1870*. Chapel Hill: University of North Carolina Press, 1978.

Kielbowicz, Richard B. *News in the Mail: The Press, Post Office, and Public Information, 1700–1860s*. New York: Greenwood Press, 1989.

Kierner, Cynthia A. *Scandal at Bizarre: Rumor and Reputation in Jefferson's America*. New York: Palgrave Macmillan, 2004.

Kleber, John E., et al., eds. *The Kentucky Encyclopedia*. Lexington: University Press of Kentucky, 1992.

Kline, Mary-Jo. "Aaron Burr as a Symbol of Corruption in the New Republic." In *Before Watergate: Problems of Corruption in American Society*, edited by Abraham S. Eisenstadt, Ari Hoogenboom, and Hans L. Trefousse, 69–77. Brooklyn, N.Y.: Brooklyn College Press, 1978.

Knight, Peter. *Conspiracy Theories in American History: An Encyclopedia*. 2 vols. Santa Barbara, Calif.: ABC-CLIO, 2003.

Knox, J. Wendell. *Conspiracy in American Politics, 1787–1815*. New York: Arno Press, 1972.

Knudson, Jerry W. *Jefferson and the Press: Crucible of Liberty*. Columbia: University of South Carolina Press, 2006.

Knupfer, Peter B. *The Union as It Is: Constitutional Unionism and Sectional Compromise, 1787–1861*. Chapel Hill: University of North Carolina Press, 1991.

Kukla, Jon. *A Wilderness So Immense: The Louisiana Purchase and the Destiny of America*. New York: Alfred A. Knopf, 2003.

LaCroix, Alison L. *The Ideological Origins of American Federalism*. Cambridge, Mass.: Harvard University Press, 2010.

Lancaster, Clay. *Vestiges of the Venerable City: A Chronicle of Lexington, Kentucky*. Lexington, Ky.: Lexington-Fayette County Historic Commission, 1978.

Larson, Edward J. *A Magnificent Catastrophe: The Tumultuous Election of 1800, America's First Presidential Campaign*. New York: Free Press, 2007.

Lathem, Edward C., comp. *Chronological Tables of American Newspapers, 1690–1820*. Barre, Mass.: American Antiquarian Society and Barre Publishers, 1972.

Leonard, Thomas C. *News for All: America's Coming-of-Age with the Press*. New York: Oxford University Press, 1995.

Lepore, Jill. *New York Burning: Liberty, Slavery, and Conspiracy in Eighteenth-Century Manhattan*. New York: Alfred A. Knopf, 2005.

Lester, Malcolm. *Anthony Merry Redivivus: A Reappraisal of the British Minister to the United States, 1803–1806*. Charlottesville: University Press of Virginia, 1978.

Leventhal, Herbert. *In the Shadow of the Enlightenment: Occultism and Renaissance Science in Eighteenth-Century America*. New York: New York University Press, 1976.

Levy, Leonard W. *Jefferson and Civil Liberties: The Darker Side*. Cambridge, Mass.: Belknap Press of Harvard University Press, 1963.

Lewis, James E., Jr. *The American Union and the Problem of Neighborhood: The United States and the Collapse of the Spanish Empire, 1783–1829*. Chapel Hill: University of North Carolina Press, 1998.

———. *The Louisiana Purchase: Jefferson's Noble Bargain?* Charlottesville, Va.: Thomas Jefferson Foundation, 2003.

Lewis, Jan. "The Republican Wife: Virtue and Seduction in the Early Republic." *William and Mary Quarterly*, 3rd ser., 44 (October 1987): 689–721.

Lewis, William Draper, ed. *Great American Lawyers: The Lives and Influence of Judges and Lawyers Who Have Acquired Permanent National Reputation and Have Developed the Jurisprudence of the United States: A History of the Legal Profession in America*. 8 vols. Philadelphia: J. C. Winston, 1907–9.

Linklater, Andro. *An Artist in Treason: The Extraordinary Double Life of General James Wilkinson*. New York: Walker & Company, 2009.

Lomask, Milton. *Aaron Burr*. 2 vols. New York: Farrar Straus Giroux, 1979–82.

Lowther, Minnie Kendall. *Blennerhassett Island in Romance and Tragedy: The Authentic Story of Blennerhassett Island, with the Burr Episode Entwined About It; The Romance and Mystery of the Blennerhassetts; Burr Under Footlights and Shadows; Tragedy of Theodosia Burr*. Rutland, Vt.: Tuttle, 1936.

Lukasik, Christopher J. *Discerning Characters: The Culture of Appearance in Early America*. Philadelphia: University of Pennsylvania Press, 2010.

Malone, Dumas. *Jefferson and His Time*. 6 vols. Boston: Little, Brown and Company, 1948–77.

Matson, Cathy D., and Peter S. Onuf. *A Union of Interests: Political and Economic Thought in Revolutionary America*. Lawrence: University Press of Kansas, 1990.

Mayo, Bernard. *Henry Clay: Spokesman of the New West*. Boston: Houghton Mifflin, Company, 1937.

McCaleb, Walter Flavius. *The Aaron Burr Conspiracy; and, A New Light on Aaron Burr*. Expanded ed. New York: Argosy-Antiquarian Ltd., 1966.

McConnell, Roland C. *Negro Troops of Antebellum Louisiana: A History of the Battalion of Free Men of Color*. Baton Rouge: Louisiana State University Press, 1968.

McCurdy, John Gilbert. *Citizen Bachelors: Manhood and the Creation of the United States*. Ithaca, N.Y.: Cornell University Press, 2009.

McDonald, Forrest. *The Presidency of Thomas Jefferson*. Lawrence: University Press of Kansas, 1976.

McDonald, Robert M. S. *Confounding Father: Thomas Jefferson's Image in His Own Time*. Charlottesville: University of Virginia Press, 2016.

McDowell, R. B. "The Personnel of the Dublin Society of United Irishmen, 1791–4." *Irish Historical Studies* 2 (March 1940): 12–53.

Melton, Buckner F., Jr. *Aaron Burr: Conspiracy to Treason*. New York: John Wiley & Sons, 2000.

———. *The First Impeachment: The Constitution's Framers and the Case of Senator William S. Blount*. Macon, Ga.: Mercer University Press, 1998.

Melton, Tracy Matthew. *Hanging Henry Gambrill: The Violent Career of Baltimore's Plug Uglies, 1854–1860*. Baltimore: Maryland Historical Society, 2005.

Merrell, James H. *Into the American Woods: Negotiators on the Pennsylvania Frontier*. New York: W. W. Norton & Company, 1999.

Merrill, Jane, and John Endicott. *Aaron Burr in Exile: A Pariah in Paris, 1810–1811*. Jefferson, N.C.: McFarland & Company, 2016.

Miles, Ellen G. *Saint-Mémin and the Neoclassical Profile Portrait in America*. Washington, D.C.: National Portrait Gallery and Smithsonian Institution Press, 1994.

Mitchell, Jennie O'Kelly, and Robert Dabney Calhoun. "The Marquis de Maison Rouge, the Baron de Bastrop, and Colonel Abraham Morhouse—Three Ouachita Valley Soldiers of Fortune: The Maison Rouge and Spanish Land 'Grants.'" *Louisiana Historical Quarterly* 20 (April 1937): 289–462.

Morgan, Winifred. *An American Icon: Brother Jonathan and American Identity*. Newark: University of Delaware Press, 1988.

Mott, Frank Luther. *American Journalism: A History of Newspapers in the United States through 250 Years: 1690–1940*. New York: Macmillan Company, 1941.

Murrin, John M. "Escaping Perfidious Albion: Federalism, Fear of Aristocracy, and the Democratization of Corruption in Postrevolutionary America." In *Virtue, Corruption, and Self-Interest: Political Values in the Eighteenth Century*, edited by Richard K. Matthews, 103–47. Bethlehem, Pa.: Lehigh University Press, 1994.

Mushkat, Jerome. "Matthew Livingston Davis and the Political Legacy of Aaron Burr." *New-York Historical Society Quarterly* 59 (April 1975): 123–48.

Nagel, Paul C. *One Nation Indivisible: The Union in American Thought, 1776–1861*. New York: Oxford University Press, 1964.

Narrett, David E. "Geopolitics and Intrigue: James Wilkinson, the Spanish Borderlands, and Mexican Independence." *William and Mary Quarterly* 69 (January 2012): 101–46.

Newmyer, R. Kent. *John Marshall and the Heroic Age of the Supreme Court*. Baton Rouge: Louisiana State University Press, 2001.

———. *The Treason Trial of Aaron Burr: Law, Politics, and the Character Wars of the New Nation*. Cambridge: Cambridge University Press, 2012.

Newton, Michael. *The Encyclopedia of Conspiracies and Conspiracy Theories*. New York: Facts on File, 2006.

Nicholls, Michael L. *Whispers of Rebellion: Narrating Gabriel's Conspiracy*. Charlottesville: University of Virginia Press, 2012.

Nolan, Charles Joseph, Jr. *Aaron Burr and the American Literary Imagination*. Westport, Conn.: Greenwood Press, 1980.

Norfleet, Fillmore. *Saint-Mémin in Virginia: Portraits and Biographies*. Richmond, Va.: Dietz Press, Publishers, 1942.

O'Brien, Michael. *Conjectures of Order: Intellectual Life and the American South, 1810–1860*. 2 vols. Chapel Hill: University of North Carolina Press, 2004.

Onuf, Peter S. "The Expanding Union." In *Devising Liberty: Preserving and Creating Freedom in the New American Republic*, edited by David Thomas Konig, 50–80. Stanford, Calif.: Stanford University Press, 1995.

———. "Federalism, Republicanism, and the Origins of American Sectionalism." In Edward L. Ayers, et al., *All Over the Map: Rethinking American Regions*, 11–37. Baltimore, Md.: Johns Hopkins University Press, 1996.

———. *Jefferson's Empire: The Language of American Nationhood*. Charlottesville: University Press of Virginia, 2000.

———. *The Origins of the Federal Republic: Jurisdictional Controversies in the United States, 1775–1787*. Philadelphia: University of Pennsylvania Press, 1983.

———. *Statehood and Union: A History of the Northwest Ordinance*. Bloomington: Indiana University Press, 1987.

Owens, Robert M. "Law and Disorder North of the Ohio: Runaways and the Patriarchy of Print Culture, 1793–1815." *Indiana Magazine of History* 103 (September 2007): 265–89.

Owsley, Frank L., Jr. "Albert J. Pickett: Planter-Historian of the Old South." *Louisiana Studies* 8 (Summer 1969): 158–84.

Palmer, Robert C. "The Federal Common Law of Crimes." *Law and History Review* 4 (Fall 1986): 267–323.

Parmet, Herbert S., and Marie B. Hecht. *Aaron Burr: Portrait of an Ambitious Man*. New York: Macmillan, 1967.

Pasley, Jeffrey L. *"The Tyranny of Printers": Newspaper Politics in the Early American Republic*. Charlottesville: University Press of Virginia, 2001.

Perkins, Bradford. *Prologue to War: England and the United States, 1805–1812*. Berkeley: University of California Press, 1961.

Perkins, Elizabeth A. *Border Life: Experience and Memory in the Revolutionary Ohio Valley*. Chapel Hill: University of North Carolina Press, 1998.

Perl-Rosenthal, Nathan. "Private Letters and Public Diplomacy: The Adams Network and the Quasi-War, 1797–1798." *Journal of the Early Republic* 31 (Summer 2011): 283–311.

Peterson, Merrill D. *The Jefferson Image in the American Mind*. New York: Oxford University Press, 1960.

———. *Thomas Jefferson and the New Nation: A Biography*. New York: Oxford University Press, 1970.

Pfau, Michael William. *The Political Style of Conspiracy: Chase, Sumner, and Lincoln*. East Lansing: Michigan State University Press, 2005.

Philbrick, Francis S. *The Rise of the West, 1754–1830*. New York: Harper & Row, Publishers, 1965.

Pitcher, M. Avis. "John Smith, First Senator from Ohio and His Connections with Aaron Burr." *Ohio Archaeological and Historical Quarterly* 45, no. 1 (1936): 68–88.

Pocock, Emil. "Slavery and Freedom in the Early Republic: Robert Patterson's Slaves in Kentucky and Ohio, 1804–1819." *Ohio Valley History* 6 (Spring 2006): 3–26.

Posey, John Thornton. "Rascality Revisited: In Defense of General James Wilkinson." *Filson Club Historical Quarterly* 74 (Fall 2000): 309–51.

Pratt, Julius W. "Aaron Burr and the Historians." *New York History* 24 (October 1945): 447–70.

Pred, Allan R. *Urban Growth and the Circulation of Information: The United States System of Cities, 1790–1840*. Cambridge, Mass.: Harvard University Press, 1973.

Presser, Stephen B. "The Supra-Constitution, the Courts, and the Federal Common Law of Crimes: Some Comments on Palmer and Preyer." *Law and History Review* 4 (Fall 1986): 325–35.

Preyer, Kathryn. "Jurisdiction to Punish: Federal Authority, Federalism and the Common Law of Crimes in the Early Republic." *Law and History Review* 4 (Fall 1986): 223–65.

Prichard, Walter. "Selecting a Governor for the Territory of Orleans." *Louisiana Historical Quarterly* 31 (April 1948): 269–393.

Quisenberry, A. C. *The Life and Times of Hon. Humphrey Marshall*. Winchester, Ky.: Sun Publishing Company, 1892.

Racine, Karen. *Francisco de Miranda: A Transatlantic Life in the Age of Revolution*. Wilmington, Del.: SR Books, 2003.

Ranck, James B. "Andrew Jackson and the Burr Conspiracy." *Tennessee Historical Magazine*, 2nd ser., 1 (October 1930): 17–28.

Randall, E. O. "Blennerhassett: An Historical Essay." *Ohio State Archaeological and Historical Quarterly* 1 (September 1887): 127–63.

Rayman, Ronald. "Frontier Journalism in Kentucky: Joseph Montfort Street and the Western World, 1806–1809." *Register of the Kentucky Historical Society* 76 (April 1978): 98–111.

Reinhold, Meyer. *The Classick Pages: Classical Reading of Eighteenth-Century Americans*. University Park: Pennsylvania State University Press, 1975.

Remini, Robert V. *Andrew Jackson and the Course of American Empire, 1767–1821*. New York: Harper & Row, Publishers, 1977.

Reps, John W. *Tidewater Towns: City Planning in Colonial Virginia and Maryland*. Williamsburg, Va.: Colonial Williamsburg Foundation, 1972.

Reynolds, Larry. "Patriots and Criminals, Criminals and Patriots: Representations of the Case of Major André." *South Central Review* 9 (Spring 1992): 57–84.

Richard, Carl J. *The Founders and the Classics: Greece, Rome and the American Enlightenment*. Cambridge, Mass.: Harvard University Press, 1994.

Ridgway, Whitman H. *Community Leadership in Maryland, 1790–1840: A Comparative Analysis of Power in Society*. Chapel Hill: University of North Carolina Press, 1979.

Risjord, Norman K. *The Old Republicans: Southern Conservatism in the Age of Jefferson*. New York: Columbia University Press, 1965.

———. *Representative Americans: The Revolutionary Generation*. 2nd ed. Lanham, Md.: Madison House, 2001.

———. "The Virginia Federalists." *Journal of Southern History* 33 (November 1967): 486–517.

Robertson, Andrew W. "'Look on This Picture . . . And on This!': Nationalism, Localism, and Partisan Images of Otherness in the United States, 1787–1820." *American Historical Review* 106 (October 2001): 1263–80.

Robertson, William S. *The Life of Miranda*. 2 vols. Chapel Hill: University of North Carolina Press, 1929.

Rockman, Seth. *Scraping By: Wage Labor, Slavery, and Survival in Early Baltimore*. Baltimore, Md.: Johns Hopkins University Press, 2009.

Rodd, Francis Rennell. *General William Eaton: The Failure of an Idea*. New York: Minton, Balch and Company, 1932.

Rosnow, Ralph L., and Gary Alan Fine. *Rumor and Gossip: The Social Psychology of Hearsay*. New York: Elsevier, 1976.

Rothman, Joshua D. *Flush Times and Fever Dreams: A Story of Capitalism and Slavery in the Age of Jackson*. Athens: University of Georgia Press, 2012.

Rotundo, E. Anthony. *American Manhood: Transformations in Masculinity from the Revolution to the Modern Era*. New York: Basic Books, 1993.

Rowland, Dunbar. *Mississippi: Comprising Sketches of Counties, Towns, Events, Institutions and Persons, Arranged in Cyclopedic Form*. 4 vols. Atlanta, Ga.: Southern Historical Publishing Association, 1907.

Royster, Charles. *The Destructive War: William Tecumseh Sherman, Stonewall Jackson, and the Americans*. New York: Alfred A. Knopf, 1991.

———. *A Revolutionary People at War: The Continental Army and American Character, 1775–1783*. Chapel Hill: University of North Carolina Press, 1979.

Samuels, Ernest. *Henry Adams: The Middle Years*. Cambridge, Mass.: Belknap Press of Harvard University Press, 1958.

Sarat, Austin, and Thomas R. Kearns, eds. *The Rhetoric of Law*. Ann Arbor: University of Michigan Press, 1994.

Savelle, Max. *George Morgan: Colony Builder*. New York: Columbia University Press, 1932.

Schachner, Nathan. *Aaron Burr: A Biography*. New York: A. S. Barnes, 1937.

Schulz, Max F. *Paradise Preserved: Recreations of Eden in Eighteenth- and Nineteenth-Century England*. Cambridge: Cambridge University Press, 1985.

Scott, Mary Wingfield. *Old Richmond Neighborhoods*. Richmond, Va.: Whittet & Shepperson, 1950.

Seelye, John. *Beautiful Machine: Rivers and the Republican Plan, 1755–1825*. New York: Oxford University Press, 1991.

Shalev, Eran. *Rome Reborn on Western Shores: Historical Imagination and the Creation of the American Republic*. Charlottesville: University of Virginia Press, 2009.

Shalhope, Robert E. *The Baltimore Bank Riot: Political Upheaval in Antebellum Maryland*. Urbana: University of Illinois Press, 2009.

Shankman, Andrew. "Malcontents and Tertium Quids: The Battle to Define Democracy in Jeffersonian Philadelphia." *Journal of the Early Republic* 19 (Spring 1999): 43–72.

Shapin, Steven. *A Social History of Truth: Civility and Science in Seventeenth-Century England*. Chicago: University of Chicago Press, 1995.

Sharp, James Roger. *The Deadlocked Election of 1800: Jefferson, Burr, and the Union in the Balance*. Lawrence: University Press of Kansas, 2010.

Shepherd, William R. "Wilkinson and the Beginnings of the Spanish Conspiracy." *American Historical Review* 9 (April 1909): 490–506.

Shibutani, Tamotsu. *Improvised News: A Sociological Study of Rumor*. Indianapolis, Ind.: Bobbs-Merrill Company, 1966.

Shields, David S. *Civil Tongues and Polite Letters in British America*. Chapel Hill: University of North Carolina Press, 1997.

Shreve, Royal Ornan. *The Finished Scoundrel: General James Wilkinson, Sometime Commander-in-Chief of the Army of the United States, Who Made Intrigue a Trade and Treason a Profession*. Indianapolis, Ind.: Bobbs-Merrill Company, 1933.

Sidbury, James. *Ploughshares into Swords: Race, Rebellion, and Identity in Gabriel's Virginia, 1730–1810*. Cambridge: Cambridge University Press, 1997.

Silver, James W. *Edmund Pendleton Gaines: Frontier General*. Baton Rouge: Louisiana State University Press, 1949.

Skelton, William B. *An American Profession of Arms: The Army Officer Corps, 1784–1861*. Lawrence: University Press of Kansas, 1992.

Slaughter, Thomas P. "Conspiratorial Politics: The Public Life of Aaron Burr." *New Jersey History* 103 (Spring/Summer 1985): 68–81.

———. "Crowds in Eighteenth-Century America: Reflections and New Directions." *Pennsylvania Magazine of History and Biography* 115 (January 1991): 3–34.

———. *The Whiskey Rebellion: Frontier Epilogue to the American Revolution*. New York: Oxford University Press, 1986.

Smelser, Marshall. "The Federalist Period as an Age of Passion." *American Quarterly* 10 (Winter 1958): 391–419.

Smith, Culver H. *The Press, Politics, and Patronage: The American Government's Use of Newspapers, 1789–1875*. Athens: University of Georgia Press, 1977.

Smith, Jean Edward. *John Marshall: Definer of a Nation*. New York: Henry Holt and Company, 1996.

Smith, Rogers M. *Civic Ideals: Conflicting Visions of Citizenship in U.S. History*. New Haven, Conn.: Yale University Press, 1997.

Smith, Thomas H. *The Mapping of Ohio*. Kent, Ohio: Kent State University Press, 1977.

Southerland, Henry deLeon, Jr., and Jerry Elijah Brown. *The Federal Road through Georgia, the Creek Nation, and Alabama, 1806–1836*. Tuscaloosa: University of Alabama Press, 1989.

Spacks, Patricia Meyer. *Gossip*. New York: Alfred A. Knopf, 1985.

Sprague, Stuart Seely. "The Louisville Canal: Key to Aaron Burr's Western Trip of 1805." *Register of the Kentucky Historical Society* 71 (January 1973): 69–86.

Stagg, J.C.A. "The Enigma of Aaron Burr." *Reviews in American History* 12 (September 1984): 378–82.

Stampp, Kenneth M. "The Concept of a Perpetual Union." *Journal of American History* 65 (June 1978): 5–33.

Stanard, Mary Newton. *Richmond: Its People and Its Story*. Philadelphia: J. B. Lippincott Company, 1923.

Stearns, Susan Gaunt. "Borderland Diplomacy: Western Elites and the 'Spanish Conspiracy.'" *Register of the Kentucky Historical Society* 114 (Summer/Autumn 2016): 371–98.

Steffen, Charles G. *The Mechanics of Baltimore: Workers and Politics in the Age of Revolution, 1763–1812*. Urbana: University of Illinois Press, 1984.

———. "Newspapers for Free: The Economies of Newspaper Circulation in the Early Republic." *Journal of the Early Republic* 23 (Fall 2003): 381–419.

Stephenson, Richard W., and Marianne M. McKee, eds. *Virginia in Maps: Four Centuries of Settlement, Growth, and Development*. Richmond: Library of Virginia, 2000.

Steward, Dick. *Frontier Swashbuckler: The Life and Legend of John Smith T*. Columbia: University of Missouri Press, 2000.

Stewart, David O. *American Emperor: Aaron Burr's Challenge to Jefferson's America*. New York: Simon & Schuster, 2011.

Stowe, Steven M. *Intimacy and Power in the Old South: Ritual in the Lives of the Planters*. Baltimore, Md.: Johns Hopkins University Press, 1987.

Swick, Ray. "Aaron Burr's Visit to Blennerhassett Island." *West Virginia History* 35 (April 1974): 205–19.

———. *An Island Called Eden: The Story of Harman and Margaret Blennerhassett*. Rev. ed. Parkersburg, W.Va.: Blennerhassett Island State Historical Park, 2000.

———. "Theodosia Burr Alston." *South Atlantic Quarterly* 74 (Autumn 1975): 495–506.

Tachau, Mary K. Bonsteel. *Federal Courts in the Early Republic: Kentucky, 1789–1816*. Princeton, N.J.: Princeton University Press, 1978.

Tackett, Timothy. *When the King Took Flight*. Cambridge, Mass.: Harvard University Press, 2003.

Tartar, Brent, and Wythe Holt. "The Apparent Political Selection of Federal Grand Juries in Virginia, 1789–1809." *American Journal of Legal History* 49 (July 2007): 257–83.

Taylor, George Rogers. "Agrarian Discontent in the Mississippi Valley Preceding the War of 1812." *Journal of Political Economy* 39 (August 1931): 471–505.

Taylor, William R. *Cavalier and Yankee: The Old South and American National Character*. New York: George Braziller, 1961.

Thornton, Tamara Plakins. *Cultivating Gentlemen: The Meaning of Country Life among the Boston Elite, 1785–1860*. New Haven, Conn.: Yale University Press, 1989.

Todd, Charles Burr. "Blennerhassett and His Island." *Magazine of History* 6 (October 1907): 236–39.

Tompkins, Hamilton Bullock. *Burr Bibliography: A List of Books Relating to Aaron Burr*. Brooklyn, N.Y.: Historical Printing Club, 1900.

Trees, Andy. "Benedict Arnold, John André, and His Three Yeomen Captors: A Sentimental Journey or American Virtue Defined." *Early American Literature* 35, no. 3 (2000): 246–73.

———. *The Founding Fathers and the Politics of Character: The Founders and National Identity*. Princeton, N.J.: Princeton University Press, 2004.

Trouillot, Michel-Rolph. *Silencing the Past: Power and the Production of History*. Boston: Beacon Press, 1995.

Tsiang, I-mien. *The Question of Expatriation in America prior to 1907*. Baltimore, Md.: Johns Hopkins Press, 1942.

Tucker, Spencer. *Stephen Decatur: A Life Most Bold and Daring*. Annapolis, Md.: Naval Institute Press, 2005.

———, and Frank T. Reuter. *Injured Honor: The* Chesapeake-Leopard *Affair, June 22, 1807*. Annapolis, Md.: Naval Institute Press, 1996.

Turner, Frederick Jackson. *Rise of the New West, 1819–1829*. New York: Harper & Brothers, 1906.

Turner, Victor R. "Harman Blennerhassett: His Rise and Fall." *Filson Club Historical Quarterly* 38 (October 1964): 316–22.

Vernet, Julien. *Strangers on Their Native Soil: Opposition to United States' Governance in Louisiana's Orleans Territory, 1803–1809*. Jackson: University Press of Mississippi, 2013.

Waldstreicher, David. *In the Midst of Perpetual Fetes: The Making of American Nationalism, 1776–1820*. Chapel Hill: University of North Carolina Press, 1997.

Wallace, Karl R., ed. *History of Speech Education in America*. New York: Appleton-Century-Crofts, 1954.

Wandell, Samuel H. *Aaron Burr in Literature: Books, Pamphlets, Periodicals, and Miscellany Relating to Aaron Burr and His Leading Political Contemporaries, with Occasional Excerpts from Publications, Bibliographical, Critical, and Historical Notes, etc.* London: K. Paul, Trench, Trubner, & Co., 1936.

———, and Meade Minnigerode. *Aaron Burr: A Biography Compiled from Rare, and in Many Cases Unpublished, Sources*. 2 vols. New York: G. P. Putnam's Sons, 1925.

Warner, Michael. *The Letters of the Republic: Publication and the Public Sphere in Eighteenth-Century America*. Cambridge, Mass.: Harvard University Press, 1990.

Warren, Elizabeth. "Benjamin Sebastian and the Spanish Conspiracy in Kentucky." *Filson Club Historical Quarterly* 20 (April 1946): 107–30.

Warren, James Perrin. *Culture of Eloquence: Oratory and Reform in Antebellum America*. University Park: Pennsylvania State University Press, 1999.

Warwick, Edward, Henry C. Pitz, and Alexander Wyckoff. *Early American Dress: The Colonial and Revolutionary Periods*. New York: Benjamin Blom, 1965.

Wass, Ann Buermann, and Michelle Webb Fandrich. *Clothing through American History: The Federal Era through Antebellum, 1786–1860*. Santa Barbara, Calif.: Greenwood, 2010.

Watlington, Patricia. *The Partisan Spirit: Kentucky Politics, 1779–1792*. New York: Atheneum, 1972.

Weber, Ralph E. *United States Diplomatic Codes and Ciphers, 1775–1938*. Chicago: Precedent Publishing, 1979.

Wensorski, John Frederick. "A Wilkinson Conspiracy." *Oklahoma State Historical Review* 4 (Spring 1983): 35–44.

Wert, Justin J. *Habeas Corpus in America: The Politics of Individual Rights*. Lawrence: University Press of Kansas, 2011.

Wheelan, Joseph. *Jefferson's Vendetta: The Pursuit of Aaron Burr and the Judiciary*. New York: Carroll & Graf Publishers, 2005.

Whitaker, Arthur P. "Harry Innes and the Spanish Intrigue, 1794–1795." *Mississippi Valley Historical Review* 15 (September 1928): 236–48.

———. *The Spanish American Frontier, 1783–1795: The Westward Movement and the Spanish Retreat in the Mississippi Valley*. Lincoln: University of Nebraska Press, 1927.

White, Ed. "The Value of Conspiracy Theory." *American Literary History* 14 (Spring 2002): 1–31.

White, Leonard D. *The Jeffersonians: A Study in Administrative History, 1801–1829*. New York: Macmillan Company, 1951.

Wiebe, Robert H. *The Opening of American Society: From the Adoption of the Constitution to the Eve of Disunion*. New York: Random House, 1984.

Wilhelmy, Robert W. "Senator John Smith and the Aaron Burr Conspiracy." *Cincinnati Historical Society Bulletin* 28 (Spring 1970): 39–60.

Wilkinson, James. *Wilkinson, Soldier and Pioneer.* New Orleans, La.: Rogers Printing Co., 1935.

Williams, Glyn. *The Death of Captain Cook: A Hero Made and Unmade.* Cambridge, Mass.: Harvard University Press, 2008.

Williams, Raymond. *The Country and the City.* New York: Oxford University Press, 1973.

Williams, Stanley T. *The Life of Washington Irving.* 2 vols. New York: Oxford University Press, 1935.

Wilson, David. *United Irishmen, United States: Immigrant Radicals in the Early American Republic.* Ithaca, N.Y.: Cornell University Press, 1998.

Wilson, George. "General Joseph Monford [*sic*] Street: A Neglected Kentucky Hero." *Register of the Kentucky State Historical Society* 4 (September 1906): 20–26.

Winship, Marion Nelson. "Kentucky *in* the New Republic: A Study of Distance and Connection." In *The Buzzel about Kentuck: Settling the Promised Land,* edited by Craig Thompson Friend, 101–23. Lexington: University Press of Kentucky, 1999.

Winterer, Caroline. *The Culture of Classicism: Ancient Greece and Rome in American Intellectual Life, 1780–1910.* Baltimore, Md.: Johns Hopkins University Press, 2002.

———. *The Mirror of Antiquity: American Women and the Classical Tradition, 1750–1900.* Ithaca, N.Y.: Cornell University Press, 2007.

Wohl, Michael. "Not Yet Saint nor Sinner: A Further Note on Daniel Clark." *Louisiana History* 24 (Spring 1983): 195–205.

Wood, Gordon S. "Conspiracy and the Paranoid Style: Causality and Deceit in the Eighteenth Century." *William and Mary Quarterly,* 3rd ser., 39 (July 1982): 401–41.

———. *The Radicalism of the American Revolution: How a Revolution Transformed a Monarchical Society into a Democratic One Unlike Any That Had Ever Existed.* New York: Alfred A. Knopf, 1991.

———. "The Real Treason of Aaron Burr." *Proceedings of the American Philosophical Society* 143 (June 1999): 280–95.

Wood, Marie Beyer. *None Called Him Neighbor: The Story of Harman Blennerhassett and the Aaron Burr Conspiracy.* Parkersburg, W.Va.: n.p., 1951.

Wright, J. Leitch, Jr. *Britain and the American Frontier, 1783–1815.* Athens: University of Georgia Press, 1975.

Wright, Louis B., and Julia H. Macleod. "William Eaton's Relations with Aaron Burr." *Mississippi Valley Historical Review* 31 (March 1945): 523–36.

Wyatt-Brown, Bertram. *Southern Honor: Ethics and Behavior in the Old South.* New York: Oxford University Press, 1982.

Yagoda, Ben. *Memoir: A History.* New York: Riverhead Books, 2009.

Yoo, John C. "The First Claim: The Burr Trial, *United States v. Nixon,* and Presidential Power." *Minnesota Law Review* 83 (May 1999): 1435–79.

Young, James Sterling. *The Washington Community, 1800–1828.* New York: Columbia University Press, 1966.

Ziff, Larzer. *Writing in the New Nation: Prose, Print, and Politics in the Early United States*. New Haven, Conn.: Yale University Press, 1991.

UNPUBLISHED

Adams, Mary P. "Jefferson's Military Policy with Special Reference to the Frontier, 1805–1809." Ph.D. diss., University of Virginia, 1958.

Blackwood, Stephen A. "The Aaron Burr Conspiracy: A Study of the Historiography of His Intentions." M.A. thesis, University of North Carolina, Greensboro, 1979.

Hamilton, Kathryn Ruth. "Villains and Cultural Change: Aaron Burr and Victorian America." M.A. thesis, California State University, Fullerton, 1985.

Lewis, James E., Jr. "'Bring Them *to Light* or Consign Them *to Oblivion*': The Strange Career of the Harman Blennerhassett Papers." Paper presented at the Society for Historians of the Early American Republic annual meeting, Ohio State University, Columbus, July 2003.

———. "'The Strongest Government on Earth' Proves Its Strength: The Jefferson Administration and the Burr Conspiracy." In *Jeffersonians in Power: Ideas in Practice*, edited by Joanne B. Freeman and Johann N. Neem. Charlottesville: University of Virginia Press, forthcoming.

Mumper, James Arthur. "The Jefferson Image in the Federalist Mind, 1801–1809: Jefferson's Administration from the Federalist Point of View." Ph.D. diss., University of Virginia, 1966.

Pasley, Jeffrey L. "Matthew Livingston Davis's Notes from the Political Underground: The Conflict of Political Values in the Early American Republic." Unpublished manuscript, 2000. Accessed 29 November 2004. http://jeff.pasleybrothers.com/writings/davisv2.htm.

Rodriguez, Junius Peter. "Ripe for Revolt: Louisiana and the Tradition of Slave Insurrection, 1803–1865." Ph.D. diss., Auburn University, 1992.

Swick, Ronald Ray. "Harman Blennerhassett: An Irish Aristocrat on the American Frontier." Ph.D. diss., Miami University, 1978.

Wohl, Michael. "A Man in the Shadow: The Life of Daniel Clark." Ph.D. diss., Tulane University, 1984.

ILLUSTRATION CREDITS

Endpapers: [Aaron Burr] to [James Wilkinson], [ca. 22–29 July 1806], Aaron Burr Letters, Everett D. Graff Collection of Americana, Call # Vault Graff 503. Image courtesy of Newberry Library, Chicago, Ill.

Figure 1: Map prepared by Jason Glatz, Western Michigan University Libraries, using information from *National Atlas of the United States*, 2004 online ed., and the National Historical Geographic Information System database, version 11.0, Minnesota Population Center, University of Minnesota, Minneapolis.

Figure 2: *List of Post-Offices in the United States; With the Counties in which They are Situated, and Their Distances from Washington, D.C.* (Washington, D.C.: 1803), in Thomas Jefferson Papers, Library of Congress, Washington, D.C. Image courtesy of the Manuscripts Division of the Library of Congress.

Figure 3: Charles Balthazar Julien Févret de Saint-Mémin, John Graham, engraving on paper, 1808. Image courtesy of National Portrait Gallery, Smithsonian Institution, Washington, D.C., gift of Mr. and Mrs. Paul Mellon.

Figure 4: John Scoles, "Kentucky Statehouse," *New York Magazine, or Literary Repository*, n.s., 1 (July 1796), 336. Image courtesy of the American Antiquarian Society, Worcester, Mass.

Figure 5: [Thomas Jefferson], *Message from the President of the United States, Transmitting a Copy of the Proceedings and of the Evidence Exhibited on the Arraignment of Aaron Burr, and Others, Before the Circuit Court of the United States, Held in Virginia, in the Year 1807* (Washington, D.C.: A. & G. Way, Printers, 1807). Image courtesy of Readex, a division of NewsBank Inc., and the American Antiquarian Society, Worcester, Mass.

Figure 6: "IN GENERAL ASSEMBLY, December 3, 1806." "An American Time Capsule: Three Centuries of Broadsides and Other Printed Ephemera" website, Library of Congress, Washington, D.C. Courtesy of the Rare Book Division of the Library of Congress.

Figure 7: Engraving based upon a painting by Sala Bosworth, William H. Safford, *The Life of Harman Blennerhassett: Comprising an Authentic Narrative of the Burr Expedition: and Containing Many Additional Facts Not Heretofore Published* (Cincinnati, Ohio: Ely, Allen & Looker, 1850). Image courtesy of the Rare Book Division, Department of Rare Books and Special Collections, Princeton University Library.

Figure 8: Cipher keys, [Ezekial Bacon], *Report of the Committee Appointed to Inquire into the Conduct of General Wilkinson, February 26, 1811* (Washington, D.C.: A. and G. Way, 1811), 292. Reproduced by permission from

Readex, a division of NewsBank Inc., and the American Antiquarian Society, Worcester, Mass.

Figure 9: John L. Boqueta de Woiseri, "A View of New Orleans Taken from the Plantation of Marigny," painting, 1803. Image courtesy of The Historic New Orleans Collection, 1958.42.

Figure 10: "Agrestis," *A Short Review of the Late Proceedings at New Orleans; and Some Remarks upon the Bill for Suspending the Privilege of the Writ of Habeas Corpus, which Passed the Senate of the United States During the Last Session of Congress. In two Letters to the Printer, by Agrestis* (Georgetown, S.C.: n.p., 1807; Reprint, Richmond, Va.: Office of the *Impartial Observer*, 1807). Image courtesy of the Rare Book Division, Department of Rare Books and Special Collections, Princeton University Library.

Figure 11: "Arrest of Aaron Burr," Orville J. Victor, *History of American Conspiracies: A Record of Treason, Insurrection, Rebellion, &c., in the United States of America, from 1760 to 1860* (New York: James D. Torrey, Publisher, 1863), opposite p. 40. Image courtesy of the Rare Book Division, Department of Rare Books and Special Collections, Princeton University Library.

Figure 12: Charles Balthazar Julien Févret de Saint-Mémin, "A View of Richmond from Below Mayo's Bridge, 1807," Christian W. Asbury, *Richmond, Her Past and Present* (Richmond, Va.: L. H. Jenkins, 1912), opposite p. 64.

Figure 13: (left) Charles Balthazar Julien Févret de Saint-Mémin, William Wirt, engraving on paper, 1808. Image courtesy of National Portrait Gallery, Smithsonian Institution, Washington, D.C., gift of Mr. and Mrs. Paul Mellon. (right) Unknown artist, Harman Blennerhassett (AL03932.tif). Image courtesy of the Ohio History Connection, Columbus.

Figure 14: "Parade of Burr's Forces," William Cullen Bryant and Sidney Howard Gay, *A Popular History of the United States from the First Discovery by the Northmen to the End of the Civil War*, 4 vols. (New York: Chas. Scribner's Sons, 1881), 4:152. Image courtesy of the Graphic Arts Collection, Department of Rare Books and Special Collections, Princeton University Library.

Figure 15: "From Baltimore Papers," *Olive Branch* (Sherburne, N.Y.), 21 November 1807. Image courtesy of Readex, a division of NewsBank Inc., and the American Antiquarian Society, Worcester, Mass.

Figure 16: Engraving based upon a painting by James Van Dyck, William K. Bixby, ed., *The Private Journal of Aaron Burr: Reprinted in Full from the Original Manuscript in the Library of Mr. William K. Bixby, of St. Louis, Mo.*, 2 vols. (Rochester, N.Y.: Genesee Press, 1903). Image courtesy of the Rare Book Division, Department of Rare Books and Special Collections, Princeton University Library.

INDEX